D1194044

Dear West Customer:

West Academic Publishing has changed the look of its American Casebook Series®.

In keeping with our efforts to promote sustainability, we have replaced our former covers with book covers that are more environmentally friendly. Our casebooks will now be covered in a 100% renewable natural fiber. In addition, we have migrated to an ink supplier that favors vegetable-based materials, such as soy.

Using soy inks and natural fibers to print our textbooks reduces VOC emissions. Moreover, our primary paper supplier is certified by the Forest Stewardship Council, which is testament to our commitment to conservation and responsible business management.

The new cover design has migrated from the long-standing brown cover to a contemporary charcoal fabric cover with silver-stamped lettering and black accents. Please know that inside the cover, our books continue to provide the same trusted content that you've come to expect from West.

We've retained the ample margins that you have told us you appreciate in our texts while moving to a new, larger font, improving readability. We hope that you will find these books a pleasing addition to your bookshelf.

Another visible change is that you will no longer see the brand name Thomson West on our print products. With the recent merger of Thomson and Reuters, I am pleased to announce that books published under the West Academic Publishing imprint will once again display the West brand.

It will likely be several years before all of our casebooks are published with the new cover and interior design. We ask for your patience as the new covers are rolled out on new and revised books knowing that behind both the new and old covers, you will find the finest in legal education materials for teaching and learning.

Thank you for your continued patronage of the West brand, which is both rooted in history and forward looking towards future innovations in legal education. We invite you to be a part of our next evolution.

Best regards,

Heidi M. Hellekson
Publisher, West Academic Publishing

CRIMINAL LAW

CASES, MATERIALS & PROBLEMS

Third Edition

■ ■ ■

By

Russell L. Weaver
Professor of Law & Distinguished University Scholar
University of Louisville
Louis D. Brandeis School of Law

Leslie W. Abramson
Frost Brown Todd Professor of Law
University of Louisville
Louis D. Brandeis School of Law

John M. Burkoff
Professor of Law
University of Pittsburgh
School of Law

Catherine Hancock
Geoffrey C. Bible & Murray H. Bring Professor of Constitutional Law
Tulane University
School of Law

AMERICAN CASEBOOK SERIES®

WEST®
A Thomson Reuters business

Mat #40745271

American Casebook Series is a trademark registered in the U.S. Patent and Trademark Office.

© West, a Thomson business, 2002, 2005
© 2009 Thomson Reuters

    610 Opperman Drive
    St. Paul, MN 55123
    1–800–313–9378

Printed in the United States of America

ISBN: 978–0–314–19419–0

TEXT IS PRINTED ON 10% POST
CONSUMER RECYCLED PAPER

*To Ben, Kate and Laurence, with love, **RLW***

*To Lisa, Sam, Shel & Will, **LWA***

*To Nancy, Amy & Sean, David & Emmy, Emma, Molly and Hannah,
with love, **JMB***

*To Lorenz Fred Koerber, Jr., and Margareta Dunne Koerber,
with love and gratitude, **CH***

*

Preface to the Third Edition

As this criminal law casebook moves into a third edition, our objectives remain unchanged. Our primary goal is to create a "teacher's book" that contains thought provoking problems designed to produce interesting classroom discussions. The problems are woven throughout each chapter and help to illuminate trends in the law. Our second goal is to provide a focus on teaching "skills." Many of the problems place students in practical situations that they are likely to encounter in litigation, and therefore encourage students to think about how they might construct arguments for their clients in these situations.

As with the prior edition, tradeoffs are necessary. In order to prevent the book from being unduly voluminous, we have chosen not to include encyclopedic notes and commentaries like those found in some other books. In the criminal law field, students have numerous high-quality secondary sources available to them. Consistent with our goal of producing a "teacher's book," we opted to limit the scope of our notes in order to supply a larger number of useful problems.

We are grateful to our research assistants and secretaries for their help in producing this book. In addition, we want to thank the many students who were subjected to earlier drafts of this book and who helped us produce a better product.

We welcome input from faculty and students who use this book. You can contact us at the following e-mail addresses: Professor Russell Weaver (russ.weaver@louisville.edu); Professor Leslie Abramson (les.abramson@louisville.edu); Professor John Burkoff (burkoff@pitt.edu); Professor Catherine Hancock (chancock@tulane.edu).

RLW, LWA, JMB, CH

December 2008

*

Summary of Contents

―――――――

TABLE OF CONTENTS

———

*

TABLE OF CASES

The principal cases are in bold type. Cases cited or discussed in the text
are roman type. References are to pages. Cases cited in principal
cases and within other quoted materials are not included.

*

CRIMINAL LAW

CASES, MATERIALS & PROBLEMS

Third Edition

*

CHAPTER 1

THE PURPOSES OF THE CRIMINAL LAW

■ ■ ■

The criminal law is unique because it is based on punishment. A convicted defendant can be fined, imprisoned, and, in rare instances, executed. In addition, a criminal conviction usually carries a moral stigma which reduces an individual's chances in life, particularly his or her employment opportunities. What function does the penalty of punishment serve? How does that function differ from the purposes served by the law of tort?

A. A CASE STUDY IN PUNISHMENT

REGINA v. DUDLEY & STEPHENS
[1884] 14 Q.B.D. 273.

Lord Coleridge, C.J. The two prisoners, Thomas Dudley and Edwin Stephens, were indicted for the murder of Richard Parker on the high seas on the 25th day of July in the present year. They were tried before my brother Huddleston at Exeter on the 6th of November, and, under the direction of my learned Brother, the jury returned a special verdict, the legal effect of which has been argued before us, and on which we are now to pronounce judgment.

The special verdict [as] finally settled before us is as follows: "That on July 5, 1884, the prisoners, Thomas Dudley and Edward Stephens, with one Brooks, all able-bodied English seamen, and the deceased also an English boy, between seventeen and eighteen years of age, the crew of an English yacht, a registered English vessel, were cast away in a storm on the high seas 16,000 miles from the Cape of Good Hope, and were compelled to put into an open boat belonging to the said yacht. That in the boat they had no supply of water and no supply of food, except two 1 lb. tins of turnips, and for three days they had nothing else to subsist upon. That on the fourth day they caught a small turtle, upon which they subsisted for a few days, and this was the only food they had up to the twentieth day when the act now in question was committed. That on the twelfth day the remains of the turtle were entirely consumed, and for the next eight days they

1

had nothing to eat. That they had no fresh water, except such rain as they from time to time caught in their oilskin capes. That the boat was drifting on the ocean, and was probably more than 1,000 miles away from land. That on the eighteenth day, when they had been seven days without food and five without water, the prisoners spoke to Brooks as to what should be done if no succor came, and suggested that some one should be sacrificed to save the rest, but Brooks dissented, and the boy, to whom they were understood to refer, was not consulted. That on the 24th of July, the day before the act now in question, the prisoner Dudley proposed to Stephens and Brooks that lots should be cast who should be put to death to save the rest, but Brooks refused to consent, and it was not put to the boy, and in point of fact there was no drawing of lots. That on the day the prisoners spoke of their families, and suggested it would be better to kill the boy that their lives should be saved, and Dudley proposed that if there was no vessel in sight by the morrow morning, the boy should be killed. That next day, the 25th of July, no vessel appearing, Dudley told Brooks that he had better go and have a sleep, and made signs to Stephens and Brooks that the boy had better be killed. The prisoner Stephens agreed to the act, but Brooks dissented from it. That the boy was then lying at the bottom of the boat quite helpless and extremely weakened by famine and by drinking sea water, and unable to make any resistance, nor did he ever assent to his being killed. The prisoner Dudley offered a prayer asking forgiveness for them all if either of them should be tempted to commit a rash act, and that their souls might be saved. That Dudley, with the assent of Stephens, went to the boy, and telling him that his time was come, put a knife unto his throat and killed him then and there; that the three men fed upon the body and blood of the boy for four days; that on the fourth day after the act had been committed the boat was picked up by a passing vessel, and the prisoners were rescued, still alive, but in the lowest state of prostration. That they were carried to the port of Falmouth, and committed for trial at Exeter. That if the men had not fed upon the body of the boy they would probably not have survived to be so picked up and rescued, but would within the four days have died of famine. That the boy, being in a much weaker condition, was likely to have died before them. That at the time of the act in question there was no sail in sight, nor any reasonable prospect of relief. That under these circumstances there appeared to the prisoners every probability that unless they then fed or very soon fed upon the boy or one of themselves they would die of starvation. That there was no appreciable chance of saving life except by killing some one for the others to eat. That assuming any necessity to kill anybody, there was no greater necessity for killing the boy than any of the other three men. But whether upon the whole matter by the jurors found the killing of Richard Parker by Dudley and Stephens be felony and murder the jurors are ignorant, and pray the advice of the Court thereupon, and if upon the whole matter the Court shall be of opinion that the killing of Richard Parker be felony and murder, then the jurors say that Dudley and Stephens were each guilty of felony and murder as alleged on the indictment." . . .

From these facts, stated with the cold precision of a special verdict, it appears sufficiently that the prisoners were subject to terrible temptation, to sufferings which might break down the bodily *symp.* power of the strongest man, and try the conscience of the best. Other details yet more harrowing, facts still more loathsome and appalling, were presented to the jury, and are to be found recorded in my learned Brother's notes. But nevertheless this is clear, that the prisoners put to death a weak and unoffending boy upon the chance of preserving their own lives by feeding upon his flesh and blood after he was killed, and with the certainty of depriving *him* of any possible chance of survival. The verdict finds in terms that "if the men had not *special verdict* fed upon the body of the boy they would *probably* not have survived," and that "the boy being in a much weaker condition was *likely* to have died before them." They might possibly have been picked up next day by a passing ship; they might possibly not have been picked up at all; in either case it is obvious that the killing of the boy would have been an unnecessary and profitless act. It is found by the verdict that the boy was incapable of resistance, and, in fact, made none; and it is not even suggested that his death was due to any violence on his part attempted against, or even so much as feared by, those who killed him. Under these circumstances the jury say that they are ignorant whether those who killed him were guilty of murder, and have referred it to this Court to determine what is the legal consequence which follows from the facts which they have [found].

[The] real question in the case [is] whether killing under the *ISSUE* circumstances set forth in the verdict be or not be murder. The contention that it could be anything else was, to the minds of us all, both new and strange, and we stopped the Attorney General in his negative argument in order that we might hear what could be said in support of a proposition which appeared to us to be at once dangerous, immoral, and opposed to all legal principle and analogy. [It] is said that it follows from various definitions of murder in books of authority, [that] in order to save your own life you may lawfully take away the life of another, when that other is neither attempting nor threatening yours, nor is guilty of any illegal act whatever towards you or any one else. But if these definitions be looked at they will not be found to sustain this contention.

It is [clear] that the doctrine contended for receives no support from the great authority of Lord Hale. It is plain that in his view the [only] necessity which justified homicide is that [which] has always been and is now considered a justification[, namely,] what is commonly called "self-defence."

Is there, then, any authority for the proposition that has been presented to us? Decided cases there are none.... The American case [*United States v. Holmes*, 26 F.Cas. 360 (C.C.E.D.Pa. 1842),] in which it was decided, correctly indeed, that sailors had no right to throw passengers overboard to save themselves, but upon the somewhat strange ground that the proper mode of determining who would be sacrificed was to vote upon the subject by ballot, can hardly ... be an authority satisfactory to a court in this country....

Now it is admitted that the deliberate killing of this unoffending and unresisting boy was clearly murder, unless the killing can be justified by some well-recognised excuse admitted by the law. It is further admitted that there was in this case no such excuse, unless the killing was justified by what has been called "necessity." But the temptation to the act which existed here was not what the law has ever called necessity. Nor is this to be regretted. Though law and morality are not the same, and many things may be immoral which are not necessarily illegal, yet the absolute divorce of law from morality would be of fatal consequence; and such divorce would follow if the temptation to murder in this case were to be held by law and absolute defence of it. It is not so. To preserve one's life is generally speaking a duty, but it may be the plainest and the highest duty to sacrifice it. War is full of instances in which it is a man's duty not to live, but to die. The duty, in case of shipwreck, of a captain to his crew, of the crew to the passengers, of soldiers to women and children ...; these duties impose on men the moral necessity, not of the preservation, but of the sacrifice of their lives for others, for which there is no country, least of all, it is to be hoped, in England, will men ever shrink, as indeed, they have not shrunk. It is not correct, therefore, to say that there is any absolute or unqualified necessity to preserve one's life. *Necesse est ut eam, non ut vivam*, is a saying of a Roman office quoted by [Lord Bacon]. It would be a very easy and cheap display of commonplace learning to quote from Greek and Latin authors[,] passage after passage, in which the duty of dying for others has been laid down in glowing and emphatic language as resulting from the principles of heathen ethics; it is enough in a Christian country to remind ourselves of the Great Example whom we profess to follow. It is not needful to point out the awful danger of admitting the principle which has been contended for. Who is to be the judge of this sort of necessity? By what measure is the comparative value of lives to be measured? Is it to be strength, or intellect, or what? It is plain that the principle leaves to him who is to profit by it to determine the necessity which will justify him in deliberately taking another's life to save his own. In this case the weakest, the youngest, the most unresisting, was chosen. Was it more necessary to kill him than one of the grown men? The answer must be "No," [in the words of Milton in *Paradise Lost*]—

So spake the Fiend, and with necessity The Tyrant's
plea, excused his devilish deeds.

It is not suggested that in this particular case the deeds were "devilish," but it is quite plain that such a principle once admitted might be made the legal cloak for unbridled passion and atrocious crime. There is no safe path for judges to tread but to ascertain the law to the best of their ability and to declare it according to their judgment; and if in any case the law appears to be too severe on individuals, to leave it to the Sovereign to exercise that prerogative of mercy which the Constitution has intrusted to the hands fittest to dispense it.

It must not be supposed that in refusing to admit temptation to be an excuse for crime it is forgotten how terrible the temptation was; how awful the suffering; how hard in such trials to keep the judgment straight and the conduct pure. We are often compelled to set up standards we cannot reach ourselves, and to lay down rules which we could not ourselves satisfy. But a man has no right to declare temptation to be an excuse, though he might have yielded to it, nor allow compassion for the criminal to change or weaken in any manner the legal definition of the crime. It is therefore our duty to declare that the prisoners' act in this case was willful murder, that the facts as stated in the verdict are no legal justification of the homicide; and to say that in our unanimous opinion the prisoners are upon this special verdict guilty of murder.

[The Court then proceeded to pass sentence of death upon the prisoners].

NOTES

1. *Maritime cannibalism.* How does a court decide what punishment to impose? Should it consider the customs of the time or public opinion? In fact, there was widespread acceptance of maritime cannibalism at the time of this case as explained in A.W. BRIAN SIMPSON, CANNIBALISM AND THE COMMON LAW: THE STORY OF THE TRAGIC LAST VOYAGE OF THE *MIGNONETTE* AND THE STRANGE LEGAL PROCEEDINGS TO WHICH IT GAVE RISE 95–145 (1984). One scholar summarized Simpson's findings as follows:

> [If] a sailing ship foundered, those it carried usually drowned. If they managed to take to the boats—assuming there were any boats— they frequently died of hunger and thirst instead. There were no radios to summon help, no helicopters for search missions, and the chances of rescue were remote. In these circumstances, the survivors were often reduced to eating the bodies of those who had died, and there are a number of well-authenticated instances of survivors actually killing one of their number in order to eat him.
>
> [Originally,] if sailors ate one another, nobody cared. For most of the days of sail, [they] inhabited a harsh and barbarous world of their

own[,] left [to] their own vices and devices. On the one hand, sailors were often hideously exploited, with unseaworthy ships, inadequate food, and wages often unpaid. If the ship sank, no one except the owner wanted to know why—and not even the owner if it was adequately insured. On the other hand, what sailors did to one another on the high seas was largely their own business. Except for piracy, nobody much troubled about crimes on the high seas. . . .

J.R. Spencer, *Book Review*, CANNIBALISM AND THE COMMON LAW, 51 U. CHI. L. REV. 1265, 1268 (1984). Public acceptance of cannibalism was so widespread that Dudley "frankly described the whole ordeal to his rescuers and, on arriving in England, to government officials. Clearly, Captain Dudley's attitude was that such things happen. . . ." Robert C. Berring, *Book Review*, CANNIBALISM AND THE COMMON LAW, 73 CALIF. L. REV. 252, 253 (1985). Public opinion was very much on the defendant's side:

> So long and entrenched was the tradition of cannibalism on the seas that public sympathy in the sailing ports was unquestionably behind Dudley and Stephens. Even the consumed Mr. Parker's older brother sought out the defendants in jail to shake their hands in a symbolic gesture of understanding. The only point that troubled the public mind was the failure to cast lots to determine the victim. The use of this impartial system instead of Dudley's more practical criterion of health would have even further legitimized the enterprise. Even so, opinion much favored Dudley and Stephens.

Id. at 256–57. Should the public's acceptance of cannibalism, and the public's opinion of the case, have any bearing on the result?

2. *Choosing Parker.* Should it matter how Parker was chosen as the victim? Consider the view of John Friedl, *Book Review*, A.W. BRIAN SIMPSON, CANNIBALISM AND THE COMMON LAW: THE STORY OF THE TRAGIC LAST VOYAGE OF THE MIGNONETTE AND THE STRANGE LEGAL PROCEEDINGS TO WHICH IT GAVE RISE, 83 MICH. L. REV. 702, 704 (1985):

> Yet another aspect of the case, one upon which legal proceedings might have turned (but in the end did not), was the selection of Parker as the victim. It was Captain Dudley who killed young Parker, although surely he would have died soon on his own. The point of killing him before he died a natural death was to save as much blood as possible to drink. But why Parker and not one of the others? Indeed, it was later argued by some that this "social Darwinist" approach was the ultimate immoral act, and that had the four chosen a victim by drawing straws or by some other random method it would have constituted a more "civilized" approach that the courts would have sanctioned. Although Dudley had earlier suggested that lots be drawn, this was never carried out. [Simpson] argues convincingly that the decision to kill Parker was a rational one, based not only on his physical condition and the belief that he would die no matter what, but also on the important consideration that Parker was a seventeen-year-old orphan, whereas Dudley and

Stephens were both family men whose death would condemn their wives and children to a lifetime of destitution. Brooks was apparently a bachelor, although the evidence is unclear on that point.

3. *Death sentence*. Was the death sentence appropriate for Dudley and Stephens? If not, what punishment should the defendants have received? The death sentence was later commuted to six months in prison. As Simpson explains, "it had been assumed throughout that [the defendants] would promptly be pardoned," and they "expected to be released immediately." The Home Secretary initially planned to advise the Queen to commute the sentence to life imprisonment because "[a]ny further leniency would make a mockery of the judges' ruling." But he was persuaded to recommend the six months sentence by legal advisors who argued that the defendants' minds must have been unbalanced. The reaction of the press generally was to welcome "both the theoretical decision of the judges and the practical solution" of the commutation. See Simpson, supra note 1, at 240–41, 244, 246, 250. Stephens and Brooks remained in England where they died poor. Dudley emigrated to Sydney, Australia where he died of the plague in 1900. *Id.* at 288–89, 296–98.

4. *Passengers sacrificed*. In the American case mentioned in *Dudley & Stephens*, *United States v. Holmes*, 26 F.Cas. 360 (C.C.E.D.Pa. 1842), a ship struck an iceberg off Newfoundland and immediately foundered: "The captain, the second mate, 7 of the crew, and 1 passenger got into the jolly-boat. The first mate, 8 seamen, of whom the prisoner was one (these 9 being the entire remainder of the crew), and 32 passengers, in all 41 persons, got indiscriminately into the long-boat." The remaining 31 passengers were left behind to drown. When the long-boat began to leak, the crew decided to throw 16 passengers overboard. The court reasoned that:

> [The] passenger stands in a position different from that of the officers and seamen. It is the sailor who must encounter the hardships and perils of the voyage. Nor can this relation be changed when the ship is lost by tempest or other danger of the sea, and all on board have betaken themselves, for safety, to the small boats; for imminence of danger can not absolve from duty. The sailor is bound, as before, to undergo whatever hazard is necessary to preserve the boat and the passengers. Should the emergency become so extreme as to call for the sacrifice of life, there can be no reason why the law does not still remain the same. The passenger, not being bound either to labour or to incur the risk of life, cannot be bound to sacrifice his existence to preserve the sailor's. . . .

> [I]f the source of the danger have been obvious, and destruction ascertained to be certainly about to arrive, though at a future time, there should be consultation, and some mode of selection fixed, by which those in equal relations may have equal chance for their life. [When] the selection has been made by lots, the victim yields of course to his fate, or, if he resist, force may be employed to coerce submission. . . .

The defendant was convicted of manslaughter on the high seas and sentenced to six months imprisonment at hard labour and a fine of $20. The *Holmes* Court affirmed the conviction, noting that: "Considerable sympathy having been excited in favour of Holmes, by the popular press, an effort was made by several persons, and particularly by the Seamen's Friend Society, to obtain a pardon from the executive. President Tyler refused, however, to grant any pardon, in consequence of the court's not uniting in the application. The penalty was subsequently remitted."

B. PURPOSES OF THE CRIMINAL LAW

NOTES

1. *The role of social condemnation.* Is "social condemnation" an essential aspect of the criminal law? According to Henry M. Hart, Jr., *The Aims of the Criminal Law*, 23 LAW & CONTEMPORARY PROBLEMS 401, 405 (1958):

> [A crime] is conduct which, if duly shown to have taken place, will incur a formal and solemn pronouncement of the moral condemnation of the community. [The] method of the criminal law, of course, involves something more than the threat (and, on due occasion, the expression) of community condemnation of antisocial conduct. It involves, in addition, the threat (and, on due occasion, the imposition) of unpleasant physical consequences, commonly called punishment. But [these] added consequences take their character as punishment from the condemnation which precedes them and serves as the warrant for their infliction. Indeed, the condemnation plus the added consequences may well be considered, compendiously, as constituting the punishment. . . .

Support for Hart's perspective appears in Louis Michael Seidman, *Soldiers, Martyrs, and Criminals: Utilitarian Theory and the Problem of Crime Control*, 94 YALE L.J. 315, 337–38 (1984):

> [B]lame not only makes the threat of other punishment credible, but also provides a kind of deterrence that other punishment cannot achieve. [If there were] any other penalty, no matter how high, a potential criminal who valued the criminal conduct enough might always be willing to pay the price. Since, by hypothesis, society would not blame such a person, it would in effect endorse the crime on efficiency grounds. [But] moral condemnation is a unique sanction because it inflicts suffering on individuals even when the conduct is otherwise efficient. Indeed, the condemnation is moral in character precisely because we are blaming an individual for preferring pleasure to pain in a situation where he should be obeying a categorical imperative. . . .

But, why are blame and moral condemnation really appropriate? Consider Professor Seidman's additional comments:

> [Our] political institutions simply distribute the cost of crime in a manner that reflects the preferences and power of competing groups.

We then utilize the rhetoric of blameworthiness to cover our moral confusion about the justification for this distribution.

[T]he clash between cost distribution and cost minimization goals creates the potential for a second kind of inefficiency that may be more serious in the long run. This difficulty stems from the debasement of the rhetoric of blame that occurs when it is used to justify distributional outcomes. As argued above, there is no necessary contradiction between the good consequences that flow from blaming and our awareness of these consequences. But it is less clear that blaming would remain a useful tool for reducing the total social cost of crime if moral condemnation were seen merely as a method of identifying losers in a distributional struggle....

[Those] punished must also believe the rhetoric of blame and accept the legitimacy of their punishment. The system begins to unravel if deviant subgroups believe that this rhetoric serves a cost-distribution function.

If this belief ever became widespread, we might become caught in a downward cycle of violence. Because criminals would then reject the moral legitimacy of the criminal sanction, they would view themselves as soldiers who bear the risk of punishment as an occupational hazard. Worse yet, when the risk became a reality, they and their peers would perceive themselves as martyrs fighting an unjust social order.

Id. at 346–47.

2. *Is retribution a justifiable objective?* Consider the view of Herbert Wechsler, *The Challenge of a Model Penal Code*, 65 HARVARD LAW REVIEW 1097, 1105 (1952):

Civilized social thought regards the penal law as the ultimate weapon for diminishing the incidence of major injuries to individuals and institutions, with only such concessions to retaliatory passions as are practically necessary for the system to survive. In short, while invocation of a penal sanction necessarily depends on past behavior, the object is control of harmful conduct in the future....

Compare the perspective of Joshua Dressler, *Hating Criminals: How Can Something that Feels so Good be Wrong?*, 88 U. MICH. L. REV. 1448, 1448–49 (1990)[1]:

[In] moral discourse we value warm and soft emotions, such as compassion, mercy, and forgiveness. We are critical of cold, hard feelings, such as resentment, revenge, and hatred.

How then do we explain the harsh emotions expressed daily by presumably decent people? How can we account for college students standing outside a prison late at night cheering the execution of a murderer; New Yorkers greeting [a notorious] hotel owner [with] jeers

---

1. Copyright, University of Michigan. Reprinted by permission of the Michigan Law Review and Professor Joshua Dressler.

and taunts as she leaves the courthouse where she has received an unusually stiff prison sentence for tax fraud; a rabbi admitting that he cannot let go of his anger toward a genuinely repentant young man who desecrated a synagogue by painting a swastika on it; and a sign defacer calling on women to be a little less gentle and a lot more angry in response to their collective victimization?

Perhaps these cases tell us only the obvious: that "good" people sometimes have "bad" emotions. But perhaps there is more to it than this. If these emotions are bad, why do they often feel good when we experience them, and why does holding on to them often seem right? Could it be that, in fact, hatred is not as bad as we say it is, and that forgiveness and mercy are not so good?

Jeffrie Murphy's thesis is that "[r]esentment (perhaps even some hatred) is a good thing", that forgiveness of wrongdoers is overvalued in our culture, and that there is little room for mercy in the sentencing of wrongdoers (or, as Murphy bluntly suggests: those involved in sentencing and punishing offenders should "keep their sentimentality to themselves for use in their private lives with their families and pets")....

3. *Should punishment be abolished in favor of treatment of offenders?* Consider the arguments of Henry M. Hart, Jr., *The Aims of the Criminal Law*, 23 LAW & CONTEMPORARY PROBLEMS 401, 406–08 (1958):

[Perhaps] the leading alternative [to criminalization], to judge from contemporary criticism of the penal law, would be to provide that people who behave badly should simply be treated as sick people to be cured, rather than as bad people to be condemned and punished....

[Professors] Hall and Glueck [point out that]:

It is the opinion of many of those who have studied both the causes of crime and the results of its treatment by means of the death penalty and the usual forms of incarceration, that for the vast majority of the general rule of delinquents and criminals, the corrective theory, based upon a conception of multiple causation and curative-rehabilitative treatment, should clearly predominate in legislation and in judicial and administrative practices. No other single theory is as closely related to the actual conditions and mechanisms of crime causation; no other gives as much promise of returning the offender to society not with the negative vacuum of punishment-induced fear but with the affirmative and constructive equipment—physical, mental and morality—for law-abidingness. Thus, in the long run, no other theory and practice gives greater promise of protecting society....

Precisely because of the difficulties of relating the content of the law's commands to the need for reformation of those who violate them, a curative rehabilitative theory of criminal justice tends always to depreciate, if not to deny, the significance of these general formulations and to focus attention instead on the individual defendant at the time of his apprehension, trial, and sentence. This has in it always a double danger—to the individual and to society. The danger to the individual is that he will be punished, or treated, for what he is or is believed to be, rather than for what he has done. If his offense is minor but the possibility of his reformation is thought to be slight, the other side of the coin of mercy can become cruelty. The danger to society is that the effectiveness of the general commands of the criminal law as instruments for influencing behavior so as to avoid the necessity for enforcement proceedings will be weakened.

This brings us to the crux of the issue confronting [us]. [W]ill the public interest be adequately protected if the legislature is allowed only to say to people, "If you do not comply with any of these commands, you will merely be considered to be sick and subjected to officially-imposed rehabilitative treatment in an effort to cure you"? Can it be adequately protected if the legislature is required to say, "If you do not comply, your own personal need for cure and rehabilitation will be the predominating factor in determining what happens to you"? Or should the legislature be enabled to say, "If you violate any of these laws and the violation is culpable, your conduct will receive the formal and solemn condemnation of the community as morally blameworthy, and you will be subjected to whatever punishment, or treatment, is appropriate to vindicate the law and to further its various purposes"?

most pragmatic.

On the sheerly pragmatic ground of the need for equipping the proposed social order with adequate tools to discourage undesired conduct, a responsible [policy]-maker assuredly would hesitate long before rejecting the third of these possibilities in favor of either of the first two. . . .

4. *Should deterrence govern the criminal law?* Consider the critique of Henry M. Hart, Jr., *The Aims of the Criminal Law*, 23 LAW & CONTEMPORARY PROBLEMS 401, 409–10 (1958):

... Deterrence, it is ventured, ought not to be thought of as the overriding and ultimate purpose of the criminal law, important though it is. For deterrence is negative, whereas the purposes of law are positive. And the practical fact must be faced that many crimes, as just recognized, are undeterrable. The grim negativism and the frequent seeming futility of the criminal law when it is considered simply as a means of preventing undesired behavior no doubt help to explain why sensitive people, working at close hand with criminals, tend so often to embrace the more hopeful and positive tenets of a curative-rehabilitative philosophy.

Would it have been possible to deter Dudley and Stephens? Consider the following comments penned by Dudley in prison:

I can assure you I shall never forget the sight of my two unfortunate companions over that gastly [sic] meal we all was like mad wolfs who should get the most and for men fathers of children to commit such a deed we could not have our right reason.

Book Review, CANNIBALISM AND THE COMMON LAW, 98 HARV. L. REV. 1100, 1101 (1985). Is it possible to deter individuals in such circumstances?

Consider Professor Hart's additional comments as they relate to *Dudley & Stephens*:

> [The] criminal law has an obviously significant, and indeed, a fundamental role to play in creating the good society. For it is the criminal law which defines the minimum conditions of [our] responsibility to [others] and holds [us] to that responsibility. The assertion of social responsibility has value in the treatment even of those who become criminals. It has far greater value as a stimulus to the [vast majority] to abide by the law and to take pride in so abiding.

5. *Should the criminal law be based on economics?* In the view of Richard A. Posner, *An Economic Theory of the Criminal Law*, 85 COLUM. L. REV. 1193, 1194, 1196, 1201–05, 1212–13 (1985):

> [T]he substantive doctrines of the criminal law, as of the common law in general, can be given an economic meaning and can indeed be shown to promote efficiency....
>
> When transaction costs are low, the market is, virtually by definition, the most efficient method of allocating resources. Attempts to bypass the market will therefore be discouraged by a legal system bent on promoting efficiency. If I covet my neighbor's car, it is more efficient to force me to negotiate with my neighbor—to pay him his price—than it is to allow me to take his car subject to being required by a court to pay the neighbor whatever the court decides the car is worth. If I happen to have no money but want a car, it would be inefficient to let me just take a car. Indeed, [this] transfer cannot possibly improve the allocation of resources—that is, it cannot move resources from a less to a more valuable employment—because value is a function of willingness to pay. Since I am unwilling (because unable—but it does not matter why) to pay my neighbor's price for the car, it follows that the car would be less valuable in an economic sense in my hands than in his. Moreover, if I am allowed to take the car I will have an incentive to expend resources on taking it and my neighbor will have an incentive to expend resources on preventing it from being taken, and these expenditures considered as a whole, yield no social product. [In] short, it is inefficient to allow pure coercive transfers of wealth—"pure" implying that the transfer is not an incident of a productive act....
>
> Although the major criminal prohibitions seem explicable as measures for discouraging inefficient behavior rather than for achieving moral objectives that economics may not be able to explain—the major exception being the prohibition of victimless crimes—this does not explain why there is a criminal law, given that there is a law of torts and that it predates criminal law....

[The] proper sanction for a pure coercive transfer is something greater than the law's estimate of the victim's loss—the extra something being designed to confine transfers to the market whenever market-transaction costs are not prohibitive. We can be a little more precise: the extra something should be the difference between the victim's loss and the offender's gain, and then some. To understand this, assume first that the gain is greater than the loss: B has a jewel worth $1000 to him, but worth $10,000 to A, who steals it ("converts" it, in tort parlance). We want to channel transactions in jewelry into the market, and this requires that the coerced transfer be a losing proposition to A. If A is risk neutral, if the probability of B's getting and collecting a judgment against A is one (an important assumption, to be relaxed shortly), and if legal proceedings are costless, then making A liable for damages of only $1000 will not do the trick, and even making him pay $10,000 (restitution) will not quite do it, but will just make him indifferent between stealing and buying. We shall have to add something on, and make the damages, say, $11,000.

[With] regard to crimes of violence, such as murder, battery, and rape, which inflict nonpecuniary as well as or instead of pecuniary loss, it is not so easy to set a money value on the victim's loss, although tort law does of course make such estimates. Quite properly, they often are very high. For a crime that creates a substantial probability of death, the optimal damages may in fact be astronomical. This is clearest in the case where one person deliberately kills another. If the average person (someone not extraordinarily altruistic toward his heirs) were asked how much money he would demand to surrender his life on the spot, his answer would be that no finite offer would be high enough, since he would get no utility out of the money. For similar reasons, the average person would demand a very high price to incur a substantial risk of death even though he might demand only a small premium to take a small risk of death. This nonlinearity suggests why tort law may be adequate for many small risks of death (for example, the risk of being killed in an automobile accident caused by negligence), but not for the large risks that are created by crimes of violence.

[In] cases where tort remedies, including punitive damages, are an adequate deterrent because they do not strain the potential defendant's ability to pay, there is no need to invoke criminal penalties—penalties which [are] costlier than civil penalties even when just a fine is imposed. In such cases, the misconduct probably will be deterred. If in a particular case it is not, even though the tort remedy is set at the correct level and there is no solvency problem to interfere with it, so that the tort remedy must actually be applied to maintain the credibility of the tort deterrent, there still is no social gain from using a criminal sanction. Although in some [cases,] affluent defendants are both prosecuted criminally and sued civilly, criminal sanctions generally are reserved, as theory predicts, for cases where the tort remedy bumps up against a solvency limitation.

This means that the criminal law is designed primarily for the nonaffluent; the affluent are kept in line, for the most part, by tort law. This may seem to be a left-wing kind of suggestion ("criminal law keeps the lid on the lower classes"), but it is not. It is efficient to use different sanctions depending on an offender's wealth. The suggestion is not refuted by the fact that fines are a common criminal penalty. They are much lower than the corresponding tort damage judgments, and hence usable even against relatively nonaffluent offenders, for two reasons. The government invests resources in raising the probability of criminal punishment above that of a tort suit, which makes the optimal fine lower than the punitive damages that would be optimal in the absence of such an investment. Second, a fine is a more severe punishment than its dollar cost. Almost every criminal punishment imposes some nonpecuniary disutility in the form of a stigma, enhanced by such rules as forbidding a convicted criminal to vote. There is no corresponding stigma to a tort judgment.

stigma

[If] society must continue to rely heavily on imprisonment as a criminal sanction, there is an argument—subject to caveats that should be familiar to the reader by now, based on risk aversion, overinclusion, avoidance and error costs, and (less clearly) marginal deterrence—for combining heavy prison terms for convicted criminals with low probabilities of apprehension and conviction. . . .

A contrasting view is provided by Louis Michael Seidman, *Soldiers, Martyrs, and Criminals: Utilitarian Theory and the Problem of Crime Control*, 94 YALE L.J. 315, 315–17, 323, 325–26, 329 (1984):

The law and economics literature on criminal law is laced with statements like the following: "Presumably, we could have as little crime as we wanted if we were willing to spend enough on police, court, jails and so on to make probabilities of arrest very, very high for most crimes." But one might fairly ask, if we could, why don't we?

Of course, a utilitarian utopia would not be crime-free. A central tenet of the utilitarian theory of crime control is that resources should be devoted to crime prevention only up to the point at which the marginal cost of prevention equals the marginal cost of the crime prevented. Victims of criminal violence would remain, but these victims could take solace from the knowledge that their victimization was "efficient"—that, in other words, society as a whole would be worse off if we had taken the measures necessary to prevent them from being mugged in dark alleys.

I suppose that utilitarians of a Panglossian bent are prepared to defend the view that the present level of crime is optimal in this sense. If it were not, the argument goes, we would incur the additional costs necessary to make it so. If one truly believes that we can have as little crime as we want, it follows that we want as much crime as we have.

This tautology provides an answer of sorts to our question. But it is an answer that ignores an obvious reality: Many Americans are dissatisfied with the level of crime and would gladly pay in the currency of harsher sentences for more peace in our streets. . . .

Utilitarians can escape the charge of irrelevance by [insisting] that they are advancing a prescriptive rather than a descriptive [theory]. On this view, the reason we have too much crime is quite simple: The people who formulate our crime control strategy are either not utilitarians or are inept at performing utilitarian calculations. . . .

The simplest utilitarian objection to a regime of exceedingly harsh punishments is that it is inefficient because it overdeters crime. . . .

[This] argument has some limited force. It must be remembered, however, that such overdeterrence would occur only in those instances where criminal and noncriminal conduct are closely allied and easily confused. For example, it is hard to imagine what socially useful activity would be deterred by extremely harsh sanctions for armed robbery. Moreover, while higher penalties may increase the importance of avoiding error, we could choose to invest the resources saved from fewer trials in more expensive but more accurate procedures.

Ironically, the more serious problem posed by very severe sanctions may be that they leave crime underdeterred. Optimal deterrence can be achieved only by maintaining a cost for more serious crimes higher than that for less serious ones. Thus, we would not want to make robbery punishable by death, since, if we did so, the robber might as well murder his victim. . . .

[It] is true that deterrence requires maintenance of higher levels of punishment for more serious crimes. But so long as the marginal effectiveness of punishment remains constant, no inefficiency would result from the upward adjustment of all penalty levels. The argument therefore fails to explain why we do not simply shift our entire penalty structure upward while maintaining the marginal differences between crimes. . . .

[This] analysis, however, raises an additional question. Assuming punishment ought to be limited to those who are blameworthy, whom should we blame? [A] utilitarian's answer to this question is relatively straightforward: We should blame individuals when doing so will maximize utility—*i.e.*, when the suffering imposed upon those who are blamed is counterbalanced by the social benefit resulting from the change in behavior.

But it is here that utilitarian theory begins to contradict itself. As argued above, blaming is a unique sanction in that it is conferred on moral rather than consequentialist grounds. Thus, an awareness that blame is being distributed in order to maximize utility seems bound to undercut the deterrent effect that justifies the distribution.

By itself, this objection need not be fatal to the theory. In the first place, it may well be possible through acoustic separation to conceal the utilitarian justification for blame. As long as criminals continue to believe that condemnation is deserved, it will retain the deterrent efficacy that justifies it.

6. *Conflicting purposes.* Consider the insight of Paul H. Robinson, *Hybrid Principles for the Distribution of Criminal Sanctions*, 82 NORTHWESTERN U. L. REV. 19 (1988)*:

> Most criminal codes, and most criminal law courses, begin with the "familiar litany" of the purposes of criminal law sanctions—just punishment, deterrence, incapacitation of the dangerous, and rehabilitation. [The] purposes frequently [conflict]. [Ultimately] a choice must be made to follow one purpose at the expense of another. Yet when faced with conflicting purposes, judges, legislators, and sentencing-guideline drafters have no principle to guide that decision.

7. *M.P.C. statement of objectives.* What objectives are we trying to achieve with the criminal law? According to the MODEL PENAL CODE § 1.02, Explanatory Note, at 14 (1980):

> [The] major goal [of the criminal law] is to forbid and prevent conduct that threatens substantial harm to individual or public interests and that at the same time is both unjustifiable and inexcusable. Subsidiary themes are to subject those who are disposed to commit crimes to public control, to prevent the condemnation of conduct that is without fault, to give fair warning of the conduct declared to be criminal, and to differentiate between serious and minor offenses on reasonable grounds. [Subsidiary] goals [are] to promote the correction and rehabilitation of offenders, within a scheme that safeguards them against excessive, disproportionate or arbitrary punishment, to give fair warning of the possible dispositions for criminal offenses, and to differentiate among offenders with a view to just individualization of treatment. . . .

PROBLEM

Punishment for Various Types of Killings. Given the purposes of the criminal law, should different "killings" be treated differently for purposes of punishment? More to the point, might the principal justifications for punishment (retribution, restraint, rehabilitation, general deterrence and special deterrence) justify different sentences based on factual differences? What punishment should be imposed on the following defendants who kill:

a. *Torture Murder.* Defendant brutally tortures and murders an elderly woman during a robbery and rape. In killing her, he is motivated by a desire to eliminate a potential witness to his crimes.

b. *Driving Accident.* Defendant is driving down a residential street at the speed limit, when a little boy unexpectedly darts out in front of

---

* Copyright, Professor Paul Robinson. Reprinted by permission.

her. Although defendant makes a valiant effort to stop her car, she is unable do so and kills the boy.

c. *Speeding Car.* In the prior problem, would you treat defendant differently for purposes of punishment if she were proceeding at a speed that was 25 mph over the speed limit? 35 mph? 50 mph?

d. *Discovery of Adultery.* Defendant comes home early from work to find his wife in bed with another man. In a fit of rage, defendant kills the other man.

e. *Assisted Suicide.* Defendant's husband is suffering from a severe, painful, debilitating fatal disease. Day after day, the husband begs the wife to help him end his life and thereby end his suffering. The wife repeatedly refuses. Finally, unable to deal with her husband's desperate plight, she administers poison to him with his consent, and he dies.

f. *Killing Children.* Defendant drowns her infant daughter and 4-year-old son in the ocean after she learns that her husband has a mistress. She attempts to drown herself, too, but she survives. Defendant is an immigrant from Japan who has lived in the United States for 15 years; she has no malicious intent, but wants only to save her children the shame their father's infidelity has brought on the family. There is an ancient practice in Japan of a parent committing suicide with her children in such circumstances (*oyaku shinju*). *See People v. Fumiko Kimura*, No. A–091133 (Cal. Super. Ct. L.A. County Nov. 21, 1985).

g. *Hot Car Manslaughter.* On a hot day in mid-summer, a father is supposed to take his infant child to day care on the way to work. The father forgets about the child and leaves the child buckled into his car seat. Since no one happens to notice, the baby dies of suffocation. The father, who truly loved the child (despite an appalling level of absent-mindedness), is devastated by the child's death and falls into a deep depression. The mother, unable to forgive the father, divorces him. Suppose that you are the prosecutor and you must decide how to handle the case. Of course, the father can be prosecuted for negligent homicide. Is such a criminal prosecution appropriate? If so, what purpose(s) would it serve? If you decide to prosecute, what punishment would you seek?

h. *Dudley and Stephens.* Finally, after deciding what should happen to all these defendants, reconsider the facts in *Regina v. Dudley & Stephens*. What punishment did the defendants deserve?

EXERCISE

Under Duress. The defendant is charged with illegally selling narcotics. The facts reveal that she was not regularly engaged in the sale of narcotics. However, earlier this year, she borrowed money from a loan shark at an exorbitant interest rate. When she was unable to repay the money, the loan shark ordered her to "handle" a narcotic transaction for him. With a gun lying on his lap, the loan shark threatened to harm the defendant and her family. Because of this threat, the defendant agreed to "handle" the transaction. Unfortunately for her, the police "got wind" of the transaction and arrested her. Given the purposes of the criminal law, does it make sense to punish the defendant?

CHAPTER 2

THE REQUIREMENT OF A "VOLUNTARY ACT"

∎ ∎ ∎

An essential element of just punishment is the requirement of a voluntary "act" or "omission." If the alleged act was involuntary, there may be not any justification for imposing punishment. For example, if "one person physically forces another person into bodily movement, as where A by force causes B's body to strike C; under these circumstances, there is no voluntary act by B."[1]

A.   THE ACT REQUIREMENT

MARTIN v. STATE

17 So.2d 427 (Ala.App. 1944).

SIMPSON, JUDGE.

Procedure

Appellant was convicted of being drunk on a public highway, and appeals. Officers of the law arrested him at his home and took him onto the highway, where he allegedly committed the proscribed acts, viz., manifested a drunken condition by using loud and profane language.

statute

The pertinent provisions of our statute are: "Any person who, while intoxicated or drunk, appears in any public place where one or more persons are present, [and] manifests a drunken condition by boisterous or indecent conduct, or loud and profane discourse, shall, on conviction, be fined."

Under the plain terms of this statute, a voluntary appearance is presupposed. The rule has been declared, and we think it sound, that an accusation of drunkenness in a designated public place cannot be established by proof that the accused, while in an intoxicated condition, was involuntarily and forcibly carried to that place by the arresting officer.

Conviction of appellant was contrary to this announced principle and, in our view, erroneous. It appears that no legal conviction can be

---

1.   WAYNE R. LAFAVE, CRIMINAL LAW § 6.1(c) (4th Ed. 2006).

sustained under the evidence, [so] the judgment of the trial court is reversed and one here rendered discharging appellant.

Reversed and rendered.

NOTES

1. *M.P.C. and voluntary acts.* In the Explanatory Note to § 2.01, the Model Penal Code provides: "[T]he law cannot hope to deter involuntary movement or to stimulate action that cannot physically be performed; the sense of personal security would be undermined in a society where such movement or inactivity could lead to formal social condemnation of the sort that a conviction necessarily entails." The M.P.C. codifies these ideas as follows:

> **Section 2.01. Requirement of Voluntary Act; Omission as Basis of Liability; Possession as an Act.**
>
> (1) A person is not guilty of an offense unless his liability is based on conduct that includes a voluntary act or the omission to perform an act of which he is physically capable.
>
> (2) The following are not voluntary acts within the meaning of this Section:
>
> > (a) a reflex or convulsion;
> >
> > (b) a bodily movement during unconsciousness or sleep;
> >
> > (c) conduct during hypnosis or resulting from hypnotic suggestion;
> >
> > (d) a bodily movement that otherwise is not a product of the effort or determination of the actor, either conscious or habitual.

2. *Being carried.* In *State v. Boleyn*, 328 So.2d 95 (La. 1976), a prisoner was subjected to rape. Afterwards, he voluntarily intoxicated himself with pills and beer. While in an unconscious and drugged condition, defendant was "carried away" from the prison by another prisoner. The court concluded that "evidence of the state of consciousness of defendant and of his intoxicated or drugged condition should have been submitted to the jury." Likewise, in *People v. Shaughnessy*, 66 Misc.2d 19, 319 N.Y.S.2d 626 (1971), defendant was found not guilty of violating an ordinance prohibiting entry upon private property. The state's evidence failed to show a voluntary act by the defendant who was merely a passenger in a trespassing car.

3. *Brake failure.* In *State v. Kremer*, 262 Minn. 190, 114 N.W.2d 88 (1962), the court held that a defendant could not be guilty of violating a city ordinance requiring all traffic to stop at a flashing red light when the evidence showed that his brakes failed with no prior warning. However, in *Kettering v. Greene*, 9 Ohio St.2d 26, 222 N.E.2d 638 (1966), the Ohio Supreme Court reached the opposite result, even though defendant had no prior warning of any defect in the brakes. The court concluded that the

statutory requirement to stop at a stop sign is mandatory and brake failure is not a legal excuse.

4. *Possession.* A voluntary act can include "possession" of an item. M.P.C. § 2.01(4) provides: "Possession is an act, within the meaning of this Section, if the possessor knowingly procured or received the thing possessed or was aware of his control thereof for a sufficient period to have been able to terminate his possession."

PROBLEMS

1. *Manifesting Drunken Condition.* Was *Martin* correctly decided? Although Martin was involuntarily placed in the street, did he commit the act of being loud and boisterous? Is that "act" sufficient for conviction under the relevant statute?

2. *Cruise Control Systems and Involuntariness.* In virtually every state, speeding is a strict liability offense which requires no mental state. It does require the "actus reus" of speeding. Suppose that a defendant is charged with travelling seventy-seven miles per hour in a fifty-five miles per hour zone. He testifies that he wanted to travel at the speed limit, and was trying to do so, but his cruise control stuck in the "accelerate" position, causing the car to exceed the posted speed limit. Defendant attempted to deactivate the cruise control by pushing the "off" and "coast" buttons, and by tapping the brakes. None of these actions was successful. Eventually, defendant switched the car's ignition to the "off" position and the car came to a stop. Subsequently, defendant had the defective cruise control repaired. Did defendant commit the actus reus of speeding? How would you argue this case for the defendant? How might the prosecutor respond? *See State v. Baker*, 1 Kan. App.2d 568, 571 P.2d 65 (1977).

FULCHER v. STATE

633 P.2d 142 (Wyo. 1981).

BROWN, JUSTICE.

[On] November 17, 1979, the appellant consumed seven or eight shots of whiskey over a period of four hours in a Torrington bar, and had previously had a drink at home.

Appellant claims he got in a fight in the bar restroom, then left the bar to find a friend. According to his testimony, the last thing he remembers until awakening in jail, is going out of the door at the bar.

Appellant and his friend were found lying in the alley behind the bar by a police officer who noted abrasions on their fists and faces. Appellant and his friend swore, were uncooperative, and combative. They were subsequently booked for public intoxication and disturbing the peace. During booking appellant continued to swear, and said he and his friend were jumped by a "bunch of Mexicans." Although his

possible consciousness

speech was slurred, he was able to verbally count his money, roughly $500 to $600 in increments of $20, and was able to walk to his cell without assistance.

Appellant was placed in a cell with one Martin Hernandez who was lying unconscious on the floor of the cell. After the jailer left the cell, he heard something that sounded like someone being kicked. He ran back to the cell and saw appellant standing by Hernandez. When the jailer started to leave again, the kicking sound resumed, and he observed appellant kicking and stomping on Hernandez's head. Appellant told the officer Hernandez had fallen out of bed. Hernandez was bleeding profusely and was taken to the hospital for some 52 stitches in his head and mouth. He had lost two or three teeth as a result of the kicking.

π not guilty

[Appellant] testified that [a] doctor diagnosed [him with] a concussion, although there is no evidence in the record of medical treatment. [A]ppellant [entered] a plea of not guilty.

Dr. testimony that π was in a state of traumatic automatism after suffering a brain injury.

In preparation for trial, appellant was examined by Dr. Breck LeBegue, a forensic psychiatrist. The doctor reviewed the police report and conducted a number of tests. [At] the trial Dr. LeBegue testified that in his expert medical opinion appellant suffered brain injury and was in a state of traumatic automatism at the time of his attack on Hernandez. Dr. LeBegue defined traumatic automatism as the state of mind in which a person does not have conscious and willful control over his actions, and lacks the ability to be aware of and to perceive his external environment. Dr. LeBegue further testified that another possible symptom is an inability to remember what occurred while in a state of traumatic automatism.

Dr. LeBegue was unable to state positively whether or not appellant had the requisite mental state for aggravated assault and battery, but thought appellant did not because of his altered state of mind. He could not state, however, that the character of an act is devoid of criminal intent because of mind alteration.

holding

[We] hold that the trial court properly received and considered evidence of unconsciousness absent a plea of "not guilty by reason of mental illness or deficiency."

automatism ≠ free will, intent, knowledge

The defense of unconsciousness perhaps should be more precisely denominated as the defense of automatism. Automatism is the state of a person who, though capable of action, is not conscious of what he is doing. While in an automatistic state, an individual performs complex actions without an exercise of will. Because these actions are performed in a state of unconsciousness, they are involuntary. Automatistic behavior may be followed by complete or partial inability to recall the actions performed while unconscious. Thus, a person who acts automatically does so without intent, exercise of free will, or knowledge of the act.

Automatism may be caused by an abnormal condition of the mind capable of being designated a mental illness or deficiency. Automatism may also be manifest in a person with a perfectly healthy mind. In this opinion we are only concerned with the defense of automatism occurring in a person with a healthy mind. To further narrow the issue to be decided in this case, we are concerned with alleged automatism caused by concussion.

The defense of automatism, while not an entirely new development in the criminal law, has been discussed in relatively few decisions by American appellate courts, most of these being in California where the defense is statutory. Some courts have held that insanity and automatism are separate and distinct defenses, and that evidence of automatism may be presented under a plea of not guilty. Some states have made this distinction by statute. In other states the distinction is made by case law.

> "A defense related to but different from the defense of insanity is that of unconsciousness, often referred to as automatism: one who engages in what would otherwise be criminal conduct is not guilty of a crime if he does so in a state of unconsciousness or [semi-consciousness]." LaFave & Scott, Criminal Law, § 44, p. 337 (1972).

> "The defenses of insanity and unconsciousness are not the same in nature, for unconsciousness at the time of the alleged criminal act need not be the result of a disease or defect of the mind. As a consequence, the two defenses are not the same in effect, for a defendant found not guilty by reason of unconsciousness, as distinct from insanity, is not subject to commitment to a hospital for the mentally ill." State v. Caddell, 287 N.C. 266, 215 S.E.2d 348, 360 (1975).

The principal reason for making a distinction between the defense of unconsciousness and insanity is that the consequences which follow an acquittal, will differ. The defense of unconsciousness is usually a complete defense. That is, there are no follow-up consequences after an acquittal; all action against a defendant is concluded. [I]n the case of a finding of not guilty by reason of insanity, the defendant is ordinarily committed to a mental institution.

[The] mental illness or deficiency plea does not adequately cover automatic behavior. Unless the plea of automatism, separate and apart from the plea of mental illness or deficiency is allowed, certain anomalies will result. For example, if the court determines that the automatistic defendant is sane, but refuses to recognize automatism, the defendant has no defense to the crime with which he is charged. If found guilty, he faces a prison term. The rehabilitative value of imprisonment for the automatistic offender who has committed the offense unconsciously is nonexistent. The cause of the act was an uncontrollable physical disorder that may never recur and is not a moral deficiency.

If, however, the court treats automatism as insanity and then determines that the defendant is insane, he will be found not guilty. He then will be committed to a mental institution for an indefinite period. The commitment of an automatistic individual to a mental institution for rehabilitation has absolutely no value. Mental hospitals generally treat people with psychiatric or psychological problems. This form of treatment is not suited to unconscious behavior resulting from a bump on the head.

It may be argued that evidence of unconsciousness cannot be received unless a plea of not guilty by reason of mental illness or deficiency is made pursuant to Rule 15, W.R.Cr.P [Wyoming Rules of Criminal Procedure]. We believe this approach to be illogical.

It does not seem that the definition of "mental deficiency" in § 7–11–301(a)(iii), which includes "brain damage," encompasses simple brain trauma with no permanent after effects. It is our view that the "brain damage" contemplated in the statute is some serious and irreversible condition having an impact upon the ability of the person to function. It is undoubtedly something far more significant than a temporary and transitory condition. The two defenses are merged, in effect, if a plea of "not guilty by reason of mental illness or deficiency" is a prerequisite for using the defense of unconsciousness.

The committee that drafted Wyoming Pattern Jury Instructions Criminal, apparently recognized mental illness or deficiency and unconsciousness as separate and distinct defenses. Admittedly the instructions in Wyo. P.J.I.Cr. are not authoritative, because they were not approved by the Wyoming Supreme Court, and this was a matter of design. Still they are the product of a distinguished group of legal scholars, including judges, attorneys and teachers of the law. The comment to this pattern jury instruction notes that it is limited to persons of sound mind, and the comment distinguishes persons suffering from "mental deficiency or illness." In this respect, it tracks the case law from other jurisdictions, which authorities hold that unconsciousness and insanity are completely separate grounds of exemption from criminal responsibility.

Although courts hold that unconsciousness and insanity are separate and distinct defenses, there has been some uncertainty concerning the burden of proof. We believe the better rule to be that stated in *State v. Caddell, supra*, at 363, 215 S.E.2d 348:

> "We now hold that, under the law of this state, unconsciousness, or automatism, is a complete defense to the criminal charge, separate and apart from the defense of insanity; that it is an affirmative defense; and that the burden rests upon the defen-

dant to establish this defense, unless it arises out of the State's own evidence, to the satisfaction of the jury."

The rationale for this rule is that the defendant is the only person who knows his actual state of consciousness.

Our ruling on the facts of this case is that the defense of unconsciousness resulting from a concussion with no permanent brain damage is an affirmative defense and is a defense separate from the defense of not guilty by reason of mental illness or deficiency.

The appellant's conviction must, nevertheless, be affirmed. Dr. LeBegue was unable to state positively whether or not appellant had the requisite mental state for aggravated assault. He could not state that the character of the act was devoid of criminal intent because of the mind alteration. The presumption of mental competency was never overcome by appellant and the evidence presented formed a reasonable basis on which the trial judge could find and did find that the State had met the required burden of proof.

[handwritten margin note: Dr testimony inconclusive]

Further, the trial judge was not bound to follow Dr. LeBegue's opinion. The trier of the facts is not bound to accept expert opinion evidence in the face of other substantial and credible evidence to the contrary. There was an abundance of other credible evidence that appellant was not unconscious at the time of the assault and battery for which he was convicted.

Affirmed.

RAPER, JUSTICE, specially concurring, with whom ROONEY, JUSTICE, joins.

[I] am not concerned with the fact that unconsciousness may be a defense in the case but am distressed that the procedure for taking advantage of it has been cast aside. . . .

[handwritten margin note: procedure concern]

[The] term "deficiency" means "defect." Defect means the want or absence of something necessary for completion, perfection, or adequacy in form or function. Webster. It is this shortcoming in appellant's mind that brought him within the sweep of § 7–11–304(a) . . . [which requires] commitment for examination [and a] plea of "not guilty by reason of mental illness or deficiency." [When a] defendant claims automatism, society and the State [should not] be deprived of [the] preliminary psychiatric examination [that] is a good [way] to wash out the phony claims of mental . . . deficiency and identify the legitimate as well.

[Wyoming] did not adopt that part of the ALI Model Penal Code which would consider automatism as a separate defense [in Section 2.01]:

"(1) A person is not guilty of an offense unless his liability is based on conduct which includes a voluntary act or the omission to perform an act of which he is physically capable."

Wyoming adopted language which embraced the alternative suggested in the comments to § 2.01, *supra*:

> Any definition must exclude a reflex or convulsion. The case of unconsciousness is equally clear when unconsciousness implies collapse or coma, as perhaps it does in ordinary usage of the term. There are, however, states of physical activity where self-awareness is grossly impaired or even absent, as in epileptic fugue, amnesia, extreme confusion and equivalent conditions. How far these active states of automatism should be assimilated to coma for this legal purpose presents a difficult issue. There is judicial authority supporting the assimilation. An alternative approach, however, is to view these cases as appropriate for exculpation on the ground of mental disease or defect excluding responsibility. This view has also had support in the decisions. It offers the advantage that it may facilitate commitment when the individual is dangerous to the community because the condition is recurrent. By the same token, however, it bears more harshly on the individual whose condition is non-recurrent, as in the case where an extraordinary reaction follows the administration of a therapeutic drug. And there may be a difficulty in regarding some of these conditions as " 'mental disease or defect,' within the meaning of section 4.01 of the draft or as 'insanity' under prevailing law, although cognition is sufficiently impaired to satisfy that aspect of the test."

The Wyoming legislature clearly defined "mental deficiency" to unquestionably include appellant's alleged condition (brain damage). . . .

NOTES

1. *Traumatic amnesia.* In accord with the *Fulcher* majority is *People v. Cox*, 67 Cal.App.2d 166, 153 P.2d 362 (1944), in which defendant was charged with homicide. He claimed that he was hit over the head with a bottle and was unconscious when he committed the homicide. The evidence showed that he suffered from traumatic amnesia. The court held:

> [Medical] testimony was introduced showing that defendant had four cuts on his forehead, evidence of bleeding from the right ear, and superficial bruises on his abdomen; that it seemed as though defendant had a brain injury and an opinion was expressed that defendant had a loss of memory or traumatic amnesia caused by a blow on the head, and that defendant, at the time of trial, was still suffering therefrom. . . .

> [It] must be said here as it was said in *People v. Sameniego, supra*, 118 Cal.App. at page 173, 4 P.2d at page 812: "Where there is evidence of the existence of that state of the mind wherein the individual's conscious mind has ceased to operate and his actions are controlled by the

subconscious or subjective mind, it would be error to refuse instructions as to the legal effect of such unconsciousness. . . ."

See also State v. Mercer, 275 N.C. 108, 165 S.E.2d 328 (1969).

2. *Reflex shock reaction.* Also in accord with *Fulcher* is *People v. Newton*, 8 Cal.App.3d 359, 87 Cal.Rptr. 394 (1970), in which defendant was shot by a police officer. Afterwards, defendant shot and killed the officer. Defendant claimed that he was unconscious during the killing. Defense witnesses testified that "defendant's recollections were 'compatible' with the gunshot wound he had received; and that '[a] gunshot wound which penetrates in a body cavity, the abdominal cavity or the thoracic cavity is very likely to produce a profound reflex shock reaction, that is quite different than a gunshot wound which penetrates only skin and muscle and it is not at all uncommon for a person shot in the abdomen to lose consciousness and go into this reflex shock condition for short periods of time up to half an hour or so.' " The court concluded that defendant was entitled to an instruction on unconsciousness.

PROBLEMS

1. *The Sleeping Driver.* Defendant, a shuttle operator, was dispatched to pick up some passengers at the local airport. On the way to the airport, she became drowsy. She opened the windows for a breeze to combat this feeling, and drove on. At some point, she fell asleep, ran off the road, and killed a pedestrian. She is charged with involuntary manslaughter. When she killed the pedestrian, did she commit a voluntary act? *See State v. Olsen*, 108 Utah 377, 160 P.2d 427 (1945).

2. *Voluntariness and Epilepsy.* James Rambo is driving to work when he has an epileptic seizure which causes him to completely black out and lose control of his car. Rambo's car runs off the road, and he kills a pedestrian. In killing the pedestrian, has Rambo committed a voluntary act? Would it matter whether Rambo had suffered seizures in the past? If he had suffered several epileptic seizures a year for some years, how would the prosecutor argue that Rambo has committed a voluntary act? How might the defense counsel respond? *See People v. Decina*, 2 N.Y.2d 133, 138 N.E.2d 799, 157 N.Y.S.2d 558 (1956).

3. *Meeting the "Actus Reus" Requirement.* A police officer was driving along when he found a car stuck in a snow-filled ditch. The headlights were on, but the motor was off. Sandra Starfield was sitting in the driver's seat. From the odor of alcohol on her breath and her bloodshot eyes, the officer inferred that Starfield was intoxicated. She refused to submit to a blood alcohol test. While in the squad car, when asked if she was operating the car, she replied, "Nope," but did not elaborate. At the jail, the police found a set of car keys in her pocket. While being booked, Starfield stated that she was not driving the car; but was waiting in the car for her son (the driver) who had gone for help after the car went into the ditch. Defendant is charged under a statute making it a crime to "drive, operate, or be in physical control

of any motor vehicle [when] the person is under the influence of alcohol." Under the circumstances, was Starfield in "physical control" of the vehicle? If you are the prosecutor, what evidence would you use to establish "control?" If you are the defense counsel, how would you rebut this evidence? *See State v. Starfield*, 481 N.W.2d 834 (Minn. 1992); *Williams v. City of Petersburg*, 216 Va. 297, 217 S.E.2d 893 (1975); *State v. Bugger*, 25 Utah 2d 404, 483 P.2d 442 (1971).

4.   *Hypnosis and Mind Control*. Defendant is 18 years old, and she shot and almost killed two United States Marshals in an attempt to help her husband (Buster) escape from custody. The shooting occurred as the marshals brought Buster into the federal building for trial on a bank robbery charge. As they did so, the defendant drew a revolver from her purse, and stood there indecisively. When Buster yelled "shoot 'em', baby, shoot 'em'," defendant opened fire. After the shootings, defendant went out the door and stood on the steps of the courthouse, again indecisively. At that point Buster gave up the struggle and commanded defendant, "run, baby, run." Defendant fled down the street and was captured without a struggle a few minutes later. At defendant's trial, Buster testified in her defense and portrayed himself as a "Svengali" who had induced defendant to commit the offense under hypnosis. Buster had been hypnotizing defendant since she was 15 years old, and made her believe that he was her mother and father, and her Lord and God. He implanted in her mind a "memory" of his having held her immediately after her birth, and of his having rescued her from drowning when she was nine years old (a time before he met her). She claimed to have seen him be crucified, die, and rise again, and she believed he was her savior and redeemer. His claim was, that since defendant believed he was God, she was unable to distinguish right from wrong, since "if God tells you to do something, you think it's right." He had instructed her (during her visits to him while he was held prior to trial in the local jail) how to manage the escape in the manner described above. He had, he claimed, implanted in her mind the compulsion to meet him and the marshals each morning, as he was brought in for trial, to have a gun ready, and to respond to his commands as to when to use it.

    a.   If Buster's claims are true, did defendant commit a voluntary act when she fired on the officers?

    b.   If you are the prosecutor, what types of evidence would you use to rebut the defendant's claim of involuntariness?

    c.   How might the defense counsel respond to your arguments?

See United States v. Phillips, 515 F.Supp. 758 (E.D.Ky. 1981).

5.   *More on Hypnosis and Mind Control*. Defendant McCollum entered a bank, approached a bank employee, and handed him an envelope without comment. The employee asked defendant about the envelope, and defendant simply replied, "Open it. I was told to bring it here. I don't know what is in it." The employee opened the note and found that it contained a demand for $100,000, and stated that the person who had delivered it was

under a hypnotic spell. The employee asked McCollum to sit down. McCollum complied, and remained seated while the bank was evacuated and police officers entered to apprehend him. McCollum failed to respond to the officers' initial questions and commands, but accompanied them to a police car. Later, while seated in the car, McCollum shook violently for a period of ten to fifteen seconds and then asked one of the officers, "What are you doing? Why am I here?" Assuming that defendant really was under hypnosis, can he be convicted of attempted bank robbery? In other words, did he commit a voluntary act? Could the person who hypnotized defendant and gave him the note be convicted of attempted bank robbery? *See United States v. McCollum*, 732 F.2d 1419 (9th Cir. 1984).

6. *Voluntariness and Multiple Personalities.* Defendant was charged with driving under the influence of alcohol. At the time of the offense, she was dissociated from her primary personality (Robin) and in the state of consciousness of a secondary personality (Jennifer). She claims that she was suffering from psychological trauma which caused her to dissociate into the personality of Jennifer, who is impulsive, angry, fearful and anxious. Jennifer has a drinking problem. Defendant contends that when she is Jennifer, Robin is unaware of what is going on, has no control over Jennifer's actions, and no memory of what Jennifer did later on when she is restored to the primary personality of Robin. As a result, the defendant argues that "she" did not commit the "act" of driving under the influence. Do you agree with defendant? Are the actions of a person with a multiple personality disorder voluntary when she is dissociated from her primary personality and in the state of consciousness of a secondary personality? *See State v. Grimsley*, 3 Ohio App.3d 265, 444 N.E.2d 1071 (1982).

7. *Somnambulism.* Defendant Bradley was living with the deceased, Ada Jenkins. One Lawrence Williams was an enemy, and had made some threats against the defendant. After retiring to bed on the night of the homicide, the deceased and the defendant discussed Williams. Deceased gave the appellant information which tended to alarm him, and put him in fear of a secret attack by Williams. During the conversation and thereafter, while reflecting upon it, defendant became more and more alarmed, and, as he expressed it, he felt "jubious and jubiouser," and took from a table which was near his bed a pistol, which he put under the pillow upon which his head was lying. Then, the following happened:

> I goes off to sleep. I never waked up any more till I was disturbed by a noise in the house. I went to sleep with that on my mind. The last I remembered was that the door was not fastened. After the noise in the house disturbed me, I was nervous, and I was not reconciled to the noise in the house. I was scared. I just jumped up with my gun and commenced shooting. I made a couple of shots, about two shots or three. And so then, when I found myself and got reconciled I was standing up in the floor. Then I turned to the library table at the head of the bed where I slept and lit the lamp. When I lit the lamp I found [Ada] laying there dead. She was laying at the foot of the bed next to the

partition wall when I lit the lamp; she was laying there. As to knowing whether I killed her or not, well, I was shooting; I couldn't say I killed her because I didn't know what I was doing. When I lit the lamp she was there dead. As to my intentionally killing Ada Jenkins, or knowing I did so, I was shooting is all I can say. I was not trying to kill her; no, sir. I would not have killed her if I had known it was her for nothing in the world.

Defendant was diagnosed with somnambulism. Under the circumstances, can we say that the homicide he committed was a voluntary act? *See Bradley v. State*, 102 Tex.Crim. 41, 277 S.W. 147 (1925).

8. *Automatism.* Defendant was a patron at a tavern known as the "Watering Place" where he consumed four drinks consisting of whisky during a 2.5 hour period. The defendant then witnessed an altercation between another patron and the tavern owner. The police were called to the scene and they forcibly escorted the other patron outside where he continued to resist arrest. A hostile crowd of approximately forty persons accompanied the police and patron as they exited from the tavern and approached the officers' automobile. The crowd was cheering for the patron. Suddenly, the defendant burst through the crowd, and, using a parking meter for leverage, leaped into the air, striking one of the officers twice in the face. Thereafter, the officer placed the defendant under arrest for aggravated battery. Defendant was very upset and great force was required to place defendant in the officer's automobile. Defendant was excited, agitated and upset. Defendant was then transported to jail and placed in a cell. Approximately one hour after being arrested, one of the jailers discovered the defendant lying on his cot gasping for breath. Defendant's eyes were fixed and his back formed a rigid reversed arch, typical symptoms of a grand mal convulsive seizure. The defendant was immediately transported to a hospital where he remained for some time. The record shows that the defendant has a complicated legal and medical history. The defendant suffers from an illness known as psychomotor epilepsy. This history includes a number of violent attacks on other persons which have varied in severity. In some attacks, physical assistance from others was required to subdue the defendant. Once, when he used a knife during an assault in a hospital, a police officer seeking to restrain the defendant was forced to use a weapon. The affray ended only when the defendant was shot in the pelvis and kidney. His past history is replete with emotional outbursts and he has been convicted on separate occasions of involuntary manslaughter and aggravated assault. Defendant claims that he suffered from "automatism" defined as the state of a person who, though capable of action, is not conscious of what he is doing. Did he act voluntarily when he attacked the police officer outside the tavern? *See People v. Grant*, 46 Ill.App.3d 125, 360 N.E.2d 809, 4 Ill.Dec. 696 (1977), *rev'd, People v. Grant*, 71 Ill.2d 551, 377 N.E.2d 4, 17 Ill.Dec. 814 (1978). *See also United States v. Phillips*, 515 F.Supp. 758 (E.D. Ky. 1981).

9. *Proving Involuntariness.* Defendant was indicted for kidnapping and raping Catherine Sutton. The State provided incontrovertible proof that defendant committed the crime. Defendant claims that he is unable to remember anything about the events surrounding the crime. In addition, defendant states that: "I never did a degrading thing like this before. I have been charged with nothing like this. I don't believe it. And if I did this, there is something wrong." However, defendant admits that photographs of the automobile in which Ms. Sutton was carried away from her home and assaulted were pictures of his car. Because he cannot remember what happened, defendant claims that he was unconscious during the assault and therefore that his acts were involuntary. If you represent the defendant, what proof might you use to show that he acted involuntarily? If you are the prosecutor, how would you prove that he acted voluntarily? *See State v. Caddell*, 287 N.C. 266, 215 S.E.2d 348 (1975).

10. *Sleep–Deprived Driving.* In 2003, New Jersey adopted a new law which prohibits drivers from operating automobiles while drowsy. The law authorizes a conviction of vehicular homicide, punishable by up to 10 years in jail and a $100,000 fine, for anyone who causes a deadly car accident due to drowsiness. Was the new law needed? In other words, is it possible to convict a motorist (who becomes drowsy and falls asleep) of homicide without using the new law? See M.P.C. §§ 210.4(1), 2.02(2)(d).

ROBINSON v. CALIFORNIA

370 U.S. 660 (1962).

MR. JUSTICE STEWART delivered the opinion of the Court.

A California statute makes it a criminal offense for a person to "be addicted to the use of narcotics." [A]ppellant was convicted after a jury trial in the Municipal Court of Los Angeles. The evidence against him was given by two Los Angeles police officers. Officer Brown testified that he had occasion to examine the appellant's arms one evening on a street in Los Angeles some four months before the trial. The officer testified that at that time he had observed "scar tissue and discoloration on the inside" of the appellant's right arm, and "what appeared to be numerous needle marks and a scab which was approximately three inches below the crook of the elbow" on the appellant's left arm. The officer also testified that the appellant under questioning had admitted to the occasional use of narcotics.

Officer Lindquist testified that he had examined the appellant the following morning in the Central Jail in Los Angeles. The officer stated that at that time he had observed discolorations and scabs on the appellant's arms, and he identified photographs which had been taken of the appellant's arms shortly after his arrest the night before. Based upon more than ten years of experience as a member of the Narcotic Division of the Los Angeles Police Department, the witness gave his opinion that "these marks and the discoloration were the result of the injection of hypodermic needles into the tissue into the vein that was not sterile." He stated that the scabs were several days old at the time of his examination, and that the appellant was neither under the influence of narcotics nor suffering withdrawal symptoms at the time he saw him. This witness also testified that the appellant had admitted using narcotics in the past.

[The] trial judge instructed the jury that the statute made it a misdemeanor for a person "either to use narcotics, or to be addicted to the use of [narcotics]. That portion of the statute referring to the 'use' of narcotics is based upon the 'act' of using. That portion of the statute referring to 'addicted to the use' of narcotics is based upon a condition or status. They are not identical. [To] be addicted to the use of narcotics is said to be a status or condition and not an act. It is a continuing offense and differs from most other offenses in the fact that [it] is chronic rather than acute; that it continues after it is complete and subjects the offender to arrest at any time before he reforms. The existence of such a chronic condition may be ascertained from a single examination, if the characteristic reactions of that condition be found present."

The judge further instructed the jury that the appellant could be convicted under a general verdict if the jury agreed either that he was of the "status" or had committed the "act" denounced by the statute. "All that the People must show is either that the defendant did use a narcotic in Los Angeles County, or that while in the City of Los Angeles he was addicted to the use of [narcotics]." [T]he jury returned a verdict finding the appellant "guilty of the offense charged."
. . .

It would be possible to construe the statute under which the appellant was convicted as one which is operative only upon proof of the actual use of narcotics within the State's jurisdiction. But the California courts have not so construed this law. Although there was evidence in the present case that the appellant had used narcotics in Los Angeles, the jury were instructed that they could convict him even if they disbelieved that evidence. The appellant could be convicted, they were told, if they found simply that the appellant's "status" or "chronic condition" was that of being "addicted to the use of narcotics." And it is impossible to know from the jury's verdict that the defendant was not convicted upon precisely such a finding.

[This] statute, therefore, is not one which punishes a person for the use of narcotics, for their purchase, sale or possession, or for antisocial or disorderly behavior resulting from their administration. It is not a law which even purports to provide or require medical treatment. Rather, we deal with a statute which makes the "status" of narcotic addiction a criminal offense, for which the offender may be prosecuted "at any time before he reforms." California has said that a person can be continuously guilty of this offense, whether or not he has ever used or possessed any narcotics within the State, and whether or not he has been guilty of any antisocial behavior there.

It is unlikely that any State at this moment in history would attempt to make it a criminal offense for a person to be mentally ill, or a leper, or to be afflicted with a venereal disease. A State might determine that the general health and welfare require that the victims of these and other human afflictions be dealt with by compulsory treatment, involving quarantine, confinement, or sequestration. But, in the light of contemporary human knowledge, a law which made a criminal offense of such a disease would doubtless be universally thought to be an infliction of cruel and unusual punishment in violation of the Eighth and Fourteenth Amendments.

We cannot but consider the statute before us as of the same category. In this Court counsel for the State recognized that narcotic addiction is an illness. Indeed, it is apparently an illness which may be contracted innocently or involuntarily.[9] We hold that a state law which imprisons a person thus afflicted as a criminal, even though he has never touched any narcotic drug within the State or been guilty of any irregular behavior there, inflicts a cruel and unusual punishment in violation of the Fourteenth Amendment. To be sure, imprisonment for ninety days is not, in the abstract, a punishment which is either cruel or unusual. But the question cannot be considered in the abstract. Even one day in prison would be a cruel and unusual punishment for the "crime" of having a common cold.

We are not unmindful that the vicious evils of the narcotics traffic have occasioned the grave concern of government. There are, as we have said, countless fronts on which those evils may be legitimately attacked. We deal in this case only with an individual provision of a particularized local law as it has so far been interpreted by the California courts.

Reversed.

MR. JUSTICE DOUGLAS, concurring.

[The] first step toward [drug] addiction may be as innocent as a boy's puff on a cigarette in an alleyway. It may come from medical prescriptions. Addiction may even be present at birth. Earl Ubell recently wrote:

In Bellevue Hospital's nurseries, Dr. Saul Krugman, head of pediatrics, has been discovering babies minutes old who are heroin addicts. More than 100 such infants have turned up in the last two years, and they show all the signs of drug withdrawal: irritability, jitters, loss of appetite, vomiting, diarrhea, sometimes

---

9. Not only may addiction innocently result from the use of medically prescribed narcotics, but a person may even be a narcotics addict from the moment of his birth.

convulsions and death. Of course, they get the drug while in the womb from their mothers who are addicts.'

The addict is under compulsions not capable of management without outside help. [Some] say the addict has a disease. [Others] say addiction is not a disease but "a symptom of a mental or psychiatric disorder." [Some] States punish addiction, though most do not. Nor does the Uniform Narcotic Drug Act, first approved in 1932 and now in effect in most of the States....

[We] know that there is "a hard core" of "chronic and incurable drug addicts who, in reality, have lost their power of self-control." ...

The impact that an addict has on a community causes alarm and often leads to punitive measures. Those measures are justified when they relate to acts of transgression. But I do not see how under our system being an addict can be punished as a crime. If addicts can be punished for their addiction, then the insane can also be punished for their insanity. Each has a disease and each must be treated as a sick person....

[The] command of the Eighth Amendment, banning "cruel and unusual punishments," stems from the Bill of Rights of 1688. And it is applicable to the States by reason of the Due Process Clause of the Fourteenth Amendment.

The historic punishments that were cruel and unusual included "burning at the stake, crucifixion, breaking on the wheel", quartering, the rack and thumbscrew, and in some circumstances even solitary confinement.

[The] Eighth Amendment expresses the revulsion of civilized man against barbarous acts—the "cry of horror" against man's inhumanity to his fellow man.

By the time of Coke, enlightenment was coming as respects the insane. Coke said that the execution of a madman "should be a miserable spectacle, both against law, and of extreme inhumanity and cruelty, and can be no example to others." Blackstone endorsed this view of Coke.

We should show the same discernment respecting drug addiction. The addict is a sick person. He may, of course, be confined for treatment or for the protection of society. Cruel and unusual punishment results not from confinement, but from convicting the addict of a crime. The purpose of § 11721 is not to cure, but to penalize. Were the purpose to cure, there would be no need for a mandatory jail term of not less than 90 days. Contrary to my Brother Clark, I think the means must stand constitutional scrutiny, as well as the end to be achieved. A prosecution for addiction, with its resulting stigma and irreparable damage to the good name of the accused, cannot be justified as a means of protecting society, where a civil commitment would do as well. [This] age of enlightenment cannot tolerate such barbarous action.

MR. JUSTICE HARLAN, concurring.

[Insofar] as addiction may be identified with the use or possession of narcotics within the State (or, I would suppose, without the State), in violation of local statutes prohibiting such acts, it may surely be reached by the State's criminal law. But in this case the trial court's instructions permitted the jury to find the appellant guilty on no more proof than that he was present in California while he was addicted to narcotics. Since addiction alone cannot reasonably be thought to amount to more than a compelling propensity to use narcotics, the effect of this instruction was to authorize criminal *procedural* punishment for a bare desire to commit a criminal act.

If the California statute reaches this type of conduct, and for present purposes we must accept the trial court's construction as binding, it is an arbitrary imposition which exceeds the power that a State may exercise in enacting its criminal law. Accordingly, I agree that the application of the California statute was unconstitutional in this case and join the judgment of reversal.

MR. JUSTICE CLARK, dissenting.

[The] majority acknowledges, as it must, that a State can punish persons who purchase, possess or use narcotics. Although none of these acts are harmful to society in themselves, the State constitutionally may attempt to deter and prevent them through punishment because of the grave threat of future harmful conduct which they pose. Narcotics addiction—including the incipient, volitional addiction to which this provision speaks—is no different. California courts have taken judicial notice that "the inordinate use of a narcotic drug tends to create an irresistible craving and forms a habit for its continued use until one becomes an addict, and he respects no convention or obligation and will lie, steal, or use any other base means to gratify his passion for the drug, being lost to all considerations of duty or social position." Can this Court deny the legislative and judicial judgment of California that incipient, volitional narcotic addiction poses a threat of serious crime similar to the threat inherent in the purchase or possession of narcotics? And if such a threat is inherent in addiction, can this Court say that California is powerless to deter it by punishment?

It is no answer to suggest that we are dealing with an involuntary status and thus penal sanctions will be ineffective and unfair. The section at issue applies only to persons who use narcotics often or even daily but not to the point of losing self-control. When dealing with involuntary addicts California moves only through § 5355 of its Welfare Institutions Code which clearly is not penal. Even if it could be argued that § 11721 may not be limited to volitional addicts, the petitioner in the instant case undeniably retained the power of self-control and thus to him the statute would be constitutional....

Nor is the conjecture relevant that petitioner may have acquired his habit under lawful circumstances. There was no suggestion by him to this effect at trial, and surely the State need not rebut all possible lawful sources of addiction as part of its prima facie case.

The argument that the statute constitutes a cruel and unusual punishment is governed by the discussion above. Properly construed, the statute provides a treatment rather than a punishment. But even if interpreted as penal, the sanction of incarceration for 3 to 12 months is not unreasonable when applied to a person who has voluntarily placed himself in a condition posing a serious threat to the State. Under either theory, its provisions for 3 to 12 months' confinement can hardly be deemed unreasonable when compared to the provisions for 3 to 24 months' confinement under § 5355 which the majority approves.

I would affirm the judgment.

MR. JUSTICE WHITE, dissenting.

[I] do not consider appellant's conviction to be a punishment for having an illness or for simply being in some status or condition, but rather a conviction for the regular, repeated or habitual use of narcotics immediately prior to his arrest and in violation of the California law. As defined by the trial court, addiction is the regular use of narcotics and can be proved only by evidence of such use. To find addiction in this case the jury had to believe that appellant had frequently used narcotics in the recent past....

Nor do I find any indications in this record that California would apply § 11721 to the case of the helpless addict. I agree with my Brother Clark that there was no evidence at all that appellant had lost the power to control his acts....

The Court clearly does not rest its decision upon the narrow ground that the jury was not expressly instructed not to convict if it believed appellant's use of narcotics was beyond his control. The Court recognizes no degrees of addiction. The Fourteenth Amendment is today held to bar any prosecution for addiction regardless of the degree or frequency of use, and the Court's opinion bristles with indications of further consequences. If it is "cruel and unusual punishment" to convict appellant for addiction, it is difficult to understand why it would be any less offensive to the Fourteenth Amendment to convict him for use on the same evidence of use which proved he was an addict....

The Court has not merely tidied up California's law by removing some irritating vestige of an outmoded approach to the control of narcotics. At the very least, it has effectively removed California's power to deal effectively with the recurring case under the statute where there is ample evidence of use but no evidence of the precise location of use. Beyond this it has cast serious doubt upon the power of any State to forbid the use of narcotics under threat of criminal punishment. . . .

NOTES

1. *The crime of "being found in a state of intoxication in a public place."* In *Powell v. Texas*, 392 U.S. 514 (1968), appellant contended that he was "afflicted with the disease of chronic alcoholism," that "his appearance in public [while drunk was] not of his own volition," and therefore "that to punish him criminally for that conduct would be cruel and unusual, in violation of the Eighth and Fourteenth Amendments to the United States Constitution." The Court disagreed:

[The] present case does not fall within [*Robinson*'s] holding, since appellant was convicted, not for being a chronic alcoholic, but for being in public while drunk on a particular occasion. The State of Texas thus has not sought to punish a mere status, as California did in *Robinson*; nor has it attempted to regulate appellant's behavior in the privacy of his own home. Rather, it has imposed upon appellant a criminal sanction for public behavior which may create substantial health and safety hazards, both for appellant and for members of the general public, and which offends the moral and esthetic sensibilities of a large segment of the community. This seems a far cry from convicting one for being an addict, being a chronic alcoholic, being "mentally ill, or a [leper]."

[It] is suggested in dissent that *Robinson* stands for the "simple" but "subtle" principle that "[c]riminal penalties may not be inflicted upon a person for being in a condition he is powerless to change." [The] entire thrust of *Robinson's* interpretation of the Cruel and Unusual Punishment Clause is that criminal penalties may be inflicted only if the accused has committed some act, has engaged in some behavior, which society has an interest in preventing, or perhaps in historical common law terms, has committed some actus reus. It thus does not deal with the question of whether certain conduct cannot constitutionally be punished because it is, in some sense, "involuntary" or "occasioned by a compulsion."

[We] are unable to conclude [that] chronic alcoholics in general, and Leroy Powell in particular, suffer from such an irresistible compulsion to drink and to get drunk in public that they are utterly unable to control their performance of either or both of these acts and thus cannot be deterred at all from public intoxication. . . .

Mr. Justice Black concurred: "[P]unishment of such a defendant can clearly be justified in terms of deterrence, isolation, and treatment." "[E]ven if we were to limit any holding in this field to 'compulsions' that are 'symptomatic' of a 'disease,' [the] sweep of that holding would still be startling. Such a ruling would make it clear beyond any doubt that a narcotics addict could not be punished for 'being' in possession of drugs or, for that matter, for 'being' guilty of using them. A wide variety of sex offenders would be immune from punishment if they could show that their conduct was not voluntary but part of the pattern of a disease...." Mr. Justice White also concurred: "Powell's conviction was for the different crime of being drunk in a public place. [M]any chronic alcoholics drink at home and are never seen drunk in public. [The] alcoholic is like a person with smallpox, who could be convicted for being on the street but not for being ill, or, like the epileptic, who would be punished for driving a car but not for his disease." Mr. Justice Fortas dissented:

> This case does not raise any question as to the right of the police to stop and detain those who are intoxicated in public, whether as a result of the disease or otherwise; or as to the State's power to commit chronic alcoholics for treatment. Nor does it concern the responsibility of an alcoholic for criminal acts. We deal here with the mere condition of being intoxicated in public.

> [The] essential constitutional defect here is the same as in *Robinson*, for in both cases the particular defendant was accused of being in a condition which he had no capacity to change or avoid. The trial judge [found] upon the medical and other relevant testimony, that Powell is a "chronic alcoholic." He defined appellant's "chronic alcoholism" as "a disease which destroys the afflicted person's will power to resist the constant, excessive consumption of alcohol." He also found that "a chronic alcoholic does not appear in public by his own volition but under a compulsion symptomatic of the disease of chronic alcoholism." I read these findings to mean that appellant was powerless to avoid drinking; that having taken his first drink, he had "an uncontrollable compulsion to drink" to the point of intoxication; and that, once intoxicated, he could not prevent himself from appearing in public places.

> [T]he findings of the trial judge call into play the principle that a person may not be punished if the condition essential to constitute the defined crime is part of the pattern of his disease and is occasioned by a compulsion symptomatic of the disease. This principle, narrow in scope and applicability, is implemented by the Eighth Amendment's prohibition of "cruel and unusual punishment," as we construed that command in *Robinson* . . . .

2. *Duty to register with police.* In *Lambert v. California*, 355 U.S. 225 (1957), a Los Angeles ordinance required "any convicted person" to register with the police within five days of arriving in the city. Defendant failed to register and was charged for her failure. The Court overturned her conviction, reasoning as follows:

> [W]e deal here with conduct that is wholly passive—mere failure to register. It is unlike the commission of acts, or the failure to act under circumstances that should alert the doer to the consequences of his

deed. The rule that "ignorance of the law will not excuse" is deep in our law, as is the principle that of all the powers of local government, the police power is "one of the least limitable." On the other hand, due process places some limits on its exercise. Engrained in our concept of due process is the requirement of notice. [Notice] is required in a myriad of situations where a penalty or forfeiture might be suffered for mere failure to act. [The] principle is equally appropriate where a person, wholly passive and unaware of any wrongdoing, is brought to the bar of justice for condemnation in a criminal case.

[The] present ordinance is entirely different. Violation of its provisions is unaccompanied by any activity whatever, mere presence in the city being the test. Moreover, circumstances which might move one to inquire as to the necessity of registration are completely lacking. At most the ordinance is but a law enforcement technique designed for the convenience of law enforcement agencies through which a list of the names and addresses of felons then residing in a given community is compiled. [A]ppellant on first becoming aware of her duty to register was given no opportunity to comply with the law and avoid its penalty, even though her default was entirely innocent. She could but suffer the consequences of the ordinance, namely, conviction with the imposition of heavy criminal penalties thereunder. We believe that actual knowledge of the duty to register or proof of the probability of such knowledge and subsequent failure to comply are necessary before a conviction under the ordinance can stand. . . .

Mr. Justice Frankfurter dissented: "The present laws of the United States and of the forty-eight States are thick with provisions that command that some things not be done and others be done, although persons convicted under such provisions may have had no awareness of what the law required or that what they did was wrongdoing."

PROBLEMS

1. *Analyzing Robinson.* How far does *Robinson's* logic extend? Suppose that Robinson has been convicted of *using* narcotics in the State of California and is now on probation. Following his release, a narcotics detective notices that Robinson has extensive needle marks on his arms (indicative of drug use). Rather than charging Robinson with "being addicted to the use of narcotics" (under the unconstitutional section of the law), the officer charges Robinson again with actually *using* narcotics in California. The prosecutor seeks to use Robinson's past history, and the recent needle marks, to prove the recent drug use. Is a conviction appropriate under these circumstances?

2. *Homeless Chronic Alcoholics.* Would it be constitutional to punish a homeless chronic alcoholic (who is destitute and unable to afford housing) for being drunk in a public place under the statute in *Powell*?

3. *Drug Addicts and Drug Use.* If the state cannot make it a crime to be "addicted to drugs," how can it punish the addict for using them? Can the

state make it a crime for a drug addict to use illegal narcotics? If it is permissible to punish the use of drugs, is it also permissible to punish the addict for prior acts of drug use that led to the addiction (assuming, of course, that the prior acts took place within the state)? *See State v. Bridges*, 360 S.W.2d 648 (Mo. 1962).

4. *Homeless Campers.* The City of Santa Ana (Santa Ana) banned "camping" and storage of personal property, including camping equipment, in designated public areas. The ordinance was designed to preserve public streets and public areas in a clean and accessible condition. Plaintiffs believe that the ordinance was part of an effort to expel homeless persons from the City. Previously, the City had tried to expel "vagrants" by creating early park closing times, disposing of sleeping bags and accessories, confiscating abandoned shopping carts, monitoring providers of free food, and turning on sprinklers frequently in city parks. This effort led to a lawsuit which the city settled. At that point, the City adopted the anti-camping ordinance. At that time the city had 3,000 homeless persons and shelter for only about 330 of them.

Wilfred J. is a 58-year-old who became homeless when his truck was stolen, and he lost the ability to obtain jobs hauling freight. Mr. J. receives no "general relief" or social security and is looking for work. He was ticketed for "camping" near a building opposite the police station, even though he obeyed police orders to move on. He now sleeps on "God's Land," a ramp at a Methodist Church. Mildred B. is a 35-year-old homeless person who suffers from schizophrenia. She elected to stay in the Santa Ana Civic Center Plaza (Civic Center) area to be near the police station for her safety. In bad weather she sleeps in a public parking garage. She was at that location, "soaking wet," with a blanket over her legs as she read "a Bible tract" when police officers cited her under the camping ordinance. After they left she "decided to stay there. It was pourin' down rain. I didn't have anywhere to go." She stated, "You can't leave your belongings even to eat. The police will take them the minute you leave them. I've seen them do that to other people numerous times." Jack K. is 52, homeless, and has lived in the Civic Center for the past two years. The only public assistance he receives is food stamps. The last time he attempted to stay at the armory, he was turned away. He was cited under the camping ordinance while reading a book in his sleeping bag in the doorway of a public building. He chose that location for lack of any other place to go and for reasons of personal safety.

Does the anti-camping ordinance unfairly punish indigents for their homeless status? *See Tobe v. City of Santa Ana*, 27 Cal.Rptr.2d 386 (Cal.App. 1994), *rev'd*, *Tobe v. City of Santa Ana*, 9 Cal.4th 1069, 892 P.2d 1145, 40 Cal.Rptr.2d 402 (1995).

5. *Possession and Knowledge.* Defendant was charged with possession of marijuana. Defendant was a prisoner at a county honor farm who shared living quarters in a bunkhouse with thirty other prisoners. The prison issued a metal box to the defendant in which he kept his toilet articles and small personal effects. The box was unlocked and was placed on the floor near his

bed. During the day, when the prisoners were engaged in other duties, one inmate was left in charge of the bunkhouse to "keep the inmates from monkeying with other people's property." During a search of the bunkhouse, guards opened defendant's metal box and found marijuana loose in the box. The guard then searched defendant's person, but found nothing. Defendant stated that he had never seen the marijuana before the officers removed it from the box. Can defendant commit the actus reus of possession without knowing about the existence of the marijuana? As defense counsel, how do you support your claim of lack of knowledge? How might the prosecution respond? *See People v. Gory*, 28 Cal.2d 450, 170 P.2d 433 (1946).

B. OMISSIONS

Even though criminal liability must be based on a voluntary act, the term "act" is defined broadly enough to include an "omission" to act. M.P.C. § 2.01 provides that liability can be based on an "omission to perform an act of which [a person] is physically capable."

JONES v. UNITED STATES

308 F.2d 307, 113 U.S.App.D.C. 352 (D.C.Cir. 1962).

WRIGHT, CIRCUIT JUDGE.

Appellant, together with one Shirley Green, was tried on a three-count indictment charging them jointly [with] involuntary manslaughter through failure to perform their legal duty of care for Anthony Lee Green, which failure resulted in his death. [A]ppellant was convicted of involuntary manslaughter. Shirley Green [is the mother of Anthony Lee Green and she] was found not guilty. [A]ppellant argues that there was insufficient evidence as a matter of law to warrant a jury finding of breach of duty in the care she rendered Anthony Lee. Alternatively, appellant argues that the trial court committed plain error in failing to instruct the jury that it must first find that appellant was under a legal obligation to provide food and necessities to Anthony Lee before finding her guilty of manslaughter in failing to provide them. The first argument is without merit. Upon the latter we reverse.

[In] late 1957, Shirley Green became pregnant, out of wedlock, with a child, Robert Lee, subsequently born August 17, 1958. Apparently to avoid the embarrassment of the presence of the child in the Green home, it was arranged that appellant [Jones], a family friend, would take the child to her home after birth. Appellant did so, and the child remained there continuously until removed by the police on August 5, 1960. Initially appellant made some motions toward the adoption of Robert Lee, but these came to nought, and shortly thereafter it was agreed that Shirley Green was to pay appellant $72 a month for his care. According to appellant, these payments were made for only five months. According to Shirley Green, they were made up to July, 1960.

Early in 1959 Shirley Green again became pregnant, this time with the child Anthony Lee, whose death is the basis of appellant's conviction. This child was born October 21, 1959. Soon after birth, Anthony Lee developed a mild jaundice condition, attributed to a blood [incompatibility] with his mother. The jaundice resulted in his retention in the hospital for three days beyond the usual time, or until October 26, 1959, when, on authorization signed by Shirley Green, Anthony Lee was released by the hospital to appellant's custody. Shirley Green, after a two or three day stay in the hospital, also lived with appellant for three weeks, after which she returned to her parents' home, leaving the children with appellant. She testified she did not see them again, except for one visit in March, until August 5, 1960. Consequently, though there does not seem to have been any specific monetary agreement with Shirley Green covering Anthony Lee's support,[5] appellant had complete custody of both children until they were rescued by the police.

With regard to medical care, the evidence is undisputed. In March, 1960, appellant called a Dr. Turner to her home to treat Anthony Lee for a bronchial condition. Appellant also telephoned the doctor at various times to consult with him concerning Anthony Lee's diet and health. In early July, 1960, appellant took Anthony Lee to Dr. Turner's office where he was treated for "simple diarrhea." At this time the doctor noted the "wizened" appearance of the child and told appellant to tell the mother of the child that he should be taken to a hospital. This was not done.

On August 2, 1960, two collectors for the local gas company had occasion to go to the basement of appellant's home, and there saw the two children. Robert Lee and Anthony Lee at this time were age two years and ten months respectively. Robert Lee was in a "crib" consisting of a framework of wood, covered with a fine wire screening, including the top which was hinged. The "crib" was lined with newspaper, which was stained, apparently with feces, and crawling with roaches. Anthony Lee was lying in a bassinet and was described as having the appearance of a "small baby monkey." One collector testified to seeing roaches on Anthony Lee.

On August 5, 1960, the collectors returned to appellant's home in the company of several police officers and personnel of the Women's Bureau. At this time, Anthony Lee was upstairs in the dining room in the bassinet, but Robert Lee was still downstairs in his "crib." The officers removed the children to the D.C. General Hospital where

_____

5. It was uncontested that during the entire period the children were in appellant's home, appellant had ample means to provide food and medical care.

Anthony Lee was diagnosed as suffering from severe malnutrition and lesions over large portions of his body, apparently caused by severe diaper rash. Following admission, he was fed repeatedly, apparently with no difficulty, and was described as being very hungry. His death, 34 hours after admission, was attributed without dispute to malnutrition. At birth, Anthony Lee weighed six pounds, fifteen ounces—at death at age ten months, he weighed seven pounds, thirteen ounces. Normal weight at this age would have been approximately 14 pounds.

Appellant argues that nothing in the evidence establishes that she failed to provide food to Anthony Lee. She cites her own testimony and the testimony of a lodger, Mr. Wills, that she did in fact feed the baby regularly. At trial, the defense made repeated attempts to extract from the medical witnesses opinions that the jaundice, or the condition which caused it, might have prevented the baby from assimilating food. The doctors conceded this was possible but not probable since the autopsy revealed no condition which would support the defense theory. It was also shown by the disinterested medical witnesses that the child had no difficulty in ingesting food immediately after birth, and that Anthony Lee, in the last hours before his death, was able to take several bottles, apparently without difficulty, and seemed very hungry. This evidence, combined with the absence of any physical cause for nonassimilation, taken in the context of the condition in which these children were kept, presents a jury question on the feeding issue.

Moreover, there is substantial evidence from which the jury could have found that appellant failed to obtain proper medical care for the child. Appellant relies upon the evidence showing that on one occasion she summoned a doctor for the child, on another took the child to the doctor's office, and that she telephoned the doctor on several occasions about the baby's formula. However, the last time a doctor saw the child was a month before his death, and appellant admitted that on that occasion the doctor recommended hospitalization. Appellant did not hospitalize the child, nor did she take any other steps to obtain medical care in the last crucial month. Thus there was sufficient evidence [for the prosecution] to go to the jury on the issue of medical care, as well as failure to feed.

Appellant also takes exception to the failure of the trial court to charge that the jury must find beyond a reasonable doubt, as an element of the crime, that appellant was under a legal duty to supply food and necessities to Anthony Lee. [The] problem of establishing the duty to take action which would preserve the life of another has not often arisen in the case law of this country. The most commonly cited statement of the rule is found in *People v. Beardsley*, 150 Mich. 206, 113 N.W. 1128, 1129:

> The law recognizes that under some circumstances the omission of a duty owed by one individual to another, where such omission

results in the death of the one to whom the duty is owing, will make the other chargeable with manslaughter. [This] rule of law is always based upon the proposition that the duty neglected must be a legal duty, and not a mere moral obligation. It must be a duty imposed by law or by contract, and the omission to perform the duty must be the immediate and direct cause of death.

There are at least four situations in which the failure to act may constitute breach of a legal duty. One can be held criminally liable: first, where a statute imposes a duty to care for another; second, where one stands in a certain status relationship to another; third, where one has assumed a contractual duty to care for another; and fourth, where one has voluntarily assumed the care of another and so secluded the helpless person as to prevent others from rendering aid.

It is the contention of the Government that either the third or the fourth ground is applicable here. [However,] the instructions given in the case failed even to suggest the necessity for finding a legal duty of care. The only reference to duty in the instructions was the reading of the indictment which charged, inter alia, that the defendants "failed to perform their legal duty." A finding of legal duty is the critical element of the crime charged and failure to instruct the jury concerning it was plain error.

[Reversed and remanded for a new trial with correct instructions.]

NOTES

1. *M.P.C. and legal duties.* M.P.C. § 2.01(3) provides as follows:

(3) Liability for the commission of an offense may not be based on an omission unaccompanied by action unless:

(a) the omission is expressly made sufficient by the law defining the offense; or

(b) a duty to perform the omitted act is otherwise imposed by law.

2. *Contractual duty.* In *Commonwealth v. Pestinikas*, 421 Pa.Super. 371, 617 A.2d 1339 (1992), Joseph Kly was hospitalized with a serious illness. When he was about to be discharged, Kly expressed a desire to live with the Pestinikas (appellants) in their home. Arrangements were made for appellants to care for Kly in their home. When appellants came for Kly, they were instructed by medical personnel regarding the care which was required and were given a prescription to have filled. Appellants agreed orally to follow the medical instructions and to supply Kly with food, shelter, care and the medicine which he required. The prescription was never filled. Instead of giving Kly a room in their home, appellants placed him in a rural house which had no insulation, no refrigeration, no bathroom, no sink and no

telephone. The walls contained cracks which exposed the room to outside weather conditions. Kly's predicament was compounded by defendants' affirmative efforts to conceal his whereabouts. They gave misleading information in response to inquiries, telling members of Kly's family that they did not know where he had gone and others that he was living in their home.

At some point, appellants took Kly to the bank and had their names added to his savings account. Bank records reveal that from May, 1982, to July, 1983, appellants withdrew amounts roughly consistent with the three hundred ($300) dollars per month which Kly had agreed to pay for his care. Beginning in August, 1983 and continuing until Kly's death in November, 1984, however, appellants withdrew much larger sums so that when Kly died, a balance of only fifty-five ($55) dollars remained. In the interim, appellants had withdrawn in excess of thirty thousand ($30,000) dollars. When Kly died, emergency personnel found that he was emaciated and that his ribs and sternum were greatly pronounced. Mrs. Pestinikas told police that she had given him cookies and orange juice that morning. A subsequent autopsy, however, revealed that Kly may have been dead for as many as thirty-nine (39) hours before his body was found. The cause of death was determined to be starvation and dehydration. The Court affirmed the Pestinikas' conviction for murder:

> [Because] there was evidence in the instant case that Kly's death had been caused by appellants' failure to provide the food and medical care which they had agreed by oral contract to provide for him, their omission to act was sufficient to support a conviction for criminal homicide. [The] jury was required to find that appellants, by virtue of contract, had undertaken responsibility for providing necessary care for Kly to the exclusion of the members of Kly's family. This would impose upon them a legal duty to act to preserve Kly's life. If they maliciously set upon a course of withholding food and medicine and thereby caused Kly's death, appellants could be found guilty of murder.

See also People v. Montecino, 66 Cal.App.2d 85, 152 P.2d 5 (1944).

PROBLEMS

1. *Applying Jones.* If Jones had a duty toward Anthony Lee Green, when did that duty arise? When did she violate that duty? Did Anthony's mother likewise have a duty towards him? Was it permissible for the mother to leave the child with Jones, or did she violate her duty simply by leaving the boy with her? If there was no breach of duty simply by leaving the child with Jones, when (and how) did a breach of duty by the mother occur?

2. *A Duty to Help?* Every year, in every major city, people die of cold and starvation. If we impose a legal duty on all citizens to help others in distress, would that mean that an affluent citizen could be criminally prosecuted for refusing to help an indigent person in need—if that person dies from starvation? Explain the policy issues at stake here.

3. *Duty to Rescue in Emergencies.* Rhode Island requires those present at the scene of an emergency to render assistance to those exposed to "grave physical harm" if those present can do so "without danger or peril to himself or herself or to others...."[6] Vermont has a similar law.

12 V.S.A. § 519. Emergency Medical Care

(a) A person who knows that another is exposed to grave physical harm shall, to the extent that the same can be rendered without danger or peril to himself or without interference with important duties owed to others, give reasonable assistance to the exposed person unless that assistance or care is being provided by others.

(b) A person who provides reasonable assistance in compliance with subsection (a) of this section shall not be liable in civil damages unless his acts constitute gross negligence or unless he will receive or expects to receive remuneration. Nothing contained in this subsection shall alter existing law with respect to tort liability of a practitioner of the healing arts for acts committed in the ordinary course of his practice.

(c) A person who willfully violates subsection (a) of this section shall be fined not more than $100.00.

Other states have similar laws including Wisconsin[7] and California.[8] Do these laws go far enough in imposing a duty to help? Do they go too far? Identify

---

6. R.I. Gen. Law § 11–56–1:

Any person at the scene of an emergency who knows that another person is exposed to, or has suffered, grave physical harm shall, to the extent that he or she can do so without danger or peril to himself or herself or to others, give reasonable assistance to the exposed person. Any person violating the provisions of this section shall be guilty of a petty misdemeanor and shall be subject to imprisonment for a term not exceeding six (6) months or by a fine of not more than five hundred dollars ($500), or both.

7. Duty to aid victim or report crime:

(1)(a) Whoever violates sub. (2)(a) is guilty of a Class C misdemeanor.

(b) Whoever violates sub. (2)(b) is guilty of a Class C misdemeanor and is subject to discipline under § 440.26(6).

(2)(a) Any person who knows that a crime is being committed and that a victim is exposed to bodily harm shall summon law enforcement officers or other assistance or shall provide assistance to the victim.

(b) Any person licensed as a private detective or granted a private security permit under § 440.26 who has reasonable grounds to believe that a crime is being committed or has been committed shall notify promptly an appropriate law enforcement agency of the facts which form the basis for this belief.

. . .

(d) A person need not comply with this subsection if any of the following apply:

1. Compliance would place him or her in danger.

2. Compliance would interfere with duties the person owes to others.

3. In the circumstances described under par. (a), assistance is being summoned or provided by others.

4. In the circumstances described under par. (b) or (c), the crime or alleged crime has been reported to an appropriate law enforcement agency by others.

. . .

(m) If a person is subject to sub. (2)(b) or (c), the person need not comply with sub. (2)(b) or (c) until after he or she has summoned or provided assistance to a victim.

particular aspects of these laws that should be reformed and explain the changes that could be made.

4. *The Kitty Genovese Case.* Consider the murder of Kitty Genovese which was described in *Moseley v. Scully*, 908 F.Supp. 1120 (E.D.N.Y. 1995), as follows:

> This case involves one of the most infamous and brutal murders committed this century, which shocked the nation when it was committed in 1964, and continues to trouble the public today. [T]he 1964 murder of Katherine "Kitty" Genovese ("Genovese") in Queens, New York "symbolized urban apathy [since] 38 people heard her screams but did nothing." . . .
>
> [Defendant] left his house in the early morning hours [with] a hunting knife for the purpose of "finding a woman and killing her." [About] 3:00 a.m., he spotted a red car, driven by Genovese, which he followed for approximately ten blocks. When Genovese [exited her car,] Moseley . . . "stabbed her twice in the back." Because someone had called out from an open window, Moseley returned to his car and moved it, but he "could see that [Genovese] had gotten up and that she wasn't dead." Since he "did not think that the person that called would come down to help [Genovese] regardless [of] the fact that she had screamed, [he] came back [and] look[ed for her] in the Long Island [R]ailroad station." Not finding her there, Moseley looked in some nearby apartment buildings, where he found her in a hallway.... [He admitted that,] "As soon as she saw me, she started screaming[,] so I stabbed her a few other times to stop her from screaming, and I had stabbed her once in the neck. [S]he only moaned after that."
>
> During [this] brutal attack, Moseley could hear that he had awakened residents of the apartment building. He heard a door open "at least twice, maybe three times, but when [he] looked [up], there was nobody up there." Since he "didn't feel that these people were coming down the stairs anyway," he decided to rape Genovese. . . . [and later] left Genovese dead.

(3) If a person renders emergency care for a victim, § 895.48(1) applies. Any person who provides other reasonable assistance under this section is immune from civil liability for his or her acts or omissions in providing the assistance. This immunity does not apply if the person receives or expects to receive compensation for providing the assistance.

8. California's law provides as follows:

Cal. Penal Code § 368. Elder or dependent adults; infliction of pain or mental suffering or endangering health; theft or embezzlement of property; penalties; definitions

. . .

(b) Any person who, under circumstances or conditions other than those likely to produce great bodily harm or death, willfully causes or permits any elder or dependent adult, with knowledge that he or she is an elder or a dependent adult, to suffer, or inflicts thereon unjustifiable physical pain or mental suffering, or having the care or custody of any elder or dependent adult, willfully causes or permits the person or health of the elder or dependent adult to be injured or willfully causes or permits the elder or dependent adult to be placed in a situation in which his or her person or health may be endangered, is guilty of a misdemeanor.

Can the state bring homicide prosecutions against those who heard the incident, but who did nothing to help? If not, should the law be changed to allow prosecution of those who heard the victim's screams? If so, how would you formulate the new homicide law?

5. *Overdosing Addict.* Yates met defendant at a party in defendant's apartment. Marijuana was in use, and defendant was flirting with Yates at the party. Yates spent the night in defendant's apartment and the two of them shared some cocaine. Defendant then had to go out. When he returned, defendant found Yates on his bed, naked from the waist up, and in severe convulsions from the cocaine. She was hemorrhaging from her nose and mouth, and the hemorrhaging blocked the passage of air to her lungs. Does defendant have a "legal duty" to seek assistance for Yates so that, if she dies, he could be charged with homicide? *See Herman v. State*, 472 So.2d 770 (Fla.App. 1985).

6. *Overdose Reprise.* Defendant, a married man, worked as a bartender at a hotel. While his wife was away, defendant had an affair with a woman named Blanche Burns. The two had been acquainted for some time. Both went to defendant's ground-floor apartment where they drank steadily for two days. Then Burns obtained morphine in quarter-grain tablets. Defendant saw Burns consume three or four tablets before he could stop her. She went into a stupor and could not be roused. Before defendant's wife returned, he moved Burns to a basement apartment occupied by a friend who agreed to "look after" her. At the time, the victim was passed out. Burns died that evening. Under the circumstances, did defendant have a "duty" to obtain medical assistance for Burns? *See People v. Beardsley*, 150 Mich. 206, 113 N.W. 1128 (1907).

7. *Defendant's Burning Building.* Due to no fault of his own, defendant's building caught on fire. Since defendant wanted to collect insurance on the building, he made no effort to put the fire out. In addition, he failed to report the fire to the fire department. Can defendant be convicted of burning a building with the intention of collecting the insurance proceeds? *See Commonwealth v. Cali*, 247 Mass. 20, 141 N.E. 510 (1923).

8. *The Rapist and His Victim.* Defendant attacked and raped twelve-year-old Edith Barton in his car. Immediately afterwards, she jumped out of the car, ran to a bridge over a stream, and either fell off the bridge or jumped off into the stream. Defendant made no attempt to rescue her even though he could have done so easily with no risk to himself. Edith Barton drowned. Did defendant have a legal duty to rescue Barton? *See Jones v. State*, 220 Ind. 384, 43 N.E.2d 1017 (1942).

9. *The Gateman.* Defendant was employed by a railroad company as a crossing gateman. Although a train was approaching, defendant failed to lower the crossing gate. Dan Goble, not realizing that a train was coming, drove across the tracks in his automobile and his car was hit by the train. Goble was killed. Did defendant have a legal duty to lower the gate so that

he can be prosecuted criminally for his failure to do so? *See State v. Harrison,* 107 N.J.L. 213, 152 A. 867 (1931).

10. *Duty to Summon Medical Assistance for Spouse.* Reverend Flaherty was a teacher, counselor, and chaplain at United Wesleyan College. Flaherty was a thirty-four year old diabetic who had, for seventeen years, administered to himself daily doses of insulin. Following an encounter on campus with a visiting evangelist speaker, Reverend Flaherty publicly proclaimed his desire to discontinue insulin treatment in reliance on the belief that God would heal his diabetic condition. One day, Flaherty fell ill and requested insulin, but his wife discouraged him from taking it, and reminded him of his vow. As the day progressed, Reverend Flaherty experienced increasing illness, and vomited intermittently. The next day he remained in bed all day except for trips to the bathroom. As the Reverend's condition worsened and he became restless, his wife and a friend did not summon medical aid, in order to help the Reverend keep his vow. The couple's eleven-year-old daughter then inquired as to why a doctor had not been summoned but Mrs. Flaherty responded that her husband was "going to be getting better." Late that night everyone in the household fell asleep. The next morning at approximately 6:00 a.m., while the others were still asleep, Reverend Flaherty died of diabetic ketoacidosis. Under the circumstances, did Mrs. Flaherty have a legal duty to summon medical assistance for her husband? *See Commonwealth v. Konz,* 498 Pa. 639, 450 A.2d 638 (1982).

11. *Care for an Ailing Parent.* As a general rule, a child is under no duty to care for an ailing parent. What facts might trigger such a duty? What if the parent is senile and lives with the adult child? What if the child is named as the parent's authorized representative for the purpose of receiving food stamps and social security checks? *See Davis v. Commonwealth,* 230 Va. 201, 335 S.E.2d 375 (1985).

12. *Psychotic Episodes.* A mother called 911 just after midnight and stated that, "I've just killed my boys." She also stated that God ordered her to do it. When they arrived at the scene, police officers found a 6 year-old and 8 year-old boy in the front yard with their skulls smashed. They also found a 14-month-old baby alive in his crib with a fractured skull. At trial, the evidence reveals that the mother had suffered from delusional psychotic disorder and had been through three major psychotic episodes over the prior three years. The evidence also reveals that the father was aware of the psychotic episodes, but nonetheless left the children alone with the mother every day. On the night of the murders, the father was asleep and heard nothing. Did the father have a duty to protect the children against the mother? Did he violate that duty?

STATE v. WILLIQUETTE

129 Wis.2d 239, 385 N.W.2d 145 (1986).

STEINMETZ, JUSTICES.

[Terri] Williquette, the defendant, was charged with two counts of child abuse. Count one was based on the defendant's alleged failure to take any action to prevent her husband, Bert Williquette, from repeatedly "sexually abusing, beating, and otherwise mistreating" her seven year old son, B.W. Count two was based on the defendant's alleged failure to take any action to prevent her husband from committing similar acts against the defendant's eight year old daughter, C.P.

[B.W.] reported being forced by his father to stand on one foot and one hand in an unbalanced position. In that position, his father would strike him. [B.W.] told his mother on many occasions that he had been beaten with the metal stick by Bert Williquette, but the defendant never did anything about it. He also reported telling his mother about the incident on November 10, 1983, when he had been struck on the foot with the metal stick. At that time, his mother told him "not to worry about it." [Dr.] Ferrin Holmes, a pediatrician at the Door County Medical Center, examined B.W. [and] observed numerous bruises on the child's feet, upper and lower legs, lower and upper back, left arm and the side of his chest. Dr. Holmes stated that, in his professional opinion, B.W. had been beaten on at least four separate occasions in the fairly recent past, and that the beatings were inflicted with a metal stick or instrument.

[C.P.], defendant's daughter, stated that Bert Williquette regularly beat her and her brother at their home in Door county, on occasion using a metal stick with a hook on its end. C.P. stated that Bert Williquette would beat her and B.W. so hard that the children would wet their pants. He allegedly would also make the children balance on one hand and one leg, and then he would take the hook end of the metal stick and trip them, causing them to fall down. C.P. told Sergeant Bies that some time after Halloween in 1983, Bert Williquette hit her on the top of the head with the metal stick so hard that she bled. Sergeant Bies examined the area of C.P.'s head where she claimed Bert Williquette had struck her, and he could still feel a lump there. C.P. indicated that she had told the defendant about the incident, and that the defendant had given her an ice pack for her head. [Williquette also sexually abused both children.]

C.P. said that she had told the defendant about all of the sexual abuse incidents involving her and B.W. but that her mother did not do anything about it. She also indicated to a social worker that she had told her mother on many occasions about the times she and B.W. were beaten by Bert Williquette. Her mother allegedly told C.P. that she would do something about it, but she never did.

[The] parties disagree as to whether [the statute] requires a person to directly inflict child abuse in order to violate the statute. The defendant contends that the legislature intended the statute to apply only to persons who directly abuse children. She maintains that the statute does not impose a duty on her to protect her own children from abuse. The state, however, argues that the statute is susceptible to an interpretation which includes persons having a special relationship to children who expose them to abuse. The state relies on the statutory language "subjects a child to cruel maltreatment." The state urges the court to construe this language to cover situations in which a parent knowingly exposes a child to abuse by placing the child in a situation where abuse has occurred and is likely to recur.

[A] person exposes a child to abuse when he or she causes the child to come within the influence of a foreseeable risk of cruel maltreatment. Causation in this context means that a person's conduct is a substantial factor in exposing the child to risk, and there may be more than one substantial causative factor in any given case. In this case, Bert Williquette's conduct obviously was a direct cause of the abuse his children suffered. However, the defendant's alleged conduct, as the mother of the children, also was a contributing cause of risk to the children. She allegedly knew that the father abused the children in her absence, but she continued to leave the children and to entrust them to his exclusive care, and she allegedly did nothing else to prevent the abuse, such as notifying proper authorities or providing alternative child care in her absence. We conclude that the defendant's conduct, as alleged, constituted a substantial factor which increased the risk of further abuse.

The defendant disputes that an omission to act may constitute a crime. Although the court disagrees with this argument, we specifically note that the alleged conduct in this case involves more than an omission to act. The defendant regularly left the children in the father's exclusive care and control despite allegedly knowing that he abused the children in her absence. We consider leaving the children in these circumstances to be overt conduct. Therefore, even assuming that an overt act is necessary for the commission of a crime, the allegations support the charges in this case.

The court, however, also expressly rejects the defendant's claim that an act of commission, rather than omission, is a necessary element of a crime. The essence of criminal conduct is the requirement of a wrongful "act." This element, however, is satisfied by overt acts, as well as omissions to act where there is a legal duty to act. LaFave and Scott, Criminal Law sec. 26 at 182, states the general rule applicable to omissions:

> "Some statutory crimes are specifically defined in terms of omission to act. With other common law and statutory crimes which are defined in terms of conduct producing a specified result, a person may be criminally liable when his omission to act produces that result, but only if (1) he has, under the circumstances, a legal duty to act, and (2) he can physically perform the act. The trend of the law has been toward enlarging the scope of duty to act."

The comments to this section then state the traditional rule that a person generally has no duty to rescue or protect an endangered person <u>unless a special relationship exists</u> between the persons which imposes a legal duty to protect:

> For criminal liability to be based upon a failure to act it must first be found that there is a duty to act—a legal duty and not simply a moral duty. As we have seen, some criminal statutes themselves impose the legal duty to act, as with the tax statute and the hit-and-run statute. With other crimes the duty must be found outside the definition of the crime itself—perhaps in another statute, or in the common law, or in a contract.
>
> Generally, one has no legal duty to aid another person in peril, even when that aid can be rendered without danger or inconvenience to himself. He need not shout a warning to a blind man headed for a precipice or to an absent-minded one walking into a gunpowder room with a lighted candle in hand. He need not pull a neighbor's baby out of a pool of water or rescue an unconscious person stretched across the railroad tracks, though the baby is drowning or the whistle of an approaching train is heard in the distance. A doctor is not legally bound to answer a desperate call from the frantic parents of a sick child, at least if it is not one of his regular patients. A moral duty to take affirmative action is not enough to impose a legal duty to do so. But there are <u>situations which do give rise to a duty to act</u>:
>
> > (1) Duty based upon relationship. <u>The common law imposes affirmative duties upon persons standing in certain personal relationships to other persons</u>—upon parents to aid their small children, upon husbands to aid their wives, upon ship captains to aid their crews, upon masters to aid their servants. Thus a parent may be guilty of criminal homicide for failure to call a doctor for his sick child, a mother for failure to prevent the fatal beating of her baby by her lover, a husband for failure to aid his imperiled wife, a ship captain for failure to pick up a seaman or passenger fallen overboard, and an employer for failure to aid his endangered employee. Action may be required to thwart the threatened perils of nature (e.g., to combat sickness, to ward off starvation or the elements); or it may be required to protect against threatened acts by third persons. LaFave and Scott, Criminal Law at 183–84.

The requirement of a legal duty to act is a policy limitation which prevents most omissions from being considered the proximate cause of a prohibited consequence. In a technical sense, a person's omission, i.e., whether the person fails to protect, warn or rescue, may be a substantial factor in exposing another person to harm. The concept of causation, however, is not solely a question of mechanical connection between events, but also a question of policy. A particular legal cause must be one of which the law will take cognizance. The rule that persons do not have a general duty to protect represents a public policy choice to limit criminal liability.

limit criminal liability.

The requirement of an overt act, therefore, is not inherently necessary for criminal liability. Criminal liability depends on conduct which is a substantial factor in producing consequences. Omissions are as capable of producing consequences as overt acts. Thus, the common law rule that there is no general duty to protect limits criminal liability where it would otherwise exist. The special relationship exception to the "no duty to act" rule represents a choice to retain liability for some omissions, which are considered morally unacceptable.

[Like] most jurisdictions, Wisconsin generally does not require a person to protect others from hazardous situations. When a special relationship exists between persons, however, social policy may impose a duty to protect. The relationship between a parent and a child exemplifies a special relationship where the duty to protect is imposed. We stated the rule applicable to the parent and child relationship in *Cole v. Sears Roebuck & Co.*, 47 Wis.2d 629, 634, 177 N.W.2d 866 (1970):

> "It is the right and duty of parents under the law of nature as well as the common law and the statutes of many states to protect their children, to care for them in sickness and in health, and to do whatever may be necessary for their care, maintenance, and preservation, including medical attendance, if necessary. An omission to do this is a public wrong which the state, under its police powers, may prevent. The child has the right to call upon the parent for the discharge of this duty, and public policy for the good of society will not permit or allow the parent to divest himself irrevocably of his obligations in this regard or to abandon them at his mere will or pleasure...."

From the above discussion, we conclude that a parent who fails to take any action to stop instances of child abuse can be prosecuted as a principal for exposing the child to the [abuse]. [When] liability [depends] on a breach of the parent's duty to protect, the parent must knowingly act in disregard of the facts giving rise to a duty to act. ...

Finally, we reject the defendant's claim that § 940.201, is unconstitutionally vague if it is construed to apply to a parent's knowing failure to protect a child from abuse. [Our] holding in this case is that a parent who knowingly exposes a child to the risk of such abhorrent conduct violates the statute. This construction of § 940.201 gives the defendant notice that she has an affirmative duty to protect her

holding

children from a foreseeable risk of cruel maltreatment. The statute is not unconstitutionally vague.

[The] decision of the court of appeals is affirmed.

Heffernan, Chief Justice (dissenting).

[The] question for a court is whether the legislature has made criminal the action with which Terri Williquette has been charged. The question is not whether a court, were it sitting as a legislature, would have proscribed the conduct. [A]lthough it points to no legislative intent contemporaneous with the passage of the law that would make Terri Williquette's conduct a felony, the majority finds that the statute means that conduct which occurred almost three years ago is now to be definitively declared criminal. In the absence of some indicia supporting that interpretation stemming from the time of the law's passage, the best that can be said of the law which the majority now promulgates, assuming it is otherwise appropriate, is that it is unconstitutional as ex post facto. [I] dissent.

NOTES

1. *Terminating life support.* In *Barber v. Superior Court*, 147 Cal.App.3d 1006, 195 Cal.Rptr. 484 (1983), a doctor was charged with murder for terminating life support to a patient in a persistent vegetative state. The court treated the act as an "omission," but concluded that the doctor acted permissibly:

> There is no criminal liability for failure to act unless there is a legal duty to act. Thus the critical issue becomes one of determining the duties owed by a physician to a patient who has been reliably diagnosed as in a comatose state from which any meaningful recovery of cognitive brain function is exceedingly unlikely.

> [A] physician has no duty to continue treatment, once it has proved to be ineffective. Although there may be a duty to provide life-sustaining machinery in the immediate aftermath of a cardio-respiratory arrest, there is no duty to continue its use once it has become futile in the opinion of qualified medical personnel.

> If it is not possible to ascertain the choice the patient would have made, the surrogate ought to be guided in his decision by the patient's best interests. Under this standard, such factors as the relief of suffering, the preservation or restoration of functioning and the quality as well as the extent of life sustained may be considered. Finally, since most people are concerned about the well-being of their loved ones, the surrogate may take into account the impact of the decision on those people closest to the patient.

2. *Spiritual treatment.* In *Walker v. Superior Court*, 222 Cal.Rptr. 87 (Cal.App. 1986), defendant's daughter died of acute purulent meningitis which had been present in her body for at least two weeks at the time of

death. Defendant knew that her daughter was ill, but chose to treat her daughter by spiritual healing rather than the use of medical specialists or practitioners. The court upheld a conviction for manslaughter: "[The] point at which parents may incur liability for substituting prayer treatment for medical care for their child is clear—when the lack of medical attention places the child in a situation endangering its person or health."

PROBLEMS

1. *Detecting Gangrenous Infection.* Defendants, husband and wife, had a 17-month-old son. The father was a laborer with only a sixth-grade education. The mother had an 11th grade education. The father's 85-year-old mother cared for the baby when the parents were at work. Both parents professed to love and care for the boy. However, when the boy developed an abscessed tooth that developed into a gangrenous infection of the mouth and cheeks, neither parent took the boy to the doctor even though they had the means to do so. A court summarized the evidence as follows:

> This condition, accompanied by the child's inability to eat, brought about malnutrition, lowering the child's resistance and eventually producing pneumonia, causing death. Dr. Wilson testified that in his opinion the infection had lasted for approximately 2 weeks, and that the odor generally associated with gangrene would have been present for approximately 10 days before death. He also expressed the opinion that had medical care been first obtained in the last week before the baby's death, such care would have been obtained too late to have saved the baby's life.... The defendant husband testified that he noticed the baby was sick about 2 weeks before the baby died. The defendant wife testified that she noticed the baby was ill about a week and a half or 2 weeks before the baby died. The evidence showed that in the critical period the baby was fussy; that he could not keep his food down; and that his cheek started swelling up. The swelling went up and down, but did not disappear. In that same period, the cheek turned "a bluish color...."

The defendants, not realizing that the baby was as ill as it was or that the baby was in danger of dying, attempted to provide some relief to the baby by giving the baby aspirin and continued to do so until the night before the baby died. The defendants thought the swelling would go down and were waiting for it to do so; and defendant husband testified, that from what he had heard, neither doctors nor dentists pull out a tooth "when it's all swollen up like that."

There was an additional explanation for not calling a doctor given by each defendant. Both parents testified that "the way the cheek looked, [and] that stuff on his hair, they [the Welfare Department] would think we were neglecting him and take him away from us and not give him back." Defendant wife testified that she "was so scared of losing him." They testified that they had heard that the defendant husband's cousin lost a child that way. The evidence showed that the defendants did not understand the significance or seriousness of the baby's symptoms. Under the circumstances, have defendants committed a violation of their duty to obtain medical assistance for their child? Are they guilty of "ordinary negligence" because of a failure to exercise "ordinary caution"? Or did they ignore a "substantial" risk of death and act in a way that represents a "gross deviation" from the conduct of a reasonable person? *See State v. Williams*, 4 Wash.App. 908, 484 P.2d 1167 (1971). Compare *People v. Sealy*, 136 Mich.App. 168, 356 N.W.2d 614 (1984).

2. *The Engineer and the Locomotive.* The engineer of a locomotive was returning the locomotive to the roundhouse when he realized that the incoming track was "spiked" (in other words, it had been nailed up and put out of service). In violation of company rules, the engineer continued inward on the outgoing track. The locomotive had gone perhaps half a mile on this wrong track, when it collided with an oncoming train. Two railroad employees were killed. Under company rules, the locomotive's foreman is responsible for insuring that the train is on the right track. Can the foreman be convicted of reckless manslaughter if he failed to realize that the engineer had the train on the wrong track? *See State v. Irvine*, 126 La. 434, 52 So. 567 (1910).

CHAPTER 3

MENS REA

■ ■ ■

A second element of just punishment is the mens rea requirement. Traditionally, the criminal law looked to a person's mental state (his or her "mens rea") and the associated notion of that person's presumed "blameworthiness" in assessing the existence or absence of criminal culpability. From this perspective, intentional criminal conduct has classically been viewed as more serious—more wicked, more immoral, more blameworthy—than unintentional criminal conduct. Indeed, Oliver Wendell Holmes made this same point more than a century ago when he observed that "even a dog distinguishes between being stumbled over and being kicked." Oliver Wendell Holmes, Jr., The Common Law 3 (1881).

A. LEGISLATIVE PATTERNS OF CRIMINAL INTENTION

At common law, a wide variety of mental states were applied. In addition to the mental state used in the following case ("maliciously"), courts applied a variety of other mental states, including "fraudulently," "corruptly," "wantonly," "willfully," "intentionally," "feloniously," "unlawfully," and "intent to steal."

REGINA v. FAULKNER
13 Cox Crim. Cas. 550 (1877).

[The prisoner was indicted for setting fire to the ship Zemindar, on the high seas, on June 26, 1876. The indictment charged that he "feloniously, unlawfully, and maliciously" burned a ship with the intent "to prejudice the owner of the ship and the owners of certain goods and chattels then laden, and being on board said ship." The ship was carrying a cargo of rum, sugar, and cotton, worth 50,000 £. The facts showed that prisoner, a seaman on the ship, went into the bulk head, and forecastle hold, opened the sliding door in the bulk head, to steal rum. The facts further showed that he bored a hole in the cask with a gimlet, that the rum ran out, that when trying to put a

57

spile in the hole out of which the rum was running, he had a lighted match in his hand; that the rum caught fire; that the prisoner himself was burned on the arms and neck; and that the ship caught fire and was completely destroyed. At the close of the Crown's case, counsel for the prisoner asked for a direction of an acquittal on the ground that on the facts proved the indictment was not sustained, nor the allegation that the prisoner had unlawfully and maliciously set fire to the ship proved. The Crown contended that inasmuch as the prisoner was at the time engaged in the commission of a felony, the indictment was sustained, and the allegation of the intent was immaterial].

At the second hearing of the case before the Court for Crown Cases Reserved, the learned judge made the addition of the following paragraph to the case stated by him for the court.

"It was conceded that the. prisoner had no actual intention of burning the vessel, and I was not asked to leave any question as to the jury as to the prisoner's knowing the probable consequences his act, or as to his reckless conduct."

The learned judge told the jury that although the prisoner had no actual intention of burning the vessel, still if they found he was engaged in stealing the rum, and that the fire took place in the manner above stated, they ought to find him guilty. The jury found the prisoner guilty on both counts, and he was sentenced to seven years penal servitude. The question for the court was whether the direction of the learned judge was right, if not, the conviction should be quashed. . . .

DOWSE, B., gave judgment to the effect that the conviction should be quashed.

BARRY, J.—A very broad proposition has been contended for by the Crown, namely, that if, while a person is engaged in committing a felony, or, having committed it, is endeavouring to conceal his act, or prevent or spoil waste consequent on that act, he accidently does some collateral act which if done wilfully would be another felony either at common law or by statute, he is guilty of the latter felony, I am by no means anxious to throw any doubt upon, or limit in any way, the legal responsibility of those who engage in the commission of felony, or acts *mala in se;* but I am not prepared without more consideration to give my assent to so wide a proposition. No express authority either by way of decision or dictum from judge or text writer has been cited in support of it. . . . [I consider myself bound] by the authority of *Reg. v. Pembliton* (12 Cox C. C. 607). That case must be taken as deciding that to constitute an offence under the Malicious Injuries to Property Act, sect. 51, the act done must be in fact intentional and wilful, although the intention and will may (perhaps) be held to exist in, or be proved by, the fact that the accused knew that the injury would be the probable result of his unlawful act, and yet did the act reckless of such consequences. The present indictment charges the offence to be under the 42nd section of the same Act, and it is not disputed that the same construction must be applied to both sections. . . . The jury [were] directed to give a verdict of guilty upon the simple ground that the firing of the ship, though accidental, was caused by an act done in the course of, or immediately consequent upon, a felonious operation, and no question of the prisoner's malice, constructive or otherwise, was left to the jury. I am of opinion that, according to *Reg. v. Pembliton*, that direction was erroneous, and that the conviction should be quashed.

FITZGERALD, J.—I concur in opinion with my brother Barry, and for the reasons he has given, that the direction of the learned judge cannot be sustained in law, and that therefore the conviction should be quashed. [In] order to establish the charge of felony under sect. 42, the intention of the accused forms an element in the crime to the extent that it should appear that the defendant intended to do the very act with which he is charged, or that it was the necessary consequence of some other felonious or criminal act in which he was engaged, or that having a probable result which the defendant foresaw, or ought to have foreseen, he, nevertheless, persevered in such other felonious or criminal act. The prisoner did not intend to set fire to the ship; the fire was not the necessary result of the felony he was attempting; and if it was a probable result, which he ought to have foreseen, of the felonious transaction on which he was engaged, and from which a malicious design to commit the injurious act with which he is charged might have been fairly imputed to him, that view of the case was not submitted to the jury. . . . Counsel for the prosecution in effect insisted that the defendant, being engaged in the commission of, or in an attempt to commit a felony, was criminally responsible for every result that was occasioned thereby, even though it was not a probable consequence of his act or such as he could have reasonably foreseen or intended. No authority has been cited for a proposition so extensive, and I am of opinion that it is not warranted by law. . . .

O'BRIEN, J.—I am also opinion that the conviction should be quashed. . . . [A]t the trial, the Crown's counsel conceded that the prisoner had no intention of burning the vessel, or of igniting the rum; and raised no questions as to prisoner's imagining or having any ground for supposing that the fire would be the result or consequence of his act in stealing the rum. . . . The reasonable inference from the evidence is that the prisoner lighted the match for the purpose of putting the spile in the hole to stop the further running of the rum, and that while he was attempting to do so the rum came in contact with the lighted match and took fire. . . .

KEOGH, J.—I have the misfortune to differ from the other members of the Court. . . . [I am] of opinion, that the conviction should stand, as I consider all questions of intention and malice are closed by the finding of the jury, that the prisoner committed the act with which he was charged whilst engaged in the commission of a substantive felony. . . .

PALLES, C.B.—I concur in the opinion of the majority of the Court. . . . The Lord Chief Justice of the Common Pleas, who, in consequence of illness, has been unable to preside to-day, has authorized me to state that he considers that the case before us is concluded by *Reg. v. Pembliton*.

DEASY, B., and LAWSON, J., concurred.

Conviction quashed.

NOTES

1. *M.P.C. mental states.* The drafters of the Model Penal Code chose to abandon most common law vocabulary for mental states, and to focus on only four mental states. *See* M.P.C. § 2.02(2):

§ 2.02. **General Requirements of Culpability.**

(1) **Minimum Requirements of Culpability.** Except as provided in Section 2.05, a person is not guilty of an offense unless he acted purposely, knowingly, recklessly or negligently, as the law may require, with respect to each material element of the offense.

(2) **Kinds of Culpability Defined.** *PKRN*

(a) **Purposely.** A person acts purposely with respect to a material element of an offense when:

(i) if the element involves the nature of his conduct or a result thereof, it is his conscious object to engage in conduct of that nature or to cause such a result; and

(ii) if the element involves the attendant circumstances, he is aware of the existence of such circumstances or he believes or hopes that they exist.

(b) **Knowingly.** A person acts knowingly with respect to a material element of an offense when:

(i) if the element involves the nature of his conduct or the attendant circumstances, he is aware that his conduct is of that nature or that such circumstances exist; and

(ii) if the element involves a result of his conduct, he is aware that it is practically certain that his conduct will cause such a result.

(c) **Recklessly.** A person acts recklessly with respect to a material element of an offense when he consciously disregards a substantial and unjustifiable risk that the material element exists or will result from his conduct. The risk must be of such a nature and degree that, considering the nature and purpose of the actor's conduct and the circumstances known to him, its disregard involves a gross deviation from the standard of conduct that a law-abiding person would observe in the actor's situation.

(d) **Negligently.** A person acts negligently with respect to a material element of an offense when he should be aware of a substantial and unjustifiable risk that the material element exists or will result from his conduct. The risk must be of such a nature and degree that the actor's failure to perceive it, considering the nature and purpose of his conduct and the circumstances known to him, involves a gross deviation from the standard of care that a reasonable person would observe in the actor's situation.

(3) **Culpability Required Unless Otherwise Provided.** When the culpability sufficient to establish a material element of an offense is not prescribed by law, such element is established if a person acts purposely, knowingly or recklessly with respect thereto. *negligently?*

if no def for culp, then P k R ≠ N

(4) **Prescribed Culpability Requirement Applies to All Material Elements.** When the law defining an offense prescribes the kind of culpability that is sufficient for the commission of an offense, without distinguishing among the material elements thereof, such provision shall apply to all the material elements of the offense, unless a contrary purpose plainly appears.

(5) **Substitutes for Negligence, Recklessness and Knowledge.** When the law provides that negligence suffices to establish an element of an offense, such element also is established if a person acts purposely, knowingly or recklessly. When recklessness suffices to establish an element, such element also is established if a person acts purposely or knowingly. When acting knowingly suffices to establish an element, such element also is established if a person acts purposely.

N → P R K
R → P K
K → P

(6) **Requirement of Purpose Satisfied if Purpose Is Conditional.** When a particular purpose is an element of an offense, the element is established although such purpose is conditional, unless the condition negatives the harm or evil sought to be prevented by the law defining the offense.

(7) **Requirement of Knowledge Satisfied by Knowledge of High Probability.** When knowledge of the existence of a particular fact is an element of an offense, such knowledge is established if a person is aware of a high probability of its existence, unless he actually believes that it does not exist.

(8) **Requirement of Wilfulness Satisfied by Acting Knowingly.** A requirement that an offense be committed wilfully is satisfied if a person acts knowingly with respect to the material elements of the offense, unless a purpose to impose further requirements appears.

(9) **Culpability as to Illegality of Conduct.** Neither knowledge nor recklessness or negligence as to whether conduct constitutes an offense or as to the existence, meaning or application of the law determining the elements of an offense is an element of such offense, unless the definition of the offense or the Code so provides.

(10) **Culpability as Determinant of Grade of Offense.** When the grade or degree of an offense depends on whether the offense is committed purposely, knowingly, recklessly or negligently, its grade or degree shall be the lowest for which the determinative kind of culpability is established with respect to any material element of the offense.

2. *Variations in mental states.* Although there can be similarities between the definitions of various mens rea terms in different jurisdictions and, although some terms may have been borrowed (at least initially) from the Model Penal Code, it is nonetheless important for criminal law practitioners to discern the precise meaning—and judicial interpretation—of each mens rea term for each offense in the Criminal Code in his or her jurisdiction. *See* JEROME HALL, GENERAL PRINCIPLES OF CRIMINAL LAW 142 (2d ed. 1960)("there must be as many *mentes reae* as there are crimes").

STATE v. JACKOWSKI

181 Vt. 73, 915 A.2d 767 (2006).

JOHNSON, J.

Defendant Rosemarie Jackowski appeals her conviction for disorderly conduct. Defendant argues that the trial court improperly instructed the jury to consider whether defendant was "practically certain" that her conduct would cause public inconvenience or annoyance, when she was charged with intentionally causing public inconvenience or annoyance. [We] reverse and remand.

Defendant was arrested on March 20, 2003, during an anti-war demonstration at the intersection of Routes 7 and 9 in Bennington. During the demonstration, protesters blocked traffic at the intersection for approximately fifteen minutes. Defendant stood in the intersection, praying and holding a sign bearing anti-war slogans and newspaper clippings, including an article accompanied by a photograph of a wounded Iraqi child. Police officers repeatedly asked defendant to leave the intersection, and when she refused, she was arrested, along with eleven other protesters. The State charged them with disorderly conduct, alleging that defendant and the other protesters, "with intent to cause public inconvenience and annoyance, obstructed vehicular traffic, in violation of 13 V.S.A. § 1026(5)."

Defendant's intent was the only issue contested during her one-day jury trial. After several police officers testified for the State, defendant took the stand, admitting to blocking traffic, but stating that her only intention in doing so was to protest the war in Iraq, not to cause public inconvenience or annoyance. [At] the conclusion of the trial, the court instructed the jury on the issue of intent. The court first instructed the jury that the State could establish defendant's intent to cause public inconvenience or annoyance by proving beyond a reasonable doubt that she acted "with the conscious object of bothering, disturbing, irritating, or harassing some other person or persons." The court then added, "This intent may also be shown if the State proves beyond a reasonable doubt that the defendant was practically certain that another person or persons ... would be bothered, disturbed, irritated, or harassed." The jury convicted defendant of disorderly conduct. Defendant appeals.

PC = consciss of bothering

LC: if π proves "pc" then convict

Defendant ... argues that the jury charge was improper because the trial court failed to instruct the jury to consider whether defendant acted with the requisite criminal intent. [Defendant] relies on *State v. Trombley* to draw a distinction between offenses that require purposeful or intentional misconduct and those that require only knowing misconduct. 174 Vt. 459, 462, 807 A.2d 400, 404–05 (2002) (mem.). In *Trombley*, we held that it was error for the trial court to instruct the jury to consider whether the defendant in an aggravated assault case acted "knowingly" or "purposely," when he was charged with "purposely" causing serious bodily injury. The aggravated assault statute in *Trombley* had been amended in 1972 to adopt the Model Penal Code's approach to mens rea, which distinguishes among crimes that are committed "purposely," "knowingly," and "recklessly." Under this approach, a person acts "purposely" when "it is his conscious object to engage in conduct of that nature or to cause such a result." A person acts "knowingly" when "he is aware that it is practically certain that his conduct will cause such a result." [Thus,] the trial court in *Trombley* erred in instructing the jury that it could find that the defendant acted "purposely" if "he was practically certain that his conduct would cause serious bodily injury."

Defendant argues that *Trombley* controls here, as the trial court used a similarly worded jury charge, and the disorderly conduct statute was amended at the same time, and for the same reasons, as the aggravated assault statute in *Trombley*. The State attempts to distinguish *Trombley* based on differences in the language of the aggravated assault and disorderly conduct statutes. Unlike the aggravated assault statute, the disorderly conduct statute contains the words "with intent" and not "purposely." This is a purely semantic distinction, and it does not indicate a departure from the Code's approach to mens rea, the adoption of which was "the major statutory change" accomplished by the Legislature's 1972 amendments. The Code does not differentiate between "with intent" and "purposely"; instead, it uses the two terms interchangeably, explaining in its definitions that " 'intentionally' or 'with intent' means purposely." There is no indication that the Legislature used the phrase "with intent" to register disagreement with the Code's approach to disorderly conduct, and such disagreement seems unlikely in the context of an otherwise unqualified adoption of the Code's approach.

The State cites several cases supporting the proposition that both "purposely" and "knowingly" causing harm involve some element of "intent," and thus, that *Trombley's* distinction between "purposely" and "knowingly" is illusory. Each of these cases predates our decision in *Trombley*, however, and each adheres to an outmoded distinction between "specific intent" and "general intent" crimes—the distinction that the Legislature rejected in adopting the Code's approach to mens rea. At common law, crimes committed "purposely" and those committed "knowingly" would both have been specific intent offenses. [These] cases provide no basis for distinguishing or limiting *Trombley* here. It was therefore error for the trial court to charge the jury to consider whether defendant was "practically certain" that her actions would cause public annoyance or inconvenience.

[Intent] was the only issue defendant contested at trial. Defendant claimed that she intended only to protest the war in Iraq, not to cause public annoyance or inconvenience. The State is correct that defendant could have had multiple intents, and a jury could certainly have convicted defendant based on the evidence presented at trial. The law makes a distinction between intentional and knowing acts, however, and defendant was entitled to have a jury decide whether causing public annoyance or inconvenience was her conscious object. The trial court's instruction prevented the jury from considering that question, effectively removing the element of intent from the crime, if not directing a guilty verdict. [We] cannot say that this error was harmless beyond a reasonable doubt, so we must reverse defendant's conviction.

[Reversed] and remanded for further proceedings consistent with the views expressed herein.

BURGESS, J., dissenting.

Confident that the trial court's misdescription of the intent element in this particular case was harmless beyond a reasonable doubt, I respectfully dissent. The majority is correct that the trial court erred in allowing the jury the option to find defendant guilty of disorderly conduct by acting either "with the conscious object," that is "with intent," to cause public inconvenience or annoyance, or by acting with "practical certainty," or "knowingly," that public inconvenience or annoyance would result from her actions. The majority is also correct that . . . the element of "intentional" action in a criminal statute derived from the Model Penal Code, such as the disorderly conduct statute, means to act not "knowingly," but "purposely." The State was required to prove, as it expressly charged, that defendant obstructed traffic "with intent to cause," rather than "knowingly" cause, public inconvenience and annoyance. Nevertheless, given the overwhelming evidence of defendant's actual intent to cause public inconvenience by obstructing traffic, the error was harmless because "we can say beyond a reasonable doubt that the result would have been the same in the absence of the error."

[Defendant's] testimony proved the elements of disorderly conduct as charged: that she obstructed vehicular traffic "with intent to cause public inconvenience or annoyance, in violation of 13 V.S.A. § 1026(5)," and did so "purposely" under the Model Penal Code applied in *Trombley*. The Code states that a person acts "purposely" when: ["]if the element involves the nature of his conduct or a result thereof, it is his conscious object to engage in conduct of that nature or to cause such a result[."]

Defendant's intentional obstruction of traffic was not disputed. That the motorists were inconvenienced and annoyed as a result, and defendant's awareness of same, were not disputed. Having admitted that she was aware her conduct was causing public inconvenience and annoyance, defendant told the jury that she resisted the temptation to stop doing it. Defendant told the jury that, inspired by prayer, she then consciously elected to continue causing public inconvenience and annoyance by continuing to block the public way. In Model Penal Code terms, defendant admitted that, as of the time of deciding to continue obstructing traffic, the "nature of [her] conduct" in obstructing traffic was to annoy and inconvenience the public, and admitted that it was her "conscious object to engage in conduct of that nature."

Nevertheless, defendant also explained to the jury, and argued on appeal, that in blocking traffic it was not her intent to inconvenience and annoy people. Defendant denied such an intent, and testified that she only meant to show her sign, to share her anti-war information and to show resistance to the federal government. So selective and implausible is this proposition that it does not achieve even the level of sophistry. That defendant was also motivated by a noncriminal urge to communicate and show political opposition does not mutually exclude a contemporaneous and, in this case, manifest criminal intent to cause public inconvenience and annoyance.

[Accordingly,] I would affirm the conviction. . . .

PROBLEMS

1. *The Bomb.* Defendant plants a bomb on an airplane in an effort to kill an enemy. If the bomb explodes, killing the enemy, did defendant "purposely" kill the enemy? Suppose that the plane also contains 240 other people. If all 240 are also killed, can it be said that defendant "purposely" killed them? Did the defendant act "knowingly?"

2. *Tire Blow Out.* Suppose that defendant is driving on a city boulevard when his car's left front tire blows out. Despite defendant's best efforts to

control the vehicle, the car swerves off the road and kills a pedestrian. In the following situations, consider whether defendant is deserving of punishment, and whether defendant has one of the mens rea states (purpose, knowledge, recklessness or negligence) for homicide:

    a. *New Tires.* Defendant is driving at or near the speed limit (35 mph) on new tires, and has no reason to believe that there are any problems with the tires.

    b. *Old Tires.* Defendant is driving at or near the speed limit, but his tires are old and bald.

    c. *Extreme Speeding.* Defendant is driving at a speed of 65 mph in a 35 mph zone when the blow out occurs.

    3. *The Driver Redux.* Consider the following additional situations in an effort to decide whether defendant is deserving of punishment, and whether she has any of the required mens rea states for homicide, particularly recklessness or negligence:

    a. Defendant is daydreaming while driving down a city street. Her speed is at or near the speed limit, but, because she is not paying attention to detail, she runs off the road killing a pedestrian.

    b. Defendant is driving on very icy streets going the speed limit (35 mph). When the car in front of her stops unexpectedly, defendant slams on her brakes but is unable to stop because of the ice. Her car veers onto the sidewalk killing a pedestrian.

    4. *Proving Mens Rea.* If some mens rea requirements have subjective elements, how does the prosecution prove that those requirements are satisfied? For example, defendant points a gun at another person, pulls the trigger, and kills him. What type of evidence might the prosecution offer to show that defendant's purpose was to kill? Likewise, in Problems 2 and 3 *supra*, if the prosecution seeks to show that defendant was "reckless" rather than simply "negligent", what type of evidence might the prosecution offer to prove the subjective portion of the driver's mens rea? Might a jury simply infer the mens rea from the circumstances?

    5. *The Epileptic Driver.* Defendant is an epileptic who periodically has seizures. One day, while driving his car on an interstate highway, defendant has a seizure and her car runs into another car, killing the passenger. If she is charged with homicide, can a jury conclude that defendant acted with purpose, knowledge or recklessness?

    6. *Russian Roulette.* Two teenage boys are playing Russian Roulette. They place one bullet in the chamber, spin it, hold it to one of their heads, and pull the trigger. The gun discharges killing one of the boys. Can it be said that the surviving boy acted purposely, knowingly, recklessly or negligently in causing the death of the other boy?

    7. *The Artificial Heart.* Recently, a medical equipment manufacturer developed and implanted the Abiocor artificial heart. This heart is different than prior artificial hearts because it is fully implantable in the patient's body

and (like prior hearts) is designed to completely replace the patient's natural heart. The heart has been approved for experimental use, but has not been approved for implantation generally. In fact, of the first five patients who received the Abiocor heart, 40% (2) died within a matter of months and 40% (a figure which includes one of the people who died) suffered strokes. Did the manufacturer act "recklessly" in removing the patients' natural hearts and replacing them with the Abiocor heart? Would it matter that the manufacturer implanted the heart:

a.   Only in patients who were near death (i.e., patients with a life expectancy of no more than 30 days)?

b.   In healthy males (the Abiocor is too large to be implanted in females) who are nowhere near death.

8.   *Drivers in a Residential Neighborhood.* In a suburban neighborhood, where there are lots of young children, the speed limit is 20 mph. Defendant is driving 20 mph in the neighborhood when a young child suddenly runs out in front of her. Unable to stop, defendant runs over and kills the child. Did defendant's act have the mens rea of negligence or recklessness? Would your analysis be different if defendant had been driving 35 mph? 50 mph?

9.   *The Reckless Rescuer.* A man's father, who lives about a mile away from him, suffers a heart attack and calls the son on his cell phone for help. The son jumps in his car and races to his father's side. In his haste, the son exceeds the speed limit and frequently crosses the center line when traveling around turns. On the last such occasion, while crossing the center line, he collides with another car, killing the driver of that car instantly. Given the circumstances, can it be said that the son acted recklessly or negligently in causing the other driver's death?

△

STATE v. DUCKER

1999 WL 160981 (Tenn.Crim.App. 1999), *aff'd*, 27 S.W.3d 889 (Tenn. 2000).

HAYES.

The appellant, Jennie Bain Ducker, was indicted [on] two counts of first degree murder resulting from the aggravated child abuse of her two children, ages 13 months and 23 months. [A jury] found the appellant guilty of two counts of the lesser charged offense of aggravated child abuse. Concurrent sentences of eighteen years were imposed for each of the class A felony convictions.

[We affirm.]

[The] events leading to the tragic deaths of thirteen month old Dustin Ducker and twenty-three month old Devin Ducker began in the early evening hours of June 5, 1995.... At approximately 3:45 a.m., the appellant arrived at Room 222 of the Holiday Inn in McMinnville. This was the temporary residence of Micah Majors, [a] boyfriend of the appellant. With [her] children securely strapped in their car seats, the appellant closed the [car] windows and locked the doors. [Others] were already in the room with Micah when the appellant arrived. The four men were playing a Sega video golf game and drinking alcoholic beverages. The men continued to play their video game, paying little or no attention to the appellant. They did notice, however, that the appellant poured herself a glass of wine. Additionally, they observed her leave the room on two occasions, once to get ice and once to get BC powders from Micah's car. The appellant never mentioned that her children were in her car or that she needed to check on the children. All four men testified that, despite her usual "dingy" attitude, the appellant did not appear intoxicated. [The others] left Micah's room around 5:00 a.m. The appellant followed the three men to the parking lot, but never checked on her children. As they were pulling out of the parking lot, Pepper noticed that the appellant was already back on the second floor balcony near Micah's room.

[Micah] had changed into boxer shorts and gotten into bed. The appellant knocked on his door and he let her back in the room. Micah testified that he was trying to go to sleep, but the appellant sat next to him on the bed trying to talk to him about a "commitment" in their relationship. Micah then fell asleep. When his alarm went off the next afternoon around twelve or one o'clock, the appellant was still there. She patted Micah on the side of the leg and said, "I have to go." She never mentioned her children.

At 1:03 p.m., the appellant arrived at the emergency room of the River Park Hospital in McMinnville. While she was attempting to get one child out of the car, David Smith, a bystander, heard her say, "Somebody help me. My babies have been in the car for four hours." He responded to her plea for assistance. When he reached the appellant, he observed that the child she was carrying appeared lifeless. . . . The appellant told Fults that the children had been left in a car for three hours with the windows closed. She explained that she had fallen asleep at a friend's house on Lucky Road. At this point, the appellant became frantic, "she was pacing the floor," "wringing her hands," "running her hands through her hair."

[The appellant] testified that she did not see any danger in leaving her thirteen month old and twenty-three month old sons in her locked car for over nine hours while she visited with [Micah] in his motel room. [A]ppellant claimed that "[she] checked on the kids four to five times." However, she could not explain why she did not tell the others that her children were in her car or that she needed to check on them. [Based] upon this evidence, the jury returned guilty verdicts as to two counts of aggravated child abuse. . . .

The appellant [contends] that the evidence is insufficient to support her convictions for aggravated child abuse because the State failed to prove "knowing conduct" beyond a reasonable doubt, i.e., that she "was actually aware that her conduct was reasonably certain to cause the resulting injury to her children." Specifically, the appellant challenges the trial court's instructions to the jury as they relate to the requisite mental state of "knowing" as the definition of this term applies to the offense of aggravated child abuse. She argues that the erroneous charge altered the State's burden of proving the elements of the offense beyond a reasonable doubt.

[Central] to the concept of criminal liability is that, before there can be a crime, there must be an act, or *actus reus*, which must be accompanied by a criminal mind, or *mens rea*. The early concept of *mens rea* meant little more than a "general notion of blameworthiness," or an "evil meaning mind." Over time, this general concept shifted from this vague notion of wickedness to a more definite requirement of a specific state of mind to do that which is prohibited by the criminal law. Thus, no longer could the requirement of "wickedness" suffice. Rather, a different state of mind was required for each crime. This development in the common law culminated in the creation of eighty or so culpability terms. Even with a specific mental state existing for each offense, under this "offense analysis" of culpability, it was soon recognized that each specific mental state was multifaceted. In a traditional "offense analysis," offenses were referred to simply in terms of one encompassing mental state for the offense, *i.e.*, an intentional offense, a knowing offense or a reckless offense. Prior to the enactment of our 1989 code, this state employed "offense analysis." However, where different culpability requirements are appropriate for different elements, "offense analysis" fosters definitions that obscure the requisite mental state. As in the case of the offense of possession of a controlled substance with the intent to sell, proof of different mental states are required for the respective elements of (1) the knowing possession of a controlled substance and (2) the intent to sell the same.

The plethora of *mentes reae* originating from the common law created much confusion and ambiguity. Thus, in 1955, the drafters of the Model Penal Code sought to eliminate this confusion and narrowed the multitude of existing culpability terms to four: purpose, knowledge, recklessness, and negligence. In furtherance of this concept, the Model Penal Code and, subsequently the Tennessee Criminal Code, provide that, with the exception of strict liability offenses, some mental culpability "must be faced separately with respect to each material element of the crime," otherwise, no valid conviction may be obtained. Moreover, the Model Penal Code and the Tennessee Criminal Code both require that one of four levels of culpability must be proven with respect to each "material element" of the offense which may involve "(1) the nature of the forbidden conduct; (2) the attendant circumstances; or (3) the result of the conduct."

[The] first element, conduct, involves the nature of the proscribed act or the manner in which the defendant acts, *e.g.*, the physical act of committing an assault, or the physical restraint of another person (kidnapping). The second element, circumstances surrounding the conduct, refers to a situation which relates to the actor's culpability, *e.g.*, lack of victim's consent or stolen status of property. The result of the defendant's conduct constitutes the final element, in other words, the accused's conduct must at least be a physical cause of the harmful result, *e.g.*, causing the death of another.

Many crimes are made up of not only one, but of several "conduct elements," including not only an act or omission, but also some specific result of that act or omission, or some prescribed attendant circumstances, or perhaps both result and circumstances. In other words, an offense may contain one or more of these conduct elements which, alone or in combination with the others, form the overall behavior which the Legislature has intended to criminalize, and it is those essential conduct elements to which a culpable mental state must apply. Correspondingly, each culpability term is defined with respect to each of the three kinds of "conduct elements": conduct, circumstances, and result. For example, where a specific act is criminalized because of its very nature, a culpable mental state must apply to committing the act itself, *i.e.*, awareness of conduct. On the other hand, unspecified conduct which is criminalized because of the result requires culpability as to that result, *i.e.*, result of conduct. Finally, where otherwise innocent behavior is criminalized due to the circumstances under which it occurs, a culpable mental state is required as to those surrounding circumstances, *i.e.*, awareness of circumstances. In other words, the analysis of the applicable mens rea varies according to the conduct elements of the offense.

In the present offense, the applicable *mens rea* is "knowingly." Tenn.Code Ann. § 39–11–302(b) defines "knowing" as:

> [A] person who acts knowingly with respect to the conduct or to circumstances surrounding the conduct when the person is aware of the nature of the conduct or that the circumstances exist. A person acts knowingly with respect to a result of the persons conduct when the person is aware that the conduct is reasonably certain to cause the result.

When a criminal statute requires a *mens rea* of knowingly, it may speak to conduct, or to circumstances, or to result, or to any combination thereof, but not necessarily to all three. In essence, three theories of "knowingly" exist, *i.e.*, (1) conduct; (2) circumstances; and (3) result of conduct, to correspond to the three conduct elements of a criminal offense. Since a crime may consist of more than one "conduct element," there may be different *mens rea* requirements as to the different "conduct elements" that constitute the crime, even if the required culpability is the same, *e.g.* "knowingly."

Because the applicable definition of "knowing" is element specific, a blanket instruction as to each theory, generally, will invite error. In other words, the court cannot instruct the jury that it could employ either (1) conduct or (2) circumstances; or (3) result of conduct. To do so would effectively alter the State's burden of proving each element of the offense beyond a reasonable doubt. For example, the offense of second degree murder is a result of conduct offense, that is, the intent of the legislature is to punish a person for the killing of another. The trial court may only instruct the jury as to the result of conduct theory of knowingly. If the court instructed the jury as to "awareness of conduct" or "awareness of circumstances," the jury could find a defendant guilty on less proof than that needed to show that the defendant engaged in conduct with knowledge that his conduct is reasonably certain to cause the result.

[The appellant] relies upon the decision of the Texas Court of Criminal Appeals [in] *Alvarado* which held that the trial court, in instructing the jury, must limit its charge of the applicable mental state to the "conduct element" or elements of the offense charged, because to provide a blanket charge as to the applicable culpability requirement would effectively alter the State's burden of proof. We concede that Texas and Tennessee have traveled similar paths regarding culpability requirements. Furthermore, while we acknowledge that Tennessee is now at the same crossroads previously confronted by the Texas court, we decline to adopt the explicit holding in *Alvarado* as this holding may be distinguished under the circumstances of the case *sub judice*. Although we agree with the appellate court of Texas regarding the principal and theory behind element analysis, we decline to apply its holding of reversible error in the case now before us.

We agree with the appellant that to provide the jury with the option that the appellant was aware of her conduct, aware of the circumstances, or was reasonably aware that her conduct was reasonably certain to cause the result, is to relieve the State of their burden of proof. To prove that a defendant is aware of her conduct is one thing; to prove that the defendant's conduct is reasonably certain to produce a certain result is, although subtle, another. The court cannot give the jury the choice of which definition to apply to the crime charged, rather the statute defining the crime dictates which definition of "knowingly" is appropriate as to each element.

The appellant asserts that the offense of "aggravated child abuse," as defined in Tenn.Code Ann. § 39–15–402 and as charged in the present case, only contains the element of "result of conduct," as was determined in *Alvarado*. We do not agree. Upon analysis of our statutory provision, a purview into the legislative intent behind the enactment of the offense leads us to conclude that the offense, as charged in the case presently before this court, contains the elements of (1) awareness of conduct, (2) awareness of circumstances; and (3) result of conduct.

The trial court provided the jury with the following instruction:

> Any person who commits the offense of aggravated child abuse is guilty of a felony. For you to find the Defendant guilty of this offense, the State must have proven beyond a reasonable doubt the existence of the following essential elements:

Knew left in car.

> (1) The Defendant acted knowingly; AND
>
> (2) That the Defendant did:

?

> (a) Other than by accidental means, treat a child in such a manner as to inflict injury; OR

Left in car.

> (b) Other than by accidental means, neglect a child so as to adversely affect the child's health and welfare; AND

No.

> (3)(a) The Defendant used a deadly weapon to accomplish the act of abuse; OR

Death

> (b) The act of abuse resulted in serious bodily injury to the child

The requirement of "knowingly" is also satisfied if it is shown that the Defendant acted intentionally.

> A person acts "knowingly" if that person acts with an awareness either:
>
> (1) That his or her conduct is of a particular nature; or
>
> (2) That a particular circumstance exists.
>
> A person acts knowingly with respect to a result of the person's conduct when the person is aware that the conduct is reasonably certain to cause a result.

A reading of this instruction implies that, for a jury to find that the defendant acted knowingly, the jury must find that the defendant was (1) aware of her conduct or aware of the circumstances and (2) aware that the conduct was reasonably certain to cause a certain result as to each material element of the offense. Although this instruction is erroneous in that it did not charge the specific *mens rea* definition applicable to each "conduct element," we conclude that any such error is harmless.

The prejudice in not providing a "conduct element" specific definition of the applicable *mens rea* is the alteration of the State's burden of proof. The instruction in the present case did not relieve the State's burden of proof. The jury was instructed that it must find each element of the offense beyond a reasonable doubt. The definition of "knowingly" provided by the court supplied a two-prong definition of the term, resulting in an added burden of proof upon the State, for which the appellant cannot now complain. Although the *jury shd. have decided on conduct element.*

preferred instruction would be one that is "conduct element" specific, we conclude that the instruction provided in the present case did not prejudice the appellant. Accordingly, any such error in the instruction is harmless.

Convicted Defendant burden of proving insuff. evidence

Because we have determined that the jury instruction constitutes harmless error, we must determine whether the evidence is sufficient to sustain the conviction. A jury conviction removes the presumption of innocence with which a defendant is initially cloaked and replaces it with one of guilt, so that on appeal a convicted defendant has the burden of demonstrating that the evidence is insufficient. It is the appellate court's duty to affirm the conviction if the evidence viewed under these standards was sufficient for any rational trier of fact to have found the essential elements of the offense beyond a reasonable doubt. On appeal, the State is entitled to the strongest legitimate view of the evidence and all legitimate or reasonable inferences which may be drawn therefrom.

Before a jury can find a defendant guilty of aggravated child abuse as charged in the present case, the State must prove beyond a reasonable doubt that the defendant "knowingly, other than by accidental means, treats a child under eighteen (18) years of age in such a manner as to inflict injury or neglects such a child so as to adversely affect the child's health and welfare . . ." and such abuse results in serious bodily injury. "Knowing" is applicable to the situations in which the accused, while not having the actual intent to accomplish a specific wrongful purpose, is consciously aware of the existence of facts which makes his conduct unlawful. "Knowing" is ordinarily established by circumstantial evidence rather than by direct proof. The undisputed proof reveals that the appellant strapped her two children, Dustin and Devin, into their car seats, secured the windows and doors, and left her children alone in the car for over nine hours, never returning to check on them. The children died as a result of systemic hyperthermia triggered by being locked in the hot vehicle. Obviously, by returning a guilty verdict, the jury did not accredit the appellant's theory of the case that the deaths of her children were an accident. Nor did the jury accredit defense testimony of the appellant's psychological problems. We conclude that a rational trier of fact could find that the appellant knew the ages of her children (circumstances), knowingly strapped her children in the car (conduct), knowingly neglected them over the next nine hours (conduct), and was aware that her conduct was reasonably certain to cause harm or injury to her children (result of conduct). Thus, the facts are sufficient to support a conviction for aggravated child abuse on each count. This issue is without merit.

Circumstance: Ages of kids

Conduct: strapped kids in car.

result: reasonably certain that causes harm.

[Finding] no reversible error committed by the trial court, we affirm the appellant's convictions and sentences imposed for two counts of aggravated child abuse.

PROBLEMS

1. *Second–Degree Murder.* Ducker was acquitted on two counts of first-degree murder. Under Tenn. Code § 39–13–210(1), it is the offense of second-degree murder for an individual to commit "[a] knowing killing of another." If Ducker had been charged and convicted by a jury of second-degree murder on the facts set out above, would the jury verdict have been upheld? Explain.

2. *Checking on Kids.* Do you think that the result in this case would have been different if Ducker had in fact returned to her car 3 or 4 times in the night to check on her children and found that they were asleep and in good health? Explain.

3. *Ducker and Manslaughter Charges.* In *Ducker*, the mother was charged with aggravated child abuse. Suppose that the prosecutor had charged her with manslaughter (which you can assume is defined to require either "recklessness" or "negligence"). Did she have either of these requisite mental states?

4. *The Absent–Minded Father.* A man is supposed to drive his child to day care on his way to work. The man, obviously very absent minded, forgets to drop the child off at day care and leaves her in the car all day while he is at his office. The day is very hot and the child suffocates to death. Can it be said that the man purposely, knowingly, recklessly or negligently caused the child's death?

5. *Applying the M.P.C.* Applying the M.P.C. § 2.02 (set forth in Note 1 *supra*, following *Regina v. Faulkner*), identify the mens rea requirements that apply to the following statutes:

   a. A burglary statute that defines the crime as the "breaking and entering of a dwelling of another at night with the purpose of committing a felony."

   b. A statute that makes it a crime to "knowingly convert to his use or the use of another any property of the United States or any department or agency thereof."

   c. A statute that makes it a crime to "operate another's automobile, airplane, motorcycle, motorboat, or other motor-propelled vehicle without consent of the owner."

   d. A statute that defines "receiving stolen property" as "knowingly receiving stolen goods."

EXERCISE

Jury Instructions. The *Ducker* court held that the jury instructions given at trial were erroneous, but that they did not require reversal of Ducker's convictions as any error was harmless. Bearing in mind the reasoning and conclusions set forth by the court, draft a set of jury instructions that could be given in a retrial in the *Ducker* case that would pass legal muster.

UNITED STATES v. VILLANUEVA–SOTELO

515 F.3d 1234, 380 U.S.App.D.C. 11 (2008).

TATEL, CIRCUIT JUDGE:

The federal "[a]ggravated identity theft" statute imposes two additional years of imprisonment on any person who during the commission of an enumerated felony "knowingly transfers, possesses, or uses, without lawful authority, a means of identification of another person." 18 U.S.C. § 1028A(a)(1). The question before us is this: to obtain a conviction under section 1028A(a)(1), must the government prove the defendant knew the "means of identification" he "transfer[red], possesse[d], or use[d]" actually belonged to "another person," or is it sufficient for the government to show that the means of identification happened to belong to another person? Based on the statute's text, purpose, and legislative history—and mindful that the rule of lenity comes into play when, after resort to the traditional tools of statutory interpretation, reasonable doubt remains as to the statute's meaning—we hold that section 1028A(a)(1)'s mens rea requirement extends to the phrase "of another person," meaning that the government must prove the defendant actually knew the identification in question belonged to someone else.

Defendant Gustavo Villanueva–Sotelo, a Mexican national, has entered the United States illegally three times and has been deported twice. In August 2006, District of Columbia Metropolitan Police approached Villanueva–Sotelo and asked him for identification. Villanueva–Sotelo presented the officers with what appeared to be a permanent resident card—an official document issued by the Department of Homeland Security proving its holder is authorized to stay or work in the United States. Villanueva–Sotelo's card displayed his own name and photograph, listed Mexico as his country of origin, and included an alien registration number. Villanueva–Sotelo admits he knew the card was a fake. Although the government can prove that the alien registration number displayed on the card belonged to another individual, it concedes—critically for this case—that it lacks any evidence that Villanueva–Sotelo actually knew this.

The government charged Villanueva–Sotelo with unlawful entry of a removed alien in violation of 8 U.S.C. § 1326(a) and (b)(1) (count one), possession of a fraudulent document prescribed for authorized stay or employment in the United States in violation of 18 U.S.C. § 1546(a) (count two), and aggravated identity theft in violation of 18 U.S.C. § 1028A(a)(1) (count three). In full, the identity theft statute reads: "Whoever, during and in relation to any felony violation enumerated in subsection (c), *knowingly transfers, possesses, or uses, without lawful authority, a means of identification of another person* shall, in addition to the punishment provided for such felony, be sentenced to a term of imprisonment of 2 years." (Emphasis added).

Villanueva–Sotelo pled guilty to the first two counts but moved to dismiss count three, the aggravated identity theft charge, arguing that section 1028A(a)(1) requires the government to prove he actually knew the alien registration number belonged to another person. Agreeing with the defendant, [the trial court] held that the word "knowingly" in section 1028A(a)(1) must "modify both the verbs and the object, that is, 'means of identification of another person.'" In reaching this conclusion, the [court] found the following exchange with the prosecutor particularly illuminating:

> [PROSECUTOR]: [I]t is stealing in the sense that if I make up a number and it belongs to someone else, I have taken that person's number that was rightfully assigned by a U.S. agency.
>
> THE COURT: If you make up the number?
>
> [PROSECUTOR]: Yes. If I—
>
> THE COURT: What if you make up a number that doesn't belong to anybody?
>
> [PROSECUTOR]: Then you don't charge the offense, there is no offense because it's not a means of identification of another person.
>
> THE COURT: So if the defendant picked a number out of the air and it was [your] number, he's guilty, but if he picked a number out of the air and [Immigration and Customs Enforcement] hasn't assigned it to anybody, he's not guilty?
>
> [PROSECUTOR]: That's correct.

Unable to conclude that a scenario like this amounts to identity theft, [the court] granted Villanueva–Sotelo's motion to dismiss count three.

[Our] interpretive task begins with the statute's language. We must first "determine whether the language at issue has a plain and unambiguous meaning with regard to the particular dispute in the case." If it does, our inquiry ends and we apply the statute's plain language. But if we find the statutory language ambiguous, we look beyond the text for other indicia of congressional intent. *See Staples v. United States*, 511 U.S. 600, 605, 114 S.Ct. 1793, 128 L.Ed.2d 608 (1994) ("[D]etermining the mental state required for commission of a federal crime requires 'construction of the statute and ... inference of the intent of Congress.'")

Reduced to its essence, section 1028A(a)(1) reads as follows: "Whoever ... knowingly ... uses, without lawful authority, a means of identification of another person shall ... be sentenced to a term of imprisonment of 2 years." According to the government, this text is unambiguous: the statute's knowledge requirement extends only so far as "means of identification," requiring no proof the defendant knew the identification belonged to "another person." For his part, Villanueva–Sotelo contends the statute is ambiguous and that the provision's title, purpose, and legislative history reveal Congress's intent to extend the mens rea requirement throughout the entire sentence, namely all the way to "of another person." We agree with the defendant. Although the government's interpretation is plausible, nothing suggests it represents the only possible—or even the most plausible—reading of section 1028A(a)(1).

The parties focus on the word "knowingly," debating whether that adverb modifies the phrase "of another person." But a simple diagram of the relevant statutory text readily demonstrates that, from a grammatical point of view, this is not the correct question:

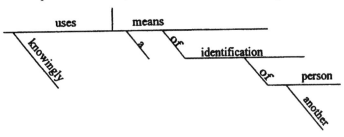

The word "knowingly" technically modifies only the verb that follows it ("uses"). It modifies neither the direct object ("means") nor the two prepositional phrases that follow ("of identification of another person").

In the end, this grammatical observation is beside the point given that the parties, as well as relevant case law interpreting similarly structured statutes (cases we discuss below), are best understood as using the word "modify" more loosely, equating it with words such as "apply," "extend," or "attach." Thus, framing the question in terms of statutory interpretation, we ask how far section 1028A(a)(1)'s mens rea requirement—"knowingly"—reaches in the statute.

That question requires us to focus on the statute's direct object, "means." "Means" is modified by the prepositional phrase "of identification," which, in turn, is modified by a second prepositional phrase, "of another person." As the government concedes, the mens rea requirement must extend at least to the direct object's principal modifier, "of identification." Were it otherwise, a person could be convicted for "knowingly us[ing] or transfer[ring]," without lawful authority, anything at all that happened to contain a means of identification. As one district court explained:

> If during a bank fraud conspiracy, I hand a defendant a sealed envelope asking her to transfer it and its contents to another and she knowingly does so, she has knowingly transferred the envel-

ope and its contents. But if she believes my statement that the envelope contains only a birthday card when in fact it contains a forged social security card, the government surely would not contend that she should receive the enhanced penalty.

United States v. Godin, 476 F.Supp.2d 1, 2 (D.Me. 2007). And it goes without saying that the mens rea requirement must also reach beyond the bare direct object "means" to its first modifying phrase "of identification," lest the sentence become gibberish: "knowingly using a means" means nothing.

But what of the second and crucial prepositional phrase "of another person"? Does section 1028A(a)(1)'s mens rea requirement apply to it as well? The government is certainly correct that the statute's knowledge requirement might apply only to the direct object's first prepositional phrase, thereby criminalizing "knowingly transfer[ing], possess[ing], or us[ing] . . . a means of identification" that happens to belong to another. [But] with regard to section 1028A(a)(1), the defendant's view—that the statute's mens rea requirement extends all the way to "of another person"—is at least equally plausible. [The government does not offer] a convincing reason, nor are we aware of one, demanding that the statute's mens rea requirement halt after "of identification" rather than proceed to "of another person." Indeed, the Model Penal Code adopts as a general principle of construction a rule under which, absent evidence to the contrary, the mens rea requirement encompasses all material elements of an offense.

[Having] found section 1028A(a)(1) ambiguous, "we seek guidance in the statutory structure, relevant legislative history, [and] congressional purposes expressed in the [statute]." According to the government, the legislative history demonstrates that "Congress intended to criminalize the knowing possession of fraudulent identity documents, even if the defendants lacked the specific knowledge that they possessed a real person's means of identification." [Reading] the legislative history differently, Villanueva–Sotelo argues that Congress intended to target identity theft and the thieves who perpetrate it, rather than to create a sentencing enhancement for individuals who use fraudulent identifying information belonging purely by happenstance to someone else. Again, we agree with Villanueva–Sotelo.

We begin with section 1028A's title: "[a]ggravated identity theft." As that title demonstrates, the statute concerns "theft," i.e., "the felonious taking and removing of personal property with intent to deprive the rightful owner of it." Yet Villanueva–Sotelo, having had no idea that his forged alien registration number belonged to anyone at all, couldn't possibly have had the intent to deprive another person of his or her identity. True, Villanueva–Sotelo had a guilty mind—he knowingly presented a fake permanent resident card to D.C. police officers—but he pled guilty to precisely that charge in the indictment's second count and is being punished accordingly.

[The trial court's] colloquy with the prosecutor reveals just how far the government's interpretation departs from the statute's focus on "theft." As the government argued in the district court and reiterated at oral argument here, a defendant could pick a series of numbers out of the air and win two extra years in prison if those numbers happened to coincide with an assigned identification number, yet escape punishment under section 1028A(a)(1) had he picked a slightly different string of random numbers. That's not theft. Judge Friedman could not square the government's position with congressional intent, nor can we.

That Congress intended section 1028A(a)(1) to single out thieves—in the traditional sense of the word—for enhanced punishment finds additional support in the statute's legislative history. [There] is a salient difference between theft and accidental misappropriation. While Villanueva–Sotelo surely misappropriated someone else's alien registration number, no evidence shows he stole it in any meaningful sense. ["Theft"] is precisely what Congress targeted when it passed section 1028A(a)(1). Because Congress intended to express "the moral condemnation of the community" by enhancing penalties for thieves who steal identities, we hold that section 1028A(a)(1)'s mens rea requirement extends to the "[a]ggravated identity theft" statute's defining element—that the means of identification used belongs to another person.

Even if we harbored any doubt about this—that is, were we unable to find "an unambiguous intent on the part of Congress"—we would "turn to the rule of lenity to resolve the dispute." Although "[t]he rule of lenity is not invoked by a grammatical possibility" and "does not apply if the ambiguous reading relied on is an implausible reading of the congressional purpose," the defendant's reading is quite plausible. Thus, even if the legislative history failed to resolve the statute's ambiguity, the rule of lenity would forbid us from "interpret[ing] a federal criminal statute so as to increase the penalty that it places on an individual when such an interpretation can be based on no more than a guess as to what Congress intended."

[We affirm.]

KAREN LeCRAFT HENDERSON, CIRCUIT JUDGE, dissenting:

[Both] the majority and I spill a lot of ink on dueling canons of statutory construction. Perhaps our exchange illustrates little more than that, in construing statutes, courts have a variety of interpretive aids to choose from. The first principle of statutory construction, however, is to apply common sense in the reading of language. Common sense tells me that the Congress, seeking to stop a type of crime that is increasing on an almost daily basis, enhanced the penalty to effect its purpose. And it is anything but common sense to conclude that the same Congress intended to gut that enhanced penalty, as the majority's reading does. . . .

NOTE

The Supreme Court will resolve the conflict in the circuits over the issue in *Villanueva-Sotelo* when it decides *Flores-Figueroa v. United States* in the 2008 Term. The Eighth Circuit upheld the conviction in the latter case. See 274 Fed.Appx. 501 (April 23, 2008) (holding that government not required to prove defendant knew means of identification belonged to another person).

EXERCISE

Amending Identity Theft Statute. Draft a proposed amendment to 18 U.S.C. § 1028A(a)(1) that would effectively "reverse" the *Villanueva-Sotelo* majority's ruling, i.e. propose language that would make it absolutely clear that the Congressional intent was that the government need only prove that someone accused under this provision did not need to know that the "means of identification" he or she "transfer[red], possesse[d], or use[d]" actually belonged to "another person."

B. STRICT LIABILITY

STAPLES v. UNITED STATES
511 U.S. 600 (1994).

JUSTICE THOMAS delivered the opinion of the Court.

[The] National Firearms Act (Act), 26 U.S.C. §§ 5801–5872, imposes strict registration requirements on statutorily defined "firearms." The Act includes within the term "firearm" a machine gun, and further defines a machine gun as "any weapon which shoots, [or] can be readily restored to shoot, automatically more than one shot, without manual reloading, by a single function of the trigger," § 5845(b). Thus, any fully automatic weapon is a "firearm" within the meaning of the Act. Under the Act, all firearms must be registered in the National Firearms Registration and Transfer Record maintained by the Secretary of the Treasury. Section 5861(d) makes it a crime, punishable by up to 10 years in prison for any person to possess a firearm that is not properly registered.

Upon executing a search warrant at petitioner's home, local police and agents of the Bureau of Alcohol, Tobacco and Firearms (BATF) recovered, among other things, an AR–15 rifle. The AR–15 is the civilian version of the military's M–16 rifle, and is, unless modified, a semiautomatic weapon. The M–16, in contrast, is a selective fire rifle that allows the operator, by rotating a selector switch, to choose semiautomatic or automatic fire. Many M–16 parts are interchangeable with those in the AR–15 and can be used to convert the AR–15 into an automatic weapon. No doubt to inhibit such conversions, the AR–15 is manufactured with a metal stop on its receiver that will prevent an M–16 selector switch, if installed, from rotating to the fully automatic position. The metal stop on petitioner's rifle, however, had been filed away, and the rifle had been assembled with an M–16 selector switch and several other M–16 internal parts, including a hammer, disconnector, and trigger. Suspecting that the AR–15 had been modified to be capable of fully automatic fire, BATF agents seized the weapon. Petitioner subsequently was indicted for unlawful possession of an unregistered machine gun in violation of § 5861(d).

At trial, BATF agents testified that when the AR–15 was tested, it fired more than one shot with a single pull of the trigger. It was undisputed that the weapon was not registered as required by § 5861(d). Petitioner testified that the rifle had never fired automatically when it was in his possession. He insisted that the AR–15 had operated only semiautomatically, and even then imperfectly, often requiring manual ejection of the spent casing and chambering of the next round. According to petitioner, his alleged ignorance of any automatic firing capability should have shielded him from criminal liability for his failure to register the weapon. He requested the District Court to instruct the jury that, to establish a violation of § 5861(d), the Government must prove beyond a reasonable doubt that the defendant "knew that the gun would fire fully automatically."

The District Court rejected petitioner's proposed instruction and instead charged the jury as follows: "The Government need not prove the defendant knows he's dealing with a weapon possessing every last characteristic [which subjects it] to the regulation. It would be enough to prove he knows that he is dealing with a dangerous device of a type as would alert one to the likelihood of regulation."

Petitioner was convicted and sentenced to five years' probation and a $5,000 fine. The Court of Appeals affirmed. [T]he court concluded that the Government need not prove a defendant's knowledge of a weapon's physical properties to obtain a conviction under § 5861(d). We granted certiorari to resolve a conflict in the Courts of Appeals concerning the *mens rea* required under § 5861(d).

Whether or not § 5861(d) requires proof that a defendant knew of the characteristics of his weapon that made it a "firearm" under the Act is a question of statutory construction. As we observed in *Liparota v. United States,* 471 U.S. 419 (1985), "[t]he definition of the elements of a criminal offense is entrusted to the legislature, particularly in the case of federal crimes, which are solely creatures of statute." Thus, we have long recognized that determining the mental state required for commission of a federal crime requires "construction of the statute and ... inference of the intent of Congress." *United States v. Balint,* 258 U.S. 250, 253 (1922).

The language of the statute, the starting place in our inquiry, provides little explicit guidance in this case. Section 5861(d) is silent concerning the *mens rea* required for a violation. It states simply that "[i]t shall be unlawful for any person ... to receive or possess a firearm which is not registered to him in the National Firearms Registration and Transfer Record." 26 U.S.C. § 5861(d). Nevertheless, silence on this point by itself does not necessarily suggest that Congress intended to dispense with a conventional *mens rea* element, which would require that the defendant know the facts that make his conduct illegal. On the contrary, we must construe the statute in light of the background rules of the common law, in which the requirement of some *mens rea* for a crime is firmly embedded. As we have observed, "[t]he existence of a *mens rea* is the rule of, rather than the exception to, the principles of Anglo–American criminal jurisprudence."

There can be no doubt that this established concept has influenced our interpretation of criminal statutes. Indeed, we have noted that the common-law rule requiring *mens rea* has been "followed in regard to statutory crimes even where the statutory definition did not in terms include it." Relying on the strength of the traditional rule, we have stated that offenses that require no *mens rea* generally are disfavored, and have suggested that some indication of congressional intent, express or implied, is required to dispense with *mens rea* as an element of a crime. *Morissette v. United States,* 342 U.S. 246, 250 (1952).

According to the Government, [the] nature and purpose of the Act suggest that the presumption favoring *mens rea* does not apply to this case. The Government argues that Congress intended the Act to regulate and restrict the circulation of dangerous weapons. Consequently, in the Government's view, this case fits in a line of precedent concerning what we have termed "public welfare" or "regulatory" offenses, in which we have understood Congress to impose a form of strict criminal liability through statutes that do not require the defendant to know the facts that make his conduct illegal. In construing such statutes, we have inferred from silence that Congress did not intend to require proof of *mens rea* to establish an offense.

For example, in *Balint,* we concluded that the Narcotic Act of 1914, which was intended in part to minimize the spread of addictive drugs by criminalizing undocumented sales of certain narcotics, required proof only that the defendant knew that he was selling drugs, not that he knew the specific items he had sold were "narcotics" within the ambit of the statute. Cf. *United States v. Dotterweich,* 320 U.S. 277, 281 (1943) (stating in dicta that a statute criminalizing the shipment of adulterated or misbranded drugs did not require knowledge that the items were misbranded or adulterated). As we explained in *Dotterweich, Balint* dealt with "a now familiar type of legislation whereby penalties serve as effective means of regulation. Such legislation dispenses with the conventional requirement for criminal conduct—awareness of some wrongdoing."

Such public welfare offenses have been created by Congress, and recognized by this Court, in "limited circumstances." Typically, our cases recognizing such offenses involve statutes that regulate potentially harmful or injurious items. Cf. *United States v. International Minerals & Chemical Corp.*, 402 U.S. 558, 564–565 (1971) (characterizing *Balint* and similar cases as involving statutes regulating "dangerous or deleterious devices or products or obnoxious waste materials"). In such situations, we have reasoned that as long as a defendant knows that he is dealing with a dangerous device of a character that places him "in responsible relation to a public danger," he should be alerted to the probability of strict regulation, and we have assumed that in such cases Congress intended to place the burden on the defendant to "ascertain at his peril whether [his conduct] comes within the inhibition of the statute." *Balint, supra*, 258 U.S., at 254. Thus, we essentially have relied on the nature of the statute and the particular character of the items regulated to determine whether congressional silence concerning the mental element of the offense should be interpreted as dispensing with conventional *mens rea* requirements. See generally *Morissette, supra*, at 252–260, 72 S.Ct., at 244–248.[3]

The Government argues that § 5861(d) defines precisely the sort of regulatory offense described in *Balint*. In this view, all guns, whether or not they are statutory "firearms," are dangerous devices that put gun owners on notice that they must determine at their hazard whether their weapons come within the scope of the Act. On this understanding, the District Court's instruction in this case was correct, because a conviction can rest simply on proof that a defendant knew he possessed a "firearm" in the ordinary sense of the term.

---

3. By interpreting such public welfare offenses to require at least that the defendant know that he is dealing with some dangerous or deleterious substance, we have avoided construing criminal statutes to impose a rigorous form of strict liability. See, *e.g., United States v. International Minerals & Chemical Corp.*, 402 U.S. 558, 563–564 (1971) (suggesting that if a person shipping acid mistakenly thought that he was shipping distilled water, he would not violate a statute criminalizing undocumented shipping of acids). True strict liability might suggest that the defendant need not know even that he was dealing with a dangerous item. Nevertheless, we have referred to public welfare offenses as "dispensing with" or "eliminating" a *mens rea* requirement or "mental element," and have described them as strict liability crimes, *United States v. United States Gypsum Co.*, 438 U.S. 422, 437 (1978). While use of the term "strict liability" is really a misnomer, we have interpreted statutes defining public welfare offenses to eliminate the requirement of *mens rea; that is,* the requirement of a "guilty mind" with respect to an element of a crime. Under such statutes we have not required that the defendant know the facts that make his conduct fit the definition of the offense. Generally speaking, such knowledge is necessary to establish *mens rea,* as is reflected in the maxim *ignorantia facti excusat.* Cf. *Queen v. Tolson,* 23 Q.B. 168, 187 (1889) (Stephen, J.) ("[I]t may, I think, be maintained that in every case knowledge of fact [when not appearing in the statute] is to some extent an element of criminality as much as competent age and sanity").

The Government seeks support for its position from our decision in *United States v. Freed*, 401 U.S. 601 (1971), which involved a prosecution for possession of unregistered grenades under § 5861(d). The defendant knew that the items in his possession were grenades, and we concluded that § 5861(d) did not require the Government to prove the defendant also knew that the grenades were unregistered. To be sure, in deciding that *mens rea* was not required with respect to that element of the offense, we suggested that the Act "is a regulatory measure in the interest of the public safety, which may well be premised on the theory that one would hardly be surprised to learn that possession of hand grenades is not an innocent act." Grenades, we explained, "are highly dangerous offensive weapons, no less dangerous than the narcotics involved in *United States v. Balint*." But that reasoning provides little support for dispensing with *mens rea* in this case.

As the Government concedes, *Freed* did not address the issue presented here. In *Freed*, we decided only that § 5861(d) does not require proof of knowledge that a firearm is *unregistered*. The question presented by a defendant who possesses a weapon that is a "firearm" for purposes of the Act, but who knows only that he has a "firearm" in the general sense of the term, was not raised or considered. And our determination that a defendant need not know that his weapon is unregistered suggests no conclusion concerning whether § 5861(d) requires the defendant to know of the features that make his weapon a statutory "firearm"; different elements of the same offense can require different mental states. See *Liparota*, 471 U.S., at 423, n. 5. Moreover, our analysis in *Freed* likening the Act to the public welfare statute in *Balint* rested entirely on the assumption that the defendant *knew* that he was dealing with hand grenades—that is, that he knew he possessed a particularly dangerous type of weapon (one within the statutory definition of a "firearm"), possession of which was not entirely "innocent" in and of itself. The predicate for that analysis is eliminated when, as in this case, the very question to be decided is *whether* the defendant must know of the particular characteristics that make his weapon a statutory firearm.

Notwithstanding these distinctions, the Government urges that *Freed's* logic applies because guns, no less than grenades, are highly dangerous devices that should alert their owners to the probability of regulation. But the gap between *Freed* and this case is too wide to bridge. In glossing over the distinction between grenades and guns, the Government ignores the particular care we have taken to avoid construing a statute to dispense with *mens rea* where doing so would "criminalize a broad range of apparently innocent conduct." In *Liparota*, we considered a statute that made unlawful the unauthorized acquisition or possession of food stamps. We determined that the statute required proof that the defendant knew his possession of food

[handwritten margin note top right: Liparota: Δ d'd know that FS was fake.]

stamps was unauthorized, largely because dispensing with such a *mens rea* requirement would have resulted in reading the statute to outlaw a number of apparently innocent acts. Our conclusion that the statute should not be treated as defining a public welfare offense rested on the commonsense distinction that a "food stamp can hardly be compared to a hand grenade."

Neither, in our view, can all guns be compared to hand grenades. Although the contrast is certainly not as stark as that presented in *Liparota*, the fact remains that there is a long tradition of widespread lawful gun ownership by private individuals in this country. Such a tradition did not apply to the possession of hand grenades in *Freed* or to the selling of dangerous drugs that we considered in *Balint*. In fact, in *Freed* we construed § 5861(d) under the assumption that "one would hardly be surprised to learn that possession of hand grenades is not an innocent act." Here, the Government essentially suggests that we should interpret the section under the altogether different assumption that "one would hardly be surprised to learn that owning a gun is not an innocent act." That proposition is simply not supported by common experience. Guns in general are not "deleterious devices or products or obnoxious waste materials," that put their owners on notice that they stand "in responsible relation to a public danger."

[handwritten margin note: ≠ grenade. guns have lawful tradition.]

[handwritten margin note: Guns are not deleterious]

The Government protests that guns, unlike food stamps, but like grenades and narcotics, are potentially harmful devices. Under this view, it seems that *Liparota*'s concern for criminalizing ostensibly innocuous conduct is inapplicable whenever an item is sufficiently dangerous—that is, dangerousness alone should alert an individual to probable regulation and justify treating a statute that regulates the dangerous device as dispensing with *mens rea*. But that an item is "dangerous," in some general sense, does not necessarily suggest, as the Government seems to assume, that it is not also entirely innocent. Even dangerous items can, in some cases, be so commonplace and generally available that we would not consider them to alert individuals to the likelihood of strict regulation. As suggested above, despite their potential for harm, guns generally can be owned in perfect innocence....

[handwritten margin note: ≠ Liparota Guns are potentially harmful]

[handwritten margin note: potential harm is not sufficient]

On a slightly different tack, the Government suggests that guns are subject to an array of regulations at the federal, state, and local levels that put gun owners on notice that they must determine the characteristics of their weapons and comply with all legal requirements. But regulation in itself is not sufficient to place gun ownership in the category of the sale of narcotics in *Balint*. The food stamps at issue in *Liparota* were subject to comprehensive regulations, yet we did not understand the statute there to dispense with a *mens rea* requirement. Moreover, despite the overlay of legal restrictions on gun ownership, we question whether regulations on guns are sufficiently *just b/c sub to regulation, dsn't mean it's the same as narc.*

slippery slope.

intrusive that they impinge upon the common experience that owning a gun is usually licit and blameless conduct. Roughly 50 percent of American homes contain at least one firearm of some sort, and in the vast majority of States, buying a shotgun or rifle is a simple transaction that would not alert a person to regulation any more than would buying a car.[9]

If we were to accept as a general rule the Government's suggestion that dangerous and regulated items place their owners under an obligation to inquire at their peril into compliance with regulations, we would undoubtedly reach some untoward results. Automobiles, for example, might also be termed "dangerous" devices and are highly regulated at both the state and federal levels. Congress might see fit to criminalize the violation of certain regulations concerning automobiles, and thus might make it a crime to operate a vehicle without a properly functioning emission control system. But we probably would hesitate to conclude on the basis of silence that Congress intended a prison term to apply to a car owner whose vehicle's emissions levels, wholly unbeknownst to him, began to exceed legal limits between regular inspection dates.

Here, there can be little doubt that, as in *Liparota,* the Government's construction of the statute potentially would impose criminal sanctions on a class of persons whose mental state—ignorance of the characteristics of weapons in their possession—makes their actions entirely innocent. The Government does not dispute the contention that virtually any semiautomatic weapon may be converted, either by internal modification or, in some cases, simply by wear and tear, into a machinegun within the meaning of the Act. But in the Government's view, any person who has purchased what he believes to be a semiautomatic rifle or handgun, or who simply has inherited a gun from a relative and left it untouched in an attic or basement, can be subject to imprisonment, despite absolute ignorance of the gun's firing capabilities, if the gun turns out to be an automatic.

Agree w/ 5th Circuit, Gov't didn't mean to intend that Δ wd get 10 yrs if he didn't know he had weapon

We concur in the Fifth Circuit's conclusion on this point: "It is unthinkable to us that Congress intended to subject such law-abiding, well-intentioned citizens to a possible ten-year term of imprisonment if . . . what they genuinely and reasonably believed was a conventional semi-automatic [weapon] turns out to have worn down into or been secretly modified to be a fully automatic weapon." *Anderson, supra,* at 1254. As we noted in *Morissette,* the "purpose and obvious effect of doing away with the requirement of a guilty intent is to ease the prosecution's path to conviction." 342 U.S., at 263, 72 S.Ct., at 249.[11]

---

9. For example, as of 1990, 39 States allowed adult residents, who are not felons or mentally infirm, to purchase a rifle or shotgun simply with proof of identification (and in some cases a simultaneous application for a permit).

11. The Government contends that Congress intended precisely such an aid to obtaining convictions, because requiring proof of knowledge would place too heavy a burden on the

We are reluctant to impute that purpose to Congress where, as here, it would mean easing the path to convicting persons whose conduct would not even alert them to the probability of strict regulation in the form of a statute such as § 5861(d).

The potentially harsh penalty attached to violation of § 5861(d)—up to 10 years' imprisonment—confirms our reading of the Act. Historically, the penalty imposed under a statute has been a significant consideration in determining whether the statute should be construed as dispensing with *mens rea*. Certainly, the cases that first defined the concept of the public welfare offense almost uniformly involved statutes that provided for only light penalties such as fines or short jail sentences, not imprisonment in the state penitentiary. See, *e.g., Commonwealth v. Raymond*, 97 Mass. 567 (1867) (fine of up to $200 or six months in jail, or both).

As commentators have pointed out, the small penalties attached to such offenses logically complemented the absence of a *mens rea* requirement: In a system that generally requires a "vicious will" to establish a crime, imposing severe punishments for offenses that require no *mens rea* would seem incongruous. Indeed, some courts justified the absence of *mens rea* in part on the basis that the offenses did not bear the same punishments as "infamous crimes," and questioned whether imprisonment was compatible with the reduced culpability required for such regulatory offenses. Similarly, commentators collecting the early cases have argued that offenses punishable by imprisonment cannot be understood to be public welfare offenses, but must require *mens rea*.

In rehearsing the characteristics of the public welfare offense, we, too, have included in our consideration the punishments imposed and have noted that "penalties commonly are relatively small, and conviction does no grave damage to an offender's reputation." *Morissette*, 342 U.S., at 256. We have even recognized that it was "[u]nder such considerations" that courts have construed statutes to dispense with *mens rea*.

Our characterization of the public welfare offense in *Morissette* hardly seems apt, however, for a crime that is a felony, as is violation of § 5861(d). After all, "felony" is, as we noted in distinguishing certain common-law crimes from public welfare offenses, " 'as bad a word as you can give to man or thing.' " *Id.,* at 260 (quoting 2 F.

Government and obstruct the proper functioning of § 5861(d). Cf. *United States v. Balint*, 258 U.S. 250, 254 (1922) (difficulty of proving knowledge suggests Congress did not intend to require *mens rea*). But knowledge can be inferred from circumstantial evidence, including any external indications signaling the nature of the weapon. And firing a fully automatic weapon would make the regulated characteristics of the weapon immediately apparent to its owner. In short, we are confident that when the defendant knows of the characteristics of his weapon that bring it within the scope of the Act, the Government will not face great difficulty in proving that knowledge. Of course, if Congress thinks it necessary to reduce the Government's burden at trial to ensure proper enforcement of the Act, it remains free to amend § 5861(d) by explicitly eliminating a *mens rea* requirement.

Pollock & F. Maitland, History of English Law 465 (2d ed. 1899)). Close adherence to the early cases described above might suggest that punishing a violation as a felony is simply incompatible with the theory of the public welfare offense. In this view, absent a clear statement from Congress that *mens rea* is not required, we should not apply the public welfare offense rationale to interpret any statute defining a felony offense as dispensing with *mens rea.*

We need not adopt such a definitive rule of construction to decide this case, however. Instead, we note only that where, as here, dispensing with *mens rea* would require the defendant to have knowledge only of traditionally lawful conduct, a severe penalty is a further factor tending to suggest that Congress did not intend to eliminate a *mens rea* requirement. In such a case, the usual presumption that a defendant must know the facts that make his conduct illegal should apply.

In short, we conclude that the background rule of the common law favoring *mens rea* should govern interpretation of § 5861(d) in this case. Silence does not suggest that Congress dispensed with *mens rea* for the element of § 5861(d) at issue here. Thus, to obtain a conviction, the Government should have been required to prove that petitioner knew of the features of his AR–15 that brought it within the scope of the Act.

We emphasize that our holding is a narrow one. As in our prior cases, our reasoning depends upon a commonsense evaluation of the nature of the particular device or substance Congress has subjected to regulation and the expectations that individuals may legitimately have in dealing with the regulated items. In addition, we think that the penalty attached to § 5861(d) suggests that Congress did not intend to eliminate a *mens rea* requirement for violation of the section. As we noted in *Morissette:* "Neither this Court nor, so far as we are aware, any other has undertaken to delineate a precise line or set forth comprehensive criteria for distinguishing between crimes that require a mental element and crimes that do not." We attempt no definition here, either. We note only that our holding depends critically on our view that if Congress had intended to make outlaws of gun owners who were wholly ignorant of the offending characteristics of their weapons, and to subject them to lengthy prison terms, it would have spoken more clearly to that effect.

For the foregoing reasons, the judgment of the Court of Appeals is reversed, and the case is remanded for further proceedings consistent with this opinion.

So ordered.

JUSTICE GINSBURG, with whom JUSTICE O'CONNOR joins, concurring in the judgment.

The statute petitioner Harold E. Staples is charged with violating, 26 U.S.C. § 5861(d), makes it a crime for any person to "receive or possess a firearm which is not registered to him." Although the word "knowingly" does not appear in the statute's text, courts generally assume that Congress, absent a contrary indication, means to retain a *mens rea* requirement. See *Liparota v. United States,* 471 U.S. 419, 426 (1985).

Conviction under § 5861(d), the Government accordingly concedes, requires proof that Staples "knowingly" possessed the machine gun. The question before us is not *whether* knowledge of possession is required, but what level of knowledge suffices: (1) knowledge simply of possession of the object; (2) knowledge, in addition, that the object is a dangerous weapon; (3) knowledge, beyond dangerousness, of the characteristics that render the object subject to regulation, for example, awareness that the weapon is a machine gun.

Recognizing that the first reading effectively dispenses with *mens rea,* the Government adopts the second, contending that it avoids criminalizing "apparently innocent conduct," because under the second reading, "a defendant who possessed what he thought was a toy or a violin case, but which in fact was a machinegun, could not be convicted." The Government, however, does not take adequate account of the "widespread lawful gun ownership" Congress and the States have allowed to persist in this country. Given the notable lack of comprehensive regulation, "mere unregistered possession of certain types of [regulated weapons]—often [difficult to distinguish] from other, [non-regulated] types," has been held inadequate to establish the requisite knowledge.

The Nation's legislators chose to place under a registration requirement only a very limited class of firearms, those they considered especially dangerous. The generally "dangerous" character of all guns, the Court therefore observes did not suffice to give individuals in Staples' situation cause to inquire about the need for registration. Only the third reading, then, suits the purpose of the *mens rea* requirement—to shield people against punishment for apparently innocent activity.

The indictment in Staples' case charges that he "knowingly received and possessed firearms." "Firearms" has a circumscribed statutory definition. The "firear[m]" the Government contends Staples possessed in violation of § 5861(d) is a machine gun. The indictment thus effectively charged that Staples *knowingly possessed a machinegun.* "Knowingly possessed" logically means "possessed and knew that he possessed." The Government can reconcile the jury instruction with the indictment only on the implausible assumption that the term "firear[m]" has two different meanings when used once in the same charge—simply "gun" when referring to what petitioner knew, and "machinegun" when referring to what he possessed.

For these reasons, I conclude that conviction under § 5861(d) requires proof that the defendant knew he possessed not simply a gun, but a machinegun. The indictment in this case, but not the jury instruction, properly described this knowledge requirement. I therefore concur in the Court's judgment.

Justice Stevens, with whom Justice Blackmun joins, dissenting.

To avoid a slight possibility of injustice to unsophisticated owners of machine guns and sawed-off shotguns, the Court has substituted its views of sound policy for the judgment Congress made when it enacted the National Firearms Act (or Act). Because the Court's addition to the text of 26 U.S.C. § 5861(d) is foreclosed by both the statute and our precedent, I respectfully dissent.

The Court is preoccupied with guns that "generally can be owned in perfect innocence." This case, however, involves a semiautomatic weapon that was readily convertible into a machine gun—a weapon that the jury found to be " 'a dangerous device of a type as would alert one to the likelihood of regulation.' " These are not guns "of some sort" that can be found in almost "50 percent of American homes." They are particularly dangerous—indeed, a substantial percentage of the unregistered machineguns now in circulation are converted semiautomatic weapons.

The question presented is whether the National Firearms Act imposed on the Government the burden of proving beyond a reasonable doubt not only that the defendant knew he possessed a dangerous device sufficient to alert him to regulation, but also that he knew it had all the characteristics of a "firearm" as defined in the statute. Three unambiguous guideposts direct us to the correct answer to that question: the text and structure of the Act, our cases construing both this Act and similar regulatory legislation, and the Act's history and interpretation.

Contrary to the assertion by the Court, the text of the statute does provide "explicit guidance in this case." The relevant section of the Act makes it "unlawful for any person . . . to receive or possess a firearm which is not registered to him in the National Firearms Registration and Transfer Record." Significantly, the section contains no knowledge requirement, nor does it describe a common-law crime.

The common law generally did not condemn acts as criminal unless the actor had "an evil purpose or mental culpability," and was aware of all the facts that made the conduct unlawful. In interpreting statutes that codified traditional common-law offenses, courts usually followed this rule, even when the text of the statute contained no such requirement. Because the offense involved in this case is entirely a creature of statute, however, "the background rules of the common law," do not require a particular construction, and critically different rules of construction apply.

In *Morissette,* Justice Jackson outlined one such interpretive rule: "Congressional silence as to mental elements in an Act merely adopting into federal statutory law a concept of crime already ... well defined in common law and statutory interpretation by the states may warrant quite contrary inferences than the same silence in creating an offense new to general law, for whose definition the courts have no guidance except the Act."

Although the lack of an express knowledge requirement in § 5861(d) is not dispositive, its absence suggests that Congress did not intend to require proof that the defendant knew all of the facts that made his conduct illegal.

proof not necessary

The provision's place in the overall statutory scheme confirms this intention. In 1934, when Congress originally enacted the statute, it limited the coverage of the 1934 Act to a relatively narrow category of weapons such as submachineguns and sawed-off shotguns—weapons characteristically used only by professional gangsters like Al Capone, Pretty Boy Floyd, and their henchmen. At the time, the Act would have had little application to guns used by hunters or guns kept at home as protection against unwelcome intruders. Congress therefore could reasonably presume that a person found in possession of an unregistered machinegun or sawed-off shotgun intended to use it for criminal purposes. The statute as a whole, and particularly the decision to criminalize mere possession, reflected a legislative judgment that the likelihood of innocent possession of such an unregistered weapon was remote, and far less significant than the interest in depriving gangsters of their use.

In addition, at the time of enactment, this Court had already construed comparable provisions of the Harrison Anti–Narcotic Act not to require proof of knowledge of all the facts that constitute the proscribed offense. Indeed, Attorney General Cummings expressly advised Congress that the text of the gun control legislation deliberately followed the language of the Anti–Narcotic Act to reap the benefit of cases construing it. Given the reasoning of *Balint,* we properly may infer that Congress did not intend the Court to read a stricter knowledge requirement into the gun control legislation than we read into the Anti–Narcotic Act.

Like the 1934 Act, the current National Firearms Act is primarily a regulatory measure. The statute establishes taxation, registration, reporting, and recordkeeping requirements for businesses and transactions involving statutorily defined firearms, and requires that each firearm be identified by a serial number. The Secretary of the Treasury must maintain a central registry that includes the names and addresses of persons in possession of all firearms not controlled by the Government. Congress also prohibited certain acts and omissions, including the possession of an unregistered firearm.

As the Court acknowledges, to interpret statutory offenses such as § 5861(d), we look to "the nature of the statute and the particular character of the items regulated" to determine the level of knowledge required for conviction. An examination of § 5861(d) in light of our precedent dictates that the crime of possession of an unregistered machinegun is in a category of offenses described as "public welfare" crimes. Our decisions interpreting such offenses clearly require affirmance of petitioner's conviction.

"Public welfare" offenses share certain characteristics: (1) they regulate "dangerous or deleterious devices or products or obnoxious waste materials," (2) they "heighten the duties of those in control of particular industries, trades, properties or activities that affect public health, safety or welfare," and (3) they "depend on no mental element but consist only of forbidden acts or omissions." Examples of such offenses include Congress' exertion of its power to keep dangerous narcotics, hazardous substances, and impure and adulterated foods and drugs out of the channels of commerce.

Public welfare statutes render criminal "a type of conduct that a reasonable person should know is subject to stringent public regulation and may seriously threaten the community's health or safety." Thus, under such statutes, "a defendant can be convicted even though he was unaware of the circumstances of his conduct that made it illegal." Referring to the strict criminal sanctions for unintended violations of the food and drug laws, Justice Frankfurter wrote:

> "The purposes of this legislation thus touch phases of the lives and health of people which, in the circumstances of modern industrialism, are largely beyond self-protection. Regard for these purposes should infuse construction of the legislation if it is to be treated as a working instrument of government and not merely as a collection of English words. The prosecution . . . is based on a now familiar type of legislation whereby penalties serve as effective means of regulation. Such legislation dispenses with the conventional requirement for criminal conduct—awareness of some wrongdoing. In the interest of the larger good it puts the burden of acting at hazard upon a person otherwise innocent but standing in responsible relation to a public danger." *United States v. Dotterweich*, 320 U.S. 277, 280–281 (1943).

The National Firearms Act unquestionably is a public welfare statute. Congress fashioned a legislative scheme to regulate the commerce and possession of certain types of dangerous devices, including specific kinds of weapons, to protect the health and welfare of the citizenry. To enforce this scheme, Congress created criminal penalties for certain acts and omissions. The text of some of these offenses—including the one at issue here—contains no knowledge requirement. [We have] read a knowledge requirement into public welfare crimes, but not a requirement that the defendant know all the facts that make his conduct illegal. Although the Court acknowledges this standard, it nevertheless concludes that a gun is not the type of dangerous device that would alert one to the possibility of regulation.

Both the Court and Justice Ginsburg erroneously rely upon the "tradition[al]" innocence of gun ownership to find that Congress must have intended the Government to prove knowledge of all the characteristics that make a weapon a statutory "firear[m]." We held in *Freed*, however, that a § 5861(d) offense may be committed by one with no awareness of either wrongdoing or of all the facts that constitute the offense. Nevertheless, the Court, asserting that the Government "gloss[es] over the distinction between grenades and guns," determines that "the gap between *Freed* and this case is too wide to bridge." As such, the Court instead reaches the rather surprising conclusion that guns are more analogous to food stamps than to hand grenades. Even if one accepts that dubious proposition, the Court founds it upon a faulty premise: its mischaracterization of the Government's submission as one contending that "*all guns* . . . are dangerous devices that put gun owners on notice. . . ." Accurately identified, the Government's position presents the question whether guns such as the one possessed by petitioner " 'are highly dangerous offensive weapons, no less dangerous than the narcotics' "in *Balint* or the hand grenades in *Freed*.

Thus, even assuming that the Court is correct that the mere possession of an ordinary rifle or pistol does not entail sufficient danger to alert one to the possibility of regulation, that conclusion does not resolve this case. Petitioner knowingly possessed a semiautomatic weapon that was readily convertible into a machinegun. The " 'character and nature' "of such a weapon is sufficiently hazardous to place the possessor on notice of the possibility of regulation. No significant difference exists between imposing upon the possessor a duty to determine whether such a weapon is registered, and imposing a duty to determine whether that weapon has been converted into a machinegun.

[The] enforcement of public welfare offenses always entails some possibility of injustice. Congress nevertheless has repeatedly decided that an overriding public interest in health or safety may outweigh that risk when a person is dealing with products that are sufficiently dangerous or deleterious to make it reasonable to presume that he either knows, or should know, whether those products conform to special regulatory requirements. The dangerous character of the product is reasonably presumed to provide sufficient notice of the probability of regulation to justify strict enforcement against those who are merely guilty of negligent, rather than willful, misconduct.

The National Firearms Act is within the category of public welfare statutes enacted by Congress to regulate highly dangerous items. The Government submits that a conviction under such a statute may be supported by proof that the defendant "knew the item at issue was highly dangerous and of a type likely to be subject to regulation." It is undisputed that the evidence in this case met that standard. Nevertheless, neither Justice Thomas for the Court nor Justice Ginsburg has explained why such a knowledge requirement is unfaithful to our cases or to the text of the Act. Instead, [they] have simply explained why, in their judgment, it would be unfair to punish the possessor of this machinegun.

The history and interpretation of the National Firearms Act supports the conclusion that Congress did not intend to require knowledge of all the facts that constitute the offense of possession of an unregistered weapon. During the first 30 years of enforcement of the 1934 Act, consistent with the absence of a knowledge requirement and with the reasoning in *Balint,* courts uniformly construed it not to require knowledge of all the characteristics of the weapon that brought it within the statute. In a case decided in 1963, then-Judge Blackmun reviewed the earlier cases and concluded that the defendant's knowledge that he possessed a gun was "all the scienter which the statute requires."

Congress subsequently amended the statute twice, once in 1968 and again in 1986. Both amendments added knowledge requirements to other portions of the Act, but neither the text nor the history of either amendment discloses an intent to add any other knowledge requirement to the possession of an unregistered firearm offense. Given that, with only one partial exception, every federal tribunal to address the question had concluded that proof of knowledge of all the facts constituting a violation was not required for a conviction under § 5861(d), we may infer that Congress intended that interpretation to survive.

In short, petitioner's knowledge that he possessed an item that was sufficiently dangerous to alert him to the likelihood of regulation would have supported a conviction during the first half century of enforcement of this statute. Unless application of that standard to a particular case violates the Due Process Clause, it is the responsibility of Congress, not this Court, to amend the statute if Congress deems it unfair or unduly strict....

This case presents no dispute about the dangerous character of machine guns and sawed-off shotguns. Anyone in possession of such a weapon is "standing in responsible relation to a public danger." In the National Firearms Act, Congress determined that the serious threat to health and safety posed by the private ownership of such firearms warranted the imposition of a duty on the owners of dangerous weapons to determine whether their possession is lawful. Semiautomatic weapons that are readily convertible into machineguns are sufficiently dangerous to alert persons who knowingly possess them to the probability of stringent public regulation. The jury's finding that petitioner knowingly possessed "a dangerous device of a type as would alert one to the likelihood of regulation" adequately supports the conviction.

Accordingly, I would affirm the judgment of the Court of Appeals.

Note

M.P.C. view of strict liability. Consider M.P.C. § 2.05:

§ 2.05. When Culpability Requirements Are Inapplicable to Violations and to Offenses Defined by Other Statutes; Effect of Absolute Liability in Reducing Grade of Offense to Violation.

(1) The requirements of culpability prescribed by Sections 2.01 and 2.02 do not apply to:

(a) offenses that constitute violations, unless the requirement involved is included in the definition of the offense or the Court determines that its application is consistent with effective enforcement of the law defining the offense; or

(b) offenses defined by statutes other than the Code, insofar as a legislative purpose to impose absolute liability for such offenses or with respect to any material element thereof plainly appears.

(2) Notwithstanding any other provision of existing law and unless a subsequent statute otherwise provides:

(a) when absolute liability is imposed with respect to any material element of an offense defined by a statute other than the Code and a conviction is based upon such liability, the offense constitutes a violation; and

(b) although absolute liability is imposed by law with respect to one or more of the material elements of an offense defined by a statute other than the Code, the culpable commission of the offense may be charged and proved, in which event negligence with respect to such elements constitutes sufficient culpability and the classification of the offense and the sentence that may be imposed therefor upon conviction are determined by Section 1.04 and Article 6 of the Code.

Problems

1. *Demonstrating at the White House.* Political activist Cindy Sheehan was arrested in September 2005 for demonstrating without a permit on the White House sidewalk during an antiwar protest involving more than 200 people. She was charged with violating 36 C.F.R. § 7.96(g)(2), a National Park Service regulation governing demonstrations in all park areas in the National Capital Region, including the White House sidewalk. Following a

bench trial, Sheehan was convicted and assessed a $50 fine and a $25 administrative fee.

The relevant language in 36 C.F.R. § 7.96(g)(2) provides that "[d]emonstrations and special events may be held only pursuant to a permit issued in accordance with the provisions of this section." Under applicable regulations, demonstrations involving more than 25 people may be held only pursuant to a permit. The term "demonstrations" is defined as "includ[ing] demonstrations, picketing, speechmaking, marching, holding vigils or religious services and all other like forms of conduct which involve the communication or expression of views or grievances, engaged in by one or more persons, the conduct of which has the effect, intent or propensity to draw a crowd or onlookers. This term does not include casual park use by visitors or tourists which does not have an intent or propensity to attract a crowd or onlookers."

At trial, the judge allowed the Government to prosecute the case against Sheehan on the premise that the disputed regulations imposed strict liability for her alleged expressive activity, and sustained the prosecutor's objections when defense counsel for Sheehan sought to advance a defense based on her lack of knowledge and intent. On appeal, Sheehan argued that she was entitled to a new trial because the Government was required to prove a culpable mens rea on her part, and because the judge's rulings and instructions eliminated the prosecutor's burden to prove this mens rea and barred her from presenting a defense on that issue. Should Sheehan's conviction be reversed? What arguments—if any—can she make based on the *Staples* opinion to support her contentions? *See United States v. Sheehan*, 512 F.3d 621, 379 U.S.App.D.C. 187 (2008).

2. *The Exxon Valdez Incident.* Captain Joseph Hazelwood ran his ship aground off Bligh Reef in Alaska and reported that he was "leaking some oil." In fact, eleven million gallons poured into Prince William Sound in what came to be known as the Exxon Valdez incident. Hazelwood was charged under an Alaska statute that provided as follows:

> A person may not discharge, cause to be discharged, or permit the discharge of petroleum [into], or upon the waters or land of the state except in quantities, and at times and locations or under circumstances and conditions as the department may by regulation permit. . . .

The statute carries a penalty of 30 days in jail or a $1,000 fine. Using the logic of *Staples*, should this statute be construed to impose strict liability? Under the M.P.C., should strict liability be imposed? *See Alaska v. Hazelwood*, 946 P.2d 875 (Alaska 1997).

3. *Strict Liability and Drug Crimes.* Congress passed a law that provided that those dealing in the production, importation, manufacture, compounding, dealing in, dispensing, selling, distributing, or giving away of opium or coca leaves must register with the Internal Revenue Service and pay a tax. The act read as follows:

It shall be unlawful for any person to sell, barter, exchange, or give away any opium or coca leaves except in pursuance of a written order of the person to whom such article is sold, bartered, exchanged, or given, on a form to be issued in blank for that purpose by the Commissioner of Internal Revenue. Every person who shall accept any such order, and in pursuance thereof shall sell, barter, exchange, or give away any of the aforesaid drugs, shall preserve such order for a period of two years for inspection by any officer, agent, or employee of the Treasury Department duly authorized for that purpose, and the state, territorial, district, municipal, and insular officials who are similarly authorized.

Defendant admits that she sold an opium-based substance, but denies that she knew its content contained opium. Assuming that the jury believes defendant, can she be convicted under the above statute? In other words, should the statute be construed to impose strict liability? What weight would you attach to evidence that Congress considered this to be a "dangerous" drug and desired for the Commissioner of Internal Revenue to keep close tabs on its distribution? On the other hand, what if the courts construed the Act as taxing act with the incidental purpose of minimizing the spread of addiction to the use of poisonous and demoralizing drugs? *See United States v. Balint*, 258 U.S. 250 (1922).

4. *Air Pollution.* Defendant company was charged with two counts of "air pollution," a misdemeanor, under a law which read as follows:

No person shall cause, suffer, allow or permit the discharge into the atmosphere from any single source of emission whatsoever any air contaminants for a period or periods aggregating more than three minutes in any one hour which is:

    a. As dark as or darker in shade than that designated as No. 2 on the Ringelmann Chart as published by the U.S. Bureau of Mines, or

    b. Of an opacity equal to or greater than an air contaminant designated as No. 2 on the Ringelmann Chart.

If allowed, defendant will argue that it did not purposely or knowingly permit the omission, and that it did not act recklessly or negligently. In addition, defendant will offer proof that it has spent large amounts of money installing pollution control equipment and taking precautions to avoid pollution. The state argues that the consequences of "unabated air pollution" imposes severe consequences on public health, and that strict liability is appropriate. Should the law be construed to contain a mens rea requirement? Should the nature of the penalty (incarceration versus fine) and the size of the penalty (small fine versus very large one) be relevant to this determination? *See State v. Arizona Mines Supply Co.*, 107 Ariz. 199, 484 P.2d 619 (1971).

5. *The Economic Effects of Strict Liability.* In the prior problem, if the court decides to impose strict liability, what economic consequences will result? Will the imposition of strict liability encourage the company to go to

even greater lengths to avoid pollution, or will it tend to discourage additional safeguards? How will the nature of and size of the penalty affect the company's actions? What if the penalty is very low (to compensate for the fact that there is no mens rea)? What if it is extremely high?

6. *Spent Bomb Casings.* On a large tract of uninhabited and untilled land in a wooded and sparsely populated part of Michigan, the United States government established a practice bombing range over which the Air Force dropped simulated bombs at ground targets. These bombs consisted of a metal cylinder about forty inches long and eight inches wide filled with sand and enough black powder to cause a smoke puff by which the strike could be located. Signs read "Danger—Keep Out—Bombing Range." Despite the signs, the range was known as deer country and was extensively hunted. Spent bomb casings were cleared from the targets and thrown into piles "so that they would be out of the way." They were not sacked or piled in any order but were dumped in heaps, some of which had been accumulating for four years or upwards, were exposed to the weather and rusting away. Jackson went hunting in this area but did not get a deer. He decided to meet his expenses by salvaging some of the casings. He loaded three tons of them on his truck and took them to a nearby farm, where they were flattened by a tractor, and then trucked to Flint where they were sold for $84. Defendant was indicted under a federal law which provided that:

> Whoever embezzles, steals, purloins, or knowingly converts to his use or the use of another, or without authority, sells, conveys or disposes of any record, voucher, money, or thing of value of the United States or of any department or agency thereof, or any property made or being made under contract for the United States or any department or agency thereof;

> Shall be fined not more than $10,000 or imprisoned not more than ten years, or both; but if the value of such property does not exceed the sum of $100, he shall be fined not more than $1,000 or imprisoned not more than one year, or both.

Jackson wants to testify that, based on their appearance, he believed the casings were cast-off and abandoned, and that he took them with no wrongful or criminal intent. The government argues that the statute should not be construed to require a mens rea. Defendant argues that crimes like "stealing" and "conversion" must necessarily contain a mens rea. Should the statute be construed to require that "knowing conversion of government property includes the mens rea of knowingly taking the property of another?" *See Morissette v. United States*, 342 U.S. 246 (1952).

C. INTOXICATION & DRUGGED CONDITION

It is not uncommon for criminal defendants to commit criminal acts while "high" on alcohol and/or drugs. Where a criminal offense is *not* a strict liability offense, it is easy to imagine situations where such a defendant does not (sometimes, virtually cannot) possess the *mens rea* required for the criminal offense in question. Nonetheless, courts have been extremely reluctant to acquit on this basis. Common law jurisdictions have traditionally taken the position that intoxication or drugged condition can negative the *mens rea* for a "specific intent" crime, but does not negative the *mens rea* of a "general intent" crime. Just what general and specific intent means in this setting has been the subject of considerable controversy.

PEOPLE v. ATKINS

25 Cal.4th 76, 18 P.3d 660, 104 Cal.Rptr.2d 738 (2001).

CHIN, J.

Is evidence of voluntary intoxication admissible [on] the issue of whether defendant formed the required mental state for [arson]? We conclude that such evidence is not admissible because arson is a general intent crime. Accordingly, we reverse the judgment of the Court of Appeal.

[On] September 26, 1997, defendant told his friends that he hated Orville Figgs and was going to burn down Figgs's house.

On the afternoon of September 27, defendant and his brother David drove by Figgs's home on the Ponderosa Sky Ranch. Defendant "flipped the bird" at Figgs as they passed by.

Later that day, around 5:00 p.m., a neighbor saw David drive a white pickup truck into the Ponderosa Sky Ranch canyon, but could not tell if he had a passenger. Around 9:00 p.m., the same neighbor saw the pickup truck drive out of the canyon at a high rate of speed. A half-hour later, a fire was reported. Shortly after 10:00 p.m., Figgs was awakened by a neighbor. Because the fire was rapidly approaching his house, Figgs set up a fire line. The fire came within 150 feet of his house.

At 9:00 or 9:30 p.m., one of defendant's friends saw defendant at David's apartment. He was angrily throwing things around. When asked if defendant was heavily intoxicated, the friend replied, "Yes. Agitated, very agitated."

The county fire marshall, Alan Carlson, responded to the fire around 1:30 a.m. and saw a large fire rapidly spreading in the canyon below the ranch. He described fire conditions on that night as "extreme." Both the weather and the vegetation were particularly dry. The wind was blowing from 12 to 27 miles per hour, with gusts up to 50 miles per hour. The canyon had heavy brush, trees, grass, and steep sloping grades. The fire could not be controlled for three days and burned an area from 2.5 to 2.8 miles long.

The fire marshall traced the origin of the fire to an approximately 10 foot-square area that was completely burned and smelled of "chainsaw mix," a combination of oil and gasoline. A soil sample taken from that area tested positive for gasoline. About 40 feet away, the marshall found defendant's wallet, which was near a recently opened beer can, and tire tracks. He also found a disposable lighter nearby and two more beer cans in other parts of the canyon. All the cans had the same expiration date.

Several days later, defendant spoke with the fire marshall. After waiving his *Miranda* rights, defendant told the marshall that he and his brother had spent much of the day drinking. They then drove in David's white pickup to the Ponderosa Sky Ranch canyon, where they drank some more and stayed between three and one-half to five hours. Defendant saw that the area was in poor condition and decided to burn some of the weeds. His family had once lived there. He pulled out the weeds, placed them in a small pile in a cleared area, retrieved a plastic gasoline jug from David's truck, and from the jug poured "chainsaw mix" on the pile of weeds. Defendant put the jug down a few feet away and lit the pile of weeds with a disposable lighter. The fire quickly spread to the jug and got out of hand. He and David tried to put the fire out, unsuccessfully. They panicked and fled while the jug was still burning. Defendant told the marshal that he meant no harm, claimed the fire was an accident, but admitted that he and his family had hard feelings with the Figgs family.

The marshall testified that the fire had not been started in a cleared area. The area was covered with vegetation, and there was no evidence that the fire started accidentally during a debris burn or that someone had tried to put it out. The marshall opined that the fire was intentionally set.

An information charged defendant with arson of forest land. The trial court instructed on arson and on the lesser offenses of arson to property, unlawfully causing a fire of forest land, and misdemeanor unlawfully causing a fire of property. It described arson and all lesser offenses as general intent crimes and further instructed that voluntary intoxication is not a defense to arson and the lesser crimes and does not relieve defendant of responsibility for the crime. The jury found defendant guilty as charged.

Defendant appealed, arguing that evidence of voluntary intoxication was admissible to show that he lacked the requisite mental state for arson. The Court of Appeal agreed. It reasoned that [the] mens rea for arson is the intent to set fire to or burn or cause to be burned forest land, a specific mental state, as to which voluntary intoxication evidence is admissible under section 22, subdivision (b). The court reversed because the instruction that voluntary intoxication was not a defense to arson "denied defendant the opportunity to prove he lacked the required mental state."

We granted the People's petition for review on the issue of whether evidence of voluntary intoxication is admissible, under section 22, to negate the required mental state for arson.

[Section] 22 provides, as relevant:

"(a) No act committed by a person while in a state of voluntary intoxication is less criminal by reason of his or her having been in that condition. Evidence of voluntary intoxication shall not be admitted to negate the capacity to form any mental states for the crimes charged, including, but not limited to, purpose, intent, knowledge, premeditation, deliberation, or malice aforethought, with which the accused committed the act.

"(b) Evidence of voluntary intoxication is admissible solely on the issue of whether or not the defendant actually formed a required specific intent, or, when charged with murder, whether the defendant premeditated, deliberated, or harbored express malice aforethought."

Evidence of voluntary intoxication is inadmissible to negate the existence of general criminal intent. In *People v. Hood* (1969) 1 Cal.3d 444, 82 Cal.Rptr. 618, 462 P.2d 370, we first addressed the question whether to designate a mental state as a general intent, to prohibit consideration of voluntary intoxication or a specific intent, to permit such consideration. There, we held that intoxication was relevant to negate the existence of a specific intent, but not a general intent, and that assault is a general intent crime for this purpose. We stated:

"The distinction between specific and general intent crimes evolved as a judicial response to the problem of the intoxicated offender. That problem is to reconcile two competing theories of what is just in the treatment of those who commit crimes while intoxicated. On the one hand, the moral culpability of a drunken criminal is frequently less than that of a sober person effecting a like injury. On the other hand, it is commonly felt that a person who voluntarily gets drunk and while in that state commits a crime should not escape the consequences.

"Before the nineteenth century, the common law refused to give any effect to the fact that an accused committed a crime while intoxicated. The judges were apparently troubled by this rigid traditional rule, however, for there were a number of attempts during the early part of the nineteenth century to arrive at a more humane, yet workable, doctrine. The theory that these judges explored was that evidence of intoxication could be considered to negate intent, whenever intent was an element of the crime charged. As Professor Hall notes, however, such an exculpatory doctrine could eventually have undermined the traditional rule entirely, since some form of mens rea is a requisite of all but strict liability offenses. To limit the operation of the doctrine and achieve a compromise between the conflicting feelings of sympathy and reprobation for the intoxicated offender, later courts both in England and this country drew a distinction between so-called specific intent and general intent crimes."

Although we noted in *Hood* that specific and general intent have been notoriously difficult terms to define and apply, we set forth a general definition distinguishing the two intents: "When the definition of a crime consists of only the description of a particular act, without reference to intent to do a further act or achieve a future consequence, we ask whether the defendant intended to do the proscribed act. This intention is deemed to be a general criminal intent. When the definition refers to defendant's intent to do some further act or achieve some additional consequence, the crime is deemed to be one of specific intent." The basic framework that *Hood* established in designating a criminal intent as either specific or general for purposes of determining the admissibility of evidence of voluntary intoxication has survived.

Defendant argues that arson requires the specific intent to burn the relevant structure or forest land, a mental state that may be negated by evidence of voluntary intoxication. The People argue that arson is a general intent crime with a mental state that cannot be negated by such evidence. The Courts of Appeal have disagreed on the intent requirement for arson.

[In] this case, the Third Appellate District [held] that the mens rea for arson, [the] intent to set fire to or burn or cause to be burned forest land—is a "required specific intent" for which evidence of voluntary intoxication is admissible under section 22, subdivision (b).

[We] agree with the People that arson requires only a general criminal intent and that the specific intent to set fire to or burn or cause to be burned the relevant structure or forest land is not an element of arson.

[As] relevant here, the proscribed acts within the statutory definition of arson are to: (1) set fire to; (2) burn; or (3) cause to be burned, any structure, forest land, or property. Language that typically denotes specific intent crimes, such as "with the intent" to achieve or "for the purpose of" achieving some further act, is [absent]. "A crime is characterized as a 'general intent' crime when the required mental state entails only an intent to do the act that causes the harm; a crime is characterized as a 'specific intent' crime when the required mental state entails an intent to cause the resulting harm." The statute does not require an additional specific intent to burn a "structure, forest land, or property," but rather requires only an intent to do the act that causes the harm. This interpretation is manifest from the fact that the statute is implicated if a person "causes to be burned ... any structure, forest land, or property." Thus, the intent requirement for

Arson + further consequence

arson fits within the *Hood* definition of general intent, i.e., the description of the proscribed act fails to refer to an intent to do a further act or achieve a future consequence....

Defendant reasons that, since arson is the more serious crime, it should have a more culpable mental state than the recklessness requirement of [the lesser offense of recklessly causing a fire]. From that premise, he infers that the more culpable mental state of arson must be a specific intent. However, the lesser offense requires mere recklessness; arson requires the general intent to perform the criminal act. This is a continuum that does not support specific intent. The fact that a crime requires a greater mental state than recklessness does not mean that it is a specific intent crime, rather than a general intent crime. The fact that reckless burning is a lesser offense of arson is also not dispositive....

Arson's malice requirement ensures that the act is "done with a design to do an intentional wrongful act ... without any legal justification, excuse or claim of right." Its willful and malice requirement ensures that the setting of the fire must be a deliberate and intentional act, as distinguished from an accidental or unintentional ignition or act of setting a fire; " 'in short, a fire of incendiary origin.' " "Because the offensive or dangerous character of the defendant's conduct, by virtue of its nature, contemplates such injury, a general criminal intent to commit the act suffices to establish the requisite mental state." Thus, there must be a general intent to willfully commit the act of setting on fire under such circumstances that the direct, natural, and highly probable consequences would be the burning of the relevant structure or property. On the other hand, the offense of unlawfully causing a fire covers reckless accidents or unintentional fires, which, by definition, is committed by a person who is "aware of and consciously disregards a substantial and unjustifiable risk that his or her act will set fire to, burn, or cause to burn a structure, forest land, or property." For example, such reckless accidents or unintentional fires may include those caused by a person who recklessly lights a match near highly combustible materials.

Defendant argues that, because the Legislature expressly made voluntary intoxication inadmissible to negate the recklessness required for the lesser offense, but did not expressly do so for arson, it intended that voluntary intoxication evidence is admissible to negate the mental state of arson. We disagree. Unlawfully causing a fire was a new crime added by the 1979 recodification of arson. The Legislature chose expressly to state its intent as to the new offense, one without an interpretative history. On the other hand, the Legislature did not redefine the basic definition of arson in the 1979 recodification; it retained the same "willful and malicious" language in section 451. [We] decline to infer an intent, which is contrary to the weight of legislative history, prior judicial interpretation, and statutory text, from legislative silence.

[Defendant] further argues that, because the mental state for arson, as with assault, can be characterized as general intent or specific intent, like *Hood*, the decision whether or not to give effect to evidence of intoxication must rest on policy considerations. He emphasizes that, as a matter of policy, allowing intoxication evidence to negate the mental state element for arson would not necessarily result in complete acquittal, since a defendant could still be held accountable for a reckless burning, to which intoxication evidence is irrelevant. However, as explained above, arson's mental state can be classified clearly as a general intent. In any event, policy considerations do not support defendant's claim. Although the policy consideration advanced by defendant may be valid, the policy considerations expressed in *Hood* itself appear to be more consistent with the legislative intent to exclude voluntary intoxication evidence from negating the mental state of arson. There, we stated:

> "A compelling consideration is the effect of alcohol on human behavior. A significant effect of alcohol is to distort judgment and relax the controls on aggressive and anti-social impulses. Alcohol apparently has less effect on the ability to engage in simple goal-directed behavior, although it may impair the efficiency of that behavior. In other words, a drunk man is capable of forming an intent to do something simple, such as strike another, unless he is so drunk that he has reached the stage of unconsciousness. What he is not as capable as a sober man of doing is exercising judgment about the social consequences of his acts or controlling his impulses toward anti-social acts. He is more likely to act rashly and impulsively and to be susceptible to passion and anger. It would therefore be anomalous to allow evidence of intoxication to relieve a man of responsibility for the crimes of assault with a deadly weapon or simple assault, which are so frequently committed in just such a manner"

[In] arson, as with assault, there is generally no complex mental state, but only relatively simple impulsive behavior. A typical arson is almost never the product of pyromania, it often is an angry impulsive act, requiring no tools other than a match or lighter, and possibly a container of gasoline. "Arson is one of the easiest crimes to commit on the spur of the moment . . . it takes only seconds to light a match to a pile of clothes or a curtain."

The apparent legislative policy concerns are consistent with studies that have shown the following: that revenge and vindictiveness are principal motives for; that there is a strong relationship between alcohol intoxication and arson; and that recidivist arsonists committing chronic or repetitive arson have high levels of alcohol. Thus, the motivations for most arsons, the ease of its commission, and the strong connection with alcohol reflect the crime's impulsiveness. "It would therefore be anomalous to allow evidence of intoxication to relieve a man of responsibility for the crime[ ] of [arson], which [is] so frequently committed in just such a manner."

[We] reverse the judgment of the Court of Appeal and remand the cause to the Court of Appeal for further proceedings consistent with this opinion.

Concurring Opinion by MOSK, J.

[Although] they apparently recognize that "general intent" should be affixed to the crime of arson because arson is itself closely linked to voluntary intoxication in its commission, the majority deny that the mental state required could readily be deemed to be one of specific intent. Their denial is inexplicable. It is also incorrect. They seem to rest on the premise that the perpetrator's intent must be inceptive, aiming to start a fire, and apparently need not be resultative, aiming to burn down an indicated object. Even if their premise is sound, it gives them no aid. For, even if the perpetrator's intent must be inceptive rather than resultative, the required mental state could readily be deemed to be one of specific intent—again, an intent to engage in proscribed conduct involving setting fire to an indicated object, burning it, or causing it to be burned, for the purpose of bringing about, or allowing, a proscribed result involving any other wrong, including vexation, fraud, annoyance, or injury to another person. At the end of the day, all that the majority have to justify their denial seems to be an assumption that the perpetrator's intent must be resultative rather than inceptive. *Hood* itself is plain: "When" a crime "refers to" the perpetrator's "intent to do some further act or achieve some additional consequence" beyond the "description of a particular act," the "crime is deemed to be one of specific intent." The majority's assumption is that, beyond referring to the perpetrator's setting fire to an indicated object, burning it, or causing it to be burned, arson must refer to an intent on his part to achieve a particular additional consequence, that is, to burn the object down, as opposed to doing any other wrong, including vexation, fraud, annoyance, or injury to another person. Their assumption is unsupported. Hence, it falls of its own weight.

In sum, although I cannot join in the majority's analysis, I do indeed join in their conclusion that evidence of voluntary intoxication is inadmissible to disprove the mental state required for the crime of arson. Because I do so, I concur in the result.

NOTES

1. *M.P.C. and intoxication.* Consider the M.P.C.'s approach to the problem of intoxication and drugged condition:

§ 2.08. Intoxication.

unless it negates an element - "can" [handwritten annotation]

(1) Except as provided in Subsection (4) of this Section, intoxication of the actor is not a defense unless it negatives an element of the offense.

(2) When recklessness establishes an element of the offense, if the actor, due to self-induced intoxication, is unaware of a risk of which he would have been aware had he been sober, such unawareness is immaterial.

(3) Intoxication does not, in itself, constitute mental disease within the meaning of Section 4.01.

(4) Intoxication that (a) is not self-induced or (b) is pathological is an affirmative defense if by reason of such intoxication the actor at the time of his conduct lacks substantial capacity either to appreciate its criminality [wrongfulness] or to conform his conduct to the requirements of law.

(5) **Definitions.** In this Section unless a different meaning plainly is required:

> (a) "intoxication" means a disturbance of mental or physical capacities resulting from the introduction of substances into the body;

> (b) "self-induced intoxication" means intoxication caused by substances that the actor knowingly introduces into his body, the tendency of which to cause intoxication he knows or ought to know, unless he introduces them pursuant to medical advice or under such circumstances as would afford a defense to a charge of crime;

> (c) "pathological intoxication" means intoxication grossly excessive in degree, given the amount of the intoxicant, to which the actor does not know he is susceptible.

2. *Involuntary intoxication.* Involuntary intoxication or drugged condition is typically considered a viable and complete defense. Generally, this defense is treated as an involuntary act rather than as bearing on defendant's mental state.

3. *Degree of intoxication.* Where an intoxication or drugged condition defense exists, it is *not* sufficient simply to demonstrate the use of alcohol or drugs or even the fact that a defendant was demonstrably "high." Rather, to be able to successfully use this defense, the defendant must be so intoxicated and/or drugged that he or she is not capable of possessing the specific intent at issue.

PROBLEMS

1. *Limiting Intoxication Defense.* Some jurisdictions have eliminated (or virtually eliminated) intoxication or drugged condition as a defense. *See, e.g.,* 18 Pa. C.S. A. § 308 ("Neither voluntary intoxication nor voluntary drugged condition is a defense to a criminal charge, nor may evidence of such conditions be introduced to negative the element of intent of the offense,

except that evidence of such intoxication or drugged condition of the defendant may be offered by the defendant whenever it is relevant to reduce murder from a higher degree to a lower degree of murder."). Is this a sensible approach? Doesn't this approach mean that some defendants who truly do not possess the *mens rea* specified for the offense with which they are charged will be convicted in any event? If so, is that a problem?

2. *The Drunken Umbrella Thief.* Upon leaving a bar, defendant picks up another customer's umbrella. Defendant is so intoxicated that she does not realize that she has an umbrella, much less that it is not her own. Defendant is charged with theft of movable property which state law defines in the following way: "A person is guilty of theft if he unlawfully takes, or exercises unlawful control over, movable property of another with purpose to deprive him thereof." Can defendant be convicted of this crime? How does her intoxication affect her liability?

3. *Seeing Bears.* While heavily intoxicated, defendant shoots two people with a high-powered rifle. The evidence reveals that defendant was so drunk that he perceived that the people were bears rather than people. Did defendant "purposely" or "knowingly" kill his victims? Did defendant act "recklessly" or "negligently" within the meaning of the M.P.C.?

4. *Intoxicated Partygoers.* In the following situations, did defendant act "recklessly" or "negligently" as those terms are defined in M.P.C. § 2.02 as modified by M.P.C. § 2.08, if he or she causes a wreck that kills a passenger in another car:

a. Defendant, who commonly consumes alcoholic beverages to excess, drinks too much in a bar. As is his custom, defendant staggers out of the bar, climbs into his car, and attempts to drive home. Defendant is so drunk that he does not realize that his intoxicated state presents a risk to the lives of others.

b. Defendant attends a party at which she consumes only non-alcoholic beverages. Another person at the party slips drugs into her drink. In a hallucinatory state, in which she does not realize what she is doing, defendant gets into her car and drives away.

c. Defendant, who has never consumed alcoholic beverages before, takes a few sips of a gin and tonic at a party. Defendant is so drunk that he does not realize that his intoxicated state presents a risk to the lives of others.

d. Defendant, who like the defendant in the prior problem has never consumed alcoholic beverages, takes a few sips of a gin and tonic at a party. Defendant realizes that she is very drunk and should not be driving. However, desperate to get home and "sleep it off," defendant enters her car and attempts to drive home.

5. *The Intoxicated Robber.* Defendant entered a convenience store, pulled his shirt over his face with one hand, walked directly to the counter and fired a shot at the store clerk. The gun then jammed. Defendant cleared the jam

and then leaned over the counter and fired another shot before pulling his shirt over his face again and leaving the store. The store clerk died from the gunshot wounds. Defendant contends that he was intoxicated at the time that these events occurred as a result of ingesting an indeterminate amount of tequila and cocaine. The videotape of the shooting showed him walking over to the clerk and shooting him, with no unsteadiness or loss of balance, even when leaning over the counter to shoot him a second time. Defendant also drove away from the scene and the witnesses to his driving did not observe any driving problems. The officers who apprehended defendant shortly after the shooting detected no odor of alcohol or any other signs of intoxication. Upon arrest, defendant told an officer he was not drunk and did not like beer. None of the officers who observed defendant, from the time he was arrested until his confession several hours later, detected any odor of alcohol about defendant or any other signs of intoxication. Moreover, his confession contained a detailed account of the murder, but no mention about ingesting alcohol or drugs. After his conviction for first-degree murder, defendant contends that the trial court erred in not giving the jury a voluntary intoxication instruction. Was he entitled to such an instruction? *State v. Rios*, 610 S.E.2d 764 (N.C.App. 2005).

D. MISTAKE OF FACT

NEW JERSEY v. SEXTON
160 N.J. 93, 733 A.2d 1125 (1999).

OHERN.

"Once again, we must reconcile anomalies and ambiguities that inhere in the Code of Criminal Justice . . . occasioned by the Legislature's selective inclusion and omission of provisions of its conceptual source, the Model Penal Code (M.P.C.)."

The "anomalies and ambiguities" presented in this appeal concern the meaning of N.J.S.A. 2C:2–4, governing the so-called mistake-of-fact defense to a criminal charge. Specifically, the question is how to explain to the jury the effect of a mistake of fact on a charge of reckless conduct. The context is that of an accusation of aggravated or reckless manslaughter, after a gun went off, killing the seventeen-year-old victim, Alquadir Matthews. From the evidence, a jury could have found that the then fifteen-year-old defendant had pointed a gun at another and pulled the trigger. Defendant claims that he mistakenly believed the gun was not loaded.

[On] May 10, 1993, Shakirah Jones, a seventeen-year-old friend of defendant and decedent, overheard the two young men having what she described as a "typical argument." The two young men walked from a sidewalk into a vacant lot. Jones saw defendant with a gun in his hand, but she did not see defendant shoot Matthews.

Jones heard Matthews tell defendant, "there are no bullets in that gun," and then walked away. Defendant called Matthews back and said, "you think there are no bullets in this gun?" Matthews replied, "yeah." Jones heard the gun go off. A single bullet killed Matthews.

[A] ballistics expert testified that there was a spring missing from the gun's magazine, which prevented the other bullets from going into the chamber after the first bullet was discharged. In this condition, the gun would have to be loaded manually by feeding the live cartridge into the chamber prior to firing.

The expert later clarified that, if the magazine had been removed after one round had been inserted into the chamber, it would be impossible to see whether the gun was loaded without pulling the slide that covered the chamber to the rear. The expert agreed that, for someone unfamiliar with guns, once the magazine was removed, it was "probably a possible assumption" that the gun was unloaded.

Defendant's version was that when the two young men were in the lot, Matthews showed defendant a gun and "told me the gun was empty." Defendant "asked him was he sure," and "he said yes." When Matthews asked if defendant would like to see the gun, defendant said "yes." Defendant "took the gun and was looking at it," and "it just went off." He never unloaded the gun or checked to see if there were any bullets in the gun. He had never before owned or shot a gun.

A grand jury indicted defendant for purposeful or knowing murder, possession of a handgun without a permit, and possession of a handgun for an unlawful purpose. At the close of the State's case, defendant moved to dismiss the murder charge because the victim had told him that the gun was not loaded. The court denied the motion.

The court charged murder and the lesser-included offenses of aggravated manslaughter and reckless manslaughter. Concerning defendant's version of the facts, the court said:

> Defense contends this was a tragic accident. That Alquadir [Matthews], says the defense, handed the gun to Ronald [defendant]. Alquadir told Ronald, you know, the gun was not loaded. Ronald believed the gun was not loaded. Ronald did not think the gun was pointed at Alquadir when it went off. But the gun went off accidentally and, says the defense, that is a very tragic and sad accident but it is not a crime.

> If, after considering all the evidence in this case, including the evidence presented by the defense as well as the evidence presented by the State, if you have a reasonable doubt in your mind as to whether the State has proven all the elements of any of these crimes: murder, aggravated manslaughter, or reckless manslaughter, you must find the defendant not guilty of those crimes.

The jury found defendant not guilty of murder, aggravated manslaughter, or possession of a handgun for an unlawful purpose, but guilty of reckless manslaughter and unlawful possession of a handgun without a permit.

On the charge of reckless manslaughter, the court sentenced defendant to the presumptive term of seven years, three of which were parole ineligible.

[On] appeal, the Appellate Division [held] that the trial court should have charged the jury that the State bore the burden of disproving beyond a reasonable doubt defendant's mistake-of-fact defense, and that the failure to do so was plain error.

[We] granted the State's petition for certification, limited to the issue of whether "mistake of fact was a defense to the charge of reckless manslaughter."

On an earlier occasion, the Court wrote: "Twelve centuries of debate have yet to resolve the law's attitude about the criminal mind." At common law, proof of an actus reus and mens rea sufficed to establish criminal liability. Today's statutes require a voluntary act and a culpable state of mind as the minimum conditions for liability. At its earliest stages, the common law imposed liability without regard to a mens rea or culpable state of mind. "If someone caused harm, the person was accountable for it without any consideration of intent." At early common law, all homicides were capital. By examining the mental states involved, such as deliberation, premeditation, or malice, English common law gradually sought to distinguish homicides that were murder from those that were manslaughter, differentiating "criminal from non-criminal homicides, and [capital] homicides from those that were not." The common law had frequently focused on the conduct of the reasonable person as the measure of responsibility. To resolve the variety, disparity, and confusion concerning the mental elements of crime, the drafters of the M.P.C. attempted to establish distinct levels of culpability applicable to all criminal offenses. The M.P.C. "obliterated ill-defined, confusing common law language and concepts and replaced them with four specifically defined hierarchial levels of culpability in relation to the three objective element types used to define crimes."

[The] M.P.C. also contains an express provision for mistake-of-fact defenses. [The] M.P.C. provides that, "Ignorance or mistake as to a matter of fact or law is a defense if: (a) the ignorance or mistake negatives the purpose, knowledge, belief, recklessness or negligence required to establish a material element of the offense; or (b) the law provides that the state of mind established by such ignorance or mistake constitutes a defense."

Whether a mistake would negate a required element of the offense, depended, of course, on the nature of the mistake and the state of mind that the offense required. This led commentators to observe:

> Technically, such provisions [for a mistake of fact defense] are unnecessary. They simply confirm what is stated elsewhere: "No person may be convicted of an offense unless each element of such offense is proven beyond a reasonable doubt." If the defendant's ignorance or mistake makes proof of a required culpability element impossible, the prosecution will necessarily fail in its proof of the offense.

[The] Commentary to the Hawaii Criminal Code gives an easy example of how, under the M.P.C., a mistake of fact may negate culpability.

> [I]f a person is ignorant or mistaken as to a matter of fact ... the person's ignorance or mistake will, in appropriate circumstances, prevent the person from having the requisite culpability with respect to the fact ... as it actually exists. For example, a person who is mistaken (either reasonably, negligently, or recklessly) as to which one of a number of similar umbrellas on a rack is the person's and who takes another's umbrella should be afforded a defense to a charge of theft predicated on either intentionally or knowingly taking the property of another. . . .

[State] legislatures, however, "in emulating the Model Penal Code's three culpability provisions (its culpability definitions, its guidelines for resolving the requisite culpable mental state, and its mistake of fact doctrine), have not always understood their interrelationship. Hence, these states have failed to coordinate the enactment of these three types of culpability provisions." States have restricted the mistake-of-fact doctrine by imposing a reasonableness requirement. By thinking in terms of the reasonable person while failing to appreciate that the M.P.C.'s mistake-of-fact and culpability provisions are interrelated, these states have undermined the structure of the M.P.C.

To explain, we may consider again the case of the absent-minded umbrella thief. If only a reasonable mistake will provide a defense to the charge of theft, the absent-minded but careless restaurant patron will have no defense to a charge of theft. . . .

How then shall we resolve the problem created by the selective inclusion and exclusion of the culpability provisions of the M.P.C.?

[The] issue posed by our grant of certification was whether a mistake of fact was a defense to the charge of reckless manslaughter. The short answer to that question is: "It depends." The longer answer requires that we relate the type of mistake involved to the essential elements of the offense, the conduct proscribed, and the state of mind required to establish liability for the offense. Defendant insists that the State is required to disprove, beyond a reasonable doubt, his mistake-of-fact defense. Most states would agree with that statement. [We] must begin by examining the language of the statute.

N.J.S.A. 2C:2–4a allows a defense of ignorance or mistake "if the defendant reasonably arrived at the conclusion underlying the mistake and" the mistake either "negatives the culpable mental state required to establish the offense" or "[t]he law provides that the state of mind established by such ignorance or mistake constitutes a defense." The crime of manslaughter is a form of criminal homicide. "A person is guilty of criminal homicide if [the actor] purposely, knowingly [or] recklessly . . . causes the death of another human being." Criminal homicide constitutes aggravated manslaughter, a first-degree offense with special sentencing provisions, when the actor "recklessly causes death under circumstances manifesting extreme indifference to human life." Criminal homicide constitutes manslaughter, a second-degree crime, "when . . . [i]t is committed recklessly," that is, when the actor has recklessly caused death.

In this case, the jury has acquitted defendant of aggravated manslaughter. He can be retried only for reckless manslaughter. The culpable mental state of the offense is recklessness. N.J.S.A. 2C:2–2b(3) states:

> A person acts recklessly with respect to a material element of an offense when [the actor] consciously disregards a substantial and unjustifiable risk that the material element exists or will result from [the actor's] conduct. The risk must be of such a nature and degree that, considering the nature and purpose of the actor's conduct and the circumstances known to [the actor], its disregard involves a gross deviation from the standard of conduct that a reasonable person would observe in the actor's situation. . . .

The State argues that "[i]t is obvious that the firing of a gun at another human being without checking to see if it is loaded disregards a substantial risk." The State argues that at a minimum there must be some proof establishing that defendant "reasonably arrived at the conclusion underlying the mistake." To return to the language of N.J.S.A. 2C:2–4a, does the mistake about whether the gun was loaded "negative [ ] the culpable mental state required to establish the offense", or does "the law provide[ ] that the state of mind established by such ignorance or mistake constitutes a defense"? Of itself, a belief that the gun is loaded or unloaded does not negate the culpable mental state for the crime of manslaughter. Thus, one who discharges a gun, believing it to be unloaded, is not necessarily innocent of manslaughter.

[Correctly] understood, there is no difference between a positive and negative statement on the issue—what is required for liability versus what will provide a defense to liability. What is required in order to establish liability for manslaughter is recklessness (as defined by the Code) about whether death will result from the conduct. A faultless or merely careless mistake may negate that reckless state of mind and provide a defense.

How can we explain these concepts to a jury? We believe that the better way to explain the concepts is to explain what is required for liability to be established. The charge should be tailored to the factual circumstances of the case. The court should explain precisely how the offered defense plays into the element of recklessness. Something along the following lines will help to convey to the jury the concepts relevant to a reckless manslaughter charge:

> In this case, ladies and gentlemen of the jury, the defendant contends that he mistakenly believed that the gun was not loaded. If you find that the State has not proven beyond a reasonable doubt that the defendant was reckless in forming his belief that the gun was not loaded, defendant should be acquitted of the offense of manslaughter. On the other hand, if you find that the State has proven beyond a reasonable doubt that the defendant was reckless in forming the belief that the gun was not loaded, and consciously disregarded a substantial and unjustifiable risk that a killing would result from his conduct, then you should convict him of manslaughter.

[To] sum up, evidence of an actor's mistaken belief relates to whether the State has failed to prove an essential element of the charged offense beyond a reasonable doubt. As a practical matter, lawyers and judges will undoubtedly continue to consider a mistake of fact as a defense. When we do so, we must carefully analyze the nature of the mistake in relationship to the culpable mental state required to establish liability for the offense charged. Despite the complexities perceived by scholars, the limited number of appeals on this subject suggests to us that juries have very little difficulty in applying the concepts involved. We may assume that juries relate the instructions to the context of the charge. For example, in the case of the carelessly purloined umbrella, we are certain that juries would have no difficulty in understanding that it would have been a reasonable mistake (although perhaps a negligent mistake) for the customer to believe that he or she was picking up the right umbrella.

To require the State to disprove beyond a reasonable doubt defendant's reasonable mistake of fact introduces an unnecessary and perhaps unhelpful degree of complexity into the fairly straightforward inquiry of whether defendant "consciously disregard[ed] a substantial and unjustifiable risk" that death would result from his conduct and that the risk was "of such a nature and degree that, considering the nature and purpose of the actor's conduct and the circumstances known to him, its disregard involve[d] a gross deviation from the standard of conduct that a reasonable person would observe in the actor's situation."

The judgment of the Appellate Division is affirmed. . . .

PROBLEMS

1. *The Circus Performer.* As part of a circus act, a clown is supposed to point a gun at another clown and pull the trigger. However, the gun is supposed to be loaded with blanks and the idea is simply to make a lot of noise. One day, rather than being loaded with blanks, the gun contains real bullets. As a result, one of the clowns is killed. If the clown who shot the gun can prove that he did not realize that it was loaded with real bullets, how does his ignorance affect his criminal responsibility?

2. *Mistake and the Purloined Umbrella.* With respect to the carelessly purloined umbrella hypothetical discussed in *Sexton*, the court finds that criminal culpability would be inappropriate as "it would have been a reasonable mistake (although a negligent mistake) for the customer to believe that he or she was picking up the right umbrella." Would this still be true if the umbrella taken was a different color (pink rather than black) than the umbrella deposited? In other words, would it matter that the defendant's belief was unreasonable? As you think about these issues, consider the language of M.P.C. §§ 223.2 and 223.1(3)(a).

3. *The Gambling Ex–Girlfriend.* Charles Thomas Anderson was convicted of false imprisonment by means of violence after he dragged his intoxicated former girlfriend, Sylvia Olsen, out of the Chicken Ranch Casino while she was fighting and resisting him because she did not want to leave. Olsen later explained that she wanted the charges dropped against Anderson because they had just broken up over her gambling problem the day before and she and Anderson had made an agreement a month earlier that, "[i]f he caught me in the casino, he was to take me home." Anderson knew Olsen had a limited amount of money that she was to use for her son's birthday, and that she was gambling it away. Although Olsen was clearly not actually consenting to being dragged out of the casino at the time that this event occurred, Anderson argues that he was entitled to a mistake-of-fact instruction on the issue whether or not he reasonably believed Olsen was consenting to his actions based on their earlier agreement. Was he entitled to such an instruction? *See People v. Anderson*, 2008 WL 570798 (Cal.App. 5 Dist. 2008).

IOWA v. FREEMAN
450 N.W.2d 826 (Iowa 1990).

McGIVERIN, CHIEF JUSTICE.

The facts of this case are not disputed. The defendant, Robert Eric Freeman, agreed to sell a controlled substance, cocaine, to Keith Hatcher. Unfortunately for Freeman, Hatcher was cooperating with the government. Hatcher gave Freeman $200, and Freeman gave Hatcher approximately two grams of what was supposed to be cocaine. To everyone's surprise, the "cocaine" turned out to be acetaminophen. Acetaminophen is not a controlled substance.

Freeman was convicted at a bench trial of delivering a simulated controlled substance with respect to a substance represented to be cocaine.... The sole question presented by Freeman's appeal is whether he can be convicted of delivering a simulated controlled substance when, in fact, he believed he was delivering and intended to deliver cocaine.

Our review is to determine whether any error of law occurred. Finding no error, we affirm the conviction.

[Iowa] Code section 204.401(2) provides, in relevant part:

[I]t is unlawful for a person to create, deliver, or possess with intent to deliver ... a simulated controlled substance....

The term "simulated controlled substance" is defined by Iowa Code section 204.101(27):

"Simulated controlled substance" means a substance which is not a controlled substance but which is expressly represented to be a controlled substance, or a substance which is not a controlled substance but which is impliedly represented to be a controlled substance and which because of its nature, packaging, or appearance would lead a reasonable person to believe it to be a controlled substance.

[Our] cases indicate that knowledge of the nature of the substance delivered is an imputed element of section 204.401(1) offenses[, offenses involving real, non-simulated controlled substances].... Proof of such knowledge has been required to separate those persons who innocently commit the overt acts of the offense from those persons who commit the overt acts of the offense with *scienter*, or criminal intent. In general, only the latter are criminally responsible for their acts.

The Iowa Code prohibits delivery of controlled substances and imitation controlled substances, as well as delivery of counterfeit substances, in language nearly identical to that prohibiting delivery of simulated controlled substances. The distinctions between these statutory classifications are not relevant to this case.

Seizing upon the similarity of the statutory prohibitions, Freeman argues that he cannot be convicted of delivering a simulated controlled substance because he mistakenly believed he was delivering and intended to deliver an actual controlled substance.

We disagree. Freeman's construction of section 204.401(2) would convert the offense of delivery of a simulated controlled substance into one requiring knowing misrepresentation of the nature of the substance delivered. The statute clearly does not require knowing misrepresentation of the nature of the substance delivered.

[The] gist of the [204.401(2)] offense is knowing representation of a substance to be a controlled substance and delivery of a noncontrolled substance, rather than knowing misrepresentation and delivery.

[Freeman's] mistaken belief regarding the substance he delivered cannot save him from conviction. Mistake of fact is a defense to a crime of *scienter* or criminal intent only where the mistake precludes the existence of the mental state necessary to commit the crime. In this case, Freeman would not be innocent of wrongdoing had the situation been as he supposed; rather, he would be guilty of delivering a controlled substance. His mistake is no defense. The *scienter* required to hold him criminally responsible for committing the overt acts of the charged offense is present regardless of the mistake. Freeman knowingly represented to Hatcher that the substance he delivered was cocaine.

In conclusion, we hold that a person who delivers a substance that is not a controlled substance, but who knowingly represents the substance to be a controlled substance, commits the offense of delivery of a simulated controlled substance regardless of whether the person believed that the substance was controlled or not controlled.

[Freeman] attempted and intended to sell cocaine. The fact that Freeman was fooled as much as his customer is no defense to the charge in this case.

Affirmed.

PROBLEMS

1. *Freeman Mental State.* A mistake-of-fact defense is inapplicable to strict liability offenses as no mens rea is required, hence, a mistaken intention is simply irrelevant. Did the *Freeman* court interpret the simulated controlled substances statute as a strict liability crime? Explain.

2. *Actual Controlled Substances.* After *Freeman*, can a mistake-of-fact defense be presented where an accused is charged with sale of controlled substances? Explain.

3. *Attempt Crime.* Could Freeman have been convicted of attempted sale of a controlled substance? If so, why did the prosecutor not charge that offense?

RHODE ISLAND v. YANEZ
716 A.2d 759 (R.I. 1998).

GOLDBERG, JUSTICE.

The principal issue presented by this case is whether a reasonable mistake of fact concerning a complainant's age may be asserted as a defense to a charge of statutory-rape. For the reasons articulated in this opinion, we hold that with respect to the age requirement first-degree child-molestation sexual assault is a strict-liability offense.

Consequently a defendant charged with this offense may not introduce evidence that he or she was mistaken regarding the child's age, nor is a defendant entitled to a jury instruction regarding the same.

[The] defendant, Alejandro Yanez (Yanez), was eighteen-years-old when he engaged in consensual sexual intercourse with Allison (a fictitious name), the victim in this case, who was thirteen-years-old at the time. The two were first introduced to each other, albeit ever so briefly, in August 1992, nearly a year before this incident. Allison testified that she was attending a Portuguese festival with a girlfriend when she saw her aunt's boyfriend, Victor Yanez (Victor), defendant's brother. According to Allison, who at that time was only twelve-years-old, Victor introduced her to Yanez. For the next eleven months Allison and Yanez had virtually no contact with each other except for the obligatory "Hello" in passing. Then one day in mid-July 1993, while Allison was walking to the local park to meet friends, she saw Yanez cruise by in his white Trans Am convertible with the top down. She testified that she waved to Yanez, who proceeded to turn the Trans Am around and offer her a ride. Since the park was only across the street, Allison declined Yanez's invitation, but when he persisted, Allison acceded. The two briefly talked during the quarter-mile trip. Yanez gave Allison his name and telephone number, and the two conversed again briefly that night on the telephone.

The next day Allison received a telephone message from either her mother or her sister that Yanez had called her and asked that she call him back. Allison returned Yanez's telephone call, and the two made arrangements to meet in the parking lot behind St. Joseph's Church in West Warwick. From the church the two left in Yanez's car and went for a ride. According to Allison, they proceeded to the home of a friend of Yanez's where they engaged in consensual sexual intercourse on the floor in a back bedroom.

Following the conclusion of their first "date" Allison returned home quite late. After entering the house, Allison proceeded directly to the bathroom to shower whereupon she was subsequently confronted by her mother. While in the bathroom, Allison's mother noticed her underwear on the floor and asked if she had engaged in sexual intercourse. Allison initially denied having had sexual intercourse that evening but later admitted the truth.... A subsequent police investigation revealed that Yanez admitted having had sexual intercourse with Allison but insisted that Allison had told him that she was sixteen-years-old. Allison denied having told Yanez that she was sixteen years of age and, in fact, testified that on the two or three occasions when Yanez had inquired about her age, she had responded that she was only thirteen.

Yanez was indicted on one count of first-degree child-molestation sexual assault, although the trial testimony would later reveal that this was not an isolated incident and that there were two more equally sordid, uncharged encounters. At trial defense counsel made numerous attempts to introduce evidence not only demonstrating Yanez's mistaken belief concerning Allison's age but also evidence concerning Allison's apparent maturity in light of her appearance, physical development, and demeanor. The trial justice rejected this evidence and determined that in cases in which conduct is made criminal because the victim is a minor, the defense of ignorance or mistaken belief with respect to the victim's age is not available. The trial justice further indicated that he intended to charge the jury with respect to the unavailability of this defense and consequently declined to charge in accordance with Yanez's requested mistake of fact instructions. The pertinent portion of the trial justice's charge to the jury reads as follows:

> "The defendant is accused that on a day and dates between July 14, 1993 and July 15, 1993, at West Warwick, Alejandro Yanez did engage in sexual penetration, to wit sexual intercourse, with [Allison], a person under 14 years of age, in violation of the laws of the State of Rhode Island. Now a person is guilty of first degree child molestation, sexual assault, if he or she engages in sexual penetration with a person 14 years of age or under. Sexual penetration includes sexual intercourse. By law, sexual intercourse is defined as the penetration of the vagina by the penis. There are two essential elements to first degree child molestation sexual assault. First, the defendant must engage in sexual intercourse with the alleged victim. And second, the victim is under the age of 14 years.

> "Now under the terms of this law, the State need not prove that the act of sexual intercourse was committed against the wishes of the victim. Thus, in order for you to return a verdict of guilty, the State is required to prove, number one, that this defendant, Alejandro Yanez; two, on or about July 15, 1993, at West Warwick; three, did in fact engage in sexual intercourse with [Allison]; and four, that at the time, if you are satisfied he did engage in sexual intercourse with [Allison], at the time she was under the age of 14 years. The law also states when conduct is made criminal because the victim is a minor, and in Rhode Island [in the context of this case] that age being 14, it is no defense that the defendant was ignorant of or mistaken as to the victim's age. And it matters not that his mistaken belief was reasonable."

Following deliberations a Superior Court jury convicted Yanez of first-degree child-molestation sexual assault. The trial justice sentenced Yanez to the minimum twenty year sentence but suspended eighteen years of the sentence with probation. The trial justice also ordered that Yanez have no contact with Allison for twenty years and, as required by law, that Yanez register with the local police authorities as a convicted sex offender.

[The] crime of statutory-rape was legislatively created in England during the thirteenth century in order to afford special protection to those society had deemed too young to appreciate the consequences of their actions. Thus English courts, which had generally recognized the mistake of fact defense in criminal prosecutions since 1638, did not begin to discuss this defense in the context of statutory-rape cases until the later half of the nineteenth century. At that time, the mistake of fact defense was rejected by courts both in England and in the United States.

Characterizing statutory-rape as a strict-liability offense remained the law in every American jurisdiction until 1964. [We] note that our research involving statutory-rape cases has revealed that the highest appellate courts of only four states have judicially recognized the mistake of fact defense. All four of these cases, however, are distinguishable from the case at bar.

The courts in *People v. Hernandez*, 39 Cal.Rptr. 361, 393 P.2d 673 (1964), and *State v. Elton*, 680 P.2d 727 (Utah 1984), both expressly relied upon the text of their respective criminal codes, which required the concurrence of an act and a mental state in order to constitute a crime, as well as language in their codes that unless otherwise provided, ignorance or mistake of fact negates a culpable mental state. Furthermore the *Elton* court relied upon a provision of the Utah Criminal Code, which stated that an offense may be a strict-liability crime only if a statute expressly provides that a mental state is not required. Our General Laws are entirely devoid of any provisions similar to those relied upon in *Hernandez* and *Elton*; therefore, these cases are of no aid to Yanez.

The other two cases in which the mistake of fact defense was judicially recognized are *State v. Guest*, 583 P.2d 836 (Alaska 1978), and *Perez v. State*, 803 P.2d 249 (N.M. 1990). In both of these cases, however, the age of the victims (fifteen) closely approached the age of consent (sixteen). In addition the court in *Perez* observed that even though the mistake of fact defense is available if the victim is between the ages of thirteen and sixteen, a defendant is precluded from raising this defense when the victim is under the age of thirteen.

["It] is well established that the Legislature may, pursuant to its police powers, define criminal offenses without requiring proof of a specific criminal intent and so provide that the perpetrator proceed at his own peril regardless of his defense of ignorance or an honest mistake of fact." As the final arbiter on questions of statutory interpretation, we have it as our purpose to establish and to effectuate the Legislature's intent. "[I]n the absence of an ambiguity, this [C]ourt must give the words of the statute 'their literal and plain meaning.'" Against this backdrop we examine our first-degree child-molestation sexual assault statute.

Section 11–37–8.1 provides that:

> "[a] person is guilty of first degree child molestation sexual assault if he or she engages in sexual penetration with a person fourteen (14) years of age or under."

The term "sexual penetration" is defined in § 11–37–1(8) as follows:

> " 'Sexual penetration'—sexual intercourse, cunnilingus, fellatio, and anal intercourse, or any other intrusion, however slight, by any part of a person's body or by any object into the genital or anal openings of another person's body, but emission of semen is not required."

Clearly the plain words and meaning of § 11–37–8.1 prohibit the sexual penetration of an underaged person and make no reference to the actor's state of mind, knowledge, or belief. In our opinion this lack of a *mens rea* results not from negligent omission but from legislative design.

Yanez correctly asserts that this Court has previously declared the existence of an implied *mens rea* element with respect to the term "sexual contact" in cases of second-degree sexual assault, and to some but not all acts of "sexual penetration" in cases of first-degree child-molestation sexual assault. These opinions represent our determination that conduct that the Legislature has included within the definitions of "sexual contact" or "sexual penetration," other than sexual intercourse, anal intercourse, cunnilingus, or fellatio, may in the absence of a *mens rea* element embrace conduct that is intended for an innocent purpose and not for purposes of sexual arousal or gratification.

[However,] this debate concerning penetration but not gratification should in no way suggest our willingness to imply an element of *mens rea* with respect to the child's age. We decline to permit a defendant charged with the sexual penetration of a child fourteen years of age or younger to escape responsibility on the basis of the purported consent of the victim or a defendant's mistaken, albeit reasonable, belief that the child was over the age of consent. Our position has both historical and legislative support.

The Rhode Island General Assembly has divided sexual offenses into two main categories—sexual assault and child-molestation sexual assault. An examination of the pertinent provisions reveals that the Legislature has carefully distinguished between the two, explicitly requiring a *mens rea* for sexual assaults that were either unknown at common law or for those acts of sexual abuse that did not involve sexual intercourse, anal intercourse, cunnilingus, or fellatio while electing to maintain the common law's strict-liability for child-molestation sexual assault. . . . Conversely, when the Legislature drafted the child-molestation sexual assault statutes, it utilized essentially the same language without reference to intent.

[It] can be inferred from this statutory classification that the child-molestation sexual assault statutes' silence with regard to a *mens rea* "is designed to subserve the state interest of protecting female children from the severe physical and psychological consequences of engaging in coitus before attaining the age of consent in the statute." Had the Legislature intended not only to punish the act of child-molestation sexual assault but also to require a mental state, the Legislature could easily have provided for such an element. But its decision to include a *mens rea* requirement in the sexual assault statutes while declining to provide a *mens rea* requirement in the child-molestation sexual assault statutes, demonstrates that the Legislature's omission was intentional. This is a sensible and pragmatic objective with which we shall not interfere by engrafting a *mens rea* requirement where one was not intended.

[We] recognize that the dissent firmly believes that the General Assembly intended for jurors "to sort out true cases of child molestation from those involving consensual premarital sex between teenagers based upon a mistaken but reasonably held belief that both were old enough to do so legally." We observe, however, the social and policy considerations such a defense would engender in future prosecutions for child-molestation.

First, it would open the door to the introduction of evidence concerning a victim's past sexual conduct, evidence that the General Assembly has already sought to restrict through the enactment of the rape-shield statute. This protection was designed to encourage rape victims to come forward and report crimes; thus we have limited the use of a victim's past sexual history to questions relating to a complaining witness' credibility and have specifically held that such an inquiry is not relevant to the issue of consent. Therefore if a victim, in this case Allison, is to be subject to cross-examination, as the dissent suggests, concerning her "evident sexual experience," as well as her "developed physical appearance, her poise, [and] her association with older teenagers," in order for a defendant to establish his or her reasonable belief that the victim was at least sixteen-years-old, we conclude that such action should come from the Legislature and not from this Court. This is a door best left closed until it is opened, if at all, by those who are better able to debate all the consequences.

Second, we are mindful that were we to adopt a mistake of age defense in cases of child-molestation sexual assault, this defense would be available to all persons charged with engaging in sexual contact with children under the age of fourteen and not only this eighteen-year-old defendant. The availability of this defense would, of course, inevitably lead to the presentation of evidence concerning the issue of consent. In order to avail oneself of the mistake of age defense, the accused, like Yanez in this case, would be required to allege not only that he or she reasonably believed the victim to have been at least sixteen years of age but also that the victim consented to the act. This defense would result in the prosecution having the burden of proving beyond a reasonable doubt the fact that the victim did not consent to a crime in which the Legislature has decreed that consent is irrelevant.

[For] the reasons articulated, we deny the defendant's appeal and affirm the judgment of conviction. . . .

FLANDERS, JUSTICE, dissenting.

I respectfully dissent. I cannot believe that the Legislature intended that Rhode Island's statutory-rape law—carrying a mandatory-minimum sentence of twenty years in jail—should be construed by the Judiciary to bar an accused teenager's reasonable mistake-of-age defense to charges based upon his engaging in consensual sexual acts with his teenaged girlfriend. The unavoidable result of such a draconian interpretation of this law is the imposition on this defendant, Alejandro Yanez (Alex)—a young man who was barely eighteen years old at the time of this incident—of an uncommonly brutal, harsh, and undeserved punishment that is so out of whack with reality that it is virtually without parallel in any jurisdiction of the United States.

If any legislative intent is apparent in the language used in § 11–37–8.1 to criminalize sex with children, it is the intent manifest in its title to outlaw sexual abuse of children by adults and to punish severely those who commit such "child molestation." But there is a world of difference between a crime involving intentional child molestation and a situation like this one in which two teenage lovers engage in a fully consensual act (or acts) of sexual intercourse in the mistaken belief on the part of one of them that they are both of a legal age to do so. Although their exuberant sexual behavior may be sniffed at by a tongue-clucking majority as "sordid," it is certainly not "child molestation" within the meaning of Rhode Island's statutory-rape law. Any criminal statute that carries a mandatory twenty-year jail sentence and imposes a lifelong stigma as a sexual predator on any violator should be rationally interpreted to draw a distinction between these two very different scenarios—especially when, as here, the sexual conduct in question would have been unquestionably legal if Alex's sexual partner had been sixteen years old, as she allegedly said she was.

[I] would hold that in this type of situation the General Assembly intended that a jury—not judges or prosecutors—is the appropriate body to sort out true cases of child molestation from those involving consensual premarital sex between teenagers based upon a mistaken but reasonably held belief that both were old enough to do so legally. To this end, a criminal defendant indicted under § 11–37–8.1 should

be afforded the opportunity to defend against such charges by showing a reasonable and good-faith mistake concerning the age of his or
her consenting sexual partner....

PROBLEMS

1. *Yanez Debate.* Which of these views—the majority's or the dissenter's—appears most sensible based upon the plain text of the statute? Which
is most sensible public policy? Should a judge's notions of appropriate public
policy play any rule in statutory interpretation? Explain.

2. *Legislative Intent.* If the majority is correct that the legislative intention was the protection of *female* minors, rather than the protection of *both*
male and female minors, do you find this statute to be inappropriately sexist?
Whatever your answer to that question, does it—should it—make any
difference to the lawfulness of such a statute what the intention of its
legislative drafters was? Explain.

3. *Mistake and the Babysitter.* Andre Knap was in bed, asleep in a
darkened bedroom, when he felt someone massaging his genitals. Assuming
that this person was his girlfriend, Knap began engaging in sexual relations
with her. At some point, however, he realized that the person with whom he
was having sex was not his girlfriend, but was instead the 13 year-old
babysitter, who had come into his bed naked while he was sleeping. As soon
as Knap realized this fact, he desisted. Is Knap guilty of statutory rape?
Commonwealth v. Knap, 412 Mass. 712, 592 N.E.2d 747 (1992).

E.   MISTAKE OF LAW

UNITED STATES v. SCARMAZZO

554 F.Supp.2d 1102 (E.D.Cal. 2008).

OLIVER W. WANGER, DISTRICT JUDGE.

The following orders on motions in limine and for clarification of
and addressing supplemental motions in limine have been heard and
decided [.] The following rulings are set forth for the benefit of and as
guidance to the parties.

[Defendants] are ordered not to introduce any evidence, questioning, or testimony, either expert or lay opinion testimony, or to
argue in the presence of the jury, to suggest: ... Defendants' "good
faith" belief that marijuana is of medical value ...

[Erroneous] Belief Conduct Was Lawful (Irrelevant).

It is unlawful for an individual knowingly or intentionally to
manufacture, distribute, dispense, or possess with intent to manufacture, distribute, or dispense a controlled substance.

Knowledge of, or intent to violate the law is not an element of
this offense. A good faith defense does not apply where the law does

not require as part of its mens rea element, proof of a Defendant's knowledge of the legal duty. A mistake of law element does not apply because ignorance or mistake of law is not a defense to a crime that does not require a showing the Defendant knew the illegality of conduct of which he is charged.

Where the crime requires only knowledge, not willfulness, the government need only prove the Defendants knew they were performing an act, not that they knew the act was unlawful or criminalized by statute.

[Ignorance] of the law is no defense, as statutes relating to the use and possession of drugs do not require proof of intent to violate the law. [There] is no requirement of knowledge of the unlawfulness of Defendant's acts under the crimes charged. The general rule, "deeply rooted in the American legal system" is "that ignorance of the law or a mistake of law is no defense to criminal prosecution."

The government is not required to prove that Defendant was aware of or intended to violate the law. [A] mistaken belief regarding what the law allows is a mistake of law, not a mistake of fact, and is not a defense to a criminal charge.

[Good] faith reliance on the advice of a counsel is not relevant because such advice can only be shown to negate a specific intent to violate the law. Here, neither good faith nor mistake as to the enforceability of the law is a defense. An attorney's advice about what the law is, medical necessity, the benefits of marijuana . . . would only be confusing, misleading, time consuming, and prejudicial. Fundamentally, advice of counsel is irrelevant.

[For] the reasons stated above, the government's motions in limine are granted.

PROBLEMS

1. *Belief in Lawful Conduct.* Should it matter that the defendants in *Scarmazzo*, who owned a medical marijuana dispensary that was organized lawfully under California law, believed that they were acting lawfully in possessing and distributing marijuana in reliance relying upon a California law which permits medicinal marijuana use? Why or why not?

2. *Advice of Attorney.* Why do you think that the *Scarmazzo* Court concluded that a person is not entitled to rely on the advice of his or her attorney as a defense to criminal charges? Does that make sense? If a person can't rely on an attorney to figure out what the law requires, how are people supposed to find out what the law is? Research it on their own?

HAWAII v. DeCASTRO

81 Haw. 147, 913 P.2d 558 (Ct.App. 1996).

BURNS, CHIEF JUDGE.

Defendant Robert DeCastro (DeCastro) appeals the October 7, 1992 Judgment entered by the District Court of the First Circuit convicting him of Resisting an Order to Stop a Motor Vehicle, Hawaii Revised Statutes (HRS) § 710–1027(1) (1985), which states as follows:

> (1) A person commits the offense of resisting an order to stop a motor vehicle if he intentionally fails to obey a direction of a peace officer, acting under color of his official authority, to stop his vehicle.

The district court sentenced DeCastro to probation for one year and ordered him to contribute $100 to the State General Fund.

[We] affirm.

[DeCastro] owns Town and Country Moving headquartered in Kalihi. On Wednesday, December 18, 1991 at about 12:30 p.m., while returning to his warehouse from a delivery in Wahiawa, DeCastro drove his van (Van) in the Koko Head (southeasterly) direction on the H–2 freeway. DeCastro's employee, Westley Damas (Damas), was a passenger in DeCastro's Van. Near the Mililani exit, DeCastro and Damas observed police officer Derek Rodrigues (Officer Rodrigues) in a Honolulu Police Department blue and white vehicle (No. 734) nearly cause a "four car accident" while pursuing a speeding motorist later identified as George Hernandez (Hernandez). Hernandez had no passenger in his vehicle. After Officer Rodrigues had stopped Hernandez to issue him a citation for speeding, Officer Rodrigues noticed a white van stop about four car lengths behind his patrol car. Officer Rodrigues saw DeCastro in the driver's seat and Damas in the passenger's seat of the Van.

DeCastro testified that he stopped because he believed Officer Rodrigues had driven his police car in a reckless manner. DeCastro remained in the Van and noted the license plate numbers of Officer Rodrigues' and Hernandez' vehicles.

The Van's presence aroused Officer Rodrigues' suspicions that its occupants were friends of Hernandez. This prompted Officer Rodrigues to approach the driver's side of the Van and ask, "Oh. You with those guys up there?" DeCastro replied, "No. Do we look like we're with those guys?"

At this point, the State and DeCastro dispute what happened. DeCastro and Damas testified that, while holding his baton or nightstick in his hand, Officer Rodrigues made the following statement: "Oh, you getting pretty cocky, aren't you? You want to get cocky …

Eh, you [f _ _ _ _ _], you like beef? You like beef, you [f _ _ _ _ _]? Step out. Both of you. Come on, step out." DeCastro admitted that at no point did Officer Rodrigues strike DeCastro or the Van with his baton. Nor did Officer Rodrigues wave his baton in the air or swing it at DeCastro. DeCastro testified that upon hearing Officer Rodrigues' statement, both he and Damas chuckled.

Nevertheless, DeCastro contends Officer Rodrigues' statement led him to be concerned for his and Damas' safety. Thereafter, Officer Rodrigues demanded DeCastro's license, and vehicle registration and insurance card, which DeCastro willingly provided. Officer Rodrigues then ordered DeCastro to "wait" while Officer Rodrigues returned to his patrol car.

Immediately after Officer Rodrigues walked away, DeCastro dialed 911 on his cellular phone. Unable to get through, DeCastro called his wife, Lisa Rodrigues, to arrange a conference call with the 911 operator. The transcript of the "911" conversation between the 911 operator and DeCastro discloses the following:

OPERATOR: You need a police?

DeCASTRO: No, I no need a police. I'm being harassed by a policeman.

OPERATOR: Hah?

DeCASTRO: I'm being harassed by a policeman.

OPERATOR: Where is the policeman?

DeCASTRO: Where are we in between?

OTHER: Waipio [Waipi'o] and Mililani.

DeCASTRO: Waipio [Waipi'o] and Mililani, and he's—I hope someone comes fast. He went ask us if, uh, we like fight with him.

OPERATOR: You have his license number?

DeCASTRO: H–P–D 734. He was reckless driving. We went go pull off on the side of the road—

OPERATOR: What's his number?

DeCASTRO:—to get his, uh, license plate.

OPERATOR: What is it?

DeCASTRO: And now he's out here with his nightstick.

OPERATOR: What is it?

DeCASTRO: You know what, I just—I should just go to my warehouse already.

OPERATOR: What's the license number?

DeCASTRO: His—his number is H–P–D—

[OPERATOR:] "D?"

DeCASTRO: H–P–D 734. This guy wants to fight us.

OPERATOR: You want the police right now?

DeCASTRO: Uh, well, I like just go to my warehouse, and you can send a policeman over there.

OPERATOR: Okay. When you get to the warehouse, call back.

DeCASTRO: You know what, he's gonna chase me once I leave.

OPERATOR: No, go ahead and just, uh, we got the license.

DeCASTRO: You got 'um?

OPERATOR: Yeah. Just go to the warehouse, and then call back.

DeCASTRO: Okay.

OPERATOR: Okay.

911 operator told him to leave — 3 times.

. . .

DeCASTRO: Now he's in back of me, and he wants to pull me over. And this guy wants to fight with me.

OPERATOR: Is he—is—is—well, do you wanna stay on the line?

DeCASTRO: Yeah, I wanna stay on the line. I want another police-man. I want another policeman at my warehouse 'cause I'm not gonna pull over.

. . .

I'm afraid if I pull over, he's—he's gonna arrest me, or what do you want me to do?

OPERATOR: I don't know. Is he in a blue-and-white?

. . .

DeCASTRO: He's in a blue-and-white. I want a policeman at 94–478 Ukee ['Uke'e] Street.

OPERATOR: But are you there now?

DeCASTRO: No, I'm on the freeway.

. . .

SUPERVISOR: This is the 911 Supervisor. May I help you?

DeCASTRO: Yeah, about an officer who I pulled over on the side of the road. I pulled him on the side of the road to take his license-plate number down. He asked me if I wanted to fight, and he came out with his nightstick.

SUPERVISOR: He couldn't be an officer.

. . .

DeCASTRO: Now there's three of 'um.

. . .

DeCASTRO: Now, now they're all coming out with their clubs. All of them have their clubs.

. . .

[DeCASTRO:] Now they're arresting me. Get—get the—get the chief—get the chief over here.

The State's evidence showed that before Officer Rodrigues returned to the Van, DeCastro drove it off in the same direction he was heading before he had stopped. Officer Rodrigues gave chase, using his automobile's horn, siren, and flashing lights, while maintaining a distance of about two car lengths behind DeCastro. Officer Rodrigues simultaneously called dispatch to inform them that he was pursuing DeCastro and asked for a backup unit to assist him. During the chase, Officer Rodrigues observed DeCastro "look in his rearview mirror at least ten times."

[Upon] stopping DeCastro, Officer Rodrigues and Sergeant Dow approached the driver's side and Officer Grilho approached the passenger's side. DeCastro refused to open the door, the window remained locked, and he continued talking on his cellular phone. Officer Rodrigues kept knocking on the window telling DeCastro to open the door. DeCastro eventually did step out of his Van. Officer Rodrigues testified that the first remark that DeCastro made was "the chief told" him "not to stop." While being handcuffed, DeCastro put up a slight struggle.

[DeCastro] contends that he lacked the requisite specific intent to commit the crime because he consulted with and relied on the 911 telephone operator's permission to leave the scene.

HRS § 702–220 (1985) states in relevant part as follows:

Ignorance or mistake of law; belief that conduct not legally prohibited. In any prosecution, it shall be an affirmative defense that the defendant engaged in the conduct or caused the result alleged under the belief that the conduct or result was not legally prohibited when he acts in reasonable reliance upon an official statement of the law, afterward determined to be invalid or erroneous, contained in:

. . .

(3) An . . . administrative grant of permission; or

(4) An official interpretation of the public officer or body charged by law with responsibility for the interpretation, administration, or enforcement of the law defining the offense.

Clearly, a 911 telephone operator is not "the public officer or body charged by law with responsibility for the interpretation, administration, or enforcement of the law defining the offense" of Resisting an Order to Stop a Motor Vehicle. Therefore, the HRS § 702–220(4) affirmative defense is not applicable.

The district court found that "the Court does not see anything in the information that could lead a reasonable person to conclude that somehow he was being given permission to leave the scene[;]" and "[DeCastro's] attempt to make a phone call via 911 was a rather calculating act, and, actually, an attempt to bootstrap some sort of defense." In contrast, DeCastro asserts, as an HRS § 702–220(3) affirmative defense, that the 911 telephone operator authorized him to proceed to his warehouse and he acted on the belief that he was legally authorized to leave.

[handwritten margin note: DC says: — ≠ reasonable to leave scene — 911 call was calculated]

[handwritten margin note: acted on belief that he was auth.]

Assuming DeCastro's assertion is true, the dispositive question is whether DeCastro has introduced evidence in satisfaction of his burden of proving that a 911 telephone operator's authorization is an "official statement of the law, . . ., contained in: . . . [a]n administrative grant of permission[.]" Our answer is no.

[The] affirmative defense stated in HRS § 702–220 is a relatively recent limited exception to the following very old general rule.

> A defendant's error as to his authority to engage in particular activity, if based upon a mistaken view of legal requirements (or ignorance thereof), is a mistake of law. Typically, the fact that he relied upon the erroneous advice of another is not an exculpatory circumstance. He is still deemed to have acted with a culpable state of mind.

[handwritten margin note: Erroneous advice ≠ negate MR]

United States v. Barker, 546 F.2d 940, 946–47 (D.C.Cir. 1976).

In his concurring opinion in *Barker*, District Judge Merhige explained the rationale of the rule in relevant part as follows:

> The district judge advised the jury that a mistake of law is no excuse, and, therefore, that a mistake as to the legality of the search in issue was not a defense to the charges contained in the indictment. In that regard, the district judge was applying the general rule on mistake of law that has long been an integral part of our system of jurisprudence. The most commonly asserted rationale for the continuing vitality of the rule is that its absence would encourage and reward public ignorance of the law to the detriment of our organized legal system, and would encourage universal pleas of ignorance of the law that would constantly pose confusing and, to a great extent, insolvable issues of fact to juries and judges, thereby bogging down our adjudicative system.

[handwritten margin note: mistake as to the legality of the search issue ≠ defense]

[handwritten margin note: absence of rule would mean rewarding ignorance]

[Assuming] a 911 telephone operator's authorization is a "statement of the law . . . contained in . . . [a]n . . . administrative grant of permission[,]" there is nothing on the record or in the law that supports a conclusion that it is an "official statement of the law[.]" There is nothing on the record or in the law that supports the conclusion that a 911 telephone operator is officially authorized to permit a motor vehicle operator to fail to obey a police officer's order. Thus, we do not reach the question of whether a 911 telephone operator's authorization is an "administrative grant of permission[.]"

[Accordingly,] we affirm the District Court's October 7, 1992 Judgment convicting DeCastro of Resisting an Order to Stop a Motor Vehicle.

Nᴏᴛᴇꜱ

1. *Ignorance of law.* In general, the old maxim, "ignorance of the law is no excuse" (*"ignorantia legis neminem excusat"*), is a perfectly accurate statement of the prevailing law, unless the criminal statute in question expressly prescribes that knowledge of the unlawfulness of one's conduct is an element of the offense.

2. *Reliance on statute or case law.* The Hawaii mistake-of-law statute, H.R.S. § 702–220, also contains provisions, not at issue in *DeCastro*, taken from the Model Penal Code, that provide a further mistake-of-law defense where an individual acts in reasonable reliance upon an official (albeit erroneous) statement of the law contained in "(1) [a] statute or other enactment; [or] (2) [a] judicial decision, opinion, or judgment."

Pʀᴏʙʟᴇᴍ

Police Authority. Do you think that the result in *DeCastro* would have— should have—been different if the 911 operator was, as is true in some states, a deputized police officer? What if DeCastro had actually talked to the Chief of Police and he or she told him to continue on to his warehouse? Explain.

KIPP v. DELAWARE

704 A.2d 839 (Del. 1998).

Hᴏʟʟᴀɴᴅ, Jᴜꜱᴛɪᴄᴇ:

This is an appeal following a bench trial in the Superior Court. The defendant-appellant, Hugh A. Kipp, Jr. ("Kipp"), was convicted of three counts of Possession of a Deadly Weapon by a Person Prohibited. The State has confessed error on appeal and submits that Kipp's judgments of conviction should be reversed.

[On] the morning of September 17, 1995, several police officers went to Kipp's home in Wilmington. They were investigating a "man with a gun" complaint from Kipp's girlfriend, Lisa Zeszut ("Zeszut"). At first, Kipp refused to come out of his house, but eventually surrendered to the police.

[The] police searched the house for other weapons. The police found a handgun and two unloaded shotguns. The police discovered ammunition for those weapons scattered on the bedroom floor. The police also found two hunting bows, with arrows. Upon checking Kipp's criminal record, police ascertained that he was a person prohibited from possessing deadly weapons.

Kipp was ... charged with five counts of Possession of a Deadly Weapon by a Person Prohibited.

[The] only defense offered by Kipp at trial was that he was unaware of his status as a "person prohibited." Kipp was a "person prohibited" as a result of his guilty plea to Assault in the Third Degree in 1990. Kipp testified he was told that he would not be prohibited from possessing weapons as a result of the plea.

The 1990 guilty plea form, which was submitted into evidence, has a space which provides that a guilty plea will result in loss of the right to possess deadly weapons. That portion of the form was marked "N/A." Kipp testified that "N/A" meant the provision did not apply to him. The completed guilty plea form was provided to the judge during the 1990 plea colloquy. Neither the prosecutor nor the judge, however, brought the error on the guilty plea form to Kipp's attention.

After hearing all of the evidence, the Superior Court concluded that the two hunting bows were not deadly weapons. [The] Superior Court found Kipp guilty of three counts of Possession of a Deadly Weapon by a Person Prohibited in connection with his possession of the three firearms.

[Under] 11 Del.C. § 1448(b), "[a]ny prohibited person ... who knowingly possesses, purchases, owns or controls a deadly weapon while so prohibited shall be guilty of possession of a deadly weapon by a person prohibited." A person is a "prohibited person" for purposes of § 1448(b) when, inter alia, he or she has "been convicted in this State or elsewhere of a felony or a crime of violence involving physical injury to another...." Assault in the Third Degree is a misdemeanor crime of violence involving physical injury to another. A person who has been convicted of a violent misdemeanor is prohibited from possessing a deadly weapon for the five-year period from the date of conviction.

[The] State has confessed error in Kipp's case on appeal. Under the facts presented, the State concedes that Kipp presented a valid mistake of law defense. This Court has held that, in very narrow circumstances, mistake of law can be a defense to a criminal charge. That defense is cognizable when the defendant: (1) erroneously concludes in good faith that his particular conduct is not subject to the operation of the criminal law; (2) makes a "bona fide, diligent effort, adopting a course and resorting to sources and means at least as appropriate as any afforded or under our legal system, to ascertain and abide by the law;" (3) "act[s] in good faith reliance upon the results of such effort;" and (4) the conduct constituting the offense is "neither immoral nor anti-social."

Kipp presented evidence that he was misled in connection with his plea to Assault in the Third Degree. His 1990 guilty plea form, which was introduced at trial, and his testimony indicated he was told that the prohibition against possession of a deadly weapon which would result from a guilty plea was "not applicable" to the plea which he was entering. Kipp testified that he was told that prohibition was not applicable to him because he was pleading to a misdemeanor.

Kipp's plea agreement and truth-in-sentencing guilty plea form were submitted to the judge in 1990 at the plea colloquy before his guilty plea to Assault in the Third Degree was accepted. Apparently, the prosecutor and the judge who accepted his guilty plea failed to notice the "not applicable" notation on the guilty plea form. The judge referred to the plea agreement in the plea colloquy, but never informed Kipp that the "not applicable" notation was incorrect with respect to the prohibition against future possession of a deadly weapon which would result from the plea.

Under 11 Del.C. § 1448, a person is guilty of possession of a deadly weapon by a person prohibited when he is: (a) a person prohibited; and (b) knowingly possesses a deadly weapon. Thus, to be guilty of the offense, the defendant need only know that he or she possessed the weapon. Section 1448 does not require the defendant to know that it was criminal to do so.

Ignorance of the law is not a defense to crime. But "[a] defendant is not charged with knowledge of a penal statute if he is misled concerning whether the statute is not being applied." A mistake of law defense is appropriately recognized where the defendant demonstrates that he has been misled by information received from the State.

Under the unique circumstances of this case, the State concedes on appeal that Kipp presented a proper and complete mistake of law defense. In relying on the advice of counsel, memorialized in an official guilty plea document presented to and not corrected by either the prosecutor or the judge, Kipp had "made a bona fide, diligent effort, adopting a course and resorting to sources and means at least as appropriate as any afforded under our legal system, to ascertain and abide by the law...." The State submits that Kipp's three convictions for possession of a deadly weapon by a person prohibited should be reversed.

[The] mistake of law defense is based upon principles of fundamental fairness. A review of the record and the applicable law supports the State's confession of error. The State's confession of error "is in accordance with the highest tradition of the Delaware Bar and the prosecutor's unique role and duty to seek justice within an adversary system."

The judgments of conviction are reversed. . . .

PROBLEM

Protesting the Right to Vote. On November 5, 1872, Susan B. Anthony and thirteen other women voted in an election in Rochester, New York. A federal statute made it a crime for any person to vote "without the lawful right to vote." Although the State of New York did not permit women to vote at that time (the XIX Amendment to the U.S. Constitution did not go into effect until 1920), Anthony argued that she had a "moral" and "God given" right to vote under the Fourteenth Amendment. The courts rejected her claim. Assuming that Anthony honestly believed that she was morally entitled to vote, did she have a tenable mistake of law claim? *See United States v. Anthony,* 24 Fed. Cas. 829 (C.C.N.D.N.Y. 1873).

Some crimes *a*a only require that it's committed
w/ req'd MR.
But result-crimes require that Δ *caused* result.

CHAPTER 4

CAUSATION

■ ■ ■

Some crimes require only an actus reus committed with the required mens rea. Other crimes are "result" crimes which require that defendant "cause" some result. In some instances, it is not difficult to determine that a defendant caused a particular result, as when defendant fires twelve bullets into his victim who falls over dead. In other instances, the "cause" of death may be less clear, as when "intervening" factors intrude between the act and the death.

STEPHENSON v. STATE

205 Ind. 141, 179 N.E. 633 (1932).

PER CURIAM.

[The] victim of this homicide is Miss Madge Oberholtzer, who was a resident of the city of Indianapolis and lived with her father and [mother]. She was twenty-eight years of age; weighed about 140 pounds, and had always been in good health; was educated in the public primary and high school and Butler College. Just prior to the time of the commission of the alleged acts in the indictment, [she] was employed by the state superintendent of public instruction as manager of the Young People's Reading Circle.

[After inviting Miss Oberholtzer on several dinner dates, Stephenson lured her to his home and kidnapped Miss Oberholtzer. He forced her to drink liquor, and then took her to Hammond by train, along with two men who assisted him. On the way,] appellant took hold of the bottom of her dress and pulled it over her head, against her wishes, and she tried to fight him away, but was weak and unsteady. Then Stephenson took hold of her two hands and held her, but she did not have strength to get away, because what she had drunk was affecting her. Then Stephenson took off all her clothes and pushed her into the lower berth. After the train started, Stephenson got into the berth with her and attacked her. [He] chewed her all over her body; bit her neck and face; chewed her tongue; chewed her breasts until they bled and chewed her back, her legs, and her ankles, and mutilated her all over her body. [At Hammond, Stephenson,

forced into
made her
drunk,

mutilated
her body

134

flourishing a revolver, took her to a hotel. Later that day, the victim obtained some bichloride of mercury tablets and took six of them, which made her very ill. Stephenson and his assistants drove the victim back to Indianapolis and she was kept confined overnight. Finally, twenty-four hours after taking the tablets, she was returned to her home and a doctor was summoned. The victim died some weeks later from the combined effect of the poison and her wounds.]

[Appellant] very earnestly argues that the evidence does not show that he is guilty of murder. He points out in his brief that, after they reached the hotel, Madge Oberholtzer left the hotel and purchased a hat and the poison, and voluntarily returned to his room, and at the time she took the poison she was in an adjoining room to him, and that she swallowed the poison without his knowledge, and at a time when he was not present. From these facts he contends that she took her life by committing suicide; that her own act in taking the poison was an intervening responsible agent which broke the causal connection between his acts and the death; that his acts were not the proximate cause of her death, but the taking of the poison was the proximate cause of death....

[In] the case at bar, appellant is charged with having caused the death of Madge Oberholtzer while engaged in the crime of attempted rape. The evidence shows that appellant, together with Earl Gentry and the deceased, left their compartment on the train and went to a hotel about a block from the depot, and there appellant registered as husband and wife, and immediately went to the room assigned to them. This change from their room on the train to a room in the hotel is of no consequence, for appellant's control and dominion over the deceased was absolute and complete in both cases. The evidence further shows that the deceased asked for money with which to purchase a hat, and it was supplied her by "Shorty," at the direction of appellant, and that she did leave the room and was taken by Shorty to a shop and purchased a hat and then, at her request, to a drug store where she purchased the bichloride of mercury tablets, and then she was taken back to the room in the hotel, where about 10 o'clock a.m. she swallowed the poison.

Appellant argues that the deceased was a free agent on this trip to purchase a hat, etc., and that she voluntarily returned to the room in the hotel. This was a question for the jury, and the evidence would justify them in reaching a contrary conclusion. Appellant's chauffeur accompanied her on this trip, and the deceased had, before she left appellant's home in Indianapolis, attempted to get away, and also made two unsuccessful attempts to use the telephone to call help. She was justified in concluding that any attempt she might make, while purchasing a hat or while in the drug store to escape or secure assistance, would be no more successful in Hammond than it was in Indianapolis. We think the evidence shows that the deceased was at all times from the time she was entrapped by the appellant at his home on the evening of March 15th till she returned to her home two days later, in the custody and absolute control of appellant.

Neither do we think the fact that the deceased took the poison some four hours after they left the drawing-room on the train or after the crime of attempted rape had been committed necessarily prevents it from being a part of the attempted rape. Suppose they had not left the drawing-room on the train, and, instead of the deceased taking poison, she had secured possession of appellant's revolver and shot herself or thrown herself out of the window of the car and died from the fall. We can see no vital difference. At the very moment Madge Oberholtzer swallowed the poison she was subject to the passion, desire, and will of appellant. She knew not what moment she would be subjected to the same demands that she was while in the drawing-room on the train. What would have prevented appellant from compelling her to submit to him at any moment? The same forces, the same impulses, that would impel her to shoot herself during the actual attack or throw herself out of the car window after the attack had ceased, was pressing and overwhelming her at the time she swallowed the poison.

The evidence shows that [the victim] was so weak that she staggered as she left the elevator to go to the room in the hotel, and was assisted by appellant and Gentry. That she was very ill, so much so that she could not eat, all of which was the direct and proximate result of the treatment accorded her by appellant. [To] say that there is no causal connection between the acts of appellant and the death of Madge Oberholtzer, and that the treatment accorded her by appellant had no causal connection with the death of Madge Oberholtzer would be a travesty on justice. The whole criminal program was so closely connected that we think it should be treated as one [transaction]. We therefore conclude that the evidence was sufficient and justified the jury in finding that appellant by his acts and conduct rendered the deceased distracted and mentally irresponsible, and that such was the natural and probable consequence of such unlawful and criminal treatment, and that the appellant was guilty of murder in the second degree as charged in the first count of the indictment.

We think the evidence justified the court in submitting the question to the jury, as there was evidence that the deceased died from the joint effect of the injuries inflicted on her, which, through natural cause and effect, contributed mediately to the death. We think the proposition of law stated in this instruction is well supported by authority:

> "The general rule, both of law and reason, is, that whenever a man contributes to a particular result, brought about, either by sole volition of another, or by such volition added to his own, he is to be held responsible for the result, the same as if his own

unaided hand had produced it. The contribution, however, must be of such magnitude and so near the result that sustaining to it the relation of cause and effect, the law takes it within its cognizance. Now, these propositions conduct us to the doctrine, that whenever a blow is inflicted under circumstances to render the party inflicting it criminally responsible, if death follows, he will be holden for murder or manslaughter, though the person beaten would have died from other causes, or would not have died from this one, had not others operated with it; provided, that the blow really contributed mediately or immediately to the death as it actually took place in a degree sufficient for the law's notice." Bishop on Criminal Law, § 653.

[We] have examined all of appellant's alleged errors, and find none that would justify a reversal of this cause.

Judgment affirmed.

Martin, J. (dissenting in part, concurring in part, dissenting in the conclusion). → EVIL ASSHOLE.

[Where] a wound is inflicted by one person on another, which is not in itself dangerous or necessarily fatal, and death results, not from such wound directly, nor from such wound indirectly "through a chain of natural effects and causes, unchanged by human action," but death results from some cause subsequently arising not at the direction or connivance of the one inflicting the first wound, and but for such subsequently arising cause death would not have resulted, the infliction of the first wound is not the proximate cause of death, but the supervening cause is the proximate cause and the one responsible for the death.

[Where,] upon deliberation, one commits suicide because of shame, humiliation, or remorse, the one who caused such mental state, although he may be morally responsible for the death in the sight of God, is not guilty of murder under the law, unless he in some way procured, advised, compelled, assisted, or exercised control over the person performing the act. . . .   JACK ASS!

≠ guilty as matter of law

Notes

1. *Year and a day rule.* At common law, defendant's conduct could not be deemed to be the "cause" of a homicide unless the victim died within a year and a day following the defendant's acts.

2. *M.P.C. and causation.* M.P.C. § 2.03 provides as follows:

Causal Relationship Between Conduct and Result; Divergence Between Result Designed or Contemplated and Actual Result or Between Probable and Actual Result

(1) Conduct is the cause of a result when:

(a) it is an antecedent but for which the result in question would not have occurred; and

(b) the relationship between the conduct and result satisfies any additional causal requirements imposed by the Code or by the law defining the offense.

(2) When purposely or knowingly causing a particular result is an element of an offense, the element is not established if the actual result is not within the purpose or the contemplation of the actor unless:

(a) the actual result differs from that designed or contemplated, as the case may be, only in the respect that a different person or different property is injured or affected or that the injury or harm designed or contemplated would have been more serious or more extensive than that caused; or

(b) the actual result involves the same kind of injury or harm as that designed or contemplated and is not too remote or accidental in its occurrence to have a [just] bearing on the actor's liability or on the gravity of his offense.

(3) When recklessly or negligently causing a particular result is an element of an offense, the element is not established if the actual result is not within the risk of which the actor is aware or, in the case of negligence, of which he should have been aware unless:

(a) the actual result differs from the probable result only in the respect that a different person or different property is injured or affected or that the probable injury would have been more serious or more extensive than that caused; or

(b) the actual result involves the same kind of injury or harm as the probable result and is not too remote or accidental in its occurrence to have a [just] bearing on the actor's liability or on the gravity of his offense.

(4) When causing a particular result is a material element for which absolute liability is imposed by law, the element is not established unless the actual result is a probable consequence of the actor's conduct.

3. *Independent actors.* Defendant's act may be the "cause" of death even though in the absence of that act, the death would have occurred anyway. For example, assume that two independent actors simultaneously shoot revolvers at a single victim and each inflicts a wound which would be fatal in and of itself. Neither actor is the "but for" cause of death as, absent the conduct of either actor, the victim would have died anyway. Nevertheless, both actors are held responsible for the victim's death. Otherwise, both defendants would be able to escape liability. *See, e.g., Jones v. Commonwealth,* 281 S.W.2d 920 (Ky.App. 1955): "[The] law will not stop, in such a case, to measure which wound is the more serious, and to speculate upon which actually caused the death."

4. *Russian roulette.* In *Commonwealth v. Atencio*, 345 Mass. 627, 189 N.E.2d 223 (1963), two defendants and the deceased decided to play a game of "Russian roulette." The deceased was the third to play. The gun fired a bullet and he fell over dead. The court concluded that both defendants "caused" the death: "[That] the defendants participated [in the game of Russian roulette] could be found to be a cause and not a mere condition [of] death. [The] testimony does not require a ruling that when the deceased took the gun from Atencio it was an independent or intervening act not standing in any relation to the defendants' acts which would render what he did imputable to them. It is an oversimplification to contend that each participated in something that only one could do at a time. There could be found to be a mutual encouragement in a joint enterprise."

PROBLEMS

1. *The Startled Horse.* Johnson is a passenger in a horse-drawn carriage which is sitting still. Defendant slaps the horse in a very hard manner that startles the horse and causes it to run away wildly. Johnson, unable to gain control of the horse, is killed when the carriage turns over. Did defendant cause Johnson's death under the common law principles described in *Stephenson*? Under M.P.C. § 2.03?

2. *The Detouring Victim.* Wyman is driving home from work when defendant fires three shots at her. Defendant's shots miss and Wyman escapes unharmed. Wyman, afraid to go home because defendant might be lying in wait for her, decides to spend the night at a friend's house. Changing her route (since she is no longer going home but rather to her friend's house), Wyman is killed while driving on the way to the friend's house. Consider the following scenarios and decide whether defendant "caused" the victim's death:

    a. The death resulted from lightning which struck and killed Wyman.

    b. The death resulted from an automobile accident, which is totally the fault of another driver; Wyman just "happened" to be in the wrong place at the wrong time.

    c. The death resulted because Wyman was very upset by defendant's conduct and was paying insufficient attention to her driving.

In each instance, argue the case for the prosecutor. How might defense counsel respond? How would you rule?

3. *The Heart Attack.* Defendant throws a stone at a house, breaking a window. The noise is heard by only one member of the household (a teenage son). He informs his mother (who did not hear the stone hit the house) about what had happened. On hearing the news, the mother collapses and dies. Did defendant "cause" the mother's death? What arguments can be made by the prosecutor? How might defense counsel respond? *See Commonwealth v. Colvin*, 340 Pa.Super. 278, 489 A.2d 1378 (1985).

4. *The Heart Attack Redux.* In the prior problem, would the result be different if defendant had been attempting to rob a convenience store with a gun (rather than breaking a window), and the owner of the store suffered a heart attack. Assume that the defendant said, "Just give me the money and you won't get hurt," and pointed the gun at the owner.

5. *The Double-parked Truck Driver.* Defendant, a truck driver, double parked his truck in violation of a local ordinance. Because of the double parking, a young girl was forced to walk in the street to get past the truck. The girl was struck by a car and killed. Did the truck driver "cause" the girl's death? *See Marchl v. Dowling & Co.*, 157 Pa.Super. 91, 41 A.2d 427 (1945).

6. *The Freezing Wife.* Suppose that a wife is forced out into freezing weather by her husband during an argument. The wife goes to her father's home because it is safe and warm. However, for unknown reasons, she decides not to enter the house. She freezes to death outside the house on the porch. Has the husband "caused" the wife's death? Argue the case for the defendant husband. How might the prosecutor respond to these arguments? *See State v. Preslar*, 48 N.C. 421 (1856).

7. *The Fatally Wounded Victim.* Defendant #1 and John Taylor got into a fight, and defendant fatally wounded Taylor. The wound severed the mesenteric artery, and medical witnesses testified that it was necessarily mortal, and that death would ensue within the hour. Internal hemorrhaging occurred and Taylor was suffering intense pain. While he lay dying, defendant #2 (a long-time enemy) inflicted a knife wound on Taylor. The wound was severe enough that it killed Taylor within five minutes. Medical witnesses agreed that, even though death was inevitable from the initial wound, it was accelerated by the later wound. Which defendant is responsible for "causing" the death? Argue the case for defendant #1. Argue the case for defendant #2. How might the prosecutor respond to these arguments? *See Henderson v. State*, 11 Ala.App. 37, 65 So. 721 (1914); *People v. Lewis*, 124 Cal. 551, 57 P. 470 (1899).

8. *The Driver and the Jogger.* Jane, a jogger, was trying to cross a busy street when she was struck by defendant's vehicle. Jane survived the impact, but was thrown into the middle of the northbound lane of Haggerty Road with her head pointing east toward the curb, and her feet pointing west toward the road. A second car was fast approaching. A witness tried to flag the second car down, but was unable to do so. The second car drove over Jane, causing severe internal injuries. Jane died two hours later. Expert testimony indicated that both sets of injuries were severe and independently could have resulted in Jane's death. Who is responsible for "causing" Jane's death? *See People v. Tims*, 449 Mich. 83, 534 N.W.2d 675 (1995).

9. *The Burglar and the Well.* Defendant took a gun and broke into a house with the intent to rob the owner. The frightened owner ran out of the house and jumped into a well; he remained there until he died from exposure. Did defendant "cause" the death? *See Gipe v. State*, 165 Ind. 433, 75 N.E. 881 (1905).

10. *The Failure to Rescue.* Defendants went to the home of Pepper armed with revolvers, forcibly took possession of Pepper, bound his arms so as to render him helpless, and in the presence of Pepper, they avowed their purpose to kill him. Then defendants placed Pepper in an automobile and started to drive away. When the car reached the banks of a river, Pepper leaped from the car into the water and drowned. Defendants stood by and made no effort to rescue Pepper. Are defendants responsible for "causing" Pepper's death? Argue the case for the prosecutor. How might defense counsel respond? *See State v. Shelledy,* 8 Iowa 477 (1859).

11. *The Burglary and the Suicidal Jump.* Jane Munson, the village nurse, lived alone. Late one night, the defendant broke into Munson's house. He went upstairs and found the bedroom door locked. Defendant threatened to break the door down if Munson did not let him in. Munson refused. As defendant tried to break-in, Munson jumped out the window and fell two stories to her death. Is defendant criminally responsible for "causing" Munson's death? *See State v. Lassiter,* 197 N.J.Super. 2, 484 A.2d 13 (1984); *Rex v. Beech,* (1912) 23 Cox Cr. Law Cas. 181.

12. *The Harasser.* The defendant "intentionally made threats, statements and accusations against said deceased for the purpose of harassing, embarrassing, and humiliating him in the presence of friends, relatives and business associates." Because of these threats, the victim became physically and mentally disturbed and as a direct result, he committed suicide. Defense counsel argues that the victim's suicide is an independent intervening cause that breaks the chain of legal causation and absolves the defendant from criminal responsibility. Is this true? *See Tate v. Canonica,* 180 Cal.App.2d 898, 5 Cal.Rptr. 28 (1960).

PEOPLE v. ACOSTA

284 Cal.Rptr. 117 (Cal.App. 1991).

WALLIN, ASSOCIATE JUSTICE.

[At] 10 p.m. on March 10, 1987, Officers Salceda and Francis of the Santa Ana Police Department's automobile theft detail saw Acosta in Elvira Salazar's stolen Nissan Pulsar parked on the street. The officers approached Acosta and identified themselves. Acosta inched the Pulsar forward, then accelerated rapidly. He led Salceda, Francis and officers from other agencies on a 48–mile chase along numerous surface streets and freeways throughout Orange County. The chase ended near Acosta's residence in Anaheim.

During the chase, Acosta engaged in some of the most egregious driving tactics imaginable. He ran stop signs and red lights, and drove on the wrong side of streets, causing oncoming traffic to scatter or swerve to avoid colliding with him. Once, when all traffic lanes were blocked by vehicles stopped for a red light, he used a dirt shoulder to circumvent stationary vehicles and pass through the intersection.

When leaving the freeway in Anaheim, he drove over a cement shoulder.

Throughout the pursuit, Acosta weaved in and out of traffic, cutting in front of other cars and causing them to brake suddenly. At one point on the freeway, he crossed three lanes of traffic, struck another car, jumped the divider between the freeway and a transition lane, and passed a tanker truck, forcing it to swerve suddenly to avoid a collision.

Acosta generally drove at speeds between 60 and 90 miles per hour, slowing only when necessary. During several turns, his wheels lost traction. When an officer was able to drive parallel to the Pulsar for a short distance, Acosta looked in his direction and smiled. Near the end of the chase, one of the Pulsar's front tires blew out, but Acosta continued to drive at 55 to 60 miles per hour, crossing freeway traffic lanes.

Police helicopters from Anaheim, Costa Mesa, Huntington Beach, and Newport Beach assisted in the chase by tracking Acosta. During the early part of the pursuit, the Costa Mesa and Newport Beach [helicopters] were used, pinpointing Acosta's location with their high beam spotlights. The Costa Mesa helicopter was leading the pursuit, in front of and below the Newport Beach helicopter. As they flew into Newport Beach, the pilots agreed the Newport Beach craft should take the lead. The normal procedure for such a maneuver is for the lead helicopter to move to the right and swing around clockwise behind the other craft while climbing to an altitude of 1,000 feet. At the same time, the trailing helicopter descends to 500 feet while maintaining a straight course.

At the direction of the Costa Mesa pilot, the Newport Beach helicopter moved forward and descended while the Costa Mesa helicopter banked to the right. Shortly after commencing this procedure, the Costa Mesa helicopter, having terminated radio communication, came up under the Newport Beach helicopter from the right rear and collided with it. Both helicopters fell to the ground. Three occupants in the Costa Mesa helicopter died as a result of the crash.

Menzies Turner, a retired Federal Aviation Administration (FAA) investigator, testified as an expert and concluded the accident occurred because the Costa Mesa helicopter, the faster of the two aircraft, made a 360-degree turn and closed too rapidly on the Newport Beach helicopter. He opined the Costa Mesa helicopter's pilot violated an FAA regulation prohibiting careless and reckless operation of an aircraft by failing to properly clear the area, not maintaining communication with the Newport Beach helicopter, failing to keep the other aircraft in view at all times, and not changing his altitude. He also testified the Costa Mesa pilot violated another

FAA regulation prohibiting operation of one aircraft so close to another as to create a collision hazard.

Turner could not think of any reason for the Costa Mesa helicopter's erratic movement. The maneuver was not a difficult one, and was not affected by the ground activity at the time. He had never heard of a midair collision between two police helicopters involved in tracking a ground pursuit, and had never investigated a midair collision involving helicopters.

After his arrest Acosta told the police he knew the Pulsar was stolen and he fled the police to avoid arrest. He also saw two helicopters with spotlights, and turned off the Pulsar's lights to evade them. Acosta knew that his flight was dangerous "to the bone," but he tried to warn other cars by flashing the car lights and by otherwise being "as safe as possible."

Acosta claims there was insufficient evidence [that] he proximately caused the deaths of the [three victims].

[Acosta] argues that although a collision between ground vehicles was a foreseeable result of his conduct, one between airborne helicopters was not, noting his expert had never heard of a similar incident. He also contends the Costa Mesa helicopter pilot's violation of FAA regulations was a superseding cause. Because the deaths here were unusual, to say the least, the issue deserves special scrutiny.

Proximate cause in criminal cases is determined by ordinary principles of causation. It is initially a question of fact for the jury to decide. [To] determine whether Acosta's conduct was not, as a matter of law, a proximate cause of death of the Costa Mesa helicopter's occupants, [we] enter a legal realm not routinely considered in published California cases. . . .

"Proximate cause" is the term historically used[6] to separate those results for which an actor will be held responsible from those not carrying such responsibility. The term is, in a sense, artificial, serving matters of policy surrounding tort and criminal law and based partly on expediency and partly on concerns of fairness and justice. Because such concerns are sometimes more a matter of "common sense" than pure logic, the line of demarcation is flexible, and attempts to lay down uniform tests which apply evenly in all situations have failed. That does not mean general guidelines and approaches to analysis cannot be constructed.

The threshold question in examining causation is whether the defendant's act was an "actual cause" of the victim's injury. It is a *sine qua non* test: But for the defendant's act would the injury have

---

6. The American Law Institute has urged the use of "legal cause" instead. Although there is some merit to its arguments, I abide with the traditional term, "proximate cause."

occurred? Unless an act is an actual cause of the injury, it will not be considered a proximate cause.

The next inquiry is whether the defendant's act was a "substantial factor" in the injury. This test excludes those actual causes which, although direct, play only an insignificant role in the ultimate injury.[8] Although there is no strict definition, the RESTATEMENT SECOND OF TORTS, *supra*, section 433, lists considerations in determining whether a factor is "substantial": (1) the number and extent of other factors contributing to the harm; (2) whether the forces created by the actor are continuous in producing the harm or merely create a condition upon which independent forces act; and (3) any lapse of time between the act and the harm.

In California, the substantial factor issue has arisen most often where multiple causes act concurrently, but independently,[9] to produce the harm. The test is one of exclusion only. Unless a cause is a substantial factor in the harm it will not be considered a proximate cause, but some substantial factor causes may not be deemed proximate causes.

A related concept which may lead to a refusal to treat an actual cause as a proximate cause is where a force set in motion by the defendant has "'come to rest in a position of apparent safety.'" Perkins and Boyce give the example of the actor who dislodges a rock which comes to rest against a tree. If the tree bends or breaks six months later, releasing the rock, the original action is not considered the proximate cause of any resulting harm.

To this point I have spoken only of direct causes, "[causes] which produce [a] result without the aid of any intervening [cause]." Because it is tautological, the definition is of little value in identifying a cause in the absence of a working definition of an indirect cause. However, Perkins and Boyce list several examples of direct causation, headed by the observation that, "If sequences follow one another in such a customary order that no other cause would commonly be thought of as intervening, the causal connection is spoken of as direct for juridical purposes even though many intervening causes might be recognized by a physicist."

The critical concept at this juncture is that a direct cause which is a substantial factor in the ensuing injury is almost always a proximate cause of it. This is so even if the result is exacerbated by a latent condition in the victim or caused by a third party. *People v. Stamp*

---

8. [An] independent intervening cause could be explained by saying it rendered the defendant's act "insubstantial." However, the traditional approach has been to determine only whether the defendant's act is substantial in the abstract or in comparison with a contributory or concurrent cause. If it is not, the analysis goes no further. If it is, the question becomes whether there is an intervening cause which should relieve the defendant of responsibility.

9. If the actors are acting in concert, both would be culpable using an aiding and abetting theory, even if only one directly caused the death.

People v. Stamp: heart attack during robbery

(1969) 2 Cal.App.3d 203, 210–211, 82 Cal.Rptr. 598 [(affirming conviction where defendant triggered heart attack of store clerk during armed robbery)]. The only exception is where the result is "highly extraordinary" in view of its cause.

However, the defendant is not always the direct cause of the harm. Sometimes forces arise between the act of the defendant and the harm, called "intervening causes." They are of two types, dependent and independent, and include acts of God.

An intervening cause is dependent if it is a normal or involuntary response to, or result of, the defendant's act. These include flight and other voluntary or involuntary responses of victims, as well as defense, rescue and medical treatment by third parties. Even where such responses constitute negligent conduct, they do not supersede the defendant's act; *i.e.*, they are nevertheless considered proximate causes of the harm. *People v. Armitage, supra*, 194 Cal.App.3d at p. 420, 239 Cal.Rptr. 515 [(affirming conviction where victim foolishly chose to attempt to swim to shore after defendant capsized the boat)].[15]

Conversely, when the defendant's conduct merely places the eventual victim in a position which allows some other action to cause the harm, the other action is termed an independent intervening cause. It usually supersedes the defendant's act; *i.e.*, precludes a finding of proximate cause. 1 LaFave & Scott, *supra*, at pp. 406–407 [(distinguishing matters of "response" from matters of "coincidence")]. The issue usually arises when the victim has been subjected to the independent harm after being disabled by the defendant, or is somehow impacted by the defendant's flight. *See People v. Pike, supra*, 197 Cal.App.3d at pp. 747–748, 243 Cal.Rptr. 54 [(affirming conviction where officer killed when struck by another while pursuing defendant)].

An independent intervening variable will not be superseding in three instances: (1) where it is merely a contributing cause to the defendant's direct cause; (2) where the result was intended; or (3) where the resultant harm was reasonably foreseeable when the act was done. As to the third exception, " '[t]he consequence need not have been a strong probability; a possible consequence which might reasonably have been contemplated is [enough]. The precise consequence need not have been foreseen; it is enough that the defendant should

---

15. The refusal to allow "contributory negligence" to be a bar to a proximate cause finding need not be the product of any mechanical policy rule. It can be grounded in the notion that it is not "abnormal" for people to react less "reasonably" under stress than if the stress were not present. For purposes of ascribing causal responsibility it may be said that a negligent or foolish response is "normal."

To the extent that a dependent intervening cause is thought to "directly" carry through the act of the defendant to a harmful result, this analysis comports well with the rule that a defendant's act is the proximate cause of any harm caused directly by his act unless the result is "highly extraordinary." It also allows the court to find that a negligent, but highly extraordinary response precludes a finding of proximate cause, while a reckless but predictable response does not. The focus is properly on the objective conditions present at the time the defendant perpetrated the causal act and the predictable, albeit sometimes unreasonable, responses of human beings to them.

have foreseen the possibility of some harm of the kind which might result from his act.' "

As Perkins and Boyce put it, " 'Foreseeability' is not a 'test' which can be applied without the use of common sense; it presents one of those problems in which 'we must rely on the common sense of the common man as to common things.' It is employed in the sense of 'appreciable probability.' It does not require such a degree of probability that the intervention was more likely to occur than not; and on the other hand it implies more than that someone might have imagined it as a theoretical possibility. It does not require that the defendant himself actually thought of it. For the purposes of proximate cause 'an appreciable probability is one which a reasonable [person] in ordering [his or her] conduct in view of [his or her] situation and [his or her] knowledge and means of knowledge, should, either consciously or unconsciously, take into account in connection with the other facts and probabilities then apparent.' "

Prosser and Keeton, in an in-depth discussion of the dynamics of foresight, conclude that although it is desirable to exclude extremely remarkable and unusual results from the purview of proximate cause, it is virtually impossible to express a logical verbal formula which will produce uniform results. I agree. The standard should be simply stated, exclude extraordinary results, and allow the trier of fact to determine the issue on the particular facts of the case using " 'the common sense of the common man as to common things.' " As with other ultimate issues, appellate courts must review that determination, giving due deference to the trier of fact.

The "highly extraordinary result" standard serves that purpose. It is consistent with the definition of foreseeability used in California. It does not involve the defendant's state of mind, but focuses upon the objective conditions present when [he or she] acts.[19] Like numerous other legal definitions, what it means in practice will be determined as case law develops. Limitations arising from the mental state of the actor can be left to concepts like malice, recklessness and negligence.

Because the highly extraordinary result standard is consistent with the limitation on direct causes, it simplifies the proximate cause inquiry. The analysis is: (1) was the defendant's conduct the actual cause of the harm (but for [defendant's] actions would it have occurred as it did)? (2) was the result an intended consequence of the act? (3) was the defendant's action a substantial factor in the harm?

---

19. The Model Penal Code takes a similar approach, focusing on whether the result is "too remote or accidental in its occurrence to have a [just] bearing on the actor's liability or on the gravity of his offense." Model Pen.Code, § 2.03(2)(b). LaFave and Scott also appear to look to the extraordinary nature of the result in determining causal responsibility, although they discuss it in terms of foreseeability.

and (4) was the result highly extraordinary in light of the circumstances?

If the first question is answered no, proximate cause is lacking. If answered yes, the next question must be examined. If the second question is answered yes, proximate cause is established. If answered no, the next question must be examined. If the third question is answered no, proximate cause is lacking. If answered yes, proximate cause is established unless the fourth question is answered yes, in which case it is lacking. The analysis does away with the need to consider the distinction between direct, concurrent, contributory, and dependent and independent intervening causes. It focuses, as it should, upon the role the defendant's act played in the harm, limiting culpability only where the conduct was de minimis or the result highly extraordinary.

Here, but for Acosta's conduct of fleeing the police, the helicopters would never have been in position for the crash. However, there was no evidence he intended the harm, so I must examine questions three and four.

Although an extremely close question, Acosta's conduct was a substantial factor in causing the crash. He was fleeing when the accident occurred, and there was no lapse of time between his flight and the crash—his action had not "come to rest." The only other factor operating at the time was the improper flight pattern of the Costa Mesa pilot. Although Acosta's horrendous driving did not cause the helicopter's improper maneuver, his flight undoubtedly infused excitement and tension into the situation, which can be considered to be a substantial factor. No similar case has held otherwise, although the third party collisions all have involved accidents on the ground.

The result was not highly extraordinary. Although a two-helicopter collision was unknown to expert witness Turner and no reported cases describe one, it was " 'a possible consequence which reasonably might have been contemplated.' " Given the emotional dynamics of any police pursuit, there is an "appreciable probability" that one of the pursuers, in the heat of the chase, may act negligently or recklessly to catch the quarry. That no pursuits have ever before resulted in a helicopter crash or midair collision is more a comment on police flying skill and technology than upon the innate probabilities involved.

Justice Crosby's opinion parts company with this analysis, reasoning that "neither the intervening negligent conduct nor the risk of harm was foreseeable." He justifies this conclusion by reference to the well-traveled opinion of Justice Cardozo in *Palsgraf v. Long Island R. Co.* (1928) 248 N.Y. 339, 162 N.E. 99, 100. Reliance on *Palsgraf* reveals the error in the analysis. Justice Cardozo approached the problem from the perspective of duty, concluding that the defendant owed no duty of care to an unforeseeable plaintiff. Although the interesting facts and novel analysis of *Palsgraf*[24] have made it a favorite in law school texts, the four-to-three decision is not the gospel on proximate cause. Because of its confusion between foreseeability as it relates to negligence and as it relates to causation, I have eliminated it from the proximate cause analysis.

Doing so avoids the undesirable risk of completely absolving a defendant of all liability on causation grounds when morally he should suffer some punishment for the consequences. When a defendant is the actual and substantial cause of the harm, the consequences of the act should depend upon the mens rea involved.

Neither concurring opinion offers case law "on all fours," suggesting this case is unique and presents a close question. Partly because this is so, it is appropriate to rely on two compelling factors: the jury found proximate cause based on proper instructions, and the dearth of case law to support a rejection of that finding. Given these circumstances, a finding of proximate cause is appropriate.

The judgment is reversed on the murder counts and is affirmed in all other respects.

MOORE, ACTING PRESIDING JUSTICE, concurring in part and dissenting.

The events leading up to the helicopter collision were set in motion by appellant's decision to flee from the police. It was predictable that, in response, the police would pursue appellant and use whatever means available to them to locate and capture him. The possibility that during the chase the pursuing police vehicles might be operated in a negligent manner thereby causing a collision was sufficiently foreseeable to establish appellant's conduct as the proximate cause of the accident. Therefore, I conclude the evidence is sufficient to support the jury's finding of proximate cause. [The] judgment should be affirmed.

CROSBY, ASSOCIATE JUSTICE, concurring and dissenting.

[To] be sure, defendant represented a threat to everyone traveling the same roads and would have been responsible for any injury directly or indirectly caused by his actions in those environs; but to extend that responsibility to persons in the air, whose role was merely to observe his movements, a simple enough task in far speedier helicopters, defies common sense. It was perfectly foreseeable that someone would be hurt on the ground via some sort of causal chain connecting to defendant's conduct; the opposite is true of the airborne observers. They were not in the zone of danger in this case by any stretch of the imagination, and the manner and circumstances of the collision could hardly have reasonably been foreseen. [Although]

---

24. The defendant's railway attendants accidentally knocked a package of fireworks from a passenger's arms while boarding a train, causing a concussive explosion which overturned scales on the platform which struck the plaintiff.

less remote than a dispatcher suffering a coronary, perhaps, this was a "highly extraordinary result" by any measure and, properly viewed, beyond the long arm of the criminal law. . . .

PROBLEMS

1. *Howard Beach and the Fleeing Victim.* In the Howard Beach case, several white teenagers assaulted and threatened three black men. In the course of the assault, which was "motivated solely by the color of the victims' skin", the defendants relentlessly chased Michael Griffith. Griffith was forced to retreat by jumping a barricade and attempting to cross a well-traveled, six-lane highway. A passing motorist collided with Griffith, killing him. Defendants argued that the evidence on causation was legally insufficient because the motorist's intervention rendered their conduct too remote a cause of death to warrant criminal liability. How would the prosecutor respond? *See People v. Kern*, 149 A.D.2d 187, 212–213, 545 N.Y.S.2d 4, 20 (1989).

2. *The KKK Rally.* Defendant, a Ku Klux Klan member, gave a racist speech in a city square. Throughout the speech, defendant was confronted by a large and hostile crowd. As the crowd became angry and potentially violent, defendant randomly fired his gun towards the crowd. Although defendant did not hit anyone, Harriett Burnett was killed when a crowd member (Joe Howard) accidentally discharged his own gun while seeking refuge from defendant's gunfire. The bullet from Howard's gun struck and killed Harriett, who ironically, was Howard's close friend. Upon seeing Harriett on the ground, Howard immediately tried to revive her. When his efforts proved unsuccessful, Howard fired four shots in defendant's direction but missed. Who "caused" the victim's death? Defendant? Howard? Both? *See Hodges v. State*, 661 So.2d 107 (Fla.App. 1995).

3. *Sterno and the Skid Row Addicts.* Defendant owned and operated a cigar store in the skid-row section of the city. One of the products he sold was Sterno, a jelly-like substance composed primarily of methanol and ethanol and designed for cooking and heating purposes. Sterno was manufactured and sold in two types of containers, one for home use and one for industrial use. Previously, both types of Sterno contained approximately 3.75% Methanol, or wood alcohol, and 71% Ethanol, or grain alcohol; of the two types of alcohols, methanol is far more toxic if consumed internally. Assume that a few months ago, the Sterno Corporation began manufacturing a new type of industrial Sterno which was 54% Methanol. The cans containing the new industrial Sterno were identical to the cans containing the old industrial Sterno except in one crucial aspect: on the lids of the new 54% Methanol Sterno were imprinted the words "Institutional Sterno. Danger. Poison. For use only as a Fuel. Not for consumer use. For industrial and commercial use. Not for home use." A skull and crossbones symbol also appeared on the lid. The cartons in which the new Sterno cans were packaged and shipped did not indicate that the contents differed in any respect from the old industrial Sterno.

According to its records, Sterno Corporation sent only one shipment of the new Sterno to the city; that shipment went to a company that made only one sale of the new industrial Sterno, and that was to defendant. Defendant sold approximately 400 cans of the new industrial Sterno at his retail cigar store. Thirty-one persons died in the skid-row area as a result of methanol poisoning, and the source of the methanol was traced to the new industrial Sterno. Since defendant owned the only retail outlet selling this type of Sterno in the area, he was arrested and indicted on thirty-one counts charging reckless manslaughter.

Assuming that defendant had the necessary mens rea for reckless manslaughter, can it be said that he "caused" the death of skid row residents who used the sterno? How would you argue the case as defense counsel? How might the prosecutor respond? *See Commonwealth v. Feinberg*, 433 Pa. 558, 253 A.2d 636 (1969).

4. *The Malicious Neighbor.* Defendant and Murdock, who lived close to each other, cursed and threatened each other repeatedly over their citizen's band radios. One evening, Murdock was legally intoxicated. Defendant knew that Murdock had a problem with night vision. Defendant also knew that Murdock owned a handgun and had boasted "about how he would shoot it to scare people off." Defendant knew further that Murdock was easily agitated and that he became especially angry if anyone disparaged his hero, General George S. Patton. During the conversation in question that evening, defendant taunted Murdock by stating that General Patton and Murdock himself were "cowards." Also during the conversation, defendant persistently demanded that Murdock arm himself with his handgun and wait on his front porch for defendant to come and injure or kill him. Murdock responded that he would be waiting on his front porch, and he told defendant to "kiss [his] mother or [his] wife and children good-bye because [he would] never go back home." Defendant then made an anonymous telephone call to the police department. Defendant identified Murdock by name and told the dispatcher that Murdock had "a gun on the porch," had "threatened to shoot up the neighborhood," and was "talking about shooting anything that moves." Three uniformed police officers were dispatched to Murdock's home. None of the officers knew that Murdock was intoxicated or that he was in an agitated state of mind. The officers observed Murdock come out of his house with "something shiny in his hand." Murdock sat down on the top step of the porch and placed the shiny object beside him. One officer approached Murdock from the side of the porch and told him to "[l]eave the gun alone and walk down the stairs away from it." Murdock then reached for the gun, stood up, advanced in the officer's direction, and opened fire. The officer retreated and was not struck. All three officers returned fire, and Murdock was shot. Lying wounded on the porch, he said several times, "I didn't know you was the police." He died from the gunshot wound. Did defendant's conduct "cause" Murdock's death? *See Bailey v. Commonwealth*, 229 Va. 258, 329 S.E.2d 37 (1985).

5. *The Firefighter*. Defendant intentionally set fire to a couch, causing a serious fire on the fifth floor of an abandoned building. The fire department, responding to the conflagration, sent a team of firefighters who arrived to find the rear portion of the fifth and sixth floors burning. The firefighters attempted to bring the situation under control, but were unable to do so and decided to withdraw from the building. At that point, the firefighters were suddenly enveloped by a dense smoke, which was later discovered to have arisen from another independent fire that had broken out on the second floor. Although this fire was caused by arson, there is no evidence that the defendant started it. However, the thick smoke from the second-floor fire became combined with the thick smoke from the fifth-floor fire, and made evacuation from the premises extremely hazardous. One firefighter sustained injuries during the evacuation, and subsequently died from those injuries. Did defendant "cause" the death of the firefighter? How would the prosecutor argue that he did cause the death? How might defense counsel respond? *See People v. Arzon*, 92 Misc.2d 739, 401 N.Y.S.2d 156 (1978).

6. *The Gun Dealer*. Defendant, who runs a firearms business, illegally sold several gun cartridges to a minor named Todd (under the age of 16 years old) in violation of state law. Todd used the cartridges to kill someone else. Can the defendant be said to have "caused" the death so that he can be charged with negligent homicide or manslaughter? *See Mautino v. Piercedale Supply Co.*, 338 Pa. 435, 13 A.2d 51 (1940).

7. *The Bar Owner and the Drunk*. Defendant, who owned a bar, continued serving drinks to a customer who was in a visibly intoxicated condition. An hour or so later, after consuming several more drinks, the customer left the bar, and then attacked and killed someone on the street. Is the defendant's conduct the "cause" of the death? *See Schelin v. Goldberg*, 188 Pa.Super. 341, 146 A.2d 648 (1958). Would your answer change if, instead of attacking someone, the drunken customer had left the bar, started his car, and then after driving only a few blocks, had crashed into another car, killing the other driver?

8. *Child Suicide*. In 2003, in Connecticut, a child committed suicide and his single mother was charged with contributing to his death. The evidence reveals that the mother kept a filthy home. The house had a foul odor, and it was filled with so much debris that it was virtually impossible to move around the home; the kitchen was full of dirty dishes and evidence of stains and spills. The evidence also revealed that the mother failed to wash the child's clothes and failed to teach the child about hygiene. As a result, the child had bad breath and body odor. He was constantly teased and sometimes attacked by other children in his school, but the mother failed to get him medical or psychological help. The boy eventually killed himself at the age of twelve. Was the mother a "cause" of the death?

COMMONWEALTH v. ROOT
403 Pa. 571, 170 A.2d 310 (1961).

CHARLES ALVIN JONES, CHIEF JUSTICE.

The appellant was found guilty of involuntary [reckless] man-slaughter for the death of his competitor in the course of an automo-bile race between them on a highway. [We accepted this appeal to decide] the important question present[ed] as to whether the defen-dant's unlawful and reckless conduct was a sufficiently direct cause of the death to warrant his being charged with criminal homicide.

The testimony [discloses] that, on the night of the fatal accident, the defendant accepted the deceased's challenge to engage in an automobile race; that the racing took place on a rural 3-lane highway; that the night was clear and dry, and traffic light; that the speed limit on the highway was 50 miles per hour; that, immediately prior to the accident, the two automobiles were being operated at varying speeds of from 70 to 90 miles per hour; that the accident occurred in a no-passing zone on the approach to a bridge where the highway nar-rowed to two directionally-opposite lanes; that, at the time of the accident, the defendant was in the lead and was proceeding in his right hand lane of travel; that the deceased, in an attempt to pass the defendant's automobile, when a truck was closely approaching from the opposite direction, swerved his car to the left, crossed the high-way's white dividing line and drove his automobile on the wrong side of the highway head-on into the oncoming truck with resultant fatal effect to himself.

This evidence would of course amply support a conviction of the defendant for speeding, reckless driving and, perhaps, other viola-tions of The Vehicle Code. In fact, it may be noted, in passing, that [a recent] Act [makes] automobile racing on a highway an independent crime punishable by fine or imprisonment or both up to $500 and three years in jail. [In] any event, unlawful or reckless conduct is only one ingredient of the crime of involuntary manslaughter. Another essential and distinctly separate element of the crime is that the unlawful or reckless conduct charged to the defendant was the direct cause of the death in issue. The first ingredient is obviously present in this case but, just as plainly, the second is not.

While precedent is to be found for application of the tort law concept of "proximate cause" in fixing responsibility for criminal homicide, the want of any rational basis for its use in determining criminal liability can no longer be properly disregarded. When proxi-mate cause was first borrowed from the field of tort law and applied to homicide prosecutions in Pennsylvania, the concept connoted a much more direct causal relation in producing the alleged culpable result than it does today. Proximate cause, as an essential element of a tort founded in negligence, has undergone in recent times, and is still undergoing, a marked extension. More specifically, this area of civil law has been progressively liberalized in favor of claims for damages for personal injuries to which careless conduct of others can in some way be associated. To persist in applying the tort liability concept of proximate cause to prosecutions for criminal homicide after the marked expansion of civil liability of defendants in tort actions for negligence would be to extend possible criminal liability to persons chargeable with unlawful or reckless conduct in circumstances not generally considered to present the likelihood of a resultant death.

[Legal] theory which makes guilt or innocence of criminal homicide depend upon such accidental and fortuitous circumstances as are now embraced by modern tort law's encompassing concept of proximate cause is too harsh to be just.

[Even] if the tort liability concept of proximate cause were to be deemed applicable, the defendant's conviction of involuntary manslaughter in the instant case could not be sustained under the evidence. The operative effect of a supervening cause would have to be taken into consideration. But, the trial judge refused the defendant's point for charge to such effect and erroneously instructed the jury that "negligence or want of care on the part of [the deceased] is no defense to the criminal responsibility of the [defendant]."

The Superior Court, in affirming the defendant's conviction in this case, approved the charge above mentioned, despite a number of decisions in involuntary manslaughter cases holding that the conduct of the deceased victim must be considered in order to determine whether the defendant's reckless acts were the proximate (i.e., sufficiently direct) cause of his death. The Superior Court [did] so on the ground that there can be more than one proximate cause of death. The point is wholly irrelevant. Of course there can be more than one proximate cause of death just as there can also be more than one direct cause of death. For example, in the so-called "shield" cases where a felon interposes the person of an innocent victim between himself and a pursuing officer, if the officer should fire his gun at the felon to prevent his escape and fatally wound the person used as a shield, the different acts of the policeman and the felon would each be a direct cause of the victim's death.

If the tort liability concept of proximate cause were to be applied in a criminal homicide prosecution, then the conduct of the person whose death is the basis of the indictment would have to be considered, not to prove that it was merely an additional proximate cause of the death, but to determine, under fundamental and long recognized law applicable to proximate cause, whether the subsequent wrongful act superseded the original conduct chargeable to the defendant. If it did in fact supervene, then the original act is so insulated from the ensuing death as not to be its proximate cause.

Under the uncontradicted evidence in this case, the conduct of the defendant was not the proximate cause of the decedent's death as a matter of law. In *Kline v. Moyer and Albert*, 1937, 325 Pa. 357, 364, 191 A. 43, 46, the rule is stated as follows: "Where a second actor has become aware of the existence of a potential danger created by the negligence of an original tort-feasor, and thereafter, by an independent act of negligence, brings about an accident, the first tort-feasor is relieved of liability, because the condition created by him was merely a circumstance of the accident and not its proximate cause."

[In] the case now before us, the deceased was aware of the dangerous condition created by the defendant's reckless conduct in driving his automobile at an excessive rate of speed along the highway but, despite such knowledge, he recklessly chose to swerve his car to the left and into the path of an oncoming truck, thereby bringing about the head-on collision which caused his own death.

To summarize, the tort liability concept of proximate cause has no proper place in prosecutions for criminal homicide and more direct causal connection is required for conviction. In the instant case, the defendant's reckless conduct was not a sufficiently direct cause of the competing driver's death to make him criminally liable therefor.

The judgment of sentence is reversed and the defendant's motion in arrest of judgment granted.

EAGEN, JUSTICE (dissenting).

[D]efendant, at the time of the fatal accident involved, was engaged in an unlawful and reckless course of conduct. Racing an automobile at 90 miles per hour, trying to prevent another automobile going in the same direction from passing him, in a no-passing zone on a two-lane public highway, is certainly all of that. Admittedly also, there can be more than one direct cause of an unlawful death. To me, this is self-evident. But, says the majority opinion, the defendant's recklessness was not a direct cause of the death. With this, I cannot agree.

If the defendant did not engage in the unlawful race and so operate his automobile in such a reckless manner, this accident would never have occurred. He helped create the dangerous event. He was a vital part of it. The victim's acts were a natural reaction to the stimulus of the situation. The race, the attempt to pass the other car and forge ahead, the reckless speed, all of these factors the defendant himself helped create. He was part and parcel of them. That the victim's response was normal under the circumstances, that his reaction should have been expected and was clearly foreseeable, is to me beyond argument. That the defendant's recklessness was a substantial factor is obvious. All of this, in my opinion, makes his unlawful conduct a direct cause of the resulting collision.

[The] majority opinion states, "Legal theory which makes guilt or innocence of criminal homicide depend upon such accidental and fortuitous circumstances as are now embraced by modern tort law's encompassing concept [is] too harsh to be just." If the resulting death had been dependent upon "accidental and fortuitous circumstances" or, as the majority also say, "in circumstances not generally considered to present the likelihood of a resultant death," [I] would agree that the defendant is not criminally responsible. However, acts should be judged by their tendency under the known circumstances, not by the actual intent which accompanies their performance. Every day of the year, we read that some teen-agers, or young adults, somewhere in this country, have been killed or have killed others, while racing their automobiles. Hair-raising, death-defying, law-breaking rides, which encompass "racing" are the rule rather than the exception, and endanger not only the participants, but also every motorist and passenger on the road. To call such resulting accidents "accidental and fortuitous," or unlikely to result in death, is to ignore the cold and harsh reality of everyday occurrences. Root's actions were as direct a cause of Hall's death as those in the "shield" cases. Root's shield was his high speed and any approaching traffic in his quest to prevent Hall from passing, which he knew Hall would undertake to do, the first time he thought he had the least opportunity.

[handwritten margin note: shouldn't ignore reality that behavior]

[While] the victim's foolhardiness in this case contributed to his own death, he was not the only one responsible and it is not he alone with whom we are concerned. It is the people of the Commonwealth who are harmed by the kind of conduct the defendant pursued. Their interests must be kept in mind.

I, therefore, dissent and would accordingly affirm the judgment of conviction.

PROBLEMS

1. *Was Root Correctly Decided?* Consider *Jacobs v. State*, 184 So.2d 711 (Fla.App. 1966), which involved similar facts, but in which the innocent driver of an oncoming vehicle was killed. Jacobs was convicted of manslaughter and the conviction was upheld on appeal based upon "proximate cause":

> The evidence clearly shows that appellant, together with others, was engaged in what is commonly known as a "drag race" of motor vehicles on a two-lane public highway in Marion County. The race entailed the operation of three motor vehicles traveling in the same direction at excessive and unlawful rates of speed contrary to the laws of this state. While engaged in such unlawful activity one of the three vehicles actively participating in the race was negligently operated in such manner as to cause the death of the person who drove that vehicle, as well as another innocent party who had no connection with the race. The deaths which proximately resulted from the activities of the three persons engaged in

the unlawful activity of drag racing made each of the active participants equally guilty of the criminal act which caused the death of the innocent party. . . .

Is the holding in *Jacobs* preferable to the holding in *Root*? Does it matter that an innocent person was killed in *Jacobs* rather than a participant in the race as in *Root*? Explain.

2. *The Drag Race.* Defendant and Osborne engaged in a drag race on Jennings Road in Genesee County. After the drag race ended and defendant had stopped at the side of the road, Osborne continued to drive extremely fast on the wrong side of the road. A mile or so down the road, Osborne ran head on into an oncoming car and killed the driver. Is defendant the "cause" of that driver's death?

3. *Another Drag Race.* Defendant and another driver (Alvarez) participated in a drag race. Both drivers completed the race course without incident. However, at the end, Alvarez made a 180 degree turn and headed back towards the starting line at a speed of 123 m.p.h., while defendant followed at a speed of 98 m.p.h.; Alvarez was not wearing a seat belt and subsequent investigation revealed that he had a blood alcohol level between .11 and .12. At some point, Alvarez crashed through a guard rail, was thrown from his car, and was killed when his vehicle landed on top of him. Defendant also crashed through the guard rail, but escaped uninjured. Should defendant be held criminally responsible as the "cause" of Alvarez's death? *See Velazquez v. State*, 561 So.2d 347 (Fla.App. 1990).

4. *Spectator Liability.* In the prior problem, if the defendant can be held criminally liable for the death of Alvarez because he participated in the race, can spectators (who were lined up along the race route to cheer the two participants) be said to have "caused" the death as well?

5. *The Game of Chicken.* Defendant Abe and his friend Bob entered into a suicide pact which was supposed to be carried out by driving a car off a cliff. The "cliff" was on a car turnout on a curve overlooking a 350–foot precipice on a country road. The two men drove a car up the hill past the cliff, turned around, and drove down around the curve and over the steep cliff at a speed in excess of 50 mph. No one saw brake lights flash. The impact of the crash killed Bob and caused severe injuries to Abe, resulting in the amputation of his foot. The State has charged Abe with the homicide of Bob. How would the prosecutor argue that defendant caused Bob's death? How might defense counsel respond to these arguments? How should the case be resolved? *See Forden v. Joseph G.*, 34 Cal.3d 429, 667 P.2d 1176, 194 Cal.Rptr. 163 (In Bank 1983).

6. *The Drug Addicts.* David Groleau, who was an alcoholic and who previously had used depressants such as Valium and Percocet, "had been drinking and doing pills" throughout the course of a day. By early evening, Groleau was visibly inebriated. Defendant prepared one "bag" of heroin and injected the heroin into his own arm. Defendant exclaimed that the heroin was "very, very good," which meant that it was particularly potent. Defen-

dant then gave another bag of heroin to Groleau, who injected the heroin into his own arm. Groleau, who was approximately thirty to forty pounds heavier than the defendant, injected the same amount of heroin as had the defendant. Approximately fifteen seconds later, Groleau lost consciousness, collapsed onto the floor, and died. The evidence revealed that the level of heroin alone was "potentially life-threatening," and that Groleau would not have died but for the administration of the heroin. Was defendant's conduct the "cause" of Groleau's death? *See State v. Wassil*, 233 Conn. 174, 658 A.2d 548 (1995); *Shirah v. State*, 555 So.2d 807 (Ala.Crim.App. 1989); *People v. Cline*, 270 Cal.App.2d 328, 75 Cal.Rptr. 459 (1969); *Ureta v. Superior Court*, 199 Cal.App.2d 672, 18 Cal.Rptr. 873 (1962).

7. *The "Eggshell" Victim.* In torts, an actor must take his victim as he finds him. Is the same thing true in the criminal law? Assume that Joe Compton is a hemophiliac, or "bleeder"—he suffers from a hereditary condition of the blood that prevents coagulation and permits hemorrhages to continue unchecked. Defendant struck Compton on the jaw once with his fist. The injury would have caused only minor injuries to a normal person because it created only a slight laceration on the inside of the mouth. However, since Compton was a hemophiliac, the blow produced a hemorrhage lasting ten days and ending in death. Defendant testified that he was unaware that the deceased was a hemophiliac. Defendant argued that Compton's death was not caused by the blow, but by his disease. Given the victim's hemophilia, is defendant's conduct the "cause" of the death? *See State v. Frazier*, 339 Mo. 966, 98 S.W.2d 707 (1936); *Fine v. State*, 193 Tenn. 422, 246 S.W.2d 70 (1952). What if the victim had a heart condition and died as a result of excitement caused by a robbery? *See People v. Stamp*, 2 Cal.App.3d 203, 82 Cal.Rptr. 598 (1969).

8. *The Cancer Patient.* The victim was 70 years old at the time of her death and had been in the ranching and cattle business. The victim was suffering from stomach cancer and was receiving chemotherapy. Defendant came to the ranch and shot the victim, following which she was hospitalized for the abdominal wound. Although the chemotherapy had been effective in inhibiting the stomach cancer, it interfered with the healing of the abdominal wound and had to be discontinued for some time. While the chemotherapy treatment was withheld from the victim, there was a rebound and rapid growth of the cancer, and the victim remained hospitalized until her death. Her death certificate listed the primary cause of death as tumor cachexia, a terminal state of cancer in which the body has a negative nitrogen balance, marked weight loss, propensity to infections, loss of strength, and a markedly diminished host resistance. The cancer had effectively overwhelmed the body's defenses. Was defendant the "cause" of the victim's death? *See In re Eliasen*, 105 Idaho 234, 668 P.2d 110 (1983).

9. *The Thieves and Their Victim.* Defendants robbed Stafford of his money and car. Afterwards, they compelled him to lower his trousers and to take off his shoes; and when they were satisfied that Stafford had no more money on his person, they forced him to exit his vehicle. As he was thrust

from the car, Stafford fell onto the shoulder of the rural two-lane highway on which they had been traveling. His trousers were still down around his ankles, his shirt was rolled up towards his chest, he was shoeless, and he had also been stripped of his jacket. Before the defendants pulled away, one defendant placed Stafford's shoes and jacket on the shoulder of the highway. Although Stafford's eyeglasses were in the vehicle, the defendants, either through inadvertence or perhaps by specific design, did not give them to Stafford before they drove away. The temperature was near zero, and, although it was not snowing at the time, visibility was occasionally obscured by heavy winds, which intermittently blew previously fallen snow into the air and across the highway. There was snow on both sides of the road as a result of previous plowing operations. About an hour later, two cars approached from opposite directions. Immediately after passing the other car, a driver of one car saw Stafford sitting in the road in the middle of the northbound lane with his hands up in the air. The driver was operating his car at a speed of approximately 50 miles per hour, and he "didn't have time to react" before his vehicle struck Stafford. After he brought his car to a stop and returned to try to be of assistance to Stafford, the driver observed that the man's trousers were down around his ankles and his shirt was pulled up around his chest. Stafford was not wearing shoes or a jacket. At the trial, the Medical Examiner of Monroe County testified that Stafford's death had occurred quickly because of massive head injuries. In addition, he found evidence of a high degree of alcohol concentration in Stafford's blood. Who is the "cause of" Stafford's death? The two defendants who robbed Stafford? The passing driver? *See People v. Kibbe*, 35 N.Y.2d 407, 321 N.E.2d 773, 362 N.Y.S.2d 848 (1974).

10. *The Screaming Woman.* Defendant and Mary Berry got into a fight in a bar. Berry left the bar and got into a cab, which was parked outside and which she drove for a living. Defendant followed her, got into the driver's seat where Berry was sitting, shoved her into the passenger's seat, and drove away. Berry was hanging out of the passenger window, screaming "Help me, he's trying to kill me!" Defendant was holding on to Berry, beating her and pulling her hair, while continuing to drive. Berry, by "fighting and kicking", had managed to get one leg out of the passenger window, but all the while the defendant was "trying to pull her back in by her hair." Berry struggled away from defendant and fell out of the passenger window. Berry then ran towards the oncoming cars, finally stopping as a station wagon approached. Berry grabbed at the window of the station wagon for about a minute, but then fell beneath the wheels of the station wagon to her death. The driver of the station wagon, Vito Michielli, was driving home from a shopping trip with his wife and two small children. Berry was screaming "help me" and "let me in" and attempted to crawl through the window of the station wagon. Michielli and his wife were frightened and the children began to cry. The Michiellis' reaction was to lock all the doors and attempt to close the windows of the car. Mr. Michielli reached out of his window, pushed Berry away and sped off. Not until several days later, when a local newspaper

reported Berry's tragic death, did Michielli realize that in leaving the scene his car had run over Berry. Who "caused" her death? *See Commonwealth v. Rementer*, 410 Pa.Super. 9, 598 A.2d 1300 (1991).

11. *The "Suicide."* Eighteen-year-old Rachelle Cazin was pregnant with defendant's child. Cazin asked defendant to meet her in the woods near their home and to bring his gun. The couple met as planned and agreed to commit suicide together. Defendant testified that Cazin put the gun in her mouth and he counted to three, but nothing happened. Defendant claims that he then tried to talk Cazin out of shooting herself, and told her that he would not go through with their pact. As he walked away from her, he heard a gunshot. Bauer hid Cazin's body under a layer of brush, ran home, changed his clothes, unloaded the gun, threw the remaining shells outside and cleaned the gun. Did defendant "cause" Cazin's death? *See State v. Bauer*, 471 N.W.2d 363 (Minn.App. 1991).

12. *The Mother and the Abusive Lover.* Defendant, who had a daughter, moved in with Ed McCue. McCue sometimes severely and brutally whipped the child. He would order the child to hold out her hand, and then he would slap her. Then he would say, "Where's your baby doll?" When the child reached for it, there would be a loud slap. A neighbor testified that his tone of voice was "crafty, nauseatingly." One night, McCue whipped the child until 11:00 p.m. Defendant asked McCue to stop, but the whipping continued and he dragged "the child up and down the hall beating her." Defendant pleaded with the neighbors not to call the police, telling them that she loved "Eddie" and that they must have been imagining that the beatings were more severe than they actually were. Defendant explained that McCue was worried over some difficulty at work and was bothered by the heat. One day, McCue struck the child with blows which ripped the child's liver and tore the mesentery, a fatty, vascular tissue supporting the colon. Hemorrhaging ensued and the child began vomiting. Defendant took her daughter to the hospital, where she died. The child had multiple bruises from head to foot, both arms, both legs, back, front and face. Defendant stated that she loved the child and was never unkind to her, and, if she had thought McCue's discipline of the child was too severe, she would have left him. Did defendant "cause" the death? *See Palmer v. State*, 223 Md. 341, 164 A.2d 467 (1960).

13. *The Asphyxiated Widow.* Defendant beat and raped Elizabeth Winslow, an 85-year-old widow, for whom he had previously done yard work. She suffered a broken arm, a broken rib, bruises on her face, neck, arms, trunk and inner thighs, and then she seemingly lost her will to live. A day or so later, Mrs. Winslow was being served lunch in the hospital. For approximately 20 minutes a nurse's aide was feeding her small portions of puréed food on a spoon, which Mrs. Winslow was accepting without choking or gagging in any way. She eventually spit out some vegetables, which the aide interpreted to mean that Mrs. Winslow did not want any more. The aide then noticed that Mrs. Winslow had stopped moving her mouth. The aide summoned other nurses who determined that Mrs. Winslow had died. The

autopsy revealed that Mrs. Winslow died of asphyxiation, which resulted from six ounces of food being aspirated into her trachea. There were internal abdominal bruises around the colon and kidney, a broken rib, and facial bruises from the beating, but none of these injuries caused her death. However, the mechanics of clearing the trachea when food enters it by mistake requires a sufficient volume of air in the lungs to push the food out of the trachea and spit it out, thus preventing asphyxiation. The pain associated with a broken rib generally inhibits deep breathing, which limits the amount of air available to the lungs. The volume of food lodged in Mrs. Winslow's trachea was very large and would have been difficult for even a normal, healthy person to expel. Is defendant criminally responsible for "causing" Mrs. Winslow's death? How would you argue the case for the prosecutor? How might defense counsel respond? *See People v. Brackett*, 117 Ill.2d 170, 510 N.E.2d 877, 109 Ill.Dec. 809 (1987).

14. *The Inmate.* As Charles Gardner, an inmate at the California Medical Facility, walked down a first-floor corridor, he was stabbed 11 times by defendant. Nevertheless, Gardner was able to grab a knife that his assailant had left on the floor. In pursuit of defendant, Gardner ran or staggered some distance up a flight of stairs to the second floor, where he plunged the knife into the chest of a prison guard, Officer Patch. Patch died within the hour at the prison clinic, and Gardner died shortly afterward. Is defendant criminally responsible for "causing" Officer Patch's death? Argue the case for the prosecutor. How would defense counsel respond? *See People v. Roberts*, 2 Cal.4th 271, 826 P.2d 274, 6 Cal.Rptr.2d 276 (1992).

15. *The Obstructed Fire Escape.* A fire erupted in a six-story warehouse operated by the defendant Deitsch Textile Corporation in Brooklyn. The source of the fire was never discovered. While those who were working on the ground floor escaped to safety, two employees were trapped on the sixth floor. One was eventually rescued. The other died. On the day of the fire, a shipment of elastic material was delivered to the warehouse and employees were in the process of carrying it up to the sixth floor. Fire escapes were available, but they were blocked with bales of stored materials. Can it be said that the supervisors, who allowed the bales to be placed in front of the fire escapes, caused the victim's death? *See People v. Deitsch*, 97 A.D.2d 327, 470 N.Y.S.2d 158 (1983); *People v. Warner–Lambert Co.*, 51 N.Y.2d 295, 414 N.E.2d 660, 434 N.Y.S.2d 159 (1980).

PEOPLE v. McGEE
31 Cal.2d 229, 187 P.2d 706 (1947).

SCHAUER, JUSTICE.

Defendant [and] Linck went to the club rooms of a fraternal organization in San Pedro. They had two drinks at the bar, then entered the card room. Linck joined in a card game (with persons with whom defendant apparently had no previous acquaintance) for 15 or 20 minutes. Defendant took Linck's place at the card table when

Linck went to the bar, where he remained for about 15 minutes. Defendant then [left] the card room and he and Linck went out of the club. They immediately returned to the card room because Linck believed he had left $40 on the card table. Linck asked, "Gentlemen, do you know what became of the money I left on the table?" One of the players pointed to defendant. Linck asked defendant, "Hank, did you take it?" or "Did you play?" Linck "understood him (defendant) to say yes" and Linck and defendant left the card room. As they walked through the bar, which was dimly lighted, [Rypdahl] came from the card room ... toward defendant [and] "pulled his hand around from back of him." At this point ... defendant shot [Rypdahl] in the abdomen. As a result of hemorrhage from the bullet wound [Rypdahl] died the next day.

[Defendant] contends that the trial court erred [by] excluding evidence which [would] have tended to show that the proximate cause of Rypdahl's death was not the bullet wound but the manner in which the wound was treated. In 8 A.L.R. at page 516 the general rule as to criminal responsibility of one who wounds another, for the death of the victim, is stated as follows: "When a person inflicts a wound on another which is dangerous, or calculated to destroy life, the fact that the negligence, mistake, or lack of skill of an attending physician or surgeon contributes to the death affords no defense to a charge of homicide." Following this general rule it has been held that where the wound inflicted by the accused operates as a cause of death, the fact that the malpractice of attending surgeons may have had some causative influence will not relieve the accused from full responsibility for the ultimate result of his act. On the other hand, in qualification of the rule, it is said that "Where a person inflicts on another a wound not in itself calculated to produce death, and the injured person dies solely as a result of the improper treatment of the wound by an attending physician or surgeon, the fact that the death was caused by medical mistreatment is a good defense to a charge of homicide." On this subject it has been said to be "the proper", and probably generally accepted, view [that] mere negligence (in the treating of a wound) is no defense even though it is the sole cause of death because it is a foreseeable intervening cause. But death caused by grossly improper treatment is not the proximate consequence of the defendant's injury unless the injury is an actual contributing factor at the time of death, because such treatment is an unforeseeable intervening cause. The evidence as to the nature of the wound inflicted by defendant and the treatment thereof is as follows[.]

An autopsy was performed on July 19 at 10:45 a.m., after the body had been embalmed. The autopsy surgeon [testified] that the bullet had grazed the liver, gone through the pancreas and spleen, and come to rest behind the upper pole of the left kidney; that there was "profuse hemorrhage throughout the course of the wound"; and that such hemorrhage was the immediate cause of death. In the opinion of the autopsy surgeon the gunshot wound was such that "If it was not controlled (by hemostasia, gauze packing, etc.) it would be only a matter of an hour, or an hour and a half, before there would be a profuse hemorrhage sufficient to cause death" and the anterior incision permitting such control was made "Within at least two hours after the wound." (It will be remembered that the hospital records show that such incision was not made until some 12 hours after deceased was shot and 11 hours after his admission to the hospital.) The autopsy surgeon also found a posterior incision starting two inches to the left of the spine and following the course of the lower rib for 4 inches. The purpose and time of making this incision and the person by whom it was made, do not appear from the record.

[The evidence] disclosed the following situation: Defendant, without aiming and without intending to shoot Rypdahl, unlawfully, or "without due caution and circumspection," discharged a pistol which was pointed toward Rypdahl. The immediate result of this unlawful or incautious act was the wounding of Rypdahl. The direct result of the wound was "profuse hemorrhage" which would be "sufficient to cause death" if it was not promptly controlled. Having thus set in motion the events which culminated in Rypdahl's death, defendant departed. The surgeon in whose care Rypdahl was promptly placed neglected for more than ten hours, grossly contrary to good surgical practice, to control the hemorrhage. We assume further that Rypdahl's life might have been saved by prompt and proper surgical treatment. But defendant cannot complain because no force intervened to save him from the natural consequence of his criminal act. The factual situation is in legal effect the same, whether the victim of a wound bleeds to death because surgical attention is not available or because, although available, it is delayed by reason of the surgeon's gross neglect or incompetence. The delay in treatment is not in fact an intervening force; it cannot in law amount to a supervening cause.

For the reasons above stated the judgment and the order denying defendant's motion for new trial are affirmed. The attempted appeal from the order denying his motion in arrest of judgment is dismissed.

PROBLEMS

1. *Negligent Medical Intervention.* Defendant stabbed Danielle Smith in the abdomen. Smith was rushed to the hospital. During the initial stages of the operation, the surgeons discovered that Smith also had an incarcerated hernia. After they had sutured the wounds and completed the operation on the stomach, the surgeons proceeded to correct the hernia. During this phase of the operation "it was noted that the body was turning blue and there was no pulse, which means the person went into cardiac arrest." Smith

then suffered a loss of oxygen to the brain and massive brain damage. She died a month later without ever regaining consciousness. At the time of death, the stomach wound had completely healed. Dr. Di Maio conceded that the chances were that if the hernia operation had not been performed, the patient would have survived. Under the circumstances, should defendant's stab wound be regarded as the legal cause of death? How would defense counsel argue the case? How might the prosecutor respond? How should the case be resolved? *See People v. Stewart*, 40 N.Y.2d 692, 358 N.E.2d 487, 389 N.Y.S.2d 804 (1976).

2. *The Irrational Patient.* The victim was stabbed in the abdomen by the defendant during a robbery. The stabbing necessitated an operation which resulted in complications including abdominal distention. As a result of the victim's post-operative condition, tubes were inserted through the victim's nostrils and into his stomach. The victim was disoriented, uncooperative and confused, and pulled out the tubes on several occasions. Finally, he pulled out a tube, gagged and asphyxiated. How would you argue as the prosecutor that defendant caused the victim's death? How might defense counsel respond? *See Commonwealth v. Cheeks*, 423 Pa. 67, 223 A.2d 291 (1966); *United States v. Hamilton*, 182 F.Supp. 548 (D.D.C. 1960).

3. *Organ Donation and Death.* Defendant inflicted a mortal wound on Charles Cronkite. When he arrived at the hospital emergency room, Cronkite was comatose, but had some slight reaction to noxious stimuli. Within minutes his condition deteriorated. He became totally unresponsive and remained so thereafter. He was placed on a respirator and various drug therapies were undertaken without result. On the following day, he was totally areflexic—completely unresponsive to all stimuli. His respiration and blood pressure were artificially supported. Two electroencephalograms (EEGs) were reported to be "flat". Dr. Rosenberg, chief of neuro-surgery at the hospital, pronounced Cronkite's condition to be cerebral death. Shortly thereafter, the victim's mother signed a consent form so that his kidneys and spleen could be removed for donation and his life support systems disconnected. Defendant contends that the doctor's actions were the cause of death and that he is not criminally responsible. How will the prosecutor respond to this argument? *See People v. Bonilla*, 95 A.D.2d 396, 467 N.Y.S.2d 599 (1983).

4. *Euthanasia.* Defendant stabbed Amelia Robinson with a three inch pocket knife following a fist fight on the victim's front porch. On arrival at the hospital, Robinson was found to be suffering from a stab wound to the upper abdomen and was in respiratory distress, with unstable vital signs and severe internal bleeding. After being transferred to an operating table, she suffered cardiac arrest attributable to an extreme loss of blood. Her left chest was opened, intravenous blood was supplied, and a heart massage was successful in re-establishing a heart beat. Robinson languished for days until the surgical team and the I.C.U. physician decided that, despite all extraordinary measures, Robinson was beyond medical help and would surely die within three to five days. That same evening, however, some 70 days after her initial wounding, Robinson died. Later, a nurse admitted, "in sum and

substance ... that she turned off the ventilator and the drips ... because somebody had to have the balls to do it ..." Does the nurse's action relieve defendant of liability for "causing" the death? *See People v. Vaughn*, 152 Misc.2d 731, 579 N.Y.S.2d 839 (1991).

5. *More on Negligent Medical Care.* Defendant was charged in the savage beating of Albea, a member of a drug ring headed by defendant Bowie in the Bronx. Essentially, defendant beat Albea with a baseball bat for 20–30 minutes, breaking several of his bones, and he later died at the hospital of complications stemming from this beating. Subsequent negligent treatment at the hospital may have contributed to Albea's death. When Albea developed malignant hyperthermia, a "possibly hereditary" reaction to anesthesia, his blood pressure dropped precipitously. Surgeons rushed to open his chest and perform cardiac massage. In doing so, they inadvertently punctured his lung, requiring three sutures to close the wound. Albea never recovered consciousness. The cause of death, four days later, was septicemia, a bacterial infection resulting from "bl[unt] force injuries of the h[e]ad and extremities with surgical intervention." Was defendant's beating the "cause" of Albea's death? Argue the case for the prosecutor? How would defense counsel respond? *See People v. Bowie*, 200 A.D.2d 511, 607 N.Y.S.2d 248 (1994).

6. *The Suicide Machine.* Marjorie Miller suffered from multiple sclerosis, and her condition had deteriorated to the point that she used a wheelchair and had to be carried from place to place and put into the chair. As a result, she was confined either to bed or to a wheelchair, did not have the use of her legs or her right arm, had only limited use of her left arm, and had problems talking and breathing. Miller contacted defendant, a champion of physician-assisted suicide, and he agreed to assist her in taking her life by hooking her up to his "suicide machine." The machine consisted of a needle to be inserted into a blood vessel that could convey various chemicals into the bloodstream. One of the chemicals was methohexital, a fast-acting barbituate that quickly depresses respiration. A large dose can cause the recipient to stop breathing. After defendant inserted the needle into a vein in Ms. Miller's arm, he tied strings to two of her fingers. The strings were attached to clips on the tubing connected to the needle. Defendant instructed Ms. Miller how to pull the strings attached to the clips so as to allow the drugs to flow into her bloodstream. Ms. Miller followed defendant's instructions and died as a result of a lethal dose of methohexital. Is defendant criminally responsible for "causing" her death by providing deceased with the means by which she killed herself, even though she performed the fatal final act? *See People v. Kevorkian*, 205 Mich.App. 180, 517 N.W.2d 293 (1994).

Common Law Parties
① first degree
② second degree : @ scene, helped
③ accessory before fact
④ accessory after.

CHAPTER 5

COMPLICITY

■ ■ ■

A. ACCOMPLICE LIABILITY

Whether they are referred to as accomplices, accessories, or aiders-and-abettors, every jurisdiction possesses statutory provisions that serve to punish actors whose only relationship to a criminal offense was the provision of assistance to the principal offender.

1. PRINCIPALS & ACCESSORIES

a. MERGER OF PRINCIPALS & ACCESSORIES

STANDEFER v. UNITED STATES
447 U.S. 10 (1980).

Mr. Chief Justice Burger delivered the opinion of the Court.

[At] common law, the subject of principals and accessories was riddled with "intricate" distinctions. In felony cases, parties to a crime were divided into four distinct categories: (1) principals in the first degree who actually perpetrated the offense; (2) principals in the second degree who were actually or constructively present at the scene of the crime and aided or abetted its commission; (3) accessories before the fact who aided or abetted the crime, but were not present at its commission; and (4) accessories after the fact who rendered assistance after the crime was complete. By contrast, misdemeanor cases "d[id] not admit of accessories[sic] either before or after the fact"; instead, all parties to a misdemeanor, whatever their roles, were principals.

COMMON LAW
1. first°
2. second
3. before
4. after.

MISDEMEANOR
—principles

Because at early common law all parties to a felony received the death penalty, certain procedural rules developed tending to shield accessories from punishment. Among them [was] the rule that an accessory could not be convicted without the prior conviction of the principal offender. Under this rule, the principal's flight, death, or acquittal barred prosecution of the accessory. And if the principal were pardoned or his conviction reversed on appeal, the accessory's conviction could not stand. In every way "an accessory follow[ed], like a shadow, his principal."

This procedural bar applied only to the prosecution of accessories in felony cases. In misdemeanor cases, where all participants were deemed principals, a prior acquittal of the actual perpetrator did not prevent the subsequent conviction of a person who rendered assistance. And in felony cases a principal in the second degree could be convicted notwithstanding the prior acquittal of the first-degree principal. Not surprisingly, considerable effort was expended in defining the categories—in determining, for instance, when a person was "constructively present" so as to be a second-degree principal. In the process, justice all too frequently was defeated.

To overcome these judge-made rules, statutes were enacted in England and in the United States. In 1848 the Parliament enacted a statute providing that an accessory before the fact could be "indicted, tried, convicted, and punished in all respects like the Principal." As interpreted, the statute permitted an accessory to be convicted "although the principal be acquitted." Several state legislatures followed suit. In 1899, Congress joined this growing reform movement with the enactment of a general penal code for Alaska which abrogated the common-law distinctions and provided that "all persons concerned in the commission of a crime, whether it be felony or misdemeanor, and whether they directly commit the act constituting the crime or aid and abet in its commission, though not present, are principals, and to be tried and punished as such."

The enactment of 18 U.S.C. § 2 in 1909 was part and parcel of this same reform movement. The language of the statute, as enacted, unmistakably demonstrates the point:

> "Whoever directly commits any act constituting an offense defined in any law of the United States, or aids, abets, counsels, commands, induces, or procures its commission, is a principal."

The statute "abolishe[d] the distinction between principals and accessories and [made] them all principals." Read against its common-law background, the provision evinces a clear intent to permit the conviction of accessories to federal criminal offenses despite the prior acquittal of the actual perpetrator of the offense. It gives general effect to what had always been the rule for second-decree principals and for all misdemeanants.

[With] the enactment of that section, all participants in conduct violating a federal criminal statute are "principals." As such, they are punishable for their criminal conduct; the fate of other participants is irrelevant....

NOTE

Accessories after the fact. The merger of principals and accessories has occurred in all American jurisdictions. One significant exception, however, is accessories after the fact. When an actor assists another *only* after the substantive criminal offense has taken place, e.g. harboring a fugitive after a bank robbery, that offense does *not* merge with the principal offense, bank robbery.

PROBLEMS

1. *Discrepancies in Result.* In *Standefer*, the Supreme Court concluded that an aider-and-abettor could be held culpable for a criminal offense (bribery) for which the principal had previously been acquitted. Does this make sense to you? Is it fair? The *Standefer* Court dismissed these concerns, observing that "[w]hile symmetry of results may be intellectually satisfying, it is not required."

2. *The Responsibility of Accomplices.* Is it fair to treat accomplices as if they had actually committed the criminal act in question themselves? Is a "getaway driver" just as culpable as a bank robber? How about the actor who simply arranges to provide the getaway car? Is the conduct of all accomplices (and principals) really *equally* blameworthy?

b. SIGNIFICANCE OF THE MERGER OF PRINCIPALS & ACCESSORIES

The merger of principals and accessories has created some significant procedural problems in criminal trials and criminal pretrial procedure. For example, what kind of notice (if any at all) must a defendant receive as to whether or not he or she is going to be tried for his or her principal and/or accessorial acts? And when must or should that notice be received?

BAKER v. ALASKA

905 P.2d 479 (Alaska Ct.App. 1995).

MANNHEIMER, JUDGE.

[Baker] and two friends, John Stanfill and Jason Frazier, decided to get some free pizzas by telephoning a Pizza Hut restaurant, ordering pizzas for home delivery, and then robbing the delivery person when he came to deliver their order. Baker's first attack on his conviction concerns the issue of whether he acted as a principal or an accessory in this robbery.

[Stanfill,] testifying under a grant of immunity, admitted taking part in the robbery. He described the planning of the robbery and the role each person played in the crime. Stanfill testified that he phoned in the pizza order and that he told the restaurant to deliver the pizzas to a neighboring apartment building. The three friends then stationed themselves near the entrance to this neighboring building. Stanfill waited on the stairs, Frazier near the door, and Baker in the hallway. Stanfill and Frazier had bandannas over their faces for concealment; Baker wore a dark blue ski mask.

The delivery person, James Seymour, arrived with the pizzas but was unable to find the person who had placed the order. As Seymour turned to leave the building, the three robbers made their move. Seymour testified he was struck by a man who emerged from beneath a set of stairs. He described his assailant as a light-complexioned [man] wearing a one-holed dark blue ski mask and dark gloves. Upon being struck, Seymour fell to the ground, dropping the pizzas. The man continued to hit Seymour. After the third blow, Seymour shouted to his assailant that he could take the pizzas. In a blur, Seymour saw someone kneel down, take the pizzas, and flee the building. Seymour was never able to positively identify the person who hit him.

Seymour's testimony that he was struck by a man who emerged from underneath the stairs, in combination with Stanfill's description of where each of the three men waited (Stanfill on the stairs, Frazier near the door, and Baker in the hallway), tended to identify Baker as the robber who struck Seymour—the robber whom Seymour saw emerge from "beneath . . . the stairs". Moreover, when Stanfill was asked, "What happened right when the robbery took place?", Stanfill replied that he "saw the pizzas fall to the ground" and that he and Frazier grabbed the pizzas and ran. This response again raised the inference that Baker had been the one who physically accosted Seymour. However, Stanfill was never asked directly whether Baker was the one who hit Seymour.

[Frazier, who testified as part of a plea bargain], also admitted taking part in the robbery. He recounted that it was Baker who first proposed the robbery and that it was Stanfill who left the apartment and placed the call to Pizza Hut. Frazier corroborated Stanfill's description of each man's location as they waited for the pizza delivery person to arrive. Like Stanfill, Frazier never directly testified that it was Baker who struck Seymour. Frazier did say that, as Seymour turned to leave the building with the undelivered pizzas, Frazier and Stanfill "grabbed the pizza, and we ran. Then all three of us ran back to [Stanfill's] apartment." Frazier stated that the three men [set] about eating the pizzas until Stanfill's mother returned home and told the men to leave.

Baker did not testify at trial. . . . Baker's attorney suggested that Baker had not participated in the robbery. [T]he defense attorney argued that Stanfill and Frazier might be lying about Baker's involvement in order to shield an unidentified friend and in order to obtain favorable treatment [for] their own crimes. . . . Toward the end of Baker's trial, [the] question arose whether the jury should be instructed on accomplice liability. Included among [the jury instructions was instruction number] "9". [T]his instruction described the law relating to accomplice liability.... The jurors were told that, if they found that one or more of the witnesses [were] accomplices to the crime under consideration, then they should view the testimony of these witnesses with distrust.

[Baker's] attorney voiced no objection when the trial judge declared his intention to give the jury this accomplice liability instruction. Nevertheless, Baker now argues on appeal that the jury's receipt of this instruction prejudiced the fairness of his trial.

Baker points out that the accomplice liability instruction could be expected to play two roles during jury deliberations. First, the instruction informed the jury of the circumstances under which Stanfill and Frazier should be considered "accomplices", thus obliging the jury to view their testimony with distrust. Second, the instruction informed the jury of the circumstances under which Baker could be held accountable for Stanfill's and Frazier's conduct. To the extent that Instruction 9 filled the first of these roles, Baker contends that it was unnecessary. And, to the extent that Instruction 9 filled the second of these roles, Baker contends that it deprived him of a fair trial [by allowing] the jury to convict him of robbery under a complicity theory even after the prosecutor announced that the State viewed Baker as a "principal", not an "accomplice". [Baker] asserts that the fairness of his trial was prejudiced when the prosecutor, during final argument, suggested to the jury that Baker could be convicted of robbery even if the State failed to prove that Baker was the man who struck Seymour, so long as the State proved that Baker was one of the three robbers....

The common-law distinction between principals and accessories was abrogated in Alaska almost 100 years ago.... At common law, a person who personally committed the actus reus of the crime was a "principal in the first degree". Any person who was present at the commission of the crime and who aided or abetted the commission of the crime was a "principal in the second degree". Anyone who aided or abetted the crime before it was committed and who was not present at the commission of the crime was an "accessory before the fact".

At common law, "the distinction between principals in the first degree and those in the second degree [was] one of fact rather than of legal consequence". A defendant who was indicted as a principal in the first degree could be convicted even though the proof established that he acted as a principal in the second degree, and vice-versa. It [was] not necessary for the [indictment] to disclose whether the defendant [was] a principal in one degree or the other. [Conviction could be obtained] although the proof establishe[d] that the one charged as abettor was in fact the perpetrator, while the other was present aiding and abetting him.

However, the common law required that an indictment clearly specify whether a defendant acted as a principal or an accessory. A defendant might escape criminal liability altogether by creating a reasonable doubt as to whether he had been a principal or an accessory (i.e., whether he had been present at the commission of the crime or not). The statutory abrogation of the distinction between principals and accessories was intended to change this rule of pleading and to avoid this potential result.

Applying these common-law definitions to Baker's case, if Baker was one of the three men who waited in ambush for the pizza delivery person, then he was a principal in the robbery. If Baker either struck the delivery person or helped to carry away the pizzas, he was a principal in the first degree—since the actus reus of robbery requires both an assault and the taking (or attempted taking) of property. If Baker was present but only provided aid or encouragement to the enterprise, then he was a principal in the second degree.

As just explained, the common law saw no legal distinction here. A common-law indictment would not have needed to specify which of these roles Baker played. And at trial, as long as the State established that Baker was present at the commission of the robbery and either personally performed some part of the actus reus or aided or abetted those who did, Baker could be convicted of the robbery.

[For] almost a century, Alaska law has recognized no distinction between principals and accessories—no distinction in the manner they are charged, tried, or punished. Both this court and the Alaska Supreme Court have repeatedly declared "that a defendant charged as a principal may be convicted as an [accessory, and] the converse is also true." [When] the Alaska Legislature revised the criminal code in 1980, it abandoned the labels "principal" and "accessory" in favor of a more straightforward approach. Former AS 12.15.010, the statute abrogating the distinction between principals and accessories, was repealed. In its place, AS 11.16.100 states the general rule of criminal liability without reference to the terms "principal" and "accessory":

> A person is guilty of an offense if it is committed by the person's own conduct[,] or by the conduct of another for which the person is legally accountable under AS 11.16.110, or by both.

The legislative commentary to this statute explains:

> AS 11.16.100 restates the basic principle of criminal law that criminal liability is based upon conduct. When liability exists, it is immaterial whether the elements of the crime are satisfied by the defendant's own behavior, or by the behavior of another person for which he is accountable[,] or by both.

Thus, while Alaska law no longer uses the terms "principal" and "accessory" to describe the theories under which a person may be held responsible for a crime, [the] revised criminal code was not intended to reintroduce the distinctions between principals and accessories before the fact. [W]hen an indictment alleges that the defendant personally committed the acts constituting the crime, the defendant is on notice that he or she may also be convicted under a theory of accomplice liability if the State establishes that the defendant is responsible for the acts of others under AS 11.16.110.

Baker nevertheless argues that once the prosecutor announced his theory of the case, (that Baker was the one who struck the robbery victim), Baker was entitled to have his case submitted to the jury without reference to any theory of accomplice liability. Baker relies [on] *Michael v. State*, 805 P.2d 371 (Alaska 1991). [In that case,] defendant and his wife were indicted for assaulting their child. Because it was unclear which spouse actually attacked the child, Michael was indicted both as a principal and, alternatively, as an accessory. At trial, the State relied on yet another theory of culpability: that even though Michael did not strike the child and even though he neither aided nor abetted his wife's abuse of the child, [he could] be convicted of assault for failing to perform his parental duty to protect the child from the assaults of others.... Michael objected that this theory of liability varied materially from the theories considered by the grand jury. The superior court overruled Michael's objection and, ultimately, convicted him under this theory.... The supreme court [overturned the conviction]. The court ruled that, even though "Michael's failure to carry out his parental duty was clear from the [grand jury] evidence", "[t]he fact remains [that] the grand jury made no such charge in the indictment" [*Michael's*] indictment could not be construed to include this theory.

Baker's case, however, presents no issue outside traditional notions of accomplice liability. Under either of the State's theories of this case—that is, whether Baker personally struck the pizza delivery man or was present only to help carry away the pizzas—Baker was a "principal" in the commission of the robbery. Even at common law[,] Baker would have no variance claim. He certainly has none now. We reject Baker's argument that the indictment failed to put him on notice that he might be convicted under the rules of accomplice liability codified in AS 11.16.110(2).

As a fall-back position, Baker asserts that [he was] misled when the prosecutor announced at trial that the State viewed Baker as a principal, not an "accomplice". There are [two] problems with this argument.... First, Baker's trial attorney never suggested that he was surprised or prejudiced when the jury was asked to consider Baker's accomplice liability.... Second, [even] under the State's primary theory of the crime[,] to evaluate Baker's guilt, the jury would necessarily have to receive instruction on the rules governing Baker's liability for Stanfill's and Frazier's acts of taking the property.

[For] these reasons, we hold that it was not error for the trial judge to instruct the jury on accomplice liability and it was not error for the prosecutor to argue that theory of liability to the jury.

[The] judgement of the superior court is Affirmed.

PROBLEMS

1. *Principals and Accessories.* Is it fair for a defendant who has been indicted as a principal to be convicted as an accessory? Is that what happened in this case? Was there fair notice to the defendant, Baker, that this might happen?

2. *Distinguishing the Michael Decision.* Do you think that the *Baker* Court did an adequate job of distinguishing the *Michael* decision where the defendant was held not to have had sufficient notice of the theory under which he was going to be prosecuted? Why is this case different from the situation presented in *Michael*?

3. *Prejudice to Baker?* The *Baker* Court held that "[u]nder either of the State's theories of this case—that is, whether Baker personally struck the pizza delivery man or was present only to help carry away the pizzas—Baker was a 'principal' in the commission of the robbery." If that is true, why wasn't Baker prejudiced when it was argued to the jury that he might be guilty as an *accessory*—not as a principal?

NEW HAMPSHIRE v. SINBANDITH
143 N.H. 579, 729 A.2d 994 (1999).

BROCK, C.J.

The defendant, Bounleuth "Pheng" Sinbandith, was convicted after a jury trial in Superior Court [on] seven indictments relating to the sale of a controlled drug. We affirm.

In July 1996, Corporal Nightingale, an undercover narcotics detective for the State Police, conducted an investigation in Laconia. In the course of that investigation, Nightingale made arrangements with the defendant for several purchases of crack cocaine. On four occasions, Nightingale gave the defendant a sum of money, and the defendant drove to a separate location. On all but one of these occasions either Elizabeth Begin, the defendant's girlfriend, or Velvet Weeks, another associate of the defendant, accompanied the defendant to the other location. Upon the defendant's return, Weeks would hand Nightingale or another undercover officer a quantity of crack cocaine. On one [occasion,] defendant, apparently unable to acquire the cocaine, returned the money to Nightingale.

A grand jury returned seven indictments against the defendant. Three of the indictments (sale indictments) alleged that the defendant

"DID, IN CONCERT WITH AND AIDED BY ANOTHER, KNOW-INGLY SELL OR DISPENSE A QUANTITY OF THE CON-TROLLED DRUG, CRACK COCAINE." Each of these indictments contained a caption at the top corner of the page that read "ACCOM-PLICE TO SALE OF A CONTROLLED DRUG."

[The defendant] argues that the trial court should have dismissed the sale indictments for failure to allege the proper mens rea. At the close of the State's case, the defendant moved to dismiss the accom-plice indictments, arguing that they were defective because they alleged that he had acted "knowingly" when accomplice liability requires the mens rea of "purposely." The State countered that the "in concert with and aided by another" language of the indictments charged the defendant either as a principal or as an accomplice, and that "knowingly" was the proper mens rea to charge the defendant as a principal. Conceding that he had notice that he was being charged as either a principal or an accomplice, the defendant asserted that the State nevertheless was required to allege that he had acted purposely. The trial court denied the motion.

An indictment is constitutionally sufficient if it provides enough information to apprise the defendant of the charges with adequate specificity to prepare a defense and to be protected against double jeopardy. To this end, the indictment must contain the elements of the offense and enough facts to notify the defendant of the specific charges.

An indictment that alleges principal liability without reference to accomplice liability sufficiently charges the defendant as an accom-plice. Neither the defendant nor the State contests that an indictment charging the defendant solely as an accomplice must allege the appropriate elements of [the accomplice liability statute], including the proper mens rea. The defendant does not argue on appeal that "purposely" is the proper mens rea[.] Rather, acknowledging that the jury could have convicted him as an accomplice had the State charged him as a principal, he argues that the State chose to charge him as an accomplice, and as such was required to allege purposeful conduct.

We have consistently stated, however, that language in an indict-ment alleging that a defendant acted "in concert with" another is sufficient to charge the defendant both as a principal and as an accomplice. Thus, the indictments in this case provided sufficient notice to the defendant that he was being charged as a principal. Indeed, the defendant conceded that he had such notice. That they were captioned as accomplice charges does not alter the explicit language of the indictments that put the defendant on notice that he could be convicted as either a principal or an accomplice. Having sufficiently charged the defendant as a principal, the indictments provided the defendant adequate notice to prepare a defense to principal or accomplice liability. Therefore, we affirm the trial court's denial of the motion to dismiss.

Affirmed.

PROBLEMS

1. *Was Sinbandith an Accomplice?* The *Sinbandith* Court held that the defendant was charged *both* as a principal and an accomplice. If that was *not* the case—if Sinbandith had been charged *only* as an accomplice—what result should the court have reached?

2. *Accomplices and Notice.* Do you think that the court was correct in concluding that the language "in concert with" gave the defendant adequate notice that he was being charged as a principal when the indictment was captioned "ACCOMPLICE TO SALE OF A CONTROLLED DRUG"?

3. *The Scope of Accomplice Responsibility.* Defendant is charged with being an accomplice to murder. The evidence showed that the perpetrator used defendant's shotgun in committing the murder, and that defendant loaned him the shotgun just prior to the murder. Is defendant complicit to murder if defendant loaned the gun based on the perpetrator's assertion that he was going duck hunting? Suppose, instead, that defendant knew that the perpetrator was going to commit a murder?

4. *Jury Instructions.* Ronald Soares and Hollie Suratt were each charged with a *separate* count of assault resulting from their *separate* altercations with a store detective and a store clerk, respectively, who observed them shoplifting. The trial court, *inter alia*, gave the jury an accomplice instruction as to each defendant, *i.e.* the jury was instructed that it could find that each defendant acted as an accomplice in the other defendant's assault. Since each charge involved different facts with different victims, was the giving of an accomplice instruction reversible error? *State v. Soares*, 72 Haw. 278, 815 P.2d 428 (1991).

2. THE ACT OF AIDING OR ENCOURAGING

It is critically important—but often difficult—to determine just how much participatory or encouraging activity on the part of an alleged accomplice is necessary to establish the *actus reus* of aiding or encouraging a principal. It is clear that an individual's "mere presence" at the scene of a crime does not (in and of itself) suffice to make an actor an accomplice. The cases that follow explore what more is required.

LANE v. TEXAS
991 S.W.2d 904 (Tex.Ct.App. 1999).

PER CURIAM.

Appellant James William Lane was convicted of the offense of aggravated robbery of an elderly person, and he appealed.... The

Patricia Shank Eason

Shank & Eason Encouraged by LANE

issue before us [is] whether the trial court erred in refusing Lane's request to instruct the jury that a particular witness, Patricia R., was an accomplice as a matter of fact. [T]he State's evidence revealed that on October 27, 1993, Patricia and Kris Shank, who lived together, went to Lane's house. Lane quickly recruited Patricia, Shank and Anna Eason to rob 71-year-old Hillard Doss. . . . Lane drove Shank and Eason to the scene of the robbery. Patricia was a passenger in Lane's truck at the time. Lane and Patricia waited in the truck while Shank and Eason went to commit the crime. At first the pair returned to the truck without having carried out the plan, but after encouragement from Lane, they went back to Doss's home, again gained entrance, committed the robbery, and returned to Lane's truck for their get-a-way.

At trial, both Patricia and Eason testified against Lane. Shank's testimony from a prior writ hearing was also introduced against Lane. The jury was instructed that Shank and Eason were accomplices as a matter of law. Therefore, the only testimony linking Lane to the crime, except Patricia's, came from accomplices. Because a conviction cannot be had on uncorroborated accomplice testimony, and the only evidence corroborating [Eason's] and Shank's testimony came from Patricia, the issue of whether she is an accomplice is crucial to the case. Were the jury to have found that Patricia was an accomplice, there would be no corroborating evidence upon which a conviction in this case could be upheld against a sufficiency challenge.

The court of criminal appeals set out the general requirements for a finding that a witness is an accomplice witness:

> A person who is merely present at the scene of the offense is not an accomplice; an affirmative act or omission is required. An accomplice participates before, during, or after the commission of the crime—presence at the scene of the offense is not required— though one is not an accomplice for knowing about a crime and failing to disclose it, or even concealing it.

We have also repeatedly stated that a person is an accomplice if he or she could be prosecuted for the same offense as the defendant, or a lesser included offense.

[To] make the determination under the above criteria, the entire record is examined for evidence raising the issue of whether or not a particular witness is an accomplice. In doing so, we eliminate from our consideration the evidence from the accomplice witness and examine the remaining evidence to ascertain if there is inculpatory evidence, that is, evidence of incriminating character, which tends to connect the defendant with the commission of the offense. An accomplice witness charge is required if raised by the evidence. . . .

Patricia was present when Lane told Shank and Eason that he knew of an old man who carried lots of money in cash. Patricia was present when Lane, Shank and Eason planned the crime. Patricia was a passenger in Lane's truck as he drove Shank and Eason to the scene of the crime and let them out of the truck to commit the crime. Patricia remained present in the truck when Shank and Eason returned the first time without committing the robbery, traveled back to Lane's residence in the truck, and were there encouraged by Lane to begin anew and carry out the robbery plan. Patricia was a passenger in the truck when Lane again drove Shank and Eason to the crime scene. Patricia was present when the pair returned to the truck after committing the robbery, and accompanied the trio back to Lane's residence. At the residence, she was present when the other three divided up the cash taken from Doss. She also saw Shank toss his dirty clothing into the bathtub.

Taking these facts as a whole and measuring them against the criteria espoused by the court of criminal appeals, we do not believe that an issue as to whether Patricia was an accomplice was raised by the evidence.... Patricia was present during the entire series of events that night and knew full well what the other three actors were doing. However, Patricia committed no affirmative act in furtherance of the crime. Further, her omission of not stopping the crime and not alerting anyone about the crime was not an omission that our laws have criminalized so that she would become an accomplice by omission. In sum, we disagree with Lane's characterization of the facts as outlined in his brief. There was simply no accomplice witness fact issue raised for the jury to decide. We therefore hold that the trial judge did not err in denying Lane's request for an instruction on Patricia's status as an accomplice.

[The] judgment of the trial court is affirmed.

UNITED STATES v. SANTANA

524 F.3d 851 (8th Cir. 2008).

BENTON, CIRCUIT JUDGE.

[On] May 3, 2006, an Iowa state trooper stopped a vehicle near Onawa, Iowa. Alberto Maldonado–Gutierrez was driving. Negrete was the only passenger. The car was registered to Carlos Lima, an alias of Maldonado. The trooper immediately noticed several air fresheners, which can signal the presence of narcotics. The trooper interviewed Maldonado and Negrete separately. Although both stated they were driving from Omaha to Sioux City, Iowa, they gave inconsistent statements about the purpose of the trip, the specific destination within Sioux City, and their relationship to each other. While being questioned, Negrete appeared extremely nervous—his hands were shaking, he held and repeatedly looked at a religious card, and his heart was beating quickly. After a drug-detection dog alerted to narcotics, officers searched the vehicle. They found meth concealed within the center console (not visible without lifting its plastic liner). A small amount of meth was also found in Negrete's sock. Maldonado and Negrete were arrested.

After Negrete was in custody, Officer Salvador Sanchez questioned him (in Spanish). Negrete said he had made two previous trips to Sioux City with Maldonado, receiving $100 per trip. During one trip, Negrete wrote street names, in English, on a map of Sioux City (found during the search of the vehicle). Negrete said the purpose of the current trip was to collect drug money, and that he expected again to be paid $100. He stated that he did not know their specific destination within Sioux City, and that on the two prior trips, he had been dropped off at public places before Maldonado collected money. Although he had been warned that Maldonado was involved in drugs, Negrete repeatedly insisted that he had never seen Maldonado with drugs and denied knowing meth was in the vehicle roughly 19 times.

Negrete was charged with one count of possession with intent to distribute meth. At trial, the government presented the testimony of the trooper, Officer Sanchez, and another officer who assisted with the search of the vehicle. Negrete was the only defense witness. [He] reiterated he had no knowledge that the meth was in the vehicle.

The jury found Negrete guilty. The district court granted his motion for judgment of acquittal, finding insufficient evidence to prove beyond a reasonable doubt that Negrete knew meth was in the vehicle. The government appeals.

[The] government argues that the evidence at trial was sufficient for a reasonable jury to find Negrete guilty of possession of meth with intent to distribute, based on an aiding-and-abetting theory. "To sustain a conviction for aiding and abetting with intent to distribute drugs, the government must prove: (1) that the defendant associated himself with the unlawful venture; (2) that he participated in it as something he wished to bring about; and (3) that he sought by his actions to make it succeed." Mere association between a principal and the defendant is not sufficient, nor is mere presence at the scene and knowledge that a crime was to be committed. However, "jurors can be assumed to know that criminals rarely welcome innocent persons as witnesses to serious crimes and rarely seek to perpetrate felonies before larger-than-necessary audiences."

[Negrete,] echoing the district court, asserts there is no evidence that he knowingly acted to aid possession-with-intent-to-distribute (the second element), or that he intended to possess controlled substances with the intent to distribute (the third element).

[The] government focuses on the traditional elements of aiding-and-abetting: the defendant (1) associated himself with the unlawful venture; (2) participated in it as something he wished to bring about; and (3) sought by his actions to make it succeed. [The] government is not required to prove that the defendant possessed the controlled substance. [In] this aiding-and-abetting case, the government must prove Negrete associated himself with the unlawful venture, participated in it as something he wished to bring about, and sought by his actions to make it succeed. The evidence must show that Negrete shared in Maldonado's criminal intent.

Viewing the evidence most favorably to the verdict, there was sufficient circumstantial evidence for a reasonable jury to conclude that Negrete aided and abetted possession with intent to distribute meth. The government presented evidence that Negrete: (1) knew Maldonado was a drug dealer; (2) knew the purpose of the trip to Sioux City was to collect drug money; (3) was to receive $100 for the trip; (4) had previously accompanied Maldonado on two trips to Sioux City, receiving payment for each; (5) lied to officers at the scene (at Maldonado's request) and in post-*Miranda* statements; (6) appeared extremely nervous during the entire stop; and (7) had meth in his sock. This evidence was sufficient for a reasonable jury to conclude that Negrete shared Maldonado's criminal intent by associating with and participating in the unlawful venture and attempting to make it succeed.

The judgment is reversed, and the case remanded to reinstate the jury verdict.

PROBLEMS

1. *Reconciling Santana and Lane.* Is the analysis of the law in the *Lane* and *Santana* decisions consistent with respect to the determination whether a passenger in a car can be an accomplice? What accounts for the difference in result in the two decisions?

2. *Patricia's Participation.* Do you agree that in *Lane* there is no evidence that Patricia did *anything* other than be present as the robbery took place? Does it matter that the court acknowledged that Lane "recruited" Patricia to participate in the robbery and that she "went along for the ride?" Explain.

3. *Uncorroborated Accomplice Testimony.* Why do you suppose that Texas follows the rule that "a conviction cannot be had on uncorroborated accomplice testimony?" Does that rule make sense? What if there were no eyewitnesses? Does that mean that there could be no conviction? Explain.

4. *Accomplice Conviction for Patricia.* Do you think that it made any difference in the disposition of the *Lane* case that the reason the court was deciding Patricia's accomplice status was only to determine whether her testimony was admissible to uphold Lane's conviction? If Patricia had been charged and convicted as an accomplice as Negrete was in *Santana*, do you think that—on this same evidence—the appellate court would have upheld her conviction?

5. *The Judge and the Seducer.* R.C. Ross seduced Annie Skelton, a sister of the Skelton brothers (Robert, John, James and Walter), as well as Judge Tally's wife. The Skeltons and Tally learned about the seduction from letters written by Ross to Annie Skelton. The Skelton brothers immediately decided to kill Ross. In an effort to escape, Ross left town in a hack headed for Stevenson (18 miles away), intending to catch a train to Chattanooga. The Skelton brothers set off in pursuit of Ross and eventually succeeded in killing him. When the Skelton brothers left, Judge Tally knew that they intended to kill Ross. Is Judge Tally guilty of complicity under any of the following facts:

a. He silently wishes and hopes that the Skelton brothers kill Ross, but does nothing to help.

b. He tells other friends that he hopes that the Skelton brothers kill Ross.

c. He paid for the rental of a horse on which one of the Skelton brothers rode.

d. He spent several hours at the telegraph office in order to prevent others from sending a telegraph to Stevenson to warn Ross. However, no one showed up or tried to send a telegram to warn Ross.

e. He actually prevented Ross' brother from sending a telegram warning Ross that the Skelton brothers were pursuing him.

f. He sent a telegram to friends in Stevenson asking them to make sure that Ross was not warned that the Skeltons were in pursuit.

State ex rel. Martin v. Tally, 102 Ala. 25, 15 So. 722 (1894).

6. *Accomplice Liability and Ineffective Assistance.* In the prior problem, for any acts which you deem sufficient to impose accomplice liability on Judge Tally, does it matter whether the acts actually helped the Skelton brothers bring about Ross' death? For example, suppose that:

a. Judge Tally spent several hours at the telegraph office (in an effort to prevent anyone from sending a telegram to warn Ross), but no one tried to send a telegram.

b. Although Judge Tally sent a telegram to friends urging them to make sure that Ross was not warned about the Skelton brothers, the friends never tried to warn Ross.

7. *Accomplice Liability for Mothers?* Defendant's boyfriend brutally shook her 3–month old son for three minutes, thereby causing the boy's death. During the shaking, defendant stood by doing nothing. In regard to defendant's liability:

a. Is she an accomplice to manslaughter (defined as a reckless homicide)?

b. Might she be responsible for the death on a non-accomplice theory?

See State v. Walden, 306 N.C. 466, 293 S.E.2d 780 (1982).

8. *More on Accomplice Liability.* Defendant shot at his girlfriend and then threw the gun away near his apartment complex. Later, he returned to retrieve the gun, but he could not find it. He blamed a security guard for taking it. Defendant told two of his friends, Richardson and Waller, while he was visiting Richardson's apartment in the same complex, that he was angry at the security guard for taking his gun, and that he was "going to kill his ass." Defendant asked them to go with him to shoot the guard, but neither of them would do so. In fact, Richardson tried to talk defendant out of shooting the security guard. Defendant then left Richardson's apartment while Richardson and Waller stayed in the apartment. At around 2:00 a.m., they heard shots being fired outside. Defendant then returned to the apartment, holding a rifle, which was smoking. Defendant said, "I got him," and "That's the lowest I can ever go." Defendant was charged with first-degree murder for shooting the security guard to death. Were Richardson and Waller the defendant's accomplices? *California v. Hypolite*, 2005 WL 758440 (Cal.App. 2 Dist. 2005).

NOTE

The M.P.C. and complicity. Consider the M.P.C.'s provisions relating to accomplice liability:

§ 2.06. Liability for Conduct of Another; Complicity.

(1) A person is guilty of an offense if it is committed by his own conduct or by the conduct of another person for which he is legally accountable, or both.

(2) A person is legally accountable for the conduct of another person when:

(a) acting with the kind of culpability that is sufficient for the commission of the offense, he causes an innocent or irresponsible person to engage in such conduct; or

(b) he is made accountable for the conduct of such other person by the Code or by the law defining the offense; or

(c) he is an accomplice of such other person in the commission of the offense.

(3) A person is an accomplice of another person in the commission of an offense if:

(a) with the purpose of promoting or facilitating the commission of the offense, he

(i) solicits such other person to commit it, or

(ii) aids or agrees or attempts to aid such other person in planning or committing it, or

(iii) having a legal duty to prevent the commission of the offense, fails to make proper effort so to do; or

(b) his conduct is expressly declared by law to establish his complicity.

(4) When causing a particular result is an element of an offense, an accomplice in the conduct causing such result is an accomplice in the commission of that offense if he acts with the kind of culpability, if any, with respect to that result that is sufficient for the commission of the offense.

(5) A person who is legally incapable of committing a particular offense himself may be guilty thereof if it is committed by the conduct of another person for which he is legally accountable, unless such liability is inconsistent with the purpose of the provision establishing his incapacity.

(6) Unless otherwise provided by the Code or by the law defining the offense, a person is not an accomplice in an offense committed by another person if:

(a) he is a victim of that offense; or

(b) the offense is so defined that his conduct is inevitably incident to its commission; or

(c) he terminates his complicity prior to the commission of the offense and

(i) wholly deprives it of effectiveness in the commission of the offense; or

(ii) gives timely warning to the law enforcement authorities or otherwise makes proper effort to prevent the commission of the offense.

(7) An accomplice may be convicted on proof of the commission of the offense and of his complicity therein, though the person claimed to have committed the offense has not been prosecuted or convicted or has been convicted of a different offense or degree of offense or has an immunity to prosecution or conviction or has been acquitted.

NEW HAMPSHIRE v. MERRITT

143 N.H. 714, 738 A.2d 343 (1999).

BRODERICK, J.

[In] December 1995, the defendant [Kevin Merritt] and his girlfriend, Kelly Higgins, had been living together for eighteen months. Higgins was in dire financial straits and did not have any source of income. On December 18, 1995, they went shopping and Higgins made numerous, expensive purchases with credit cards belonging to Frances Driscoll and Marjorie Dannis.

That afternoon, at approximately 2:00 p.m., Driscoll noticed that her purse, which contained her Jordan Marsh and Visa credit cards, was missing. Driscoll was the only person authorized to use the cards.

At 2:30 p.m., Higgins used Driscoll's Jordan Marsh card to buy jewelry at the store in the Fox Run Mall. Several days later, a sales clerk gave a written statement to the police that "[o]n 12/18, in the fine jewelry department in Jordan Marsh, [Higgins] was accompanied by [the defendant] and made a purchase using a credit card" belonging to Driscoll. There was no other evidence concerning the jewelry purchase.

Around 3:17 p.m. on December 18, after the defendant tried on clothes at American Eagle Outfitters in the mall, Higgins purchased men's pants and shirts with Driscoll's Visa card. The sales clerk testified that the defendant "was standing right next to [Higgins]" while the sale was taking place and that the defendant basically "did all the talking." Later that afternoon, the defendant and Higgins looked at a men's gold bracelet at Hannoush Jewelers in the mall. The sales clerk testified that she had "a long conversation" with the defendant about the bracelet and that they "went back and forth" over the price for twenty-five minutes. The defendant successfully negotiated a lower price, and Higgins bought the bracelet with the Visa card. Subsequently, Higgins and the defendant patronized Whitehall Jewelers [and] said they were interested in buying the defendant a gold bracelet. The sales clerk testified that she interacted principally with the defendant and that he was interested in negotiating a lower price. The clerk obtained the manager's approval to reduce the price, which made the defendant "very, very excited." He shook her hand "for helping him pick out such a real nice piece that he was very, very anxious to have." At 3:52 p.m., Higgins bought the bracelet with Driscoll's Visa card.

The defendant and Higgins then proceeded to Prelude Jewelers in downtown Portsmouth. The store owner testified that the defendant and Higgins had been in the store previously and admired a women's diamond ring. During the December 18 visit, the owner heard the defendant tell Higgins he wanted to buy her the ring but that he would need to use her credit card. At 4:53 p.m., Higgins again used Driscoll's Visa card and purchased the ring.

Around 5:30 p.m., a short distance from Prelude Jewelers, a man stole Marjorie Dannis' purse from her car. Her purse contained her Visa and Mastercard, which only she was authorized to use.

At 7:30 p.m., a male matching the defendant's description tried on a pair of men's work boots at J.C. Penney in the Fox Run Mall, and the woman with him purchased them with Dannis' Mastercard. At 7:44 p.m., the defendant and Higgins purchased a men's diamond ring from the store's jewelry department, with Higgins using Dannis' Mastercard. The sales clerk spoke mainly with the defendant. When the sale was completed, the clerk gave the defendant, who identified himself as "Kevin Johnson," a diamond certificate. At trial, the clerk explained that the individual named in the certificate was entitled to free diamond cleanings and to trade the diamond for one of greater value in the future. When Dannis' purse was later recovered at a gas station in Portsmouth, it contained a torn diamond certificate and part of a receipt.

Based on this evidence, the defendant was indicted on four charges of fraudulent use of credit cards, alleging that he acted in concert with Higgins: the first count was for the Jordan Marsh jewelry; the second count was for the purchases at American Eagle, Hannoush Jewelers, and Whitehall Jewelers; the third count related to the ring purchased at Prelude Jewelers; and the fourth count identified the ring bought at J.C. Penney. The jury found the defendant guilty on all four counts, and this appeal followed.

[The] indictments alleged that the defendant "act[ed] in concert" with Higgins in the fraudulent use of the Driscoll and Dannis credit cards. The trial court instructed the jury that "acting in concert" meant accomplice liability. Under our Criminal Code, a person may be legally accountable for the conduct of another person if "[h]e is an accomplice of such other person in the commission of [an] offense." A person is an accomplice if, "[w]ith the purpose of promoting or facilitating the commission of [an] offense, he . . . aids or agrees or attempts to aid such other person in planning or committing it."

In reviewing the sufficiency of the evidence, "we must determine whether, based upon all the evidence and all reasonable inferences from it, when considered in a light most favorable to the State, any rational trier of fact could have found beyond a reasonable doubt that the defendant was a voluntary and active participant" in each of the fraudulent credit card transactions.

The defendant first contends that no rational jury could have found him guilty as an accomplice for the Jordan Marsh jewelry purchase because he was merely present in the store and did not take affirmative steps to satisfy the actus reus requirement. We agree. The crime of accomplice liability necessitates "some active participation by the accomplice." Mere presence at the scene of a crime is insufficient. The defendant's presence, however, can be sufficient if it was intended to, and does, aid the primary actor. Thus, the defendant's presence may constitute aiding and abetting when it is shown to encourage the perpetrator or facilitate the perpetrator's unlawful deed. Moreover, the circumstances surrounding the defendant's presence at the scene may warrant a jury inference beyond a reasonable doubt that he sought to make the crime succeed.

The State relies on *State v. Laudarowicz*, 142 N.H. 1, 694 A.2d 980 (1997), to argue that the defendant's act of accompanying Higgins to Jordan Marsh, given the relationship between the two, was sufficient to constitute "encouragement" and trigger accomplice liability. *Laudarowicz*, however, is inapplicable because the defendant in that case conceded that he aided the principal and challenged only the evidence of his intent. Moreover, we relied upon substantial evidence other than the defendant's presence at the scene to support his convictions. Here, there is no evidence that the defendant did anything other than accompany Higgins to the Jordan Marsh store. The record does not indicate where the defendant was when the jewelry was purchased, nor does it reflect that he did or said anything which could be construed as aiding Higgins.

The State also relies on evidence of the defendant's other conduct on the day in question to support the inference that he engaged in similar conduct at Jordan Marsh. Assuming that the defendant's subsequent conduct might be relevant to his intent, we conclude that the State failed to present sufficient facts to satisfy the actus reus element of accomplice liability. Accordingly, we reverse the defendant's conviction with respect to count one.

The defendant next contends that no rational jury could have found him guilty as an accomplice for the remaining transactions because he did not participate in them. He asserts no actus reus was proven. [We] disagree.

With respect to actus reus, the jury could have found that the defendant aided Higgins in these other transactions. In each transaction, the defendant dominated the exchange with the sales clerk, especially at the moment the sale was completed. Moreover, the defendant selected, or assisted Higgins in selecting, the merchandise that was ultimately purchased. Although the evidence shows that the defendant did not present the cards or sign any of the credit card slips, we are satisfied that the jury could have found he aided Higgins in committing fraud by picking out the merchandise and distracting the sales clerks from closely examining the credit cards while the merchandise was being purchased.

[Furthermore,] we conclude that a rational jury could have reasonably decided, viewing the totality of the evidence in the State's favor, that all rational inferences other than guilt had been excluded beyond a reasonable doubt. The defendant and Higgins had a relationship and were living together. Moreover, the credit cards were used six times in six stores, over a period of about five and a quarter hours, for merchandise totaling over $2,600. In addition, jewelry and clothes purchased fit the defendant or were items the defendant expressed an intent to give to Higgins. Finally, the defendant gave a false name on the diamond certificate that accompanied the purchase of a men's diamond ring.

[Affirmed] in part; reversed in part; remanded.

PROBLEMS

1. *Merritt as Accomplice.* Do you agree that there is no evidence of an accomplice actus reus sufficient to tie Merritt to the Jordan Marsh episode? Isn't the evidence clear (or, put another way, couldn't a reasonable jury find from the evidence) that Merritt and Higgins were on a shopping spree together with stolen credit cards? Explain.

2. *Merritt's Ignorance.* With respect to the other transactions, would Merritt be guilty if he simply did not know that Higgins was using stolen credit cards? Is there any evidence at all that he did know? Does it matter in this analysis that Merritt and Higgins were living together? Should it matter? Explain.

3. *Unused Burglary Tools.* Washington Tazwell and Wilson Kealey were convicted of the burglary of a barn with intent to steal, and Zeke Hall was charged as an accessory before the fact. The evidence shows that Hall provided Tarwell and Kealey with burglary tools before they went to the barn, but that the two found more convenient and more suitable tools when they arrived. As a result, they did not use Hall's tools. Is Hall nonetheless an accomplice to the burglary? Suppose that defendant claims that he was not involved in a burglary, but simply "happened" to be on the premises (in a way that looked suspicious)? *State v. Tazwell,* 30 La. Ann. 884 (1878).

4. *The Intoxicated Driver and the Borrowed Car.* Defendant loaned his car to a friend who he knew was legally intoxicated, and then went to bed for the evening. An hour later, while defendant was sound asleep in his bed, the friend caused an accident that resulted in the death of a passenger in another car. Consider whether defendant is an accomplice to the crime of:

   a. Murder (defined as a purposeful or knowing homicide).

   b. Manslaughter (defined as a reckless or negligent homicide).

See People v. Marshall, 362 Mich. 170, 106 N.W.2d 842 (1961).

5. *Narcotics Information.* An undercover police officer told defendant that he was interested in buying "hash." In an effort to be helpful, defendant told the officer that a man by the name of Craig "deals quite heavily in narcotics." Defendant gave the officer Craig's address and told the officer to go to that address. The officer succeeded in purchasing narcotics from Craig who was arrested and charged with narcotics trafficking. Can defendant be convicted of complicity? Would it make any difference regarding defendant's criminal liability whether:

   a. Defendant was working with the seller and receiving a kickback on all sales?

   b. Defendant was simply trying to help the buyer find what he wanted?

See People v. Gordon, 32 N.Y.2d 62, 295 N.E.2d 777, 343 N.Y.S.2d 103 (App. 1973).

6. *The Illegal Saxophonist.* A foreign national, a famous saxophonist, is given permission to enter England on condition that he take no employment, paid or unpaid. In violation of the condition, the saxophonist performs for compensation at a local night club. Which of the following people have committed the actus reus of accomplice liability (assuming, of course, that they have the necessary mens rea):

    a. Customers who go to the club, pay the admission price, and applaud between sets.

    b. A magazine owner and editor who attends the concert as a spectator, having paid for his ticket, who does not applaud, but does not protest. Afterwards he published in his magazine a most laudatory description, fully illustrated, of this concert.

See Wilcox v. Jeffrey [1951] 1 All E.R. 464.

EXERCISE

Accomplices to Rape. You are an assistant district attorney in Allegheny County (Pittsburgh), Pennsylvania. Pittsburgh police officers have reported to you that a victim, Jane Roe, was raped in a pool hall by two men: John Smith and Joe Doe. While the rapes were taking place, three other individuals were present: a bartender, Jerry Ames, and two individuals drinking at the bar, Sally Baker and Bruce Cox. Ames watched the rapes take place and yelled at the rapists to "stop," but when they did not listen to him, he did absolutely nothing to stop them from committing these crimes nor did he make any attempt to call the police; Baker watched the rapes and yelled at Smith and Doe to encourage them to commit the assaults (e.g., "Give it to her!"; "Hey, pals, she's lovin' that!"; etc.); Cox watched the rapes and said nothing. Prepare a short (2–3 pages) memorandum to the District Attorney recommending to her whether or not (and why) Ames, Baker and Cox should be charged as accessories in the rape of Roe.

3. THE INTENT TO PROMOTE OR FACILITATE A CRIME

The *mens rea* of accomplice liability is often described in the case law as having two separate (and independent) components: (1) the intent to assist a principal actor in committing the target act; and (2) the intent that the principal actually commit that act. In most jurisdictions, this intent can be (and often is) implied from a person's actions.

HAWAII v. SOARES
72 Haw. 278, 815 P.2d 428 (1991).

LUM, CHIEF JUSTICE.

[On] August 22, 1989, Holiday Mart store detective Mitchell Tam (Tam) observed appellants [Ronald Soares and Hollie Suratt] placing several cartons of cigarettes into a shopping cart. Tam then saw Soares place the cigarettes into a large handbag. Appellants left the store, with Suratt carrying the bag, without paying for the cigarettes.

Outside of the store, Tam approached appellants, identified himself, showed his badge, and told appellants that they were under citizen's arrest for shoplifting. As Soares turned towards him, Tam grabbed Soares. During their struggle, the back of Soares' head hit Tam in the mouth causing Tam to release Soares. Soares then fled.

While struggling with Soares, Tam instructed Conway Marks (Marks), a Holiday Mart clerk who was assisting Tam, to stop Suratt from leaving the area. Marks blocked Suratt's escape by standing directly in front of her path. After unsuccessfully attempting to push Marks out of her way, Suratt tricked Marks into looking the other direction and then fled with the bag.

[We] conclude that the court's accomplice jury instruction was a misstatement of Hawaii law. The accomplice instruction provided:

> All persons who are present and participate in the commission of a crime [are] responsible for the acts of each other done or made in furtherance of the crime.

> It is not necessary to prove that each one committed all of the acts of the crime.

> Each person who does one act which is an ingredient of the crime or immediately connected with it is as guilty as if he or she committed the whole crime with his or her own hands.

[Section] 702–222 requires that to be guilty as an accomplice, a person must act with the intent of promoting or facilitating the commission of the crime. The court's accomplice instruction clearly does not contain such a mens rea element. The court's instruction implies that a person merely needs to be present and participate in an act of the crime to be guilty as an accomplice. Under the court's accomplice instruction, the State is relieved from its burden of proving that appellants acted with the requisite intent.

[Accordingly,] appellants' convictions are reversed and the cases are remanded for new trials.

PROBLEMS

1. *Soares Result.* If the jury in *Soares* had been properly instructed on intent, what do you think the result would have been in this case? Explain.

2. *Criminal Intent.* What acts, if any, gave rise to an implication of criminal intent in *Soares*? Explain.

MARSHALL v. MORGAN

260 Fed.Appx. 789 (6th Cir. 2008), *cert. denied*, 129 S.Ct. 90 (Oct. 6, 2008).

DAMON J. KEITH, CIRCUIT JUDGE.

Petitioner, Tyrone P. Marshall, appeals from the April 17, 2006 decision of the United States District Court for the Western District of Kentucky denying his petition for a writ of habeas corpus. For the reasons stated below, we Affirm.

Petitioner Marshall was convicted in the Oldham County Circuit Court (Kentucky) for murder, criminal attempt to commit murder, and first-degree burglary. He was sentenced to life in prison without the possibility of parole for twenty-five years for the murder conviction. He was also sentenced to twenty years each on the attempted murder and first-degree burglary convictions, each to run concurrently with the life sentence.

On April 5, 1996, three men—the Petitioner, Mark Downey, and Richard Strode—broke into the home of Joseph and Sharon Fink in Trimble County, Kentucky. Mr. Downey and Petitioner entered through the front door and knocked over Mr. Fink, who was sitting in a chair watching television. Mr. Strode entered the residence through the back door after cutting the phone line. When Mrs. Fink emerged from her bedroom, she was taken to the kitchen, where her arms were bound behind her back with duct tape. Downey and one of the other men then led Mr. Fink around the house, forcing him to show them where he kept his jewelry and cash.

After finding the cash and jewelry, the men took Mr. Fink into the kitchen and bound his hands in front of him with duct tape. Downey placed a pillow over Mr. Fink's head and shot him when Fink attempted to get up. He then shot Mrs. Fink. Mr. Fink survived; Mrs. Fink did not.

[The] three men and Mark Downey's wife, Sharon, who had driven them to the Finks's home, were all indicted . . . for murder, attempted murder, and first-degree burglary. [Mark] Downey pled guilty to the charged offenses . . . and was sentenced to life in prison without the possibility of parole for twenty-five years on the murder charge and twenty years each on the burglary and attempted murder charges, each to run concurrently with the life sentence. Petitioner waived his right to a jury trial. He was found guilty of intentional murder, attempted murder, and first-degree burglary and was given the same sentences as Mark Downey.

The Supreme Court of Kentucky affirmed[.]

Petitioner commenced this habeas action in the United States District Court for the Western District of Kentucky[.] Because Petitioner did not fire the shots that resulted in the murder of the victim, he disputes whether the facts in the record below are sufficient to warrant a murder conviction. [Judge] John G. Heyburn adopted the report and dismissed the habeas petition. Petitioner then appealed to this Court.

This Court evaluates petitions for writ of habeas corpus to determine whether the state court decision was either (1) contrary to clearly established federal law as determined by the Supreme Court of the United States or (2) involved an unreasonable application of clearly established federal law as determined by the Supreme Court of the United States.

[Petitioner] contends that because he did not fire the gun at the murder scene and because he did not know Downey would shoot Mr. and Mrs. Fink, he should not have been found guilty of intentional murder.

[The] trial court applied KRS 502.020, which provides that a defendant can be held liable for actions of another under two circumstances: (1) a defendant is criminally liable for "complicity to the result" when he acts with the same degree of culpability with respect to the result that would be sufficient for the commission of the offense; and (2) a defendant can be found criminally liable for "complicity to the act" if he intended that the victim be killed. The fact-finder may infer intent from the actions of the defendant or the circumstances surrounding those actions, or from the defendant's knowledge.

The record in this case indicates that (1) Marshall agreed to participate in the burglary, (2) Marshall knew Downey had a gun and may have himself been armed; (3) Marshall told his daughters' babysitter that he and Mark Downey entered through the front door and Richard Strode came in through the back door and "they cut the phone lines, they taped them up, and they shot them;" (4) Marshall admitted knocking Mr. Fink out of his chair and kicking him in the head when Fink tried to grab a gun; and (5) Kim Long, Mr. Strode's girlfriend, testified that Marshall told Downey that he did not want to be present when the couple was shot and that he did not want to see it.

Based on this evidence, it was reasonable for the Supreme Court of Kentucky to conclude that a rational trier of fact could be convinced beyond a reasonable doubt that Marshall intended that Mrs. Fink be killed. The trial judge reasonably inferred from Marshall's actions and statements that he knew and intended that the victims would be shot. Under Kentucky law, circumstantial evidence is sufficient to determine complicity.

[Because] the record in the instant case shows that Petitioner acted in complicity with the results of the burglary, we uphold the decision of the lower court.

PROBLEMS

1. *The Burglary.* David Vaillancourt and a friend, Richard Burhoe, were seen standing on the front porch of a home, ringing the doorbell and conversing with one another for ten minutes. When there was no answer at the door, the pair walked around the side of the house where Burhoe allegedly attempted to break into a basement window. Tipped off by a suspicious neighbor, the police arrived and arrested Vaillancourt and Burhoe as they were fleeing the scene. Burhoe is charged with attempted burglary. If you are the prosecutor, what kind of proof would you use to show that Vaillancourt was an accomplice? If you are the defense attorney, how might you respond to that evidence? *See New Hampshire v. Vaillancourt,* 122 N.H. 1153, 453 A.2d 1327 (1982).

2. *The Mother and the Murdering Husband.* Carol Hoffman, was murdered by her husband David Hoffman because she refused to have sexual relations with him. While he was choking her, he began to believe he was "doing the right thing" and that, to get "the evil out of her," he had to dismember her body. After Carol was dead, David decided to dismember her body in the bathtub. Is David's mother an accomplice if:

> a. She had strained relations with Carol and told friends that she hated her. On the morning of the murder, David told his mother that he was going to "put Carol to sleep" and then he would have to dispose of the body. The mother replied that it would "be for the best." (Suppose further that David later testified that his mother thought that he was "kidding.")

> b. During the actual murder, the mother was asleep. However, after Carol was dead, the mother was adamant about shielding her granddaughter (the couple's older daughter) from witnessing the dismembering should she awake and want to use the bathroom. As a result, the mother decided to lie on a couch near the bathroom and keep watch.

> c. Suppose that, instead of trying to protect the granddaughter from the trauma of witnessing the dismemberment, the mother was trying to protect her son by preventing her granddaughter from becoming a witness to the crime. As a result, the mother decided to sleep on a couch near the granddaughter's room in case she awoke.

State v. Ulvinen, 313 N.W.2d 425 (Minn. 1981).

3. *Proof Problems.* In the prior problem, what kinds of proof might suffice to implicate the mother as an accomplice? What kinds of proof might tend to exonerate her from accomplice liability?

4. *The Murdered Father and Husband.* Defendant Virginia's husband, Joe Davis, died of a shotgun wound outside his home. Although Will Day, defendant's acquaintance, committed the killing, defendant was charged with complicity. The evidence revealed that defendant had repeatedly expressed a

desire to have her husband killed (claiming that he beat her), and that she offered Day money to do the killing. Defendant's daughter, Angel, who was sexually involved with Day, independently asked Day to kill Davis because he was sexually assaulting her. When asked why he killed Davis, Day said: "Well, some of me wants to say about what he done to Angel, but I can't say that was the only reason. I don't believe if Virginia and them would have kept pressuring me about killing Joe or having someone kill Joe, I don't think I would have done it." An inmate at the jail testified that he asked defendant whether Virginia had anything to do with the killing of her husband. Day said, "No. She didn't have anything to do with it." On these facts, is defendant guilty as an accomplice? *State v. Davis*, 319 N.C. 620, 356 S.E.2d 340 (1987).

    5. *Customers and Spectators.* Reconsider the case of the famous saxophonist who was given permission to enter England on condition that he take no employment, paid or unpaid. In violation of the condition, the saxophonist performs for compensation at a local night club. If the state wants to charge customers with "complicity" in the immigration violation, what will it need to show in terms of their mens rea? Does it seem fair or appropriate to impose accomplice liability on customers and spectators? But, in some or many instances, is the customer's participation a necessary predicate to the event? In some areas, although cock fighting is illegal (because it is deemed to be cruel to the animals who are bloodied and injured by the fights), some individuals still stage cock fights. Are they likely to do so without the customer base that pays for the tickets and, in many cases, engages in illegal betting? *See Wilcox v. Jeffrey* [1951] 1 All E.R. 464.

    6. *The Housekeeper.* Gudelia Ramirez was found in a residence with a large amount of heroin when police arrived executing a lawful search warrant for evidence related to a large-scale heroin-distribution operation. The State's evidence showed that Ramirez was aware of the existence of the operation and cooked and cleaned for the group that ran it. She was, for example, cooking dinner in the kitchen when heroin was cut and packaged on the kitchen table.

    a. Is this sufficient to establish her culpability (through constructive possession) as an accomplice to the crime of possession of heroin?

    b. What if, instead of paying Ramirez an hourly rate, she is paid a percentage of the profits?

Washington v. Amezola, 49 Wash.App. 78, 741 P.2d 1024 (1987).

PEOPLE v. KAPLAN
76 N.Y.2d 140, 556 N.E.2d 415, 556 N.Y.S.2d 976 (1990).

TITONE, JUDGE.

    Defendant Murray Kaplan was convicted of first degree criminal sale of a controlled substance because of his involvement in a narcotics network which operated out of a garment business office located in the Empire State Building. His primary contention on appeal is that although the culpable state required for the commission of this crime is "knowledge," the trial court should have instructed the jury that defendant could not be held liable as an accomplice unless he acted with the specific intent to sell a controlled substance. We conclude that such an instruction is not required and that, accordingly, the conviction should be affirmed.

From May 1, 1986 to February 17, 1987, the police investigated a cocaine ring which apparently operated out of an office maintained by defendant's cousin, Mike Kaplan, in the Empire State Building. Detective Janis Grasso, posing as a drug courier for someone named "Ronnie" from Atlantic City, engaged in a series of transactions, primarily with Mike Kaplan. The charges against defendant were based on his actions on October 15, 1986, when, pursuant to a prior phone call, Grasso went to Kaplan's office to purchase 10 ounces of cocaine and found Kaplan, Kaplan's brother and defendant present. After introducing Grasso to the other two men, Mike Kaplan told defendant "to take care of the young lady." Defendant got off the couch, walked to a file cabinet in the room, removed a manila envelope from it, and placed it on the desk in front of Grasso. She in turn took out $15,000 in prerecorded buy money and placed it on the table. Defendant picked up the money, took it over to the table and began counting it. At the same time, Grasso opened the manila envelope, took out a zip-lock plastic bag, and placed the drugs into her purse remarking that "it looks nice."

Defendant was subsequently charged with, inter alia, criminal sale of a controlled substance. Before the case was submitted to the jury, defense counsel asked the court to instruct the jurors that in order to convict defendant as an accomplice they must find that he had "specific intent" to sell a controlled substance, and that he had to "share the intent or purpose of the principal actors." The court denied defendant's request, noting that the mental culpability required for criminal sale was not "intent" but "knowledge" and, further, that the standard charge for accomplice liability requires proof that the defendant "intentionally aided" the other participants. Following the court's charge, which tracked the language of the applicable statutes, the jury found defendant guilty of criminal sale. The Appellate Division, First Department, affirmed defendant's conviction, without opinion, and leave to appeal was granted by a Judge of this court.

Penal Law § 20.00 provides that a person may be held criminally liable as an accomplice when he performs certain acts and does so "with the mental culpability required for the commission" of the substantive crime. Despite this language, defendant argues [that] even though the substantive crime with which he was charged—criminal sale of a controlled substance—requires only knowledge,[3] the statute should be construed to require proof of a more exacting mens rea, namely specific intent to sell.

Under section 2 of the former Penal Law, a person could be convicted as a principal if he "aid[ed and abetted in the commission of a crime]". The former Penal Law, however, did not specifically state what type of acts were required for conviction. Consequently, in order to prevent the imposition of criminal liability for the principal's crime on someone who may have been merely present, the courts required proof that the aider or abetter " 'share[d] the intent or purpose of the principal actor'."

Defendant's argument is that this "shared intent or purpose" test required proof [that] he acted with the specific intent to sell cocaine. However, any lack of clarity that previously existed under section 2 of the former Penal Law was eliminated by the adoption of section 20.00 of the revised Penal Law, which specifies that an accomplice must have acted with the "mental culpability required for the commission" of the particular crime. Further, we have already construed section 20.00 as not requiring specific intent within the meaning of Penal Law § 15.05(1) when the substantive crime does not involve such intent. Finally, the "shared intent or purpose" language from our earlier cases [cannot] be read for the proposition, advanced by defendant, that a specific wish to commit the principal's substantive crime is required in all circumstances, including those involving substantive crimes with mental states other than that defined in Penal Law § 15.05(1). Indeed, the "shared intent or purpose" test set forth in the case law merely establishes that acts undertaken in relative innocence and without a conscious design to advance the principal's crime will not support a conviction for accomplice liability. The same conclusion, however, is implicit in the specific requirement in Penal Law § 20.00 that the accomplice "solicit, request, command, importune, or intentionally aid" the principal, since all of the delineated acts import goal-directed conduct.

The distinction made here is a subtle, but important, one. It is well illustrated by our holding in *People v. Flayhart*[, 72 N.Y.2d 737, 536 N.Y.S.2d 727, 533 N.E.2d 657], in which we concluded that the defendants could be guilty as accomplices to the crime of criminally negligent homicide under Penal Law § 125.10, even though neither defendant had the victim's death as a "conscious object". This result flowed naturally from the fact that both defendants could be found to have "fail[ed] to perceive a substantial and unjustifiable risk" of death—the "mental culpability required for the crime"—and that

---

3. Penal Law § 220.43 provides, in pertinent part, that "[a] person is guilty of criminal sale of a controlled substance in the first degree when he knowingly and unlawfully sells". A person acts knowingly "when he is aware that his conduct is of such nature or that such circumstance exists". In contrast, a person acts intentionally "when his conscious objective is to cause such result or to engage in such conduct".

both engaged in deliberate conduct to advance the common enterprise, i.e., the egregious neglect of the victim.

[For] the same reasons, we reject defendant's alternative argument that the crime of which he was convicted under the court's charge is indistinguishable from second degree criminal facilitation[.] A person is guilty of second degree criminal facilitation when "believing it probable that he is rendering aid to a person who intends to commit a class A felony, he engages in conduct which provides such person with means or opportunity for the commission thereof and which in fact aids such person to commit such class A felony". This statute was enacted to provide an additional tool in the prosecutorial arsenal for situations where the "facilitator" knowingly aided the commission of a crime but did not possess the mental culpability required for commission of the substantive crime. Additionally an "accomplice" and a "facilitator" are distinguishable in that the accomplice must have intentionally aided the principal in bringing forth a result, while the facilitator need only have provided assistance "believing it probable" that he was rendering aid.

In defendant's case there was sufficient evidence for the jury to find that, knowing the substance in question was cocaine, defendant intentionally aided Mike Kaplan by delivering it to Detective Grasso. The evidence established that after being asked by Mike Kaplan to "take care of" Detective Grasso, defendant immediately went to a file cabinet drawer, retrieved a package containing cocaine, and gave the package to Grasso in exchange for money which defendant immediately began to count. That defendant neither negotiated nor arranged the transactions does not affect his liability as an accomplice, and the court was not required to include specific intent to sell as an element in its charge on accessorial liability. The elements were adequately conveyed when the court told the jury that it must find both that defendant acted with the specific intent required for the substantive offense, i.e., knowledge that the substance was cocaine, and that he "intentionally aided" the sale.

[Order affirmed.]

PROBLEMS

1. *Evidence of Specific Intent.* If the court had ruled differently in *Kaplan*—if a specific intent to sell a controlled substance was required in order to support a conviction—was there sufficient evidence on the record to support a jury verdict based upon accomplice culpability? What was that evidence?

2. *Distinguishing Complicity and Facilitation.* Do you agree with the *Kaplan* Court that accomplice liability and criminal facilitation are distinguishable? How are they distinguishable?

3. *The Execution.* Following an all-night dance at which a good deal of whisky was consumed, Rowe and Colvard got into an argument which continued for some time. Twice, Rowe raised his rifle, aimed it at Colvard, and then lowered it. The third time that Rowe raised the rifle, he fired it, killing Colvard. Consider the following facts and decide whether Hicks was complicit in the murder:

    a.   Hicks sat and silently watched the entire series of events.

    b.   Each time Rowe raised the rifle, Hicks laughed.

    c.   Each time Rowe raised the rifle, Hicks not only laughed, but also yelled, "Take off your hat and die like a man."

    d.   Prior to the killing, Hicks yelled to Rowe: "Go ahead and shoot him."

Hicks v. United States, 150 U.S. 442 (1893).

4. *The Contrived Burglary.* Hayes agreed with Hill to burglarize a store. Hayes raised a store window and helped Hill slide through it. Hill handed Hayes a 45–pound piece of meat out the window. Both men were captured within a matter of minutes. Hill was not arrested because he was the brother of the store's owner. The facts showed that Hayes had originally proposed the burglary. When Hill agreed to commit the crime, he had no intent to actually burgle the store, but simply wanted to trap Hayes. To this end, Hill alerted his brother, the store's owner, about the plan. Police were waiting to apprehend Hayes, and Hill knew that they were there when he entered the store. Can Hayes be an accomplice to the crime of burglary if Hill had absolutely no intention of actually burglarizing the store and in fact acted with the knowledge and consent of the store owner? *State v. Hayes*, 105 Mo. 76, 16 S.W. 514 (1891).

5. *More on Contrived Burglaries.* Wilson and Pierce agreed to burglarize a drugstore. Pierce helped Wilson enter the store. While Wilson was inside stealing cash, Pierce called the police. Pierce then helped the police track Wilson down. Pierce later testified that the sole reason for his participation in the burglary was to get even with Wilson, and to arrange for the police to "catch Wilson in the act." Can Wilson be convicted of burglary? Can Pierce be convicted as an accomplice? *Wilson v. People*, 103 Colo. 441, 87 P.2d 5 (1939).

6. *List of Tools.* In the preceding problem, suppose that Wilson told Pierce that he planned to burglarize a store and asked Pierce for help. Pierce responded by giving Wilson a list of tools that would be needed, and by helping Wilson map out a plan. However, before the plan could be executed, Pierce told the police, who were lying in wait when Wilson arrived. Wilson is charged with attempted burglary. Can Pierce be convicted as an accomplice?

7. *Bystander or Accomplice?* Corbin and Mitchell were charged with robbery in the first degree. The evidence showed that the men agreed to drive a third man (Roosevelt) to his employer's to obtain his weekly pay. Corbin and Mitchell were to be paid $10 for their efforts. On the way back,

Corbin attacked Roosevelt and took the remainder of his paycheck. Mitchell claimed that he was just a bystander and that he did not (and never did) have any intention of robbing Roosevelt. However, following the attack, when Corbin dumped Roosevelt by the side of the road, Mitchell did nothing. Indeed, Mitchell was driving the car and he stopped at Corbin's request to dump Roosevelt out (and he pleaded with Corbin not to kill Roosevelt). Afterwards, Corbin and Mitchell went off to a bar to drink. When they were apprehended a few hours later, they had spent $10 on drinks. Was Mitchell complicit in the robbery? If you are the prosecutor, what type of evidence would you offer to show that defendant had the mens rea for accomplice liability? *State v. Corbin*, 186 S.W.2d 469 (Mo. 1945).

8. *Prostitutes and Condom Sellers.* In a "red-light district," a drug store regularly sells condoms. Known prostitutes frequently purchase condoms from the store, and some have negotiated bulk discounts. The store's owner is aware that the prostitutes are using the condoms in their trade. If prostitution is illegal in the jurisdiction, is the store owner an accomplice to prostitution? Could Planned Parenthood be convicted as an accomplice if it were distributing condoms to prostitutes to protect them against STDs?

PENNSYLVANIA v. POTTS

388 Pa.Super. 593, 566 A.2d 287 (1989).

BECK, JUDGE:

[This] is a direct appeal by Ernest Potts from a judgment of sentence of life imprisonment for the offense of murder of the first degree. On March 17, 1980, at about 7:00 p.m., Ernest Potts and David Owens met and drove in a car together to the residence of Michael Cunerd as designated by Owens. This trip was being made to inquire into an alleged burglary of Potts' apartment during which two pounds of marijuana, various articles of jewelry, and $400.00 in cash had been stolen. Potts testified at trial that subsequent to the alleged burglary, Owens told him that Cunerd was the person who had burglarized his apartment. Potts and Owens successfully accosted Cunerd on a street corner near his residence. Potts contends that he then exited from his car and told Cunerd that he wanted to speak with him. At that time Cunerd allegedly excused himself by claiming that he needed to first talk with a neighbor, but that he would return to speak with Potts subsequent to that conversation. Potts and Owens waited for Cunerd's return in Potts' car. When Cunerd returned, Potts asked him to get into his car and Cunerd obliged. Potts contends that at this time, with Potts operating the car, a three-way conversation ensued during which Potts continually asked Cunerd if he had burglarized his apartment. Cunerd denied having committed the burglary, and Owens asserted his belief that Cunerd had committed [the] burglary. The three eventually reached a deserted area in southeastern Philadelphia known as the "Meadows". [T]he conversation in the car continued, with Cunerd protesting his innocence and Owens periodically grabbing Cunerd's shoulders from behind and shaking him. Eventually, Potts contends that he ordered Cunerd from the car stating that he and Cunerd "were going to fight." Potts got out from the driver's door and confronted Cunerd outside the passenger door. Ultimately, Potts pushed Cunerd up onto the front hood of the car. At this point, Owens exited the car through the passenger door. Potts testified at trial that at this time, Cunerd jumped off the hood of the car and ran from the car with Owens in pursuit. Owens caught Cunerd within 100 yards of the parked car and began to stab him in the back. When Cunerd had fallen, Owens pinned him with his knees and stabbed him many more times. During this time, Potts contends that he watched the stabbing from a distance of approximately 30 feet. After the stabbing, Potts approached Owens and told him to "See if anything is in his pockets." Owens did so, and in a statement given to the police after his eventual arrest, Potts claimed that he may have seen his wedding ring which was allegedly taken during the burglary. Owens also found a small spoon in the deceased's pocket which he placed in the deceased's mouth and thereafter kicked down his throat. Potts claims that at this point, Owens told him "Let's get the hell out of here. The _____ f _____ is dead." During the course of this incident, Potts was armed with a pen-gun and Owens with a knife with a seven-inch blade. Potts contends that as he drove Owens back to his home, Owens advised that "If anything ever comes down on this, you don't know anything."

[Appellant] first contends that since his stated intention was to beat up the deceased, rather than to kill him, there was insufficient evidence to establish his intention to kill Cunerd, as required for conviction of murder of the first degree.

[The] Pennsylvania Crimes Code provides that for liability to attach for an offense, the offense must be committed by the person's own conduct or by the conduct of another person for which he is legally accountable, or both. A person is legally accountable for the conduct of another if "he is an accomplice of such other person in the commission of the offense." A person is an accomplice of another person if "with the intent of promoting or facilitating the commission of the offense, he: . . . aids or agrees or attempts to aid such other person in planning or committing it . . . . ."

Thus, to be convicted as an accomplice of the crime of murder of the first degree, a two-step analysis is required. The first step is to consider whether an accused possessed the requisite criminal intent. An accomplice's conduct need not result in the ultimate criminal offense. Rather, an accomplice is equally criminally liable for the acts of another if he acts "with the intent of promoting or facilitating the commission of an offense," and agrees or aids or attempts to aid such other person in either planning or committing the criminal offense.

Thus in the instant case, because the appellant has been convicted of murder of the first degree, the Commonwealth must have presented sufficient evidence to establish that he possessed the specific intent to facilitate the crime of murder.

The next step is to examine the actions of the accused to determine whether such actions rise to the level of criminal activity, such that the accused has promoted or facilitated the commission of the crime, and, thus, may be held responsible as an accomplice to another's acts and the consequences of such acts. In order to establish the appellant's guilt on an accomplice theory, no agreement is required. Rather, the only requirement is that the accomplice have aided the principal. It is well settled that this requirement is satisfied by "[t]he least degree of concert or collusion" between the accomplice and the principal.

Turning to the facts, in evaluating whether there was sufficient evidence to establish beyond a reasonable doubt that the appellant possessed the intent to promote or facilitate Cunerd's death, the evidence presented and the inferences which follow from that evidence must be viewed in the light most favorable to the Commonwealth as the verdict winner below. From this record there was sufficient evidence for the fact finder to reject the appellant's contention that he merely intended to beat up the deceased, and to instead find that based upon appellant's actions, he intended to facilitate the killing of Cunerd. Appellant suggests that because he testified to wanting merely to beat Cunerd up and not to kill him, and since there was no evidence to the contrary, that the Commonwealth has failed to carry its burden of proving intent. However, the Commonwealth did offer contrary evidence through the testimony of William Dales, who testified that approximately two days prior to Cunerd's death, appellant told him that he was going to kill Cunerd. It is a firmly established principle of law that where conflicting evidence is presented, it is the fact finder's duty to assess the credibility of the proponents of such evidence. It is clearly within the fact finder's province "to believe all, part, or none of the evidence presented." The jury thus was free to disbelieve that portion of appellant's confession which suggested that he only intended to hurt Cunerd and not to facilitate his death. Viewed in this light, and based upon the additional evidence adduced at trial regarding the events which occurred on the evening of March 17, 1980, the fact finder could have found beyond a reasonable doubt that appellant entertained the intent to promote or facilitate Cunerd's death.

We turn now to the second step of the analysis. The focus at this stage is whether appellant's conduct was sufficient to satisfy the mandates of accomplice liability delineated in the Crimes Code. It is also clear that the jury could have found beyond a reasonable doubt that appellant promoted or facilitated Cunerd's death by aiding or agreeing or attempting to aid Owens in the killing and thus satisfied the "least degree of concert or collusion" standard. First, appellant admitted to knowing that earlier on the day of Cunerd's death, Owens had a knife with him. In addition, appellant admitted both to carrying a pen-gun in his pocket and to driving the car to the "Meadows," which was described during the trial as a desolate, deserted area. Also, based upon the murky details presented regarding the actual stabbing, it was never proven who actually stabbed Cunerd. But even assuming that Owens stabbed Cunerd, the jury could still have found that appellant drove Cunerd to the deserted area and stood by and watched as Owens stabbed Cunerd twenty-nine times. In addition, appellant admitted that after the stabbing he suggested going through Cunerd's pockets to see if they contained any fruits from the burglary. This suggestion is clearly contrary to appellant's testimony that he feared Owens and was shocked by his killing of Cunerd.

In addition, the record discloses several contradictions between appellant's first statement to the police, his second statement to the police, and his testimony at trial. These contradictions could have persuaded the fact finder to disbelieve appellant when he contended that he only intended to beat up Cunerd and was surprised that Owens killed him. Instead, the fact finder may have believed that all of appellant's actions were in an effort to bring Cunerd to the "Meadows" so that Owens would kill him.

Finally, appellant suggested that it was not until later that he realized that he had been set-up by Owens, and that it was probably Owens and Dales who had burglarized his apartment. This is clearly inconsistent with appellant's statement to police that he may have seen his wedding ring which was stolen from his home pulled out of Cunerd's pocket when Owen's searched through it. If one of appellant's rings was in Cunerd's pocket, it does not make sense that appellant would believe that Cunerd was not involved in the burglary.

Based upon the evidence adduced at trial, Dales' testimony, and the inconsistencies contained in appellant's statements and trial testimony, there was clearly sufficient evidence, albeit circumstantial, to prove beyond a reasonable doubt that appellant facilitated or promoted Cunerd's death by providing aid to Owens in that effort.

[Judgment] of sentence affirmed.

PROBLEMS

1. *Reconciling Kaplan and Potts.* The *Potts* court concluded that, in Pennsylvania, to convict someone of murder as an accomplice, "the Commonwealth must have presented sufficient evidence to establish that [the defendant] possessed the specific intent to facilitate the crime of murder." The New York court in *Kaplan*, the previous case, rejected the applicability

of a "specific intent" requirement. Are these two decisions simply inconsistent with one another?

2. *Conspiracy in Potts.* How, if at all, is accomplice liability in this case different from an actor's culpability as a co-conspirator? Could Potts and Owens have been convicted of conspiracy on these facts?

B. VICARIOUS LIABILITY

Sometimes, an individual may be found guilty of criminal conduct as a result of the criminal actions of other persons, about which the individual is wholly unaware. This "vicarious liability" is most commonly employed against corporations and corporate agents. There are, however, limits to the scope of such culpability.

UNITED STATES v. PARK

421 U.S. 658 (1975).

MR. CHIEF JUSTICE BURGER delivered the opinion of the Court.

[Acme] Markets, Inc., is a national retail food chain with approximately 36,000 employees, 874 retail outlets, 12 general warehouses, and four special warehouses. Its headquarters, including the office of the president, respondent Park, who is chief executive officer of the corporation, are located in Philadelphia, Pa. In a five-count information filed in the United States District Court for the District of Maryland, the Government charged Acme and respondent with violations of the Federal Food, Drug and Cosmetic Act. Each count of the information alleged that the defendants had received food that had been shipped in interstate commerce and that, while the food was being held for sale in Acme's Baltimore warehouse following shipment in interstate commerce, they caused it to be held in a building accessible to rodents and to be exposed to contamination by rodents.

[Acme] pleaded guilty to each count of the information. Respondent pleaded not guilty. The evidence at trial demonstrated that in April 1970 the Food and Drug Administration (FDA) advised respondent by letter of insanitary conditions in Acme's Philadelphia warehouse. In 1971 the FDA found that similar conditions existed in the firm's Baltimore warehouse. An FDA consumer safety officer testified concerning evidence of rodent infestation and other insanitary conditions discovered during a 12–day inspection of the Baltimore warehouse in November and December 1971. He also related that a second inspection of the warehouse had been conducted in March 1972. On that occasion the inspectors found that there had been improvement in the sanitary conditions, but that 'there was still evidence of rodent activity in the building and in the warehouses and we found some rodent-contaminated lots of food items'.

The Government also presented testimony by the Chief of Compliance of the FDA's Baltimore office, who informed respondent by letter of the conditions at the Baltimore warehouse after the first inspection.[4] There was testimony by Acme's Baltimore division vice president, who had responded to the letter on behalf of Acme and respondent and who described the steps taken to remedy the insanitary conditions discovered by both inspections. The Government's final witness, Acme's vice president for legal affairs and assistant secretary, identified respondent as the president and chief executive officer of the company and read a bylaw prescribing the duties of the chief executive officer. He testified that respondent functioned by delegating 'normal operating duties,' including sanitation, but that he retained 'certain things, which are the big, broad, principles of the operation of the company,' and had 'the responsibility of seeing that they all work together.'

At the close of the Government's case in chief, respondent moved for a judgment of acquittal on the ground that 'the evidence in chief has shown that Mr. Park is not personally concerned in this Food and Drug violation.' The trial judge denied the motion, stating that *United States v. Dotterweich*, 320 U.S. 277 (1943), was controlling.

Respondent was the only defense witness. He testified that, although all of Acme's employees were in a sense under his general direction, the company had an 'organizational structure for responsibilities for certain functions' according to which different phases of its operation were 'assigned to individuals who, in turn, have staff and departments under them.' He identified those individuals responsible for sanitation, and related that upon receipt of the January 1972 FDA letter, he had conferred with the vice president for legal affairs, who informed him that the Baltimore division vice president 'was investigating the situation immediately and would be taking corrective action and would be preparing a summary of the corrective action to reply to the letter.' Respondent stated that he did not 'believe there was anything (he) could have done more constructively than what (he) found was being done.'

On cross-examination, respondent conceded that providing sanitary conditions for food offered for sale to the public was something that he was 'responsible for in the entire operation of the company,' and he stated that it was one of many phases of the company that he assigned to 'dependable subordinates.' Respondent was asked about

---

4. The letter, dated January 27, 1972, included the following:

"We note with much concern that the old and new warehouse areas used for food storage were actively and extensively inhabited by live rodents. Of even more concern was the observation that such reprehensible conditions obviously existed for a prolonged period of time without any detection, or were completely ignored. . . .

"We trust this letter will serve to direct your attention to the seriousness of the problem and formally advise you of the urgent need to initiate whatever measures are necessary to prevent recurrence and ensure compliance with the law."

and, over the objections of his counsel, admitted receiving, the April 1970 letter addressed to him from the FDA regarding insanitary conditions at Acme's Philadelphia warehouse. [Finally,] in response to questions concerning the Philadelphia and Baltimore incidents, respondent admitted that the Baltimore problem indicated the system for handling sanitation 'wasn't working perfectly' and that as Acme's chief executive officer he was responsible for 'any result which occurs in our company.'

At the close of the evidence, respondent's renewed motion for a judgment of acquittal was denied.... Respondent's counsel objected to the instructions on the ground that they failed fairly to reflect our decision in *United States v. Dotterweich* and to define "responsible relationship." The trial judge overruled the objection. The jury found respondent guilty on all counts of the information, and he was subsequently sentenced to pay a fine of $50 on each count.

The Court of Appeals reversed the conviction and remanded for a new trial. That court viewed the Government as arguing 'that the conviction may be predicated solely upon a showing that ... (respondent) was the President of the offending corporation,' and it stated that as 'a general proposition, some act of commission or omission is an essential element of every crime.'

[The] question presented by the Government's petition for certiorari in *United States v. Dotterweich* and the focus of this Court's opinion, was whether 'the manager of a corporation, as well as the corporation itself, may be prosecuted under the Federal Food, Drug, and Cosmetic Act of 1938 for the introduction of misbranded and adulterated articles into interstate commerce.' In *Dotterweich*, a jury had disagreed as to the corporation, a jobber purchasing drugs from manufacturers and shipping them in interstate commerce under its own label, but had convicted Dotterweich, the corporation's president and general manager. The Court of Appeals reversed the conviction on the ground that only the drug dealer, whether corporation or individual, was subject to the criminal provisions of the Act, and that where the dealer was a corporation, an individual connected therewith might be held personally only if he was operating the corporation "as his 'alter ego.'"

In reversing the judgment of the Court of Appeals and reinstating Dotterweich's conviction, this Court looked to the purposes of the Act and noted that they 'touch phases of the lives and health of the people which, in the circumstances of modern industrialism, are largely beyond self-protection.' It observed that the Act is of 'a now familiar type' which 'dispenses with the conventional requirement for criminal conduct—awareness of some wrongdoing. In the interest of the larger good it puts the burden of acting at hazard upon a person otherwise innocent but standing in responsible relation to a public danger.'

Central to the Court's conclusion that individuals other than proprietors are subject to the criminal provisions of the Act was the reality that 'the only way in which a corporation can act is through the individuals who act on its behalf.'

[At] the same time, however, the Court was aware of the concern which was the motivating factor in the Court of Appeals' decision, that literal enforcement 'might operate too harshly by sweeping within its condemnation any person however remotely entangled in the proscribed shipment.' A limiting principle, in the form of 'settled doctrines of criminal law' defining those who 'are responsible for the commission of a misdemeanor,' was available. In this context, the Court concluded, those doctrines dictated that the offense was committed 'by all who [have] a responsible share in the furtherance of the transaction which the statute outlaws.'

[The] rule that corporate employees who have 'a responsible share in the furtherance of the transaction which the statute outlaws' are subject to the criminal provisions of the Act was not formulated in a vacuum. Cases under the Federal Food and Drugs Act of 1906 reflected the view both that knowledge or intent were not required to be proved in prosecutions under its criminal provisions, and that responsible corporate agents could be subjected to the liability thereby imposed. Moreover, the principle had been recognized that a corporate agent, through whose act, default, or omission the corporation committed a crime, was himself guilty individually of that crime. The principle had been applied whether or not the crime required 'consciousness of wrongdoing,' and it had been applied not only to those corporate agents who themselves committed the criminal act, but also to those who by virtue of their managerial positions or other similar relation to the actor could be deemed responsible for its commission.

In the latter class of cases, the liability of managerial officers did not depend on their knowledge of, or personal participation in, the act made criminal by the statute. Rather, where the statute under which they were prosecuted dispensed with 'consciousness of wrongdoing,' an omission or failure to act was deemed a sufficient basis for a responsible corporate agent's liability. It was enough in such cases that, by virtue of the relationship he bore to the corporation, the agent had the power to prevent the act complained of.

Thus *Dotterweich* and the cases which have followed reveal that in providing sanctions which reach and touch the individuals who execute the corporate mission—and this is by no means necessarily confined to a single corporate agent or employee—the Act imposes not only a positive duty to seek out and remedy violations when they occur but also, and primarily, a duty to implement measures that will insure that violations will not occur. The requirements of foresight and vigilance imposed on responsible corporate agents are beyond question demanding, and perhaps onerous, but they are no more stringent than the public has a right to expect of those who voluntarily assume positions of authority in business enterprises whose services and products affect the health and well-being of the public that supports them.

The Act does not, as we observed in *Dotterweich*, make criminal liability turn on 'awareness of some wrongdoing' or 'conscious fraud.' The duty imposed by Congress on responsible corporate agents is, we emphasize, one that requires the highest standard of foresight and vigilance, but the Act, in its criminal aspect, does not require that which is objectively impossible. The theory upon which responsible corporate agents are held criminally accountable for 'causing' violations of the Act permits a claim that a defendant was 'powerless' to prevent or correct the violation to 'be raised defensively at a trial on the merits.' If such a claim is made, the defendant has the burden of coming forward with evidence, but this does not alter the Government's ultimate burden of proving beyond a reasonable doubt the defendant's guilt, including his power, in light of the duty imposed by the Act, to prevent or correct the prohibited condition.

[We] cannot agree with the Court of Appeals that it was incumbent upon the District Court to instruct the jury that the Government had the burden of establishing 'wrongful action' in the sense in which the Court of Appeals used that phrase. The concept of a 'responsible relationship' to, or a 'responsible share' in, a violation of the Act indeed imports some measure of blameworthiness; but it is equally clear that the Government establishes a prima facie case when it introduces evidence sufficient to warrant a finding by the trier of the facts that the defendant had, by reason of his position in the corporation, responsibility and authority either to prevent in the first instance, or promptly to correct, the violation complained of, and that he failed to do so. The failure thus to fulfill the duty imposed by the interaction of the corporate agent's authority and the statute furnishes a sufficient causal link. The considerations which prompted the imposition of this duty, and the scope of the duty, provide the measure of culpability.

Turning to the jury charge in this case, it is of course arguable that isolated parts can be read as intimating that a finding of guilt could be predicated solely on respondent's corporate position. But this is not the way we review jury instructions, because 'a single instruction to a jury may not be judged in artificial isolation, but must be viewed in the context of the overall charge.'

Reading the entire charge satisfies us that the jury's attention was adequately focused on the issue of respondent's authority with respect to the conditions that formed the basis of the alleged violations. Viewed as a whole, the charge did not permit the jury to find guilt solely on the basis of respondent's position in the corporation; rather, it fairly advised the jury that to find guilt it must find respondent 'had a responsible relation to the situation,' and 'by virtue of his position ... had ... authority and responsibility' to deal with the situation. The situation referred to could only be 'food ... held in unsanitary conditions in a warehouse with the result that it consisted, in part, of filth or ... may have been contaminated with filth.'

[We] conclude that, viewed as a whole and in the context of the trial, the charge was not misleading and contained an adequate statement of the law to guide the jury's determination. Although it would have been better to give an instruction more precisely relating the legal issue to the facts of the case, we cannot say that the failure to provide the amplification requested by respondent was an abuse of discretion.

[Reversed.]

MR. JUSTICE STEWART, with whom MR. JUSTICE MARSHALL and MR. JUSTICE POWELL join, dissenting.

[As] I understand the Court's opinion, it holds that in order to sustain a conviction under § 301(k) of the Federal Food, Drug, and Cosmetic Act the prosecution must at least show that by reason of an individual's corporate position and responsibilities, he had a duty to use care to maintain the physical integrity of the corporation's food products. A jury may then draw the inference that when the food is found to be in such condition as to violate the statute's prohibitions, that condition was 'caused' by a breach of the standard of care imposed upon the responsible official. This is the language of negligence, and I agree with it.

To affirm this conviction, however, the Court must approve the instructions given to the members of the jury who were entrusted with determining whether the respondent was innocent or guilty. Those instructions did not conform to the standards that the Court itself sets out today.

The trial judge instructed the jury to find Park guilty if it found beyond a reasonable doubt that Park 'had a responsible relation to the situation. [The] issue is, in this case, whether the Defendant, John R. Park, by virtue of his position in the company, had a position of authority and responsibility in the situation out of which these charges arose.' Requiring, as it did, a verdict of guilty upon a finding of 'responsibility,' this instruction standing alone could have been construed as a direction to convict if the jury found Park 'responsible' for the condition in the sense that his position as chief executive officer gave him formal responsibility within the structure of the corporation. But the trial judge went on specifically to caution the jury not to attach such a meaning to his instruction, saying that 'the fact that the Defendant is pres(id)ent and is a chief executive officer of the Acme Markets does not require a finding of guilt.' 'Responsibility' as used by the trial judge therefore had whatever meaning the jury in its unguided discretion chose to give it.

The instructions, therefore, expressed nothing more than a tautology. They told the jury: 'You must find the defendant guilty if you find that he is to be held accountable for this adulterated food.' In other words: 'You must find the defendant guilty if you conclude that he is guilty.'

[Before] a person can be convicted of a criminal violation of this Act, a jury must find—and must be clearly instructed that it must find—evidence beyond a reasonable doubt that he engaged in wrongful conduct amounting at least to common-law negligence. There were no such instructions, and clearly, therefore, no such finding in this case.

For these reasons, I cannot join the Court in affirming Park's criminal conviction.

NOTES

1. *Mental state for corporate liability.* While the *Park* decision describes constitutional limits on the extent of vicarious strict liability of corporate officers, a number of jurisdictions have, by statute, legislated higher mens rea requirements. *See, e.g.,* 18 Pa. C. S. § 307(e)(2)("Whenever a duty to act is imposed by law upon a corporation or an unincorporated association, any agent of the corporation or association having primary responsibility for the discharge of the duty is legally accountable for a reckless omission to perform the required act to the same extent as if the duty were imposed by law directly upon himself.").

2. *M.P.C. and corporate liability.* Consider also the Model Penal Code's provisions relating to corporate liability:

§ 2.07. Liability of Corporations, Unincorporated Associations and Persons Acting, or Under a Duty to Act, in Their Behalf.

(1) A corporation may be convicted of the commission of an offense if:

 (a) the offense is a violation or the offense is defined by a statute other than the Code in which a legislative purpose to impose liability on corporations plainly appears and the conduct is performed by an agent of the corporation acting in behalf of the corporation within the scope of his office or employment, except that if the law defining the offense designates the agents for whose conduct the corporation is accountable or the circumstances under which it is accountable, such provisions shall apply; or

 (b) the offense consists of an omission to discharge a specific duty of affirmative performance imposed on corporations by law; or

(c) the commission of the offense was authorized, requested, commanded, performed or recklessly tolerated by the board of directors or by a high managerial agent acting in behalf of the corporation within the scope of his office or employment.

(2) When absolute liability is imposed for the commission of an offense, a legislative purpose to impose liability on a corporation shall be assumed, unless the contrary plainly appears.

(3) An unincorporated association may be convicted of the commission of an offense if:

(a) the offense is defined by a statute other than the Code that expressly provides for the liability of such an association and the conduct is performed by an agent of the association acting in behalf of the association within the scope of his office or employment, except that if the law defining the offense designates the agents for whose conduct the association is accountable or the circumstances under which it is accountable, such provisions shall apply; or

(b) the offense consists of an omission to discharge a specific duty of affirmative performance imposed on associations by law.

(4) As used in this Section:

(a) "corporation" does not include an entity organized as or by a governmental agency for the execution of a governmental program;

(b) "agent" means any director, officer, servant, employee or other person authorized to act in behalf of the corporation or association and, in the case of an unincorporated association, a member of such association;

(c) "high managerial agent" means an officer of a corporation or an unincorporated association, or, in the case of a partnership, a partner, or any other agent of a corporation or association having duties of such responsibility that his conduct may fairly be assumed to represent the policy of the corporation or association.

(5) In any prosecution of a corporation or an unincorporated association for the commission of an offense included within the terms of Subsection (1)(a) or Subsection (3)(a) of this Section, other than an offense for which absolute liability has been imposed, it shall be a defense if the defendant proves by a preponderance of evidence that the high managerial agent having supervisory responsibility over the subject matter of the offense employed due diligence to prevent its commission. This paragraph shall not apply if it is plainly inconsistent with the legislative purpose in defining the particular offense.

(a) A person is legally accountable for any conduct he performs or causes to be performed in the name of the corporation or an unincorporated association or in its behalf to the same extent as if it were performed in his own name or behalf.

(b) Whenever a duty to act is imposed by law upon a corporation or an unincorporated association, any agent of the corporation or association having primary responsibility for the discharge of the duty is legally accountable for a reckless omission to perform the required act to the same extent as if the duty were imposed by law directly upon himself.

(c) When a person is convicted of an offense by reason of his legal accountability for the conduct of a corporation or an unincorporated association, he is subject to the sentence authorized by law when a natural person is convicted of an offense of the grade and the degree involved.

PROBLEMS

1. *The Coal Sample Switch.* Richard Schomaker, an attorney, entered into a business venture with Robert Todd, a client, and Stephen Levitt. They formed a coal brokerage firm called American International Company ("AIC"), which contracted to supply West Penn Power Company ("Utility Company") with low-sulfur coal. The contract provided that if the average sulfur content for any month's shipment exceeded a specified level, Utility Company could cancel the remainder of the contract and pay only half the $120,000–per–month contract price for the nonconforming shipment. To measure sulfur content, Utility Company accumulated samples of pulverized coal for each 10–day period, stored them in a shed, and subsequently tested them before making payment. AIC's first twenty days of shipment drastically exceeded the specified sulfur level. Schomaker met several times with Todd and Levitt to discuss the problem. Soon thereafter, Todd and Levitt went to Utility Company's shed and replaced the last 10–day sample from their company with a similar quantity of extra-low sulfur coal. Although Todd told Schomaker about the sample switch the following day, the testimony conflicts as to whether Schomaker actually believed Todd. In any event, Schomaker did not notify the Utility Company. As a result of the switch, the month's sulfur content was within specified levels, and a few weeks later, Schomaker accepted Utility Company's full payment of $120,000 on behalf of AIC. Is Schomaker guilty of theft by deception under M.P.C. § 2.07? *Commonwealth v. Schomaker*, 501 Pa. 404, 461 A.2d 1220 (1983).

2. *Ford Motor Co. and the Exploding Gas Tank.* At one point, the Ford Motor Company (Ford) manufactured the Pinto, a compact car. The Pinto suffered from a major gas tank defect that would cause the vehicle to explode when it was hit from behind. As a result, lots of people were killed or seriously injured. There was evidence suggesting that Ford's officers were aware of the problem, and could have remedied the problem rather cheaply, but chose not to spend the money. What would it take to impose criminal liability on Ford or its officers for these deaths or injuries? If you are the prosecutor in the case, what types of evidence might you offer against the officers?

EXERCISE

Park in Pennsylvania. Assume that the *Park* facts occurred in Pennsylvania (where a version of M.P.C. § 2.07 applies) and assume further that Park was convicted at trial in a Pennsylvania trial court under a Pennsylvania law similar to the federal Food, Drug and Cosmetic Act. After being assigned the role either of prosecutor or defense attorney, be prepared to argue on appeal to an intermediate appellate court in Pennsylvania the lawfulness of such a conviction.

SOUTH DAKOTA v. HY VEE FOOD STORES, INC.

533 N.W.2d 147 (S.D. 1995).

KONENKAMP, JUSTICE.

A corporation appeals its misdemeanor conviction for selling an alcoholic beverage to a person under age twenty-one. We affirm.

As part of an undercover sting operation Sioux Falls police sent a nineteen-year-old college student into a Hy Vee grocery store on March 19, 1993 to attempt to purchase liquor. Wearing a college sweatshirt and football jacket, the police infiltrator carried a bottle of whiskey to the checkout counter. Too young to sell liquor herself[,] the cashier asked an older employee to scan the item. The cashier then took the purchase money and rang up the sale. Neither employee asked for identification to verify the purchaser's age.

Based upon the actions of these two employees, Hy Vee Food Stores, Inc. was charged with and found guilty in magistrate court [of] selling an alcoholic beverage to a person under twenty-one. The magistrate imposed a $200 fine. Neither employee was charged with committing a crime. Hy Vee appealed to circuit court seeking to have the statute declared unconstitutional. The circuit court upheld the conviction. Hy Vee asserts that the individual employees committed the wrongful acts, not the corporation, and appeals on the following issue:

> Did Hy Vee's conviction [violate] its substantive due process rights by imposing vicarious criminal liability on the company for the illegal acts of its employees?

[Hy Vee] concedes its employees sold alcohol to an underage person in violation of SDCL 35–4–78(1): "No licensee may sell any alcoholic beverage: (1) To any person under the age of twenty-one years...." A violation of this section is a Class 1 misdemeanor punishable by one year in jail or a one thousand dollar fine, or both. Hy Vee avers that the imposition of criminal penalties on [it] for acts of its employees constitutes an impermissible infringement upon Hy Vee's substantive due process rights in violation of both Article VI of the South Dakota Constitution and the 14th Amendment of the

United States Constitution. The question is whether criminal liability can be imposed against an alcoholic beverage corporate licensee for the unlawful acts of its employees?

All legislative enactments arrive before us with a presumption in favor of their constitutionality; Hy Vee bears the burden of proving beyond a reasonable doubt that the law is unconstitutional. [Under] this criterion we determine if the statute as applied to Hy Vee has "a real and substantial relation to the objects sought to be attained." "Whenever within the bounds of reasonable and legitimate construction, an act of the legislature can be construed so as not to violate the constitution, that construction should be adopted."

The law disfavors statutes which impose criminal liability without fault, much less those enactments which impose such liability vicariously. Yet states "have power to legislate against what are found to be injurious practices in their internal commercial and business affairs, so long as their laws do not run afoul of some specific federal constitutional prohibition. . . ."

Hy Vee notes certain "state supreme courts have directly addressed the constitutionality of similar statutes and have found them to be in violation of the liquor licensee's due process rights under the state and federal constitutions." *Commonwealth v. Koczwara*, 155 A.2d 825 (Pa. 1959), *cert. denied*, 363 U.S. 848 (1960); *Davis v. City of Peachtree City*, 304 S.E.2d 701 (Ga. 1983); *State v. Guminga*, 395 N.W.2d 344 (Minn. 1986). In *Koczwara*, an individual owner-licensee was fined $500 and sentenced to three months in jail for the actions of an employee who sold liquor to a minor. Holding that imprisonment under these facts deprives the defendant of due process, the Court made an observation germane to our case:

> Were this the defendant's first violation of the Code, and the penalty solely a minor fine of from $100–$300, we would have no hesitation in upholding such a judgment. Defendant, by accepting a liquor license, must bear such a financial risk.

The *Koczwara* court overturned the jail sentence, but upheld the $500 fine. In *Davis v. City of Peachtree City*, the court held that a violation of due process occurred when the president of a convenience store chain was fined $200 and given 60 days in jail with conditions for a suspended sentence when an employee sold wine to a minor. Georgia's Supreme Court held that imposing even a slight fine violates due process.

After one of his employees sold an alcoholic beverage to a minor, the restaurant owner in *State v. Guminga* faced imprisonment and a fine under Minnesota law. Citing *Davis*, the Court declared that criminal penalties based upon vicarious liability under Minnesota law violated Guminga's due process rights: "Even if there is no prison sentence imposed, under the new statutory guidelines, a gross misdemeanor conviction will affect his criminal history score were he to be convicted of a felony in the future ... only civil penalties would be constitutional."

We begin our analysis with the rather mundane observation that a corporation cannot act but through its agents. Well settled is the basic principle that criminal liability for certain offenses may be imputed to corporate defendants for the unlawful acts of its employees, provided that the conduct is within the scope of the employee's authority whether actual or apparent.

Koczwara, Guminga, and *Davis* involved individuals subjected to vicarious liability for illegal liquor sales. We must leave for some future time, consequently, whether those precedents will guide us when an individual licensee comes before us to constitutionally challenge a conviction for the acts of an employee. Almost six decades ago this Court sustained vicarious criminal liability against a licensee for an employee's illegal sale to a minor, but the constitutional issues raised now were not dealt with then.

Here, a corporate entity, not an individual, was charged with violating SDCL 35–4–78(1) and upon conviction only a fine was imposed. Pennsylvania's highest court in *Koczwara,* discerning the contrast, was "extremely careful to distinguish [its facts] from the question of corporate criminal liability." [Corporations] have been held criminally accountable in numerous circumstances involving a variety of crimes.

Hy Vee urges us to avert constitutional entanglement by reading into the statute a knowledge or *scienter* requirement and hold that a corporate superior must know that an employee is selling liquor to an underage person and either consent to or ratify the act. We decline to do so in this instance because "[l]egislative acts which are essentially public welfare regulatory measures may omit the knowledge element without violating substantive due process guarantees." Where "penalties commonly are relatively small, and conviction does no grave damage to an offender's reputation" under such circumstances statutes dispensing with a *mens rea* component have been upheld.

Hy Vee asserts that criminal liability should not be imputed here because it adopted a firm, oft-reiterated policy that its employees, new and old, must not sell liquor to underage persons.

[Constitutional] questions aside for the moment, the general rule is that merely stating or promulgating policies will not insulate a corporation from liability. Moreover, corporations may be held responsible for violations "even though its employees or agents acted contrary to express instructions when they violated the law, so long as they were acting for the benefit of the corporation and within the scope of their actual or apparent authority."

As the statute provides for a potential one year jail sentence, Hy Vee argues that the enactment goes beyond being a mere regulatory measure with minor consequences for its violation. If the defendant was not a corporation, this argument might carry serious merit. In this case, however, a fine was all that could have been imposed; corporations cannot be imprisoned. We will not speculate over the law's applicability to persons not before us or assume that some future court will impose a jail sentence upon such persons. Hy Vee's maximum criminal exposure was a $1,000 fine. . . .

South Dakota's alcoholic beverage laws manifest an unwavering public interest in prohibiting liquor sales to persons under twenty-one. The serious problems associated with youth who abuse alcohol justify stringent enforcement against those who dispense it. By establishing vicarious liability against a corporate alcoholic beverage licensee, our laws hold accountable the true beneficiary of illegal sales and encourage such licensees to exercise intensified supervision over employees delegated with liquor sale responsibilities. Thus, the challenged statute has a real and substantial relation to the objects sought to be attained.

Was Hy Vee's $200 fine a constitutionally permissible sanction under the circumstances? Wayne R. LaFave & Austin W. Scott, Jr., HANDBOOK ON CRIMINAL LAW § 32, at 227 (1972), supports the view that:

> [I]mposition of a fine is consistent with the rationale behind vicarious criminal liability. Vicarious liability is imposed because of the nature and inherent danger of certain business activities and the difficulties of establishing actual fault in the operation of such businesses. A fine, unlike imprisonment, is less personal and is more properly viewed as a penalty on the business enterprise.

[The] magistrate's imposition of a $200 fine was consistent with the nature of regulatory offenses and did not offend Hy Vee's state and federal constitutional due process rights.

Affirmed.

AMUNDSON, JUSTICE (dissenting).

The fact that there may be serious problems in our society with abuse of alcohol by our youth does not warrant the imposition of a criminal conviction where there is no showing of knowledge or authorization of the crime by the employer/Hy Vee.

Discussing vicarious liability in the criminal arena, the court in *Davis v. City of Peachtree City* stated:

> In balancing this burden against the public's interests, we find that a [criminal conviction] cannot be justified under the due process clauses of the Georgia or United States Constitutions, regardless of Peachtree City's admittedly legitimate interests of

deterring employers from allowing their employees to break the law and of facilitating the enforcement of these laws. This is especially true, when, as here, there are other, less onerous alternatives which sufficiently promote these interests. The Model Penal Code recommends that civil violations providing civil penalties such as fines or revocation of licenses be used for offenses for which the individual was not morally blameworthy and does not deserve the social condemnation 'implicit in the concept "crime".' . . . The availability of such sanctions renders the use of criminal sanctions in vicarious liability cases unjustifiable. . . .

Similarly, commentators LaFave and Scott have written in opposition to criminal sanctions based on vicarious liability:

> [I]t must be recognized that the imposition of criminal liability for faultless conduct is contrary to the basic Anglo–American premise of criminal justice that crime requires personal fault on the part of the accused. Perhaps the answer should be the same as the answer proposed in the case of strict-liability crimes: it is proper for the legislature to single out some special areas of human activity and impose vicarious liability on employers who are without fault, but the matter should not be called a 'crime'. . . . As the law now stands, however, in almost all jurisdictions imprisonment and the word 'criminal' may be visited upon perfectly innocent employers for the sins of their employees.

Adopting this vicarious liability/respondeat superior theory to brand a corporation/employer as a criminal, does not comport with the precept of criminal jurisprudence that guilt is personal and individual. Whether or not one should be so branded, should not rest on whether an employee commits a mistake in judgment. Even the court, which found Hy Vee guilty, understood the fact that employees can make mistakes and will intentionally violate the law notwithstanding the store policy on training and handling mistaken sale of alcohol to underage persons.

In this case, as in others, there are appropriate mechanisms to civilly deal with liquor-sale violations if a license holder violates the law; namely, regulatory revocation or suspension of the license. . . .

I would reverse this conviction.

PROBLEM

The Proper Standard. Do you agree with the analysis of the majority or the dissenter in this South Dakota decision? If the dissenting position became the accepted law in South Dakota, wouldn't this create a deterrent *disincentive* for Hy Vee to adopt policies restricting the sale of alcohol to underage persons? Explain.

IOWA v. CASEY'S GENERAL STORES, INC.

587 N.W.2d 599 (Iowa 1998).

TERNUS, JUSTICE.

This consolidated appeal involves simple misdemeanor convictions of two corporations whose employees sold alcoholic beverages to underage customers during a "sting" operation by the local police. The corporations argue they cannot be held criminally responsible for their employees' actions under the circumstances presented. We agree and so reverse their convictions and remand for dismissal of the criminal charges.

[The] factual predicate for the charges at issue here is undisputed. Both appellants, Casey's General Stores, Inc. and Hy–Vee, Inc., operate stores in Oskaloosa, Iowa. On October 26, 1996, cashiers in both stores sold alcoholic beverages to underage customers without requiring identification or attempting to ascertain the customer's age. These sales violated policies and procedures established by the corporations to prevent the sale of alcoholic beverages to minors.

Both corporations were charged with the crime of selling alcoholic beverages to an underage person.... These simple misdemeanor charges were tried to the court and both defendants were found guilty. Their convictions were affirmed on appeal to the district court.

[Casey's] and Hy–Vee argue that there is no evidence that they, as corporate entities, engaged in culpable conduct.... The State does not contest this assertion, but rather relies on the corporations' alleged vicarious responsibility for their employees' actions.

[The] precise claim in this appeal is based on the alleged insufficiency of the evidence to support the verdict. We review the record in the light most favorable to the State in assessing the sufficiency of the evidence. The determinative question, however, is whether the statutes in question render corporate defendants criminally responsible for the actions of their employees in selling alcoholic beverages to a minor in contravention of company policies and procedures.

[The] primary rule of statutory interpretation is to give effect to the intention of the legislature. To ascertain that intent, we look to the language of the statute. We consider not only the commonly understood meaning of the words used in the statute, but also the context within which they appear. Finally, we construe statutes that relate to the same or a closely allied subject together so as to produce a harmonious and consistent body of legislation. We turn now to a review of the pertinent statutes.

[Section] 123.47 prohibits the sale of alcohol to a minor:

A person shall not sell ... alcoholic liquor, wine, or beer to any person knowing or having reasonable cause to believe that person to be under the age of eighteen....

Section 123.49(2)(h) contains a similar prohibition:

A person or club holding a liquor control license or retail wine or beer permit under this chapter, and the person's or club's agents or employees, shall not. . . .

. . .

h. Sell, give, or otherwise supply any alcoholic beverage, wine, or beer to any person, knowing or failing to exercise reasonable care to ascertain whether the person is under legal age. . . .

The State argues that the evidence supports the defendants' convictions for violating these statutes under the following rationale.

The State first points out that the statutory prohibitions apply to a "person," and that word is defined to include a corporation. Because a corporation can act only through an employee, the State reasons that the legislature must have contemplated criminal liability for corporations based on the acts of their employees. We find this analysis unpersuasive because these statutes do not impose vicarious liability.

Vicarious liability occurs when "one [person] is made liable, though without personal fault, for the bad conduct of someone else." This doctrine is contrary to the "basic premise of criminal justice that crime requires personal fault."

As [Professor] LaFave explains in his treatise on criminal law,

It is a general principle of criminal law that one is not criminally liable for how someone else acts, unless of course he directs or encourages or aids the other so to act. Thus, unlike the case with torts, an employer is not generally liable for the criminal acts of his employee even though the latter does them in furtherance of his employer's business. In other words, with crimes defined in terms of harmful acts and bad thoughts, the defendant himself must personally engage in the acts and personally think the bad thoughts, unless, in the case of a statutory crime, the legislature has otherwise provided.

Thus, if a statutory crime requires mental fault, "it is the rule that the employer must personally know or be wilful or have the requisite intention [before he will] be liable for the criminal conduct of his employee. . . ."

We begin, therefore, with an examination of the statutes to determine whether they require mental fault or whether they impose strict liability. Such an examination reveals that a *mens rea* element is included in both crimes.

We had the opportunity to consider whether section 123.47 required mental fault in *Bauer v. Cole*, 467 N.W.2d 221 (Iowa 1991), a negligence case premised on a violation of section 123.47. In that case, the plaintiffs, an injured minor and his parents, sued the hosts of a New Year's Eve party for injuries sustained by the minor in an automobile accident. The plaintiffs alleged the defendants had provided liquor to the minor driver causing his intoxication, which in turn caused the accident. The plaintiffs appealed from an adverse jury verdict, claiming error in the instruction submitting the plaintiffs' negligence claim based on section 123.47.

In the challenged instruction, the trial court had required the plaintiffs to prove the defendants had knowingly supplied alcohol to the minor driver. The plaintiffs argued that knowledge was not an element of the offense. In ruling that the instruction was correct, this court held that section 123.47 requires proof of the defendants criminal intent: "[W]e conclude that defendants' knowledge of the transaction must be shown to prove a criminal violation under section 123.47."

We think the same conclusion is appropriate with respect to section 123.49(2)(h). Section 123.49(2)(h) requires that the defendant sell the alcoholic beverage "knowing or failing to exercise reasonable care to ascertain whether the person is under legal age." Similarly, section 123.47 requires that the defendant "know[ ] or hav[e] reasonable cause to believe" that the person buying the alcoholic beverage is under the age of eighteen. The similar language of section 123.49(2)(h) calls for the same interpretation given to section 123.47 in *Bauer*, namely, that proof of the defendant's criminal intent is required for a criminal violation. Thus, a licensee or permittee cannot be held strictly criminally liable for the illegal sale of alcohol to a minor; there must be proof that the sale to a minor was made "with the knowledge, or by the direction, sanction, or approval of the defendant."

Because sections 123.47 and 123.49(2)(h) specifically require fault, we will not read vicarious liability into these criminal statutes, but must first find a legislative expression of an intent to impose vicarious liability. Clearly, there is no expression of such an intent in the statutory language.

[We] now consider the State's contention that the defendants can be held vicariously liable for the conduct of their employees under section 703.5(1). Section 703.5 provides for the vicarious liability of a corporation in two different situations:

> A ... private corporation ... shall have the same level of culpability as an individual committing the crime when any of the following are true:
>
> 1. The conduct constituting the offense consists of an omission to discharge a specific duty or an affirmative performance imposed on the accused by the law.

2. The conduct or act constituting the offense is committed by an agent, officer, director, or employee of the accused while acting within the scope of the authority of the agent, officer, director or employee and in behalf of the accused and when said act or conduct is authorized, requested, or tolerated by the board of directors or by a high managerial agent. . . .

We think the first subsection of this statute addresses crimes of omission, ones in which the criminal statute imposes an obligation on the corporation to do something, as opposed to criminal statutes prohibiting certain conduct. The second subsection of the statute addresses criminal conduct that consists of the commission of a prohibited act. With this distinction in mind, we now consider the application of this statute to the case before us.

The State does not rely on section 703.5(2) to support the defendants' convictions. Indeed, there is no evidence in the record that these sales of alcohol to minors were "authorized, requested, or tolerated" by the companies' boards of directors or any high managerial agents of the defendants. Therefore, we must focus on the requirements of section 703.5(1) and decide whether there is sufficient evidence of those requirements to support the application of this statute in this case. To determine whether section 703.5(1) applies, we must identify the "conduct constituting the offense" and then consider whether that conduct constitutes "an omission to discharge a specific duty or an affirmative performance imposed on the accused by the law."

The State argues that the conduct constituting the offense is the failure to use reasonable care to ascertain the purchaser's age. But a defendant can be convicted of a violation of sections 123.47 and 123.49(2)(h) in the absence of such evidence, for example, where the defendant knew the purchaser was a minor. Thus, the requirement of reasonable care is merely a substitute for the *mens rea* or knowledge element of the crime. We think "the conduct constituting the offense," as contemplated by section 703.5(1), is not the *mens rea* element of the crime, but rather is the core conduct of selling alcohol to a minor.

We next consider whether this conduct is "an omission to discharge a specific duty or an affirmative performance imposed on the accused by law" within the meaning of section 703.5(1). The sale of alcohol to a minor is the commission of a prohibited act; it is not the omission of a specific duty or affirmative obligation. Therefore, section 703.5(1) does not apply.

[Sections] 123.47 and 123.49(2)(h) do not impose vicarious liability on licensees and permittees for illegal sales made by their employees. Therefore, the criminal culpability of Casey's and Hy–Vee's employees does not provide a basis for the convictions of these corporations. In addition, the factual prerequisites of the statute providing for a corporation's vicarious liability, section 703.5, are not satisfied under the facts before us.

We conclude, therefore, that there is insufficient evidence to support a finding that the corporate defendants violated sections 123.47 and 123.49(2)(h). Accordingly, we reverse the defendants' convictions and remand for dismissal of the charges.

CHAPTER 6

ATTEMPT

■ ■ ■

Although the criminal law does not punish citizens merely for "bad thoughts," the state does have an interest in intervening early before a suspect actually commits a crime. The goal is to prevent the defendant from actually causing harm. The proof requirements for the attempt crime, both as to the mens rea and the actus reus, can vary from state to state.

A. MENS REA

STATE v. MAESTAS

652 P.2d 903 (Utah 1982).

Δ robbed a bank, as escaping, shot at by officer. Δ fired back.

HALL, CHIEF JUSTICE:

[D]efendant allegedly robbed a bank and attempted to escape in a black van.... Sergeant Cecil Throckmorton of the Salt Lake City Police Department [had] stationed his car on [an] island in the center of the street and was standing beside the car awaiting defendant's approach. As defendant's van passed[,] Sergeant Throckmorton fired a shot [in] an unsuccessful attempt to disable it. [As he drove away,] defendant allegedly leaned out of the van window holding a 38–caliber revolver and fired it at the officer. Defendant drove several blocks further before crashing into a parked car, at which time he was apprehended by other police officers.

Defendant was [found guilty of] attempted first degree murder. [The] court granted defendant's motion [to dismiss] on the ground that "specific intent to kill could not properly be inferred from the evidence." U.C.A., 1953, 76–5–202(1) describes the elements of first degree murder:

Δ guilty of attempted 1st murder. Court granted Δ dismiss.

> Criminal homicide constitutes murder in the first degree if the actor intentionally or knowingly causes the death of another under any of the following circumstances:
>
> . . .
>
> (d) The homicide was committed while the actor was engaged in the commission of, or an attempt to commit, or flight

after committing or attempting to commit, aggravated robbery, robbery, rape, forcible arson, aggravated burglary, burglary, aggravated kidnapping or kidnapping.

> (e) The homicide was committed for the purpose of avoiding or preventing an arrest by a peace officer acting under color of legal authority or for the purpose of effecting an escape from lawful custody.

[I]n order to find defendant guilty of attempted first degree murder, the jury was required to determine beyond a reasonable doubt that he "intentionally or knowingly" attempted to kill Sergeant Throckmorton under one of the circumstances listed above.

Defendant [argues] that the crime of attempted murder requires a stronger showing of intent than does the crime of murder itself. This theory derives from the common law rule that intent is a necessary element of every "attempt" crime even where the corresponding completed crime does not require intent.... As an example, defendant cites cases which discuss the common law rule that there is no crime of "attempted felony murder" because of the fact that felony murder requires no specific intent to kill, while an "attempt" crime must always consist of an intent to commit the corresponding completed crime accompanied by a substantial step toward realization of that crime. Defendant then attempts to carry this rule one step further by asserting that the crime of attempted first degree murder with which he is charged requires a "specific intent" beyond that which would have been required in order to prove first degree murder itself if an actual death had occurred. Defendant does not argue that the evidence concerning intent would have failed to support a first degree murder conviction in the event of actual death, but rather that such evidence fell short of establishing the stronger "specific intent" allegedly required for the crime of attempted first degree murder.

[The] statute makes it clear that regardless of any requirements which the common law may impose concerning "attempt" crimes, Utah law requires only "the kind of culpability otherwise required for the commission of the [completed] offense." Thus, there can be no difference between the intent required as an element of the crime of attempted first degree murder and that required for first degree murder itself.

Even if the common law rule of attempt governed this Court's interpretation of the elements of that crime, that rule would not require the result urged by defendant here. That rule differentiates between the intent requirements for an attempted and a completed crime only where the completed crime may be committed without the intent to commit that crime in particular, as in the case of felony murder. Where an intent to commit the particular crime committed is an element of the completed crime, the same intent requirement applies to the corresponding "attempt" crime, even at common law. Thus, Utah's first degree murder statute, which does contain such an intent requirement, would not fall within the rule cited by defendant even under common law principles.

[There was] "substantial evidence" from which the jury could have concluded not only that defendant aimed and fired a revolver at Sergeant Throckmorton, but also that he did so "intentionally or knowingly." Because of the near impossibility of proving intent directly, Utah law clearly permits the inference of such intent from the actions of a defendant considered in light of surrounding circumstances.

[I]n order to determine defendant's intent, the jury might have considered further evidence concerning his conduct and the circumstances surrounding the alleged gunshot, including testimony that he had just committed a bank robbery, that he had attempted to avoid capture by throwing money out of the van window[,] and that he had demonstrated an indifference to the safety of others by driving erratically and on the wrong side of the traffic divider in his efforts to elude pursuers. We therefore hold that substantial evidence supported the jury in finding that the state had established both the act and the intent components of attempted first degree murder by defendant.

[Reversed.]

NOTE

M.P.C. revisions of attempt. The Model Penal Code defines the crime of attempt in the following way:

Section 5.01. Criminal Attempt

(1) *Definition of Attempt.* A person is guilty of an attempt to commit a crime if, acting with the kind of culpability otherwise required for commission of the crime, he:

(a) purposely engages in conduct that would constitute the crime if the attendant circumstances were as he believes them to be; or

(b) when causing a particular result is an element of the crime, does or omits to do anything with the purpose of causing or with the belief that it will cause such result without further conduct on his part; or

(c) purposely does or omits to do anything that, under the circumstances as he believes them to be, is an act or omission constituting a substantial step in a course of conduct planned to culminate in his commission of the crime.

PROBLEMS

1. *Intent to Scare or Kill.* In the prior case, suppose defendant testified that his intention was not to kill Officer Throckmorton, but simply to scare him. Defendant hoped that this would force the officer to duck and stop shooting. If you were the prosecutor, how would you rebut defendant's testimony? If the jury believed the defendant, should he be convicted of attempted murder? *See People v. Harris,* 72 Ill.2d 16, 377 N.E.2d 28, 17 Ill.Dec. 838 (1978).

2. *Attempt and Recklessness.* Defendant's brakes were not working. Fully aware of this fact, as well as of the danger posed to others, defendant decides to drive to the grocery store. Defendant drives safely, buys groceries, and drives home without incident. A police officer, who was aware that defendant's brakes did not work, charged defendant with attempted manslaughter. Given these facts, does defendant have the mens rea for attempted manslaughter?

3. *Accidental Shooting.* Two defendants entered a shoe store, wearing masks and armed with loaded handguns. One defendant ordered the owner to open the cash register. A second defendant jumped over the counter, and emptied the drawer of its money. Defendants then ordered the owner to open a second register. Upon finding it empty, defendants demanded to know where the money could be found. When the owner said "that's all there is," one defendant pointed his gun right in the owner's face and said "I'm going to kill you" in a very serious voice. At that point, the store owner tried to escape. In doing so, he banged into the defendant who had been pointing the gun earlier and the gun accidentally discharged. The store owner was hospitalized for five weeks from a gunshot wound to his stomach. Did the defendant whose gun discharged have the mens rea for the crime of attempted murder? How would you argue the case for the state? How might the defense respond? *See Bruce v. State,* 317 Md. 642, 566 A.2d 103 (Md.App. 1989).

4. *Homicide Tools.* In February 2007, NASA Astronaut Lisa Marie Nowak was charged with attempted murder for an attack on another woman, an Air Force captain and a love rival. The prosecution alleged that Nowak drove 900 miles from Houston to Florida, and that she carried a wig to disguise her appearance, a steel mallet, a knife, pepper spray, four feet of rubber tubing, latex gloves and garbage bags with her. The prosecution also alleged that she wore a diaper during her drive so that she would not have to take rest breaks. Nowak claims that she did not intend to murder the captain, or even to hurt her, but only to talk to her and perhaps intimidate her. However, she did approach the captain's car in a parking lot in Florida and a minor altercation with the captain ensued before Nowak drove off. If you are the prosecutor, how do you go about proving the intent to murder?

PEOPLE v. GIBSON

94 Cal.App.2d 468, 210 P.2d 747 (1949).

MOORE, PRESIDING JUSTICE.

[After midnight,] appellant crossed an alley [carrying] a 14–foot wooden ladder which he placed horizontally by the fence in the rear of a department store. The darkness [was marred only by street lights that] reflected into the alley. Having deposited his burden, he stood erect, looked upward and walked along the edge of the building. [Appellant] then proceeded easterly for 120 feet when commanded to halt. As he stood in the beam of [a police] officer's flashlight he stated that he was considering whether he could use the ladder at his home and that he might steal it. [The officer noticed that appellant] wore brown cotton gloves, placed him under arrest[,] directed him to the police station [and] returned to the scene[;] he found a burlap sack which contained various tools and burglars' equipment, including an eight pound sledge hammer, bits, braces, flashlights, gloves and 30 feet of quarter-inch, white rope ladder of about 15 steps. In [appellant's pockets were] two flashlights, wire cutters and a coil of small brown copper wire. . . . At the station appellant [said] that he was fixing to commit a burglary. While he had not yet selected a building, "he said after I got on top I was going to see which was the most likely looking spot. . . ."

[Two elements are] essential to an attempted crime, namely, a specific intent and an ineffectual overt act directed at its consummation. [Of] course, the intent of any person at the time of his attempt to offend [is] a question of fact. It may be inferred from the circumstances in evidence. [If] a man traveled 25 miles from his home by the seashore to Burbank north of the Hollywood hills to find a store to burglarize and thereafter was detected by an officer at midnight bearing a ladder down a dark alley and placing it at the rear of a department store and if he is equipped with all the tools commonly used by burglars, there could be no doubt that he was attempting to commit a burglary. [It] could not reasonably be said that he was out to improve his health or the condition of the merchant on San Fernando Road. Even without his admissions, his criminal purpose was clearly evident. With such admissions in evidence his attempt to commit burglary was positively established.

Judgment affirmed.

PROBLEMS

1. *Proving Intent.* In the absence of direct and unequivocal evidence of a defendant's intent, a court must infer intent from the circumstances. Note how the *Gibson* court puts together a series of objective facts to infer that defendant intended to commit a burglary. Would the same result have been reached if:

a. These events had occurred during the middle of the day rather than at night?

b. Defendant had not been in possession of burglar's tools?

2. *More on Proving Intent.* Defendant was charged with attempt to commit assault with intent to rape. When Joy Allen left the "Tiny Diner," she noticed defendant sitting in a truck. According to Allen, as she passed, defendant said something unintelligible, opened the door and placed his foot on the running board. He then followed her, walking behind her down the street until she stopped by a friend's house. By this time, defendant was within two or three feet of her. She waited inside the house ten minutes for defendant to pass. When she proceeded on her way, defendant came toward her from behind a telephone pole. When defendant saw Mr. Simmons unexpectedly emerge from his house, defendant immediately turned and went back to his truck. Defendant gave a different version of the facts. He testified that, on the evening in question, he was carrying a load of junk-iron with a partner, and happened to park near the diner. When the partner disappeared, defendant walked up the street looking for him. As he did, he saw Allen. He turned around and walked up the street; then he stopped at the telephone pole, and waited until she had gone. He remained there for 25 or 30 minutes to see if his partner might come by. He denied that he followed Allen or made any gesture toward molesting her. Under the circumstances, is there sufficient evidence to conclude that defendant had the mens rea for the crime of attempted assault with intent to commit rape? *See McQuirter v. State*, 36 Ala.App. 707, 63 So.2d 388 (1953).

B. ACTUS REUS

Even if a defendant has the required mens rea for an attempt, defendant must commit the actus reus. Some jurisdictions continue to use demanding common law standards of proximity to the completed crime, whereas others use the "substantial step" concept.

COMMONWEALTH v. PEASLEE

177 Mass. 267, 59 N.E. 55 (1901).

HOLMES, C.J.

[Defendant was indicted for] an attempt to burn a building and certain goods therein, with intent to injure the insurers of the same. The defense is that the overt acts alleged and proved do not amount to an offense. . . .

[Defendant] constructed and arranged combustibles in the building in such a way that they were ready to be lighted, and if lighted would have set fire to the building and its contents. To be exact, the plan would have required a candle which was standing on a shelf six feet away to be placed on a piece of wood in a pan of turpentine and lighted. The defendant offered to pay a younger man [to] go to the building, seemingly some miles [away], and carry out the plan. This was refused. Later the defendant and the young man drove towards the building, but when within a quarter of a mile the defendant said that he had changed his mind, and drove away. This is as near as he ever came to accomplishing what he had in contemplation.

The question [is] whether the defendant's acts come near enough to the accomplishment of the substantive offense to be punishable. The statute does not punish every act done towards the commission of a crime, but only such acts done in an attempt to commit it. The most common types of an attempt are either[: 1)] an act which is intended to bring about the substantive crime, and which sets in motion natural forces that would bring it about in the expected course of events, but for the unforeseen interruption, as in this case, if the candle had been set in its place and lighted, but had been put out by the police[;] or [2)] an act which is intended to bring about the substantive crime, and would bring it about but for a mistake of judgment in a matter of nice estimate or experiment, as when a pistol is fired at a man, but misses him, or when one tries to pick a pocket which turns out to be empty. In either case the would-be criminal has done his last act.

[N]ew considerations come in when further acts on the part of the person who has taken the first steps are necessary before the substantive crime can come to pass. In this class of cases there is still a chance that the would-be criminal may change his mind. In strictness, such first steps cannot be described as an attempt, because that word suggests an act seemingly sufficient to accomplish the end, and has been supposed to have no other meaning. That an overt act, although coupled with an intent to commit the crime, commonly is not punishable if further acts are contemplated as needful, is expressed in the familiar rule that preparation is not an attempt. But some preparations may amount to an attempt. It is a question of degree. If the preparation comes very near to the accomplishment of the act, the intent to complete it renders the crime so probable that the act will be a misdemeanor, although there is still a *locus poenitentiae*, in the need of a further exertion of the will to complete the crime. [T]he degree of proximity held sufficient may vary with circumstances, including, among other things, the apprehension which the particular crime is calculated to excite.

As a further illustration, when the servant of a contractor had delivered short rations by the help of a weight, which he had substituted for the true one, intending to steal the meat left over, it was held by four judges that he could be convicted of an attempt to steal. *Cheeseman's Case*, Leigh & C. 140, 10 Wkly. Rep. 255. So, lighting a match with intent to set fire to a haystack, although the prisoner desisted on discovering that he was watched. So, getting into a stall with a poisoned potato, intending to give it to a horse there, which the prisoner was prevented from doing by his arrest . . . . .

[In this case,] a majority of the court is of opinion that the exceptions must be sustained. A mere collection and preparation of materials in a room for the purpose of setting fire to them, unaccompanied by any present intent to set the fire, would be too remote. If the accused intended to rely upon his own hands to the end, he must be shown to have had a present intent to accomplish the crime without much delay, and to have had this intent at a time and place where he was able to carry it out. We are not aware of any carefully considered case that has gone further than this. [The indictment] would have been proved if, for instance, the evidence had been that the defendant had been frightened by the police as he was about to light the candle. On the other hand, if the offense is to be made out by showing a preparation of the room, and a solicitation of some one else to set the fire, which solicitation, if successful, would have been the defendant's last act, the solicitation must be alleged as one of the overt acts. [If] the indictment had been properly drawn, we have no question that the defendant might have been convicted.

Exceptions sustained.

Notes

1. *Definitions of actus reus of attempt.* At common law, the actus reus of the attempt crime was defined in different ways. Consider the following common law tests as summarized by the drafters of the M.P.C.:

(1) The physical proximity doctrine under which defendant must have committed an overt act that was proximate to the completed crime, or directly tending toward the completion of the crime, or amounting to the commencement of the consummation.

(2) The dangerous proximity doctrine under which the court considers the gravity and probability of the offense, and the nearness of the act to the crime.

(3) The indispensable element test (similar to the proximity tests) which emphasizes whether an indispensable aspect of the criminal endeavor remains over which the actor has not yet acquired control.

(4) The probable desistance test which focuses on whether, in the ordinary and natural course of events, without interruption from an outside source, defendant's conduct will result in the crime intended.

(5) The abnormal step approach under which the focus is on whether defendant's conduct has gone beyond the point where the normal citizen would think better of his conduct and desist.

(6) The *res ipsa loquitur* or unequivocality test under which the defendant's conduct manifests an intent to commit a crime.

United States v. Mandujano, 499 F.2d 370, 376 (5th Cir. 1974).

2. *M.P.C. and substantial step.* Consider the M.P.C.'s definition of a "substantial step" that may be sufficient as the actus reus for attempt:

§ 5.01. Criminal Attempt.

. . .

(2) **Conduct That May Be Held Substantial Step Under Subsection (1)(c).** Conduct shall not be held to constitute a substantial step under Subsection (1)(c) of this Section unless it is strongly corroborative of the actor's criminal purpose. Without negativing the sufficiency of other conduct, the following, if strongly corroborative of the actor's criminal purpose, shall not be held insufficient as a matter of law:

(a) lying in wait, searching for or following the contemplated victim of the crime;

(b) enticing or seeking to entice the contemplated victim of the crime to go to the place contemplated for its commission;

(c) reconnoitering the place contemplated for the commission of the crime;

(d) unlawful entry of a structure, vehicle or enclosure in which it is contemplated that the crime will be committed;

(e) possession of materials to be employed in the commission of the crime, that are specially designed for such unlawful use or that can serve no lawful purpose of the actor under the circumstances;

(f) possession, collection or fabrication of materials to be employed in the commission of the crime, at or near the place contemplated for its commission, if such possession, collection or fabrication serves no lawful purpose of the actor under the circumstances;

(g) soliciting an innocent agent to engage in conduct constituting an element of the crime.

(3) **Conduct Designed to Aid Another in Commission of a Crime.** A person who engages in conduct designed to aid another to commit a crime that would establish his complicity under Section 2.06 if the crime were committed by such other person, is guilty of an attempt to commit the crime, although the crime is not committed or attempted by such other person.

PROBLEMS

1. *Close Enough.* According to the *Peaslee* court, what additional acts would have been required to convict the defendant of attempt? What if he had:

a. Purchased the materials, arranged them in a combustible manner, struck the match, and lit the candle?

b. Agreed with another person that this person would light the candle?

c. Would it be enough if the other person went to the room with the intention of setting fire to the materials, or would he or she have to actually strike the match?

2. *Solicitation as Substantial Step.* Should solicitation to commit a crime constitute an attempt? In *Peaslee*, the defendant clearly solicited another person to help him commit the crime. Why was this act not sufficient for conviction? Under the M.P.C.'s "substantial step" test, does the solicitation by itself (in other words, considered without reference to the other preparatory acts) constitute an attempt? Should it?

3. *Resolving Peaslee.* How would the *Peaslee* case have been resolved under the other common law tests listed in Note 1 *supra*, as well as under the M.P.C.'s "substantial step" test in § 5.01(2)?

4. *Applying Tests.* Consider the following problems under the various common law tests (referred to in Note 1 *supra*) and the M.P.C. "substantial step" test (described in Note 2 *supra*) to decide whether the actus reus of attempt has been committed. As you think about how these tests apply, consider whether one test is preferable to the others. Is one test more consistent with particular justifications for punishment? Does a particular test allow the police to intervene too early or too late?

a. *Agreement.* Defendant agrees with another person to burn a building. The two do nothing more than agree and take no further actions.

b. *Looking for Victim.* Carrying a firearm and ammunition, several members of the Ortiz family left their father's apartment in search of Jose Rodriguez. The Ortiz and Rodriguez families were feuding, and the Ortizes believed that Rodriguez had gone to their father's apartment earlier that day with a gun. The Ortizes drove through Rodriguez's neighborhood six times hoping to find him. When they could not find him, the Ortizes drove back to their father's apartment. As their vehicle arrived at the apartment, the police stopped it. Upon being questioned, the Ortiz family members admitted that they wanted to "hurt" Rodriguez. They are charged with attempted assault and battery with a dangerous weapon on Jose Rodriguez. *See Commonwealth v. Ortiz*, 408 Mass. 463, 560 N.E.2d 698 (1990).

c. *Loading Rifle.* Defendant, who had threatened to kill Jeans for annoying his wife, went in an intoxicated condition to a field where Jeans was working. Carrying a rifle, defendant walked in a direct line toward Jeans who was 250 yards away. When defendant was 100 yards away, he stopped to load his rifle. At no time did he take aim. When Jeans saw defendant, he fled. Defendant started after Jeans, but another man stepped in and took the rifle away from him. Defendant offered no resistance. The gun was loaded with a .22–caliber long, or high-speed, cartridge. Defendant is charged with attempted murder. *See People v. Miller*, 2 Cal.2d 527, 42 P.2d 308 (1935).

d. *Carrying Cash*. The police conducted a "reverse sting operation," in which undercover police officers posed as drug sellers and actively solicited drug transactions. Joyce had twenty thousand dollars that she was interested in using to purchase cocaine. An informant took Joyce to a hotel room where an undercover officer (Sam) offered her a duct-tape wrapped package said to contain a kilogram of cocaine. Joyce refused because she could not see the cocaine. Sam then unwrapped half of the package. Joyce again returned the package and asked Sam to completely open it. Sam refused unless Joyce produced the purchase money. Joyce replied that she would not produce any money until Sam opened the package. Joyce left with no apparent intention of returning. As she left the hotel, she was arrested. A subsequent search revealed twenty thousand dollars in cash. Joyce is charged with attempt to purchase cocaine with the intent to distribute. *See United States v. Joyce*, 693 F.2d 838 (8th Cir. 1982).

e. *Looking to Buy Later*. An informant ("SKH") met with defendant, to whom he had previously sold cocaine, at a hotel. Defendant said that he wanted to purchase one-half pound of cocaine, and SKH agreed that he would make it available. The next day, SKH and his "source"—an undercover police officer—met with defendant in the same hotel. After discussing the quality, defendant agreed to purchase eight ounces at $2,050 per ounce. The transaction was not consummated because the "source" had only six ounces of cocaine, and defendant did not have the money with him. Moreover, defendant wanted the cocaine wrapped in two-ounce packages, and defendant did not want to receive the cocaine at the hotel. The three men agreed to meet elsewhere the next day. Before the meeting ended, at defendant's request the "source" showed the cocaine to the defendant so he could examine it. At this point, police officers entered the room and arrested defendant for attempted possession of a controlled substance. *See People v. Warren*, 66 N.Y.2d 831, 489 N.E.2d 240, 498 N.Y.S.2d 353 (1985).

f. *Dictating Terms*. Defendant, an inmate in a penitentiary, solicited another inmate to help him murder three people who were not in prison. The other inmate, who was working undercover, told defendant that he could arrange for "Gunther" to do the killings for $5,000. Defendant agreed to the price, but stipulated the time when the killings could be done, how the bodies could be disposed of, and the condition that nothing was to be done in front of the defendant's son. Defendant is charged with attempted murder. Under the circumstances, should he be convicted? *See State v. Molasky*, 765 S.W.2d 597 (Mo. En Banc 1989).

g. *Catching Hack Saws*. Defendant, a prison inmate, convinced a former inmate to throw a bundle of hack saws to him as he sat behind the bars of a prison window. The former inmate did throw the hack saws and defendant caught them. However, a jail official witnessed the event and immediately ordered defendant to drop the saws. Defendant was charged with attempting to break out of jail (defined as "the purposeful or knowing breaking out of a place of imprisonment"). *See State v. Hurley*, 79 Vt. 28, 64 A. 78 (1906).

5. *Robbery Note.* The police observed defendant acting suspiciously in front of a bank. Police questioned him. Following a consensual search, police found a note in defendant's backpack which stated: "I want $10,000 in $100 bills. Don't push no buttons, or I'll shoot you." Did defendant commit the *actus reus* of attempt?

6. *Boots and Uniforms as Attempt.* In 2006, federal authorities charged seven men with plotting to blow-up the Sears Tower in Chicago. The prosecution claimed that the men adhered to a militant (but vague) form of Islamic ideology, and had attempted to make contact with al Qaeda. The men provided a supposed al Qaeda representative (actually, an undercover federal officer) with a list of needed supplies (*e.g.*, uniforms, boots, machine guns, radios and vehicles), and claimed that their objective was to "wage Jihad" and to "kill all the devils we can" in a 9/11-style mission. In fact, the group never made contact with al Qaeda although it did manage to obtain some boots and uniforms. Eventually, the plot just "petered out." Did the men commit the actus reus of attempt?

PEOPLE v. RIZZO

246 N.Y. 334, 158 N.E. 888 (1927).

CRANE, J.

[Defendant] has been convicted of an attempt to commit the crime of robbery in the first degree.... There is no doubt that he had the intention to commit robbery, if he got the chance. An examination [of] the facts is necessary to determine whether his acts were in preparation to commit the crime if the opportunity offered, or constituted a crime in itself, known to our law as an attempt to commit robbery in the first degree. [Defendant Rizzo,] with three others, planned to rob Charles Rao of a pay roll [which] he was to carry from the bank for the United Lathing Company. [D]efendants, two of whom had firearms, started out in an automobile, looking for Rao.... They went to the bank from which he was supposed to get the money and to various buildings being constructed by the United Lathing Company. At last they came to One Hundred and Eightieth street and Morris Park Avenue. By this time, they were watched and followed by two police officers. As Rizzo jumped out of the car and ran into the building, all four were arrested ..... The four men intended to rob the pay roll man, whoever he was. They were looking for him, but they had not seen or discovered him up to the time they were arrested.

Does this constitute the crime of an attempt to commit robbery in the first degree? The Penal Law, § 2, prescribes:

An act, done with intent to commit a crime, and tending but failing to effect its commission, is "an attempt to commit that crime."

The word "tending" is very indefinite.... "Tending" means to exert activity in a particular direction. Any act in preparation to commit a crime may be said to have a tendency towards its accomplishment. The procuring of the automobile, [and the] searching [of] the streets looking for the desired victim, were in reality acts tending toward the commission of the proposed crime. The law, however, has recognized that many acts in the way of preparation are too remote to constitute the crime of attempt. The line has been drawn between those acts which are remote and those which are proximate and near to the consummation. The law must be practical, and therefore considers those acts only as tending to the commission of the crime which are so near to its accomplishment that in all reasonable probability the crime itself would have been committed, but for timely interference. The cases which have been before the courts express this idea in different language, but the idea remains the same. The act or acts must come or advance very near to the accomplishment of the intended crime....

In *Hyde v. U.S.*, 225 U. S. 347 [(1912)], it was stated that the act amounts to an attempt when it is so near to the result that the danger of success is very great. "There must be dangerous proximity to success." Halsbury in his "Laws of England," says:

An act in order to be a criminal attempt must be immediately and not remotely connected with an directly tending to the commission of an offense.

[The] method of committing or attempting crime varies in each case, so that the difficulty, if any, is not with this rule of law regarding an attempt, which is well understood, but with its application to the facts. As I have said before, minds differ over proximity and the nearness of the approach.

How shall we apply this rule of immediate nearness to this case? [To] constitute the crime of robbery, the money must have been taken from Rao by means of force or violence, or through fear. The crime of attempt to commit robbery was committed, if these defendants did an act tending to the commission of this robbery. Did the acts above described come dangerously near to the taking of Rao's property? Did the acts come so near the commission of robbery that there was reasonable likelihood of its accomplishment but for the interference? [T]hese defendants had planned to commit a crime, and were looking around the city for an opportunity to commit it, but the opportunity fortunately never came. Men would not be guilty of an attempt at burglary if they had planned to break into a building and were arrested while they were hunting about the streets for the building not knowing where it was.... So here these defendants were not guilty of an attempt to commit robbery in the first degree when they had not found or reached the presence of the person they intended to rob.

For these reasons, the judgment of conviction of this defendant appellant must be reversed and a new trial granted.

PROBLEM

Applying M.P.C. in Rizzo. Did the Court reach the correct result in this case according to any of the common law tests in Note 1 after *Peaslee*? If the court had applied the M.P.C.'s "substantial step" test, would there have been an "attempt?"

UNITED STATES v. JACKSON
560 F.2d 112 (2d Cir. 1977).

FREDERICK VAN PELT BRYAN, SENIOR DISTRICT JUDGE:

[Vanessa] Hodges wanted to meet someone who would help [her rob a] Manufacturers Hanover branch [in] Brooklyn, and she invited [Martin] Allen to join her. Hodges proposed that the bank be robbed the next Monday [at] 7:30 A.M. [They would] enter with the bank manager[,] grab the weekend deposits, and leave. Allen agreed to rob the bank[,] and told her he had access to a car, two sawed-off shotguns, and a .38 caliber revolver.

The following Monday, June 14, Allen arrived at [Hodges'] house about 7:30 A.M. in a car driven by appellant Robert Jackson. A suitcase in the back seat of the car contained a sawed-off shotgun, shells, materials intended as masks, and handcuffs to bind the bank manager. While Allen picked up Hodges[,] Jackson filled the car with gas. The trio then left for the bank.

When they arrived, it was almost 8:00 A.M. It was thus too late to effect the first step of the plan, viz., entering the bank as the manager opened the door. They rode around for a while[,] and then went to a restaurant to get something to eat and discuss their next move. After eating, the trio drove back to the bank. Allen and Hodges left the car and walked over to the bank. They peered in and saw the bulky weekend deposits, but decided it was too risky to rob the bank without an extra man.

Consequently, Jackson, Hodges, and Allen drove to Coney Island in search of another accomplice. [T]hey found appellant William Scott, who promptly joined the team. Allen added to the arsenal another sawed-off shotgun, [and] the group drove back to the bank.

When they arrived again, Allen entered the bank to check the location of any surveillance cameras, while Jackson placed a piece of cardboard with a false license number over the authentic license plate of the car. Allen reported [that] a single surveillance camera was over the entrance door. After further discussion, Scott left the car and entered the bank. He came back and informed the group that the tellers were separating the weekend deposits and that a number of patrons were now in the bank. [Hodges] suggested that they [reschedule] for the following Monday, June 21. Accordingly, they left the vicinity of the bank and returned to Coney Island where, before splitting up, they purchased a pair of stockings for Hodges to wear over her head as a disguise and pairs of gloves for Hodges, Scott, and Allen to don before entering the bank.

Hodges was arrested on Friday, June 18, [on] an unrelated bank robbery charge, and immediately began cooperating with the Government. After relating the events on June 14, she told FBI agents that [the robbery] was now scheduled [for] June 21. [At] the request of the agents, Hodges called Allen on Saturday [and] and asked if he were still planning to do the job. He said that he was ready. On Sunday she called him again. This time Allen said that he was not going to rob the bank [because] Hodges had been arrested and he feared that federal agents might be watching. Hodges nevertheless advised the agents that [the] robbery might still take place as planned. . . .

[On June 21,] FBI agents took various surveilling positions in the area of the bank. At about 7:39 A.M., the agents observed a brown four-door Lincoln, with a New York license plate on the front and a cardboard facsimile of a license plate on the rear, moving in an easterly direction on Flushing Avenue past the bank. . . . The front seat of the Lincoln was occupied by [a] male driver and [a] male passenger. . . . The Lincoln circled the block and came to a stop at a fire hydrant situated at the side of the bank. . . . A [third] male, who appeared to have an eye deformity, got out of the passenger side rear door of the Lincoln[,] and stood on the sidewalk in the vicinity of the bank's entrance. He then walked south [only] to return a short time later with [coffee]. He stood again on the corner [in] front of the bank, drinking the coffee and looking around, before returning to the parked Lincoln.

The Lincoln pulled out, made a left turn onto Flushing[,] and proceeded [one] block to Waverly Avenue. It stopped, made a U-turn, and parked on [the] same side of the street as the bank entrance. . . . After remaining parked [for] five minutes, it [cruised] past the bank again[,] made a right [turn and] headed south. It stopped halfway down the block [and] remained there for several minutes. During this time Jackson was seen working in the front of the car, which had its hood up. [When the] Lincoln was next sighted[, its front license plate was] missing. [It] began moving [in] the direction of the bank.

At some point[,] appellants detected the presence of the surveillance agents. The Lincoln accelerated [and] turned south. . . . It was overtaken by FBI agents who ordered the appellants out of the car and arrested them. The agents [found] a black and red plaid suitcase in the rear of the car. The zipper of the suitcase was partially open and exposed two loaded sawed-off shotguns, a toy nickel-plated revolver, a pair of handcuffs, and masks. A New York license plate was seen lying on the front floor of the car. All of these items were seized.

[The trial judge applied] the following two-tiered inquiry formulated in *United States v. Mandujano*, 499 F.2d 370, 376 (5th Cir. 1974), *cert. denied*, 419 U.S. 1114 (1975):

> First, the defendant must have been acting with the kind of culpability otherwise required for the commission of the crime which he is charged with attempting....

> Second, the defendant must have engaged in conduct which constitutes a substantial step toward commission of the crime. A substantial step must be conduct strongly corroborative of the firmness of the defendant's criminal intent.

[The judge] concluded that on June 14 and again on June 21, the defendants took substantial steps, strongly corroborative of the firmness of their criminal intent, toward commission of the crime of bank robbery and found the defendants guilty on each of the two attempt counts. These appeals followed.

[Fed.R.Crim.P. 31(c)] provides in pertinent part that a defendant may be found guilty of "an attempt to commit either the offense charged or an offense necessarily included therein if the attempt is an offense." 18 U.S.C. § 2113(a)[1] specifically makes attempted bank robbery an offense.

Appellant Scott argues that the very wording of 18 U.S.C. § 2113(a) precludes a finding that the actions charged in counts two and three reached the level of attempts. [H]e contends that since the statute only mentions attempted taking and not attempted force, violence, or intimidation, it clearly contemplates that actual use of force, violence, or intimidation must precede an attempted taking in order to make out the offense of attempted bank robbery.

[The court in *United States v. Stallworth*, 543 F.2d 1038 (2d Cir. 1976),] faced a similar statutory construction argument.... In re-

---

1. The subsection provides:

Whoever, by force and violence, or by intimidation, takes, or attempts to take, from the person or presence of another any property or money or any other thing of value belonging to, or in the care, custody, control, management, or possession of, any bank, credit union, or any savings and loan association; or

Whoever enters or attempts to enter any bank, credit union, or any savings and loan association, or any building used in whole or in part as a bank, credit union, or as a savings and loan association, with intent to commit in such bank, credit union, or in such savings and loan association, or building, or part thereof, so used, any felony affecting such bank or such savings and loan association and in violation of any statute of the United States or any larceny

Shall be fined not more than $5,000 or imprisoned not more than twenty years, or both.

sponse to the assertion that the defendants in that case could not be convicted of attempted bank robbery because they neither entered the bank nor brandished weapons, Chief Judge Kaufman stated:

> We reject this wooden logic. Attempt is a subtle concept that requires a rational and logically sound definition, one that enables society to punish malefactors who have unequivocally set out upon a criminal course without requiring law enforcement officers to delay until innocent bystanders are imperiled.

We conclude that Scott's argument is foreclosed by this *Stallworth* holding, with which we are in entire accord.

Appellants Jackson and Allen [seek] to distinguish the instant case from *Stallworth*. They claim that while the conduct of the defendants in that case could properly support a finding of attempted bank robbery, this is not true in the case at bar.... In *Stallworth*, the [robbers] pulled up directly in front of the bank and Sellers, armed with the sawed-off shotgun and positioned at an adjacent liquor store, started to approach the bank. Campbell said "let's go," and the occupants of the car reached for the doors. Immediately, FBI agents and New York City policemen who had staked out the parking lot and were monitoring the gang's conversations moved in and arrested the men.

Chief Judge Kaufman [used] the two-tiered inquiry of *Mandujano*, [which] "conforms closely to the sensible definition of an attempt proffered by the American Law Institute's Model Penal Code." ... The [drafters] of the Model Penal Code recognized the difficulty of arriving at a general standard for distinguishing acts of preparation from acts constituting an attempt. They found general agreement that when an actor committed the "last proximate act," *i.e.*, when he had done all that he believed necessary to effect a particular result which is an element of the offense, he committed an attempt. They also concluded, however, that while the last proximate act is sufficient to constitute an attempt, it is not necessary to such a finding. The problem then was to devise a standard more inclusive than one requiring the last proximate act before attempt liability would attach, but less inclusive than one which would make every act done with the intent to commit a crime criminal.

The [drafters] considered and rejected the [common law] approaches to distinguishing preparation from attempt.... The formulation upon which the [drafters] ultimately agreed required, in addition to criminal purpose, that an act be a substantial step in a course of conduct designed to accomplish a criminal result, and that it be strongly corroborative of criminal purpose in order for it to constitute such a substantial step. The following differences between this test and previous approaches to the preparation-attempt problem were noted:

First, this formulation shifts the emphasis from what remains to be done the chief concern of the proximity tests to what the actor has already done. The fact that further major steps must be taken before the crime can be completed does not preclude a finding that the steps already undertaken are substantial. It is expected, in the normal case, that this approach will broaden the scope of attempt liability.

Second, although it is intended that the requirement of a substantial step will result in the imposition of attempt liability only in those instances in which some firmness of criminal purpose is shown, no finding is required as to whether the actor would probably have desisted prior to completing the crime. Potentially the probable desistance test could reach very early steps toward crime depending upon how one assesses the probabilities of desistance but since in practice this test follows closely the proximity approaches, rejection of probable desistance will not narrow the scope of attempt liability.

Finally, the requirement of proving a substantial step generally will prove less of a hurdle for the prosecution than the *res ipsa loquitur* approach, which requires that the actor's conduct must itself manifest the criminal purpose. The difference will be illustrated in connection with the present section's requirement of corroboration. Here it should be noted that, in the present formulation, the two purposes to be served by the *res ipsa loquitur* test are, to a large extent, treated separately. Firmness of criminal purpose is intended to be shown by requiring a substantial step, while problems of proof are dealt with by the requirement of corroboration (although, under the reasoning previously expressed, the latter will also tend to establish firmness of purpose).

Model Penal Code § 5.01, Comment at 47 (Tent. Draft No. 10, 1960).

The [drafters] concluded that, in addition to assuring firmness of criminal design, the requirement of a substantial step would preclude attempt liability, with its accompanying harsh penalties, for relatively remote preparatory acts. At the same time, however, by not requiring a "last proximate act" or one of its various analogues it would permit the apprehension of dangerous persons at an earlier stage than the other approaches without immunizing them from attempt liability.

Applying the *Mandujano* test, which in turn was derived in large part from the Model Penal Code's standard, Chief Judge Kaufman concluded that since the *Stallworth* appellants had intended to execute a successful bank robbery and took substantial steps in furtherance of their plan that strongly corroborated their criminal intent, their attempted bank robbery convictions were proper.

[As] in *Stallworth*, the criminal intent of the[se] appellants was beyond dispute. The question remaining then is the substantiality of the steps taken on the dates in question, and how strongly this corroborates the firmness of their obvious criminal intent. This is a matter of degree.

On two separate occasions, appellants reconnoitered the place contemplated for the commission of the crime and possessed the paraphernalia to be employed in the commission of the crime loaded sawed-off shotguns, extra shells, a toy revolver, handcuffs, and masks which was specially designed for such unlawful use and which could serve no lawful purpose under the circumstances. Under the Model Penal Code formulation, approved by the *Stallworth* court, either type of conduct, standing alone, was sufficient as a matter of law to constitute a "substantial step" if it strongly corroborated their criminal purpose. Here both types of conduct coincided on both June 14 and June 21, along with numerous other elements strongly corroborative of the firmness of appellants' criminal intent. The steps taken toward a successful bank robbery thus were not "insubstantial" as a matter of law, and [the trial judge] found them "substantial" as a matter of fact. We are unwilling to substitute our assessment of the evidence . . . and thus affirm the convictions for attempted bank robbery on counts two and three.

[The] judgments of conviction are affirmed.

NOTE

Possession of tools. In addition to the crime of attempt, most criminal codes also prohibit possession of burglar tools or other tools that might be used in the commission of a crime. *See Moore v. State*, 197 Ga.App. 9, 397 S.E.2d 477 (1990) (upholding conviction for possession of tools for the commission of a crime).

PROBLEM

Applying Tests. When considering the following problems, decide whether the actus reus of attempt has been committed under the various common law tests, or under the M.P.C.'s substantial step test:

a. *Gun and Mask.* At 6:15 a.m., the police were informed that two armed men were hiding behind a service station. When a police officer arrived, he saw defendant crouching in the weeds in an empty lot 20 to 30 feet from the station. Then defendant jumped up, climbed a fence, and ran down an adjoining street. Defendant threw away a gun before he scaled the fence. Minutes later, defendant was found hiding in the weeds behind a company some 200 feet from the service station. Defendant had removed his shirt, and had a black nylon stocking with a knot in the end. Although defendant claimed that he went to the gas station to buy cigarettes, defendant had no money. On these facts, can defendant be convicted of the crime of attempted robbery? How would you argue the case for the prosecution? How might defense counsel respond? *See People v. Terrell*, 99 Ill.2d 427, 459 N.E.2d 1337, 77 Ill.Dec. 88 (1984).

b. *Instructing Patient.* Defendant agreed to perform an illegal abortion for an undercover police officer who went to defendant's apartment. The officer saw a table with a sheet and cover; a large folding screen (for privacy); a chair at one end of the table; a stove with a covered pan on the burner that contained instruments commonly used in performing abortions; and various medicines, medical instruments and books. Defendant gave the officer two sedative pills which she pretended to swallow, and she paid him the agreed-upon price. Defendant then explained the operation, and told her he would have to examine her. The officer removed her shoes and suit jacket and had unbuttoned two buttons on her blouse when she revealed her true identity and arrested the defendant. Did defendant commit the crime of attempted abortion? *See People v. Woods*, 24 Ill.2d 154, 180 N.E.2d 475 (1962).

c. *Looking for Store.* Defendant hired a taxi cab and directed the driver to take him to Genesee Street to a jewelry store. The driver pointed out a jewelry store, but defendant told him that was "not the one." The driver then noticed a police car and asked defendant if they should ask for directions. Defendant declined to do so, and then exited the taxi. Her suspicions being raised, the taxi driver notified the police who quickly apprehended the defendant. He admitted that he intended to rob an unidentified jewelry store on Genesee Street. Although defendant did not know the name of the jewelry store, he did know what the building looked like. Has defendant committed the crime of attempted robbery of the jewelry store? *See People v. Smith*, 148 Ill.2d 454, 593 N.E.2d 533, 170 Ill.Dec. 644 (1992).

d. *Running with Tools.* Defendant left his home and drove approximately twenty miles to a nearby city; he was followed by several unmarked police cars. After driving slowly down several residential streets, he parked his car at an apartment complex and turned his lights off. Defendant then exited the car and walked a short distance. When a police car appeared, he crossed the street, and began running behind a group of homes. Shortly thereafter, he was arrested. He was dressed in dark clothing, and carried a heavy-gauge screwdriver, a ten-inch pry bar, two flashlights, a knit cap, and a pair of gloves. There was no evidence that any nearby house had been burglarized. Did defendant take a "substantial step" towards the commission of a burglary? *See Commonwealth v. Melnyczenko*, 422 Pa.Super. 363, 619 A.2d 719 (1992).

e. *Arranging for Theft.* Defendant insured her collection of gold and silver Persian antiquities with Lloyd's of London for $18.5 million. She then traveled to New York where she rented a vault at a long-term storage facility, and arranged to have two men (experienced in burglaries of art storage facilities) steal the art. The men tried to burglarize the facility, but were apprehended by police. Defendant was charged with staging the theft of her Persian antiquities with the objective of recovering insurance proceeds (*i.e.*, attempted grand larceny). Did she commit the actus reus if she never submitted a false claim to his insurer? *See People v. Mahboubian*, 74 N.Y.2d 174, 543 N.E.2d 34, 544 N.Y.S.2d 769 (1989).

f. *HIV Exposure.* Defendant, who had been diagnosed with the Human Immunodeficiency Virus (HIV), was incarcerated in the county jail. Defendant knew that if he had sex with others, he would expose them to the risk of becoming infected with HIV. After his release, defendant committed a rape. If defendant failed to use a condom when he committed the rape, has he committed the actus reus of assault with intent to commit murder? *See Smallwood v. State*, 106 Md.App. 1, 661 A.2d 747 (1995).

g. *Locked Bank.* The police received information that three male defendants planned to rob a bank and that one of them would be dressed as a woman. On the day of the robbery, defendants (two men and a third person appearing to be a woman) entered the shopping center parking lot in a car. Defendants drove slowly past the bank, exited the parking lot, made a U-turn, drove past the bank again, and parked by a nearby store. One defendant left the car, entered the store, and walked to a window which provided a view of the bank. He stood there for 3 minutes, but did no shopping. The other two defendants exited the car, and stood facing the bank. Then a power outage hit the shopping center area, and a bank teller locked the door. All three defendants returned to the car and began to leave the parking lot. A police officer stopped the vehicle and found a revolver on the person of one of the defendants and another revolver on the floor of the car. Defendants were arrested. Did they commit attempted bank robbery? *See United States v. Buffington*, 815 F.2d 1292 (9th Cir. 1987).

h. *Talked Out of Robbery.* Defendants went to a gasoline station to purchase gasoline. After they purchased the gas, they decided to rob the station with a .410 shotgun. One defendant pointed the gun at the owner of the station and told him that it was a "stick-up." The owner tried to talk them out of it, and they told him they needed more gas. The owner then offered to give them $2 worth of gas if they would abandon the robbery. They agreed, took the gas, and left the station without robbing it. Did they commit attempted robbery? *See People v. Crary*, 265 Cal.App.2d 534, 71 Cal.Rptr. 457 (1968).

i. *The Bill Trap.* Defendants were found in a rented car near a bank with two loaded handguns, a roll of duct tape, a stun gun, and two pairs of latex surgical gloves. One defendant carried a stolen Automated Teller Machine (ATM) card which he had used to request a twenty-dollar withdrawal, without removing the cash from the cash drawer. This omission created a "bill trap." In other words, the ATM shut itself down, causing the company to send a service technician to repair it.

These facts about the bill trap were known to defendant who had previously worked for an ATM service company. The prosecution argues that defendant intentionally caused the bill trap to summon the ATM service technicians who would have to open the ATM, and that defendants planned to rob the technicians of the money in the ATM. Did defendants cross the line between preparation and attempt? *See United States v. Harper*, 33 F.3d 1143 (9th Cir. 1994).

j. *Failing to Call.* Dillon, an undercover FBI agent, agreed to hire defendant to protect him during an alleged drug transaction. After the transaction was completed, Dillon claimed that he was shortchanged by the buyer. At that point, defendant offered to kill the buyer for $10,000. So Dillon and the defendant met at a lounge near the motel where the buyer was staying. They decided that defendant should go to the lobby of the motel, call the buyer and convince him to come down to the lobby where defendant would then shoot him. Defendant went to the lobby with a loaded gun, but did not call the buyer's room. The defendant left the lobby, and sheriff's deputies arrested him. Defendant contends that he was collecting evidence to build a case against Dillon and that he thought he was following police procedures. Did the defendant commit attempted murder? *See State v. Pacheco*, 125 Wash.2d 150, 882 P.2d 183 (En Banc 1994).

C. ABANDONMENT

If the prosecution's evidence can satisfy the mens rea and actus reus of attempt, should it matter if a defendant subsequently "abandons" the attempt?

STATE v. WORKMAN
90 Wash.2d 443, 584 P.2d 382 (En Banc 1978).

HOROWITZ, JUSTICE.

[Defendants] Lawrence Dean Workman and Steven Lynn Hughes [spent] the evening of July 22, 1976 drinking and dancing with their wives in State Line, Idaho. On the way home to Moses Lake, Washington after the taverns closed, the defendants decided to commit a robbery. Taking the freeway exit for Spokane, they spotted the Fill-em' Fast Gas Station and chose it as their target. They parked their car in an alley behind the station. Leaving their wives asleep, they took a .22 caliber rifle from the trunk of the car and loaded it. They also took a gunny sack with holes punched in it for eyeholes, and a stocking cap, both intended for use as masks. Then they walked up the alley to a fence behind the station and waited. This was normally a busy time at the station. After about 15 minutes, they moved to a hiding place just behind the pay booth, where they waited again.

At about 2:30 a.m., when business at the station was slack, the attendant took a short walk to get some fresh air and saw the defendants, unmasked, behind the pay booth. He returned to the booth and called the police. Defendant Workman later appeared at the window without a mask or gun and asked for a cigarette and match. The attendant refused, and Workman rejoined defendant Hughes. During this period, according to defendants' testimony, they were trying to summon the "courage" to commit the robbery and decide how to do it.

Sometime after the cigarette episode, an unmarked police car took up a position across the street from the station. The police officer could see both the defendants and a second police car which had turned into the alley behind the station. The first car then pulled into the station.

At that time, the defendants, having decided not to go through with their plans, started walking away from the station. They testified at their trials that they had not seen the police [cars] before they decided to leave. They were stopped and arrested in the alley behind the station. Defendant Hughes was found to have the sawed-off rifle concealed under his clothes.

The defendants were each charged with attempted first degree robbery while armed with a deadly weapon. At their separate trials, each defendant was found guilty. [At] trial, defendants tried to show they abandoned their plan before the crime of attempt was committed. They proposed an instruction on abandonment derived essentially from a New York statute which sets up abandonment of criminal purpose as an affirmative defense to the crime of attempt. The trial courts both rejected the proposed instruction and gave an instruction properly based on our attempt statute.

The instruction, given correctly, stated that a person is guilty of attempt if, with intent to commit a specific crime, he does any act which is a substantial step towards the commission of the crime. The instruction qualified the meaning of a "substantial step" by stating that the conduct must be more than mere preparation. [Defendants] contend, however, that the statutory language, "substantial step," is unconstitutionally vague unless further defined, that an instruction on abandonment is necessary in order to properly define it, and that without the requested instruction, they were precluded from arguing their theory of the case to the jury.

We must disagree. The question of what constitutes a "substantial step" under the particular facts of the case is clearly for the trier of fact. The instruction given informed the jury that mere preparation would not be sufficient, that something more must be present in order to constitute a substantial step. When preparation ends and an attempt begins, we have held, always depends on the facts of the particular case. We cannot agree that the instruction given was unconstitutionally vague.

Furthermore, an instruction relating to abandonment is neither necessary, [nor] particularly helpful in defining the meaning of a substantial step. Once a substantial step has been taken, and the crime of attempt is accomplished, the crime cannot be abandoned. The defendants' attempt to show they abandoned their plan is thus relevant only if the abandonment occurred before a substantial step was taken. Through arguing their theory at trial, they could only have hoped to show they never took a substantial step toward the specific crime. Abandonment is not, however, a true defense to the crime of attempt under our statute that is, a showing of abandonment does not negate the State's allegation that a substantial step occurred. Thus, pursuing the theory of abandonment could only be a strategy for showing why a substantial step was never taken. Defendants could not thereby show whether such a step was taken. We therefore conclude an instruction on abandonment is not necessary as a matter of law to properly define a "substantial step."

[It is so ordered.]

NOTE

M.P.C. and abandonment. The M.P.C., § 5.01(4) takes the following position regarding abandonment:

(4) *Renunciation of Criminal Purpose.* When the actor's conduct would otherwise constitute an attempt under Subsection (1)(b) or (1)(c) of this Section, it is an affirmative defense that he abandoned his effort to commit the crime or otherwise prevented its commission, under circumstances manifesting a complete and voluntary renunciation of his criminal purpose. The establishment of such defense does not, however, affect the liability of an accomplice who did not join in such abandonment or prevention.

Within the meaning of this Article, renunciation of criminal purpose is not voluntary if it is motivated, in whole or in part, by circumstances, not present or apparent at the inception of the actor's course of conduct, that increase the probability of detection or apprehension or that make more difficult the accomplishment of the criminal purpose. Renunciation is not complete if it is motivated by a decision to postpone the criminal conduct until a more advantageous time or to transfer the criminal effort to another but similar objective or victim.

PROBLEMS

1. *Encouraging Renunciation.* Does *Workman's* holding make sense in terms of policy concerns? As the court recognizes, the defendants committed a "substantial step" towards commission of the crime. Thus, why were they not deserving of punishment considering the justifications for punishment, i.e., deterrence, restraint, rehabilitation and retribution? On the other hand,

should the law encourage renunciation? If a defendant has already passed the point of no return, in the sense that he can be convicted of "attempt" based on a substantial step, does this fact reduce his incentive to desist if no abandonment defense is allowed?

2. *Workman and the M.P.C.* How would the *Workman* case be resolved under M.P.C. § 5.01(4)? Although the defendants took a "substantial step," would the M.P.C. still permit them to assert the defense of renunciation? In fact, is it clear that their renunciation was "complete and voluntary" and unrelated to a fear of detection?

3. *Cutting Wire.* Shortly after midnight, a guard heard an alarm which indicated that someone was attempting an escape from a prison recreation area. The alarm could not be heard in the recreation area. Guards immediately checked the prison population, but found no one missing. In the recreation area, they found that a piece of barbed wire had been cut, and they also found a prison laundry bag filled with civilian clothing. The next morning, without prompting, defendant voluntarily told a guard that, "I was gonna make a break last night, but I changed my mind because I thought of my family, and I got scared of the consequences." Defendant testified that he was depressed prior to his decision to escape because he had been denied a Christmas furlough. Defendant is charged with attempted prison escape. On these facts, should defendant be convicted? Under the M.P.C. § 5.01(4), did he sufficiently renounce the attempt? What would you argue as defense counsel? How might the prosecution respond? *See Commonwealth v. McCloskey,* 234 Pa.Super. 577, 341 A.2d 500 (1975).

4. *Threats and Loaded Gun.* Defendant went to the laundry of a hotel where his wife, from whom he was separated, was employed. Defendant approached his wife. He had been in the same laundry room the previous Saturday and had called her a "yellow-bellied son of a bitch" and had also said, "I'll give you just twenty-four hours to live." This time he told his wife: "This is it." She ran to an adjoining office where she tried to phone the police. Defendant followed her, took the phone, tore it loose from the wall and threw it at her. He missed. The wife then ran to another room where she did call the police. At this point, defendant retrieved a loaded 12–gauge shotgun from his car. He returned to the laundry room with the gun positioned to shoot directly in front of him. As he entered, he said, "Don't move anyone or I'll shoot you." Shortly after that, defendant turned around and walked away. As he was leaving the building, he was apprehended by a police officer who responded to the wife's phone call. Did defendant commit attempted murder? Did he renounce the attempt under § 5.01(4)? *See State v. Wilson,* 218 Or. 575, 346 P.2d 115 (1959).

5. *Demanding Big Bills.* Defendant, who had been drinking very heavily, stopped at a store to buy a pack of cigarettes. Defendant approached the cashier and demanded money. The cashier thought defendant was joking until he demanded money again in a "firmer tone". The cashier then began fumbling with the one-dollar bills until defendant directed her to the "big bills." The cashier testified that defendant then said, "I won't do it to you;

you're good-looking, but if you're here next time, it won't matter." Defendant's girlfriend then came into the store, put a hand on defendant's shoulder, and directed him out of the store. Did defendant attempt to rob the liquor store? Did he renounce the attempt? *See People v. Kimball*, 109 Mich.App. 273, 311 N.W.2d 343 (1981).

6. *Drilling into Bank.* While his wife was away, defendant rented an office directly over the vault of a bank. Defendant placed drilling tools, acetylene gas tanks, a blow torch, a blanket, and a linoleum rug in the office. Subsequently, defendant drilled two groups of holes in the floor above the vault. He came back to the office several times to drill down, covering the holes with the linoleum rug. The holes did not go through the floor. At some point, defendant's landlord became aware of his activities and notified the police. At trial, defendant testified that he had planned to rob the bank, but that he "began to realize that, even if I were to succeed, a fugitive life of living off of stolen money would not give me enjoyment of life. I still had not given up my plan however. I felt I had made a certain investment of time, money, effort and a certain psychological commitment to the concept. I came back several times thinking I might slowly drill down. When my wife came back, my life as bank robber seemed more and more absurd." Under the circumstances, should the defense of abandonment be available to defendant? *See People v. Staples*, 6 Cal.App.3d 61, 85 Cal.Rptr. 589 (1970).

7. *Carrying Arson Tools.* Lombardi, an undercover detective, arrested defendant for receiving stolen goods and he was released on bail. One night, Lombardi saw a late-model car bearing a license plate assigned to defendant's automobile agency. The driver went down the street, turned left, came back on a perpendicular street, stopped directly across from Lombardi's residence, and extinguished its lights. Lombardi radioed for help. When the police arrived, the driver backed up, made a U-turn, and headed away. The police caught the defendant, and a search revealed that the car contained a can of gasoline; a rag; matches; an aluminum baseball bat; and a note that read, "Hi, Sal, it's my turn asshole." Defendant was charged with attempting knowingly and maliciously to dissuade a police officer from giving testimony. On these facts, is conviction appropriate? If an attempt occurred, did defendant abandon it? *See State v. Latraverse*, 443 A.2d 890 (R.I. 1982).

8. *Ordering Victim with Gun.* Henley and her seven-year-old daughter lived in a trailer. One day when Henley was alone, she answered the door to find defendant asking for directions. Then defendant pointed a handgun at her, ordered her into the house, told her to undress, and shoved her onto the couch. He also threatened to kill her. Henley described herself as frightened and crying. She attempted to escape from defendant by telling him that her daughter would be home from school at any time. She testified: "I started crying and talking about my daughter, that I was all she had because her daddy was dead, and then he said if I had a little girl he wouldn't do anything, for me just to go outside the trailer and turn my back." Defendant then departed. Did defendant abandon the attempted

rape? *See Ross v. State*, 601 So.2d 872 (Miss. 1992); *People v. McNeal*, 152 Mich.App. 404, 393 N.W.2d 907 (1986).

9. *Rejecting Cocaine.* Defendant negotiated with Rojas to purchase cocaine. Rojas called defendant and asked, "are you ready?" Defendant replied "yes." Defendant called an associate, and told him that Rojas would be "coming over [here]. Right now." Officers staked out defendant's apartment because they suspected that he would buy drugs from a "delivery" person. They saw a man pull up in a car, remove a plastic bag from the trunk, and enter the building. The bag's handles were stretched, indicating that the contents were heavy. A half hour later, the man emerged from the building, carrying the same plastic bag which still appeared to be heavy. He placed the bag back in the trunk and drove off. The evidence showed that defendant intended to purchase the contents of the bag (cocaine) from Rojas (who was arrested), but declined to do so because of its inferior quality. On these facts, does the defense of abandonment apply? *See People v. Acosta*, 80 N.Y.2d 665, 609 N.E.2d 518, 593 N.Y.S.2d 978 (1993).

10. *Victim Breaks Free.* M.B. and J.G. skipped school and were drinking sodas outside a liquor store. Smith approached the boys, asked about their absence from school, and demanded identification. He had a gun and a badge on his hip and told the boys he was a police officer. The boys started to walk back to school, but Smith told them he would drive them back. When the boys refused the ride, Smith threatened to use handcuffs to escort them to school. The boys then entered the car. Smith drove them to a wooded area, handcuffed M.B. to a tree, and ordered J.G. to exit the car. Smith held J.G.'s arm behind his back and shoved him into the woods. Smith asked whether J.G. "ever had sex with a boy" and commanded him to disrobe. When J.G. refused, Smith placed his gun to J.G.'s throat and again told him to remove his clothes. J.G. still refused. Smith was startled by the sound of a branch snapping, which was M.B. breaking free from the tree. Smith then took J.G. back to the car and released him. Meanwhile, M.B. ran to a nearby home and called the police. Smith was arrested for attempted sexual assault. Was there abandonment? *See Smith v. State*, 636 N.E.2d 124 (Ind. 1994).

11. *Remorse after Stabbing.* Defendant and his uncle were drinking heavily and began quarreling. Defendant stabbed his uncle in the chest twice. The uncle then fled, pursued by defendant. The uncle collapsed a block away. Defendant was remorseful and wept. Defendant then dragged his uncle to his car, threw away the knife, "floored the accelerator," and sped towards the local hospital. Examination by physicians at the hospital revealed that the uncle had suffered two deep stab wounds between his ribs and close to his heart which had penetrated and collapsed both lungs. But he survived. Should defendant be convicted of attempted murder? *See State v. Smith*, 409 N.E.2d 1199 (Ind.App. 1980).

D. IMPOSSIBILITY

Suppose a defendant tries to commit a crime which it turns out is impossible to commit. Should defendant be punished with a conviction for attempt?

STATE v. GUFFEY

262 S.W.2d 152 (Mo.App. 1953).

VANDEVENTER, PRESIDING JUDGE.

Appellants were convicted of violating Section 252.040, V.A.M.S. [The] information charges that [defendants] did "willfully and unlawfully hunt, pursue, and attempt to take, with the use of firearms, a deer during the prescribed closed [season]," contrary to the statute and the wild life code....

The State's evidence shows that Conservation agents [procured] the hide of a 2 1/2 year old doe which had been killed by an automobile.... They had taken it to a taxidermist, who soaked it to soften it, stuffed it with excelsior and boards, inserted rods in the legs so it would stand upright and used the doe's skull in the head part of the hide so it would hold its former shape. For eyes, which had not been preserved, two small circular pieces of scotchlight reflector tape of a "white to amber color", had been placed over the eyeless sockets. [The] dummy was placed in a field about fifty yards from the north side of an old road [so] it could be seen by anyone coming along the road.... conservation agents, fully armed, then concealed themselves in the brush [and] awaited the arrival of some citizen who might come that way, see the tempting bait and with visions of odoriferous venison cooking in pot or pan, decide not to wait until the 4th of December to replenish his larder....

[A] car was observed coming from the east [at] a speed of 10 or 15 miles per hour [with] two spotlights [sweeping] the countryside and piercing the darkness with their beams. As the car neared[,] one of the beams fell on the stuffed deer and someone in the car was heard to exclaim, "Wait, there stands one." The car stopped, [a spotlight was] trained upon the dummy deer. Immediately after the car stopped, there was a blast of a shotgun [fired] by a man on the right side of the front seat.... The agents converged upon the Chevrolet and its occupants, seized the spotlights, a flashlight, the shotgun, an empty shell, and a loaded shell.... Charges were filed against the two appellants.

[It is argued] that the evidence does not show the violation of any law; that though the mountain labored, it did not even bring forth a mouse. [The] State argue[s] that [the] evidence does show that defendants did pursue a deer. The State then argues that one of the meanings of the word "pursue" is to "seek" and that the facts that defendants were going along the highway in an automobile with spotlights and a shotgun and did take a shot at the dummy deer proves that they did "seek" a deer, which being synonymous with "pursue" made them guilty of violating Section 252.040 and the regulations. . . .

[T]he State has wholly failed to make its case when it stands upon the proposition that defendants "pursued" a deer. In the first place there was no deer. The hide of a doe long since deceased, filled with boards, excelsior and rods with eyes made of a reflective scotch tape, was not a deer within the meaning of the statute and Section 33 of the "Wildlife Code of Missouri." The dummy, such as it was, was a stationary affair, it could not run, could not jump, it could not flee from the rifle slug of a hunter. It was not wild and it had no life. . . .

Undoubtedly the words "pursued" as used in the statute and "pursue" as used in Section 33 of the Code means to follow with the intention of overtaking, or to chase. A deer's part in such a pursuit or chase is clearly described by the Scottish Bard, Sir Walter Scott, in "The Lady of the Lake, Canto First, The Chase."

> The antler'd monarch of the waste Sprung from his heathery couch in haste
>
> Then, as the headmost foes appear'd with one brave bound the copse he clear'd
>
> And stretching forward free and far, sought the wild heaths of Uam–Var.

It is difficult for us to visualize the dummy with its tottering legs, synthetic eyes and vitals of shredded wood, springing from its couch, bounding a copse [and] "stretching forward free and far" seeking other fields. It could hardly stand alone and almost collapsed from loss of excelsior after it was shot.

Neither is the State's contention bolstered [by] the fact that the information contains the word "hunt" and "attempt to take." [The] State's evidence shows that one of the defendants did shoot the dummy but did they pursue, chase or follow a deer by shooting this stuffed defunct doe hide? It was not a deer. If the dummy had been actually taken, (it could not be pursued) defendants would not have committed any offense. It is no offense to attempt to do that which is not illegal. Neither is it a crime to attempt to do that which it is legally impossible to do. For instance, it is no crime to attempt to murder a corpse because it cannot be murdered.

[If] the State's evidence showed an attempt to take the dummy, it fell far short of proving an attempt to take a deer. We hold that the State wholly failed to make a case.

STATE v. CURTIS

157 Vt. 629, 603 A.2d 356 (1991).

MORSE, JUSTICE.

Defendant shot a deer decoy and was convicted of attempting to take a wild deer out of season under 10 V.S.A. § 4745. His principal argument on appeal is that the defense of legal impossibility precludes a conviction under this statute and under Vermont's attempt statute. . . .

A person is prohibited from taking "a wild deer except specified wild deer during the seasons provided by law." A person is guilty of attempting a crime by doing "an act toward [its] commission [but] by reason of being interrupted or prevented fails in the execution of the same." We have held that an "attempt consists not only of an intent to commit a particular crime, [but] some overt act designed to carry out such intent." Undoubtedly, defendant's behavior demonstrated an intent to take a wild deer out of season. He performed an overt act toward the commission of the intended crime. His conduct went as far as it could in achieving the goal of taking a wild deer out of season. Except for the fact that the "wild deer" in his sights was not real, he would be guilty of the crime prohibited by § 4745.

[Defendant] was "prevented" from shooting a wild deer because he was tricked into shooting a decoy. We see no meaningful distinction between the infeasible act of putting a bullet-proof protection on a live deer to prevent its demise and the use of a decoy to divert a hunter's attention from a live deer. Either way, live deer are given a measure of protection.

[D]efendant possessed the specific intent to take a wild deer out of season. Defendant's failure to actually take a live wild deer is of no consequence. This is not a case where defendant's conduct was equivocal. . . . There was no testimony that defendant thought the decoy was not a live deer. . . . Failure to find that defendant's actions amount to a crime would frustrate the goals underlying wildlife protection legislation. A contrary holding would oblige state and local officials to respond to illegal hunting by more cumbersome, dangerous, after-the-fact methods. Prosecution based on a fresh kill defeats the purpose of legislation drafted to preserve wildlife. The difficulties and risks associated with detecting poachers without the benefit of decoys are manifest. As stated by a game warden at trial, there is a serious concern for the safe detection of poachers, and the decoy system was established in response to those concerns.

[Affirmed].

NOTE

Stolen status of goods. In *People v. Jaffe*, 185 N.Y. 497, 78 N.E. 169 (1906), defendant was charged with attempting to receive stolen property under a statute providing "that the accused shall have known [to] have been stolen or wrongfully appropriated in such a manner as to constitute larceny." When the property was sold to defendant, the police and the owner were acting in collaboration so that the goods were not actually stolen. The court reversed the conviction: "The defendant could not know that the property possessed the character of stolen property when it had not in fact been acquired by theft...." The *Jaffe* rule was rejected in *People v. Rojas*, 55 Cal.2d 252, 358 P.2d 921, 10 Cal.Rptr. 465 (1961): "The criminality of the attempt is not destroyed by the fact that the goods, having been recovered by [the] police had, unknown to defendants, lost their 'stolen' status." *See also People v. Rollino*, 37 Misc.2d 14, 233 N.Y.S.2d 580 (1962).

PROBLEMS

1. *Comparing Deer Cases.* Which holding—*Guffey* or *Curtis*—makes more sense in terms of policy concerns? In both cases, defendant intended to kill a deer out of season, and defendant did everything he could to bring his intent to fruition. Why should it matter that the "deer" was a decoy rather than a real deer?

2. *Empty Pocket.* Defendant was observed in a crowded market and was seen to thrust his hand into the pocket of a man. Defendant found the pocket empty and withdrew his hand without obtaining anything. A police officer arrested the defendant and charged him with attempted grand larceny. Given that the pocket was empty, can defendant be convicted of attempted theft? *See People v. Twiggs*, 223 Cal.App.2d 455, 35 Cal.Rptr. 859 (1963); *People v. Moran*, 123 N.Y. 254, 25 N.E. 412 (1890).

PEOPLE v. DLUGASH

41 N.Y.2d 725, 363 N.E.2d 1155, 395 N.Y.S.2d 419 (1977).

JASEN, JUDGE.

[The] issue is whether an individual's intentions and actions, though failing to achieve a manifest and malevolent criminal purpose, constitute a danger to organized society of sufficient magnitude to warrant the imposition of criminal sanctions. Difficulties in theoretical analysis and concomitant debate over very pragmatic questions of blameworthiness appear dramatically in reference to situations where the criminal attempt failed to achieve its purpose solely because the factual or legal context in which the individual acted was not as the actor supposed them to be. Phrased somewhat differently, the concern centers on whether an individual should be liable for an attempt to commit a crime when, unknown to him, it was impossible to successfully complete the crime attempted. For years, serious studies have been made on the subject in an effort to resolve the continuing controversy when, if at all, the impossibility of successfully completing the criminal act should preclude liability for even making the futile attempt. The 1967 revision of the Penal Law approached the impossibility defense to the inchoate crime of attempt in a novel fashion. The statute provides that, if a person engages in conduct which would otherwise constitute an attempt to commit a crime, "it is no defense to a prosecution for such attempt that the crime charged to have been attempted was, under the attendant circumstances, factually or legally impossible of commission, if such crime could have been committed had the attendant circumstances been as such person believed them to be." This appeal presents to us, for the first time, a case involving the application of the modern statute. . . .

[Defendant admitted] that, on the night [in question], he, Bush and Geller had been out drinking. Bush had been staying at Geller's apartment and during [the] evening, Geller several times demanded that Bush pay $100 towards the rent on the apartment. . . . Bush [told] Geller that "you better shut up or you're going to get a bullet." All three returned to Geller's apartment [at midnight and continued to drink]. When Geller again pressed his demand for rent money, Bush drew his .38 caliber pistol, aimed it at Geller and fired three times. Geller fell to the floor. After the passage of a few minutes, perhaps two, perhaps as much as five, defendant walked over to the fallen Geller, drew his .25 caliber pistol, and fired approximately five shots in the victim's head and face. [At] the time [defendant] shot at Geller, Geller was not moving and his eyes were [closed]. . . .

The jury found the defendant guilty of murder. [A]ll three medical expert witnesses testified that they could not, with any degree of medical certainty, state whether the victim had been alive at the time the latter shots were fired by the defendant. Thus, the People failed to prove beyond a reasonable doubt that the victim had been alive at the time he was shot by the defendant. Whatever else it may be, it is not murder to shoot a dead body. Man dies but once.

[The] most intriguing attempt cases are those where the attempt to commit a crime was unsuccessful due to mistakes of fact or law on the part of the would-be criminal. A general rule developed in most American jurisdictions that legal impossibility is a good defense but factual impossibility is not. [An] example is Francis Wharton's classic hypothetical involving Lady Eldon and her French lace. Lady Eldon, traveling in Europe, purchased a quantity of French lace at a high price, intending to smuggle it into England without payment of the duty. When discovered in a customs search, the lace turned out to be of English origin, of little value and not subject to duty. The traditional view is that Lady Eldon is not liable for an attempt to smuggle.

On the other hand, factual impossibility was no defense. For example, a man was held liable for attempted murder when he shot into the room in which his target usually slept and, fortuitously, the target was sleeping elsewhere in the house that night. Although one bullet struck the target's customary pillow, attainment of the criminal objective was factually impossible. *State v. Moretti*, 52 N.J. 182, 244 A.2d 499, presents a similar instance of factual impossibility. The defendant agreed to perform an abortion, then a criminal act, upon a female undercover police investigator who was not, in fact, pregnant. The court sustained the conviction, ruling that "when the consequences sought by a defendant are forbidden by the law as criminal, it is no defense that the defendant could not succeed in reaching his goal because of circumstances unknown to him." . . .

The New York cases can be parsed out along similar lines. One of the leading cases on legal impossibility is *People v. Jaffe*, 185 N.Y. 497, 78 N.E. 169, in which we held that there was no liability for the attempted receipt of stolen property when the property received by the defendant in the belief that it was stolen was, in fact under the control of the true owner. Similarly, in *People v. Teal*, 196 N.Y. 372, 89 N.E. 1086, a conviction for attempted subornation of perjury was overturned on the theory that the testimony attempted to be suborned was irrelevant to the merits of the case. Since it was not subornation of perjury to solicit false, but irrelevant, testimony, "the person through whose procuration the testimony is given cannot be guilty of subornation of perjury and, by the same rule, an unsuccessful attempt to that which is not a crime when effectuated, cannot be held to be an attempt to commit the crime specified." Factual impossibility, however, was no defense. Thus, a man could be held for attempted grand larceny when he picked an empty pocket.

As can be seen[,] the distinction between "factual" and "legal" impossibility was a nice one indeed and the courts tended to place a greater value on legal form than on any substantive danger the defendant's actions posed for society. The approach of the [drafters] of the Model Penal Code was to eliminate the defense of impossibility in virtually all situations. Under the code provision, to constitute an attempt, it is still necessary that the result intended or desired by the actor constitute a crime. However, the code suggested a fundamental change to shift the locus of analysis to the actor's mental frame of reference and away from undue dependence upon external considerations. The basic premise of the code provision is that what was in the actor's own mind should be the standard for determining his dangerousness to society and, hence, his liability for attempted criminal conduct.

In the belief that neither of the two branches of the traditional impossibility arguments detracts from the offender's moral culpability, the Legislature substantially carried the code's treatment of impossibility into the 1967 revision of the Penal Law. Thus, a person is guilty of an attempt when, with intent to commit a crime, he engages in conduct which tends to effect the commission of such crime. It is no defense that, under the attendant circumstances, the crime was factually or legally impossible of commission, "if such crime could have been committed had the attendant circumstances been as such person believed them to be." Thus, if defendant believed the victim to be alive at the time of the shooting, it is no defense to the charge of attempted murder that the victim may have been dead.

Turning to the facts of the case before us, [the] jury could conclude that the defendant believed Geller to be alive at the time defendant fired shots into Geller's head. Defendant admitted firing five shots at a most vital part of the victim's anatomy from virtually point blank range. Although defendant contended that the victim had already been grievously wounded by another, [the] jury could conclude that the defendant's purpose and intention was to administer the coup de grace. . . .

The jury convicted the defendant of murder. Necessarily, they found that defendant intended to kill a live human being. Subsumed within this finding is the conclusion that defendant acted in the belief that Geller was alive. Thus, there is no need for additional fact findings by a jury. Although it was not established beyond a reasonable doubt that Geller was, in fact, alive, such is no defense to attempted murder since a murder would have been committed "had the attendant circumstances been as (defendant) believed them to be." The jury necessarily found that defendant believed Geller to be alive when defendant shot at him.

[T]he order of the Appellate Division should be modified and the case remitted to the Appellate Division for its review of the facts [and] for further proceedings with respect to the sentence in the event that the facts are found favorably to the People. . . .

Problems

1. *Type of Impossibility.* Over the years, commentators have offered numerous variations on the Lady Eldon hypothetical (referred to in the *Dlugash* case). The court offers the hypothetical as an example of "legal impossibility." Do you agree that the case should be characterized in that way?

2. *Scalping Tickets.* Defendant wants to scalp his tickets to the Louisville–Kentucky basketball game outside Freedom Hall in Louisville. Fearing that it is illegal to scalp tickets (in fact, it is not illegal), defendant is extremely furtive as he approaches prospective purchasers. An undercover detective, who happened to notice defendant's unusual behavior, approached defendant about the tickets. Realizing that defendant believes that it is illegal to

scalp tickets, the officer charges defendant with attempted scalping. Should he be convicted?

3. *Biting to Kill.* Defendant is an inmate and he knows that he has the human immunodeficiency virus (HIV). On several occasions, he has threatened to kill corrections officers by biting or spitting at them. One day, he bites an officer's hand, causing puncture wounds of the skin during a struggle which he precipitated. Defendant is charged with attempted murder. At trial, defendant claims that a bite cannot transmit HIV. If defendant's claim is correct, can he be convicted of attempted murder? Would it matter whether he knew that a bite could not transmit HIV? *See State v. Smith*, 262 N.J.Super. 487, 621 A.2d 493 (1993).

4. *Selling Fake P–2–P.* Defendant was convicted of attempting to distribute the drug phenyl–2–propanone (P–2–P). Both methamphetamine and P–2–P are non-narcotic controlled substances. P–2–P has no use other than in the manufacture of methamphetamine. An undercover police officer agreed to buy six pints of P–2–P from defendant at $1250 per pint. At the time of the purchase, defendant was arrested. After chemical testing, it was learned that the liquid was not P–2–P but merely liquid bleach. Under these circumstances was the defendant's conviction appropriate? *See United States v. Everett*, 700 F.2d 900 (3d Cir. 1983); *United States v. Oviedo*, 525 F.2d 881 (5th Cir. 1976).

5. *Bullet–proof Glass.* McKinley, a gasoline station employee, was at the cashier's window when defendant gave him $4 for gasoline. After defendant pumped gasoline worth $3.99, he insisted that he had given McKinley "cinco dollars." McKinley denied he had been given that much money and both men began yelling. Defendant fired three shots at McKinley. Since McKinley was protected by bullet-proof glass, the bullets marred the glass but did not penetrate it. Defendant claims that he cannot be convicted of attempted murder because the glass made murder impossible. How will the prosecutor respond? *See People v. Valdez*, 175 Cal.App.3d 103, 220 Cal.Rptr. 538 (1985).

6. *Non–deceived Victim.* An undercover officer called on defendant (a doctor) and told him that his sister was in failing health. In fact, the officer had no sister. Defendant told the officer to write her name on a piece of paper, and the officer wrote a fictitious name. Defendant placed the paper on what appeared to be an electrical instrument and rubbed it. He then told the officer that his sister was suffering from sarcoma, a blood clot on the brain, had beef worms, and was anemic. When the officer offered to bring his sister to see defendant, the doctor replied that it was unnecessary. The doctor claimed that he had cured patients he had never seen. Defendant asked for a fee of $65 a month for twelve months. The officer gave a down payment of $25 in marked bills. The officer then arrested defendant. The instrument on which defendant placed the handwriting (which he had rubbed for the apparent purpose of diagnosing the supposed sister's ailments) was found on investigation not to be wired to any electric current. Can the doctor be convicted of attempting to obtain money by false pretenses when the undercover officer was not deceived as to the legitimacy of the

treatment? *See Harwei, Inc. v. State*, 459 N.E.2d 52 (Ind.App. 1984); *Commonwealth v. Johnson*, 312 Pa. 140, 167 A. 344 (1933).

7. *Fake Victim Photos.* Defendant paid an undercover officer a $100 finder's fee to procure a young girl for sexual intercourse. He chose a young girl, represented to be six years of age, from a collection of photographs supplied by the officer; and prepared for sexual intercourse with the young girl by arranging for a room and purchasing vaseline to use as a lubricant. Defendant was charged with attempted sexual assault. Does it matter that the undercover officer did not have a young girl available to have sexual intercourse with defendant? *See Van Bell v. State*, 105 Nev. 352, 775 P.2d 1273 (1989).

8. *Buying Talcum Powder.* Defendant proposed to pay a police deputy, a member of the narcotics detail, to the chief of police, if she would supply him with narcotics. The deputy reported the conversation and was instructed to go along with defendant. She asked defendant, "Were you serious about what we were talking about the other day?" Defendant said, "Yes." A day later, the deputy told defendant that she "had the stuff." The deputy gave defendant a package containing white powder. Defendant put the package in his pocket. When defendant opened his safe to get the money, the deputy arrested him. The package did not contain heroin, but only talcum powder. Can defendant be convicted of attempted possession of narcotics? *See United States v. McDowell*, 714 F.2d 106 (11th Cir. 1983); *People v. Siu*, 126 Cal. App.2d 41, 271 P.2d 575 (1954).

9. *Dead Victim.* Defendant is charged with attempted rape. Defendant was bar hopping with friends when a woman collapsed in his arms while the two of them were dancing. Defendant offered to take her home and placed her in his car. Believing that she was drunk and unconscious, defendant had sexual intercourse with her. It was later determined that she was dead, and that she had died when she collapsed on the dance floor. Can defendant be convicted of attempted rape? *See United States v. Thomas*, 32 C.M.R. 278, 13 USCMA 278, 1962 WL 4490 (1962).

10. *Bribe for Nothing.* A labor union owned fourteen acres of land on which it planned to develop a recreational facility for its members. The union began to dig a lake on the property, but stopped at the request of the County Commission. Believing that a county permit was required, a union official tried to bribe a county commissioner. As it turned out, no permit was required. Can the official be convicted of attempted bribery? *See Nell v. State*, 277 So.2d 1 (Fla. 1973).

11. *Bribe to Person without Authority.* In an attempt to evade induction into the U.S. armed forces, defendant tried to bribe an induction official to help him. The officer refused. After consulting with his superiors, who wanted to catch defendant, the official returned to defendant and offered to take the bribe. Defendant agreed that $450.00 was a fair price and paid it. Shortly afterwards, defendant was arrested. It was later shown that the official had nothing to do with the actual induction process, nor could he

make any recommendation as to whether a prospective inductee should be accepted or rejected for military service. Under the circumstances, can defendant be convicted of attempted bribery, given that the official could not prevent defendant's induction into the armed forces, and did not intend to do so? *See Hurley v. United States*, 192 F.2d 297 (4th Cir. 1951).

12. *Warden's Knowledge.* Father Philip Berrigan and Sister Elizabeth McAlister were convicted of attempting to violate 18 U.S.C. § 1791 for sending seven letters out of a federal prison "without the knowledge and consent of the warden." The evidence shows that defendants did send the letters. However, the warden knew that they were trying to send the letters and allowed the letters to pass out of the institution. Given the warden's knowledge, can defendants be convicted of attempt? *See United States v. Berrigan*, 482 F.2d 171 (3d Cir. 1973).

13. *Belief Gun Is Loaded.* Defendant points a gun at his wife's head and pulls the trigger. Defendant incorrectly believes that the gun is loaded. Can defendant be convicted of attempted murder? *See State v. Damms*, 9 Wis.2d 183, 100 N.W.2d 592 (1960).

CHAPTER 7

CONSPIRACY

■ ■ ■

In theory, conspiracy statutes respond to the special danger to society posed by group criminal activity, *e.g.,* it is more likely that a group will succeed in its criminal endeavors than will a lone individual. As a result, most criminal codes contain a "general" conspiracy offense, *i.e.* a statute that prohibits individuals from agreeing to commit any other criminal offense. However, a few codes do not contain this offense, and some codes limit conspiracy to agreements to commit particular crimes.

Given the expansion of the conspiracy offense over the last few decades in some jurisdictions, and the fact that some conspiracy offenses overlap the coverage of other inchoate and substantive offenses, some commentators have argued that the conspiracy offense as it is currently defined in modern criminal codes no longer serves a useful or sensible function. *See, e.g.,* Philip E. Johnson, *The Unnecessary Crime of Conspiracy,* 61 Cal. L. Rev. 1137 (1973); Neal Kumar Katyal, *Conspiracy Theory,* 112 Yale. L.J. 1307 (2003); Paul Marcus, *Criminal Conspiracy Law: Time to Turn Back From an Ever Expanding, Ever More Troubling Area,* 1 Wm. & Mary Bill of Rts. J. 1 (1992). As you review the cases and materials that follow, you should ask yourself whether there still is an appropriate place for the offense of conspiracy in our criminal justice system.

A. UNILATERAL–BILATERAL CONSPIRACIES

At common law, a conspiracy consisted of an agreement *between two or more persons* to commit, by concerted action, an unlawful act or a lawful act by unlawful means (the "bilateral" approach). Today, in contrast, most jurisdictions follow the approach of the Model Penal Code, and focus on the act of a *single* individual who is or believes that he or she is agreeing with another person to commit a criminal act (the "unilateral" approach).

This "unilateral" or "bilateral" distinction is quite significant. Given the extensive use of undercover agents by law enforcement agencies, the trend toward adoption of a unilateral—broader and more inclusive—conspiracy offense has resulted in harsher punishment for many defendants who are accused and convicted of conspiracy in addition to other inchoate and/or substantive offenses.

MILLER v. WYOMING

955 P.2d 892 (Wyo. 1998).

THOMAS, JUSTICE.

[James Miller] was confined in the minimum security wing of the Wyoming State Penitentiary [where] he became acquainted with Steven Ingersoll, another inmate. Ingersoll told Miller that he had access to some firearms, and Miller endeavored to arrange to purchase [them]. Ingersoll contacted his friend, James Powell, [to] see if Powell could get the firearms. Powell said that he could, and their arrangement called for the weapons to be delivered to Rawlins. Powell then would be paid $2,500. Miller's plans expanded beyond the weapons transaction, however, and he decided to pay Powell to "watch somebody." That proposal developed into a scheme for Powell to kidnap Miller's ex-wife and children.

Miller offered to let Ingersoll escape from prison with him in exchange for Ingersoll's help with the kidnapping. Ingersoll again contacted Powell by telephone and asked Powell if he would be interested in the kidnapping, advising him that it would pay $50,000. Following a series of phone calls, Powell advised DCI [the Department of Criminal Investigation] of this plan, and, that same day, a DCI agent went to Powell's home and arranged to record future phone calls that Powell received from Ingersoll and Miller.

[The parties agree that Powell] was acting as a government agent and under the direction of law enforcement officers. [In subsequent] conversations Powell and Miller discussed the floor plan of Miller's ex-wife's home; the place where the hostages would be held; the method of financing the kidnapping; and the possibility that Miller's niece or Miller's brother would help in the abduction. During this same time frame, Ingersoll mailed floor plans to Powell, doing this for Miller who was unable to find a stamp.

[Miller] was charged with conspiring to kidnap his ex-wife [and was] convicted. The jury instructions at the first trial adopted the bilateral theory of conspiracy. The jury also was advised by those instructions that a government agent cannot be a co-conspirator. Following a reversal[,] the district court, relying on public policy reasons, adopted the unilateral theory of conspiracy and so instructed the jury.... Miller again was convicted and sentenced to a term of seven to fourteen years in the Wyoming State Penitentiary. Miller now appeals from that conviction.

[Miller argues] that the bilateral theory of conspiracy had become the law of this case. . . . If the district court was required to instruct on the bilateral theory of conspiracy, it obviously did not do so. [It] is accepted law in the jurisdictions where there has been occasion to consider the question in the last thirty years that when a new trial is granted in a criminal case, the case is tried de novo and rulings made in connection with the first trial are not binding in the second trial. [It] follows that the reliance by Miller upon the law of the case is erroneous and furnishes no basis for a claim of error upon appeal.

[While] Miller primarily relies upon his claim of entitlement to relief under the law of the case doctrine, the instruction on the unilateral theory of conspiracy poses a novel question for Wyoming. For that reason we consider whether that instruction was a correct instruction on the law. The Supreme Court of North Dakota has distinguished the bilateral theory of conspiracy from the unilateral theory in this way:

> Under a unilateral formulation, the crime is committed when a person agrees to proceed in a prohibited manner; under a bilateral formulation, the crime of conspiracy is committed when two or more persons agree to proceed in such manner. Under either approach, the agreement is all-important to conspiracy. Under the unilateral approach, as distinguished from the bilateral approach, the trier-of-fact assesses the subjective individual behavior of a defendant. . . . Under the traditional bilateral approach, there must be at least two 'guilty' persons, two persons who have agreed.

Prior to its revision in 1982, as amended in 1983, the statute making conspiracy a crime in Wyoming read:

> If two (2) or more persons conspire to (a) commit a felony in the state of Wyoming or to commit an act beyond the state of Wyoming which if done in this state would be a felony, and (b) one (1) or more of such persons do any act, within or without the state of Wyoming, to effect the object of the conspiracy, each, upon conviction, shall be fined not more than one thousand dollars ($1,000.00) or imprisoned in the penitentiary not more than ten (10) years or both. . . .

As revised in 1982, and then amended in 1983, this statute now reads:

> (a) A person is guilty of conspiracy to commit a crime if he agrees with one (1) or more persons that they or one (1) or more of them will commit a crime and one (1) or more of them does an overt act to effect the objective of the agreement. . . .

The new version was adopted from both the Model Penal Code and the laws of neighboring states. The Model Penal Code, like the new version of the Wyoming statute, defines conspiracy in the context of a single actor agreeing with another, and this language is said to adopt the unilateral approach. While federal courts have continued to follow the bilateral theory of conspiracy, the modern trend in state courts is to rule that a conspiracy count is viable even when one of the participants is a government agent or is feigning agreement. The focus under the unilateral theory is on the culpability of the defendant, without any necessity to establish the guilty mind of one or more co-conspirators.

When we compare the first sentences of the earlier and current statutes in Wyoming, we find that the old statute began "[i]f two (2) or more persons conspire to (a) commit a felony in the state of Wyoming[,]" while the new statute reads, "[a] person is guilty of conspiracy to commit a crime if he agrees with one (1) or more persons that they or one (1) or more of them will commit a crime[.]" Our research discloses that most states that have adopted this second definition of the crime of conspiracy have embraced a unilateral approach to conspiracy, and we hold that is appropriate in Wyoming.

Other states have justified the unilateral theory of conspiracy as sound public policy. A person who believes he is conspiring with another to commit a crime is a danger to the public regardless of whether the other person in fact has agreed to commit the crime. As one text writer has expressed the proposition, "such an approach is justified in that a man who believes that he is conspiring to commit a crime and wishes to conspire to commit a crime has a guilty mind and has done all in his power to plot the commission of an unlawful purpose." Miller's case furnishes a textbook example of the justification for a unilateral approach. Miller's guilty mind was not diminished by the fact that Powell had made an agreement to serve as a law enforcement informant. It is true that Miller's chance of succeeding in kidnapping his family under the circumstances was minimal, but Miller has "nonetheless engaged in conduct which provides unequivocal evidence of his firm purpose to commit a crime." It is our conclusion that we should follow the majority rule of our sister states, and we hold that valid public policy as well as the language and the legislative history of our conspiracy statute make the unilateral approach to conspiracy the law of Wyoming.

[The] Judgment and Sentence of the district court is affirmed.

NOTES

1. *Criticizing unilateral concept.* In *Washington v. Pacheco*, 125 Wash.2d 150, 882 P.2d 183 (1994), the court applied a statute similar to the one applied in *Miller*, but reached a different result. As in *Miller*, Pacheco conspired with a government agent.

[A] conspiratorial agreement necessarily requires more than one to agree because it is impossible to conspire with oneself. [B]y requiring an agreement, the Legislature intended to retain the requirement of a genuine or bilateral agreement. [T]he statute incorporates a limited form [of] unilateral conspiracy in that it is no longer necessary that agreement be proved against both conspirators. Thus[,] the failure to convict an accused's sole co-conspirator will not prevent proof of the conspiratorial agreement against the accused. However, this does not indicate the Legislature intended to abandon the traditional requirement of two criminal participants reaching an underlying agreement.

[T]he primary reason for making conspiracy a separate offense from the substantive crime is the increased danger to society posed by group criminal activity. [I]ncreased danger is nonexistent when a person "conspires" with a government agent who pretends agreement. In the feigned conspiracy there is no increased chance the criminal enterprise will succeed, no continuing criminal enterprise, no educating in criminal practices, and no greater difficulty of detection.... [I]t is questionable whether the unilateral conspiracy punishes criminal activity or merely criminal intentions. The "agreement" in a unilateral conspiracy is a legal fiction, a technical way of transforming nonconspiratorial conduct into a prohibited conspiracy....

Another concern with the unilateral approach is its potential for abuse. In a unilateral conspiracy, the State not only plays an active role in creating the offense, but also becomes the chief witness in proving the crime at trial. [T]his has the potential to put the State in the improper position of manufacturing crime. At the same time, such reaching is unnecessary because the punishable conduct in a unilateral conspiracy will almost always satisfy the elements of either solicitation or attempt. The State will still be able to thwart the activity and punish the defendant who attempts agreement with an undercover police officer.

[The] purpose of incorporating the unilateral approach into [Washington's conspiracy statute] was to obviate the prior law's implicit requirement of conviction of the co-conspirators.... [T]he State has not persuaded us the Legislature intended to abandon the traditional requirement of an actual agreement....

Justice Durham dissented: "The unilateral approach is not concerned with the content of the agreement or whether there is a meeting of minds. Its sole concern is whether the agreement, shared or not, objectively manifests the criminal intent of at least one of the conspirators. [T]he major basis of conspiratorial liability is not the group nature of the activity but the firm purpose of an individual to commit a crime which is objectively manifested in conspiring...."

2. *Expansion of conspiracy.* Consider also the following comments from *United States v. Valigura*, 50 M.J. 844 (Army Ct.Crim.App. 1999):

Two reasons have been given for making conspiratorial agreements illegal. One is to punish the special dangers inherent in group criminal activity. The second is to permit preventive steps against those who show a disposition to commit crime. The unilateral theory of conspiracy does not further the first purpose because when there is only a solo conspirator, there is perforce no "group" criminal activity. The increased danger is particularly nonexistent in a feigned conspiracy with a government agent who pretends agreement. There is no increased chance the criminal enterprise will succeed, no continuing criminal enterprise, and no greater difficulty of detection.

The unilateral theory also does not further the second purpose beyond that which already exists in other multiple actor inchoate offenses, i.e., solicitation and attempted conspiracy. The punishable conduct in a unilateral conspiracy will almost always satisfy the elements of either solicitation or attempt. The government will still be able to thwart the activity and punish the individual who attempts agreement with an undercover police officer. Thus, it is in the instant case. Although appellant dodges the conspiracy bullet, attempted conspiracy still finds its mark.

This court notes with some concern the proliferation of conspiracy charges in recent years. As eloquently stated by Judge Learned Hand, conspiracy is the "darling of the modern prosecutor's nursery." Its attraction has not diminished with the passage of years. Justice Jackson sardonically noted that the history of conspiracy exemplified Justice Cardozo's phrase, "the 'tendency of a principle to expand itself to the limit of its logic,' " and further cautioned that "loose practice as to this offense constitutes a serious threat to fairness in our administration of justice." Adoption of a "unilateral theory" of conspiracy would exacerbate this threat. Although we affirm a lesser included attempted conspiracy in this case, we do not do so to encourage any further expansion of prosecutorial overzealousness. Let us hearken back to basic principles of justice and proportionality. . . .

3. *Wharton's rule.* Some jurisdictions continue to follow the dictates of the traditional "Wharton's Rule," a rule which provides that two individuals may *not* be convicted for conspiracy where they have committed a crime that necessarily requires the participation of two individuals, e.g. adultery. *See Iannelli v. United States*, 420 U.S. 770 (1975). While infrequently applied today in any jurisdiction, this rule would appear particularly to be of questionable applicability in a unilateral conspiracy jurisdiction.

PROBLEMS

1. *Comparing Miller and Pacheco.* Since the conspiracy statutes at issue in the Colorado and Washington were both taken, in significant part, from the Model Penal Code, what, in your opinion, accounts for the differences in the judicial interpretations found in *Miller* and *Pacheco*?

2. *Pretending Co-conspirators.* Patricia Columbo solicited two people, Roman Sobczynski and Lannie Mitchell, to kill her parents and brother

because her parents were giving her and her boyfriend "a hard time." Sobczynski and Mitchell agreed with her to do the killing, but never intended to take any action. They pretended to do what Columbo wanted in order to induce her to have sexual relations with them. In a bilateral jurisdiction (as Illinois was at that time), is Columbo guilty of conspiracy to commit murder? Is she guilty in a unilateral jurisdiction (as Illinois is now)? *People v. Columbo*, 118 Ill.App.3d 882, 74 Ill.Dec. 304, 455 N.E.2d 733 (1983).

3. *Attempted Conspiracy.* Suppose that A agrees with B to scalp basketball tickets at double their face value. Both A and B believe that it is illegal to scalp tickets. In fact, although it used to be illegal to scalp them, the law changed a year ago and it is now legal. Can A and B be convicted of conspiracy? Attempted conspiracy?

B. MENS REA

The mens rea of conspiracy is often described in the case law as having two separate (and independent) components: (1) the intent to agree with another person to commit the target act; and (2) the intent to commit the target act itself.

PALMER v. COLORADO

964 P.2d 524 (Colo. 1998).

JUSTICE BENDER delivered the Opinion of the Court.

[The] defendant, Aaron Palmer, was convicted of multiple felonies for having fired gunshots at several victims. The district court sentenced Palmer to the Department of Corrections for a substantial period of time and imposed a concurrent term for the single count of conspiracy to commit reckless manslaughter.... On appeal, Palmer argued that conspiracy to commit reckless manslaughter is not a legally cognizable crime in Colorado. Noting that conspiracy is a crime requiring a specific intention to achieve the forbidden result and that reckless manslaughter is a crime requiring recklessness with respect to the result, Palmer argued that it is logically impossible to specifically intend that an unintended death occur.

The court of appeals [determined] that conspiracy does not require that the conspirator intend to cause a particular result but merely requires that the conspirator know that he or she and another are engaging in criminal conduct. Since it is possible to know that an agreement to engage in conduct creates a substantial and unjustifiable risk of death, and to disregard that risk, the court of appeals concluded that conspiracy to commit reckless manslaughter is a legally cognizable crime.

[Conspiracy] is a substantive "offense." Thus, the phrase "with [the] intent" as it appears in [the conspiracy] statute refers to and relies on the statutory definition of these words for its meaning: the defendant must have the "conscious objective [to] cause the specific result proscribed by the statute defining the offense." Since the culpable mental state for the crime of conspiracy is "with intent," conspiracy is a specific intent crime.

The crime of conspiracy requires two mental states. First, the defendant must possess the specific intent to agree to commit a particular crime. Second, the defendant must possess the specific intent to cause the result of the crime that is the subject of the agreement. Specific intent is an integral part of the crime and "must be established with the same certainty as any other material element of the crime."

[By contrast, a] criminal attempt requires that the accused act with the kind of culpability otherwise required for the commission of the underlying offense:

> A person commits criminal attempt if, acting with the kind of culpability otherwise required for commission of an offense, he engages in conduct constituting a substantial step toward the commission of the offense.

If the underlying offense is a specific intent crime, then the culpable mental state for the crime of attempt will be "intentionally;" if the underlying offense is a general intent crime, then the culpable mental state will be "knowingly." Thus, unlike conspiracy, punishment for attempt "is not confined to actors whose conscious purpose is to perform the proscribed acts or to achieve the proscribed results." Instead, it is enough that the accused knowingly engages in the risk producing conduct that could lead to the result. It is possible to be convicted of attempt without the specific intent to obtain the forbidden result.

[Unlike] attempt and conspiracy, complicity is not a separate and distinct crime under the Colorado Criminal Code. It is not a violation of, or conduct defined by, a statute for which a fine or imprisonment may be imposed. Rather, complicity is a legal theory in which a person who aids, abets, or advises another who commits an offense is liable for that offense as a principal. . . .

The complicity statute creates criminal liability only if the defendant acts "with the intent" to promote or facilitate the offense. Unlike conspiracy, however, complicity is not a substantive offense, and therefore the word "intent" in the complicity statute does not mean specific intent but rather retains its plain and ordinary meaning. . . .

To summarize, conspiracy, attempt, and complicity are distinct legal principles with different requirements for mental culpability. Conspiracy is a specific intent crime that requires the defendant to intend to agree, and to intend specifically to achieve the result of the crime. The phrase "with the intent to promote or facilitate [the] commission [of a crime]" contained in the conspiracy statute requires construction using the precise statutory definition. The accused must have the conscious objective to achieve the specific result proscribed by an offense. The culpable mental state for attempt is determined by the required mental state of the underlying crime. Hence, it is possible to commit the crime of attempt without possessing a specific intent, provided that the underlying crime does not require a specific intent. Complicity is a legal theory rather than a crime; the phrase "with the intent to promote or facilitate the commission of the offense" contained in the complicity statute retains its ordinary meaning and usage and does not require specific intent as defined by the General Assembly. With these principles in mind, we turn to the issue of whether conspiracy to commit reckless manslaughter is a cognizable crime.

[The] People argue that the crime of conspiracy to commit reckless manslaughter, if recognized, would not require the defendant to specifically intend the death of the victim, and therefore such an offense would not be a logical impossibility. We disagree. Although a superficial reading of the conspiracy statute might support the People's argument, it is necessary to analyze the statute together with the legislative definition of specific intent and with our prior case law interpreting the crime of conspiracy in Colorado. In doing so, we reach the conclusion that a crime of conspiracy to commit reckless manslaughter would indeed pose a legal and logical conflict that is irreconcilable. Thus, we hold that conspiracy to commit reckless manslaughter is not a cognizable crime.

[A] person commits reckless manslaughter if "[h]e recklessly causes the death of another person." Reckless manslaughter does not require the specific intent to cause the death of another. Rather, it requires that a person knowingly engage in risk producing acts or conduct that create a substantial and unjustifiable risk of causing a death. "One may be guilty of attempting to commit a crime of recklessness if it is shown that he was merely reckless toward the possibility that his conduct might have a certain consequence."

The culpable mental states for conspiracy and for reckless manslaughter are legally and logically inconsistent. The crime of conspiracy to commit reckless manslaughter would require that the defendant have the specific intent to commit reckless manslaughter. Crimes of recklessness are, by definition, crimes that are committed unintentionally, but with a conscious disregard for a substantial and unjustifiable risk that a result will occur. Thus, the state of mind required for reckless manslaughter is irreconcilable with the specific intent required for conspiracy. Logic dictates that one cannot agree in advance to accomplish an unintended result. Thus, we hold that conspiracy to commit reckless manslaughter is not a cognizable offense in Colorado.

[In] [*People v.*] *Thomas*[, 729 P.2d 972, 975 (Colo. 1986),] the petitioner argued that the crime of attempted reckless manslaughter was a legal impossibility. We noted that the culpable mental state for attempted reckless manslaughter is the mental state required for the commission of the underlying offense, reckless manslaughter, and that attempt liability focuses on conduct rather than results. Reckless manslaughter requires the conscious disregard of a substantial and unjustifiable risk that death will occur. Thus, we held, the culpable mental state for attempted reckless manslaughter is that the accused knowingly engage in conduct while consciously disregarding a substantial and unjustifiable risk of death. Even though death is an element of reckless manslaughter, one may commit the crime of attempted reckless manslaughter without intending that death occur. Since attempt requires the same mental culpability as the underlying crime, we held that there is no inconsistency between the mental culpability requirement for attempt and that for the underlying crime, reckless manslaughter.

Here, however, the culpability requirement for conspiracy and that for the crime of reckless manslaughter conflict. Conspiracy is always a specific intent crime, and conspiracy liability focuses on specifically intended results rather than on conduct. Unlike attempted reckless manslaughter, conspiracy to commit reckless manslaughter would require the accused to possess the specific intent to achieve an unintentional death, which we conclude is a legal and logical impossibility.

[In] summary, we hold that conspiracy to commit reckless manslaughter is not a cognizable crime under Colorado law. [Accordingly,] we reverse the judgment of the court of appeals on this issue only and remand the case with instructions to vacate the judgment of conviction for the crime of conspiracy to commit reckless manslaughter.

PROBLEMS

1. *Other Conspiracy Crime in Palmer.* Even though Palmer cannot be convicted of conspiracy to commit manslaughter, has he conspired to commit any other crime? If so, what?

2. *Attempt Mens Rea.* In some jurisdictions, attempt is a specific intent crime. Where that is true, would that change this analysis? How?

3. *Conspiracy to Commit Negligence Crime.* In Colorado, can a defendant be guilty of conspiracy to commit an offense which has the mens rea element of criminal negligence? Why or why not? In such a case, how would the prosecutor prove that the parties had agreed?

UNITED STATES v. HASSOUN

2007 WL 4180844 (S.D.Fla. 2007).

MARCIA G. COOKE, DISTRICT JUDGE.

[Following] a four-month jury trial, on August 16, 2007, defendants Adham Amin Hassoun, Jose Padilla and Kifah Wael Jayyousi were convicted of the three counts charged in the Fifth Superseding Indictment. Count One charged the defendants with violating 18 U.S.C. § 956(a)(1), conspiring to commit acts of murder, kidnaping or maiming outside of the United States, while committing one or more overt acts in furtherance thereof within the United States. Count Two charged the defendants with violating 18 U.S.C. § 371, conspiring to violate section 2339A (i.e., conspiring to provide material support to terrorists). Count Three charged the defendants with violating 18 U.S.C. § 2339A, providing material support or resources, or concealing the nature thereof, all while knowing or intending that they be used in preparation for, or in carrying out a violation of section 956 (i.e., a conspiracy to murder, kidnap or maim on foreign soil).

[Defendants] assert that the evidence at trial was insufficient to prove their intent, while in the United States, to murder, kidnap, or maim persons overseas. [The] arguments defendants offer to support [these] claims are unpersuasive [and] the defendants' Motions for Judgment of Acquittal are denied.

[Hassoun] claims that the government did not adduce sufficient evidence at trial to find beyond a reasonable doubt that he harbored the specific intent to commit any of the three objects of the conspiracy to murder, kidnap or maim. Consequently, Hassoun asserts that no reasonable jury could have found, beyond a reasonable doubt, that he possessed the requisite specific intent "which was the essential underpinning of the government's entire case." Hassoun correctly recites the well-established legal principle that a "[c]onspiracy to commit a particular substantive offense cannot exist without at least the degree of criminal intent necessary for the substantive offense itself." Thus, to find Hassoun guilty of Count One, the jury needed to find that Hassoun had the specific intent to murder, kidnap or maim. When viewing the evidence in the light most favorable to the government, a reasonable jury could have found that Hassoun harbored the specific intent to murder, kidnap or maim.

The jury was entitled to consider the evidence, and decide whether Hassoun's actions were driven by the sole desire to provide humanitarian support or the violent intent to murder, maim or kidnap. The government's evidence indicated that Hassoun distinguished between jihad which he defined as "battle for the sake of Allah" and da'wa, which he defined as building schools and teaching people. Moreover, the government presented evidence indicating that Hassoun was committed to a violent form of jihad—which he frequently referred to using the code word "tourism"—and viewed it as paramount to providing humanitarian support.[12]

It was not unreasonable for the jury to weigh the evidence and conclude that Hassoun adopted a violent concept of jihad. The government also presented evidence indicating that code words such as 'football,'[13] 'zucchini,'[14] and 'eggplant'[15] used by Hassoun were intended to cover up his participation in illicit violent activities. See, e.g., GX 28T/ 28TR (discussing the "first area"—identified as Afghanistan[16]—and how there are "football courts"[17] ready for whomever wants to train for the game); GX 86T/86TR (inquiring whether the brothers bought "the zucchini and such"); GX 92T/92TR (discussing equipping an al Qaeda affiliate in Lebanon with funds to purchase "zucchini" and "eggplant" for future violent battles).[18] Telephone conversations where Hassoun used this language could reasonably suggest that Hassoun actively sent money, recruits, and equipment overseas for use in future violent jihad conflicts. Hassoun's monetary contributions for 'tourism' must be viewed in the same light. When considered in conjunction with the other evidence at trial, these contributions could reasonably be viewed as Hassoun's attempts to equip mujahideen fighters with munitions for future battles. This support for violent jihadist activities—which had as an expected consequence, murder, kidnaping and maiming—was entitled to the jury's consideration when deciding Hassoun's specific intent.

---

12. After explaining to his co-conspirators that their roles in the conspiracy were akin to links in a chain, where "one . . . completes the other," Hassoun explained:

As to the other issues the Calling [missionary work] . . . the people who work in the Calling, God bless, there are so many of them . . . But the people who work in "tourism," they are just few, you can count them on your fingers . . . So let those people who work in the Calling, let them work in the Calling . . . do their books, newsletters, and matters . . . it's not a problem, as long as they work on it. But with regard to the field of "tourism," let us work on it . . . this is a very important issue . . . because very few work in "tourism" very few.

This discussion evidences that Hassoun appreciated the significance of both "tourism"—defined as jihad—and humanitarian aid. However, he felt it his duty—along with his co-conspirators—to furnish the latter form of support.

13. See Tr. (interpreting "football" as a code word for jihad).

14. See Tr. (defining "zucchini" as weapons and noting that support cells and radical Islamist groups commonly use this terminology).

15. Dr. Rohan Gunaratna defined "eggplant" as a rocket propelled grenade launcher ("RPG") and explained that he is familiar with this term being used in this regard through his research and study. Dr. Gunaratna added that an RPG is a standup weapon used by militant and terrorist organizations to conduct attacks. He additionally noted that, the weapon is intended to fire at and destroy its target, be it infrastructure, a vehicle or people.

16. See Tr. (interpreting "first area" as a code word for Afghanistan).

17. See Tr. 6/28/07 (noting that "football courts" was a code expression for training camps intended to "train people to conduct attacks").

18. Hassoun also discussed the status of screws—referring to bullets during this call. Kassem Daher informed Hassoun that there were a million "screws" in Lebanon that "slipped through [their] hands because there's no . . . money." After Hassoun affirms that he understood what Daher's reference to one-million screws meant, Daher adds that "the dogs . . . the ones who are with the party of the devil" came and took the screws.

[Furthermore,] with regard to having the intent to murder specifically, the jury was allowed to consider a variety of factors indicative of malice aforethought and premeditation. When drawing inferences in favor of the government, the jury was allowed to consider the lengthy time frame of the conspiracy, and how defendants observed and were informed of how their material support in America generated actual violence in various overseas locations. Furthermore, Hassoun's continued planning and involvement in these activities even after he observed the consequences of his actions is indicative of his premeditation and malice aforethought. Hassoun received news-report and first hand accounts of the jihad theaters to which he contributed, and could have disavowed the violence or extricated himself from the conspiracy if the violence did not comport with his intent. Hassoun never did this. Nor did he merely acquiesce in the violence perpetrated in these jihad areas. Rather, Hassoun continued to promote the violence in these regions and support the violence with money, equipment and recruits.

[Additionally,] Hassoun discussed dividing the labor among various members of the conspiracy and specified that "each [member of the conspiracy] has a duty and a mission . . . let him work on it and perfect it." Statements such as this, when viewed in conjunction with statements suggesting the nature of the conspiracy could reasonably be perceived by the jury as evidencing Hassoun's premeditated intent. For instance, on a call with Jayyousi and Daher, Hassoun explains:

> [T]he important thing is that each one of us completes the other . . . so if you can't finish something your brother will complete it for you, and the other brother will complete it for him, and so on . . . so we are all a connected link . . . if someone splits from this link, the link is no longer connected, and each one is on their own. We don't want to get to that point . . . especially that tourism work is a good work, because there are a lot of tourists and a lot of people who would like to go do tourism . . . so we work toward, of course to always inform them of the nice places for tourism and so on . . . and 'resort places' and so on. . . .

Accordingly, the government provided sufficient evidence that Hassoun harbored the requisite specific intent for Count One.

[In] his Motion for Judgment of Acquittal Padilla asserts that the government . . . did not adduce sufficient evidence at trial for a reasonable jury to find, beyond a reasonable doubt, that Padilla . . . engaged in a conspiracy to murder, kidnap, or maim while physically within the United States[.] [Padilla] correctly argues that the mere presence of a defendant with alleged conspirators is insufficient to support a conviction. However, the evidence at trial, when viewed most favorably to the government, does not merely show Padilla's presence among and association with his co-conspirators. Rather, the calls, testimony, and the fruit of defendants' effort—Padilla attending an al Qaeda training camp, evinced by his training camp application—prove that Padilla was an integral part of defendants' conspiratorial agreement. Specifically, the evidence demonstrated Padilla's complicity in a "specific plan to engage in violent [jihad] which had as a necessary consequence murder, kidnaping, and maiming."[26]

Padilla actively participated in planning the defendants' scheme. He discussed his intentions to train and fight with his co-conspirators, he boarded a plane fully intending to train for and fight in violent jihad abroad, and he ultimately attended an al Qaeda training camp in Afghanistan. Furthermore, Padilla even criticized and instructed his co-conspirators about how jihad should be discussed and the attributes necessary to participate in jihad. Padilla's status as one of the conspiracy's mujahideen recruits further embroiled him in the conspiracy's web by making him an instrument of the scheme itself. Padilla's involvement in the defendants' agreement went well beyond mere presence. Padilla voluntarily participated in planning aspects of the conspiracy, participated in the accomplishment of its goals, and took steps to ensure that these goals were effectuated while in the United States. Accordingly, the jury were entitled to conclude that Padilla engaged in a conspiracy to murder, kidnap, or maim and provided or concealed material support to a section 956 conspiracy to murder, kidnap, or maim, both while physically within the United States.

[Jayyousi's] general assertion that "a reasonable jury could not have returned a verdict of guilty, based solely upon the evidence presented at trial" ... does not reflect the evidence presented at trial. The government's evidence documented Jayyousi's participation in the conspiracy and furtherance of its goals. Similarly to Hassoun, the government adduced evidence indicating that Jayyousi subscribed to a violent form of jihad. The government also provided significant evidence indicating Jayyousi's complicity in the conspiratorial scheme, including participation in phone calls discussing funding violent jihad, utilizing code words to cover up illicit activity and recruiting mujahideen. See, e.g., GX 18T/18TR (discussing how each member of the conspiracy has a distinct role, similar to links in a chain, and discussing the importance of their continued work in "tourism"); GX 12T/12TR (discussing funding "football" and how "the brothers are ready to play football"); GX 28T/ 28TR (discussing the "first area" and how there are "football courts" ready for whomever wants to train for the game); GX 31T/31TR (inquiring whether "football" was being played

---

26. [The] government's evidence did not document Padilla's mere presence, passive acquiescence or knowledge of the conspiratorial scheme. Rather, the evidence proffered by the government indicated that Padilla pro-actively made himself a party to the conspiracy by agreeing to further its objectives and taking steps to ensure that these objectives were met. [The] government presented substantial evidence that Padilla was actively involved in planning and furthering the goals of the conspiracy ...

in a specific area and whether or not there was a "playground" available).

[Furthermore,] the government provided evidence documenting Jayyousi's efforts to secure communications equipment and to fund the travels of mujahideen recruits destined for training in Afghanistan or fighting in Chechnya. This evidence documented Jayyousi's ongoing, methodical and calculated complicity in the object of the conspiracy. Accordingly, the jury were entitled to conclude that Jayyousi engaged in a conspiracy to murder, kidnap, or maim and provided or concealed material support to a section 956 conspiracy to murder, kidnap, or maim, both while physically within the United States.

[For] all the foregoing reasons, and based upon the record at trial and the entirety of evidence presented by the government in this case, the defendants are not entitled to judgments of acquittal on any of the three counts in the Indictment.

PROBLEMS

1. *Charging Substantive Instead of Conspiracy Offenses.* The federal district court in *Hassoun* noted that "Hassoun correctly recites the well-established legal principle that a '[c]onspiracy to commit a particular substantive offense cannot exist without at least the degree of criminal intent necessary for the substantive offense itself.'" Since that is the case, with respect to the first charged conspiracy—conspiring to commit acts of murder, kidnaping or maiming outside of the United States, while committing one or more overt acts in furtherance thereof within the United States—why do you think that the prosecution did not simply charge and try these three co-defendants with the substantive offenses themselves (or, at least, with attempts to commit these substantive offenses) rather than simply conspiracy to commit these offenses?

2. *Conspiracy to Provide Support.* With respect to the second charged conspiracy—conspiring to provide material support to terrorists—why do you think that the prosecution did charge these co-defendants both with conspiracy and the substantive offense itself?

UNITED STATES v. BLANKENSHIP
970 F.2d 283 (7th Cir. 1992).

EASTERBROOK, CIRCUIT JUDGE.

Courts do not enforce bargains among the producers of illegal drugs or between these producers and their customers. Extra-judicial remedies tend to be violent, which makes drug running a crime of the young and vigorous. Substitutes for both legal processes and brutality are possible, however; family ties may suffice. Nancy Nietupski, a grandmother in her early 60's, ran a methamphetamine ring through her extended family. She started on the west coast, working with her nephew William Zahm. Later she moved to her sister's farm in

Illinois. While sister Violet Blankenship supplied a base of operations, nephew Robert Blankenship helped distribute the drug and collect debts.

Nietupski initially bought methamphetamine from outside sources. When these proved unreliable, Zahm helped her enter the manufacturing end of the business. "Cooking" methamphetamine is messy, and there is a risk of explosion when volatile chemicals such as acetone reach high temperatures. Nietupski and Zahm moved their laboratory frequently to reduce the risk of detection. In February 1989, Zahm leased from Thomas Lawrence a house trailer in which to set up shop for a day. Nietupski told Lawrence what Zahm planned to make and offered $1,000 or one ounce of methamphetamine; Lawrence preferred the cash and took $100 as a down payment. He covered the floor of the trailer with plastic for protection. Zahm postponed the operation when he could not find a heating control. A few days later Lawrence got cold feet, telling Marvin Bland (one of Nietupski's assistants) that he wanted the chemicals and equipment removed. Bland complied.

Zahm soon joined William Worker to set up a new methamphetamine ring. Agents of the DEA infiltrated the Zahm–Worker clique. Zahm cut his losses by turning against his aunt, whose operations collapsed. Eighteen persons from the Nietupski ring were indicted. Robert Blankenship, Thomas Lawrence, and six others were in one group, all charged in a single count with conspiring to manufacture and distribute methamphetamine. Of the six, three pleaded guilty and three were acquitted. Blankenship and Lawrence, convicted by the jury, received identical sentences of 120 months' imprisonment plus five years' supervised release. . . .

Conspiracy is agreement to violate the law. Unless Lawrence willingly joined the Nietupski venture, he did not commit the crime of conspiracy. What evidence was there that Lawrence knew, let alone joined? Nietupski and Zahm told Lawrence what they planned to do in his trailer; Zahm and Lawrence sampled some of the product scraped off the apparatus; for $1,000 he furnished the space, covered the floor with plastic, supplied refreshments, and let Zahm take a shower to wash some acid off his legs. If providing assistance to a criminal organization were the same thing as conspiracy, then Lawrence would be guilty. Yet there is a difference between supplying goods to a syndicate and joining it, just as there is a difference between selling goods and being an employee of the buyer. Cargill sells malt and barley to Anheuser Busch, knowing that they will be made into beer, without being part of Busch; by parallel reasoning, someone who sells sugar to a bootlegger knowing the use that will be made of that staple is not thereby a conspirator, *United States v. Falcone*, 311 U.S. 205 (1940), and someone who buys one load of marijuana has not conspired with the sellers, *United States v. Baker*, 905 F.2d 1100, 1106–07 (7th Cir. 1990).

Falcone illustrates the doctrine that "mere" sellers and buyers are not automatically conspirators. If it were otherwise, companies that sold cellular phones to teenage punks who have no use for them other than to set up drug deals would be in trouble, and many legitimate businesses would be required to monitor their customers' activities. Yet this does not get us very far, for no rule says that a supplier cannot join a conspiracy through which the product is put to an unlawful end. *Direct Sales Co. v. United States*, 319 U.S. 703 (1943), makes that point in holding that the jury may infer that a pharmaceutical house selling huge quantities of morphine to a physician over a seven-year span conspired with the physician to distribute the drug illegally.

Where does the "mere" sale end, the conspiracy begin? One may draw a line, as *Falcone* and *Direct Sales* did, between knowledge of other persons' crimes and intent to join them, but this restates the elements of the offense without telling us when an inference of intent to join is permissible. Selling a camera to a spy does not make one a traitor—but selling camera and film, developing the prints, enlarging the detail in the critical areas, and collecting half of the payment for the secret information would assuredly land one in prison. Stating polar cases is easy, but locating the line of demarcation is hard. Courts have a tendency in these situations to draw up a list of relevant factors, without describing necessary or sufficient conditions. Lists have burgeoned since *Falcone*.

[When] writing for the court of appeals in *Falcone*, Learned Hand concluded that a supplier joins a venture only if his fortunes rise or fall with the venture's, so that he gains by its success.... On this view the sale of a staple commodity such as sugar or telephone service does not enlist the seller in the criminal venture; in a competitive market the vendor could sell to someone else at the market price, and the buyer could turn to other sources. Anonymous transactions are the norm in markets and do not create criminal liability; when the seller has knowledge but the terms remain the same, there is no reason to infer participation in the enterprise any more than in the Cargill–Busch case we have given.

[Trailers] do not rent for $1,000 per week—not in legitimate markets, anyway. By charging a premium price, Lawrence seemingly threw in his lot with the Nietupski operation and may be convicted under Judge Hand's approach. Yet the price cannot be the end of things. What does the $1,000 represent: a piece of the action, or only a premium for the risks? Lawrence bore two. One was that the chemicals would damage his trailer. Although he took precautions by spreading plastic on the floor, an explosion would have spattered chemicals on the walls and ceiling. Lawrence would have charged for taking this risk even if the manufacture of methamphetamine were entirely legal. The other risk was the hazard of criminal liability, a cost of doing business. One who covers his own costs and no more does not share in the venture's success. Using a price calculated by reference to the risk of criminal conviction as support for that conviction would be circular. Reduce the risk of conviction, and you reduce the price. Either way, the price responds to the legal system rather than to the potential profits of the Nietupski gang and does not establish a desire to promote its success. Repeat business, as in *Direct Sales*, might show such a desire, but Lawrence did not carry through with the initial transaction and never realized even the $1,000.

[Other] cases from this court speak reverentially of Judge Hand but actually ask a different, and more functional, question. It is whether the imposition of liability on transactions of the class depicted by the case would deter crime without adding unduly to the costs of legitimate transactions.

[If] the product is itself contraband—for example, the methamphetamine Nietupski bought in California early on—the analysis differs but the result is the same: an isolated sale is not the same thing as enlisting in the venture. A sale of methamphetamine is a substantive crime. Because the substance is illegal, the seller knows that the buyer will put the drug to an illegal use, yet this does not make the sale a second, inchoate offense. To treat it as a second crime of aiding and abetting (or conspiring with) the buyer is to multiply the criminal punishment and so distort the penalty system the legislature adopted—for what is the point of setting at five years the maximum penalty for selling a given quantity of methamphetamine if every sale violates a second law and doubles the penalty?

[Some] states have statutes forbidding "criminal facilitation," an apt description of Lawrence's acts. Lawrence agreed to facilitate the manufacture of methamphetamine, but the United States Code lacks a facilitation statute. It does forbid aiding and abetting substantive offenses.

[Neither] *Direct Sales* nor any of this court's cases permits a supplier to a criminal organization to be sentenced for all of that organization's sins when he facilitated only one. If the United States Code contained a facilitation statute along the lines of New York's, Lawrence would receive a sentence proportioned to his own iniquity rather than that of Nietupski and her henchmen. So too if the Code penalized abetting criminal attempts. But it does not, and if the only options are conspiracy, with full responsibility for all of the venture's other crimes, and no crime, then no crime comes much closer to describing Lawrence's responsibility.

[Let] us be clear: we do not hold that in reforming criminal sentences Congress altered the definition of conspiracy. We come to the same conclusion as the Supreme Court did in *Falcone*. Lawrence knew what Zahm wanted to do in the trailer, but there is a gulf between knowledge and conspiracy. There is no evidence that Lawrence recognized, let alone that he joined and promoted, the full scope of the Nietupski organization's activities. He may have joined, or abetted, a more limited agreement to manufacture a quantity of methamphetamine, but he was not charged with that offense. Lawrence facilitated an attempted crime, and probably conspired to do this, but he did not subscribe to the broader agreement on which his conviction depends.

On Lawrence's appeal [the] judgment is reversed. . . .

PROBLEMS

1. *Burden on Legitimate Businesses.* Judge Easterbrook opines that a finding of conspiratorial intent in situations such as those described in *Blankenship* would lead to an undesirable "parade of horribles": "[C]ompanies that sold cellular phones to teenage punks who have no use for them other than to set up drug deals would be in trouble, and many legitimate businesses would be required to monitor their customers' activities." Is this really an undesirable result? Why or why not?

2. *Knowledge Is Not Intent.* Should there be exceptions to the proposition that "knowledge is not intent?" What if someone *knows* that an actor is about to kill his wife? Wouldn't silence be the same as a tacit agreement to assist in the homicide, i.e. assistance by not creating any impediments to the criminal act? Explain.

3. *Suspicious Buyers.* In making methamphetamine, drug producers use large quantities of legal chemicals (e.g., household and cleaning chemicals). Suppose that the owner of a large supermarket "suspects" that some customers are purchasing its chemicals and using them to create meth. Does that suspicion make the supermarket owner a co-conspirator? Would you reach a different result if:

    a. *Knowledge.* The supermarket owner is aware of the meth production and begins ordering much larger quantities of the desired chemicals?

    b. *Stopping Sales.* Because of the demand for the chemicals, the supermarket owner decides not to put them on sale.

4. *Taking Messages.* Louis Lauria operated a telephone-answering service which supplied its services to a number of prostitutes. Lauria knew that some of his customers were prostitutes (he used the services of one of them who received 500 calls a month) and he assured them of the utmost confidentiality in message-taking. When three of the prostitutes were arrested, Lauria was indicted along with them for conspiracy to commit prostitution. Is he guilty of this charge? *People v. Lauria*, 251 Cal.App.2d 471, 59 Cal.Rptr. 628 (1967).

5. *Bed Sheets.* Suppose that the owner of a local dry goods store has customers who include a known prostitute who buys bed sheets. Assuming that the store owner knows that the prostitute is using the sheets in her business, is the store owner a co-conspirator with the prostitute?

6. *Extra Charges.* In Problem 4, *supra*, should the result be different if Lauria charged the prostitute double what he charges his other customers? Should it matter whether he provides a special paging service to the prostitutes that he does not provide to other customers (for the additional fee)?

C. THE ACT OF AGREEMENT

It should come as no surprise that it is relatively uncommon for the prosecution to be able to present *direct* proof of a conspiratorial agreement. Most agreements are clandestine; they are not made in front of witnesses; nor are they made in the presence of video or audio surveillance; and, in the absence of a plea agreement, it is not in the interest of individual co-conspirators to testify to the existence of such incriminating matters. As a result, the *actus reus* element of conspiracy—the conspiratorial "agreement"—may be (and often is) established inferentially and/or circumstantially. In large part due to the nature of the proof, there is an abiding concern, particularly in large conspiracy trials, that some individuals who were not actually part of the conspiracy under scrutiny will be swept into the conspiratorial "net" simply because they have associated previously with one or more of the co-conspirators, however innocently.

UNITED STATES v. BARNES
38 M.J. 72 (Ct.Mil.App. 1993).

CRAWFORD, JUDGE:

In late September 1991, appellant was tried at Darmstadt, Germany, before a military judge sitting as a general court-martial. Contrary to her pleas, appellant was found guilty of conspiracy to kidnap, assault consummated by a battery (2 specifications), aggravated assault, and kidnapping. She was sentenced to a dishonorable discharge, confinement for 4 years, and total forfeitures. The convening authority approved the sentence. The Court of Military Review affirmed the findings and sentence. . . .

[The evidence] disclosed that the victim, Private (PVT) S, was a witness at a prior summary court-martial at which appellant was convicted of adultery, committing indecent acts, being disorderly, and absence from her appointed place of duty. During that trial, appellant was overheard threatening to "get" PVT S [who] had formerly roomed with her. PVT S also knew and was "real good friends" with PVT D, the alleged co-conspirator. The incident which led to appellant's conviction occurred in PVT D's room which adjoined appellant's room via a shared bathroom.

On the night of the activities leading to the charges[,] PVT D went to PVT S's room.... PVT S wanted "to stay there" and talk, but PVT D requested that PVT S come to her room. Later that evening PVT S went to PVT D's room. Upon PVT S's entering the room, PVT D locked the front door. PVT S and PVT D had talked for about an hour when appellant entered the room through the bathroom entrance. Thereafter an argument ensued regarding PVT S's testimony at appellant's summary court-martial. Appellant threatened to use a .9–millimeter weapon on PVT S unless she kept quiet about what was about to happen.

For the next hour or two, PVT S was subjected to various assaults. Appellant repeatedly hit PVT S in the face with her fists and a combat boot while holding on to PVT S's hair. Appellant also lit PVT S's hair and t-shirt on fire. Finally, appellant and PVT D took off all of PVT S's clothes, tied her hands and feet to the bed with shoelaces, and stuffed a sock in her mouth. Then appellant proceeded to beat PVT S with a plastic coat hanger.

During this 2–hour period, appellant and PVT D both left the room at various times. At one point appellant's roommate asked what was going on and was told by appellant that she and PVT D were messing S up. PVT S finally escaped by loosening the shoelaces when PVT D and appellant left the room to buy some beer....

[The] issue concerns the sufficiency of the evidence to support a finding of conspiracy to kidnap. A conspiracy to kidnap may be found if appellant and a co-conspirator entered into an agreement to kidnap the victim and, while the agreement continued to exist, either conspirator performed an overt act for the purpose of bringing about the kidnapping.

The existence of a conspiracy "need not take any 'particular form or be manifested in any formal words.'" The agreement to prove conspiracy can be silent, "tacit[,] or [only a] mutual understanding among the parties." [C]onspiracy is generally established by circumstantial evidence and is usually manifested by the conduct of the parties themselves. Conduct alone is sufficient to show an agreement. Finally, the conspiracy or agreement need not precede a substantive or overt act but, rather, may be "contemporaneous" with the offense.

[We] conclude that there was sufficient evidence of an implied agreement and an overt act which could, and did, lead a rational trier of fact to conclude that there was a conspiracy to commit kidnapping.

First, the victim testified that after she was in the room and the door had been locked behind her, she later overheard Barnes saying to PVT D, "Don't let her leave. I'm not done with her yet." One of the co-conspirators was also overheard saying to appellant's roommate, "We're teaching her a lesson." The other co-conspirator said, "We're beating the shit out of her for . . . what she did to us." A trier of fact could infer from these statements that the conspirators held a common purpose and intent to hold and harm PVT S, and to seek revenge against her. These statements suggest a tacit agreement to kidnap the victim.

Second, in addition to a common purpose or motive, there were ample means to carry out the agreement. Appellant and PVT D were friends whose bedrooms adjoined. They had a convenient location to hold PVT S while attracting little attention. The record shows that during the 2 hours that they held and assaulted PVT S, they played loud music so their neighbors would not suspect anything.

Finally, there were several overt acts which establish the final component of conspiracy to kidnap. The evidence reveals that appellant and PVT D worked together to tie up PVT S. PVT D also searched for and found the plastic hanger which subsequently was used by appellant to whip the victim. In addition, at one point PVT D held the victim down so she could not escape.

We conclude that a rational trier of fact could have found an implied agreement and subsequent overt acts which would prove a conspiracy to kidnap beyond a reasonable doubt.

The decision of the United States Army Court of Military Review is affirmed.

NOTE

How many agreements? Often co-conspirators have multiple criminal objectives, raising questions about how many conspiracies exist. Generally, the answer to that question can be simply answered. If co-conspirators make a single agreement to accomplish a number of criminal objectives, there is a single conspiracy. If, in contrast, co-conspirators make two agreements, each to accomplish one or more criminal objectives, there are two conspiracies. And so on. *See, e.g., Braverman v. United States,* 317 U.S. 49 (1942).

PROBLEMS

1. *Proving Conspiracy.* A and B are scalping tickets to a University of Louisville basketball game in Freedom Hall, Louisville. In Kentucky, scalping is illegal. Before the police arrested A and B, they observed them holding up tickets (suggesting that the tickets were for sale), talking with potential customers, and eventually selling tickets above face value. In addition, from time-to-time, A and B conversed with each other and were observed passing something between each other. Is there sufficient evidence of conspiracy to scalp to convict A and B? What kind of proof might the prosecutor offer to show that A and B are co-conspirators?

2. *Making Change.* In the prior problem, assume that C is A's girlfriend. While he is scalping tickets, she sits off to the side. Police observed her

getting coffee for A one time. In addition, during one sale, when A did not have exact change, C provided it to him. Is there sufficient evidence to convict C of conspiracy to scalp?

UNITED STATES v. MERCER

165 F.3d 1331 (11th Cir. 1999).

PER CURIAM:

David Mercer was convicted of conspiracy to distribute and possession with intent to distribute cocaine base. Mercer appeals only the conspiracy conviction, for which he received a mandatory life sentence. Because the government's evidence is insufficient to establish the existence of a conspiracy, we reverse.

This case began when a confidential informant told St. Petersburg, Florida detectives that he could provide information regarding an investigation of certain individuals suspected of drug activity, including Mercer's co-defendant Carol Miller. On October 3, 1995, the informant asked Miller where he could purchase one to two ounces of cocaine. Miller referred the informant to Mercer and gave him Mercer's address. In a recorded conversation, Miller told the informant that Mercer was her friend and could be trusted. Miller refused, however, to telephone Mercer or to accompany the informant to meet Mercer. The informant met with Mercer two days later, on October 5, 1995, and in recorded conversations discussed the purchase of two ounces of cocaine. The next day, Mercer sold the informant 27.98 grams of crack cocaine for $1,000. The informant attempted to arrange another purchase but was unable to contact Mercer.

Later, in January and February 1996, Mercer sold crack cocaine to an undercover police detective as the result of an unrelated drug investigation. In late January, a different informant identified Mercer to police as a drug dealer. When the detective in charge ran Mercer's name through the police computer system, he discovered Mercer was already being investigated. The detective arranged through his informant to meet with Mercer, and bought 17.6 grams of crack cocaine for $900. In February, the detective purchased 29 grams of crack cocaine for $1,200.

The government returned a superceding indictment charging David Mercer and Carol Miller with conspiracy to distribute cocaine base from about October 1, 1995 to about August 22, 1996. [Mercer] was convicted as charged. For sentencing purposes, the three transactions were grouped together in the conspiracy count. Because the aggregate amount of drugs sold was more than 50 grams and Mercer had two or more prior felony drug convictions, he received a mandatory life sentence for the conspiracy offense.

[Co-defendant,] Miller, who in addition to conspiracy was also charged with two counts of aiding and abetting the distribution of cocaine base, and with two counts of using a communication facility to facilitate the commission of drug offenses, was acquitted of all counts, including the conspiracy charge.

We must determine whether, when examined de novo in the light most favorable to the government, there is substantial evidence to support the conspiracy verdict as to David Mercer.

Mercer was convicted of violating section 846 of Title 21 of the United States Code, which provides:

> [A]ny person who attempts or conspires to commit any offense in this subchapter shall be subject to the same penalties as those prescribed for the offense, the commission of which was the object of the attempt or conspiracy.

To support a conspiracy conviction under section 846, the government must prove (1) an agreement between the defendant and one or more persons, (2) the object of which is to do either an unlawful act or a lawful act by unlawful means. The existence of the conspiracy and the defendant's participation in it may be established through circumstantial evidence.

The government contends the evidence proves Mercer conspired with his co-defendant, Carol Miller, and with unknown co-conspirators. The evidence of conspiracy arises out of Miller's conversation with the defendant and the three drug transactions. We can easily dispense with the allegation of conspiracy between Mercer and Carol Miller. The government's evidence shows that Miller met with the confidential informant to discuss what drugs Mercer could supply. Miller stated: "He got to take you to who he deal with, he deal with um, what's his . . . (Unintelligible) . . . name. He deal with somebody he got to take you, I know he do pot, I don't know what all he do it for, you need to find out." She told the confidential informant where to locate Mercer, and encouraged him to trust Mercer.

Although this evidence may be considered in reviewing the sufficiency issue even though Miller was acquitted, there is nothing here to support a finding of conspiracy between Mercer and Miller. Despite the confidential informant's repeated requests, Miller refused to telephone Mercer, or to go with the confidential informant to see Mercer. While the evidence shows that Miller referred Mercer to the informant as a source for the drug purchase, there is no evidence that she discussed with the informant or Mercer any details regarding the amount, quality or price of the cocaine or any particulars concerning the meeting. In short, there is no evidence of any agreement between Mercer and Miller.

The question then becomes whether there is sufficient evidence regarding the three drug sales to support a decision that Mercer was conspiring with unknown persons. The government relies heavily on the tape-recorded conversations in which Mercer and the police informant attempt to arrange a sale on October 5, 1995:

> MERCER: Oh boy . . . wait till my partner get in, be about 5 o'clock today.
>
> CI: Uh hum.
>
> MERCER: And I am, he got to call his boy in Tampa . . .
>
> CI: Come all the way from Tampa?
>
> MERCER: Yea.
>
> CI: Damn man.
>
> MERCER: It won't take that long . . . I got to check it out . . . get hold of some more guys around here that I know but they gonna run you where from about ah . . $750.00 to $800.00 an ounce.

After Mercer's delivery to the informant was delayed, Mercer said he was considering buying from another source if he had to wait too much longer.

> MERCER: I don't know I . . . like I said man, I am just on hold.
>
> CI: . . . that's bad business . . . . . .
>
> MERCER: I know. . . . But right now I am just waiting on him to call us and then if he don't call as soon as, uh, my old lady get home, I am going some where else.

(The actual sale did not occur until the next day, October 6, 1995).

According to the government, these conversations constitute evidence from which a jury could reasonably infer that "Mercer had an unknown source who supplied and/or cooked crack cocaine and that Mercer was involved in more than a buyer/seller relationship with his source." The government's case against Mercer appears to be based on the following syllogism: Since cocaine comes from out of the country, Mercer must know he is buying from conspirators involved in the importation and distribution of drugs, and therefore he is a member of the conspiracy. . . . Under the government's theory, anyone selling crack cocaine can be charged with conspiracy in addition to the substantive charge.

[Justice] Jackson, 50 years ago, in discussing the development of the law of conspiracy referred to Justice Cardozo's maxim about "the tendency of a principle to expand itself to the limit of its logic." This case tests the limit of the logic underlying conspiracy law. The government's position "stretches the boundaries of conspiracy law to the breaking point."

To properly decide this case, we must make the critical distinction between a conspiratorial agreement and a buyer-seller transaction. "We punish conspiracy because joint action is, generally, more dangerous than individual action." While a sale, by definition, requires two parties, the agreement is to exchange drugs for money. "The buy-sell transaction is simply not probative of an agreement to join together to accomplish a criminal objective beyond that already being accomplished by the transaction." On the other hand, "[c]onspiracies, which are really 'agreements to agree' on the multitude of decisions and acts necessary to successfully pull off a crime, pose an additional risk that the object of the conspiracy will be achieved, and so warrant additional penalties." The essence of the conspiracy, then, is an agreement, not the commission of the substantive offense. "Where the buyer's purpose is merely to buy and the seller's purpose is merely to sell, and no prior or contemporaneous understanding exists between the two beyond the sales agreement, no conspiracy has been shown."

In the case of a purchaser of narcotics, we have held that agreement may be inferred when the evidence shows a continuing relationship that results in the repeated transfer of illegal drugs to the purchaser. [In *United States v.*] *Beasley*, [2 F.3d 1551 (11th Cir. 1993),] the evidence against defendant established more than a buyer-seller relationship between defendant and seller. The seller testified that defendant purchased crack cocaine from him on several occasions during seller's short stay in Mobile and that he sometimes fronted the cocaine to defendant. The seller knew from what street corner defendant was selling the cocaine. The seller testified that he and defendant "split up" three kilograms of cocaine. From this evidence, the jury could have reasonably inferred a continuing course of conduct between the parties designed to result in the distribution of cocaine from that particular street corner.

In [*United States v.*] *Bascaro*, [742 F.2d 1335 (11th Cir. 1984), *cert. denied*, 472 U.S. 1017 (1985),] the defendants were among the selling group's best buyers, they purchased from the selling group on numerous occasions, and maintained a close relationship with the selling group. The selling group relied upon the defendant's participation and cooperation for its success. The court determined the evidence was more than sufficient to sustain the conclusion that the defendants had entered into a conspiratorial agreement with the other co-defendants.

We have held the evidence sufficient to support a conspiracy involving unknown persons where there were numerous references to other conspirators and details regarding the conspiratorial agreement.... In [*United States v.*] *Carcaise*, [763 F.2d 1328 (11th Cir. 1985),] we upheld defendant's conviction for conspiracy to possess drugs with intent to distribute based on numerous statements referring to "the guy," "my friend" and "these people" and references to the details of the drug delivery.

At the other end of the spectrum, where the evidence proved only a buy-sell transaction, this Court has reversed a conviction for drug conspiracy. Concluding that the evidence was insufficient to establish conspiracy, the Court noted that the "record reveals little conversation between [the seller] and the Appellant, and no evidence that an actual agreement was consummated."

Applying this law to the facts in this case, we can infer from Mercer's remarks that he had a buy-sell relationship with an unnamed source. The evidence is legally insufficient, however, to show a conspiratorial agreement to distribute drugs. Nor does Mercer's single reference to "my partner" establish the existence of a partnership for purposes of this case. When looked at in context, the term partner probably was used in the colloquial sense as someone with whom he had dealings with. This vague reference without more is insufficient to establish a conspiratorial agreement. In fact, Mercer's comment that he would go somewhere else if he did not hear from his supplier belies the inference that he had a conspiratorial agreement with a particular supplier.

[In] this case there is no evidence of anything other than at most a buyer-seller relationship. There was no evidence of a common design or purpose to join Mercer with anyone other than government agents. The evidence shows simply that his co-defendant Miller knew that Mercer sold drugs and that he had sources from which he could get drugs, that Mercer had a source for drugs and if that source failed he would "go somewhere else," that he bought quantities of cocaine from some unknown source and sold it to police agents presumably at a profit. Having carefully reviewed the record, we conclude that evidence is insufficient to sustain Mercer's conspiracy conviction.

Reversed.

NOTES

1. *Hearsay exception.* In establishing the existence of a conspiratorial agreement in court, prosecutors may use testimony by one co-conspirator about what another co-conspirator said, even though such testimony is ordinarily inadmissible as hearsay. The "co-conspirator hearsay exception," is justified on the ground that co-conspirators are acting as agents of one another. Under that exception, declarations made by one co-conspirator during and in furtherance of the conspiracy are admissible in court, assuming that there has been a substantial and independent showing that a conspiracy existed and that the individuals in question were a part of that conspiracy.

2. *Wheels and chains.* Some courts have used such metaphors as "wheels" and "chains" to describe the operation of common types of conspiratorial arrangements. A "wheel" conspiracy involves separate conspiracies

("the spokes") linked to each other through a common individual ("the hub"). *See, e.g., Kotteakos v. United States*, 328 U.S. 750 (1946) (holding no wheel conspiracy where spokes not connected, e.g. through knowledge by the separate conspirators of the existence of other conspirators or conspiracies). A "chain" conspiracy, in contrast, is a single conspiracy where individual members (the "links") interact only with the next link in the chain and may not know any of the other links farther up or down the chain. Narcotics importation and distribution schemes are common examples of chain conspiracies.

PROBLEMS

1. *Single Transaction.* Are you persuaded that a conspiracy does not exist in *Mercer* as a result of a single buy-sell narcotics transaction, but that a conspiracy may (does?) exist as a result of multiple transactions? Arguably, both situations involve an "agreement," with the difference being the terms of the agreement (the frequency of sales). Explain.

2. *The Lookout.* Defendant Luis Mercado leaned out a third-floor window and observed three different crack cocaine sales (all to undercover police officers) made on three different occasions by his co-defendant, Alex Colon. According to the government, Mercado was operating as a "lookout" for Colon. When the third-floor apartment was searched pursuant to a lawful search warrant, no drugs were found on Mercado, but officers found 23.7 grams of cocaine sitting out in the open on a table, as well as two plastic packets each containing 20 vials of crack cocaine, numerous clear plastic vials, caps, and packets, and a spoon and a razor, each containing white residue (which turned out to be cocaine). Is there sufficient evidence on this record to convict Mercado of conspiring with Colon to engage in the criminal sale of narcotics? *Commonwealth v. Mercado*, 420 Pa.Super. 588, 617 A.2d 342 (1992).

3. *Establishing Conspiracy.* In the prior problem, which additional facts would help the State establish the existence of a conspiratorial relationship:

    a.   The fact that Mercado and Colon were frequently seen together?

    b.   The fact that defendant was found using cocaine in the apartment when the search warrant was executed.

Commonwealth v. Rodgers, 410 Pa.Super. 341, 599 A.2d 1329 (1991).

EXERCISE

Scouts and Steerers. You are an Assistant District Attorney assigned to support a joint state-federal law enforcement Task Force which seeks to eradicate illegal narcotics sales in a particular neighborhood in your city. The Task Force hopes to arrest not only the street salespersons themselves, but also the various "scouts," "runners," "lookouts," and other individuals who are paid to support the narcotics sales operation by watching for police presence and/or steering potential customers to the sales force. Prepare a brief memorandum for the Task Force officers explaining to them when precisely such "scouts" or "steerers" may be deemed to be co-conspirators with the actual salespersons—and when they may not. Make sure to advise the officers precisely what conduct or statements they should be looking for (or waiting for) in order to make a lawful arrest for conspiracy.

D. OVERT ACT

Most (but not all) jurisdictions with general conspiracy statutes require as an element of the offense proof of an overt act on the part of one of the co-conspirators in order to establish the existence of a conspiracy. It does not usually take much, however, to establish such an overt act. Often, even a relatively insignificant action on the part of one of the co-conspirators will suffice.

KANSAS v. CROCKETT

26 Kan.App.2d 202, 987 P.2d 1101 (1999).

GERNON, J.

Raymond Crockett appeals his conviction of conspiracy to commit first-degree murder. Following the jury trial, Crockett filed a motion to arrest judgment, contending the charging document was fatally defective because it failed to include an allegation of the overt act element of conspiracy. Crockett appeals the denial of his motion to arrest judgment.

K.S.A. 21–3302(a) [proclaims] that "[n]o person may be convicted of a conspiracy unless an overt act in furtherance of such conspiracy is alleged and proved to have been committed by such person or by a co-conspirator."

The charge read:

[Raymond] J. Crockett, Jr. [and] Ronnell F. Jones did unlawfully, feloniously, intentionally and with premeditation, kill a human being, to-wit: Terrance Canada, in violation of K.S.A. § 21–3401. (First Degree Murder.)

COUNT II

At the County of Wyandotte, State of Kansas, [on] or about the 26th day of August, 1996, one Raymond J. Crockett, Jr. and one Ronnell F. Jones did unlawfully, feloniously, knowingly and willfully enter into an agreement with one another to commit a crime, to-wit: First Degree Murder, as defined by K.S.A. § 21–3401, and in furtherance of such agreement committed the following overt acts, to-wit: planning on the time, location and

manner of killing Terrance Canada, in violation of K.S.A. § 21–
3302. . . .

In *State v. Hill*, 847 P.2d 1267 (Kan. 1993), the court adopted the
following definition of overt act:

> Overt act. An open, manifest act from which criminality may be
> implied. An outward act done in pursuance and manifestation of
> an intent or design. An open act, which must be manifestly
> proved . . . . .

> An overt act which completes crime of conspiracy to violate
> federal law is something apart from conspiracy and is an act to
> effect the object of the conspiracy, and need be neither a criminal
> act, nor crime that is object of conspiracy, but must accompany or
> follow agreement and must be done in furtherance of object of
> agreement.

In *State v. Chism*, 759 P.2d 105 (Kan. 1988), the court stated: "It
must be shown the defendant took a step beyond mere preparation so
that some appreciable fragment of the crime was committed." The
Chism court went on to say: "In some cases, [it] is enough that the
defendant arrived at the scene at which he planned for the crime to
occur."

In *State v. Hobson*, 671 P.2d 1365 (Kan. 1983), Sueanne Hobson
appealed her convictions of first-degree murder of her stepson and
conspiracy to commit murder. The evidence suggested that Hobson
asked her son to help her "get rid of" her stepson. Hobson promised
her son she would buy him a car if he would kill Hobson's stepson.
The court [stated]: "The facts tending to establish the appellant hired
or procured others to kill [her stepson] would not, standing alone,
have established the additional element of an overt act required to
support the charge of conspiracy."

In *People v. Flood*, 277 N.Y.S.2d 697 (1966), the court explained
that "it is 'hornbook' law that conversations among co-conspirators in
forming and planning the conspiracy are not overt acts in furtherance
of the conspiracy."

In *People v. Russo*, 393 N.Y.S.2d 435 (App.Div. 1977), the court
reversed a conviction for conspiracy because the charging document
was fatally defective for failing to allege an overt act. The charging
document listed the following overt acts: "(1) [T]he defendant met a
certain individual and told him that he intended to have his father-in-
law murdered and (2) the defendant and his co-conspirator met
another individual and agreed to pay him $10,000 for committing the
murder." The court characterized the alleged overt acts as "nothing
more than words" and concluded they were not overt acts. Moreover,
the opinion states the overt act was required to be alleged and cites to
Penal Law, § 105.20. That statute reads, in language almost identical
to the Kansas counterpart: "A person shall not be convicted of

conspiracy unless an overt act is alleged and proved to have been committed by one of the conspirators in furtherance of the conspiracy."

[A] citation to the statute will not supply the charging document with a missing element. Incorporation by reference will not be implied or inferred. Even an instruction to the jury will not remedy a defective complaint.

Given the record before us, we conclude we are required to reverse Crockett's conviction of conspiracy to commit first-degree murder.

Reversed.

PENNSYLVANIA v. FINNEGAN

280 Pa.Super. 584, 421 A.2d 1086 (1980).

PRICE, JUDGE:

[The] incident began on April 4, 1978, when Trooper Gentile observed [an] advertisement in a Pittsburgh newspaper stating, "Anna's Health Club, membership, out-calls, 371–5440." The trooper placed a call to the number and spoke with a man who identified himself as "Tony." The trooper testified that he recognized the voice from prior experience as that of appellant. Trooper Gentile disguised his voice and identified himself as Ralph Kubic, a business man interested in an "outcall." Appellant informed him that the price was $80.00, which prompted a response from the trooper that he was not interested in it at that time but would be returning to Pittsburgh and would partake of the services at a later date.

On April 19, 1978, the trooper again placed a call to the number, identified himself as Ralph Kubic, and spoke with appellant. He informed appellant that he was interested in an outcall at his motel for the following day. Appellant agreed and instructed him to call again the next evening at 6:30 p.m. On April 20, 1978, at approximately 6:30 p.m., the trooper secured a room at a local motel and again contacted appellant by dialing the number listed in the advertisement. Upon receiving the call, appellant inquired as to the name of the motel. After receiving this information, he hung up and approximately fifteen minutes later contacted the trooper by calling the motel office and requesting to be connected to the room registered to Ralph Kubic. The trooper then stated that he wanted two girls as outcalls, and was informed that the price would be $160.00 which he should pay to the girls when they arrived at 8:30 p.m.

Trooper Gentile then departed from the motel leaving Trooper Ralph Nevala to maintain surveillance. . . . Trooper Ralph Nevala also testified at trial that at 9:50 p.m. on April 20, 1978, a female, later identified as Patricia Marshall, came to the room at the motel, identified herself as "Dee Dee," stated that she had been sent by "John," and inquired if he was "Ralph." After discussing various fees and sexual services, she disrobed and was immediately placed under arrest by the trooper. After being given her *Miranda* warnings, she stated that she shared her fees for outcalls with "John" on an equal basis. . . .

Appellant's final contention is that the evidence presented was insufficient to support the conviction for conspiracy to promote prostitution. [Under] 18 Pa.C.S. § 903(e)[,] the Commonwealth must prove the commission of an overt act in furtherance of the conspiracy. Appellant contends that the evidence was insufficient because it failed to establish both the existence of a conspiratorial scheme and an overt act in furtherance of the crime. We disagree.

Although a common agreement or understanding is at the heart of any conspiracy, it is generally difficult to prove an explicit or formal agreement. Thus, like other elements, the conspiracy may be proven by circumstantial evidence, that is, by examining the relations, conduct, circumstances and overt acts by the alleged co-conspirators. In the instant case, the evidence was sufficient to prove that appellant entered into a conspiratorial scheme with Patricia Marshall arising out of the incident on April 20, 1978. The testimony established that after Trooper Gentile placed a telephone call to appellant requesting sexual services at a motel, Miss Marshall arrived at appellant's establishment, departed shortly thereafter and arrived at the motel stating that she had been sent by "John" to fulfill the request. From this statement of facts, the jury could reasonably infer that appellant and Miss Marshall conspired to commit the crime of prostitution. Moreover, the activities by Miss Marshall in arriving at the motel and disrobing in preparation for the sexual act clearly satisfy the overt act requirement in furtherance of the conspiracy.

The judgments in the trial court are affirmed.

NOTE

Overt act creates venue. Venue for a conspiracy trial is typically deemed to be appropriate in any jurisdiction in which an overt act took place, even if that jurisdiction is not the jurisdiction in which most of the conspiratorial acts took place.

PROBLEMS

1. *Disrobing.* Is the act of disrobing in *Finnegan* the "overt act," or can the overt act be established by other conduct? If so, what?

2. *Attempt.* Did the defendant in *Finnegan* also commit an attempt?

3. *Boots and Uniforms and Overt Acts.* In 2006, federal authorities charged seven men with plotting to blow-up the Sears Tower in Chicago.

The prosecution claimed that the men adhered to a militant (but vague) form of Islamic ideology, and had attempted to make contact with al Qaeda. The men provided a supposed al Qaeda representative (actually, an undercover federal officer) with a list of needed supplies (*e.g.*, uniforms, boots, machine guns, radios and vehicles), and claimed that their objective was to wage Jihad and to "kill all the devils we can" in a 9/11-style mission. In fact, the group never made contact with al Qaeda, although it did manage to obtain some boots and uniforms. Eventually, the plot just "petered out." Did the men commit the crime of conspiracy? Did they commit a sufficient overt act?

E. RENUNCIATION OR WITHDRAWAL

Unlike acts leading to the commission of completed criminal offenses, acts leading toward the commission of inchoate offenses (like conspiracy, solicitation and attempt) may, under the proper circumstances, be "taken back" by appropriate acts of withdrawal, abandonment, renunciation, contrition, and assistance of law enforcement efforts to prevent whatever criminal enterprise may be ongoing.

CALIFORNIA v. SCONCE
228 Cal.App.3d 693, 279 Cal.Rptr. 59 (1991).

KLEIN, PRESIDING JUSTICE.

The People filed an information charging defendant and respondent David Wayne Sconce (Sconce) with conspiracy to commit murder. The trial court set the information aside because it found Sconce effectively had withdrawn from the conspiracy. The People appeal.

[This] case involves Sconce's alleged formation of a conspiracy to kill Elie Estephan (Estephan).

In 1985, Estephan and Cindy Strunk (Cindy) were separated. Cindy testified she worked for her father, Frank Strunk, at his business, the Cremation Society of California (CSC). In the course of her duties at CSC, she met Sconce whose family owned the Lamb Funeral Home (LFH) and the Pasadena Crematorium. In 1985, Cindy met Sconce's brother-in-law, Brad Sallard (Sallard). She and Sallard dated and began to live together in May 1985.

When Estephan served divorce papers on Cindy in June, 1985, Sconce offered her the services of LFH's attorney. Sconce and Sallard accompanied Cindy to the first meeting with the lawyer. One of the assets she mentioned during the meeting was a $250,000 insurance policy on Estephan's life which named her as beneficiary.

At some point thereafter, Cindy argued with Estephan at CSC in front of Frank Strunk and others including an LFH employee, John

Pollerana (Pollerana). Estephan chased Cindy and pushed her down a number of stairs. She was upset but not hurt.

Pollerana testified that in late summer of 1985, the day after the argument between Estephan and Cindy, Sconce asked Pollerana "if he gave me $10,000, would I get rid of Elie [Estephan], but, you know, I just shook my head, and we just walked by. That was the end of the conversation."

Pollerana further testified Sconce did not like Estephan because he had slapped Cindy.... Pollerana did not take Sconce's offer seriously. However, two weeks later Pollerana had a conversation with Bob Garcia (Garcia) in which Garcia said Sconce had offered him $10,000 to kill Estephan. Pollerana told Garcia, " 'I wouldn't do it.' " A few days later, Garcia showed Pollerana the address to Estephan's house and Pollerana drove Garcia there.

Garcia testified he also worked for Sconce. One day at the crematorium, Sconce asked Garcia "about someone being murdered, and if I knew anyone who would do it." Sconce told him "a friend wanted someone killed." Sconce offered Garcia $10,000 or $15,000 to commit the murder. Garcia told Sconce he would either find someone to do it or that he would do it himself.

In a telephone conversation a few days later, Sconce told Garcia that Estephan "had a large insurance policy and he just wanted him murdered to collect the insurance money."

[Approximately] one week later, Sconce and Garcia went to a Jack-in-the-Box across the street from Estephan's gas station. CSC is on another corner of the same intersection. They sat next to the window and as they ate lunch, Sconce used binoculars to point Estephan out to Garcia. Sconce later gave Estephan's address to Garcia. One night shortly thereafter, Garcia and Pollerana drove to Estephan's house.

Garcia then contacted Herbert Dutton (Dutton), an ex-convict who lived next door to him, about committing the offense. Dutton agreed to do the job for $5,000. That same night Garcia and Dutton drove to Estephan's house. On the way there they discussed whether to blow up Estephan's car or shoot him on the freeway. They settled on the former because Dutton had explosives and no one would have to pull the trigger. They intended to plant the bomb, run a wire to it from three houses away, and wait for Estephan.

Conversations between Sconce and Garcia about the matter were brief but continued over a three-week period. Sconce would ask Garcia, "Is he still walking today[?]" Garcia would respond that "we" would take care of it. Approximately three weeks after Sconce's initial conversation with Garcia, Sconce "just called it off. He said just forget about it, disregard doing it." Garcia did not see Dutton after the night they drove to Estephan's house.

[The] magistrate held Sconce to answer and the People filed an information alleging conspiracy to commit murder. The information asserted six overt acts committed between September 1 and 16, 1985. These acts consisted of Sconce's pointing out Estephan at the Jack-in-the-Box, the use of binoculars to view Estephan, Garcia's trip to the Estephan home with Pollerana, the solicitation of Hutton by Garcia, Garcia's trip to the Estephan home with Hutton, and Sconce's inquiries of Garcia to "take care of and kill" Estephan.

Thereafter, notwithstanding the trial court's finding there had been a conspiracy, it granted Sconce's motion to set the information aside. The trial court stated it could find no authority on point but "[commentators] seem to follow the general policy of encouraging withdrawal from conspiracies [and it] is a good one. It seems to me that David Sconce['s] withdrawal here was an effective one."

[The] People contend the trial court erroneously set aside the information because Sconce's withdrawal from the conspiracy, although it might insulate him from liability for future conspiratorial acts, does not constitute a defense to liability for the conspiracy itself. Further, the People assert Sconce failed to demonstrate effective withdrawal from the conspiracy.

[Conspiracy] to commit an offense consists of the unlawful agreement of two or more persons to commit an offense and an overt act in furtherance thereof. It does not require the actual completion of the substantive offense. An overt act need not be criminal in nature, and need not amount to an attempt to commit the offense or to aiding and abetting.

[Criminal] liability for conspiracy, separate from and in addition to that imposed for the substantive offense which the conspirators agree to commit, has been justified by a 'group danger' rationale. The division of labor inherent in group association is seen to encourage the selection of more elaborate and ambitious goals and to increase the likelihood that the scheme will be successful. Moreover, the moral support of the group is seen as strengthening the perseverance of each member of the conspiracy, thereby acting to discourage any reevaluation of the decision to commit the offense which a single offender might undertake. And even if a single conspirator reconsiders and contemplates stopping the wheels which have been set in motion to attain the object of the conspiracy, a return to the status quo will be much more difficult since it will entail persuasion of the other conspirators.

[" 'Once] the defendant's participation in the conspiracy is shown, it will be presumed to continue unless he is able to prove, as a matter of defense, that he effectively withdrew from the conspiracy. Although a defendant's arrest and incarceration may terminate his participation in an alleged conspiracy, his arrest does not terminate, or constitute a withdrawal from, the conspiracy as a matter of law. Withdrawal from, or termination of, a conspiracy is a question of fact.' "

Withdrawal from a conspiracy requires "an affirmative and bona fide rejection or repudiation of the conspiracy, communicated to the co-conspirators."

"A member of a conspiracy may effectively withdraw from it so as to exculpate himself from guilt for the future criminal acts of his co-conspirators."

[Under] California law, withdrawal is a complete defense to conspiracy only if accomplished before the commission of an overt act, or, where it is asserted in conjunction with the running of the statute of limitations.

["The] requirement of an overt act before conspirators can be prosecuted and punished exists[,] to provide a locus p[o]enitentiae—an opportunity for the conspirators to reconsider, terminate the agreement, and thereby avoid punishment for the conspiracy."

Obviously, the inverse of this rule is that once an overt act has been committed in furtherance of the conspiracy, the crime of conspiracy has been completed and no subsequent action by the conspirator can change that.

Thus, even if it be assumed Sconce effectively withdrew from the conspiracy or, as Sconce argues, that the People conceded withdrawal before the trial court, withdrawal merely precludes liability for subsequent acts committed by the members of the conspiracy. The withdrawal does not relate back to the criminal formation of the unlawful combination. In sum, conspiracy is complete upon the commission of an overt act.

This rule is consistent with the traditional view that the crime of conspiracy is complete with the agreement and an overt act, and no subsequent action can exonerate the conspirator of that crime. Federal law is consonant with this view. "[T]o avoid complicity in the conspiracy, one must withdraw before any overt act is taken in furtherance of the agreement."

The rationale in favor of terminating liability is the one relied upon by the trial court, i.e., the reasons for allowing withdrawal as a defense to conspiracy—encouraging abandonment and thereby weakening the group—continue to apply after the commission of an overt act.

However, the rule remains that withdrawal avoids liability only for the target offense, or for any subsequent act committed by a co-conspirator in pursuance of the common plan. "[I]n respect of the conspiracy itself, the individual's change of mind is ineffective; he cannot undo that which he has already done."[4]

Even if this court were inclined to agree with the trial court, we are bound to follow the foregoing settled rule. Any change in the law is a matter for the Legislature.

Because we conclude Sconce's withdrawal from the conspiracy is not a valid defense to the completed crime of conspiracy, we need not determine whether the evidence showed that Sconce, in fact, withdrew from the conspiracy and communicated that withdrawal to each co-conspirator. Similarly, Sconce's assertion the People conceded at the trial court level that he had withdrawn is now of no moment.

[Sconce] argues overt acts must constitute "'decisive steps'" toward the commission of the crime. He asserts none of the overt acts alleged in the information satisfies this test. He claims the meeting at the Jack-in-the-Box was "mere discussion," the trips to Estephan's home were "mere investigation," and the meetings of Garcia and Dutton "merely ... expand[ed] the agreement to Dutton." Sconce argues these acts are either the agreement itself, negotiations leading up to the agreement or verbal affirmations of the agreement.

This contention is belied by the record which abundantly satisfies the People's burden of demonstrating a reasonable suspicion a public offense had been committed. Indeed, the trial court remarked, "No doubt about it, until the time of withdrawal ... there was a conspiracy."

Sconce also complains the information must fail because he effectively communicated his withdrawal to Garcia who Sconce claims was the sole co-conspirator. He argues Pollerana rejected Sconce's offer, Sallard's involvement was not clearly shown and Dutton had not yet agreed on a price.

These assertions similarly lack factual basis in the record. Although Pollerana refused to kill Estephan, he assisted Garcia with knowledge of Garcia's criminal purpose. Sallard necessarily had to be involved in the plot since he was the link to Cindy, and Dutton clearly agreed to commit the crime. The fact no money had been paid or the existence of conflicting evidence as to the price does not negate Dutton's inclusion in the conspiracy.

[Withdrawal] from a conspiracy is not a valid defense to the completed crime of conspiracy itself. If this result is seen as anoma-

---

4. The Model Penal Code recognizes a defense which it refers to as renunciation. The Model Penal Code states: "It is an affirmative defense that the actor, after conspiring to commit a crime, thwarted the success of the conspiracy, under circumstances manifesting a complete and voluntary renunciation of his [or her] criminal purpose." (Model Pen.Code, § 5.03, subd. (6).)

The defense of renunciation is not the same as withdrawal. "One difference is immediately apparent: In renunciation, the defendant must 'thwart the success' of the conspiracy. Another important difference is that renunciation is a complete defense, relieving liability for all prior involvement in the conspiracy." Renunciation is not available as a defense in California.

lous, any change in the applicable law is for the Legislature, not this court.

The order setting the information aside is reversed.

NOTE

Voluntary withdrawal. For a withdrawal or renunciation to be effective in most jurisdictions, it must also be "voluntary and complete." An actor who desists because of the fear of apprehension is not, for example, acting "voluntarily." And an individual who simply gives up one of his or her criminal objectives, as another example, has not effected a complete withdrawal or renunciation of the criminal enterprise. Does the M.P.C. change this formulation?

PROBLEMS

1. *Withdrawal after Overt Act.* If an overt act sufficient to establish the existence of a conspiracy may consist of an inconsequential (and lawful) action on the part of a co-conspirator, wouldn't it be desirable—in the interests of *locus poenitentiae*—to permit withdrawal from a conspiracy even after such an overt act was committed? Is that possible in California under the holding in *Sconce?*

2. *M.P.C. Renunciation.* If the Model Penal Code defense of renunciation (adopted in a number of jurisdictions) were in effect, what could or should Sconce have done to make sure that he had "thwarted" the conspiracy? Would he have had to inform the police of his now-discarded criminal plan?

NEW JERSEY v. HUGHES

215 N.J.Super. 295, 521 A.2d 1295 (App.Div. 1986).

ANTELL, P.J.A.D.

At approximately 7:00 p.m. September 28, 1982 the cashier at the office of the Courier Post in Cherry Hill was robbed at gun point of a large amount of cash by two men. In connection therewith defendant was indicted for robbery, possession of a weapon for an unlawful purpose, and conspiracy to rob. After a trial by jury he was convicted of conspiracy and a jury disagreement was recorded as to the other two charges.

On this appeal defendant first argues that the trial court erred in failing to instruct the jury as to the defense of "renunciation of purpose" as an affirmative defense to the charge of conspiracy.

[The] evidence upon which defendant rests his claim to the defense of renunciation is found in the testimony of defendant himself and the testimony of Detective Beverly of the City of Camden Police Department. According to defendant, during the period of approximately one month before the robbery he had been approached on a number of occasions by Tyrone Wolley who solicited him to take part in robbing the Courier Post. On each occasion defendant rejected the invitation and answered Wolley that he was not interested in doing armed robberies. Approximately one or two weeks before the Courier Post robbery actually occurred, defendant visited Detective Beverly and told him of Wolley's solicitations. He did not, however, suggest that he had agreed to join the enterprise and, in fact, said that he told Wolley he would not do so. His purpose, he said, in giving Detective Beverly the information was to enable the police to investigate the matter.

The defense of renunciation to a charge of conspiracy is found, N.J.S.A. 2C:5–2e:

> Renunciation of purpose. It is an affirmative defense which the actor must prove by a preponderance of the evidence that he, after conspiring to commit a crime, informed the authority of the existence of the conspiracy and his participation therein, and thwarted or caused to be thwarted the commission of any offense in furtherance of the conspiracy, under circumstances manifesting a complete and voluntary renunciation of criminal purpose....

It is evident that the basic condition of the defense finds no support in the evidence. The statute presupposes an acknowledgment by the actor that he actually conspired to commit a crime and its benefits are conferred only where he informs police authority of the conspiracy's existence "and his participation therein...." Where the elements of the defense have been shown by a preponderance of the evidence one can be said to have "renounced" the conspiracy. Renunciation, after all, posits prior participation, and defendant could not renounce a conspiracy he had not joined. The defense was not available to defendant for the reason that, as he testified, he had steadfastly refused to support the criminal undertaking. His testimony to this effect as well as Detective Beverly's was relevant, not to whether he had renounced the conspiracy, but only to whether he had ever joined it in the first place. Once this issue was resolved against defendant there was nothing else in the record to support a finding of renunciation.

[Affirmed.]

PROBLEMS

1. *Consistent Defenses?* If Hughes could not renounce the conspiracy because he claimed that he was not a part of it, how could he be convicted of conspiracy in the first place? If the jury did not believe Hughes' claim that he was not a party to the conspiracy, why wasn't he entitled to a renunciation instruction?

2. *Conspiracy or Duress.* Quinton Alston attempted to hijack a truck by pointing a gun at the driver (actually a BB gun wrapped in a towel). When apprehended, he claimed that he was forced to participate in the hijacking by Bernard Short who told Alston that he would harm Alston's family if Alston didn't assist in the crime. Alston claims that he told the driver that he was being threatened and that the driver should go and call the police. (The driver denies this.) Alston has been charged, *inter alia*, with conspiracy to commit carjacking. Is Alston entitled to a renunciation instruction? *State v. Alston*, 311 N.J.Super. 113, 709 A.2d 310 (App.Div. 1998).

F. MERGER

Since the actus reus of conspiracy (a conspiratorial agreement) is different from the actus reus of the target crime itself, e.g. the illegal sale of narcotics, the rule in most jurisdictions is that a conviction for conspiracy to commit a target crime does *not* merge with a conviction for the crime itself.

NEW MEXICO v. VILLALOBOS

120 N.M. 694, 905 P.2d 732 (1995).

WECHSLER, JUDGE.

Defendant appeals his convictions for attempted trafficking by possession with intent to distribute cocaine and conspiracy to commit attempted trafficking. Defendant raises five issues on appeal [including] whether his convictions for attempt and conspiracy should merge[.] We affirm.

[On] June 23, 1992, government informant, Marcelino Ramirez, introduced Defendant to two undercover officers at a lunchtime meeting in a restaurant in El Paso, Texas, that was previously arranged by Ramirez for the sale of cocaine. The officers, posing as husband and wife, and Defendant, his wife, and their three-year-old daughter ate together. Ramirez sat at a separate table. The day before, Defendant had agreed to purchase three kilograms of cocaine for Robert Garza. Garza gave Defendant $50,000 for the cocaine and, apparently, dropped the money off at Defendant's home in Chaparral, New Mexico.

During the meeting in El Paso, Defendant inquired about purchasing three kilograms of cocaine. The undercover officers told him that they could provide the cocaine at a price of $17,000 per kilogram. After negotiations over the price, Defendant agreed to purchase the cocaine for $15,000 per kilogram for a total purchase price of $45,000, with $39,000 up front and the remaining $6000 to be paid after Defendant completed a separate marijuana transaction. At trial, Defendant testified that he intended to purchase the cocaine and transfer it to Garza and that he never intended to pay the remaining $6000.

Before making the final arrangements for the transaction, Defendant wanted to inspect the cocaine and its packaging. The undercover officers arranged a meeting with a third undercover officer at a Kmart parking lot in El Paso. The third officer brought the cocaine. Defendant inspected the package and indicated that it was acceptable. Defendant's wife did not inspect the cocaine with Defendant. Instead, she went into Kmart with one of the undercover officers to look at birthday cards. Defendant and the officers then made plans to meet at Defendant's home later in the afternoon to complete the drug purchase.

When the undercover officers arrived at Defendant's home, Defendant's wife let them in and offered them beer. Defendant asked the officers about the cocaine, and he presented them with a paper bag containing $39,000. Defendant insisted that an undercover officer count the money. The undercover officer did so and instructed his partner to get the cocaine. Defendant's wife went with the partner. At that point, the officers arrested Defendant and his wife.

[We] turn now to the question of whether Defendant's convictions for attempted trafficking and conspiracy to traffic violate the prohibition against double jeopardy and should, therefore, merge. *Swafford v. State*, 810 P.2d 1223 (N.M. 1991), provides the framework for analyzing claims that convictions under multiple statutes are the same for double jeopardy purposes. The first part of the *Swafford* test is "whether the conduct underlying the offenses is unitary, i.e., whether the same conduct violates both statutes." If the conduct is not unitary, the inquiry is complete because there is no double jeopardy violation. However, if the conduct is unitary, as the reviewing court, we must proceed to the second part of the *Swafford* test to determine whether the legislature intended to permit multiple punishments under different statutes for the same conduct.

We assume, without deciding, that the conduct forming the basis for both convictions was unitary. The second part of the *Swafford* test then requires this Court to determine whether the legislature intended to permit multiple punishments for attempt and conspiracy. In the absence of an express indication of such intent in the attempt and conspiracy statutes, we must compare the statutory elements of the separate criminal statutes and decide whether, as structured by the legislature, one crime is really only a part of, or subsumed by, another offense. If so "the inquiry is over and the statutes are the same for double jeopardy purposes—punishment cannot be had for both."

A statute stands independently and is not subsumed by another, when each crime " 'requires proof of a fact the other does not.' " The elements of conspiracy are: (1) agreement to commit the underlying offense; and (2) the intent to commit the offense. As mentioned above, the elements of attempt are: (1) an overt act in furtherance of the offense, tending but failing to effect the commission of the offense; and (2) the intent to commit the offense. Because the elements of attempt and conspiracy are not subsumed one within the other, a presumption arises that the legislature intended multiple punishments.

Defendant argues that the conspiratorial agreement can be considered an overt act in furtherance of the attempt and thus conspiracy is subsumed within attempt. We disagree. Defendant is looking beyond the elements of the offenses by continuing to focus on the particular facts of the case. Those facts have already been considered in the first part of the *Swafford* test. The second part of the test requires us to look at the elements of the statutes without regard to the facts used to prove the elements in this particular case.

The overt act for an attempt need not be an agreement with a co-conspirator. For example, offering cocaine for sale to someone who did not purchase it would unquestionably represent an attempt to traffic in cocaine. On the other hand, the agreement necessary to constitute a conspiracy need not be an act that is in furtherance of the crime and tending to effect its commission.

Although the attempt and conspiracy statutes have different elements, the presumption against merger is rebuttable. The presumption can be rebutted by showing that the statutes are designed to protect against the same social evil. A leading treatise provides the following comparison between the crimes of conspiracy and attempt:

> The crime of conspiracy ... serves two important but different functions: (1) as with solicitation and attempt, it is a means for preventive intervention against persons who manifest a disposition to criminality; and (2) it is also a means of striking against the special danger incident to group activity.

2 Wayne R. LaFave & Austin W. Scott, Jr., Substantive Criminal Law § 6.4(c), at 68 (1986) (footnote omitted). Thus, while the statutes prohibiting attempts and conspiracies may seek to protect against a similar social evil by providing a means of intervention and punishment against those who are preparing to commit a crime, only the prohibition against conspiracy seeks to protect against the additional social evil of coordinated criminal group activity. Therefore, we do not believe the presumption that the legislature intended multiple punishment is rebutted by applying the "social evils" test described in *Swafford*. Accordingly, Defendant's attempt and conspiracy convictions do not merge.

[Based] on the foregoing, we affirm Defendant's convictions.

It is so ordered.

NOTE

Merger. In some jurisdictions, there are statutory provisions mandating that multiple inchoate offenses aimed at the same target offense merge into one another. *See, e.g.,* 18 Pa. C. S. § 906 (1986)("A person may not be convicted of more than one of the inchoate crimes of criminal attempt, criminal solicitation or criminal conspiracy for conduct designed to commit or to culminate in the commission of the same crime.").

PROBLEM

Murder and Conspiracy. Defendant Jones planned with codefendants Craft and Moore to rob Haywood. The three obtained a gun, waited outside the lounge Haywood frequented until he exited, followed him to a hotel, and waited again for him to emerge. After several hours of stalking him, they followed Haywood to his home. One of Haywood's neighbors testified that she heard gunfire and looked out her window to see Jones walk from Haywood's car to an older two-door gray Chevrolet, while the victim's car slowly moved forward to rest against a tree. Haywood was found slumped over the steering wheel of his car, dead from multiple gunshot wounds. Jones was convicted of attempted armed robbery, conspiracy to commit armed robbery, and murder. Should any or all of these offenses merge with one another? *People v. Jones,* 234 Ill.App.3d 1082, 176 Ill.Dec. 382, 601 N.E.2d 1080 (1992).

G.   CULPABILITY OF CO–CONSPIRATORS

To what extent is a conspirator culpable for the criminal acts of other co-conspirators? Consider the following case.

PINKERTON v. UNITED STATES

328 U.S. 640 (1946).

M̲R̲. J̲USTICE̲ D̲OUGLAS̲ delivered the opinion of the Court.

Walter and Daniel Pinkerton are brothers who live a short distance from each other on Daniel's farm. They were indicted for violations of the Internal Revenue Code. The indictment contained ten substantive counts and one conspiracy count. The jury found Walter guilty on nine of the substantive counts and on the conspiracy count. It found Daniel guilty on six of the substantive counts and on the conspiracy count. Walter was fined $500 and sentenced generally on the substantive counts to imprisonment for thirty months. On the conspiracy count he was given a two year sentence to run concurrently with the other sentence. Daniel was fined $1,000 and sentenced generally on the substantive counts to imprisonment for thirty months. On the conspiracy count he was fined $500 and given a two year sentence to run concurrently with the other sentence. The judgments of conviction were affirmed by the Circuit Court of Appeals. The case is here on a petition for a writ of certiorari. . . .

A single conspiracy was charged and proved. Some of the overt acts charged in the conspiracy count were the same acts charged in the substantive counts. Each of the substantive offenses found was committed pursuant to the conspiracy. Petitioners therefore contend that the substantive counts became merged in the conspiracy count, and that only a single sentence not exceeding the maximum two-year penalty provided by the conspiracy statute could be imposed. Or to state the matter differently, they contend that each of the substantive counts became a separate conspiracy count but since only a single conspiracy was charged and proved, only a single sentence for conspiracy could be imposed. They rely on *Braverman v. United States*, 317 U.S. 49 [(1942)].

In the *Braverman* case the indictment charged no substantive offense. Each of the several counts charged a conspiracy to violate a different statute. But only one conspiracy was proved. We held that a single conspiracy, charged under the general conspiracy statute, however diverse its objects may be, violates but a single statute and no penalty greater than the maximum provided for one conspiracy may be imposed. That case is not apposite here. For the offenses charged and proved were not only a conspiracy but substantive offenses as well.

Nor can we accept the proposition that the substantive offenses were merged in the conspiracy. There are, of course, instances where a conspiracy charge may not be added to the substantive charge. One is where the agreement of two persons is necessary for the completion of the substantive crime and there is no ingredient in the conspiracy which is not present in the completed crime. Another is where the definition of the substantive offense excludes from punishment for conspiracy one who voluntarily participates in another's crime. But those exceptions are of a limited character. The common law rule that the substantive offense, if a felony, was merged in the conspiracy, has little vitality in this country. It has been long and consistently recognized by the Court that the commission of the substantive offense and a conspiracy to commit it are separate and distinct offenses. The power of Congress to separate the two and to affix to each a different penalty is well established. A conviction for the conspiracy may be had though the substantive offense was completed. And the plea of double jeopardy is no defense to a conviction for both offenses. It is only an identity of offenses which is fatal. A conspiracy is a partnership in crime. It has ingredients, as well as implications, distinct from the completion of the unlawful project. As stated in *United States v. Rabinowich*, 238 U.S. 78, 88 [(1915)]:

'For two or more to confederate and combine together to commit or cause to be committed a breach of the criminal laws is an offense of the gravest character, sometimes quite outweighing, in injury to the public, the mere commission of the contemplated crime. It involves deliberate plotting to subvert the laws, educating and preparing the conspirators for further and habitual criminal practices. And it is characterized by secrecy, rendering it difficult of detection, requiring more time for its discovery, and adding to the importance of punishing it when discovered.'

Moreover, it is not material that overt acts charged in the conspiracy counts were also charged and proved as substantive offenses. As stated in *Sneed v. United States*, [298 F. 911 (5th Cir. 1924),] 'If the overt act be the offense which was the object of the conspiracy, and is also punished, there is not a double punishment of it.' The agreement to do an unlawful act is even then distinct from the doing of the act.

It is contended that there was insufficient evidence to implicate Daniel in the conspiracy. But we think there was enough evidence for submission of the issue to the jury.

There is, however, no evidence to show that Daniel participated directly in the commission of the substantive offenses on which his conviction has been sustained, although there was evidence to show that these substantive offenses were in fact committed by Walter in furtherance of the unlawful agreement or conspiracy existing between the brothers. The question was submitted to the jury on the theory that each petitioner could be found guilty of the substantive offenses, if it was found at the time those offenses were committed petitioners were parties to an unlawful conspiracy and the substantive offenses charged were in fact committed in furtherance of it.

Daniel relies on *United States v. Sall*, [116 F.2d 745 (3d Cir. 1940)]. That case held that participation in the conspiracy was not itself enough to sustain a conviction for the substantive offense even though it was committed in furtherance of the conspiracy. The court held that, in addition to evidence that the offense was in fact committed in furtherance of the conspiracy, evidence of direct participation in the commission of the substantive offense or other evidence from which participation might fairly be inferred was necessary.

We take a different view. We have here a continuous conspiracy. There is here no evidence of the affirmative action on the part of Daniel which is necessary to establish his withdrawal from it. *Hyde v. United States*, 225 U.S. 347, 369 [(1912)]. As stated in that case, 'having joined in an unlawful scheme, having constituted agents for its performance, scheme and agency to be continuous until full fruition be secured, until he does some act to disavow or defeat the purpose he is in no situation to claim the delay of the law. As the offense has not been terminated or accomplished, he is still offending. And we think, consciously offending,—offending as certainly, as we have said, as at the first moment of his confederation, and consciously through every moment of its existence.' And so long as the partnership in crime continues, the partners act for each other in carrying it forward. It is settled that 'an overt act of one partner may be the act of all without any new agreement specifically directed to that act.' Motive or intent may be proved by the acts or declarations of some of the conspirators in furtherance of the common objective. A scheme to use the mails to defraud, which is joined in by more than one person, is a conspiracy. Yet all members are responsible, though only one did the mailing. The governing principle is the same when the substantive offense is committed by one of the conspirators in furtherance of the unlawful project. The criminal intent to do the act is established by the formation of the conspiracy. Each conspirator instigated the commission of the crime. The unlawful agreement contemplated precisely what was done. It was formed for the purpose. The act done was in execution of the enterprise. The rule which holds responsible one who counsels, procures, or commands another to commit a crime is founded on the same principle. That principle is recognized in the law of conspiracy when the overt act of one partner in crime is attributable to all. An overt act is an essential ingredient of the crime of conspiracy. [If] that can be supplied by the act of one conspirator, we fail to see why the same or other acts in furtherance of the conspiracy are likewise not attributable to the others for the purpose of holding them responsible for the substantive offense.

A different case would arise if the substantive offense committed by one of the conspirators was not in fact done in furtherance of the conspiracy, did not fall within the scope of the unlawful project, or was merely a part of the ramifications of the plan which could not be reasonably foreseen as a necessary or natural consequence of the unlawful agreement. But as we read this record, that is not this case.

Affirmed.

Mr. Justice Rutledge, dissenting in part.

The judgment concerning Daniel Pinkerton should be reversed. In my opinion it is without precedent here and is a dangerous precedent to establish.

Daniel and Walter, who were brothers living near each other, were charged in several counts with substantive offenses, and then a conspiracy count was added naming those offenses as overt acts. The proof showed that Walter alone committed the substantive crimes. There was none to establish that Daniel participated in them, aided and abetted Walter in committing them, or knew that he had done so. Daniel in fact was in the penitentiary, under sentence for other crimes, when some of Walter's crimes were done.

There was evidence, however, to show that over several years Daniel and Walter had confederated to commit similar crimes concerned with unlawful possession, transportation, and dealing in whiskey, in fraud of the federal revenues. On this evidence both were convicted of conspiracy. Walter also was convicted on the substantive counts on the proof of his committing the crimes charged. Then, on that evidence without more than the proof of Daniel's criminal agreement with Walter and the latter's overt acts, which were also the substantive offenses charged, the court told the jury they could find Daniel guilty of those substantive offenses. They did so.

I think this ruling violates both the letter and the spirit of what Congress did when it separately defined the three classes of crime, namely, (1) completed substantive offenses; (2) aiding, abetting or counseling another to commit them; and (3) conspiracy to commit them. Not only does this ignore the distinctions Congress has prescribed shall be observed. It either convicts one man for another's crime or punishes the man convicted twice for the same offense.

The three types of offense are not identical. Nor are their differences merely verbal. The gist of conspiracy is the agreement; that of aiding, abetting or counseling is in consciously advising or assisting another to commit particular offenses, and thus becoming a party to them; that of substantive crime, going a step beyond mere aiding, abetting, counseling to completion of the offense.

These general differences are well understood. But when conspiracy has ripened into completed crime, or has advanced to the stage of aiding and abetting, it becomes easy to disregard their differences and loosely to treat one as identical with the other, that is, for every purpose except the most vital one of imposing sentence. And thus the substance, if not the technical effect, of double jeopardy or multiple punishment may be accomplished. Thus also may one be convicted of an offense not charged or proved against him, on evidence showing he committed another.

The old doctrine of merger of conspiracy in the substantive crime has not obtained here. But the dangers for abuse, which in part it sought to avoid, in applying the law of conspiracy have not altogether disappeared. There is some evidence that they may be increasing. The looseness with which the charge may be proved, the almost unlimited scope of vicarious responsibility for others' acts which follows once agreement is shown, the psychological advantages of such trials for securing convictions by attributing to one proof against another, these and other inducements require that the broad limits of discretion allowed to prosecuting officers in relation to such charges and trials be not expanded into new, wider and more dubious areas of choice.

[Daniel] has been held guilty of the substantive crimes committed only by Walter on proof that he did no more than conspire with him to commit offenses of the same general character. There was no evidence that he counseled, advised or had knowledge of those particular acts or offenses. There was, therefore, none that he aided, abetted or took part in them. There was only evidence sufficient to show that he had agreed with Walter at some past time to engage in such transactions generally. As to Daniel this was only evidence of conspiracy, not of substantive crime.

The court's theory seems to be that Daniel and Walter became general partners in crime by virtue of their agreement and because of that agreement without more on his part Daniel became criminally responsible as a principal for everything Walter did thereafter in the nature of a criminal offense of the general sort the agreement contemplated, so long as there was not clear evidence that Daniel had withdrawn from or revoked the agreement. Whether or not his commitment to the penitentiary had that effect, the result is a vicarious criminal responsibility as broad as, or broader than, the vicarious civil liability of a partner for acts done by a co-partner in the course of the firm's business.

Such analogies from private commercial law and the law of torts are dangerous, in my judgment, for transfer to the criminal field. Guilt there with us remains personal, not vicarious, for the more serious offenses. It should be kept so. The effect of Daniel's conviction in this case, to repeat, is either to attribute to him Walter's guilt or to punish him twice for the same offense, namely, agreeing with Walter to engage in crime. Without the agreement Daniel was guilty of no crime on this record. With it and no more, so far as his own conduct is concerned, he was guilty of two. . . .

PROBLEMS

1. *Bank Robberies.* A organizes a conspiracy to rob banks. B & C are included in the conspiracy, but they never meet and they rob different banks. Each does, however, know about the existence of the other. Is B responsible for crimes committed by C and vice-versa? Would it matter if:

    a. C never robbed a bank?

    b. A, B and C all shared ideas and strategies about how to rob banks?

2. *M.P.C. Conspiracy.* What results in Problem 1 under the M.P.C.?

3. *Wheel or Chain.* In answering the preceding question, you might consider once again the notion of "wheel" and "chain" conspiratorial arrangements as described in Note 2 after *Mercer* in Part C, *supra*. Is the conspiracy described in Problem 1 a "wheel" or a "chain" or neither? What difference does this make?

4. *Scope of Agreement.* X conspires with Y to rob a bank. Y is designated to "do the job" itself. X provides support and assistance before the fact. During the robbery, Y kills bank teller. Can X be convicted of murder?

EVERRITT v. GEORGIA

277 Ga. 457, 588 S.E.2d 691 (2003).

THOMPSON, JUSTICE.

Defendant Raymond F. Everritt, John Henry McDuffie and James Wallace Weeks were indicted for the murder with malice aforethought of Roosevelt Cox. McDuffie died one month before the case was to be tried; Weeks admitted his complicity in the murder and testified at trial against Everritt, who appeals from his conviction and enumerates error upon the denial of his motion for a directed verdict of acquittal. To address this enumeration, we must answer this question: Can one who enters a successful conspiracy to commit arson be held criminally responsible for the murder of one co-conspirator by another, when the murder was committed months after the arson in order to keep the conspiracy secret?

Viewing the evidence in a light to uphold the verdict, as we are bound to do, we find the following: Everritt owned and operated a service station in Shellman, Georgia. Because he was experiencing financial problems, Everritt hired James McDuffie to burn down the station, which was insured. Everritt was to pay McDuffie $5,000 for his services out of the insurance proceeds.

McDuffie tried to burn down the station with a Molotov cocktail in June of 1992. He recruited his teenage grandson, Jamie Weeks, to help him in that attempt, but they failed—the incendiary device hit the side of the building, missing the window. Soon thereafter, McDuffie asked Cox, who worked for McDuffie, to help him burn the station. He agreed to pay Cox $1,500. Two weeks after the first, failed attempt, McDuffie and Cox burned down the station with an accelerant.

At first, Everritt's insurance company declined to pay on the policy because of the suspicious circumstances surrounding the fire. Everritt hired an attorney to press his insurance claim. But payment was not forthcoming and, as time went by, Cox remained unpaid. Cox told friends that Everritt owed him $1,500 for burning down the station; and he began to complain that he had not yet been paid by either McDuffie or Everritt. McDuffie was worried because Cox would not keep quiet. In September of 1992, he lured Cox into his shop and killed him with an axe. That day, Everritt called his attorney's office more than three times. He also called his wife, who worked at a bank which had loaned him money.

Jamie Weeks helped McDuffie dispose of Cox's body, which was discovered by hunters on September 27, 1992. Thereafter, in March of 1993, Everritt's insurance claim was settled for $123,065. Nearly nine years later Everritt, McDuffie, and Weeks were charged with the murder of Cox.

Jamie Weeks, who was 26 years old at the time of trial, testified that shortly after the murder, Everritt gave McDuffie a set of tires to conceal the fact that McDuffie used his truck to transport the victim's body. He also testified that Everritt later warned Weeks to keep his mouth shut.

Everritt asserts the evidence is insufficient to enable a rational trier of fact to find him guilty beyond a reasonable doubt of the malice murder of Roosevelt Cox. In this regard, defendant posits that the evidence fails to demonstrate that he conspired with McDuffie to kill Cox. The State counters that the evidence suffices to show a conspiracy between Everritt and McDuffie to kill Cox; that, even if it does not, it proves that Everritt, McDuffie, and Cox conspired to burn down Everritt's place of business and that McDuffie murdered Cox in furtherance of that conspiracy.

As to the State's first argument, we agree with Everritt that the evidence fails to show a conspiracy to murder Cox. Although the existence of a conspiracy can be shown by circumstantial evidence, there was absolutely no evidence tying Everritt to a conspiracy to commit murder. That Everritt placed calls to his attorney and bank on the day of the murder proves nothing one way or the other. And the fact that Everritt gave McDuffie a set of tires after the murder only shows that he was a party to the murder after the fact.

With respect to the State's second argument, we agree that the evidence was sufficient to demonstrate that Everritt entered a conspiracy to commit arson with McDuffie and Cox. But that does not end our inquiry; it merely begs the question: Having entered into a conspiracy with McDuffie and Cox to commit arson, is Everritt responsible for the murder of Cox by McDuffie? The State asserts that he is because McDuffie killed Cox to further concealment of the conspiracy. We cannot accept this assertion.

> [A] criminal conspiracy is a partnership in crime, and ... there is in each conspiracy a joint or mutual agency for the prosecution of a common plan. Thus, if two or more persons enter into a conspiracy, any act done by any of them pursuant to the agreement is, in contemplation of law, the act of each of them and they are jointly responsible therefor. This means that everything said, written, or done by any of the conspirators in execution or furtherance of the common purpose is deemed to have been said, done, or written by each of them.... And this joint responsibility extends not only to what is done by any of the conspirators pursuant to the original agreement but also to collateral acts incident to and growing out of the original purpose.

Burke v. State, 234 Ga. 512, 514, 216 S.E.2d 812 (1975). However, a defendant can be held criminally responsible for such collateral acts only if it can be said that they are a natural and probable consequence of the conspiracy.

The State argues that Cox's murder was necessary to conceal the conspiracy to commit arson and that, therefore, Everritt should be deemed responsible. This argument misses the mark because the question is not just one of necessity, but of "reasonable foreseeability." See *Pinkerton v. United States*, 328 U.S. 640, 647–648, 66 S.Ct. 1180, 90 L.Ed. 1489 (1946). Under the facts of this case, it cannot be said that the murder of Cox could be reasonably foreseen as a necessary, probable consequence of the conspiracy to commit arson. Simply put, a conspiracy to commit arson, without more, does not naturally, necessarily, and probably result in the murder of one co-conspirator by another.

[The] evidence was insufficient to enable a rational trier of fact to find Everritt guilty beyond a reasonable doubt of the malice murder of Roosevelt Cox. It follows that the trial court erred in denying Everritt's motion for a directed verdict of acquittal.

Judgment reversed.

All the Justices concur.

PROBLEMS

1. *Forseeability in Everritt.* Do you agree with the Georgia Supreme Court that Everritt was not responsible for the death of Cox? Does it make any difference in your analysis if the prosecution could have shown that Everritt knew that McDuffie wanted to kill Cox and Everritt did nothing about that information, e.g. report it to the police? Explain.

2. *Awareness of Potential Culpability.* What if Everritt's attorney revealed that Everritt had called him the day of Cox's murder to inquire about his culpability for Cox's murder by McDuffie. Would that additional fact suffice to establish Everritt's culpability for Cox's death as a co-conspirator? Explain.

CHAPTER 8

HOMICIDE

■ ■ ■

Homicide, the most serious of all criminal offenses, involves the killing of a human being by another human being. In some jurisdictions, moreover, recent statutory enactments have extended homicide culpability to an actor's unlawful acts causing the death of a fetus.

By the late Common Law period in England, homicide consisted generally of only two constituent offenses, murder and manslaughter, the former crime distinguished from the latter by the presence of "malice aforethought." Despite the terminology, the crime of murder did not actually require either "malice" or "forethought." "Malice aforethought" was a term of art which referred to a homicide committed in any of four ways: with the intent to cause death or serious bodily injury; with the knowledge that the action will cause death or serious bodily injury; when the killing occurred during the commission of a felony; or when the perpetrator intended to oppose, by force, an officer or justice of the peace in the performance of his or her duties.

Today, the various Criminal Code provisions relating to homicide found in federal law and in each of the fifty states (and the District of Columbia) are far more nuanced, more complicated, and, candidly, more idiosyncratic. Accordingly, the way in which homicide offenses are classified in this Chapter should be viewed simply as a typical—but not a universal—American homicide taxonomy. Do not assume that any particular jurisdiction follows this approach precisely.

A. INTENTIONAL KILLINGS

In general, and typically, each jurisdiction's homicide provisions can be divided into two distinct categories: intentional and unintentional killings. The most serious form of homicide is an intentional killing.

307

1. MURDER BY DEGREES

In most states, the crime of murder is divided into degrees. Homicides committed with the specific intention to kill usually are treated as first-degree murders. Consider, for example, California Penal Code, § 189, which provides as follows:

§ 189. Murder; degrees

All murder which is perpetrated by means of a destructive device or explosive, a weapon of mass destruction, knowing use of ammunition designed primarily to penetrate metal or armor, poison, lying in wait, torture, or by any other kind of willful, deliberate, and premeditated killing, or which is committed in the perpetration of, or attempt to perpetrate, arson, rape, carjacking, robbery, burglary, mayhem, kidnapping, train wrecking, . . . or any murder which is perpetrated by means of discharging a firearm from a motor vehicle, intentionally at another person outside of the vehicle with the intent to inflict death, is murder of the first-degree. All other kinds of murders are of the second-degree . . .

To prove the killing was "deliberate and premeditated," it shall not be necessary to prove the defendant maturely and meaningfully reflected upon the gravity of his or her act.

Like California, many states that divide the crime of murder into degrees specifically provide that a "willful," "deliberate" and "premeditated" homicide constitutes first-degree murder. In some of these states, courts have held that "no time is too short" for a wicked person to premeditate and deliberate upon his or her intention to kill. In other states, by contrast, premeditation and deliberation are not established unless it is shown that a cognizable period of reflection has occurred. Are these positions irreconcilable? Which position most appropriately reflects first-degree murder's status as the most heinous of homicide offenses?

STATE v. RAMIREZ

190 Ariz. 65, 945 P.2d 376 (Ct.App. 1997).

NOYES, PRESIDING JUDGE.

[A] young man named David knocked on the door of Appellant's girlfriend's townhouse. Appellant opened the door and greeted David with an aggressive handshake, as if trying to overpower him. The two struggled for a moment, then quit. As they walked into the house, Appellant pressed a gun into David's ribs and said, "I could have took you out already." Nothing more happened between them.

About a month later, Appellant walked out of the townhouse and saw David's brother walking towards him. David and his brother looked alike. Appellant went up to the brother and shook hands with him[,] greeted him, and then, for no apparent reason, pulled out a gun and shot him three times, killing him. Appellant paused between the second and third shots. There were several witnesses. As Appellant walked away, he pointed the gun at a girl and said, "Later, Vicki." Appellant said to one witness, "He started it. He deserves it." (The victim had done nothing.) Appellant said to another witness, "He showed me a gun. I gave him a bullet." (The victim had no gun.) By some accounts, Appellant appeared to be under the influence of alcohol and methamphetamine at the time. By all accounts, it was a senseless killing. Whether it was also a premeditated killing was the only contested issue in the trial.

The jury found Appellant guilty of first-degree murder. [Appellant] claims that the jury instruction on premeditation "lessened the State's burden of proving premeditation." [The statutory definition of premeditation provides]:

> "Premeditation" means that the defendant acts with either the intention or the knowledge that he will kill another human being, when such intention or knowledge precedes the killing by a length of time to permit reflection. An act is not done with premeditation if it is the instant effect of a sudden quarrel or heat of passion.

[In] *Moore v. State*, 65 Ariz. 70, 75, 174 P.2d 282, 285 (1946), [it was] stated that, " . . . deliberation and premeditation may be as instantaneous as successive thoughts of the mind." [*Moore*] also cautioned that, "[W]hile the jury may be told that the brain can function rapidly they must not be misled into thinking that an act can at the same time [be] impulsive, unstudied and premeditated." The jury was so misled in Appellant's case. The court's instruction, as mis-argued by the State, essentially told the jury that an act could be both impulsive and premeditated.

> The instruction given in Appellant's case was as follows:

> "Premeditation" means the defendant's knowledge that he will kill another person existed before the killing long enough to permit reflection. However, the time for reflection must be longer than the time required merely to form the knowledge that conduct will cause death. It may be as instantaneous as successive thoughts in the mind, and it may be proven by circumstantial evidence.

> It is this period of reflection, regardless of its length, which distinguishes first-degree murder from second-degree murder.

This instruction contains two ambiguities which turned into errors when the State mis-argued the law. . . . First, by failing to be clear that premeditation requires actual reflection, the instruction allowed the State to argue that premeditation is just a period of time. Second, because the instruction commented that this period of time can be "instantaneous as successive thoughts in the mind" but provided no balancing language to the effect that an act cannot be both impulsive and premeditated, it allowed the State to argue, in effect, that premeditation is just an instant of time. . . . The instruction says it can be as instantaneous as two thoughts in the mind.

[The] State argues that the instruction and the prosecutor were correct in Appellant's case; that premeditation is, in fact, a period of time rather than actual reflection. The State [argues] that actual reflection was not required after the 1978 enactment of A.R.S. section 13–1101(1). . . .

[Defining] premeditation as a length of time (which can be instantaneous as successive thoughts in the mind) obliterates any meaningful difference between first-and second-degree murder—other than the penalties. The legislature has not merged these two offenses; it has prescribed different elements and different penalties for them. The minimum sentence for first-degree murder is life in prison with possible release in twenty-five years; the maximum is the death penalty. The minimum sentence for second-degree murder is ten years in prison; the maximum is twenty-two years. This significant difference in penalty ranges strongly suggests that the legislature intended there to be an equally significant difference between first- and second-degree murder; something with more relevance to criminal responsibility than an instant of time.

In Appellant's case[,] the only difference between first- and second-degree murder was the element of premeditation. In this case, as in most, after defendant formed the knowledge that he would kill, he could not possibly pull the gun, and aim it, and pull the trigger faster than he could form a successive thought in his mind. Therefore, if the State's argument prevails, any murder is premeditated [unless] defendant acted faster than he could have a second thought. In real life, of course, many persons act without thinking twice, even when they have time to do so. But the State's definition of premeditation would include those unreflecting killers in the first-degree murder category, along with those who actually reflected before acting. We conclude that the first-degree murder statute has never been aimed at those who had time to reflect but did not; it has always has been aimed at those who actually reflected—and then murdered.

If the difference between first- and second-degree murder is to be maintained, premeditation has to be understood as reflection. It is fair to talk of the period of time in which reflection might occur; but it is not fair to define reflection as the period of time in which it might occur. To have meaning, the element of premeditation must describe something that defendant actually does. Just as murder requires actual killing, premeditation requires actual reflection. Premeditation can, of course, be proven by circumstantial evidence; like knowledge or intention, it rarely can be proven by any other means. The more time defendant has to reflect, the stronger the inference that he actually did reflect. This is what the statute is getting at—that actual reflection can be inferred from the length of time to permit reflection. That is the way it has always been and nothing we say here changes that. What we reject, however, is the notion that premeditation is just an instant of time.

[Because] of the premeditation instruction and argument in Appellant's case, however, the verdict merely establishes that an instant of time existed between Appellant's knowledge and his action. The verdict does not establish actual premeditation. [Appellant] claimed that he acted impulsively, without premeditation. Substantial evidence supports this claim. At sentencing, the trial court stated that defendant "impulsively and for no reason pulled out a gun and shot this person." If a properly-instructed jury viewed the evidence as the trial court did, it might have a reasonable doubt about premeditation; it might convict on second-degree murder. On the other hand, if a properly-instructed jury viewed the evidence as our dissenting colleague does, it might convict on first-degree murder.

[We] conclude that the jury instruction on premeditation, as argued by the State, obliterated the distinction between first- and second-degree murder. . . . Because substantial evidence supports both Appellant's argument for second-degree murder and the State's argument for first-degree murder, we cannot say beyond a reasonable doubt that the error in the premeditation instruction did not contribute significantly to the first-degree murder verdict.

[Reversed] and remanded for new trial.

RYAN, JUDGE, dissenting.

[I] disagree with the majority. . . . This disagreement stems from A.R.S section 13–1101(1)'s clarity: "premeditation" is intent or knowledge of killing which precedes the killing "by a length of time to permit reflection." Under this language no actual reflection is required, and the jury decides the factual question of whether adequate time for reflection existed. Except for rare cases, reflection [can] be proven only by the passage of time. The legislature clearly decided not to require the state to prove actual reflection. Instead, it determined that an objective standard of proof of a passage of some period of time would be adequate. Such a determination is a legitimate legislative prerogative. . . . Further, if the legislature had intended that actual reflection be an element of first-degree murder, it could have readily said so. [I] appreciate the majority's concern that, under the present statutory definition of premeditation, the line between first- and second-degree murder is not entirely clear. [W]hile I share the majority's concern, the answer more appropriately rests with the legislature. . . .

NOTES

1. *M.P.C. murder categories.* The Model Penal Code does not divide the crime of murder into degrees. Instead, it treats "purposeful" or "knowing" homicides as murder, as well as unpremeditated murder (which is discussed in greater detail in Part B.1. *infra*):

§ 210.2. Murder.

(1) Except as provided in Section 210.3(1)(b), criminal homicide constitutes murder when:

(a) it is committed purposely or knowingly; or

(b) it is committed recklessly under circumstances manifesting extreme indifference to the value of human life. Such recklessness and indifference are presumed if the actor is engaged or is an accomplice in the commission of, or an attempt to commit, or flight after committing or attempting to commit robbery, rape or deviate sexual intercourse by force or threat of force, arson, burglary, kidnapping or felonious escape.

(2) Murder is a felony of the first-degree [and a person convicted of murder may be sentenced to death, as provided in Section 210.6].

2. *Death penalty.* In many jurisdictions, first-degree murder can be punished by imposition of the death penalty, a sentence that is not available for conviction of any lesser degrees of murder or other homicide offense. In reviewing the problems that follow, you might consider whether—in your view—the aggravating factor of premeditation (the specific intention to kill) *should be* the dispositive factor in determining whether or not an accused killer will be executed. See Chapter 14, Part B.

PROBLEMS

1. *Proving Premeditation.* Following the *Ramirez* decision, how does a prosecutor prove "premeditation"? Obviously, the lapse of time can be a factor, but the court indicates that it is not controlling. Assuming that you are the prosecutor, what other evidence might you use to show that the defendant actually reflected?

2. *Significance of Premeditation.* Does it make sense to aggravate a conviction from second-degree murder to first-degree murder based solely on the fact of premeditation? What is the logic behind the focus on this fact to the exclusion of others? Does the fact of premeditation relate to any of the justifications for punishment (retribution, restraint, deterrence, rehabilitation)? Is someone one who commits a premeditated murder necessarily more deserving of punishment than someone who commits an unpremeditated, but intentional, murder? For example, assume that a man's wife is dying from cancer and she is in great pain. She begs him to help her end her life by providing her with poison. He repeatedly refuses. After much soul searching, he decides that the humane thing to do is to provide the poison.

He does, helps her drink it, and she dies. Was there premeditation? Is he more deserving of punishment than a person who impulsively beats a child or an elderly victim to death? Does it make sense that only the former actor may face the death penalty as a result of his actions? Why?

3. *Deterrence.* As you think about the prior problem, consider the issue of deterrence. Is someone who reflects before committing a crime more amenable to deterrence? If so, does that fact provide a reason for punishing premeditated homicides more severely? But is the possibility of punishment likely to deter the anguished spouse of the cancer patient? Does deterrence provide sufficient justification to treat the spouse more severely than the defendant who brutally beats an elderly victim?

4. *Amending Arizona Statute.* If you were a member of the Arizona legislature, do you think that legislative action would be desirable after the decision in *Ramirez* to amend the legislative definition of "premeditation"? If so, how so? If not, why not? Do you like the provision in the California Penal Code, *supra*, which provides that premeditation need not be "mature" and "meaningful?" What purpose does the premeditation requirement serve if it does not involve "mature" and "meaningful" premeditation?

5. *Impulsiveness Evidence.* The *Ramirez* majority notes that "[a]ppellant claimed that he acted impulsively, without premeditation. Substantial evidence supports this claim." Given Appellant's history of "bad blood" with the victim's brother, to what evidence was the majority referring? If it is conceded that the majority is correct that there was both evidence of impulsiveness and evidence supporting premeditation, why did the majority not simply defer to the jury's fact-finding as reflected in the conviction?

6. *Premeditated or Impulsive Attack.* Defendant became upset with his defense counsel after a jury found him guilty of the charged offenses. While the prosecutor was making his sentencing arguments to the court, defendant abruptly struck his attorney on the side of the head with his fist with such force that counsel was immediately knocked unconscious and fell to the floor. Defendant continued to punch and kick his attorney, landing at least one more forceful blow before being tackled by sheriff's deputies. After he was subdued, defendant also attempted to bite his then-unconscious attorney as the two men lay on the courtroom floor. The audio recording device used by the court reporter captured several statements defendant made during and immediately after the incident, including the following:

> "I would try to kill . . . I hope he's dead! I tried to kill him, he tried . . . he just took my life. . . . I hope you die——f——! I told you you was f——with the wrong one! . . . Oh jack ass leg [sic] lawyer. . . . [T]hey found me guilty . . . I hope you die George! You took my life, I'm gonna to take yours. . . . I hope the bastard die. You done f——the last——you gonna f—in your lifetime. . . ."

Counsel was hospitalized in intensive care. Was the defendant's conduct sufficiently premeditated to support conviction of defendant for attempted murder? (Does this case give you any second thoughts about a career as criminal defense counsel?) *See State v. Forrest*, 168 N.C.App. 614, 609 S.E.2d 241 (2005).

7. *Drunken Dream.* Defendant forcibly entered a mobile home while the residents (whom defendant did not know) were asleep. He removed his clothes, pulled four large steak knives from a knife block in the kitchen, walked to the bedroom where the residents were sleeping, and stabbed both of them in the chest. He then fled, leaving his clothing behind, and took refuge in his own nearby trailer. One victim died. The other called the police who found evidence linking defendant to the scene, including his wallet and the keys to his car and his trailer, all of which he had left behind in the kitchen when he fled the murder scene naked. When the police awakened defendant he agreed to accompany them to the police station. On the way to the station, defendant told the police that he knew why they wanted to talk with him. He said he had had a dream in which he "knifed" a couple of people and he was afraid they were dead. Defendant asked the police if this incident really happened. When told that it had, defendant started to cry. He said that he had spent the evening drinking and that he did not remember everything that happened. He did remember entering a trailer, grabbing knives, entering a bedroom, and making a swinging motion at two people. He also remembered running naked back to his trailer. He previously had fantasized about killing people whom he did not know, "like a spy" would do. Also, one or two months before the killing defendant had wondered aloud in the presence of two friends what it would be like to kill someone, and had asked them if they ever had thought about killing anyone. Was this killing "premeditated?" *See State v. Netland*, 535 N.W.2d 328 (Minn. 1995).

8. *Thinking about Gun.* Defendant's wife suffered a fractured skull which contributed to her mental disorder, diagnosed as a schizoid personality type. She complained of nervousness and told the examining doctor "I feel like hurting my children." This sentiment sometimes took the form of sadistic "discipline" toward their very young children. When defendant was selected to attend an electronics school in another city for nine days, his wife greeted the news with violent argument. Prior to his scheduled departure, he placed a *loaded* .22 calibre pistol on the window sill at the head of their common bed. He did so at the request of his wife, who claimed that the loaded weapon would make her feel safe while he was away. That same evening, a violent and protracted argument ensued and continued until four o'clock in the morning. The couple went to their bedroom a little before 3 o'clock in the morning where they continued to argue in short bursts. She laid on her back facing the wall and yelled over her shoulder at her husband. He started to think about the children: "seeing my older son's feet what happened to them. I could see the bruises on him and Michael's chin was split open, four stitches." As he testified: "I didn't know what to do. I wanted to help my boys. Sometime in there [she] called me some kind of name. I kept thinking of this. *During this time I either thought or felt—I thought of the gun, just thought of the gun.* I am not sure whether I felt my hand move toward the gun—I saw

my hand move, the next thing—the only thing I can recollect after that is right after the shots or right during the shots I saw the gun in my hand just pointed at my wife's head. She was still lying on her back—I mean her side. I could smell the gunpowder and I could hear something—it sounded like running water. I didn't know what it was at first, didn't realize what I'd done at first. Then I smelled it. I smelled blood before." When pressed on cross-examination, defendant estimated that five minutes elapsed between his wife's last remark and the shooting. Did defendant "premeditate"? *See Commonwealth v. Carroll*, 412 Pa. 525, 194 A.2d 911 (1963).

EXERCISE

Judge Ryan's Amendment. Assume that Judge Ryan, the dissenting judge in *Ramirez*, was a legislator and not an appellate judge. As his legislative assistant, draft a proposed (post-*Ramirez*) amendment to Arizona law (as discussed in that decision) which would have the effect of codifying the views expressed in his dissenting opinion.

STATE v. DAVIS

905 S.W.2d 921 (Mo.Ct.App. 1995).

CHARLES B. BLACKMAR, SENIOR JUDGE.

[On] the evening of Wednesday, December 2, 1992, Luther Blackwell, Demetrius Tabbs and the defendant were drinking copiously of beer intermingled with gin. Tabbs drove them in his newly acquired car to the central west end of St. Louis. During the ride, one of the others told Tabbs that they were going to "jack" somebody. When the car reached the vicinity of Euclid and Maryland Plaza, the group spied a couple on foot who turned out to be Natalie Hasty and Kevin Young. The defendant and Blackwell left the car and Tabbs drove one block west to Kings Highway. Tabbs testified that the defendant customarily carried a gun, which he concealed in the small of his back. He did not see him with the gun on this occasion, but did see the defendant reach for the small of his back as he left the car.

Hasty and Young were unloading groceries from their car in the parking lot at the rear of an apartment on Maryland Plaza. Blackwell approached Hasty, flourished a knife, and demanded her purse. He then grabbed the purse and she tried to hold on to it. At the same time, the defendant headed toward Young. Just as soon as Hasty saw the person later identified as the defendant, she noticed that he was carrying a handgun. Hasty heard the sound of chains rattling and assumed that the defendant and Young were wrestling. The defendant said, "I want your money. Give me your wallet." She then heard three shots. While she was thus distracted Blackwell escaped with her purse. She then went to Young, who was lying on the ground. He and the defendant moved as much as 30 feet during the struggle.

Young was mortally wounded and died before arriving at the hospital.

Blackwell was apprehended by security officers in a neighboring subdivision, carrying Hasty's purse. He was taken into custody and, after substantial equivocation and circumlocution, admitted the robbery, identifying the defendant as his companion. He testified for the State after a plea bargain. Tabbs also was apprehended at his home and testified for the State.

The defendant first argues that the evidence does not establish the element of deliberation which is essential to a first-degree murder conviction. Hasty testified, however, that the defendant was carrying a handgun as he and Blackwell approached her and Young in the parking lot. The jury could have concluded that the defendant had formed a deliberate purpose of using the gun during his criminal enterprise if necessary to accomplish his ends. Blackwell testified, furthermore, as follows:

> . . . And when I snatched her purse, I seen a [dude] jump up out of the car and wrestle with Reginald [the defendant]. And when he wrestled with Reginald, Reginald pulled the gun on him and shot him.

The defendant therefore made a decision to use the weapon he was carrying when he was confronted by his intended robbery victim. This demonstrates deliberation.

[The] deliberation essential to a conviction of first-degree murder need only be momentary. [Perhaps] the instruction language, "cool reflection" might be applied by some jurors in a manner more favorable to the defendant than the law strictly requires. The required reflection need be only momentary to establish deliberation.

[Affirmed.]

PROBLEMS

1. *Drowning Methods and Reasons.* A man crossing a bridge sees a young child standing at the bridge railing and, for no apparent reason, the man pushes the child into the water and the child drowns. Is this "premeditated" murder? Should it be? Does it make any difference if the child struggles to resist the push and it takes a couple of minutes of fighting before the man is able to push the child off the bridge? Does it make any difference if the man recognized the child as his newspaper delivery boy, and if the man had been angry at the boy for months because the morning paper was often thrown into the bushes, and if the man pushed him to teach him a lesson?

2. *Firing at Police.* Uniformed police officers were executing a no-knock search warrant at Paul Lyons's apartment. The officers yelled "Police search" outside the apartment and, at the very same moment, broke down the front

door with a battering ram. Lyons fired at the entering officers, killing one of them only a few feet inside his apartment. Is Lyons guilty of "premeditated" murder? *See State v. Lyons*, 340 N.C. 646, 459 S.E.2d 770 (1995).

3. *Arguing at Party.* Garcia and Ray Gutierrez, who had been friends, were drinking heavily at a party when they began arguing in the backyard and went to the front yard to fight. Gutierrez's girlfriend testified that she saw Garcia jabbing Gutierrez in the chest with a knife, and she saw Gutierrez fall down, his face "all sliced up." When the police arrived, Gutierrez was dead and Garcia said, "I did it. I did it. I'm not ashamed to admit it. I told my brother I did him and I'd do him again." Is Garcia's statement consistent with a simple intentional murder (perhaps of the rash and impulsive kind) or did it involve "premeditation"? Even if Garcia had not decided to kill Gutierrez before the argument, could he have premeditated while walking from the back yard to the front yard? Would it matter that, at one point while in the backyard, Garcia said, "Remove Ray away from me or you're not going to be seeing him for the rest of the day"? *See State v. Garcia*, 114 N.M. 269, 837 P.2d 862 (1992).

4. *Sixty Wounds.* Defendant, who was living with a woman, killed her ten-year-old daughter, Victoria. Prior to the killing, defendant had been drinking. The arresting officer found Victoria's body on the floor near her bed. He also found defendant's blood-spattered shorts on a chair in the living room, and a knife and defendant's socks, with blood encrusted on the soles, in the master bedroom. The victim's torn and bloodstained dress had been ripped from her, her clothes were found in various rooms of the house, there were bloody footprints matching the size of the victim's feet leading from the master bedroom to Victoria's room, and that there was blood in almost every room of the house, including the kitchen, the floor of which appeared to have been mopped. Over 60 wounds, both severe and superficial, were found on Victoria's body. Several of the wounds, including the vaginal lacerations, were post mortem. No evidence of spermatozoa was found in the victim, on her underwear, or on the bed next to which she was found. Was there sufficient evidence of "premeditation" on these facts to establish first-degree murder? *See People v. Anderson*, 70 Cal.2d 15, 447 P.2d 942, 73 Cal.Rptr. 550 (1968).

2. VOLUNTARY MANSLAUGHTER

The offense of voluntary manslaughter is also an intentional killing, but it is an intentional killing which has been mitigated from murder to manslaughter due to the presence of adequate and sufficient provocation or other appropriate sorts of excuses for engaging in an act of killing. Or, to put it another way, voluntary manslaughter is an intentional murder which includes additional circumstances that serve to negative the requisite element of malice needed to establish murder. Given its mitigating status, voluntary manslaughter is usually raised as a defense by the accused to a charge of murder, i.e. "I killed the victim but the killing was the result of circumstances which mitigate the severity of the offense from murder to manslaughter." Less frequently, the prosecution accepts the existence of these mitigating circumstances and simply charges the accused with voluntary manslaughter. In most (but not all) jurisdictions, there are two distinct types of voluntary manslaughter: (1) provocation or "heat of passion" defenses; and (2) imperfect defenses.

a. PROVOCATION OR HEAT OF PASSION DEFENSE

One justification for mitigating an intentional homicide to manslaughter is when the defendant acted under "provocation" or in the "heat of passion."

STATE v. REDMOND
937 S.W.2d 205 (Mo. 1996).

HOLSTEIN, CHIEF JUSTICE.

[Von] Michael Johnson, the victim, lived down the street from [defendant Marlon] Redmond's mother. On May 8, 1993, Redmond was washing his car in the street in front of his mother's house. Johnson was walking his dogs [with] Laura Sherwood, who was alleged to be the mother of Redmond's child. As Johnson and Sherwood walked by [, Johnson and Redmond] began to argue. Sherwood continued to walk past, and heard the men arguing behind her. Redmond testified that Johnson accused Redmond of treating Sherwood badly. [At that point, Johnson reached into his pocket. Redmond claims that he saw a gun and that he thought Johnson was going to kill him.] Redmond grabbed a baseball bat from the open trunk of the car he was washing and hit Johnson in the head, killing him.... Sherwood did not see the blow, but said that she heard a single crack.... Redmond then drove off, and was arrested later that day at his girlfriend's house. After his arrest, Redmond questioned a reserve police officer as to the victim's condition and stated "I can't believe this happened.... It just made me mad, so mad. We just had this baby. I can't believe I hit him...."

Redmond testified that he told the police about Johnson having a gun. However, according to the reserve police officer, Redmond did not mention the gun. After being read his *Miranda* rights and signing a waiver, Redmond made a voluntary written statement to the police. In that statement, Redmond also failed to mention that the victim had a gun. According to the victim's mother and an emergency room nurse, the victim did not have a weapon on his person.

[The] trial court refused Redmond's proffered instructions on voluntary [manslaughter] but submitted an instruction on self-defense. The jury found Redmond guilty of murder in the second-degree....

[Voluntary] manslaughter [is a] lesser included offense [of] second-degree murder, the crime for which Redmond was convicted. A trial court is required to instruct on a lesser included offense if the evidence, in fact or by inference, provides a basis for both an acquittal of the greater offense and a conviction of the lesser offense, and if such instruction is requested by one of the parties or the court.

[The] trial court erred in refusing Redmond's proffered instruction on voluntary manslaughter because there was sufficient evidence to support an acquittal of murder in the second-degree and a conviction of voluntary manslaughter.

The crime of voluntary manslaughter is defined as causing the death of another person under circumstances that would constitute murder in the second-degree, except that the death was caused "under the influence of sudden passion arising from adequate cause[.]" The defendant has the burden of injecting the issue of influence of sudden passion arising from adequate cause. This means the issue is not submitted to the trier of fact unless supported by the evidence.

The trial court is therefore required to give an instruction on voluntary manslaughter if there is sufficient evidence to support a finding that the defendant caused the death of the victim under the influence of sudden passion arising from adequate cause. "Sudden passion" is defined as "passion directly caused by and arising out of provocation by the victim or another acting with the victim which passion arises at the time of the offense and is not solely the result of former provocation[.]" "Adequate cause" is "cause that would reasonably produce a degree of passion in a person of ordinary temperament sufficient to substantially impair an ordinary person's capacity for self-control[.]" The offense must have been committed in sudden passion, and not after there has been time for the passion to cool. Words alone, no matter how opprobrious or insulting, are not sufficient to show adequate provocation.

The facts of the present case are similar to [*State v. Fears*, 803 S.W.2d 605 (Mo. 1991)] and *State v. Newlon*, 721 S.W.2d 89 (Mo.App. 1986), two cases in which Missouri courts have found sufficient evidence to support a finding of sudden passion arising from adequate cause. In *Fears*, the victim and the defendant were engaged in a heated quarrel, the victim poked the defendant several times with his finger, and swung at the defendant with his fist. After blocking the swing, the defendant punched the victim causing him to fall to the ground. The victim was killed by a resulting head injury. The court held that this evidence was sufficient to inject the issue of sudden passion so as to warrant a voluntary manslaughter instruction:

> The aggregate of the insulting words, offensive gestures and
> physical contacts that occurred during this encounter [was] suffi-

cient to put Fears in fear of serious bodily harm, carried out in a
time span insufficient for Fears' anger to cool, and sufficient for
reasonable persons to have found that Fears acted under "sudden passion."

Thus, the court found that a physical altercation in which the victim
swung his fist at the defendant constituted adequate provocation.

State v. Newlon is similar to the case at bar in that in both cases the
victim was alleged to have provoked the defendant by brandishing a
weapon during a heated argument. In *Newlon*, the victim and the
defendant were arguing. The defendant testified that the victim
verbally threatened her and pulled a kitchen knife, which scared the
defendant. Consequently, the defendant shot and killed the victim.
Finding evidence of sudden passion arising from adequate cause, the
court of appeals reversed the trial court for failing to submit a
voluntary manslaughter instruction.

[I]n the present case there was evidence of a heated argument, in
which the victim confronted the defendant in a threatening manner,
and scared the defendant by displaying a deadly weapon. Redmond
testified that the victim approached him in a confrontational manner
and an altercation ensued because the victim accused Redmond of
mistreating the mother of Redmond's alleged child. According to
Redmond, the victim displayed the handle of a gun. Redmond
further testified that, as a result of this confrontation, he feared for his
life and consequently struck the victim with a baseball bat.

The jury could accept Redmond's testimony, or the jury could
reject it as unbelievable. It is not, however, for the court to determine
Redmond's credibility, nor to weigh the evidence in any other respect.
The court's role is to determine whether the testimony presented
would support a finding that the defendant killed under the influence
of sudden passion arising from adequate cause.

The threatening confrontation described by Redmond along with
the showing of a gun is the type of provocation that could cause a
reasonable person to lose self-control. Thus, the evidence presented is
sufficient to inject the issue of sudden passion arising from adequate
cause. This being so, the trial court committed reversible error in
failing to submit a voluntary manslaughter instruction upon the
defendant's request.

[Because] the evidence warranted an instruction on voluntary
manslaughter, the trial court's denial of Redmond's request for such
an instruction was error. Redmond is entitled to a new trial before a
properly instructed jury. Redmond's conviction of murder in the
second-degree is, therefore, reversed, and the cause remanded for a
new trial. . . .

NOTE

M.P.C. version of voluntary manslaughter. The Model Penal Code also contains a "heat of passion" provision (although it does not refer to the provision in that way and does not limit the application to "passion" situations). Section 210.3, manslaughter, provides as follows: "Criminal homicide constitutes manslaughter when ... a homicide which would otherwise be murder is committed under the influence of extreme mental or emotional disturbance for which there is reasonable explanation or excuse. The reasonableness of such explanation or excuse shall be determined from the viewpoint of a person in the actor's situation under the circumstances as he believes them to be."

PROBLEM

Seeing a Gun. The *Redmond* court ruled that "[t]he threatening confrontation described by Redmond along with the showing of a gun is the type of provocation that could cause a reasonable person to lose self-control." Do you agree? Would a "reasonable person" ever kill someone by striking them with a baseball bat? Explain.

STATE v. CORNETT
82 Ohio App.3d 624, 612 N.E.2d 1275 (1992).

JONES, PRESIDING JUDGE.

[Appellant] had a stormy relationship with Angela Ratliff, who was either his girlfriend or common-law wife. Appellant occasionally threatened to kill Ratliff, but had never acted on those threats. In late March 1991, appellant and Ratliff had a fight and separated.

On the afternoon of March 31, 1991, appellant purchased cartridges for a handgun that he had purchased a few days earlier in a Middletown bar. According to several witnesses, appellant purchased the weapon after Ratliff's parents "put out a contract on appellant's life" through a local motorcycle gang. Upon purchasing the ammunition, appellant and a friend went to a wooded area near Hamilton where appellant practiced shooting the handgun. Appellant and two other friends then spent the remainder of the day and evening drinking at several Hamilton bars. Later that night, appellant had one of his friends drive him to Ratliff's apartment.

Appellant testified that he knocked on the door of Ratliff's apartment, but received no answer. Appellant then went to a bedroom window and looked in, whereupon he saw Ratliff having sex with the victim, Darrell Harris. Appellant went back and attempted to kick open the front door. He then returned to the bedroom window and "dove" through it onto the bed, from where he saw Ratliff and Harris heading down the hallway. Ratliff ran out the front door and appellant walked down the hallway into the living room.

According to appellant, Harris suddenly came at appellant from the kitchen with his head down and swinging his arms "with what appeared to be a knife." Appellant went for his handgun because Harris screamed he would kill appellant and appellant "didn't know what was going to happen." Appellant testified that Harris collided with him and as the two men struggled, appellant "accidentally" shot Harris once in the head, fatally wounding him. Appellant denied that he intended to kill or even shoot Harris. Police later recovered a closed pocket knife from behind a couch in the living room. There was testimony, however, that Ratliff slept on the couch earlier that week following one of appellant's threats and placed the knife there for her protection.

Ratliff testified that she and Harris were in bed and got up to investigate after hearing a noise outside the apartment. As they were in the kitchen, Ratliff heard the sound of a window breaking. She then ran out of her apartment and upstairs to the manager's unit. On her way up the stairs, Ratliff "heard [appellant's] voice [and] a loud noise [and heard Harris] scream."

[The] grand jury indicted appellant on one count of aggravated murder with a firearm specification and an additional specification charging appellant with committing the homicide while committing aggravated burglary.... The jury found appellant not guilty of aggravated murder but guilty of the lesser included offense of murder. [Appellant] claims the trial court erred by refusing to instruct the jury on the lesser offense of voluntary manslaughter when the evidence clearly warranted such an instruction. It is appellant's position that in an aggravated murder case where the defendant discovers his or her spouse in the act of adultery, the accused is entitled to a jury instruction on voluntary manslaughter....

There is no question that involuntary manslaughter may be a lesser included offense of aggravated murder. On the other hand, voluntary manslaughter, although not a lesser included offense, is an inferior degree of aggravated murder and murder since "its elements [are] contained within the indicted offense, except for one or more additional mitigating elements...." The element of provocation mitigates the offender's culpability.

Thus, even though voluntary manslaughter is not a lesser included offense of aggravated murder or murder, the test for whether a judge should give a jury instruction on voluntary manslaughter where a defendant is charged with the more serious crime is the same test to be applied as when an instruction on a lesser included offense is sought. In other words, an instruction on an inferior degree offense must be given if, under any reasonable view of the evidence, it is possible for the trier of fact to find the defendant not guilty of the greater offense and guilty of the lesser or inferior offense. A jury must find a defendant guilty of voluntary manslaughter rather than murder if the prosecution proves, beyond a reasonable doubt, that the defendant knowingly caused the victim's death, and if the defendant establishes, by a preponderance of the evidence, the existence of a mitigating circumstance. . . .

"Voluntary manslaughter" is defined in R.C. 2903.03(A) in the following terms: "No person, while under the influence of sudden passion or in a sudden fit of rage, either of which is brought on by serious provocation occasioned by the victim that is reasonably sufficient to incite the person into using deadly force, shall knowingly cause the death of another." The statute defines "voluntary manslaughter" as a single offense that, under certain circumstances, permits the defendant to mitigate a charge of aggravated murder or murder to manslaughter. The crime comprises elements that the state must prove as well as mitigating circumstances that must be established by the defendant. The mitigating circumstances are (1) sudden passion in response to serious provocation by the victim sufficient to incite the defendant to use deadly force, and (2) a sudden fit of rage in response to serious provocation by the victim sufficient to incite the defendant to use deadly force.

Under the statute, a jury must find the accused guilty of voluntary manslaughter rather than the more serious offense of murder or aggravated murder if the prosecution has proven, beyond a reasonable doubt, that the defendant knowingly caused the victim's death, and if the defendant has established by a preponderance of the evidence the existence of one or both of the mitigating circumstances. Thus, a defendant on trial for murder or aggravated murder who produces sufficient evidence of one or both of the mitigating circumstances is entitled to an instruction on voluntary manslaughter if under any reasonable view of the evidence, a reasonable jury could find that the defendant had established by a preponderance of the evidence the existence of one or both of the mitigating circumstances.

An inquiry into the mitigating circumstances requires a determination of whether there has been serious provocation by the victim. Serious provocation involves both objective and subjective components. In determining whether the provocation is reasonably sufficient to bring on a sudden passion or a fit of rage, an objective standard is applied, i.e., there must have been a reasonable provocation, and a reasonable man so provoked would not have cooled off in the interval of time between the provocation and the delivery of the fatal blow.

Appellant contends that his discovery of his common-law wife in the act of adultery is sufficient evidence of "serious provocation" and entitles him to an instruction on voluntary manslaughter. . . . Although the case at bar may be a "classic" voluntary manslaughter situation and—despite the paucity of Ohio case law on the subject— would call for a voluntary manslaughter instruction on a purely objective basis, we must still determine whether there was sufficient evidence of the subjective components of serious provocation. In addition to the objective factors, a defendant must show the following subjective factors before a voluntary manslaughter instruction will be given: (1) the defendant must have been in fact provoked, and (2) the defendant must not in fact have cooled off during the interval of time between the provocation and the delivery of the fatal blow.

Appellant testified that when he saw Ratliff and Harris having sex, "it felt like my whole life just raced in front of me. I just crumbled." Appellant ran back to the front door and then ran back to the bedroom where he dove through the window. At that point, however, appellant walked down the hallway into the living room and claimed that Harris aggressively came at appellant, stating he was going to kill appellant. Appellant further testified that he did not intend to shoot Harris, that the shooting was an accident, and that he would never intentionally shoot anyone. After shooting Harris, appellant "started running around in circles" before leaving the apartment.

A defendant on trial for aggravated murder bears the burden of showing, by a preponderance of the evidence, that he or she acted under the influence of sudden passion or in a sudden fit of rage brought on by serious provocation by the victim that was reasonably sufficient to incite the defendant into using deadly force. While appellant may have produced sufficient objective evidence to justify a jury instruction on involuntary manslaughter, a lesser included or inferior degree offense instruction is not always required simply because there is "some evidence" going to the lesser offense. Based upon his own testimony, it is questionable whether appellant was sufficiently provoked or, if so, whether he "cooled off" between the provocation and the delivery of the fatal blow. After entering the apartment, appellant walked after Ratliff and Harris; he did not run after them. Appellant claimed that Harris made an aggressive move towards appellant, that the shooting was accidental, and that he never intended to kill or even shoot Harris. This evidence would suggest that from a subjective standpoint, appellant did not present the requisite reasonably sufficient evidence of provocation in order to merit a jury instruction on voluntary manslaughter.

Finally, we believe it is inappropriate for the trial court to place a defendant in the position where he or she must choose between lesser included or inferior degree offenses. It is not the accused's responsibility to select those lesser included or inferior degree offenses that will be submitted to the jury. The defendant may request that such instructions be given to the jury. It is the duty of the trial court to determine whether the evidence presented warrants a jury instruction on a particular lesser included or inferior degree offense. [S]ince we conclude that the evidence of provocation was not reasonably sufficient and that no reasonable jury could have found appellant not guilty of the greater offense, but guilty of voluntary manslaughter, the trial court's failure to instruct the jury on voluntary manslaughter was not erroneous. . . .

Judgment affirmed.

NOTES

1. *Proving lack of provocation.* As a matter of due process, the prosecution has the burden of proving the existence of all of the elements of a crime beyond a reasonable doubt. *In re Winship*, 397 U.S. 358, 90 S.Ct. 1068, 25 L.Ed.2d 368 (1970). As a result, because the traditional provocation defense to a murder charge has been viewed as serving to negative the element of malice aforethought that is requisite for a murder conviction (thus mitigating the offense to voluntary manslaughter), in jurisdictions that use this traditional defense, the Supreme Court has held that—when provocation is offered as a (mitigating) defense—the burden of proof is upon the prosecution to prove beyond a reasonable doubt that the defendant was *not* provoked. *Mullaney v. Wilbur*, 421 U.S. 684, 95 S.Ct. 1881, 44 L.Ed.2d 508 (1975).

2. *Proving provocation.* However, in jurisdictions where a version of the provocation defense has been enacted in such a way that it does *not* serve to mitigate a finding of malice necessary to establish murder, the burden of proof of establishing provocation may be placed upon the defendant. *Patterson v. New York*, 432 U.S. 197, 97 S.Ct. 2319, 53 L.Ed.2d 281 (1977) (upholding a New York "extreme emotional disturbance" mitigating defense which placed the burden of proof on the defendant where that defense served to mitigate second-degree murder which did not have malice aforethought as an element).

PROBLEMS

1. *Evidence of Heat of Passion in Cornett.* The *Cornett* Court concluded that an instruction on voluntary manslaughter "must be given if, under any reasonable view of the evidence, it is possible for the trier of fact to find the defendant not guilty of [murder] and guilty of [voluntary manslaughter]." Do you agree that there was *no* reasonable view of the evidence that supported a finding that Cornett actually became suddenly impassioned or enraged and killed as a result of that serious provocation? Explain.

2. *Intent to Kill without Passion.* A learns that his wife is having an adulterous relationship with B. A reasonable person would have been outraged by the news. A was not outraged. However, because he hates B, A uses the news as an opportunity to kill him. Is A entitled to a reduction of his crime to voluntary manslaughter?

3. *Passion Based on Mistake.* Suppose that B tells A that he has been having an adulterous relationship with A's wife. Although A believes B, there is no such relationship. In a fit of anger, A kills B. Is A entitled to a reduction to voluntary manslaughter?

4. *Relevance of Defendant's Characteristics.* Defendant, a one-legged man, was standing next to a park bench on crutches. The victim, just prior to the killing, maliciously knocked one of defendant's crutches out from under him. In a fit of anger, defendant stabbed the victim with a knife and killed him. Was the victim's action sufficient to constitute adequate provocation? Should the jury apply a reasonable person standard, in determining whether the provocation was sufficient, or should it apply a "reasonable one-legged man on crutches" standard? *See Rex v. Raney* [1942] 29 Crim. App. 14.

5. *A "Reasonable Impotent Man" Standard?* Defendant, who was sexually impotent, tried in vain to have sex with a prostitute. She jeered at him and attempted to get away. Defendant tried to prevent her from leaving, but she slapped him in the face and punched him in the stomach. At this point, defendant took out a knife and stabbed her to death. Under the common law, is defendant be entitled to a voluntary manslaughter instruction if he is tried for murder? What about an instruction under M.P.C. § 210.3 (which provides that "Criminal homicide constitutes manslaughter when ... a homicide which would otherwise be murder is committed under the influence of extreme mental or emotional disturbance for which there is reasonable explanation or excuse")? *See Bedder v. DPP*, [1954] 2 All E.R. 801, [1954] 1 W.L.R. 1119, 38 Cr.App. 133.

6. *When Defendant Is Responsible for Circumstances Giving Rise to the "Extreme Mental or Emotional Disturbance."* A attempted to blackmail B. B became enraged and attacked A with a knife. A, who became very angry, in a fit of "white hot temper," stabbed B to death. Is A entitled to an instruction under the common law or under M.P.C. § 210.3? *See Edwards v. Regina*, [1973] A.C. 648, [1973] 1 All E.R. 152, [1972] 3 W.L.R. 893, 57 Cr.App. 157.

7. *Cultural Provocation Defense?* Oscar Trejo was quarreling with his cousin Ricardo Rosales. Both of them were intoxicated. After some friendly insults, Rosales insulted Trejo's mother by referring to her as a prostitute. Trejo broke a beer bottle on the sidewalk and threatened to "stick" Rosales unless Rosales stopped making such insults. When Rosales again called Trejo the "son of [a] whore mother", Trejo stabbed Rosales in the neck with the broken bottle. Rosales bled to death before he reached a hospital. At his trial for murder, Trejo's defense was that, although he killed his cousin, he was guilty of voluntary manslaughter, not murder. He argued that Rosales's insults aroused a heat of passion in him that negated the malice necessary for second degree murder. He presented expert evidence that accusations of prostitution by one's own mother are "the most serious insults any man can pronounce ... in most [of] Latino America" and are "fighting words" for a person of "Mexican cultural background." He also tried to argue that references to Trejo's mother as a prostitute were especially inflammatory because certain members of his family had been prostitutes. The trial judge did not, however, permit him to make the later argument, holding that it was irrelevant to a provocation defense. Did the trial judge err? *See People v. Trejo*, 2008 WL 2132367 (Cal.App. 2 Dist. 2008).

8. *Juries and Homicide Verdicts.* During the Summer of 2005, a former Klu Klux Klan member, Edgar Ray Killen, was convicted of killing three civil rights workers in 1964. The evidence shows that the victims were brutally beaten and shot, and that their bodies were buried in an earthen dam. The case was complicated by the age of the evidence and fading witness recollections. It was also complicated by the fact that no witness was able to positively place Killen at the scene of the crime. The trial ended with a conviction of manslaughter rather than murder. Given the brutal nature of the killings, how do you explain a conviction for manslaughter? *See Killen v. State*, 958 So.2d 172 (Miss. 2007).

b. IMPERFECT DEFENSE

An "imperfect defense" arises when a defendant commits an intentional murder, but does so under circumstances which he or she has an honest belief that fits within the parameters of a legal defense, except that belief is unreasonable. Most, but not all, jurisdictions recognize the existence of imperfect defenses. In those that do, when a complete defense is imperfectly established, i.e. every element is met except reasonableness, the crime is mitigated from murder to voluntary manslaughter. Often an imperfect defense arises in the context of justifications such as self-defense. See Chapter 11, Part A, *infra*.

STATE v. ORDWAY
261 Kan. 776, 934 P.2d 94 (1997).

ALLEGRUCCI, JUSTICE:

[At the Kansas home of Clarence and Betty Ordway, the police found Clarence's deceased body. He died as a result of a shotgun wound to the back that caused extensive damage to his left lung and heart. There was no evidence of defensive injuries to his hands or feet. A few days later, New York police found defendant Kim Ordway, Clarence and Betty's son, sitting in his parent's car. A loaded shotgun was found on the front passenger seat, and a serrated kitchen knife was found under the driver's seat of the car. Clarence Ordway's wallet and two rings were found in a backpack in the back seat. Betty Ordway's body, wrapped in a tarp and a blanket, was found in the trunk. She had also died as a result of shotgun wounds in her right chest and one entry wound in her back, which caused damage to her lungs, heart, liver, ribs, vertebrae, and aorta. In addition, she had bruises, lacerations, abrasions, and fractures caused by impact with a blunt object. There were bruising and swelling around the left eyebrow; five lacerations on her head; bruising, swelling, and abrasion of the left forearm; and broken bones in both forearms. The pathologist's opinion was that the injuries to her forearms were defensive wounds.]

[The] jury was instructed on the elements of first- and second-degree murder with respect to each count. Defendant's counsel requested that the jury be instructed on voluntary manslaughter, and the district court refused. [Ordway] contends that a voluntary manslaughter instruction was required [because] the evidence showed that he killed his parents without malice and for the purpose of preventing them from harming his children.

Voluntary manslaughter is defined in K.S.A. 21–3403: "Voluntary manslaughter is the intentional killing of a human being committed: (a) Upon a sudden quarrel or in the heat of passion; or (b) upon an unreasonable but honest belief that circumstances existed that justified deadly force under K.S.A. 21–3211 [...]." K.S.A. 21–3211 provides: "A person is justified in the use of force against an aggressor when and to the extent it appears to him and he reasonably believes that such conduct is necessary to defend himself or another against such aggressor's imminent use of unlawful force."

[Ordway] argues that a voluntary manslaughter instruction should have been given because the evidence showed that he killed his parents upon an unreasonable but honest belief that circumstances existed that justified the use of deadly force against them in the defense of his children. [T]here was evidence to the effect that it appeared to Ordway that his use of force against his parents was necessary to defend his children from unlawful force being used against them by his parents. There is no evidence or even contention that his belief was reasonable.

K.S.A. 21–3403(b) defines voluntary manslaughter as an intentional killing upon an unreasonable but honest belief that circumstances existed that justified deadly force under 21–3211. K.S.A. 21–3211 provides that the circumstances justify the use of force when a defendant reasonably believes that its use is necessary to defend others. When the two statutes are read together, the unreasonable belief element of 21–3403 must be reconciled with the reasonable belief element of 21–3211. It seems that this may be accomplished by a plain reading. That is, if the reasonable belief that force was necessary, which is the substance of 21–3211, is substituted for the defense-of-self-or-others as designated in 21–3403(b), the latter provides that voluntary manslaughter is an intentional killing upon a defendant's unreasonable but honest belief that he or she reasonably believed the use of force was necessary to defend others. In other words, the 21–3211 reasonableness of the belief that deadly force was justified is irrelevant because the 21–3403(b) belief is unreasonable. Although Ordway could not qualify for acquittal under the perfect defense of defense of self or others under 21–3211, the reasonableness element of 21–3211 should not prevent a trial court's giving an instruction on the lesser included offense of voluntary manslaughter.

With regard to a defense-of-others instruction, this court has stated that the evidence must support affirmative findings by a rational factfinder to the subjective question whether defendant honestly believed his action was necessary to defend others as well as to the objective question whether his belief was reasonable. In a case such as the present one, however, where the defendant is seeking an instruction on the lesser included offense of voluntary manslaughter rather than asserting the affirmative defense of defense of others, the objective component of defense of others should be immaterial. Both elements in the offense of voluntary manslaughter as defined in 21–3403(b) are subjective. The defendant's belief must be sincerely held, and it must be unreasonable. For this reason, the "objective elements" of 21–3211—an aggressor, imminence, and unlawful force—would not come in for consideration.

Legislative history of K.S.A. 21–3403 shows that the definition of voluntary manslaughter was expanded by the addition of subsection (b) in 1992. Until then, the statute defined voluntary manslaughter as an intentional killing upon a sudden quarrel or in the heat of passion. Notes on proposed criminal code revisions were attached to the minutes of the Senate Judiciary Committee from March 22, 1992, which contained the following comments about subsection (b) of 21–3403:

> "(b) 'Imperfect right to self-defense' manslaughter

> "This new subsection covers intentional killings that result from an unreasonable but honest belief that deadly force was justified in self-defense. In essence, the defendant meets the subjective, but not the objective, test for self-defense. This so-called 'imperfect right to self-defense' is recognized in various forms. Kansas apparently recognizes it for unintentional killings under involuntary manslaughter. The Model Penal Code also follows this approach. Some states, e.g. Illinois, recognize this partial defense for intentional killings.

> "Applying this partial defense to intentional killings is simply a recognition of the practical realities of plea bargaining and jury verdicts. Often it is unjust to prosecute and convict such killers of murder and it is equally unjust to acquit them. This new subsection provides a middle category that is theoretically sound and legitimizes the realities of plea bargaining and jury verdicts."

There is no express indication in the note to 21–3403(b) that there was any contemplation that the subsection's unreasonable belief might be based on psychotic delusions (or some other form of mental illness). Nor does examination of the Kansas case law cited in the note indicate that application of subsection (b) to cases where a homicide defendant denied criminal responsibility due to mental illness was envisioned.

In Illinois, the offense known as second-degree murder includes the elements of Kansas' voluntary manslaughter offense. [The] Illinois intermediate appellate court considered the "unreasonable but honest belief" mitigation provision of the statute in *People v. Aliwoli*, 238 Ill.App.3d 602, 179 Ill.Dec. 515, 606 N.E.2d 347 (1992). The defendant in that case was charged with attempted first-degree murder of three police officers when he shot and wounded them trying to avoid being stopped for a traffic violation. Defense counsel asserted an insanity defense, but defendant testified that he acted in self-defense. The appellate court affirmed the trial court's refusing to give an instruction on second-degree murder for several reasons. One reason [was] that the court found:

> no evidence of mitigation in the case at bar that justifies the giving of the instruction even if the crime of attempted second-degree murder existed in Illinois. Defendant failed to validly prove a sudden and intense passion or that he was seriously provoked by the officers' routine stop for passing a school bus. The evidence adduced at trial was that defendant was either insane or that he had a longstanding mental illness, neither of which is a mitigating factor under the statute. An unproved insanity defense was not intended to be a mitigating factor in the crime of second-degree murder. The predatory conduct of the defendant in searching out his victims would negate the notion of self-defense.

We conclude that K.S.A. 21–3403(b) has no application where a defendant raises the defense of insanity, and more specifically, the "unreasonable but honest belief" necessary to support the "imperfect right to self-defense manslaughter" cannot be based upon a psychotic delusion.

[Affirmed.]

PROBLEMS

1. *Psychotic Delusions.* Why did the court hold that Ordway's "psychotic delusions" were not included within the subset of "unreasonable" subjective beliefs which establish an imperfect (voluntary manslaughter) defense?

2. *Stupidity.* If Ordway, instead of being psychotic and delusional, had simply misinterpreted his parents' actions and honestly (but stupidly) believed that these actions were aimed at harming his children, would he be entitled to acquittal on both charges of murder due to the existence of an imperfect defense?

3. *Unreasonable Fear of Victim.* A victim was found brutally murdered and forensic evidence showed that she had been sexually assaulted before her death. Witnesses saw her leave a bar with defendant the night before. Defendant admitted that he drove her home. Supposedly, as she left his car, she took a steak knife from her purse and held it at her side. Defendant claimed that he was scared, although the victim did not actually threaten him with the knife, but mentioned something about her "old man" being around.

Defendant claimed he then "kicked" her from his car when she stated that she wanted to "hurt somebody." On these facts, does defendant have a right to an imperfect self-defense instruction when faced with first-degree murder charges? *See People v. Stitely*, 35 Cal.4th 514, 26 Cal.Rptr.3d 1, 108 P.3d 182 (2005).

B. UNINTENTIONAL KILLINGS

The typical set of unintentional killings found in an American jurisdiction's crimes code consists of second-degree murder, felony-murder, and involuntary or reckless manslaughter. Again, it is important to note that there is great variability in each state's homicide provisions. In some states, for example, the residual category of murder (sometimes called second-degree or, in some states, third-degree murder) is treated as the equivalent of an intentional killing, albeit as a lesser included offense of first-degree murder. In some states, there is no felony-murder offense. And, in some states, there are additional homicide offenses which are deemed to be equivalent in moral culpability to involuntary manslaughter or as less serious, e.g. negligent homicide or homicide by vehicle.

1. UNPREMEDITATED MURDER

At common law, the crime of murder involved a homicide committed with "malice aforethought." Malice could be express or implied. When implied, often these crimes involved unintentional killings that were committed by someone whose conduct manifested gross recklessness or an extreme indifference to the value of human life. This type of murder is called different things in different jurisdictions. Most often, it is deemed "second-degree murder." In common law terms, it is referred to as "depraved heart murder"; in Model Penal Code terms, the crime is reckless murder committed with "extreme indifference to the value of human life." Sometimes it is simply denominated "murder" (implying the absence of premeditation or the specific intent to kill found in "first-degree" or "premeditated" murder definitions).

STATE v. BURLEY
137 N.H. 286, 627 A.2d 98 (1993).

BATCHELDER, JUSTICE.

[On] January 7, 1989, the defendant was at home with his ex-wife, Debbie Glines, with whom he had reconciled. He drank at least six beers between noon and 6:00 p.m. At approximately 6:30 p.m., he telephoned 911 requesting an ambulance for a gunshot wound. The police and ambulance crews arrived to find Ms. Glines lying on the kitchen floor with a gunshot wound on the right side of her head, from which she eventually died.

The defendant told the officers on the scene that he had been cleaning a .22 caliber semi-automatic handgun when it accidentally discharged.... At the station the defendant explained that he had been keeping the handgun and a .22 caliber rifle for a friend. He stated that he retrieved the gun and a loaded clip of ammunition from a closet, placed them on tables in the living room, went to the kitchen for a beer, and took a cotton swab from the bathroom to clean the gun, which he admitted he had cleaned two weeks before. [He] loaded the gun, knowing he had made it ready to fire, before getting the beer. [A]fter watching television for twenty minutes, he picked up the gun and went to sit on the living room floor at the entryway to the kitchen. He knew that his ex-wife was in the kitchen. The gun went off, he stated, as he was cleaning excess oil from it, with the gun in his left hand and a finger in the trigger housing. He acknowledged familiarity with the operation of a .45 caliber semi-automatic, which is functionally similar to a .22.

A search of the defendant's apartment revealed two spent bullet casings in a garbage bag. No cotton swabs were found in the living room or kitchen. The defendant agreed to re-enact the shooting at his apartment.... Although at first stating that he did not know what had happened to the empty casing, when the officers told him it had been found in the trash, he admitted that he must have thrown it away. He admitted that he had occasionally "dry-fired" the gun by aiming the unloaded weapon at articles around the room. He was unable to tell the officers where they might find the clip to the .22, which they had been unsuccessful in locating.

Several days later the defendant returned to the police station after locating the clip. It had apparently been in his jacket pocket and had fallen out at his mother's house later on the night of the shooting. [At that time, he] admitted, after being told of a bullet found lodged in his wall, that the second shell found in the trash came from his having fired the rifle in the apartment two days before shooting his ex-wife. He had been "joking around with it and it discharged." Ultimately, the defendant admitted he had not been cleaning the handgun when he shot his ex-wife, although he denied he had been dry-firing it. He stated that he "was fooling around with it on the floor and it went off." In all, he gave the police three different versions of how he had been holding the gun that night.

The defendant was tried on the charge of second-degree murder. He requested and was granted a lesser included offense instruction for manslaughter and for negligent homicide.

[The] indictment charged that the "defendant [committed the crime of second-degree murder by causing the death of his wife] under circumstances manifesting an extreme indifference to the value of human life, by shooting her in the head with a pistol...."

An indictment is constitutionally sufficient if it informs a defendant of the charge with enough specificity to allow the defendant to prepare for trial and be protected against double jeopardy.... Here, the indictment alleges all of the elements of second-degree murder, as well as the date of the offense, the name of the victim, and how the defendant committed the offense, i.e., by shooting her in the head. This was sufficient to put the defendant on notice as to what he had to meet at trial. Other specific acts of the defendant or circumstances that would demonstrate his extreme indifference need not be alleged. The defendant argues that, as extreme indifference represents a greater degree of culpability than recklessness, additional factual allegations must appear in the indictment.... The indictment informed the defendant that he was charged with recklessly, under circumstances manifesting extreme indifference to the value of human life, causing his ex-wife's death on a specific date by shooting her in the head. This was constitutionally sufficient.

The defendant next argues that the evidence was insufficient to prove the element of extreme indifference. We will uphold the verdict unless, viewing the evidence and all reasonable inferences in the light most favorable to the State, no reasonable trier of fact could have found guilt beyond a reasonable doubt. In a prosecution for second-degree murder charging extreme indifference to the value of human life, "[t]he existence and extent of disregard manifested" are for the jury to determine on the facts of the case.

The evidence here showed, inter alia, that the defendant was familiar with the operation of a semi-automatic handgun, that he knew he had loaded the .22, and that he knew his ex-wife was in the next room. He had been drinking beer all afternoon and his blood alcohol content nearly five hours after the shooting was .15. At the time of the shooting, he was sitting with his elbows resting on raised knees with the barrel of a gun he knew to be loaded pointing into the kitchen where his ex-wife was located. The gun was cocked and ready to fire, and the defendant's finger was in the trigger housing. A firearms expert testified that due to its safety features the gun could not have fired without simultaneously gripping the safety on the back of the handle and squeezing the trigger. The defendant, who had told the police he knew not to point a gun at anyone, finally admitted that he had been "fooling around" with it after consistently lying by saying he had been cleaning it. On all the evidence the jury was warranted in finding that the defendant's conduct occurred under circumstances manifesting extreme indifference to the value of human life and in thereby finding him guilty of second-degree murder.

[Affirmed.]

NOTE

M.P.C. revisions of depraved heart murder. Model Penal Code § 210.2 provides that "criminal homicide constitutes murder when.... it is committed recklessly under circumstances manifesting extreme indifference to the value of human life."

PROBLEMS

1. *Russian Roulette.* Three teenage boys are playing Russian Roulette. They insert a single bullet in a gun that can be loaded with six bullets. One boy spins the cylinder, places the gun to another boy's head, and pulls the trigger. The gun discharges killing the boy. The remaining two boys, who never intended to kill their friend, are horrified. Is it possible to say that they have committed murder in the "purposeful" or "knowing" sense? Have they committed reckless murder as in *Burley*? Argue the case for the prosecution. How might the defense respond? What facts make this a "murder case?" Is it the way the gun was loaded? The way the game was played? Something else? *See Commonwealth v. Malone*, 354 Pa. 180, 47 A.2d 445, 447 (1946).

2. *Shooting to Scare.* Burkman had a stormy relationship with the victim, Kathryn Burns. On the day in question, Burkman argued with the victim over whether she was having an affair with a co-worker. At some point, Burkman retrieved a gun from the linen closet and threw it on the bed in front of Burns, who picked up the gun, looked at it, and pulled back the hammer. Burkman questioned the victim as to why she had pulled the hammer back, asking if she wanted to kill herself. The victim simply shrugged, continuing to smoke a cigarette and drink her beer. Burkman then waved the gun in front of the victim's face and yelled at her that she should go ahead and kill herself. Intending to scare Burns, Burkman aimed the gun at a pillow behind her and fired. The bullet accidentally struck and killed Burns. Is Burkman guilty of murder? *See Cook v. Maryland*, 118 Md.App. 404, 702 A.2d 971 (Ct.Spec.App. 1997).

3. *Drag Racing.* Two teenagers are drag racing on a public highway. As the racers approach a curve, one aggressively tries to pass the other by veering into the lane that would otherwise be occupied by oncoming traffic. In the middle of the curve, the passing racer runs head-on into an oncoming car, killing the driver and herself. Is the surviving racer guilty of murder? See *Commonwealth v. Root*, 403 Pa. 571, 170 A.2d 310 (1961) (from Chapter 4 on Causation).

4. *Swerving and Killing.* Johnson went to a birthday/keg party at a friend's house. Rogers, who also attended, argued with Johnson all evening. After midnight, the two threatened to attack each other with weapons, but both ultimately decided to desist. As Johnson got in his truck, Rogers banged on the window and broke off the radio antenna. Johnson reacted by shifting into reverse and squealing his tires as he backed-up about fifteen feet.

Johnson then shifted into drive and drove towards Rogers as if he were going to hit him. In fact, Johnson had no intention of hitting Rogers, but simply wanted to "scare" him. Johnson planned to swerve to the right at the last minute. Unfortunately, at the same moment that Johnson swerved, Rogers tried to evade the truck by diving to his left (Johnson's right). As a result, Johnson's truck ran over Rogers and killed him. Would it be more appropriate to convict Johnson of voluntary manslaughter or murder? Why? *Cf. State v. Powell*, 872 P.2d 1027 (Utah 1994).

5. *Abiocor Heart.* Reconsider the following problem from Chapter 3 on Mens Rea, *supra*. Recently, a medical equipment manufacturer developed and implanted the Abiocor artificial heart. This heart is different than prior artificial hearts because it is fully implantable in the patient's body and (unlike prior hearts) is designed to completely replace the patient's natural heart. The heart has been approved for experimental use, but has not been approved for general implantation. In fact, of the first five patients who received the Abiocor heart, 40% (2) died within a matter of months and 40% (a figure which includes one of the people who died) suffered strokes. Did the manufacturer commit either reckless murder or involuntary (reckless) manslaughter in removing the patients' natural hearts and replacing them with the Abiocor heart? Would it matter that the manufacturer implanted the heart:

a. Only in patients who were near death (i.e., patients with a life expectancy of no more than 30 days)?

b. In healthy males (the Abiocor is too large to be implanted in females) who are nowhere near death?

6. *Neglect and Murder or Manslaughter.* The police, investigating allegations of child abuse, found Malone sitting with five of her children in the living room of her house. In a second floor bedroom, they found her seven-month-old twin daughters who had died of starvation. Their skin was dried and wrinkled, and their stomachs were discolored. The children died from dehydration, and malnutrition, and there were signs of decay. The facts revealed that Malone was a cocaine addict who neglected her children. The defense does not deny that she neglected a "duty" to her children. The only question is whether she committed the crime of reckless manslaughter or reckless murder. Is your answer to this question affected by the fact that Malone's drug addiction made her unaware of her children's needs and therefore of the risk of death? *See Commonwealth v. Miller*, 426 Pa.Super. 410, 627 A.2d 741 (1993).

7. *High Speed Chases.* Defendant Jason McKinley was found guilty of second degree murder because he ran a red light while being chased by a police car for speeding, smashed head on into another car at between 93 and 100 miles per hour, and killed the driver. McKinley argues that while he was "admittedly reckless," the evidence did not support a murder conviction, only an involuntary (reckless) manslaughter conviction. Is he right? *See McKinley v. State*, 945 A.2d 1158 (Del.Supr. 2008).

8. *Speeding through Red Light*. Believing that a driver has committed a theft, a police officer pulls over the driver on a city street. As the officer approaches the vehicle, the driver drives off at a very high rate of speed, and attempts to go through a red light without stopping. Unfortunately, she does not make it, and smashes into another car, killing an 11–year old passenger. Did the driver commit reckless murder? Why or why not?

9. *Attempted Suicide Casualty*. A love-sick driver decides to commit suicide by crashing her vehicle, and does a "countdown" to the crash in text messages sent to the girl who spurned her affections. In the crash, the driver crosses the center line and runs head-on into an oncoming vehicle. The driver of the other vehicle is killed and the love-sick driver survives. Should the love-sick driver be charged with reckless murder or involuntary (reckless) manslaughter?

2.　FELONY–MURDER

At common law, one of the ways in which murder could be established was to demonstrate that the accused committed a homicide in the process of committing or attempting to commit a felonious act. Today, most (but not all) jurisdictions continue to recognize felony-murder as a distinct homicide offense, either as a separate component of first-degree murder, or as an entirely distinct crime, (sometimes deemed second-degree murder), or as both. Although felony-murder can be proved by establishing an unintended killing in the course of the commission of certain specified felonies, in another sense, felony-murder may be viewed as an intentional killing in which the intent to kill is imputed (or "transferred") from the accused's intent to commit the dangerous felony at issue.

MARES v. WYOMING

939 P.2d 724 (Wyo. 1997).

LEHMAN, JUSTICE.

[Marie] Bressler celebrated her 81st birthday by going to dinner with her two granddaughters. Bressler's long-time friend, 76-year-old Velma Filener, was visiting Bressler at the time but did not accompany the Bressler party to dinner. Bressler and her granddaughters left the house around 6:15 p.m. Approximately two hours later, Bressler returned to her unlocked and well-lit home and found the body of Filener lying between the laundry room and kitchen. Filener had been stabbed seventeen times, and her body had been dragged from a hallway near the entry of the home to the laundry room. The home obviously had been burglarized. The county coroner estimated Filener's time of death to be between 7:30 and 8:15 p.m.

Five months later, 16-year-old Heather Carrillo informed police and counselors at the Wyoming Girls' School that she was involved in the Bressler burglary. At Mares' trial, Carrillo testified that [she] stole her mother's car and drove Victor Madrid to Bressler's home, where they met Mares and Christine Sievers. After waiting for a car to leave the residence, the four teenagers entered the residence wearing rubber gloves provided by Madrid. Once inside, the teens split up and went to different rooms. Upon hearing a female voice confront Madrid, Carrillo became scared and left the house. Carrillo testified that as she waited in the car, Mares came out of the house, followed by Sievers, and finally Madrid. Madrid was covered in blood.

[Mares admitted that he was] in the Bressler home when Madrid stabbed Filener.... Mares told the detectives that he, Victor Madrid, Christine Sievers, and [Carrillo] entered the Bressler residence with the intent of "doing a little burglary." Mares stated that he was in a back bedroom of the house when he heard what sounded like a woman falling down stairs and screaming. He came out of the bedroom and witnessed Madrid stabbing the victim.... Mares also told the detectives that Madrid stabbed Filener with a "butterfly knife" which Mares had given Madrid a few days earlier.

[A] jury found Mares guilty of felony-murder, aggravated burglary, and conspiracy to commit burglary for his part in the burglary of the Bressler home and the murder of Filener. He received a sentence of life imprisonment for the felony-murder conviction, a concurrent term of 20 to 25 years in prison for the aggravated burglary conviction, and a consecutive term of 4 to 5 years in prison for conspiracy. He timely appeals the judgment and sentence.

[Mares] argues that because the stabbing was a purely independent act of a co-felon, the rigid application of the felony-murder doctrine, resulting in a life sentence, is unduly harsh.... Several jurisdictions have statutorily created a no-culpability-as-to-the-homicide defense, with the most common conditions being that the defendant 1) did not commit the homicidal act or in any way cause, solicit, or aid the commission thereof, 2) had no reason to believe that any other participant would engage in conduct likely to cause death or serious bodily injury, 3) was not armed with a deadly weapon, and 4) had no reason to believe that any other participant was armed with such a weapon.

The legislature abolished common law crimes in Wyoming, but chose to retain common law defenses unless provided otherwise by statute. Therefore, our first inquiry is whether the defense proposed by Mares is recognized in Wyoming by statute or judicial decision. Mares contends that although we have not explicitly adopted the defense, the defense is inherent in our prior felony-murder decisions because in each of those decisions at least one of the four elements for the affirmative defense was not satisfied. In other words, our prior cases involved situations where the defendant carried out or participated in the murderous act, was armed, or knew that one or more of the participants was armed. However, the fact that one or more elements of the defense was not satisfied does not mean that the court would have reached a different result if all the elements had been met, and we find no discussion or analysis in any of our prior felony-murder cases which would lead us to conclude otherwise.... Mares does not provide, nor does our own research reveal, any authority that the proffered defense is a recognized common-law defense in any other jurisdiction. The jurisdictions that have created a no-culpability-as-to-the-homicide defense for felony-murder have done so legislatively, not judicially.

The felony-murder rule is the subject of much criticism for its potential harshness, for instance in the circumstance where the killing is an independent act of a co-felon, as in Mares' case. Adopting an affirmative defense is but one of many mechanisms that other jurisdictions have utilized to mitigate the potential harshness of the rule. For example, the rule has been limited by permitting its use only as to certain types of felonies, by strictly interpreting the requirement of proximate or legal cause, by narrowly construing the time period during which the felony is committed, by downgrading the offense to a lesser degree crime, and by requiring a mens rea of malice. Wyoming has narrowed the scope of the felony-murder rule by limiting its application to "crimes of violence" which are enumerated in W.S. 6–2–101(a). [In] our view, the determination of whether the felony-murder doctrine should be further limited in Wyoming and, if so, the appropriate manner of so doing, are matters for the legislature. Consequently, we decline to judicially adopt appellant's suggested affirmative defense to felony-murder.

[At] the time of the offense, Wyoming's first-degree murder statute provided:

> (a) Whoever purposely and with premeditated malice, or in the perpetration of, or attempt to perpetrate, any sexual assault, arson, robbery, burglary, escape, resisting arrest or kidnapping, kills any human being is guilty of murder in the first-degree.

Under this provision, when a killing arises out of one of the enumerated felonies, it makes no difference whether or not there was an intent to kill. Mares argues that the failure to require that the State prove a defendant acted with malice violates due process. He asserts that felony-murder should require an intent to kill or the intent to do an act greatly dangerous to the lives of others or with knowledge that the act creates a strong probability of death or great bodily harm.

Mares' due process challenge appears to be based on *Sandstrom v. Montana*, 442 U.S. 510 (1979), in which defendant's conviction was reversed because of a jury instruction which stated that "[t]he law presumes that a person intends the ordinary consequences of his voluntary acts." The instruction was found to shift the burden of persuasion to the defendant and invade the factfinding function of the jury. As a result, the court held that, in the case where intent is an element of the crime charged, such an instruction violates the Fourteenth Amendment's requirement that the State prove every element of a crime beyond a reasonable doubt. Mares' argument, then, is that the felony-murder rule violates this constitutional requirement because it presumes the mental state required for murder from the intent required for the underlying felony.

Mares directs us to *State v. Ortega*, [112 N.M. 554, 817 P.2d 1196 (1991),] in which the court, relying in part on *Sandstrom*, held that New Mexico's felony-murder statute requires proof that the defendant intended to kill or was knowingly heedless that his or her acts created a strong probability of death or great bodily harm.... We find the dissent in *Ortega* persuasive and more in line with our previous holdings in Wyoming. The dissent considered *Sandstrom* inapposite because the New Mexico statute does not require an intent to kill where a killing has been committed during a felony. In *Osborn v. State*, [672 P.2d 777, 794 (Wyo. 1983)] we pointed out that viewing the commission of the statutory felony as the legal equivalent of the malice and premeditation required for first-degree murder is a legal fiction that is unnecessary under our statute:

> [T]he Wyoming Statute, § 6–4–101[,] does not relate the killing of a human being in the perpetration of robbery (or the other crimes listed) to "purposely and with premeditated malice," but separated that clause with an "or." The legislature has thus merely labeled the latter crime as first-degree murder because it is considered to be of equal wickedness justifying the ultimate penalty.

The felony-murder statute imposes a form of strict responsibility on those perpetrating the underlying felony for killings occurring during the commission of that felony; the intent to kill is not an element of the crime. Even so, the State is not relieved of establishing a mens rea. Rather, the necessary intent the State must prove to convict a person of felony-murder is the intent associated with the underlying felony.

[There] is no question the legislature has the authority to revise the current statute to include a mens rea of malice for killings occurring during the perpetration of a felony.... Our judicial task is to effectuate the statute as written. [A]ccordingly, arguments concerning the addition of elements to the statute should be addressed to the legislature, not this court.

[We] decline to judicially modify the felony-murder rule in Wyoming by adopting an affirmative defense or establishing a mens rea of malice. [Affirmed.]

NOTES

1. *M.P.C. presumption of extreme indifference.* Although the Model Penal Code rejects the felony-murder rule, it does contain the following provision concerning homicides that occur during seven specified felonies:

§ 210.2. Murder.

(1) Except as provided in Section 210.3(1)(b), criminal homicide constitutes murder when ... it is committed recklessly under circumstances manifesting extreme indifference to the value of human life. Such recklessness and indifference are presumed if the actor is engaged or is an accomplice in the commission of, or an attempt to commit, or flight after committing or attempting to commit robbery, rape or deviate sexual intercourse by force or threat of force, arson, burglary, kidnapping or felonious escape.

2. *Independent felony required.* In many jurisdictions, the triggering felony for felony murder cannot be an offense that is inherent in the act of killing itself, like assault or battery or discharging a firearm. In other words, the triggering felony must be independent of the killing itself. *See, e.g., People v. Rosenthal,* 383 Ill.App.3d 32, 321 Ill.Dec. 414, 889 N.E.2d 679 (2008).

Some state codes follow the M.P.C. approach of enumerating felonies for felony murder, and often distinguish between first and second degree types of felony murder.

PROBLEMS

1. *Acquittal of Underlying Felony.* In Pennsylvania, as in many other states, a defendant may only be convicted of felony-murder if the victim's death occurred during the commission or an attempt to commit (or flight after committing or attempting to commit) enumerated, serious felonies, which include in Pennsylvania, "robbery, rape, or deviate sexual intercourse by force or threat of force, arson, burglary or kidnapping." Pa. Cons. Stat. § 2502(b) & (d). If a defendant is charged with both robbery and felony-murder based upon the death of the robbery victim (e.g. from a heart attack), should a felony-murder conviction stand if the jury finds the defendant innocent of the robbery? Should a robbery verdict stand if the jury finds the defendant innocent of felony-murder during the commission of the robbery?

2. *Felony Dangerous to Human Life.* Some states do not enumerate an exclusive list of triggering felonies for application of the felony-murder rule, but instead apply the rule to in any situation where the facts are sufficiently dangerous to human life to justify application of the doctrine. Using that test, would a defendant be guilty of felony-murder where he and three of his friends chased their victim, tripped and kicked him, and dropped a boulder on his head, thus committing an aggravated assault that resulted in his unintended death? Or would this defendant only be guilty of reckless or negligent homicide? *See Roary v. State,* 385 Md. 217, 867 A.2d 1095 (2005).

3. *Misdemeanor Manslaughter.* At common law, a misdemeanor-man-slaughter rule also existed, imputing the offense of manslaughter to actors who committed an unlawful act not amounting to a felony which nonetheless resulted in the death of a victim. This rule was rejected by the drafters of the Model Penal Code as "objectionable on the same ground as the felony-murder rule." It has also been abolished in most states. Moreover, in those states that still retain a version of the rule, either by common law or by statute, typically the unlawful act needs to be *"malum in se"* (inherently wrong and immoral in nature in contrast to *"malum prohibitum"* offenses that are wrong simply because a legislature says so) in order to suffice to establish manslaughter. Do you think there is a place in modern American penal codes for some version of this common-law rule? Explain.

4. *Bombing a Building.* After *Mares*, would an individual who placed a bomb in a building which she believed was unoccupied, but which resulted in the unintended death of someone who was (unbeknownst to the bomber) trespassing in that building during the explosion, be guilty of first-degree murder under Wyoming law? Why or why not? How about second-degree (reckless) murder?

5. *Guns for Intimidation.* A and B decide to rob a convenience store. Both are carrying guns, but they explicitly agree that neither is to shoot anyone else. The weapons are being carried simply for intimidation pur-poses. Consider the following scenarios and decide whether A is guilty of felony-murder if the following events occur during the robbery:

     a. B becomes enraged at a recalcitrant clerk and kills him in cold blood;

     b. B accidentally drops his gun, and it discharges and kills a customer;

     c. The clerk pulls out a weapon and shoots B dead;

     d. As A and B are trying to escape, a police officer arrives and shoots B dead.

     e. On the way to commit the robbery, A fails to see a red light, smashes into another car, and kills a passenger.

How would these examples be resolved under the Model Penal Code § 210.2(1)?

6. *Faulkner's Logic.* Is the felony-murder doctrine consistent with *Regina v. Faulkner* (in Chapter 3 on Mens Rea), in which a sailor went down in the hold of a ship to steal some rum and accidentally burned the ship? The British court concluded that Faulkner could not be convicted of "malicious-ly" burning a ship. If A intends to rob a convenience store and a customer is accidentally killed when B drops his gun, is it fair or appropriate to convict A of "murder"? Is a murder conviction consistent with the justifications for punishment?

7. *Non-dangerous Felonies.* Even if you conclude that the felony-murder doctrine has some virtues, does it make sense to apply that doctrine to all

felonies? For example, under federal law, it is a felony to file a false tax return. Suppose that on the way to the post office to file a fraudulent return, A's brakes go out without warning and despite regular and diligent maintenance. Unable to stop, A hits and kills a pedestrian. Should this be treated as felony murder?

EXERCISE

Amending Wyoming Statute. The *Mares* court concluded that, "[i]n our view, the determination of whether the felony-murder doctrine should be further limited in Wyoming and, if so, the appropriate manner of so doing, are matters for the legislature." What changes do you believe are desirable and appropriate (including possibly abolition)? Acting as a legislative assistant to a Wyoming legislator, draft proposed (post-*Mares*) amendments to the Wyoming felony-murder law that would have the effect of codifying such changes.

PEOPLE v. PORTILLO

107 Cal.App.4th 834, 132 Cal.Rptr.2d 435 (2003).

HUFFMAN, ACTING P. J.

A jury convicted Coby J. Portillo of first-degree murder, forcible rape, and forcible sodomy. [The] trial court sentenced Portillo to life in prison without the possibility of parole, plus a consecutive one year for the deadly weapon use enhancement.

Portillo appeals, contending the trial court prejudicially erred in expanding the scope of felony-murder sex offenses to include a homicide that occurred after the sex offenses were complete, but before the defendant reached a place of temporary safety. [We] affirm.

[During] the summer of 2000, Portillo was a petty officer in the United States Navy stationed aboard the U.S.S. Ogden in San Diego. Due to the stress level aboard the ship, Portillo often talked with other seamen and petty officers about picking up a prostitute, raping her and then killing her. On August 25, 2000, Portillo said that when he killed a prostitute he would put her body in a seabag, which is a round, green duffel bag issued to Navy personnel. None of the other men reported his statements because they thought he was joking.

On August 27, 2000, Portillo, who lived with his wife off base in an apartment, called a professional escort service that provides strippers and nude entertainers, after he had taken his wife to work. Using a different name, he requested an "Asian girl," and offered to pay cash. The receptionist described the availability of a petite Asian escort who used the name "Monica." In agreement, Portillo gave the receptionist his telephone number and the apartment number of his neighbor who lived directly below him.

Monica, a 36-year-old licensed escort and mother of two whose real name was Natividad W. (Nancy), was given the assignment by the agency in response to Portillo's call. Less than five feet tall, Nancy was "security conscious" [and] carried a stun gun.... [When] Nancy arrived at the given address around 2:00 p.m., the man answering the door told her he was not the person she was looking for. Shortly after she [found Portillo's apartment, the neighbor] heard muffled voices upstairs and "a loud thumping sound like somebody running across the floor."

Nancy never called into the agency that day and Portillo failed to pick up his wife from work at 3:15 p.m. as arranged. A coworker drove his wife home and she obtained a key from the apartment manager to enter their apartment around 6:30 p.m. When his wife entered the apartment, she saw blood on the floor near what appeared to be Portillo's seabag, an unknown pair of women's sandals in the hallway, a purse and cloth bag which did not belong to her near the dining room table, and a hammer with blood-like stains on it. She called 911.

When San Diego deputy sheriffs arrived, they found Nancy's body covered by two seabags, secured the area, and waited for homicide detectives. [The] subsequent investigation revealed that inside the seabag near Nancy's head were her pants with a broken zipper and torn underwear. Her bra was found pulled down underneath her breasts and her sweater pulled up, exposing them. An autopsy revealed she had sustained five blows to her head consistent with being hit by a hammer, and suffered broken bone and cartilage in her neck, petechiae hemorrhages in her eyes and eyelids, which are the "hallmarks of strangulation," two black eyes, bruises and lacerations on her lip, an abrasion on her left elbow, and blunt force injuries in her vaginal area and bruising around her anus. The medical examiner opined the cause of death was manual strangulation and multiple blunt force head injuries.

Further testing revealed that Nancy's blood was on Portillo's shorts, his carpet and the hammer in his apartment. Tests also showed that Portillo's DNA was in scrapings and clippings from her fingernails and his sperm was inside her vagina and around her anus.

Portillo was brought to trial for Nancy's rape, sodomy and murder, and the above evidence was presented in the prosecution case. [The] gist of Portillo's defense was that the sex with Nancy was consensual and her killing was committed in self-defense. [According] to Portillo, after Nancy orally copulated him and had both vaginal and anal intercourse with him, he stopped any sexual activity when she complained it hurt. When he told her he did not have the money to pay her, she became angry and attacked him. In the process, she tore the underwear she was putting on. As they exchanged punches, Nancy threatened to kill him. When Portillo pushed her to the ground, she reached for an object from her bag and lunged at him. Thinking the object was a knife, Portillo grabbed a heavy hammer out of a box and "hit her like four, five times, just boom, real quick in the head." As she fell, she grabbed him and he fell on top of her with his hand on her neck, dropping the hammer on the floor nearby. He held her down as she started kicking and swinging at him. When she picked up the hammer to swing at him, he took it and threw it behind him. Nancy then "just like stopped." She was nonresponsive and not breathing.

The jury did not believe Portillo's version of the events the day Nancy was murdered.

[During] jury instruction discussions, Portillo asserted there was insufficient evidence for the court to give felony-murder instructions as an alternate theory for first-degree murder because they contemplated a continuous action, which he argued was not present in this case due to the completion of the underlying rape and sodomy offenses. The court overruled the objection, finding there was a sufficient evidentiary basis for such instruction.

[When] the court . . . instructed the jury on felony-murder, it told the jurors that in order to find Portillo guilty under such theory, they had to find beyond a reasonable doubt he committed the murder "in the course of" rape or sodomy. During deliberations, the jury sent the court the following note: "We have a question about the term[s] 'commission' and 'in the course of' rape and sodomy. We were wondering about time frame, etc. [¶] legal definition of commission of rape as it is different from course of the rape. [¶] does the victim need to die while there is penetration or can the victim die after the crime[?] [¶] As to felony-murder 1." [Over] defense counsel's objection the court then sent the following response to the jury: " 'In the commission of' is synonymous with 'in the course of'. [¶] For the purposes of determining whether an unlawful killing has occurred during the commission or attempted commission of a forcible rape or sodomy by use of force, the commission of said crime (forcible rape or sodomy by use of force) is not confined to a fixed place or a limited period of time. Such crime is still in progress while a perpetrator is fleeing in an attempt to escape or to avoid detection. The crime is complete when the perpetrator has reached a place of temporary safety. [¶] The unlawful killing need not be simultaneous with the act of forcible penetration. However, it must be proven beyond any reasonable doubt that the unlawful killing occurred during the commission or attempted commission of a forcible rape or sodomy by use of force (as defined above), and that the death of the victim did not precede the commission or attempted commission of a forcible rape or sodomy by use of force."

[On] appeal, Portillo contends the trial court prejudicially erred in essentially expanding the scope of felony-murder sex offenses to include a homicide that occurred after the sex offenses were complete, but before the defendant reached a place of temporary safety. He argues that the portion of the court's instruction telling the jury the underlying crimes of rape and sodomy continue for felony-murder purposes while the perpetrator attempts to escape or to avoid detection was wrong because the so-called "escape rule" only applies to theft offenses. We disagree.

[The] felony-murder doctrine ... eliminates the requirements of malice and premeditation for first-degree murder and provides that a killing is still murder of the first-degree, whether intentional or unintentional, if it is committed in the perpetration of, or the attempt to perpetrate, certain serious felonies, including rape and sodomy as charged in this case. Such alternative theory to premeditated murder "was adopted for the protection of the community and its residents, not for the benefit of the lawbreaker ... " and "was not intended to relieve the wrongdoer from any probable consequences of his act by placing a limitation upon the res gestae which is unreasonable or unnatural." Based on such intent and purpose, the established law of this state "has never required proof of a strict causal relationship between the felony and the homicide." Thus it has been held that "[t]he homicide is committed in the perpetration of the felony if the killing and felony are parts of one continuous transaction."

[Moreover,] because flight following a felony has also been considered as part of the same transaction, it has generally been held that a felony continues for purposes of the felony-murder rule "until the criminal has reached a place of temporary safety."

[Even] though we have found no reported felony-murder decision which has specifically applied the so-called escape rule to crimes other than robbery and burglary, we believe, as the trial court here did, that ... the ... felony-murder law support[s] the court's answer given the jury in this case which essentially encompassed the "one continuous transaction" test for the felony sex offenses as the basis for the felony-murder theory as well as the language of the escape rule. As given, the instruction left open for the jury the question as to whether Portillo had reached a place of temporary safety cutting off felony-murder liability after raping and sodomizing his victim before killing her. Although it may appear illogical to attach such flight or escape language to a crime that is itself considered complete upon penetration, we do not believe the use of such escape principles are unreasonable or unnaturally extend the felony-murder rule beyond its established application of the "one continuous transaction" analysis used to define such theory based on underlying sexual offenses.

[In] sum, we conclude the trial court's answer to the jury question on the theory of felony-murder based on rape and sodomy was legally proper.

[The] judgment is affirmed.

PROBLEM

Delayed High Speed Chase. Suppose that the police are looking for A, who is a robbery suspect, the robbery having occurred the previous day. Suddenly a police officer sees A's car on the highway, and during the high-speed car chase that follows, A runs into and kills B, a pedestrian. Is A guilty of felony-murder under California law as interpreted in *Portillo*? Under the Model Penal Code? If these events occurred in Pennsylvania with a felony-murder statute as described in Problem 1 after *Mares*, would that make a difference in your analysis?

3. INVOLUNTARY MANSLAUGHTER

The crime of involuntary manslaughter is, as the name implies, an unintentional killing. It is distinguished from unintentional murder, however, by the absence of the element of malice. The mens rea showing required to establish the existence of involuntary manslaughter varies widely by jurisdiction. In most jurisdictions, involuntary manslaughter is established when it is proved that the accused has acted with gross negligence (sometimes, in circular fashion, deemed "criminal negligence"), resulting in someone's death. In other jurisdictions, however, involuntary manslaughter is not established absent the higher showing of recklessness as required in the Model Penal Code; rarely, a lesser showing of ordinary negligence (sometimes, again, in circular fashion, called "civil negligence") is all that is required to establish this offense.

STATE v. BROOKS
163 Vt. 245, 658 A.2d 22 (1995).

ALLEN, CHIEF JUSTICE.

[D]efendant purchased a home [that] was equipped with a driveway heater. Hot water, heated by gas in the unit's boiler, flowed through a system of pipes beneath the driveway to melt snow and ice. Exhaust fumes from the system were supposed to exit through a vent located on the backside of the garage.... Defendant turned on the driveway heater before running an errand. While he was gone, another occupant, Jill McDermott, and her infant became ill from noxious fumes that had emanated from the garage. When defendant returned home, McDermott asked him to take her and the baby to the hospital. Defendant took them to the emergency room where they were examined and released....

Defendant thought the fumes were caused by a plumbing problem and called C & L Plumbing and Heating. C & L sent an employee

[to] inspect the heater [and it was] determined that a dislodged flap [was] preventing proper exhaust. [The C & L employee] explained the malfunction to defendant and told him that repairs should be made and safety features added. [A] Vermont Gas Systems (VGS) [employee also examined] the system. [B]oth [heater inspectors] decided the gas should remain off until repairs were made. The VGS employee told McDermott the system was not safe to operate and that she was lucky to be alive, "because it was carbon monoxide." McDermott relayed these comments to defendant. . . . That night, the owner of C & L called defendant and told him that the heater had been improperly installed. . . . A VGS supervisor also called and explained the dangers of the condition and agreed that it should be repaired. . . .

In May 1988, defendant hired a real estate agent to sell his home. Defendant did not mention the heater's history to the agent. Instead, defendant instructed the agent to turn the heater on, then off, when demonstrating it to prospective buyers. The heater was a highlighted feature in agent's marketing materials. . . . In July 1988, the agent showed the house to Linda Cifarelli. . . . [T]he agent explained and demonstrated the driveway heating system by turning it on for approximately five minutes. During their second showing, defendant, who was present to answer questions, explained and demonstrated the driveway heater again, but did not mention its prior problem or faulty condition. [Cifarelli purchased the house. During a professional home inspection,] defendant demonstrated the heater, but did not explain how it worked or mention its history. [At the] closing, defendant insisted that the Cifarellis return to the house with him for a more detailed showing because "he knew things [the inspector] wouldn't know." Defendant showed Linda Cifarelli and her parents the central vacuum system, the drainage system, and the driveway heater. When showing the heater, he told them it was not necessary to run it for more than two hours.

On the evening of December 9, 1988, Linda Cifarelli and her husband, John, turned on the driveway heater because it was snowing. They put their two young daughters to bed upstairs and followed shortly after. A house guest, Andrew Csermak, stayed awake to watch television. After a while, Csermak became dizzy and nauseous, and eventually vomited. Csermak cracked a window and fell asleep on the downstairs couch. When Csermak awoke at noon, he was concerned because the Cifarellis were not yet awake. He went upstairs and discovered that only the infant daughter was still breathing. Csermak called 911.

Upon arrival, the police and firemen discovered the bodies of John and Linda Cifarelli and their four-year-old daughter. The police also found the garage door dripping with condensation and the driveway heater running.... Autopsies revealed that Linda and John Cifarelli and their daughter died of carbon monoxide poisoning....

[Defendant was convicted of] involuntary manslaughter by reckless endangerment. Because the underlying unlawful act charged was reckless endangerment, defendant's conviction could only be sustained upon finding reckless intent. Defendant argues that the instruction defining recklessness was flawed because it incorporated both the criminal negligence and recklessness standards but did not distinguish between the two. Defendant maintains that while recklessness requires an actual awareness of the risk and of the resulting harm, criminal negligence requires a less stringent showing that the actor should have known of the risk and harm. According to defendant, the failure to distinguish between the two levels of intent amounted to plain error, because the jury could have convicted him if it found only that he should have known either that the heater was not repaired, or that the heater posed a risk.

We have endorsed the Model Penal Code's definition of recklessness, which explains:

> A person acts recklessly with respect to a material element of an offense when he consciously disregards a substantial and unjustifiable risk that the material element exists or will result from his conduct. The risk must be of such a nature and degree that, considering the nature and purpose of the actor's conduct and the circumstances known to him, its disregard involves a gross deviation from the standard of conduct that a law-abiding person would observe in the actor's situation.

In contrast, criminal negligence occurs when the actor should be aware that a substantial and unjustifiable risk exists or will result from his conduct. Disregarding the risk amounts to a gross deviation from the standard of care that a reasonable person would observe in the actor's situation.

Contrary to defendant's suggestion, both recklessness and criminal negligence require an objective view of the risk; the difference is one of degree. The more critical distinction between recklessness and criminal negligence is the actor's subjective awareness of the risk. Recklessness requires a conscious disregard of the risk. In contrast, criminal negligence results when an actor is unaware of the risk which the actor should have perceived.

The court properly instructed the jury to objectively assess the risk and to determine whether defendant consciously disregarded that risk. For further clarification, it referred the jury to the reckless endangerment instruction, which expressly required a finding that defendant "actually knew from the circumstances then existing that the heater had not properly been repaired." If there was any flaw in the instruction, it stemmed from the court's use of the term "reasonable-person" instead of "law-abiding person" when describing the standard for objectively assessing the nature of the risk. This does not amount to plain error.

[Defendant] challenges the court's denial of his motion for acquittal, claiming there was insufficient evidence to convict on the essential elements of recklessness and a legal duty. [W]e consider whether the evidence, taken in a light most favorable to the State and excluding modifying evidence, is sufficient to fairly and reasonably support a finding of guilt beyond a reasonable doubt. . . . Defendant contends [that] proof of both recklessness and the existence of a legal duty hinged on finding that he actually knew the driveway heater had not been repaired. Defendant argues [that] there was insufficient evidence to prove beyond a reasonable doubt that he knew the driveway heating unit had not been repaired. We disagree.

Defendant knew the heater was malfunctioning and emitting fumes when he took McDermott and her infant child to the hospital in November 1987. Representatives from C & L and VGS testified that they explained the exhaust problem to defendant and told him that the system was dangerous and needed repairs. Although there was conflicting testimony about who was responsible for the repairs, resolving this confusion was less important than determining when, and if, defendant thought the repairs were completed.

Defendant's position was that he thought the heater was fixed by VGS shortly after, if not immediately following, the November 1987 accident. Other witnesses, however, testified to conversations with defendant about repairing the heater which refute defendant's position. The C & L employee, Linden, testified that one month after the accident, defendant told him the heater was still unrepaired. Linden then told defendant he was "playing Russian roulette." Defendant suggests that he construed Linden's conversation with him to mean that Linden had fixed the problem. Linden testified, however, that a reasonable person would not have thought the problem was fixed. In the summer of 1988, at the recommendation of defendant's real estate agent, defendant spoke with Karl Sklar. According to Sklar's testimony, defendant mentioned that there was a problem with the heater and asked Sklar if he would work on it. There was no evidence that either VGS or C & L worked on the heater while the home was on the market or after Sklar's visit. In sum, there was sufficient evidence fairly and reasonably supporting a finding that defendant actually knew the heater had not been repaired when he sold his home to the Cifarellis. With this critical finding and other supporting evidence, the jury could reasonably conclude that defendant had the requisite reckless intent. There was sufficient evidence to support a finding that defendant's failure to disclose the existence of the malfunctioning heater before selling his home amounted to a conscious disregard of a substantial and unjustifiable risk.

There was also sufficient evidence that defendant breached his legal duty to disclose the heater's defect. " 'Where material facts are accessible to the vendor only, and he knows them not to be within the reach of the diligent attention, observation and judgment of the purchaser, the vendor [of real estate] is bound to disclose such facts....' " Defendant knew that the heater could emit noxious fumes into the home, if unattended, and that it was unrepaired when his home was on the market. Defendant also accompanied both Linda Cifarelli and the home inspector on their tours of the home. In each instance, he demonstrated the heater, but did not mention its history. The jury could reasonably conclude that defendant knew that the Cifarellis, despite two walk-throughs and a home inspection, were unaware of the heater's dangerous condition. Thus, there was sufficient evidence upon which the jury could find that defendant failed to disclose a material defect when he had a duty to disclose them.

[Defendant] also argues that the scope of involuntary manslaughter predicated on reckless endangerment is prone to arbitrary and discriminatory enforcement.... Although we cannot specify every set of facts which constitute reckless conduct, the recklessness standard is sufficiently precise to prevent it from being arbitrarily applied. The scope of conduct which may be deemed reckless is sufficiently narrowed by the requirement that the risk, when objectively viewed, amounts to a gross deviation from the standard of conduct that a law-abiding person would observe in the actor's situation. The statute is not unconstitutionally vague.

[Affirmed.]

NOTE

M.P.C. reckless manslaughter and negligent homicide. The Model Penal Code contains the following provisions defining manslaughter and negligent homicide. Note the difference in the applicable mens rea elements:

§ 210.3. Manslaughter.

(1) Criminal homicide constitutes manslaughter when:

(a) it is committed recklessly; or

(b) a homicide which would otherwise be murder is committed under the influence of extreme mental or emotional disturbance for which there is reasonable explanation or excuse. The reasonableness of such explanation or excuse shall be determined from the viewpoint of a person in the actor's situation under the circumstances as he believes them to be.

(2) Manslaughter is a felony of the second-degree.

§ 210.4. Negligent Homicide.

(1) Criminal homicide constitutes negligent homicide when it is committed negligently.

(2) Negligent homicide is a felony of the third degree.

PROBLEM

Forseeable Horse Escape? A horse escaped from a fenced enclosure at the Sea Horse Ranch. The fence was weather-worn, rotting, and dilapidated. The horse strayed onto an adjacent coastal highway, and while running free after dark one evening, collided with a car, killing the passenger when the impact of the collision crushed the roof of the passenger compartment. Assuming that the owners knew of the dilapidated condition of the fence and that horses had escaped from there previously (eight horses were found wandering free on the road that night), could they be prosecuted successfully for involuntary manslaughter? How about negligent homicide under the Model Penal Code formulation? *See Sea Horse Ranch, Inc. v. Superior Court*, 24 Cal.App.4th 446, 30 Cal.Rptr.2d 681 (1994).

STATE v. POWELL

336 N.C. 762, 446 S.E.2d 26 (1994).

FRYE, JUSTICE.

[Hoke] Lane Prevette, a five-foot, one and one-half inch, ninety-four pound jogger, was attacked by defendant's dogs and died as a result of multiple dog bites. The dogs were away from defendant's property and had been loose earlier that day.

Defendant [owned] two Rottweilers, "Bruno" and "Woody." Each dog was a little over one year old. Bruno weighed eighty pounds and Woody weighed one hundred pounds. [A]t approximately 9:00 p.m., Hoke Prevette[, who was five-foot, one and one-half inches tall and weighed ninety-four pounds,] left his home [to] go jogging. At about 11:00 p.m., James Fainter and his wife returned [home,] discovered Prevette's body in their front yard, and notified the police.... Prevette did not have a pulse.... Dr. John Butts, Chief Medical Examiner for the State of North Carolina, [concluded] that Prevette died as the result of multiple dog bites. Prevette's external injuries included shallow scrapes, deeper puncture wounds that extended down into tissue, evulsing skin, and skin torn away creating large holes in some places. His internal injuries included broken ribs on the left side and collapsed lungs. The cause of death was determined to be collapsed lungs, loss of blood, and choking.

David Moore, who [lived nearby], testified that he saw defendant's dogs when he arrived home at about 9:30 p.m.... One of the dogs growled but both dogs relented when Moore stamped his foot. Another neighbor [encountered] two Rottweilers he recognized as defendant's dogs earlier that evening when he drove his sister and sister-in-law home. He held the dogs at bay while the women entered the house.

After the discovery of Prevette's body[,] Police Officer Jason Swaim went to defendant's house to investigate a report that defendant's dogs had been out that evening. When Swaim advised defendant that he wanted to see his dogs, defendant responded, "Oh my God, what have they done now?" Defendant admitted that his dogs had been out twice that day and that he picked the dogs up in his automobile at approximately 9:00 p.m. at the intersection of Cascade Avenue and Dinmont Street.... The police seized the dogs, a dog dish, a portion of the wall in defendant's kitchen, the dogs' collars, and a portion of the back seat of defendant's automobile.

Robert Neill of the State Bureau of Investigation Crime Laboratory testified that six hairs removed from Prevette's clothing were canine; however, he could not match the hairs to a particular dog. An SBI forensic serologist found human blood on Woody's collar, on a sample of Woody's hair, on the dog dish, on a portion of the wall from defendant's home, and on defendant's car seat. According to the serologist, the blood could not be typed because of the presence of an inhibiting substance, possibly soap. A forensic odontologist testified that dental impressions taken from Bruno and Woody were compatible with some of the lacerations in the wounds pictured in scale photographs of Prevette's body.

Several witnesses testified to seeing Bruno and Woody running loose in the neighborhood prior to 20 October 1989 and to their aggressive behavior. Defendant's former girlfriend testified that defendant abused the dogs by kicking and hitting them. [Animal] Psychologist Donna Brown testified regarding an evaluation for aggressive propensities that she performed on Bruno and Woody in November 1989. She videotaped her testing and showed the videotape to the jury. Dr. Brown concluded that both dogs showed dominance and predatory aggression. She opined that an attack on a person would be consistent with her observations of Bruno's and Woody's behavior.

Animal Behavioralist Peter Borthelt testified for the defense that, although he had not evaluated the dogs, he had reviewed Dr. Brown's videotape and her results which he found to be ambiguous. He testified that aggressiveness was only one possible interpretation of the dogs' behavior and that some of it could be labeled "play."

Defendant presented several witnesses who testified that Bruno and Woody were friendly and playful and responded to his commands to get down or sit. Other defense witnesses testified that the dogs were not aggressive when they were loose in the neighborhood.

[The] questions presented on appeal are: (1) whether there was sufficient evidence to submit the charge of involuntary manslaughter to the jury and (2) whether the trial judge erroneously instructed the jury on the charge of involuntary manslaughter. After careful review of the record and consideration of the briefs and arguments of counsel, we conclude that there was sufficient evidence to submit the charge of involuntary manslaughter.... We also conclude that the trial judge did not err in his instructions to the jury on involuntary manslaughter. Therefore, we affirm the decision of the Court of Appeals.

By his first assignment of error, defendant contends that there was insufficient evidence to establish the essential elements of involuntary manslaughter; thus, the trial court erred in denying his motion to dismiss at the close of all the evidence. Involuntary manslaughter is the unlawful killing of a human being without malice, without premeditation and deliberation, and without intention to kill or inflict serious bodily injury. Involuntary manslaughter may also be defined as the unintentional killing of a human being without malice, proximately caused by (1) an unlawful act not amounting to a felony nor naturally dangerous to human life, or (2) a culpably negligent act or omission. "An intentional, willful or wanton violation of a statute or ordinance, designed for the protection of human life or limb, which proximately results in injury or death, is culpable negligence." A death which is proximately caused by culpable negligence is involuntary manslaughter.

[At] the time of the attack on Prevette, a Winston–Salem ordinance provided:

> (a) No dog shall be left unattended outdoors unless it is restrained and restricted to the owner's property by a tether, rope, chain, fence or other device. Fencing, as required herein, shall be adequate in height, construction and placement to keep resident dogs on the lot, and keep other dogs and children from accessing the lot. One (1) or more secured gates to the lot shall be provided.

Winston–Salem Code § 3–18 (1989).

A safety statute or ordinance is one designed for the protection of life or limb and which imposes a duty upon members of society to uphold that protection. According to the Court of Appeals and the State, Section 3–18 of the Winston–Salem Code "was designed to protect both the persons of Winston–Salem and their property, and thus is a safety ordinance." The dissenting judge, on the other hand, concluded that the ordinance was not a safety ordinance, but was designed to "protect people from the minor annoyances posed from having someone else's pets roaming through your yard." Defendant contends that the ordinance is merely a nuisance law "designed to prevent roaming dogs from trespassing, damaging property, leaving waste in neighbors' yards and interfering with traffic."

After a careful reading of the ordinance, we conclude that it is designed to protect persons as well as property.... It is without question that the ordinance has the effect of protecting property from damage by roaming dogs. However, the life and limb of pedestrians, joggers, and the public at large are protected by this ordinance as well. . . . The fact that the ordinance serves a dual purpose does not make it any less a safety ordinance. . . .

Defendant also argues that the ordinance does not promote safety because an owner may choose methods of restraint that are less effective than a fence. Assuming [that] the use of a tether, rope, chain or other device is not as effective as the use of a fence for restraining dogs, it is still far better protection than no restraint at all. Additionally, the flexibility allowed dog owners in choosing the method of restraint is a recognition that some property owners may not need to incur the greater expense of a fence in order to restrain their dogs.

Based on the foregoing reasons, we agree with the Court of Appeals that Section 3–18 "was designed to protect both the persons of Winston–Salem and their property, and thus is a safety ordinance."

The evidence that defendant intentionally, willfully, or wantonly violated the safety ordinance was aptly set out by the Court of Appeals.

> Bruno and Woody had been picked up by animal control officers on at least three occasions prior to the fatal attack. The dogs had been taken by animal control officers to the animal shelter as recently as August, 1989, two months prior to the death of Prevette. Defendant admitted that his dogs had been out twice on the day of Prevette's death. On one occasion in July, 1989, after the dogs escaped by digging out from underneath the fence, defendant simply covered the escape hole with a cooler after returning the dogs to the fence. Defendant's next-door neighbor testified that the dogs were allowed to run loose "on a regular basis," day and night, and that defendant would often "just open the door and let the dogs out." Defendant's ex-girlfriend testified that defendant let the dogs run free both day and night.

The trial judge instructed the jury that "the violation of a statute or ordinance governing the care of dogs which results in injury or death will constitute culpable negligence if the violation is willful, wanton, or intentional." Viewed in the light most favorable to the State, as we must on a motion to dismiss, we find that the State presented sufficient evidence that defendant intentionally, willfully, or wantonly violated the ordinance.

[For] the foregoing reasons, we hold that the State presented substantial evidence of each element of the offense of involuntary manslaughter based on culpable negligence where a safety ordinance is involved. Accordingly, this assignment of error is rejected.

Defendant next argues that the trial court erroneously instructed the jury on the charge of involuntary manslaughter. Defendant's request for a jury instruction regarding the elements of involuntary manslaughter in cases involving domestic animals where there is no safety statute or ordinance was denied. Instead, the trial court instructed the jury regarding culpable negligence where a safety statute or ordinance is involved. It is well settled that the trial court must give a requested instruction in substance if the instruction is correct and is supported by the evidence. Here, the instruction is not supported by the evidence as we have held that a safety ordinance is involved in this case. Therefore, the trial court committed no reversible error in refusing to instruct the jury as requested by defendant.

The decision of the Court of Appeals is affirmed.

PROBLEM

Mother's Psychosis. Andrea Yates was convicted of murder for drowning her five children in Houston, Texas. Her conviction was later overturned based on her insanity defense. The evidence revealed that, following her second pregnancy and with every pregnancy thereafter, she suffered postpartum psychosis. At the time of the murders, she claimed that she believed that the only way to get her children to heaven (and thereby escape the devil), was to kill them. Suppose that Andrea's husband, Dan, was aware that she suffered post-partum psychosis after each pregnancy, but continued having children with her. Suppose further that, at the time of the killings, it was clear that she was suffering mental problems in conjunction with postpartum psychosis following the birth of her fifth child. Nevertheless, each morning, Dan went to work and left Andrea alone with their children. Dan's mother came to help Andrea later in the day, but there was a two-hour gap during which Andrea was alone with the children. If the preceding suppositions are treated as fact, did Dan commit either reckless manslaughter or negligent homicide?

PEOPLE v. McCOY

223 Mich.App. 500, 566 N.W.2d 667 (1997).

PER CURIAM.

Defendant appeals as of right his jury trial convictions of involuntary manslaughter, felonious driving, and leaving the scene of an accident. Defendant was sentenced as a third-offense habitual offender to concurrent terms of twelve to thirty years' imprisonment for the manslaughter conviction, three to ten years' imprisonment for the felonious driving conviction, and one to four years' imprisonment for the conviction of leaving the scene of an accident. We affirm.

Defendant's first claim on appeal is that the prosecution presented insufficient evidence of gross negligence to support his convictions of manslaughter and felonious driving. We disagree.

In reviewing claims of insufficiency of the evidence to sustain a verdict, this court views the evidence in the light most favorable to the prosecution to determine if a rational factfinder could find the essential elements of the crime proved beyond a reasonable doubt. An unlawful act, committed with the intent to injure or in a grossly negligent manner, that proximately causes death is involuntary manslaughter. As with involuntary manslaughter, a conviction of felonious driving requires proof of gross negligence. The Court in [*People v.*] *Datema*, [448 Mich. 585,] 604, 533 N.W.2d 272 [(1995)], explained the distinction between criminal intent, negligence, and gross negligence:

> [T]he legally significant mental states [should be viewed] as lying on a continuum: criminal intention anchors one end of the spectrum and negligence anchors the other. Intention, as explained by Professor Hall, "emphasiz[es] that the actor seeks the proscribed harm not in the sense that he desires it, but in the sense that he has chosen it, he has decided to bring it into being." Negligence, lying at the opposite end of the spectrum, "implies inadvertence, i.e., that the defendant was completely unaware of the dangerousness of this behavior although actually it was unreasonably increasing the risk of occurrence of an injury."

> Criminal negligence, also referred to as gross negligence, lies within the extremes of intention and negligence. As with intention, the actor realizes the risk of his behavior and consciously decides to create that risk. As with negligence, however, the actor does not seek to cause harm, but is simply "recklessly or wantonly indifferent to the results."

Here, two sisters were standing on the yellow line in the middle of Greenfield Road waiting for traffic to clear when they were struck from behind by a van driven by defendant. One of the sisters was killed, and the other was injured. The accident occurred at approximately 3:00 p.m. on February 3, 1995, as the deceased was on her way home from school. The sole witness to the accident testified that the van was traveling at a speed of approximately fifty to fifty-five miles an hour when it struck the two sisters. The posted speed limit was thirty-five miles an hour. Defendant argues that this evidence was insufficient to show that he was driving in a grossly negligent manner at the time that he struck the decedent.

In order to show gross negligence, the following elements must be established:

> (1) Knowledge of a situation requiring the exercise of ordinary care and diligence to avert injury to another.

> (2) Ability to avoid the resulting harm by ordinary care and diligence in the use of the means at hand.

> (3) The omission to use such care and diligence to avert the threatened danger when to the ordinary mind it must be apparent that the result is likely to prove disastrous to another.

Here, there is no question that a jury could properly infer that defendant knew that the act of driving requires the exercise of ordinary care and diligence to avert injury to others. Similarly, there is no question that a jury could properly infer under these facts that defendant had the ability to avoid the harm that occurred by exercising ordinary care and diligence, but failed to do so. Accordingly, the only question is whether to the ordinary mind it must have been apparent that the result was likely to prove disastrous to another.

A violation of the speed limit, by itself, is not adequate to establish the element of gross negligence. However, under certain circumstances, a violation of the speed limit can be gross negligence. [A] jury could properly determine that traveling at a speed of one hundred miles an hour through a residential neighborhood is gross negligence. Similarly, given the right conditions, it is possible to drive in a grossly negligent manner even in the absence of exceeding the speed limit (e.g., in heavy traffic, on slick roads, or in fog). Accordingly, the appropriate consideration is not whether defendant was exceeding the speed limit, but rather, whether defendant acted with gross negligence under the totality of the circumstances, including defendant's actual speed and the posted speed limit. This is a question that ordinarily is for the jury.

Viewing the evidence in a light most favorable to the prosecution, a jury could reasonably find that at the time his van struck the two sisters, defendant was traveling at a speed of fifty-five miles an hour in a thirty-five miles an hour zone during heavy traffic conditions. [T]his speed was "a lot faster than the rest of traffic," and significantly faster than the average speed on that stretch of road of forty to forty-five miles an hour. Finally, the two sisters had been standing stationary at the same location for several seconds. The fact that defendant did not slow down or swerve in an attempt to avoid striking them suggests that he was traveling at a reckless speed. [A] reasonable jury could find that defendant was grossly negligent.

This conclusion is strengthened by the testimony concerning defendant's conduct immediately following the accident. [D]efendant approached the next light at a speed of fifty miles an hour. Defendant slowed down to a speed of twenty-five miles an hour to make a left turn onto Puritan against a red light. He nearly hit several cars in the process. Defendant continued on Puritan, weaving in and out of traffic, and forcing a vehicle in the oncoming lane off the road. The van then turned left[,] tires squealing, nearly hitting a grandmother and her grandchildren. It is true that evidence of immoderate speed at points remote from the scene of the accident is incompetent to establish immoderate speed at the accident scene itself. Here, however, the facts that subsequent observations took place in the immediate vicinity of the accident, and that defendant's speed did not change between the time of the accident and the time that he approached the first intersection, would allow a reasonable jury to conclude that defendant engaged in a single, continuous pattern of grossly negligent driving. Accordingly, the trial court did not err in denying defendant's motion for a directed verdict.

[Affirmed.]

NOTE

Vehicular homicide. In a number of jurisdictions, separate vehicular homicide offenses exist which apply to deaths resulting from negligent operation of a motor vehicle. Typically, these specific types of negligent homicide statutes provide for lower levels of punishment than involuntary (reckless) manslaughter statutes, but the former crimes may be established with a lesser showing of culpability.

PROBLEMS

1. *Need for Vehicular Homicide Statute.* Why do you suppose jurisdictions might prefer to enact *separate* criminal offenses to apply to vehicular homicide? Why not cover this activity under the standard involuntary manslaughter offense or under a *general* negligent homicide statute? Explain.

2. *Tire Blow Out.* (Reconsider the following problems following *Jackowski* in Chapter 3, *supra*.) Suppose that defendant is driving on a city boulevard when her car's left front tire blows out. Despite defendant's best efforts to control the vehicle, the car swerves off the road and kills a pedestrian. In the following situations, consider whether defendant is guilty of involuntary manslaughter or vehicular homicide:

　　a. *New Tires.* Defendant is driving at or near the speed limit (35 mph) on new tires, and has no reason to believe that there are any problems with the tires.

　　b. *Old Tires.* Defendant is driving at or near the speed limit, but his tires are old and bald.

　　c. *Extreme Speeding.* Defendant is driving at a speed of 65 mph in a 35 mph zone when the blow out occurs.

3. *Unexpected Events.* Consider the following additional situations in an effort to decide whether defendant has committed involuntary (reckless) manslaughter or vehicular (negligent) homicide:

　　a. *Daydreaming.* Defendant is daydreaming while driving down a city street. His speed is at or near the speed limit, but, because he is not paying attention to detail, he runs off the road killing a pedestrian.

　　b. *Icy Skid.* Defendant is driving on very icy streets going the speed limit (35 mph). When the car in front of him stops unexpectedly, defendant slams on his brakes but is unable to stop because of the ice. His car veers onto the sidewalk killing a pedestrian.

4. *Epileptic Seizure.* Defendant is an epileptic who periodically has seizures. One day, while driving his car on an interstate highway, defendant has a seizure and his car runs into another car, killing the passenger. Did defendant commit involuntary manslaughter or vehicular homicide?

CHAPTER 9

ASSAULT & BATTERY

■ ■ ■

The modern meanings of battery and assault crimes retain core elements of their common law components. In English common law, there were two types of battery crimes. Both crimes required the defendant to use actual force upon a victim; one type of battery caused bodily injury and a second type of battery caused only "offensive touching." The mental states for these crimes included either the intent to injure or touch offensively, or the state of mind described ambiguously as "criminal negligence." There was only one type of common law assault crime, which was the attempt to commit a battery. The assault could be proved only when the defendant came very close to achieving the result of battery and also had the "present ability" to do so. The mental state for assault was the immediate intention to commit the battery. Early state criminal codes often contained no definition of either battery or assault, and judges were expected to use the English precedents to interpret the meaning of these crimes.

The first important change in state codes was the invention of the felony crimes of "aggravated battery" and "aggravated assault." The crimes of battery and assault were only misdemeanors at common law, and the felony crime of mayhem punished only the causing of physical impairments affecting the ability to fight in battle. As this crime became obsolete, legislatures replaced it with more broad definitions of violent conduct that constituted "aggravated" forms of battery or attempted-battery assault. Four elements became common features that distinguished "aggravated" crimes from "simple" crimes, including: 1) the causing of serious bodily injury instead of bodily injury; 2) the use of a deadly weapon; 3) the victim's status as a law enforcement officer; and 4) the intent to commit felony crimes, such as murder, robbery, or rape.

Two other important changes occurred in state codes and case law. A majority of jurisdictions abandoned the "offensive touching" type of battery, and most states borrowed the "frightening" tort of assault to establish a second type of criminal assault. The latter crime made it possible to prosecute some defendants whose acts did not satisfy the stringent requirements for the attempted-battery type of assault. The elements of the "frightening" assault crime usually included the act of causing fear of bodily injury, accompanied by the apparent ability to cause such injury.

By the time the M.P.C. drafters proposed to reform the definitions of battery and assault, state codes exhibited a wide variety of definitions for "aggravated" and "simple" versions of both crimes. The goals of the M.P.C. revision were to simplify the elements of these crimes and to consolidate the many types of crimes into a small number of prototypes. For example, the M.P.C. drafters decided to use the term "Assault" as the name of the crime that encompassed eight types of crimes derived from common law battery and assault. Throughout this chapter, if an "assault" crime is the equivalent of common law battery, both labels will be used for clarification.

A. BATTERY

1. OFFENSIVE TOUCHING

ADAMS v. COMMONWEALTH

33 Va.App. 463, 534 S.E.2d 347 (2000).

FRANK, JUDGE.

[On] September 22, 1998, while on duty at the Gloucester County High School, Sergeant Steven Giles of the Gloucester County Sheriff's Department was struck in his right eye by a laser light owned by [Adams], who was a twelfth-grade student at the school. Giles had been talking with another [sheriff's officer] and the school nurse when he felt a "stinging sensation" in his eye. [That officer] told Giles that [Adams] had "just lit [him] up," as there was "a red dot" on him. Giles approached [Adams] and asked what he had. [Adams] said, "It can't hurt you," and handed over the laser light, which was attached to his key chain. Giles gave the laser light to the assistant principal and told [Adams] he could retrieve it later. Giles said he "felt a burning sensation" in his eye and "saw red" before looking away, but he did not know how long the laser had been pointed at him. Giles had his eye checked the next morning by a local doctor who found "heavy irritation" but no other injury. [The other officer testified that Adams was 150 feet from Giles and that Giles flinched when he was hit.]

[Adams] testified that he purchased the laser light for six dollars at a convenience store two days before the offense. He said it had no warning on it regarding use and that he had not been hurt when hit in the eye by the light. [Adams] denied hitting Giles in the face or eye and claimed he had not intended to strike Giles with the light but, instead, was "just goofing off" to get [the] attention [of the other officer, with whom Adams had a friendly relationship,] by waving the laser around. [Adams] did not get along well with Sergeant Giles. He stated that Giles had previously given him a hard time. . . .

[The trial court convicted Adams of battery on a law enforcement officer. The crime is defined in the state criminal code as follows: "any person [who] commits [a] battery against another knowing or having reason to know that such other person is a law-enforcement officer . . . engaged in the performance of his public duties . . . shall be guilty of a Class 6 felony," and "shall be sentenced to a mandatory, minimum term of six months in jail."]

"[T]he slightest touching of another . . . if done in a rude, insolent, or angry manner, constitutes a battery for which the law affords redress." *Crosswhite v. Barnes*, 139 Va. 471, 477, 124 S.E. 242, 244 (1924).

"[W]here there is physical injury to another person, it is sufficient that the cause is set in motion by the defendant, or that the [victim] is subjected to its operation by means of any act or control which the defendant exerts." "The law upon the subject is intended primarily to protect the sacredness of the person, and, secondarily, to prevent breaches of the peace."

Banovitch v. Commonwealth, 196 Va. 210, 219, 83 S.E.2d 369, 374 (1954).

Adams contends that shining the laser on Sergeant Giles was insufficient to constitute a touching for the purposes of assault and battery. Touch is defined as to be in contact or to cause to be in contact. *See Merriam–Webster's Desk Dictionary* 573 (1995).

In Virginia, it is abundantly clear that a perpetrator need not inflict a physical injury to commit a battery. The cases that guide our analysis, however, have not addressed circumstances where contact with the corporeal person was accomplished by directing a beam of light at the victim. Because substances such as light or sound become elusive when considered in terms of battery, contact by means of such substances must be examined further in determining whether a touching has occurred. Such a test is necessary due to the intangible nature of those substances and the need to limit application of such a principle (touching by intangible substances) to reasonable cases. Because the underlying concerns of battery law are breach of the peace and sacredness of the person, the dignity of the victim is implicated and the reasonableness and offensiveness of the contact must be considered. Otherwise, criminal convictions could result from the routine and insignificant exposure to concentrated energy that inevitably results from living in populated society.

Accordingly, we hold that for purposes of determining whether a battery has occurred, contact by an intangible substance such as light must be considered in terms of its effect on the victim. There need be no actual injury for a touching to have occurred. However, to prove a touching, the evidence must prove that the substance made objectively offensive or forcible contact with the victim's person resulting in some manifestation of a physical consequence or corporeal hurt.....

[Adams], by aiming the laser at the officers, effected a contact that caused bodily harm to Sergeant Giles. [Adams] argued there was no touching because the laser has no mass and, therefore, cannot physically touch Sergeant Giles. This argument is misplaced. The laser, directed by [Adams], came into contact with Sergeant Giles' eye and, as a result, there was an unlawful touching.

[Adams also contends that the evidence is not sufficient to prove his intent.] Proving intent by direct evidence often is impossible. Like any other element of a crime, it may be proved by circumstantial evidence, as long as such evidence excludes all reasonable hypotheses of innocence flowing from it. Circumstantial evidence of intent may include the conduct and statements of the alleged offender, and "[t]he finder of fact may infer that [he] intends the natural and probable consequences of his acts." *Campbell v. Commonwealth*, 12 Va. App. 476, 484, 405 S.E.2d 1, 4 (1991) (*en banc*).

The trial court, sitting as the fact finder, was entitled to reject appellant's testimony that he was "just goofing off" to attract [the] attention of [the officer standing next to Giles]. The court specifically found that [Adams] intended to hit Giles with the laser and that [a] battery occurred. That decision is not plainly wrong or without supporting evidence and must be upheld on appeal.

For the reasons stated, we affirm the judgment of the trial court.

Lemons, Judge, dissenting.

[Whether] a touching is a battery depends upon the intent of the actor, not upon the force applied. Here, the evidence does not support beyond a reasonable doubt that Adams had the intent to offensively touch Sergeant Giles. In order to have such intent, Adams would have to know or be reasonably charged with knowledge that a six-dollar novelty item attached to his key chain had the potential for offensive touching. It is not within common knowledge that such a device has such capacity. There is no evidence that Adams had specific knowledge of such capacity. That Adams had a bad relationship with Giles may explain his motive, but it does not prove intent to offensively touch. A finder of fact may infer that an actor intends the natural and probable consequences of his acts. In the absence of common knowledge of the capacity of this device, no inference may be drawn. Without inference or specific knowledge, there is no proof that Adams intended to offensively touch Giles.

Additionally, the majority redefines "touching" for the purpose of common law battery. Although the reasoning is logical, it is unwise, because the unintended consequences may reach too far. Will the next prosecution for battery be based upon failure to dim high beams in traffic, flash photography too close to the subject, high intensity flashlight beams or sonic waves from a teenager's car stereo? Rather than stretch the boundaries of the common law understanding of what is necessary for a "touching" to occur, criminalizing conduct that involves intangible objects put in motion should be left to specific legislative action rather than generalized redefinition that may sweep into the ambit of criminal behavior conduct that is not intended. *See, e.g.,* 720 Ill. Comp. Stat. 5/2–10.2, 2–10.3, 5/12–2, 12–4 (West 2000) (shining or flashing a laser gunsight near or on a person constitutes aggravated assault or aggravated battery); 720 Ill. Comp. Stat. 5/24.6/20 (West 2000) (aiming a laser pointer at a police officer is a misdemeanor); Wash. Rev.Code § 9A–49.020 (1999) (felony to discharge a laser beam at various peace officers or pilots, bus drivers or transit operators in the commission of their respective duties).

I respectfully dissent.

NOTES

1. *Majority view of offensive-touching battery.* The M.P.C. drafters supported the emerging majority consensus that only the "bodily injury" type of battery crime should be preserved, and that the "offensive touching" type of common law battery should be abandoned. Therefore, the M.P.C treats "forms of offensive but not physically endangering behavior" as minor offenses such as disorderly conduct or harassment. *See* M.P.C. § 211.1, Comment (2), at 185 (1980). However, a minority of states continue to rely on the common law of battery to criminalize acts of offensive touching as illustrated in *Adams*.

2. *Offensive touchings and police.* Some courts construe "offensive touchings" narrowly, as in *State v. Jones,* 129 N.M. 165, 3 P.3d 142 (2000), where the statute used a broad definition of battery, like the one in the *Adams* statute, to prohibit "the unlawful, intentional touching or application of force to the person of a peace officer while he is in the lawful discharge of his duties, when done in a rude, insolent or angry manner." The *Jones* Court held that "the unlawful conduct comprising a battery upon a peace officer" must "rise to the level of an actual injury, actual threat to safety, or meaningful challenge to authority." The court reasoned that without such a limiting construction, "even a mundane [tort-law] battery, such as rudely grabbing a ticket from an officer's hands, or any other touching no matter how insignificant, could, at the prosecutor's whim, become punishable as a felony."

Some statutes criminalize particular types of non-injurious challenges to police authority, such as the Indiana statute that defines "battery by body waste." This crime occurs when a person "knowingly or intentionally in a rude, insolent, or angry manner places blood or another body fluid or waste on a law enforcement officer or a corrections officer identified as such and while engaged in the performance of official duties." A higher penalty is imposed "if the person knew or recklessly failed to know that the person was infected with: (A) hepatitis B; (B) HIV; or (C) tuberculosis." See *Newman v. State*, 677 N.E.2d 590 (Ind.App. 1997). By contrast, the court in *Gilbert v. Commonwealth*, 45 Va.App. 67, 608 S.E.2d 509 (2005), held that under the *Adams* battery statute, the act of spitting on a police officer justified conviction because the "slightest touching" in an angry manner constitutes common law battery.

3. *Laser battery statutes.* The Virginia legislature enacted the following statute after *Adams* was decided:

> If any person, knowing or having reason to know another person is a law enforcement officer, a probation or parole officer, a correctional officer, or a person employed by the Department of Corrections directly involved in the care, treatment or supervision of inmates in the custody of the Department engaged in the performance of his public duties as such, intentionally projects at such other person a beam or a point of light from a laser, a laser gun sight, or any device that simulates a laser, shall be guilty of a Class 2 misdemeanor. [The penalties for such a misdemeanor are up to six months in jail and a fine of up to $1,000.]

VA. CODE ANN. § 18.2–57.01 (2000). Some other states also allow for punishment of up to six months in jail for laser battery. For example, a Louisiana statute provides:

> Unlawful use of a laser on a police officer is the intentional projection of a laser on or at a police officer without consent of the officer when the offender has reasonable grounds to believe the officer is a police officer acting in the performance of his duty and that the officer will be injured, intimidated, or placed in fear of bodily harm.

LA. REV. STAT. ANN. § 14:37.3 (1999).

4. *Outmoded types of battery.* A third type of battery crime, the "unlawful-act" battery, was recognized at common law. Some judges imposed strict liability for battery when any injury resulted from any unlawful conduct that was *malum in se*, or more broadly, from any unlawful conduct. Other judges required criminal negligence for such battery liability based on unlawful acts. The M.P.C. drafters abandoned the unlawful-act form of battery in § 211.1, and it is rare to see this crime included in a modern code. Another outmoded type of battery is the crime that punishes unwanted sexual advances. The M.P.C. treats harmful sexual touching as Sexual Assault under § 213.4, defined as "any touching of sexual or other intimate parts of [a] person for the purpose of arousing or gratifying sexual desire," accompanied by other circumstances. But some states still use the crime of common law battery to punish harmful sexual touchings. *See Perkins v. Commonwealth*, 31 Va.App. 326, 523 S.E.2d 512 (2000) (upholding battery conviction of teacher for touching a student while making sexual remarks, when touching did not occur in the ordinary course of the need to communicate or in the discharge of duties).

PROBLEMS

1. *Abolition of "Offensive Touching" Battery.* Assume that the defense counsel in *Adams* had argued that the Virginia Supreme Court should abolish the "offensive touching" type of battery. This argument could emphasize the lack of definition for the term "battery" in the Virginia statute, and the inherent authority of the state court to interpret that term as it chooses, and hence, to reverse its own precedents that recognize the "offensive touching" type of battery crime. How can the prosecutor respond to these arguments? Explain the arguments that could be made by both sides regarding the defense counsel's proposal.

2. *Laser Battery at the Movies.* Sue is a high school senior who went to the movies with a group of friends. She had purchased a small laser pointer from a store selling business products. It came in a package that described how it may be used for pointing at a screen or wall during slide show presentations. Witnesses at Sue's trial testified that she told her friends that she wanted to have some fun by pointing the laser at the movie screen during the previews. When Sue and her friends arrived at the movie theatre, it was very crowded. During the previews, Sue flashed the laser pointer at the screen, and she also happened to flash the pointer at the back of the heads of the people sitting in front of her. These people did not feel anything, but one moviegoer noticed Sue's actions and complained to the theater manager, who called the police. Sue was arrested and convicted of the crime of common law battery, which is defined under state law as including the conduct of "offensive touching." On appeal, Sue's defense counsel argues that the evidence was insufficient to support her conviction. What arguments will the prosecutor and defense counsel make on appeal? How can each side use ideas from the *Adams* majority opinion and dissent to support their arguments?

3. *Interpreting Laser Battery Statutes.* Assume that the facts of *Adams* arise in another Virginia case in 2001, and that the prosecutor decides to ignore the recent laser battery statute enacted in 2000, as described in Note 3 *supra*. Instead, the prosecutor charges the defendant with the *Adams* crime because it provides for a more severe penalty, and the defendant is convicted and appeals.

     a. *Overruling Adams.* As a policy matter, should Virginia Supreme Court decide to overrule *Adams*, and to adopt the view of the *Adams* dissent, on the ground that the enactment of the 2000 statute should be interpreted as superceding the judge-made laser battery crime in *Adams*? Explain the arguments on both sides here.

     b. *Adams in Louisiana.* Suppose that the facts of *Adams* arise in Louisiana and that the defendant is convicted of the Louisiana crime of "unlawful use of a laser on a police officer", described in Note 3 *supra*. How will each side argue the sufficiency of the evidence question on appeal?

4. *Crime of Disarming a Police Officer.* Assume that a state legislature has abolished the "offensive touching" type of battery, but that the legislature is concerned about the need to punish conduct that does not qualify for the "bodily injury" type of battery. This conduct is the disarming of a police officer, which sometimes occurs when an arrestee takes an officer's gun for the purpose of escape. What language should the legislature use to define this special kind of "touching" crime? See Wash Rev. Code § 9A.76.023. (1998).

2. BODILY INJURY

Modern battery statutes require the element of bodily injury for simple battery and use the element of serious bodily injury to define an aggravated battery. A definition of each concept may appear in a state code, but such definitions are ambiguous and require judicial interpretation. It may be difficult for courts to define the differences between serious and non-serious bodily injury and the differences between bodily injury and non-injury or mere touching.

STATE v. GORDON

560 N.W.2d 4 (Iowa 1997).

LAVARATO, JUSTICE.

[On] October 3, 1995, Gordon was in the home of Mary Johnston in Prairie City. Several other people were present, including Jeremiah Fry. Apparently unprovoked, Gordon stood up from where he was seated, spun around, and kicked Fry in the chest. As he kicked Fry, Gordon said, "Die pale-face pumpkin head." The kick left a red mark to the right of Fry's sternum.... A short time later, a Prairie City police officer saw Fry, interviewed him, and saw a heel imprint on Fry's shirt. When Fry raised his shirt, the officer saw what he described as a "reddening" on Fry's chest....

After all of the evidence was in, the State asked the court to instruct the jury that "marks" constitute [a bodily] injury for purposes of [the charged crime of] assault [the equivalent of battery]. Defense counsel objected and suggested a definition of bodily injury taken from the Model Penal Code and adopted in *State v. McKee*, 312 N.W.2d 907, 913 (Iowa 1981). Defense counsel argued that no case had recognized a red mark as a bodily injury [and the trial judge responded, "Then I'll tell the jury that a red mark on the skin is a bodily injury"]. Over defense counsel's objection, the court instructed the jury as follows: "A 'bodily' injury means a bodily or physical pain, illness, or any impairment of physical condition. A red mark or bruise on the skin would constitute an impairment of physical condition, and therefore an injury."

The jury convicted Gordon of assault [the equivalent of battery] causing bodily injury. Later the court sentenced Gordon to one year in jail, suspended all but ninety days of the sentence, put him on supervised probation for one year, and fined him [$200].

[In *McKee* we] adopted the Model Penal Code's definition of bodily injury[:] "physical pain, illness, or any impairment of physical condition." [We] explained in *McKee*:

> Bodily injury ordinarily "refers only to injury to the body, or to sickness or disease contracted by the injured as a result of injury." Injury includes "an act that damages, harms, or hurts: an unjust or undeserved infliction of suffering or [harm]." Thus the ordinary dictionary definition of bodily injury coincides with the Model Penal Code definition of the [term].

[We] agree [with] Gordon that the court went too far when it instructed the jury that "[a] red mark or bruise on the skin would constitute an impairment of physical condition, and therefore an injury." . . .

In *McKee* we also defined impairment as [follows:] "An impairment, according to common usage, includes any deviation from normal health. The term means: 'To weaken, to make worse, to lessen in power, diminish, or relax, or otherwise affect in any injurious manner.'" 312 N.W.2d at 913.

There was no direct evidence that Fry suffered any deviation from normal health because of the blow. Nor did he testify that he had any pain or illness because of the blow. Those were fact questions peculiarly within the jury's common experience and for them to decide. [The] red mark or bruise on Fry's chest was not a physical impairment per se but only evidence of such impairment.

Had the district court merely given the definition of a bodily injury and stopped, the jury could have found the red mark or bruise was not a bodily injury. The court's gratuitous addition was especially prejudicial to Gordon because . . . [t]he only direct evidence of injury was that Fry had suffered a "reddening" on his chest. . . . In effect, the district court directed a verdict in favor of the State on bodily injury, a critical element of the offense. In doing so the court invaded the province of the jury and committed [error]. . . . Because the error here was prejudicial, we reverse and remand for a new trial.

Reversed and Remanded.

NOTE

M.P.C. revisions of battery. The policy judgments of the M.P.C. drafters have had a wide influence upon modern judicial interpretations of battery and assault crimes, even though only a minority of states enacted the M.P.C definitions of these offenses. The M.P.C. condenses four definitions of battery and four definitions of assault into a package of eight crimes, all called "Assault," which is divided into simple and aggravating categories. Unlike most state codes, the M.P.C. does not use the "aggravating" crime elements of "law enforcement officer victim" or the "intent to commit" particular violent felonies. M.P.C. § 211.1 uses the following revised definitions of common law battery:

> **(1) Simple Assault.** A person is guilty of assault if he:
>
>> (a) .... purposely, knowingly or recklessly causes bodily injury to another; or
>>
>> (b) negligently causes bodily injury to another with a deadly weapon; ...
>
> **(2) Aggravated Assault.** A person is guilty of aggravated assault if he:
>
>> (a) .... causes [serious bodily] injury to another ... purposely, knowingly or recklessly under circumstances manifesting extreme indifference to the value of human life; or
>>
>> (b) .... purposely or knowingly causes bodily injury to another with a deadly weapon....

As the *Gordon* Court notes, the M.P.C. defines "bodily injury" as "physical pain, illness, or any impairment of physical condition." M.P.C. § 210.0 defines "serious bodily injury" as "bodily injury which creates a substantial risk of death or which causes serious, permanent disfigurement, or protracted loss or impairment of the function of any bodily member or organ."

PROBLEMS

1. *New Trial in Gordon.* Assume that you are the prosecutor at Gordon's new trial. How will you argue to the jury that the facts in the case present sufficient evidence of "bodily injury" defined as "physical pain, illness, or any impairment of physical condition," and therefore justify the defendant's conviction? What new testimony or evidence could you present at trial to support your arguments?

2. *Adams in Iowa.* Assume that the facts of *Adams* occurred in Iowa. Under *Gordon*'s interpretation of "bodily injury," would there be sufficient evidence to convict the *Adams* defendant of the *Gordon* crime? Explain.

3. *Dental Crowns and Mucosal Mouth.* Assume that the *Gordon* defendant's kick had landed in the victim's mouth and had damaged two teeth, and that a dentist capped these teeth with crowns. How would the prosecutor argue that this injury should qualify as "serious bodily injury" under the M.P.C definition? Explain. What if the victim also happened to develop "mucosal mouth", which is a rare chronic condition involving the blistering of mucous membranes in the mouth. How would the arguments for the prosecutor change in this scenario? Explain. Compare *People v. Conley*, 187 Ill.App.3d 234, 134 Ill.Dec. 855, 543 N.E.2d 138 (1989).

STATE v. WHITFIELD

132 Wash.App. 878, 134 P.3d 1203 (2006).

HOUGHTON, P.J.

Anthony Whitfield appeals from his conviction [and sentence for more than 178 years for] 17 counts of first degree assault [equivalent of battery] with sexual motivation ... He raises various constitutional and statutory arguments. We affirm.

Whitfield learned that he had HIV (human immunodeficiency virus) in April 1992, while incarcerated in Oklahoma.... [According to a] psychologist at the [prison,] "[r]eportedly, [Whitfield] contracted the virus through non-consensual sex while incarcerated." Whitfield's case manager also wrote: "Whitfield is well aware of the consequence of his disease and this seems to frighten him. If he becomes a threat to the public it will not be because of ignorance." After being released from prison in 1995, Whitfield moved to [the state of] Washington in 1999 and later had multiple sexual encounters with 17 women....

During [his] sexual liaisons involving oral, vaginal, and sometimes anal sex, Whitfield rarely wore a condom, even when asked to. And he never informed any of his partners that he had been diagnosed HIV-positive. When asked about his sexually transmitted disease status, he would deny having any disease or would state that he had tested negative. At least five of the 17 women became HIV-positive or ill with Acquired Immune Deficiency Syndrome (AIDS) after having sex with Whitfield.

Dr. Diana Yu, the Thurston County Public Health Officer, first became aware of Whitfield in 2002, when a person diagnosed with AIDS named him as a sex partner. Dr. Yu's office tried unsuccessfully to locate Whitfield at that time. In March 2003, another woman diagnosed with AIDS named Whitfield as her only sex partner. Diana Johnson, a supervisor of the HIV unit [of the Health Department], then located [and interviewed Whitfield,] and tested him for HIV.

Upon receiving the results, [Johnson] contacted Whitfield by telephone and met with him at the Health Department. When she told him that the test results indicated that he was HIV-positive, Whitfield broke into tears. [Johnson] then explained to Whitfield about what he needed to do to avoid infecting others, which included notifying all his sexual partners of his HIV status and using condoms to reduce the risk of infection....

In December 2003, Dr. Yu learned that a third individual diagnosed with AIDS named Whitfield as a sex partner. Dr. Yu contacted a Thurston County deputy prosecutor. [In March] 2004, Dr. Yu signed a [cease and desist order, and] Johnson served Whitfield with the [order]. The [order] required Whitfield to submit names and information about all of his sexual partners to the Health Department. It also ordered Whitfield not to engage in any activity that may involve exchange of vaginal fluid or semen and to inform all of his sexual partners that they may have been exposed to HIV. Dr. Yu then drafted a declaration under RCW 70.24.034 and sent it to the deputy prosecutor to aid the prosecutor in detaining Whitfield. [This declaration allowed the prosecutor to obtain a court order to take Whitfield into custody, and Whitfield was later arrested.] . . .

[On] October 28, 2004, the State [charged] Whitfield with 17 counts of first degree assault with sexual motivation. . . . [This crime provides that a person is guilty of first degree assault "if he or she, with intent to inflict great bodily harm . . . [a]dministers, exposes, or transmits to or causes to be taken by another, poison, the human immunodeficiency virus . . . , or any other destructive or noxious substance." The term "sexual motivation" is defined as follows: "one of the purposes for which the defendant committed the crime was for the purpose of his or her sexual gratification."] . . .

After Whitfield waived his right to a jury trial, a bench trial ensued. Dr. Yu testified that medical science currently cannot cure HIV or AIDS and that HIV eventually leads to AIDS. She also stated that the statistical risk of a female getting infected by an [act of] unprotected vaginal intercourse with an HIV-positive male is four percent but that science cannot predict who will become infected and who will not. . . . The trial court found Whitfield guilty as charged on all counts . . . [and] ruled:

> For a person prosecuted for Assault in the First Degree by exposing another to HIV, it does not matter whether the exposure resulted in transmission of the virus. Neither does it matter whether the other person was already infected with the virus from another source. . . . [R]epeated acts of exposing the same person to HIV increased the risk that transmission will occur during one of the repeated acts in a mathematical progression. Thus, 25 or more acts of exposing a person to HIV increases the risk that at least one act will transmit the virus to something near 100 percent.

After carefully analyzing all the evidence, the court concluded that Whitfield "intended to expose" all 17 victims to HIV. . . .

Whitfield [challenges his conviction] on the basis that [the first degree assault statute violates the state constitutional guarantee of equal protection because it] does not prohibit the intentional transmission of other harmful, sexually transmitted diseases such as herpes, gonorrhea, and syphilis. . . . "Under the rational basis test, a legislative classification will be upheld 'unless it rests on grounds wholly irrelevant to the achievement of legitimate state objectives'" [and] "the burden rests on the party challenging the classification to show that it is 'purely arbitrary.'" [*State* v. *Coria*, 120 Wash.2d 156, 171–172, 839 P.2d 890, 899 (1992)].

Here, the classification under [the first degree assault statute] bears a reasonable relationship to a legitimate state objective—to stop the transmission of a deadly disease. As Dr Yu testified and the trial court found, HIV is incurable and shortens the life expectancy of anyone infected. No one can question the State's interest in stopping its spread. Because Whitfield fails to show a purely arbitrary classification, his equal protection argument fails. . . .

[Next,] Whitfield argues that the State presented insufficient evidence of his intent to inflict great bodily harm. . . . [However,] the evidence proved that Whitfield knew about his HIV status before coming to Washington. . . . Moreover, Whitfield deliberately lied to all of the victims, telling them that he did not have any sexually transmitted diseases while insisting that they engage in unprotected sex with him. Whitfield's deception and unprotected sexual activities continued even after [Johnson's] counseling in August 2003, and after the March 2004 cease and desist order. . . . Finally, [on] multiple occasions, [Whitfield] told others that if he knew he had HIV he would try to infect as many people as possible. . . .

Whitfield [also argues] that the State failed to present sufficient evidence to convict him of 12 of the first degree assault charges pertaining to victims who tested HIV-negative. He asserts that he was not always capable of transmitting HIV. In making this argument, he relies on Dr. Yu's testimony that a person infected with HIV is not always contagious or capable of transmitting the disease.

Whitfield's argument, however, confuses the elements of the charged crime [which applies to a person who] "*exposes*, or transmits to . . . another . . . the human immunodeficiency virus . . ." (Emphasis added.) [The] State had to prove only that Whitfield intentionally exposed the victims to HIV. [According] to Dr. Yu, "every incidence of sexual activity would be a period of exposure," although not every exposure would necessarily transmit HIV. Dr. Yu also testified that exposure occurs with any sexual activity that involves vaginal, oral, or anal exchange of bodily fluids as occurs during unprotected sex.

Whitfield knew that he was HIV-positive when he engaged in unprotected sexual activities while deliberately concealing his HIV status. [There was] sufficient evidence [that] Whitfield intentionally exposed the 12 HIV-negative victims to the disease. . . .

Affirmed.

NOTE

HIV Exposure Crimes. The *Whitfield* Court observed that "at least 22 states have criminalized intentionally transmitting HIV". Instead of amending a battery or assault statute, some legislatures created a new crime like that enacted in Tennessee, which prohibits "Criminal Exposure of Another to HIV." That statute applies to any person who knows that he or she is infected with HIV and "knowingly engage[s] in intimate contact with another"; "intimate contact" is defined as "the exposure of the body of one person to a bodily fluid of another person in any manner that presents a significant risk of HIV transmission." It is an affirmative defense to this crime that the victim knew that the defendant was infected with HIV, knew that the intimate contact could result in infection with HIV, and consented to the contact with that knowledge. See Tenn. Code Ann. § 39–13–109(a)–(c). See *Tennessee v. Bonds*, 189 S.W.3d 249 (Tenn. 2006) (holding that "exposure" element requires only evidence that victim was subjected to risk of contact with bodily fluids in a manner that would present a significant risk of HIV transmission). The *Whitfield* Court also noted that in some states the conduct of HIV exposure may be punished as attempted murder. See, *e.g.*, *Weeks v. Texas*, 834 S.W.2d 559, 561 (1992).

PROBLEMS

1. *Refusing HIV Test.* Assume that the defendant in *Whitfield* never knew about his HIV-positive status because he was never tested for HIV after he contracted HIV from an infected sexual partner in prison before he moved to Washington. Assume that when Johnson interviewed him in 2003, he refused to be tested for HIV. Should the state legislature enact a criminal statute to punish this refusal? If such a statute is enacted, should the legislature also criminalize the refusal to be tested for other STDs, such as herpes, gonorrhea, and syphilis, under circumstances like those in the *Whitfield* case?

2. *Enacting HIV–Exposure Statute.* Assume that another state legislature is considering whether to enact a statute that is similar to the Washington first degree assault crime in *Whitfield,* in order to prosecute defendants who expose other persons to HIV. Should the mental states for this crime require the knowledge of HIV-positive status and "intent to inflict great bodily harm" as in the *Whitfield* statute? Or should the legislature also include the mental state of recklessness as to these elements? Explain the policy pros and cons concerning these options.

B. ASSAULT

ANTHONY v. UNITED STATES
361 A.2d 202 (D.C.App. 1976).

Before KELLY, FICKLING and HARRIS, ASSOCIATE JUDGES.

HARRIS, ASSOCIATE JUDGE:

Appellants are brothers appealing from their jury convictions of assault with intent to commit robbery. D.C.Code 1973, § 22–501.

Their only claim of error is that the trial court's instructions on the elements of the offense were plainly erroneous. We affirm.

Viewed in the light most favorable to the government, the record reveals that on an evening when he was assigned to an "old clothes" tactical unit, Metropolitan Police Sergeant Patrick Lanigan was being trailed by appellants through what he knew to be an area with a high incidence of robberies. After the two men followed Lanigan for awhile, appellant Aaron Anthony asked him for a cigarette. As Lanigan turned, he saw that each appellant had his hand in his pocket, with protruding bulges which were aimed at Lanigan's midsection. One of the appellants told Lanigan to "Give it up." Lanigan grabbed Aaron, and, using him as a shield, drew his service revolver and pointed it toward John [Anthony], who turned and ran. As the latter fled, Lanigan saw a shiny object in his hand. No weapon was found on Aaron. John was pursued by another plain-clothes officer, who observed him make a tossing motion and heard a "clunk" on the ground immediately thereafter. John was apprehended, and, a few minutes later, the officers found a revolver in the area through which he had run.

Both appellants testified. They denied having accosted Sergeant Lanigan, disclaimed any knowledge of the recovered pistol, and maintained that John had run because Lanigan drew his gun on them without provocation. The indictments charged appellants with [several crimes but the jury] found each appellant guilty only of assault with intent to commit robbery. . . .

In its instructions on the elements of the offense of assault with intent to commit robbery, the trial court defined an assault as "an attempt or effort with force or violence to do injury to the person of another, coupled with the *apparent* present ability to carry out such attempt or effort." (Emphasis added.) The instruction given followed the standard charge outlined in the D.C. Bar Ass'n Criminal Jury Instructions for the District of Columbia, No. 4.11 (2d ed. 1972). [The] appellants now urge that the instruction misstated the law of assault by reducing the element of present ability to inflict injury to the quality of being merely "apparent", instead of that of actual, existing ability. . . . We conclude that there was no error.

The assault which comprises an essential element of the offense of assault with intent to commit robbery is common law assault. The established definition thereof is:

> [A]n attempt with force or violence to do a corporal injury to another; and may consist of any act tending to such corporal injury, accompanied with such circumstances as denote at the time an intention, coupled with the present ability, of using actual violence against the person.

Guarro v. United States, 99 U.S.App.D.C. 97.99 (1956), quoting *Patterson v. Pillans*, 43 App.D.C. 505, 506–507 (1915).

The thrust of appellants' argument is that the "present ability" referred to in the quoted definition is an actual ability, and that absent proof of this element the crime of assault has not been established.

No prior case in this jurisdiction has decided specifically whether the crime of assault requires that the perpetrator possess the actual ability to inflict the threatened harm. There is a conflict of authority on this question in other jurisdictions. Based upon an analysis of the historical development of the offense [and] the interests intended to be protected by the criminal law, we conclude that an assailant's undisclosed present inability to do harm does not preclude a conviction for assault.

Despite historical distinctions, certain aspects of the concepts of a criminal assault and the tort of assault have merged, enlarging the criminal concept to encompass such conduct as could induce in the victim a well-founded apprehension of peril. See Perkins Criminal Law 116–122 (2d ed. 1969). Under this expanded concept of common law assault, a lack of actual ability to inflict the harm threatened is largely irrelevant, since the behavior of the assailant still might be such as would generate fright in the intended victim. Consistent with this analysis, [many] jurisdictions hold that if a defendant possesses the apparent ability to accomplish the threatened injury, an assault may be found. [The court acknowledged that "there are jurisdictions which have imposed, through statutory enactments, a more restricted definition of criminal assault, and have made actual ability to cause harm a requisite element of the crime."] . . . .

While certain conceptual aspects of tort theory have been absorbed into the criminal offense of assault, it is not necessarily the case that the victim must be shown factually to have experienced apprehension or fear in order to establish the offense. In our view the better position holds that although the question whether the defendant's conduct produced fear in the victim is relevant, the crucial inquiry remains whether the assailant acted in such a manner as would under the circumstances portend an immediate threat of danger to a person of reasonable sensibility. Contrary to appellants' contentions, application of the standard of "apparent present ability" does not elevate the victim's subjective perception to an element of the crime of assault. Rather, this standard focuses attention squarely upon the menacing conduct of the accused and his purposeful design either to engender fear in or do violence to his victim. Both the doctrine of apparent ability and the rule abrogating the necessity to show the victim's actual fear stem from a similar appreciation of the wrongfulness of the criminal conduct involved. The criminal law, designed as it is to protect public order, proscribes acts which increase "the potential for injury, and the tendency toward resistance, conflict, and violence." *Commonwealth v. Tarrant*, 326 N.E.2d 710, 714 (Mass. 1975). That appellants' conduct went far toward creating a violent disruption of order is evident, and they cannot avoid criminal responsibility on the ground that they arguably lacked the actual ability to accomplish the violence they were found by the jury to have attempted. Nor could they successfully argue, for example, that their intended victim was not actually put in fear because his training as a police officer might have made him resistant to such threats of danger. . . .

We are satisfied that the jury was properly instructed on the necessary elements of the offenses with which appellants were charged. No more than an apparent present ability to commit the threatened act of violence need be found to have an assailant's intended forcible act constitute an assault. Whether under the circumstances appellants' conduct was such as would satisfy the applicable standard was a question of fact to be resolved by the jury under appropriate instructions. . . .

Affirmed.

NOTES

1. *Limitations on attempted-battery assault.* The strict proximity requirement of the common law definition of attempted-battery assault is illustrated by one court's observation that attempted battery could not be proved by evidence of the act of pointing a gun, only by evidence of an attempt to fire it. See *Robinson v. United States*, 506 A.2d 572 (D.C.App. 1986). The M.P.C Commentary explains that this common law requirement was discarded by the M.P.C. drafters in favor of "the normal application of attempt principles", so that an assault conviction is possible when a defendant takes a "substantial step" toward the completion of a battery, and when the defendant's conduct is "strongly corroborative" of the defendant's intent to commit the battery. See M.P.C. § 211.1, Comment (2), at 184 (1980). However, some state codes continue to use a common law definition of attempted-battery assault that includes a strict proximity requirement and proof of the defendant's "present ability" to commit a battery. These requirements created an incentive for courts to expand the elements of assault by adopting the "frightening" crime with its less onerous proof requirements.

2. *Adoption of frightening assault crime.* When a legislature enacts the "frightening" version of assault, there are a variety of issues to be addressed, as illustrated by the M.P.C. definition: "attempts by physical menace to put another in fear of imminent serious bodily injury." This definition relieves a prosecutor from proving: 1) that a victim suffered actual fear, and 2) that the victim's fear was caused by a particular means such as a threat, and 3) that a defendant had the "actual present ability" to cause fear. Even so, some potentially frightening conduct has been excluded from this definition,

namely the attempt to cause fear of non-imminent and/or non-serious bodily injury.

3. *Reckless endangerment crime*. The M.P.C. drafters proposed the creation of a crime to cover conduct that is not covered by the assault crimes, which implicitly are limited because of their requirements of high-level mental states, namely the intent to cause bodily or serious bodily injury, and the intent to put another in fear of serious bodily injury. Before the M.P.C., a number of specific crimes existed to cover particular types of endangerment, and the M.P.C. drafters sought to "replace the haphazard coverage of prior law with one comprehensive provision" to reach "any kind of conduct" that places other people in danger. M.P.C. § 211.2, comment (1), at 196 (1980). The crime is defined in § 211.2 as "recklessly" engaging in "conduct which places or may place another person in danger of death or serious bodily injury." This provision also explicitly provides an additional rule: "Recklessness and danger shall be presumed where a person knowingly points a firearm at or in the direction of another, whether or not the actor believes the firearm to be loaded."

4. *M.P.C revisions of assault*. M.P.C. § 211.1 uses the following revised definitions of common law assault:

> **(1) Simple Assault.** A person is guilty of assault if he:
>
> > (a) attempts to cause ... bodily injury to another; or
> >
> > (b) attempts by physical menace to put another in fear of imminent serious bodily injury.
>
> **(2) Aggravated Assault.** A person is guilty of aggravated assault if he:
>
> > (a) attempts to cause serious bodily injury to another ...; or
> >
> > (b) attempts to cause ... bodily injury to another with a deadly weapon.

Problems

1. *Anthony and the M.P.C. Assault Crimes*. Can the defendants in *Anthony* be convicted of any of the four M.P.C. § 211.1 crimes in Note 4 *supra*, which derive from the attempted-battery and frightening types of assault? Explain.

2. *Two Types of Assault*. Bell is a patient in the ward in a Veterans Administration Hospital. He is convicted of the crime of "assault" under 18 U.S.C. § 113(a) based on his conduct toward a female geriatric patient who was suffering from a mental disease that made her unable to comprehend what was going on. Bell's defense at trial is that because the victim was unable to form a "reasonable apprehension of bodily harm," he could not be convicted of assault. The federal statute does not provide a definition of "assault." Bell is convicted and appeals. *See United States v. Bell*, 505 F.2d 539 (7th Cir. 1974).

> a. *Attempted Battery*. If the court treats Bell's crime as an attempted-battery type of assault, what elements must be proved by the prosecutor?

Will it matter if the victim was unable to comprehend what was going on?

b. *Frightening*. If the court treats Bell's crime as a frightening type of assault, what elements must be proved for this crime? Will it matter if the victim was unable to comprehend what was going on?

3. *Reasonable Fear*. Some state statutes and precedents require that a prosecutor must show that a defendant's conduct would cause a "reasonable person" to be afraid of bodily injury, in order to convict the defendant of a frightening type of assault. Assume that a state supreme court is presented with the question whether to adopt this rule. The M.P.C. does not use this requirement. What are the pros and cons policy arguments that can be made on this issue?

4. *Mental State for Frightening Assault*. A car was parked in the break-down lane on a deserted stretch of I–89 near St. Alban's, Vermont, at sunset. A police officer stopped his patrol car to check to see whether the lone driver inside the car might need assistance. The driver was sitting in the driver's seat. The driver's window was open, the interior car light was on, and the driver's door was unlocked. As the officer approached the driver's door, he saw that a handgun was placed on the passenger's seat. So the officer opened the driver's door and asked the driver, Riley, to put both his hands on the wheel. Riley did so. Then the officer asked Riley to get out of the car but Riley refused, and so the officer ordered him out. Before Riley got out, the officer saw Riley's hand move toward the gun, and so the officer drew his own weapon and said, "Hold it right there!" Riley replied, "everything is cool, don't shoot," and brushed the gun off the passenger's seat and down on to the floor of the car. Then Riley got out of the car and the officer arrested him for assault. At trial, the officer testified that he had feared for his life because of Riley's conduct. Riley testified that he assumed that the officer had not seen the gun, and that he was attempting to hide the gun from the officer when he initially refused to get out of the car and then brushed the gun off the seat. Riley explained that he was afraid that if the officer saw the gun, he would become fearful and shoot Riley. Riley insisted that he never intended to frighten the officer. *Compare State v. Riley*, 141 Vt. 29, 442 A.2d 1297 (1982).

a. *M.P.C. in Vermont*. If Vermont uses the M.P.C definition of assault, "an attempt by physical menace to put another in fear of imminent serious bodily injury", was there sufficient evidence to convict Riley? How would you argue the case for both sides?

b. *Anthony in Vermont*. If Vermont uses the definition of a frightening assault that is applied in *Anthony*, was there sufficient evidence to convict Riley? How do the arguments for each side change in this situation, when compared to the M.P.C. scenario?

5. *Reckless Endangerment and Cocaine during Pregnancy* Assume that when baby Raymond is born in the county hospital in Baltimore, he has cocaine in his bloodstream. His mother Regina admits that she used cocaine during her

pregnancy. The prosecutor charges her with the crime of reckless endangerment for "recklessly engaging in conduct which places or may place another person in danger of death or serious bodily injury." The jury convicts and on appeal, the Maryland Court of Appeals must determine whether the crime of reckless endangerment is intended to encompass the conduct of the mother in using cocaine during her pregnancy. Explain why virtually all state courts have rejected the application of this particular crime to this scenario. *Compare Kilmon v. State*, 394 Md. 168, 905 A.2d 306 (2006).

NOTE

Definition of deadly or dangerous weapon. One of the most common elements used to define aggravated battery is the use of a "deadly weapon." The M.P.C. § 210(4) defines the term as "any firearm or other weapon, device, instrument, material or substance, whether animate or inanimate, which in the manner it is used or is intended to be used is known to be capable of producing death or serious bodily injury." Some state codes and courts use other generic definitions of dangerous weapons that may give rise to difficult questions of interpretation.

One example of a controversial interpretation of the "dangerous weapon" concept appears in *Commonwealth v. Shea*, 38 Mass.App.Ct. 7, 16, 644 N.E.2d 244, 249 (1995). The defendant in *Shea* invited two women, who were sunbathing on the banks of the Charles River, to come aboard his boat for a ride. Then the defendant headed out to the open sea. About five miles off shore from Boston, he made sexual advances which the two women rejected, and then he threw them overboard and sailed away. The women managed to swim toward a passing sailboat and were rescued. The defendant was convicted of a variety of crimes including battery with a dangerous weapon, specifically, the ocean. The *Shea* Court determined that state precedents implied that a "dangerous weapon" should be "an instrumentality which the batterer controlled, either through possession of or authority over it, for use of it in the intentional application of force." Therefore, the court concluded that since "the ocean in its natural state cannot be possessed or controlled, it is not an object or instrumentality capable of use as a weapon."

The *Shea* Court's interpretation was revised by a higher court in *Commonwealth v. Sexton*, 425 Mass. 146, 149–150, 680 N.E.2d 23, 24–25 (1997). The *Sexton* Court held that *Shea* gave "too narrow a reading" of the concept of "instrumentality" that did not recognize how "ordinarily innocuous items can be considered dangerous weapons when used ... in a dangerous manner." Therefore, it is not necessary "that, to be a dangerous weapon, the defendant must be able to wield the item at issue" and it is not relevant that the weapon "was present as part of the environment in which the defendant chose to participate in" an assault or battery. The *Sexton* Court noted that the ocean could be a dangerous weapon when used to inflict great harm in a particular manner, as when a defendant holds a victim's head underwater. However, the *Sexton* Court did not disagree with the *Shea* result, opining that "the danger posed by the ocean [in *Shea*] was not a result of the defendant bringing his victims into contact with" the ocean. Instead, the danger was only a result of "the circumstances which followed when he deserted them, five miles from shore."

PROBLEMS

1. *Deadly Ocean.* Assume that the Rhode Island Supreme Court must decide whether to follow the reasoning of the *Sexton* Court and endorse the result in *Shea*, in a case with similar facts. What pro and con policy arguments can be made by the defense counsel and prosecutor concerning the need to apply the definition of "dangerous instrumentality" in the way described by the *Sexton* Court?

2. *Falling Victim.* Samuel was angry at his neighbor Gar, who was standing on his lawn next to his driveway. Gar was wearing a jacket and Samuel quickly pulled the jacket up over Gar's back and over his head so that his face was covered. Then Samuel pushed Gar so that he fell to the ground. Gar's torso landed on the lawn but his head landed on his concrete driveway. Gar sustained serious head injuries. Samuel was prosecuted for the crime of "aggravated battery" defined as "battery by means of a dangerous weapon." The code does not define the term "battery" or the terms "dangerous weapon." Samuel is convicted and appeals on the grounds that there was insufficient evidence for a conviction. What arguments will the defense counsel and prosecutor make on this issue? *Compare Commonwealth v. Sexton*, 425 Mass. 146, 680 N.E.2d 23 (1997).

3. *Special Circumstances and Dangerous Weapons.* Some legislatures choose to identify particular circumstances where the use of a dangerous weapon establishes a special crime. For example, a Maine statute punishes the crime of "assault while hunting" when a person, "while in the pursuit of wild game or game birds, with criminal negligence, causes bodily injury to another with the use of a dangerous weapon." Me. Rev. Stat. Ann., tit. 17A, § 208A (1977). Identify other circumstances where a legislature might find it necessary for policy reasons to define a particular scenario as an assault or battery crime involving a dangerous weapon.

NOTE

Consent as defense to battery or assault. Consent is rarely a defense to crimes that result in bodily injury, and one reason is because "society has an interest in punishing [such crimes] as breaches of the public peace and order so that an individual cannot consent to a wrong that is committed against the public peace." *State v. Shelley*, 85 Wash.App. 24, 29, 929 P.2d 489, 491–492 (1997). Another reason is that consent cannot be a defense to activities that are "against public policy"; thus, "a child cannot consent to hazing [and] a gang member cannot consent to an initiation beating." *State v. Hiott*, 97 Wash.App.

825, 828, 987 P.2d 135, 136–137 (1999). However, some states have codified the M.P.C.'s provision in § 211(2)(b) recognizing the consent defense when "the conduct and the injury are reasonably foreseeable hazards of joint participation in a lawful athletic contest or competitive sport." The *Shelley* Court adopted this rule as case law doctrine, because "[i]f consent cannot be a defense to [battery], then most athletic contests would need to be banned. . . ." When the consent defense is raised, the prosecutor may rebut it by arguing: 1) that the injury did not occur "as a by-product of the game itself"; or 2) that the defendant's conduct was not "foreseeable behavior in the play of the game." To make the latter determination of foreseeability, a court will look to evidence "about the nature of the game, the participants' expectations, the location where the game has been played, as well as the rules of the game." *Shelley*, 85 Wash.App. at 32–33, 929 P.2d at 493. The *Hiott* Court opined that the consent defense should be limited to games that are "accepted by society as lawful athletic contests" or "competitive sports", which "carry with them generally accepted rules, at least some of which are intended to prevent or minimize injuries", and which "commonly prescribe the use of protective devices or clothing to prevent injuries." *Hiott*, 97 Wash.App. at 828, 987 P.2d at 136.

PROBLEMS

1. *Basketball Scenarios*. Assume that Jane and Marie collide in mid-air when both of them leap up to try to snag a rebound during a pick up game of basketball on a city playground. When both fall to the ground, Jane is slightly bruised but Marie breaks her arm. If Jane is prosecuted for aggravated battery for causing serious bodily harm to Marie, what arguments can Jane's defense counsel make to obtain a consent instruction under *Shelley*? If Jane and Marie both landed on their feet without falling down, and then Jane bumped Marie hard with her hip, causing Marie to fall to the ground and break her arm, how would the defense counsel's arguments change concerning the requested consent instruction?

2. *Whitfield and Consent Defense*. In the *Whitfield* case, the trial judge denied the defense counsel's request for a jury instruction on consent, thus precluding the defendant from arguing the consent defense. On appeal, the defense counsel relied on the Washington precedent of *Shelley* to analogize HIV exposure during a consensual sexual encounter to an assault during a sporting event, arguing that "the risk of contracting a gamut of sexually transmitted diseases—including HIV—is eminently foreseeable and an inherent part of engaging in unprotected sex." The appellate court found it unnecessary to determine whether consent may sometimes be a defense to the first degree assault crime in *Whitfield*, and held that the trial judge properly refused to consider a consent defense on the facts. What reasons could the appellate court use to support this conclusion?

C. MODERN VARIANTS OF ASSAULT & BATTERY

1. STALKING

STATE v. SIMONE

152 N.H. 755, 887 A.2d 135 (2005).

DALIANIS, J.

[In] 2001, Coral Olson was employed by the U.S. Census Bureau as a field service representative. Olson traveled door-to-door to conduct census surveys. She would then re-contact the same respondents by telephone and by personal visit until she had obtained sufficient survey information. In January 2001, Olson went to the [Simone's] home to conduct a census survey. Olson gave [Simone] her business card with her home phone number, and conducted several follow-up telephone calls and one follow-up personal visit to complete the census survey. After [Simone] completed his census survey, however, he continued to call Olson. [Simone] told Olson that he was interested in her; Olson responded that she was married and not interested in him. Nevertheless [he] persisted in calling her. [She] did not initiate any of these personal telephone calls. [She] told him not to contact her. If she did not answer the telephone, [Simone] would call repeatedly and leave messages each time until she finally answered. . . .

In August 2001, Olson contacted the Temple Police Department[,] met with Officer Steven Duval [and] expressed her desire that [Simone] cease contact. On August 18, 2001, Officer Duval spoke with [Simone] about the situation. Nonetheless, [Simone] continued to pursue Olson [and so] Olson obtained a protective order prohibiting [Simone] from contacting her. Notwithstanding the protective order, [Simone] continued to call her. Olson testified that between the fall of 2001 and June 2003, [Simone] placed more unwanted calls to her than she could estimate [and] also sent [her] packages, which she did not open. As a result, Olson frequently contacted the Temple police.

On June 11, 2003, [Simone] called Olson [and] she again told [him] not to contact her [but] he called back and left [three] lengthy messages on Olson's answering machine. [In his first message, he said,] "that he had a lot of anger towards [her]." [In his second message, he] admitted that he had previously misrepresented himself to Olson's husband in order to obtain personal information about her and about her marriage. [Then he] said, "I don't care if the police come and arrest me. I don't care if I go to court. And I don't care if I get seven years or 70 years. This means so much to me to tell you that I'm terribly sorry and remorseful and I don't care if I rot in hell. And I know I will die in, in jail. . . ." [In his third message, he said:]

[I] honestly don't care and I've made the decision now. I know this is very severe and even stupid of me to call you, but I basically don't care because I, I consider on August the 13th of 2001 when you broke up with me, that my life had changed drastically. It's not gotten any better and I realize that was like, you know, that was like the nail in the coffin for me. I, I'm already dead and jail is just a place to finalize that act.

[Simone also said that even though] he "was terribly, terribly sorry over the bad things that he did . . . it was worth rotting in jail for, and [he] would do it again in a heartbeat." He said that "he had a lot of demons inside" but that . . . [he] "never entertained the thoughts of hurting [Olson]." He also admitted that he was stopped [by the police] while traveling to her home late at night.

After listening to these messages, Olson called the police department and Officer Duval came to her home. Olson received another call from [Simone] just as Officer Duval arrived. Officer Duval took the telephone and spoke with [Simone] for about 20 minutes [and then Simone] called again and left a fourth message. . . . [stating] that he would be "prosecuted and face a felony charge" and [that] he would pray for Olson every night. Officer Duval left [and] returned [30 minutes later] to respond to a 911 call made by Olson. . . .

Olson arrived home on June 17, 2003 to find twenty new messages [left by Simone during a two-hour period] on her answering machine. [In his messages, Simone said that] he was "sorry it had come to this"[,] . . . implored Olson "not to return the things that are coming in the mail"[,] . . . [and said] that he was sorry that he did not have her anymore [and] that he lost everything that he loved. . . . [In sixteen of the messages, Simone repeatedly asked Olson if she was present in her home and begged her to answer the telephone.] [Olson] immediately called the police department and Officer Duval came to her home. [On June 18] Olson called Officer Duval to report that she had received two packages from [Simone]. On June 24, Olson reported to Officer Duval that she had received yet another package and a letter from [Simone, who] continued to call. . . .

In October 2003, a [county grand jury] indicted [Simone] on one count of stalking under [a New Hampshire statute] which criminalizes "knowingly . . . engag[ing] in a course of conduct targeted at a specific person which would cause a reasonable person to fear for his or her personal safety . . . and the person is actually placed in such fear." . . . On appeal, [Simone] argues [that] the State failed to present sufficient evidence to support the jury's verdict. . . . that his conduct: (1) would cause a reasonable person to fear for his or her personal safety; and (2) actually placed Olson in fear for her personal safety. . . .

[Simone] argues that we must interpret the phrase, "fear for his or her personal safety," as used in the stalking statute, to require a fear of physical violence. We need not reach [this] argument, however, because even if [this is so,] the evidence was sufficient to [satisfy this definition].

[Simone] contends that his conduct would not cause a reasonable person to fear physical violence because he never assaulted Olson or explicitly threatened her with violence, and he "mostly apologized and expressed his continuing love" in his repeated telephone calls to her. We disagree.... [A] reasonable person could view [Simone's] unrelenting telephone calls and gifts to Olson, especially in light of [Simone's] emotional instability, as evidence that [he] was obsessed with Olson and posed a threat of physical violence to her. [He had told Olson that he had "serious personal problems" and felt suicidal and out of control.] [Simone] and Olson never had a personal relationship.... [In light of all the evidence,] we conclude that there was sufficient evidence to prove beyond a reasonable doubt that [Simone's] conduct would cause a reasonable person to fear for his or her personal safety.

Next, [Simone] argues the State failed to prove that his conduct caused Olson actually to fear for her personal safety. At trial, the State asked Olson about the impact of [Simone's] conduct upon her. Olson answered, "I live in fear every day. I don't know—I don't know what's going to happen next, or what [the defendant is] going to do." Both Olson and Officer Duval testified that Olson frequently contacted the police between August 2001 and June 2003 as a result of [Simone's] conduct. [The] trial court twice noted that Olson's testimony and demeanor on the witness stand ... gave rise to a reasonable inference that Olson actually feared the defendant. [In light of all the evidence, we conclude] that there was sufficient evidence beyond a reasonable doubt that [Simone's] conduct actually caused Olson to fear for her personal safety. Accordingly, the jury properly convicted the defendant of stalking....

NOTES

1. *History of stalking statutes.* The first stalking statute was enacted in California in 1990 after five women were murdered by their stalkers. These statutes now exist in all state criminal codes. In 1996, the crime of interstate stalking was added to the federal statute criminalizing acts of domestic violence in 18 U.S.C. § 2261. The goal of stalking statutes is to address the harmful features of stalking behavior that are not addressed by assault and related crimes. Such crimes are concerned with single incidents whereas a stalking statute focuses on repeated behavior that causes fear of bodily injury to the victim, in the absence of oral or written threats and where evidence of the intention to cause fear may be lacking. In theory, a stalking statute makes

it possible for police to intervene before a stalker takes violent action; it also imposes more serious penalties to attempt to deter stalking behavior. Legislatures have continued to amend their stalking statutes in order to take account of criticisms and enforcement problems with the earliest versions of these laws. See Jennifer L. Bradfield, Note, *Anti-Stalking Laws: Do They Adequately Protect Stalking Victims?*, 21 Harv. Women's L.J. 229, 240–245 (1998).

2.   *Behavior of stalkers.* Some stalking statutes identify particular types of unconsented contact that causes fear and emotional distress to victims. Such contact includes the conduct of: 1) communication with the victim (via telephone, mail, fax, email, and the internet); 2) following the victim; 3) appearing within sight of the victim, at a residence or workplace or in other locations; 4) approaching the victim; 5) leaving objects for the victim to find. In 1998, a report to Congress provided data suggesting that "at least one million women and 370,000 men are stalked annually—almost five times as many as previously estimated"; an estimated 87% of stalkers in this data were men and "the average stalking lasted more than eighteen months." ELIZA-BETH M. SCHNEIDER, CHERYL HANNA, JUDITH G. GREENBERG, and CLAIRE DALTON, DOMESTIC VIOLENCE AND THE LAW: THEORY AND PRACTICE 282 (2d ed. 2008). According to one estimate, "at least half the women who try to terminate abusive relationships are harassed or stalked", and "[a]n estimated ninety percent of women killed by their intimate partners have been stalked first." Lisa Nolen Birmingham, Note, *Closing the Loophole: Vermont's Legislative Response to Stalking*, 18 Vt. L. Rev. 477, 478 (1994). Some studies have divided stalkers into groups. One group includes the "erotomanic" and "love obsessional" stalkers, who have deluded beliefs that their victims love them, even though their victims have had no contact or only superficial contact with them. A second group includes the "simple obsessional" stalker, whose actual prior relationship with the victim has ended; these stalkers believe that they were wronged or mistreated by the victim and they seek revenge and control over the victim in the manner of batterers. Birmingham, *supra*, at 490.

3.   *Elements of stalking statutes.* In 1993, the National Institute of Justice developed a "Model Anti–Stalking Code" which has been influential in some states. This code identifies a variety of elements that should be addressed in any stalking statute, but most of these elements will not be defined the same way in all state codes. Most stalking statutes use these elements: a defendant's "course of conduct" is "directed at a specific person", which conduct causes "fear" in the victim, and which is "repeated" at least twice. Some states also provide a list of prohibited acts, and require a "credible threat" from the defendant, the intent to cause fear in the victim, and "reasonable fear" in the victim. However, most states take the approach of the model code, which is intended to cover "threats implied by conduct" and does not use the term "credible threat", which could be construed too narrowly to require an oral or written threat. Some states follow the code in criminalizing conduct directed toward the victim's immediate family, and in requiring only that the defendant *should* know that his or her conduct will cause fear. Critics argue

that the code's weaknesses include the failure to define "fear" to include fear of sexual assault, and failure to include conduct directed at a person in an intimate relationship with a victim who does not reside in the victim's household. Bradfield, *supra*, at 247–254.

4. *Impact of stalking statutes.* The *Simone* case illustrates some of the difficulties involved in enforcing stalking laws. Some data in a National Violence Against Women Survey shows that roughly 45% of victims may not report stalking conduct to the police, and that police reports may not generate prosecutions in 75% of cases. When victims obtain restraining orders, "69% of women and 81% of men . . . reported the stalker had subsequently violated the order." When stalking behavior stopped and victims were asked to explain why, 15% attributed this event to police warnings and 9% to the arrest of the stalker, whereas 19% of victims said that stalking stopped because they moved away and 18% said the stalker had a new partner. "Less than 2% thought that a conviction or a restraining order had ended the stalking." CLAIRE DALTON and ELIZABETH M. SCHNEIDER, BATTERED WOMEN AND THE LAW 668 (2001).

PROBLEMS

1. *Different Messages and Conduct.* Assume that the messages left by the defendant in *Simone* did not mention his personal problems, suicidal and out-of-control feelings, anger toward Olson, or comments about dying in jail. Assume also that there was no evidence that the defendant misrepresented himself to Olson's husband to obtain personal information, and that he was never stopped by the police while traveling to Olson's home at night. Based on the other evidence in the case, how would the prosecutor argue that there was sufficient evidence to convict the defendant of the stalking crime?

2. *Revising Stalking Statutes.* Mandy Petersen is eighteen-years-old and she works at a restaurant on the shift from 6:00 pm until midnight. One night when she leaves the restaurant at midnight, she notices that a man is sitting in a pick-up truck with the engine running; this truck and Mandy's car are the only vehicles in the parking lot outside the restaurant. The street is deserted. As Mandy walks to her car, the man shouts very loudly to her, "Come on, pretty baby, go down on me! Come here! Now!" Mandy ignores the man, gets into her car, and drives away. When she looks in her rear view mirror, she notices that the man has driven his car out of the parking lot and is taking the same route as Mandy. After driving for ten blocks, Mandy sees the man put on his turn signal and turn right at the next block. Then his truck disappears from view. The next evening, Mandy is working in the restaurant when the phone rings at 9:00 p.m., and Mandy's co-worker Jack picks up the phone. A voice says, "I want to speak to Mandy Petersen. This is the guy in the truck from last night." When Jack turns to Mandy to hand her the phone, he repeats what the caller said, and Mandy can hear the caller shouting, "If she doesn't get on the phone right now, tell her I will catch up with her later!" Mandy shakes her head and signals to Jack that he should

hang up the phone. At midnight when Mandy leaves the restaurant, she sees that the same man is parked in his truck again in the parking lot. So Mandy retreats into the restaurant and after a minute, the man drives away. Mandy calls the police department and when an officer arrives at the restaurant, Mandy describes the man's conduct. She also tells the officer that she is afraid that the man is stalking her and may attack her physically or rape her.

a. *1995 Statute*. Assume that the man, who is named Tony, is prosecuted for the crime of stalking under a statute that provides as follows:

> A person is guilty of stalking if he or she purposely *and* repeatedly follows another person and engages in a course of conduct *or* makes a credible threat with the intent of placing that person in reasonable fear of death or great bodily injury.
>
> > (1) "Course of conduct" means a knowing and wilful course of conduct directed at a specific person, composed of a series of acts over a period of time, however short, evidencing a continuity of purpose which alarms or annoys that person and which serves no legitimate purpose. The course of conduct must be such as to cause a reasonable person to suffer emotional distress.
> >
> > (2) "Credible threat" means an explicit *or* implicit threat made with the intent *and* the apparent ability to carry out the threat, so as to cause the person who is the target of the threat to reasonably fear for his or her safety.

Assume that Tony is convicted and that you are the law clerk for one of the judges who will hear Tony's appeal. Your judge asks you: 1) to explain whether the evidence is sufficient to convict Tony of all the elements of the 1995 stalking crime, and 2) to identify any debatable issues of statutory interpretation that may arise in this case.

b. *Amended 2005 Statute*. Assume that Tony is prosecuted instead under an amended stalking statute that provides as follows:

> A person is guilty of stalking if he or she:
>
> > (A) Purposefully engages in a course of conduct directed at a specific person that would cause a reasonable person to fear bodily injury, *and*;
> >
> > (B) Knowingly, recklessly, or negligently places the specific person in reasonable fear of bodily injury;
> >
> > > (1) "Course of conduct" means repeatedly maintaining a visual or physical proximity to a person *or* repeatedly conveying verbal or written threats or threats implied by conduct or a combination thereof directed at or toward a person;
> > >
> > > (2) "Repeatedly" means on two or more occasions.

Assume that Tony is convicted and appeals, Again, your judge asks you: 1) to explain whether the evidence is sufficient to convict Tony of all the elements of the 2005 stalking crime, and 2) to identify any debatable issues of statutory interpretation that may arise in this case.

2. DOMESTIC ASSAULT

There are many crimes that may be committed during the course of abusive behavior by a person who fits a modern definition of a "family or household member of the victim", which could include "a spouse, a person living as a spouse, or a former spouse" or other relationships. These crimes include murder or manslaughter, negligent homicide, rape or sexual assault, assault and battery (possibly with a dangerous weapon), burglary or breaking and entering, criminal trespass, disorderly conduct, disturbing the peace, willful and malicious destruction of property, harassment (including harassing phone calls), violation of a restraining order, intimidation of a witness, and a variety of attempt crimes. See ELIZABETH SCHNEIDER, CHERYL HANNA, JUDITH G. GREENBERG, and CLAIRE DALTON, DOMESTIC VIOLENCE AND THE LAW: THEORY AND PRACTICE 275–276 (2d ed. 2008).

In 1977 the California legislature enacted the separate felony crime of "domestic violence" to cover "the infliction of injury on spouse, cohabitee or parent of a child" of the defendant. Many state codes now include such crimes and define them in a variety of ways. For example, the Vermont legislature enacted a Domestic Assault statute in 1993 with three degrees of the crime. The lowest degree of the crime imposes a maximum punishment of one year in jail for attempting to cause or recklessly causing bodily injury to a family or household member, or for wilfully causing such a victim to fear imminent serious bodily injury. The aggravated second degree crime allows for a five-year prison sentence for committing a second domestic assault offense or for committing a first offense that violates a restraining order issued by the criminal court. The aggravated first degree crime applies when a person commits domestic assault while armed with a deadly weapon, commits domestic assault after having been convicted of this crime, or attempts to cause or recklessly causes serious bodily injury to the victim. See VT. STAT. ANN. tit. 13 §§ 1042, 1043, 1044 (1993).

When Congress enacted the Violent Crime Control and Law Enforcement Act of 1994, this statute included The Violence Against Women Act of 1994 (VAWA), which "federalized the enforcement of restraining orders by requiring that states provide full faith and credit to orders issued by sister states [and] also criminalized interstate violations of restraining orders." Schneider et al., *supra*, at 355. The VAWA also made "interstate domestic violence" a federal crime that encompasses all "intimate partners" and "dating partners". Interstate stalking was added to the list of crimes in this provision in 1996. *Id.* The statutory definition of interstate domestic violence in 18 U.S.C. § 2261 provides as follows:

(a) Offenses—

(1) Crossing a State line—A person who travels across a State line or enters or leaves Indian country with the intent to injure, harass, or intimidate that person's spouse, intimate partner, or dating partner and who, in the course of or as a result of such travel, intentionally commits a crime of violence and thereby causes bodily injury to such spouse or intimate partner, shall be punished [as provided].

(2) Causing the crossing of a State line—A person who causes a spouse, intimate partner, or dating partner to cross a State line or to enter or leave Indian country by force, coercion, duress, or fraud and, in the course or as a result of that conduct, intentionally commits a crime of violence and thereby causes bodily injury to the person's spouse or intimate partner, shall be punished [as provided].

The penalty for the § 2261 crime depends on the injuries to the victim. A sentence of life or any term of years may be imposed if the victim dies; a maximum sentence of 20 years is allowed if the victim suffers permanent disfigurement or life-threatening bodily injury. A maximum sentence of 10 years applies if a dangerous weapon is used or if the victim suffers serious bodily injury. Otherwise, the maximum sentence is five years. See generally Schneider et al., *supra*, at 356–358 (quoting excerpts from Michelle Easterling, *For Better or Worse: The Federalization of Domestic Violence*, 98 W. Va. L. Rev. 933 (1996)).

NOTE

"Defense of Marriage" Provisions. In some states, the enactment of "Defense of Marriage" statutes or state constitutional provisions has sparked challenges to the enforcement of the state's domestic assault statute. For example, the "Marriage Amendment" to Ohio's state constitution provides that, "Only a union between one man and one woman may be a marriage valid in or recognized by this state and its political subdivisions ... [which] shall not create or recognize a legal status for relationships of unmarried individuals that intends to approximate the design, qualities, significance or effect of marriage." Section 11, Article IV, Ohio Constitution. The Ohio criminal code's "domestic violence" crime is defined as "recklessly" causing harm to a "family or household member", which includes "a person living as a spouse." The Ohio Supreme Court held that the statute did not conflict with the Amendment in *State v. Carswell*, 114 Ohio St.3d 210, 871 N.E.2d 547 (2007).

PROBLEMS

1. *Domestic Assault Crimes.* Describe the various policy reasons that may explain why state legislatures have enacted "domestic assault" crimes like those in Vermont, and the impact that such crimes could have on the criminal justice system.

2. *Beating before Travel.* Assume that a defendant is convicted of the federal crime of "interstate domestic violence" under 18 U.S.C. § 2261, set forth in the text *supra*. The facts show that the defendant's acts of physical violence, when he beat the victim for several hours, occurred before interstate travel began. Only after the beating did the defendant put the injured and disabled victim in his car and cross a state line. The defense counsel argues that the prosecutor cannot satisfy the elements of the statute. What statutory interpretation arguments can the prosecutor make to persuade a court to uphold the conviction? See *United States v. Page*, 167 F.3d 325 (6th Cir. 1999).

CHAPTER 10

RAPE AND SEXUAL ASSAULT

■ ■ ■

The common law crime of rape was a capital offense and it was defined as an act of sexual intercourse by means of genital penetration, by a man of a woman not his wife, through the use of force or by threat of force, without the consent of the victim. This definition was reflected in the statutory law of most states until the 1970s. Courts required a prosecutor to prove that the victim resisted the sexual act "to the utmost" and reported the crime promptly. Corroborating evidence was required to support the victim's testimony, and jurors were instructed in the words of Lord Hale that they should give special scrutiny to the victim's testimony because rape "is an accusation easily to be made and hard to be proved, and harder to be defended by the party accused." Evidence of the victim's sexual reputation and prior sexual experiences could be offered by the defendant to show that her "lack of chastity" showed that she was more likely to fabricate a claim of rape or to consent to forcible sex.

In 1975 the Michigan legislature enacted the first "rape reform" statute and thereby launched a widespread movement for statutory change in the definitions of the elements of rape crimes and the evidentiary rules governing rape trials. The new statutes typically redefined the rape crime as gender neutral, and expanded the scope of the crime to include acts of sexual penetration by fingers or objects, and oral or anal sexual acts. Some statutes eliminated the "resistance" requirement and "lack of consent" element, and allowed conviction when sexual intercourse was accomplished by "fear" instead of "force." New evidence code provisions in "rape shield laws" required the exclusion of evidence of the victim's prior sexual conduct with persons other than the defendant. Courts and legislatures abolished the corroboration requirement, the prompt report requirement, and the Lord Hale instruction. Even the marital rape exemption was abandoned or limited. Many statutes established new crimes to allow convictions for lesser degrees of rape, thus expanding the scope of criminal sexual conduct. The large variety of statutory changes required courts to revise their interpretations of rape crime elements and defenses, to design new jury instructions, and to revise "sufficiency of the evidence" standards for conviction. Some statutes use the term "sexual assault" instead of "rape." In this chapter, these terms will be used synonymously unless otherwise indicated.

A. FORCIBLE RAPE

1. ACTUS REUS: FORCE AND LACK OF CONSENT

The two most important actus reus elements for the common law crime of forcible rape were "force" and "lack of consent." While it is useful to study these elements separately, it is important to recognize the historical connections between them that influence modern judicial interpretations of their meaning. Some judges define these two elements as being intertwined, as when the term "force" is described as "force used to overcome the victim's nonconsent." Evidence of one element sometimes may be treated as supplying proof of the other. Today the most serious rape crimes are likely to include the elements of "force," "threat of force," or "fear." When the "lack of consent" element is not included in a statute, courts recognize the "affirmative defense" of "consent" for the most serious rape crimes.

a. FORCE, THREAT, OR FEAR

At common law, the courts looked to the victim to supply evidence of the defendant's use of unlawful "force," as illustrated by the "utmost resistance" requirement. Proof of such resistance persuaded judges that a defendant's use of "force" was sufficiently harmful to justify conviction, and that a victim's claim of rape was credible. Without proof of resistance, judges treated the use of force to accomplish sexual intercourse as an ambiguous event that should be characterized as "seduction" rather than "rape." Over time, courts replaced the "utmost resistance" requirement with the concept of "sufficient resistance" under the circumstances, depending on the character of the "force" or "threat of force." Some judges even recognized that either violent force or a threat of violence could explain a victim's submission to sexual intercourse without resistance. This insight led to the expansion of the "force" concept to include the defendant's provocation of a victim's "reasonable fear", which could justify conviction in the absence of a victim's physical resistance. In the pre-reform era, however, courts and legislatures usually required proof of fear of imminent death or serious bodily injury.

At the outset of the rape reform era, some judges began to question the appropriateness of the resistance requirement on policy grounds, arguing that women should not be forced to risk death or injury in order to provide the prosecutor with evidence that a rape occurred. Courts began to accept proof of verbal resistance as a substitute for physical resistance, and to look more closely at the defendant's actions, rather than the victim's actions, in assessing the existence of "force." As new elements were added to the emerging range of rape definitions in statutes, courts took on the task of redefining the concepts of force, threat, fear, and resistance. Their decisions often evidenced sharp disagreements, and the subsequent codifications of contested holdings provided a continuing supply of statutory interpretation controversies, which illustrate the evolving cultural definitions of rape.

PEOPLE v. INIGUEZ

7 Cal.4th 847, 872 P.2d 1183, 30 Cal.Rptr.2d 258 (1994) (In Bank).

Opinion by ARABIAN, J., with LUCAS, C. J., MOSK, KENNARD, BAXTER and GEORGE, JJ., and Spencer J., concurring.

[The] Court of Appeal reversed the defendant's conviction for rape on the grounds that the evidence of force or fear of immediate and unlawful bodily injury was insufficient. We granted review to determine whether there was sufficient evidence to support the verdict, and to delineate the relationship between evidence of fear and the requirement under Penal Code section 261 [that] sexual intercourse be "accomplished against a person's will" in a case where lack of consent is not disputed.

[On] June 15, 1990, the eve of her wedding, at approximately 8:30 p.m., 22–year–old Mercy P. arrived at the home of Sandra S., a close family friend [who] was to stand in at [Mercy's] wedding the next day for Mercy's mother[.] Mercy was planning to spend the night at [Sandra's] home [and Mercy] met defendant, Sandra's fiancé, for the first time that evening. Defendant was scheduled to stand in for Mercy's father during the wedding. Mercy noticed that defendant was somewhat "tipsy" when he arrived. He had consumed a couple of beers and a pint of Southern Comfort.... Mercy, Sandra, and defendant celebrated Mercy's impending wedding by having dinner and drinking some wine. There was no flirtation or any remarks of a sexual nature between defendant and Mercy at any time during the evening. [Around] 11:30 p.m., Mercy went to bed in the living room. She slept on top of her sleeping bag. She was wearing pants with an attached skirt, and a shirt. She fell asleep at approximately midnight.

Mercy was awakened between 1:00 and 2:00 a.m. when she heard some movements behind her. She was lying on her stomach, and saw defendant, who was naked, approach her from behind. Without saying anything, defendant pulled down her pants, fondled her buttocks, and inserted his penis inside her. Mercy weighed 105 pounds. Defendant weighed approximately 205 pounds. Mercy was afraid, so "I just laid there.".... Less than a minute later, defendant ejaculated, got off her, and walked back to the bedroom....

Officer Fragoso, who interviewed Mercy several days after the attack, testified that she told him she had not resisted defendant's sexual assault because, "She said she knew that the man had been drinking. She hadn't met him before; he was a complete stranger to her. When she realized what was going on, she said she panicked, she froze. She was afraid that if she said or did anything, his reaction could be of a violent nature. So she decided just to [lie] still, wait until it was over with and then get out of the house as quickly as she could and get to her [fiancé] *and tell him what happened*."

Mercy immediately telephoned her fiancé Gary and left a message for him. She then telephoned her best friend Pam, who testified that Mercy was so distraught she was barely comprehensible. Mercy asked Pam to pick her up, grabbed her purse and shoes, and ran out of the apartment. Mercy hid in the bushes outside [for] approximately half an hour while waiting for Pam because she was terrified defendant would look for her.

Pam arrived about 30 minutes later, and drove Mercy to Pam's house. Mercy sat on Pam's kitchen floor, her back to the wall, and asked Pam, "Do I look like the word 'rape' [is] written on [my] face?" Mercy wanted to take a shower because she "felt dirty," but was dissuaded by Pam. Pam telephoned Gary, who called [the police]. Gary and his best man then drove Mercy to the hospital, where a "rape examination" was performed. [Blood and semen were found in Mercy's vagina and on her underpants.]

The following day, Mercy and Gary married.... Neither Sandra nor defendant participated in the wedding. [The defendant] was arrested the same day. When asked by the arresting officer if he had had sexual intercourse with Mercy, defendant replied, "I guess I did, yes."

Dr. Charles Nelson, a psychologist, testified as an expert on "rape trauma syndrome." He stated that victims respond in a variety of ways to the trauma of being raped. Some try to flee, and others are paralyzed by fear. This latter response he termed "frozen fright."

Defendant conceded at trial that the sexual intercourse was nonconsensual. However, defense counsel argued [to the jury] that the element of force or fear was absent[:] "It's a situation where it looks to him like he can get away with it and a situation where his judgment [has] flown out the window.... He keeps doing it, probably without giving much thought to it, but certainly there is nothing there to indicate using fear ever entered his mind. What he was doing was taking advantage, in a drunken way, of a situation where somebody appeared to be out of it."

The jury was instructed on both rape [and] sexual battery. [Rape was defined under Penal Code § 261(2), as "an act of sexual intercourse accomplished with a person not the spouse of the perpetrator,

[w]here it is accomplished against a person's will by means of force, violence, or fear of immediate and unlawful bodily injury on the person of another."] [The] court [also] instructed in relevant part, " '[F]ear' means, a feeling of alarm or disquiet caused by the expectation of danger, pain, disaster or the like." "Verbal threats are not critical to a finding of fear of unlawful injury, threats can be implied from the circumstances or inferred from the assailant's conduct. A victim may entertain a reasonable fear even where the assailant does not threaten by words or deed." [The] jury found defendant guilty of rape. He was sentenced to state prison for the midterm of six years.

The Court of Appeal reversed, concluding that there was insufficient evidence that the act of sexual intercourse was accomplished by means of force or fear of immediate and unlawful bodily injury. On the issue of fear, the court stated: "While the [defendant] was admittedly much larger than the small victim, he did nothing to suggest that he intended to injure her. No coarse or sexually suggestive conversation had taken place. Nothing of an abusive or threatening nature had occurred. The victim was sleeping in her aunt's house, in which screams presumably would have raised the aunt and interrupted the intercourse. Although the assailant was a stranger to the victim, she knew nothing about him which would suggest that he was violent. [The] event of intercourse [was] singularly unusual in terms of its ease of facilitation, causing no struggle, no injury, no abrasions or other marks, and lasting, as the victim testified, 'maybe a minute.' " ...

The test on appeal for determining if substantial evidence supports a conviction is whether "a reasonable trier of fact could have found the prosecution sustained its burden of proving the defendant guilty beyond a reasonable doubt." In making this determination, we "must view the evidence in a light most favorable to [the prosecution] and presume in support of the judgment the existence of every fact the trier could reasonably deduce from the evidence." *People v. Johnson*, 26 Cal. 3d 557, 576 (1980).

Prior to 1980, section 261 "defined rape as an act of sexual intercourse under circumstances where the person resists, but where 'resistance is overcome by force or violence' or where 'a person is prevented from resisting by threats of great and immediate bodily harm, accompanied by apparent power of execution....' " *People v. Barnes*, 42 Cal.3d 284 (1986). Under the former law, a person was required to either resist or be prevented from resisting because of threats.

Section 261 was amended in 1980 to eliminate both the resistance requirement and the requirement that the threat of immediate bodily harm be accompanied by an apparent power to inflict the harm. As the legislative history explains, "threat is eliminated and the victim need only fear harm. The standard for injury is reduced from great and immediate bodily harm to immediate and unlawful bodily injury."

In discussing the significance of the 1980 amendments in *Barnes*, we noted that "studies have demonstrated that while some women respond to sexual assault with active resistance, others 'freeze,'" and "become helpless from panic and numbing fear." *Barnes, supra,* 42 Cal.3d at 299. In response to this information, "For the first time, the Legislature has assigned the decision as to whether a sexual assault should be resisted to the realm of personal choice." "By removing resistance as a prerequisite to a rape conviction, the Legislature has brought the law of rape into conformity with other crimes such as robbery, kidnapping and assault, which require force, fear, and nonconsent to convict. In these crimes, the law does not expect falsity from the complainant who alleges their commission and thus demand resistance as a corroboration and predicate to conviction."

[The] deletion of the resistance language from section 261 by the 1980 amendments thus effected a change in the purpose of evidence of fear of immediate and unlawful injury. Prior to 1980, evidence of fear was directly linked to resistance; the prosecution was required to demonstrate that a person's *resistance* had been overcome by force, or that a person was prevented from resisting by threats of great and immediate bodily harm. As a result of the amendments, evidence of fear is now directly linked to the overbearing of a victim's will; the prosecution is required to demonstrate that the act of sexual intercourse was accomplished against the person's *will* by means of force, violence, or fear of immediate and unlawful bodily injury.

In *Barnes*, [we] addressed the question of the role of force or fear of immediate and unlawful bodily injury in the absence of a resistance requirement. We stated that "[a]lthough resistance is no longer the touchstone of the element of force, the reviewing court still looks to the circumstances of the case, including the presence of verbal or nonverbal threats, or the kind of force that might reasonably induce fear in the mind of the victim, to ascertain sufficiency of the evidence of a conviction under [§ 261(2)]." "Additionally, the complainant's conduct must be measured against the degree of force manifested or in light of whether her fears were genuine and reasonably grounded." "In some circumstances, even a complainant's unreasonable fear of immediate and unlawful bodily injury may suffice to sustain a conviction [under § 261(2)] if the accused knowingly takes advantage of that fear in order to accomplish sexual intercourse."

[Thus,] the element of fear of immediate and unlawful bodily injury has two components, one subjective and one objective. The subjective component asks whether a victim genuinely entertained a fear of immediate and unlawful bodily injury sufficient to induce her to submit to sexual intercourse against her will. In order to satisfy this component, the extent or seriousness of the injury feared is immaterial.

In addition, the prosecution must satisfy the objective component, which asks whether the victim's fear was reasonable under the circumstances, or, if unreasonable, whether the perpetrator knew of the victim's subjective fear and took advantage of it. The particular means by which fear is imparted is not an element of rape.

Applying these principles, we conclude that the evidence that the sexual intercourse was accomplished against Mercy's will by means of fear of immediate and unlawful bodily injury was sufficient to support the verdict in this case. First, there was substantial evidence that Mercy genuinely feared immediate and unlawful bodily injury. Mercy testified that she froze because she was afraid, and the investigating police officer testified that she told him she did not move because she feared defendant would do something violent.

The Court of Appeal stated, however, "But most importantly, the victim was unable to articulate an experience of fear of immediate and unlawful bodily injury." This statement ignores the officer's testimony as to Mercy's state of mind. Moreover, even absent the officer's testimony, the prosecution was not required to elicit from Mercy testimony regarding what precisely she feared. "Fear" may be inferred from the circumstances despite even superficially *contrary* testimony of the victim. *See People v. Renteria*, 61 Cal.2d 497, 499 (1964) [robbery case]; *People v. Borra*, 123 Cal.App. 482, 484–85 (1932)[same]. In addition, immediately after the attack, Mercy was so distraught her friend Pam could barely understand her. Mercy hid in the bushes outside the house waiting for Pam to pick her up because she was terrified defendant would find her; she subsequently asked Pam if the word "rape" was written on her forehead, and had to be dissuaded from bathing prior to going to the hospital.

Second, there was substantial evidence that Mercy's fear of immediate and unlawful bodily injury was reasonable. The Court of Appeal's statements [—] that defendant "did nothing to suggest that he intended to injure" Mercy, and that "[a]lthough the assailant was a stranger to the victim, she knew nothing about him which would suggest that he was violent" [—] ignor[e] the import of the undisputed facts. Defendant, who weighed twice as much as Mercy, accosted her while she slept in the home of a close friend, thus violating the victim's enhanced level of security and privacy.

Defendant, who was naked, then removed Mercy's pants, fondled her buttocks, and inserted his penis into her vagina for approximately one minute, without warning, without her consent, and without a reasonable belief of consent. Any man or woman awakening to find himself or herself in this situation could reasonably react with fear of immediate and unlawful bodily injury. Sudden, unconsented-to groping, disrobing, and ensuing sexual intercourse while one appears to lie sleeping is an appalling and intolerable invasion of one's personal autonomy that, in and of itself, would reasonably cause one to react with fear.

The Court of Appeal's suggestion that Mercy could have stopped the sexual assault by screaming and thus eliciting Sandra S.'s help, disregards both the Legislature's 1980 elimination of the resistance requirement and our express language in *Barnes* upholding that amendment. It effectively guarantees an attacker freedom to intimidate his victim and exploit any resulting reasonable fear so long as she neither struggles nor cries out. Moreover, it is sheer speculation that Mercy's assailant would have responded to screams by desisting the attack, and not by causing her further injury or death.

The jury could reasonably have concluded that under the totality of the circumstances, this scenario, instigated and choreographed by defendant, created a situation in which Mercy genuinely and reasonably responded with fear of immediate and unlawful bodily injury, and that such fear allowed him to accomplish sexual intercourse with Mercy against her will. . . .

The judgment of the Court of Appeal is reversed, and the case is remanded to that court for further proceedings consistent with this opinion.

NOTES

1. *Reasons for rape law reform.* The 1980 reform statute in *Iniguez* is one example of a nationwide pattern of legislative action that emerged after the enactment of the 1975 Michigan reform statute. The 1980 Revised Comments to the republished Model Penal Code of 1962 explain some of the reasons that rape law reforms were viewed as necessary in 1975 and thereafter:

> [T]here is reason to suppose that rape is the most dramatically under-reported of all violent crimes and that the incidence of rape far exceeds the number of reported crimes. This assumption certainly seems plausible in light of the ordeal that a rape victim may face upon public disclosure of the event.
>
> There are at least two other factors that may contribute to the present sense [that rape law revision is necessary]. The first is that the probability of apprehension of a suspect is not good even when the police are called. Among the factors that contribute to this result are conclusions by the police that the rape complaint is unfounded. . . . Second, arrest for rape is unlikely to result in conviction. Contributing factors to this result include the unwitting destruction of evidence by victims, special evidentiary rules relating to rape, and the difficulty of tying the offender the crime by evidence other than the testimony of a

victim who, because of the emotions surrounding the event and testimony about it, may prove especially vulnerable to disbelief.

Cumulatively, these bits of data suggest that the criminal justice system actually identifies and punishes a small fraction of the total population of rape offenders.... [Rape law reform] has also been a special target of feminist reform. There have been accusations that the law of rape reflects sexist assumptions about appropriate behavior of men and women, as well [as] insensitivity to the plight of rape victims....

Model Penal Code § 213.1, Comment (3), at 283–286 (1980).

2. *The limited Model Penal Code reforms of 1962.* In most respects, the M.P.C. drafters did not anticipate the directions that rape law would take during later decades. The M.P.C. rape crime is defined as penetration by a man who "compels [a woman] to submit by force or by threat of imminent death, serious bodily injury, extreme pain or kidnapping, to be inflicted on anyone." M.P.C. § 213.1(1)(a). The term "compulsion" "plainly implies nonconsent", and the absence of a "resistance" element does not mean that judicial "inquiry into the level of resistance by the victim cannot or should not be made." Model Penal Code § 213.1, Comment (4)(a), at 306–307 (1980). The M.P.C. crime is not gender neutral and it retains the marital rape exemption, a corroboration requirement, and a form of the Lord Hale instruction. M.P.C. § 213.6(2) & § 213.6(5). The 1980 M.P.C. Commentary criticized the 1975 Michigan reform statute as an "unacceptable" "overreaction" to the concerns of reformers. Model Penal Code § 213.1(1), Comment (3)(b)(ii), at 288–289 (1980). At the outset of the rape reform era, the drafters of the Commentary did not envision the imminent widespread abandonment of the common law concepts embedded in the M.P.C. rape crime. In hindsight, the 1975 Michigan statute provided a more enduring legacy than the M.P.C. for most subsequent rape reform statutes.

3. *Reform aspects of the 1980 Iniguez rape statute.* The 1980 California rape statute contains both common law and reform elements. The "against the will" language derives from the common law, as does the exclusive focus on the act of "sexual intercourse." The crime is gender neutral but it retains the marital rape exemption. Two noteworthy reform elements are the elimination of a resistance element and the substitution of "fear of unlawful bodily injury" for "threats of great and immediate bodily harm", although the *Iniguez* Court emphasized that common law "threat" definitions would have continuing relevance for modern definitions of "fear."

4. *The "duress" or "menace" elements in the 1990 statute.* The California rape statute was amended in 1990 after the events that led to the *Iniguez* prosecution. The amendment revived the old threat concept from the pre–1980 statute, while giving it new meanings by using the terms "duress" and "menace." The amended version of § 261 defines rape as being "accomplished against a person's will by means of force, violence, *duress, menace,* or fear of immediate and unlawful bodily injury on the person of another." The

term "menace" is defined broadly as "any threat, declaration, or act which shows an intention to inflict an injury upon another." The term "duress" is defined as "direct or implied threat of force, violence, danger, or retribution sufficient to coerce a reasonable person of ordinary susceptibilities to perform an act which otherwise would not have been performed, or acquiesce in an act to which one otherwise would not have submitted. The total circumstances, including the age of the victim and his or her relationship to the defendant, are factors to consider in appraising the existence of duress." Cal. Penal Code §§ 261 (a)(2), (7)(b) & (c) (West 2003).

5. *The meaning of "force."* The *Iniguez* Court decided that it was unnecessary to address the sufficiency of the evidence of "force" because there was sufficient evidence of "fear." Here are four definitions of the concept of "force", which illustrate the difficulties involved in defining this inherently ambiguous concept and applying it to particular facts.

a. *"Physical Force" as the equivalent of "offensive touching" for a battery.* Where the crime of sexual assault is defined as the commission of "an act of sexual penetration with another person [where] the actor uses physical force", the term "physical force" means "any amount of sexual touching brought about involuntarily." The term does not require "the application of some amount of force in addition to the act of penetration." "Physical force" is shown when "the defendant applies any amount of force ... in the absence of what a reasonable person would believe to be affirmative and freely-given permission to penetration." *State of New Jersey in the Interest of M.T.S.*, 129 N.J. 422, 443, 609 A.2d 1266, 1277 (1992).

b. *"Force" as including threats creating fear.* Where a rape statute includes element of "force," then "[f]orce is an essential element of the crime [but] no particular amount of force, either actual or constructive, is required to constitute rape. Necessarily that fact must depend on the prevailing circumstances.... [Force] may exist without violence. If the acts and threats of the defendant were reasonably calculated to create in the mind of the victim—having regard to the circumstances in which she was placed—a real apprehension, due to fear, of imminent bodily harm, serious enough to impair or overcome her will to resist, then such acts and threats are the equivalent of force." *State v. Baby*, 404 Md. 220, 260, 946 A.2d 463, 486–487 (2008), citing *Hazel v. State*, 221 Md. 464, 469, 157 A.2d 922, 925 (1960).

c. *"Force" as including psychological pressure.* Where the statutory definition of "force" includes an act that "coerces the victim to submit by threatening to use force or violence on the victim", then "force" may include a threat that "may be implied as well as express", and "force" may "consist of the imposition of psychological pressure upon a person who, under all of the circumstances, is vulnerable and susceptible to such pressure." *State v. DiPetrillo*, 922 A.2d 124, 134 (R.I. 2007).

d. *"Forcible compulsion" as uncertain degree of physical force.* Where a rape statute requires "forcible compulsion", "the precise degree of actual physical force necessary to prove" this element "is uncertain" and "relative" and "depends on the facts and circumstances." Even where there is "disparity in the weights or strengths of the parties", as long the defendant's acts are "not inconsistent with consensual sexual relations", then the potentially "coercive" effects of the defendant's conduct are "speculative" when the defendant only puts the victim on bed, straddles the victim, removes her pants and underwear, and places his body weight on top of her before penetration. Even when the victim says no repeatedly before during intercourse, such verbal resistance indicates "reluctant submission" that establishes lack of consent element, but it is not relevant to show the "forcible compulsion" element. *Commonwealth v. Berkowitz*, 415 Pa.Super. 505, 522–523, 609 A.2d 1338, 1346–1347 (1992), *aff'd*, 537 Pa. 143, 641 A.2d 1161 (1994).

PROBLEMS

1. *Sexual Battery Crime in Iniguez.* The jury in *Iniguez* was offered the options of convicting the defendant of rape or sexual battery, or of acquitting him of both crimes. The sexual battery statute applied to "[a]ny person who touches an intimate part of another person while that person is unlawfully restrained by the accused or an accomplice, and if the touching is against the will of the person touched and is for the purpose of sexual arousal, sexual gratification, or sexual abuse." If the *Iniguez* jury had acquitted the defendant of rape but convicted him of sexual battery, how could the prosecutor and defense counsel argue on appeal that there was sufficient (or insufficient) evidence for a conviction on that charge? How does the sexual battery definition illustrate an apparent gap in the California definitions of sexual assault crimes?

2. *Rusk Facts and California Rape Definitions.* Pat met Rusk at a bar where she went with a woman friend after a high school reunion. During their conversation, Pat told him that she was a single mother and had to be home soon to take care of her child. After midnight, Rusk asked her for a ride home and she agreed, telling him it was "just a ride." When they arrived at his rooming house, Pat parked but did not turn off the ignition. Rusk asked her to come up and she refused. He continued to ask her and she later testified that she became afraid. She tried to convince him that she didn't want to go with him because she was separated and it might cause her marital problems. Rusk then took her car keys out of the ignition, walked over to Pat's side of the car, opened the door and said, "Now will you come up?" Pat was afraid of being stranded in the unfamiliar neighborhood and she followed Rusk up to his room. When Rusk left the room for a few minutes to go to the bathroom, Pat did not leave. When Rusk returned, he started to pull her on to the bed and began to remove her blouse. Then he told her to take off the rest of her clothes and his clothes and she did so. Pat testified that she begged him to let her leave and he kept saying, "no." She

was frightened by Rusk's tone of voice and by the look in his eyes. She asked him, "If I do what you want, will you let me go without killing me?" She started to cry and Rusk put his hands on her throat. Pat described this act as a "light choking" but it could have been a "heavy caress." Then she said, "If I do what you want, will you let me go?" Rusk said, "yes," and sexual intercourse followed. Pat got dressed, left for home, and then reported the rape to the police. Assume that Rusk is charged with rape and convicted at trial. *Compare Rusk v. State*, 43 Md.App. 476, 406 A.2d 624 (1979) *rev'd*, *State v. Rusk*, 289 Md. 230, 424 A.2d 720 (1981).

a. *Fear Theory.* If Rusk is charged under the 1980 statute in *Iniguez*, is there sufficient evidence to convict him under the *"fear"* theory as interpreted in *Iniguez*? Argue both sides.

b. *Force Theories.* If Rusk is charged under the 1980 statute in *Iniguez*, is there sufficient evidence to convict him under a *"force"* theory? Assume that the meaning of "force" is unclear under California law. Explain the arguments that each side will make using each of the four definitions of "force" described in note 5 after *Iniguez*.

c. *Duress or Menace.* If Rusk is charged under the 1990 California statute described in note 4 after *Iniguez*, how will the prosecutor argue that there is sufficient evidence to convict Rusk under a theory of either "duress" or "menace"?

STATE v. BORTHWICK

255 Kan. 899, 880 P.2d 1261 (1994).

Davis, J.: The defendant, Donald Borthwick, appeals his conviction of one count of rape.... [The] victim, J.C., had been a student in the defendant's wife's learning disabilities classroom. J.C. has spastic hemiplegia cerebral palsy and lives with her mother. J.C. is four-feet, nine or ten inches tall and weighs about 88 pounds. She cannot walk without assistance; she cannot stand without support. At home, she moves about the house by crawling. J.C. was, at the time, 21 years old.

After J.C. graduated from high school she and Mrs. Borthwick remained friends. They occasionally would go out to dinner or for ice cream together. The defendant usually accompanied them on these outings because Mrs. Borthwick needed help getting J.C. in and out of the car. At the time charges were filed, the defendant was 71 years old.

On August 12, 1991, J.C. called the defendant's home because she and Mrs. Borthwick had made tentative plans to go out to dinner together. When the defendant told her that Mrs. Borthwick was at a meeting and would be unable to go out to dinner, J.C. invited the defendant over to watch movies. He agreed and brought some ice cream with him.

After the defendant arrived at J.C.'s home, he sat on the floor behind her. He rubbed her back, lifted her shirt and bra, and started "chewing" on her breast. She asked him to stop but he did not. He also nibbled on her ear. She asked him to stop but he did not. The defendant then laid J.C. down on the floor on her back, lifted her legs, pulled down her shorts and underpants, and put his fingers in her vagina. As J.C. testified at trial about the penetration[:] "I asked him to think about it and to think about his wife and to think about what he was doing and then I asked him to stop." She also testified that she tried to keep her legs together, "but they always come apart." J.C. testified that she was afraid and felt powerless to stop what was happening.

After the defendant stopped, he went into the bathroom to wash his hands. J.C. testified that they then ate ice cream together. J.C. testified that while they were in the kitchen she tried to use the phone to call her mother, but the defendant took it out of her hand and told her that was "not a good idea. Let's not tell your mom." When J.C. asked why she could not tell her mother, the defendant replied: " 'Cause if your mom finds out that I was here, then your mom would have a lot of questions and I don't want to run into your mom or anybody else." Before the defendant left, he told J.C.: "You better not say anything 'cause I'll get in trouble with my wife." He also asked J.C. not to report him and to make sure that nobody knew he was there. He took his ice cream with him when he left so that J.C.'s mother would not know that anyone had been at the house while she was gone. [J.C. reported the incident to her mother several days later.]

J.C. testified that she did not give the defendant permission to do any of the things he did to her and that she was afraid of him while he did these things. At trial, the defendant denied that he touched J.C., other than to give her a hug when he first arrived.

[The] defendant was charged and convicted [of rape]. [This crime is defined as "sexual intercourse with a person who does not consent to the sexual intercourse", "[w]hen the victim is overcome by force or fear"; "sexual intercourse" is defined as "any penetration of the female sex organ by a finger, the male sex organ or any object"; "[a]ny penetration, however, slight, is sufficient to constitute sexual intercourse."] [T]he jury concluded that J.C. was overcome by force or fear. In a 2–1 decision [the] Court of Appeals affirm[ed] the conviction. . . .

[We] have held that the "testimony of the [victim] alone can be sufficient to sustain a rape conviction without further corroboration as long as the evidence is clear and convincing and is not so incredible and improbable as to defy belief." *State v. Cooper*, 252 Kan. 340, 347, 845 P.2d 631 (1993). This basic principle must be viewed in the light of another important principle: "The function of weighing the evidence and passing on credibility belongs to the jury, not to us. A verdict secured on substantial competent evidence will not be disturbed on appellate review."

[The first] key question is whether J.C.'s testimony [about nonconsent], if believed, is sufficient to support a rape conviction. [We] find that J.C.'s testimony on direct does [support] an inference [of nonconsent to the defendant's acts]. In the context of her testimony about the defendant placing his fingers in her vagina, the State's attorney asked J.C. if she asked the defendant to stop. J.C. testified: "I asked him to think about it and to think about his wife and to think about what he was doing and then I asked him to stop." . . . .

Viewing the record as a whole, however, we also note that J.C.'s testimony on that particular issue was not consistent. [But this fact does] not require reversal. The record as a whole supports a conclusion that J.C. conveyed to the defendant that his advances were not welcome. She was alone in a house with a man who was married to one of her good friends. When he touched J.C.'s breast, she told him to stop and he did not. When he nibbled on her ear, she told him to stop and he did not. She testified on direct that when he laid her down, took off her pants, and began to touch her genitalia, she told him to stop. On cross-examination, she testified that she tried to get him to stop by keeping her legs together and telling the defendant to think about his wife and to think about what he was doing. Even though her testimony was inconsistent in some respects, J.C. told the defendant in various ways that she did not desire his conduct to continue. Viewing the record in the light most favorable to the prosecution, we find that a rational factfinder reasonably could conclude that the act was not accomplished with mutual consent.

The defendant next contends that even if J. C.'s testimony is believed, there was not sufficient evidence that J.C. was overcome by force or fear. . . . Recent cases make clear [that] violent assaults and life-threatening actions are not necessary to sustain a "force or fear" rape conviction. [The] defendant urges the court to look to J. C.'s testimony that he did not force or threaten her. . . . [But] J.C. testified that she was afraid, that she did not consent to the sexual intercourse, that she felt powerless to do anything to stop the assault, that she told the defendant to stop, and that he nevertheless continued. Under the circumstances of this case, a reasonable factfinder could have found J.C. was overcome by fear. Although when asked on cross-examination whether the defendant forced or threatened her, J.C. testified that he did not, she also testified that she felt powerless to stop what was happening. She also testified that she told the defendant to stop what he was doing, but that he nevertheless continued.

Finally, the defendant cites a recent opinion of the Pennsylvania Supreme Court [*Commonwealth v. Berkowitz*, 641 A.2d 1161 (Pa.1994)] to support his contention that there was insufficient evidence of force [or] fear to sustain his rape conviction. [But] the Pennsylvania legislature defined rape differently than did our legislature. [The] Pennsylvania statute [required] the State to prove that the intercourse occurred "by forcible compulsion" or "threat of forcible compulsion that would prevent resistance by a person of reasonable resolution." *Berkowitz*, 641 A.2d at 1163. The Pennsylvania legislature did not permit a rape conviction when a victim is overcome by fear, except to the extent that it is fear induced by [a] threat of forcible compulsion.... [By contrast, the Kansas statute allows conviction when the victim is "overcome by force or fear."] Fear in and of itself is inherently subjective [and] a finding that a particular victim is overcome by fear does not require proof that it is fear induced by threat of force....

[Under] Kansas law, when a victim testifies that she was overcome by fear, and her testimony is not "so incredible as to defy belief," there is sufficient evidence to present the ultimate determination [of the rape crime] to the factfinder. The reasonableness of a particular victim's fear may affect the jury's assessment of the victim's credibility in arriving at its verdict. The "force" required to sustain a rape conviction in this state does not require that a rape victim resist to the point of becoming the victim of other crimes such as battery or aggravated assault. [The Kansas statute] does not require the State to prove that a rape victim told the offender she did not consent, physically resisted the offender, and then endured sexual intercourse against her will. It does not require that a victim be physically overcome by force in the form of a beating or physical restraint. It requires only a finding that she did not give her consent and that *the victim was overcome* by force or fear to facilitate the sexual intercourse.

Viewed in a light most favorable to the prosecution, the evidence is sufficient that J.C. did not consent to the defendant's digital intercourse and that she was overcome by force or fear. Under these circumstances, we conclude that a rational factfinder could have concluded beyond a reasonable doubt that the sexual intercourse was nonconsensual and that the victim was overcome by force or fear....

ALLEGRUCCI, J. dissenting:

I cannot accept the majority's conclusion that the evidence is sufficient for a rational factfinder to find beyond a reasonable doubt that J.C. was overcome by force [or] fear. [I] agree with the majority that the evidence, taken as a whole, was sufficient to support a finding that she did not consent to the sexual intercourse. However, [the] State must also prove that J.C. was overcome by force or fear....

As stated [in] *Commonwealth v. Berkowitz*[:] "As to the complainant's testimony that she stated 'no' throughout the [encounter], we point out that, while such an allegation of fact would be relevant to the issue of consent, it is not relevant to the issue of force," and "[where] there is a lack of consent, but no showing of either physical force, a threat of physical force, or psychological coercion, the 'forcible compulsion' requirement [i]s not met."

[I] agree with the majority that "violent assaults and life-threatening actions are not necessary to sustain a 'force or fear' rape conviction." However, more than the unsupported conclusory statement of the victim is required.

J.C. testified on cross-examination: . . . .

. . . .

"Q. At no time did Mr. Borthwick threaten you, did he?

"A. No.

"Q. At no time did you tell Mr. Borthwick you were afraid; isn't that correct?

"A. No.

"Q. That's not correct or—

"A. I said, 'Yes, it's correct,' but you don't tell anybody that you're afraid of 'um.

"Q. Okay. As a matter of fact, you've testified that there was nothing you did that would give Mr. Borthwick the indication that you were afraid; isn't that correct?

"A. That's correct. . . .

. . . .

On redirect examination, the following questions were asked by the State's prosecutor and answered by J.C.: . . .

"Q. You stated that the defendant didn't force you in any way to do—for him to do these things to you.

"A. Yes.

"Q. Okay. You also said though that you held your legs together. What was the reason that you tried to hold your legs together?

"A. 'Cause he was trying to put his fingers inside of me.

"Q. And what did you think holding or trying to hold your legs together would do?

"A. Try and stop him.

. . . .

"A. I was afraid of him, yes.

"Q. What was it that you were afraid of?

"A. Well, he didn't—he didn't put his—he didn't put all of his sentences together and there was pieces and that wasn't exactly put together in my mind.

"Q. Okay. How did that frighten you?

"A. Well, he didn't tell me the truth and I didn't think it was fair of him not to tell me the truth.

"Q. You stated in your cross-examination testimony that you don't tell anyone you're afraid of them. Can you explain that?

"A. Well, if somebody's bigger than you are and you're smaller, which I am, you don't tell anybody that you're afraid of them 'cause they might hurt you."

Finally, on recross-examination, J.C. testified:

"Q. Okay. When Mr. Borthwick, according to your testimony, was putting his fingers inside you, he wasn't pinning you down, was he?

"A. No.

"Q. He didn't have his body weight on top of you, did he?

"A. No. . . .

"Q. Nothing he was doing caused you—let me rephrase that. He did not say something to you that caused you to be afraid, did he?

"A. No.

"Q. He didn't say, 'I'm going to kill you if you tell anybody about this,' correct?

"A. No.

"Q. He didn't say, 'You'll go to jail because of this,' correct?

"A. No.

"Q. The only thing Mr. Borthwick ever said to you was, according to your testimony, is that he would be in trouble, correct?

"A. Yes.

"Q. Now, he didn't say anything to you to cause you to be afraid of him, did he?

"A. No.

"Q. The only thing that you're upset about or you're afraid of is the fact that it might hurt, correct?

"A. Yes.

"Q. And that your mother would be upset, correct?

"A. Yes, there's no doubt in my mind.

. . . .

"Q. But Mr. Borthwick didn't threaten you, did he?

"A. No.

"Q. And Mr. Borthwick did not apply force to you, did he?

"A. No.

"Q. So it was nothing that Mr. Borthwick did by what he said that caused you fear; isn't that right?

"A. I was afraid of him. You don't say it out loud. You can think it. You don't tell anybody that you're afraid of him."

The majority finds this conclusory testimony of J.C. sufficient for a reasonable factfinder to find beyond a reasonable doubt that J.C. was overcome by force or fear.... [But] [t]he fact that J.C. tried to keep her legs together is not evidence that the defendant used force. J.C. is a 21–year–old with cerebral palsy. She testified she could not walk or stand unaided. Obviously, she has limited use of, or strength in, her legs. She did not testify that the defendant forced her legs apart. The fact that J.C. tried to keep her legs together tends to support that she did not consent but not that force was used. This is particularly true in light of her testimony that the defendant did nothing to force her to have sexual intercourse....

In the recent case of *People v. Iniguez*, 7 Cal.4th 847, 30 Cal. Rptr.2d 258, 872 P.2d 1183 (1994), the California Supreme Court [affirmed] the defendant's rape conviction because the evidence of force or fear was [sufficient] to support the conviction.... [The] evidence [in *Iniguez*] is in stark contrast to the evidence in the present case, particularly as to whether J.C. was overcome by fear. [Here] the majority totally ignores the objective component to the element of fear. What rendered J.C. to be immobilized by fear? That the defendant "didn't put all of his sentences together" and "he didn't tell ... the truth." J.C. testified the defendant never threatened, coerced, or used force. How can a "reasonable factfinder" find her fear to be "reasonable"? Although J.C. testified she was afraid, her fear was not of what would happen to her if she did not submit to the defendant. She testified on cross-examination that "the only thing" she was afraid of was that "it might hurt," "that [her] mother would be upset," and what defendant's wife would think....

Simply stated, the majority holds that the State need not prove beyond a reasonable doubt that the victim is overcome by force or fear but, rather, a conclusory statement from the victim to that effect is sufficient. Absent the legislature's amending [the rape statute], I cannot accept that to be the law in this state. I [would find] that the evidence is not sufficient to establish that J.C. was overcome by force or fear.

PROBLEMS

1. *Verbal and Physical Resistance in Borthwick*. The *Borthwick* defendant conceded on appeal that there was sufficient evidence of the victim's "lack of consent", and both the majority and the dissent agree with that conclusion. Describe how the reasoning of each opinion in *Borthwick* interprets the significance of the victim's verbal and physical resistance to the defendant in relation to the "force or fear" element.

2. *Comparing the Iniguez and Borthwick Facts about Fear*. Assume that the prosecutor in *Borthwick* relied on the *Iniguez* Court's interpretation of "fear" when arguing before the Kansas Supreme Court. What arguments could the prosecutor make to point out the factual analogies between *Iniguez* and *Borthwick* that support a finding of "reasonable fear" in both cases?

3. *The Berkowitz Facts and the Borthwick Statute*. Berkowitz and V. are college sophomores. He was in his dorm room when V. came looking for his roommate. He invited her to "hang out for a while" and offered to give her a back rub. She declined the back rub but sat down on his floor. Berkowitz moved down to the floor and "kind of pushed" V. with his body, straddled her and kissed her. She said she had to go and meet her boyfriend and Berkowitz lifted up her shirt and bra and fondled her. V. said, "No." He undid his pants while she said, "No," and V. could not move because his weight was over her body. Berkowitz tried to put his penis in her mouth and she said, "No, I gotta go, let me go." Then they both rose to their feet and Berkowitz locked the door so that people outside could not enter but a person inside could leave. Berkowitz put V. down on the bed, straddled her and removed her sweatpants and underwear. V. could not move because Berkowitz was on top of her. Berkowitz put his penis in the victim's vagina, and she moaned, "No, no, no" because, as she testified later, "it was just so scary." After 30 seconds, Berkowitz pulled out his penis, ejaculated on V.'s stomach, and got off her. She got up, dressed quickly, grabbed her books, and ran downstairs to find her boyfriend. V. was crying and her boyfriend called the police to report a rape. Compare *Commonwealth v. Berkowitz*, 415 Pa.Super. 505, 522–523, 609 A.2d 1338, 1346–1347 (1992), *aff'd*, 537 Pa. 143, 641 A.2d 1161 (1994).

a. *"Fear" Theories*. If Berkowitz is prosecuted under the *Borthwick* statute, is there sufficient evidence of the "fear" element as interpreted by the *Borthwick* Court? Explain the prosecutor's arguments.

b. *"Force" Theories*. The *Berkowitz* defendant's conviction was reversed because of insufficient evidence of "forcible compulsion" as described in Note 4 after *Iniguez*. But if he had been prosecuted under any of the other three definitions of "force" in Note 4, would there have been sufficient evidence to convict him? Explain the prosecutor's arguments under each definition.

b. LACK OF CONSENT

The importance of a victim's "lack of consent" casts a long shadow over modern rape law. At common law, defendants could attempt to raise a reasonable doubt about the "lack of consent" element by arguing that a victim's consent could be inferred from submission or lack of resistance. Some drafters of rape reform statutes singled out this element for elimination in the hope of easing the prosecution's path to obtaining convictions, by making it unnecessary to prove the element of lack of consent beyond a reasonable doubt. But the mere elimination of the "lack of consent" element from a statute cannot prevent jurors from taking the issue of consent into account when reaching a verdict. It is traditional for case law interpretations of such statutes to preserve the defendant's right to raise the "affirmative defense of consent." However, during the rape reform era, some legislatures and courts adopted definitions of "consent" that focused on the need for proof of affirmative conduct by the victim, rather than on inferences of consent that might be drawn from passive submission.

i. DEFINING "CONSENT"

STATE v. LEDERER

99 Wis.2d 430, 299 N.W.2d 457 (App. 1980).

Cannon, Judge.

[The defendant was convicted of third degree sexual assault and challenged the statute as being unconstitutionally overbroad.] Defendant contends that application of the definition of consent contained in [§] 940.225(4) could subject an individual to punishment for engaging in consensual sexual activities where no testimony was produced regarding acts or words which evidenced freely given consent. We do not agree.

The plain terms of [the statute define] third degree sexual assault as sexual intercourse without consent [and consent] is defined [as] "words or overt actions by a person who is competent to give informed consent indicating a freely given agreement to have sexual intercourse or sexual contact."

[We] reject defendant's contention that a defendant could be convicted [of sexual assault] for engaging in consensual sexual relations. The plain terms of the statute require that the state must prove that the act of sexual intercourse must be without consent. In *Gates v. State*, [91 Wis.2d 512, 520, 283 N.W.2d 474, 477 (Ct.App. 1979)] this court stated that for conviction of second degree sexual assault "[the] State must introduce evidence that there was no consent, and this evidence must be sufficient to convince the jury beyond a reasonable doubt." Our supreme court has also determined that "[the] plain wording of the statutory definition of consent demonstrates that failure to resist is not consent[.]" *State v. Clark*, 87 Wis.2d 804, 815, 275 N.W.2d 715, 721 (1979). We hold that these definitions of consent apply equally well to third degree sexual assault. In so defining consent the legislature has relieved the state of the burden of proving that the victim resisted in order to establish that the act was nonconsensual.

Defendant contends that two parties may enter into consensual sexual relations without manifesting freely given consent through words or acts. We reject this contention as we know of no other means of communicating consent. [We] hold that the legislature has provided a sufficient standard to distinguish criminal from noncriminal activities. We, accordingly, reject defendant's constitutional challenge on the grounds of overbreadth.

[Defendant also] asserts that the evidence offered [was] insufficient to establish that the [sexual acts] were performed without the consent of the [victim]. We do not agree. [The] record discloses that the [victim] objected when the defendant initially disrobed her and continued to object throughout the night when defendant performed the various acts of sexual intercourse. The record further discloses that the [victim] testified that when asked to open her mouth prior to the performance of the act of fellatio she did not, but instead turned her head away and only complied when the defendant took her head in his hands. These actions on the part of the [victim] can hardly be said to be manifestations of consent, particularly when viewed together with the threat of the defendant that things would be worse if she did not comply. "No" means no, and precludes any finding that the [victim] consented to any of the sexual acts performed during the night.

[Judgment] and order affirmed.

NOTES

1. *Reform goals and the "lack of consent" concept.* The views of rape law reformers about the lack-of-consent element and its functions are summarized in *State of New Jersey in the Interest of M.T.S.*, 129 N.J. 422, 432–439, 609 A.2d 1266, 1271–1274 (1992):

> Although the terms "non-consent" and "against her will" were often treated as equivalent under the traditional definition of rape, both formulations squarely placed on the victim the burden of proof and of action. Effectively, a woman who was above the age of consent had actively and affirmatively to withdraw that consent for the intercourse to be against her will.

> The presence or absence of consent often turned on credibility. [Courts] and commentators historically distrusted the testimony of victims, "assuming that women lie about their lack of consent for various reasons: to blackmail men, to explain the discovery of a consensual affair, or because of psychological illness." Evidence of resistance was viewed as a solution to the credibility problem; it was the "outward manifestation of nonconsent, [a] device for determining whether a woman actually gave consent." ...

> [To] refute the misguided belief that rape was not real unless the victim fought back, reformers emphasized empirical research indicating that women who resisted forcible intercourse often suffered far more serious injury as a result. [Reformers also] criticized the conception of

rape as a distinctly sexual crime rather than a crime of violence. They emphasized that rape had its legal origins in laws designed to protect the property rights of men to their wives and daughters. [They] argued that vestiges of the old law remained, particularly in the understanding of rape as a crime against the purity or chastity of a woman. The burden of protecting that chastity fell on the woman, with the state offering its protection only after the woman demonstrated that she had resisted sufficiently. . . .

Critics of rape law agreed that the focus of the crime should be shifted from the victim's behavior to the defendant's [conduct]. [There] were, however, differences over the best way to redefine the crime. Some reformers advocated a standard that defined rape as unconsented-to sexual intercourse, others urged the elimination of any reference to consent from the definition of rape. Nonetheless, all proponents of reform shared a central premise: that the burden of showing non-consent should not fall on the victim of the crime. In dealing with the problem of consent the reform goal was not so much to purge the entire concept of consent from the law as to eliminate the burden that had been placed on victims to prove they had not consented.

2. *Modern "consent" definitions.* Like the Wisconsin statute in *Lederer*, some reform statutes define consent in "positive" or "affirmative" terms. The *Iniguez* statute defined consent for rape crimes as follows: "[P]ositive cooperation in act or attitude pursuant to an exercise of free will. The person must act freely and voluntarily and have knowledge of the nature of the act or transaction involved." Calif. Penal Code § 261.6. Some courts have created similar case law definitions of "consent" when interpreting that term or other elements in a rape statute. For example, even when a sexual assault statute did not include a reference to "consent", the *M.T.S.* court decided to incorporate the consent concept into the definition of "physical force", by defining the latter element as the application of "any amount of force against another person in the absence of what a reasonable person would believe to be affirmative and freely-given permission to the act of sexual penetration." The court also noted that such "permission" "may be inferred either from acts or statements reasonably viewed in light of the surrounding circumstances" and that "permission" "can be and indeed often is indicated through physical actions rather than words." *M.T.S.*, 129 N.J. at 443, 609 A.2d at 1277.

ii.   WITHDRAWAL OF CONSENT

STATE v. BABY

404 Md. 220, 946 A.2d 463 (2008).

[This case] presents this Court principally with the task of determining whether it was error for a trial court, during a rape trial, to respond to jury questions concerning the effect of post-penetration withdrawal of consent by referring the jury to previously provided instructions on the elements of first degree rape, without further clarification. [The defendant was convicted of first degree rape, defined as engaging in vaginal intercourse with another "by force, or the threat of force, without the consent of the other" "while aided and abetted by another."] . . . .

In this case, the [lower court] held that if a woman "consents [to sexual intercourse] prior to penetration and withdraws the consent following penetration, there is no rape", [and] relied on what it characterized as a holding in *Battle* [*v. State*,] 287 Md. 675, 414 A.2d 1266 [(1980)]. . . . [But the] sole issue [in] *Battle* was whether withdrawal of consent before penetration, followed by vaginal intercourse accomplished through force or threat of force, constituted rape. [The] analysis in *Battle* [was] not extensive enough to be applicable to the issue of post-penetration withdrawal of consent.

The gravamen of the distinction between our analysis in *Battle* and that of the [lower court here] lies in the historical importance that the [latter] court placed on the notions of virginity, the harm of deflowering a virgin, and the importance of penetration to the crime of rape. Pivotal to this analysis is the [court's] reliance on [the proposition] that the English common law was based upon the "cultural mores" of the laws of the Old Testament and the Middle Assyrian Laws of Mesopotamia "which undergird[ed] the notion that the crime of rape was complete upon penetration" and which characterized the rape of a virgin as "an illegal trespass upon the father's property" [*quoting* Ricki Lewis Tannen, *Setting the Agenda for the 1990s: The Historical Foundations of Gender Bias in the Law: A Context for Reconstruction*, 42 Fla. L. Rev. 163, 172 (1990)]. The [lower court asserted] that it was the act of penetration that was the essence of the crime of rape [at common law]; after this initial infringement upon the responsible male's interest in a woman's sexual and reproductive functions, any further injury was considered to be less consequential. [The lower court assumed that it] was this view[,] that the moment of penetration was the point in time after which a woman could never be "re-flowered," that gave rise to the principle that, if a woman consents prior to penetration and withdraws consent following penetration, there is no rape. . . .

[A] search of early English case law and scholarship reveals that by the time Maryland expressly adopted "the rules of the common law of England" in 1639, the English law of rape had evolved beyond the understanding of rape as merely a trespass upon a man's property. Before Maryland adopted the English common law, penetration could no longer be said to represent the completion of the harm caused by rape, although it was still focused on as sufficient evidence for the required element of vaginal intercourse. [Bracton's 13th century treatise, Hale's 17th century writings, and Blackstone's Commentaries provide authority that the English common law "criminalized the rape of any woman, including prostitutes, regardless of whether she was a 'deflowered' virgin."]

[After] the Revolution, in the American States there is a paucity of cases addressing the issue of withdrawal of consent [and the issue] arises infrequently in early American case law, and never directly presents the issue of post-penetration withdrawal of consent.... In more recent years, the courts in many [states] have directly considered whether withdrawal of consent after penetration can constitute rape. Of these, only one court has held that it does not ... without any further analysis or citation of authority, [and so] we do not find [the] decision to be persuasive. [See *State v. Way*, 297 N.C. 293, 254 S.E.2d 760 (1979).]

In *State v. Robinson*, 496 A.2d 1067 [(Maine 1985)], the [c]ourt [upheld the] jury instruction [that] "if a couple consensually engages in sexual intercourse and one or the other changes his or her mind, and communicates the revocation or change of mind of the consent, and the other partner continues the sexual intercourse by compulsion of the party who changes his or her mind, then it would be rape [and] the critical element there is the *continuation under compulsion*." *Id.* [at 1069] (emphasis in original). [The] [c]ourt further stated that "[the] ongoing intercourse, initiated we here assume with the [victim's] consent, did not become rape merely because she revoked her consent. It became rape if and when the [victim] thereafter submitted to the defendant's sexual assault only because [of force or threat of force]." *Id.* at 1070.

In *State v. Bunyard*, 31 Kan.App.2d 853, 75 P.3d 750 (2003), [the defendant contended] that the moment of penetration is the crucial point at which to determine the presence or absence of consent. [T]he court concluded that nowhere in its statutory definition of rape or sexual intercourse was it stated that intercourse ended with penetration, but rather that penetration "merely establishes a minimum amount of contact necessary to prove the offense." *Id.* at 756....

In *State v. Siering*, [35 Conn.App. 173,] 644 A.2d 958 [(1994)], the court upheld [a *Robinson*-style] instruction [and] noted that the Connecticut statute did not suggest that, [as the defendant argued,] " 'intercourse is complete' upon penetration; rather, it provides that 'penetration, however, slight, [is sufficient] to complete ... intercourse.' " *Id.* at 962. [The court observed that the] defendant's argument would mean that the act that commences intercourse is also the act that simultaneously concludes intercourse.

It is axiomatic that statutes are not to be interpreted to arrive at bizarre or absurd results. The defendant's construction of the statute would mean that if intercourse is continued by force after the victim withdrew consent, it would not constitute sexual assault unless the victim, upon revoking consent and struggling against the defendant, succeeds in momentarily displacing the male organ, followed by an act of repenetration by the defendant.

The absurdity of this construction is demonstrated not only by the difficulty involved in the close evidentiary determination required but also because it protects from prosecution a defendant whose physical force is so great or so overwhelming that there is no possibility of the victim's causing even momentary displacement of the male organ. . . .

We find that the analyses [of *Robinson*, *Bunyard*, and *Siering]* to be persuasive. We conclude, utilizing a similar framework, that our own rape statute punishes the act of penetration, which persists after the withdrawal of consent. [A]fter consent has been withdrawn, the continuation of vaginal intercourse by force or the threat of force may constitute rape.

[In] responding to the jury's questions [in the present case], the trial court should have directly addressed the jurors' confusion on the effect of withdrawal of consent during intercourse, rather than simply referring the jurors to previously provided instructions on the elements of rape. . . . Referring the jury to the legal definition of rape that the court had previously provided was not sufficient to address either of the jury's questions as the definition makes no reference to the issue of post-penetration withdrawal of consent which was central to the jury's questions.

We cannot determine that the trial court's error [was] harmless beyond a reasonable doubt.

NOTE

Rejected Rationales. The holding in *Baby* was endorsed earlier in *In re John Z.*, 29 Cal.4th 756, 60 P.3d 183, 128 Cal.Rptr.2d 783 (2004), where the court rejected two arguments against the position that "withdrawal of consent after penetration can constitute rape." The first argument was that in such a scenario, "the sense of outrage to [the] person and feelings" of a female, "when a male ignores her wishes", "could hardly be of the same magnitude as that resulting from an initial nonconsensual violation of her womanhood." *People v. Vela*, 172 Cal.App.3d 237, 243, 218 Cal.Rptr. 161, 165 (1985). The *John Z* Court repudiated this idea, noting that "we have no way of accurately measuring the level of outrage the victim suffers" and that "[w]e must assume the sense of outrage is substantial" in the withdrawal-of-consent scenario. The court cited Alaska precedent criticizing the *Vela* reasoning as based on "archaic and outmoded social conventions"; the court also emphasized that "outrage by the victim is not an element of forcible rape", and concluded that under the California statute, "it is immaterial at what point the victim withdraws her consent, so long as that withdrawal is communicated to the male and he thereafter ignores it." *In re John Z*, 29 Cal.4th at 761, 60 P.3d at 186, 128 Cal.Rptr.2d at 787. The second rejected argument was the defendant's proposal that "the male should be permitted a 'reasonable amount of time' in which to withdraw" after "the female raises an objection to further intercourse", because it is "unreasonable" for "the law to expect a male to cease having sexual intercourse immediately" without some time "in which to quell his primal urge." The court found no supporting authority for this theory, and observed that "nothing in the language" of the forcible rape statute "suggests that the defendant is entitled to persist in intercourse once his victim withdraws her consent." *In re John Z*, 29 Cal.4th at 762–63, 60 P.3d at 187, 128 Cal.Rptr.2d at 788.

PROBLEM

Facts of Baby and New Trial. The 18-year-old victim, J.L. testified that one night, when she drove her friend Lacey to a fast food restaurant, they encountered Baby and Mike, friends of Lacey's brother. J.L. agreed to give the men a ride to first one destination and then another, until Lacey left the group, and J.L. was alone with the men. Lacey had given her cell phone to J.L. and one of the men took it away from J.L. They told J.L. to park the car. Then Baby put his hand between J.L's legs and Mike tried to put J.L.'s hand down his pants. They talked to her about having sex, and when she ignored them, Baby began to fondle her breast. Then he tried to remove J.L's pants while Mike tried to place his penis in her mouth, and J.L. told them to stop. They told J.L. that she wouldn't be able to leave until they were done. Baby held her arms as Mike attempted to have intercourse unsuccessfully, and Baby inserted his fingers into J.L.'s vagina. Then Baby got out of the car, leaving Mike alone with J.L., and Mike inserted his fingers and then his penis into J.L.'s vagina. When Mike left the car, he told Baby that he just had sex with J.L., and then Baby got into the car and told J.L "it's my turn now." Baby said, "Are you going to let me hit it?," and "I don't want to rape you." J.L. told Baby that "as long as he stopped when she told him to, he could." After Baby put on a condom, J.L testified that he "got on top of me and he tried to put it in and it hurt. So I yelled stop, that it hurt, and that's when he kept pushing it in and I was pushing his knees to get [him] off me." When asked how long Baby kept pushing, J.L. said "about five or so seconds." When Baby did stop, he took off his condom and put it in his pocket. Then Mike got in the car and drove it back to the neighborhood near the restaurant without J.L.'s permission. One of the men gave Lacey's cell phone back to J.L., and so J.L. called Lacey, the men left, and J.L. found Lacey again. They found Lacey's mother and told her what occurred; the police were called and J.L. went to the hospital to be examined.

Baby's testified that neither he nor Mike touched J.L. before Baby got out of the car and left Mike and J.L. together. Baby also said that when he told J.L. that "I don't want to rape you", this was "kind of like to confirm the permission" he thought he had when she told him, "I could as long as I stop when she says to." Baby denied that J.L. ever yelled, "Stop." He testified that, "I tried to put it in once, it wouldn't go in, and I tried a couple more times and it wouldn't go in. I didn't feel nothing there." Baby said that J.L. sat up at that point and said, "It's not going to go in." That is when he took off the condom.

Assume that the jury at Baby's new trial will receive an instruction that even if J.L. consented to sexual intercourse with Baby before penetration, continuation of intercourse "by force or threat of force" after consent is withdrawn may constitute rape. What arguments will be made by each side that there is (or is not) sufficient evidence to convict Baby? If J.L. testified that she yelled, "I want to go home" instead of "stop, it hurts", how would the arguments change for each side?

iii.   CONSENT AS AN AFFIRMATIVE DEFENSE

STATE v. KOPERSKI
254 Neb. 624, 578 N.W.2d 837 (1998).

GERRARD, JUSTICE.

David Koperski was convicted by a jury of first degree sexual assault and sentenced [to] 4 years' probation and 60 days in jail. [The crime was defined as the act of subjecting "another person to sexual penetration" and overcoming the victim "by force, threat of force, express or implied, [or] coercion."] The Nebraska Court of Appeals affirmed the [conviction]. [W]e reverse the judgment [and] remand this cause to the district court for a new trial.

[The defendant's] theory at trial was that he reasonably believed that K.O. had consented to sexual penetration and that he did not use force to overcome K.O. beyond that force normally employed when two consenting adults engage in sexual intercourse. To this end, Koperski tendered [two] instructions. [The first instruction declared, in part, that "voluntary consent is a defense," and the second instruction defined "consent" as "positive cooperation in an act or attitude as an exercise of free will." The district court rejected both requested instructions.]

[T]he district court was incorrect to conclude that the jury need only receive instruction over the elements of the offense and not Koperski's theory or theories of defense. [T]he issues before this court are whether consent is a defense to a charge of first degree sexual assault[,] and if so, whether any evidence was adduced in support of a legally cognizable theory of defense regarding [consent].

[Although] lack of consent is not an element of [the crime], it can hardly be said that consent is not an issue in regard to a charge of first degree sexual assault. Generally, the law may only proscribe nonconsensual sexual conduct, in other words, sexual conduct which is forced upon a person by another without the consent of such person, or where one person is incapable of consenting, or where, although there is consent, such consent is invalid due to, for example, the victim's minority or diminished mental capacity. However, it is evident that consent may well be an issue in a prosecution for first degree sexual assault even though lack of consent is not an express, substantive element of the crime.

Our cases certainly reveal that this court has, subsequent to the 1975 and 1977 revisions to our sexual assault statutes, considered consent to be an issue in regard to a charge of sexual assault. [It] is true that consent is not a statutorily defined affirmative [defense]. [Nonetheless], consent can operate as a defense to a charge of first degree sexual assault [for] two reasons. First, consent may operate as a failure of proof in regard to the essential element of the use of force, or in regard to the essential element that the victim must be overcome. [Second], consent becomes a defense to a charged crime when consent precludes the infliction of the harm or evil sought to be prevented by the law defining the offense. See Model Penal Code § 2.11(1) (1985). [Accordingly], we conclude that consent may be a defense to a charge of first degree sexual assault[.] . . .

[If], by examining the facts and circumstances of the accused's conduct, it is objectively reasonable to conclude that the alleged victim consented to sexual penetration, then the accused should be free from criminal culpability. The [court] reached a similar conclusion in *State v. Smith*, 210 Conn. 132, 554 A.2d 713 (1989). Like [the Nebraska statute, the Connecticut statute] did not expressly make lack of consent an element of the crime of first degree sexual assault. Nevertheless, the court held that consent was a defense because it negated the statutory element of force. The court went on to explain how the defense of consent operates:

> While the word "consent" is commonly regarded as referring to the state of mind of the complainant in a sexual assault case, it cannot be viewed as a wholly subjective concept. Although the actual state of mind of the actor in a criminal case may in many instances be the issue upon which culpability depends, a defendant is not chargeable with knowledge of the internal workings of the minds of others except to the extent that he should reasonably have gained such knowledge from his observations of their [conduct]. [W]hether a complainant has consented to intercourse depends upon her manifestations of such consent as reasonably construed.

Likewise, in *State v. Ayer*, 136 N.H. 191, 195–96, 612 A.2d 923, 926 (1992), the New Hampshire Supreme Court stated:

> The defendant argues that the purported lack of consent must be communicated to a defendant in some way in order for him to be guilty. To the extent he means by this that the victim must manifest her unwillingness objectively, the defendant is correct.

If, however, the victim objectively communicates lack of consent and the defendant subjectively fails to receive the message, he is guilty. The appropriate inquiry is whether a reasonable person in the circumstances would have understood that the victim did not consent.

In this regard, we agree with the reasoning of the Connecticut and New Hampshire courts [in *Smith* and *Ayer*]. Accordingly, for criminal prosecutions [for first degree sexual assault] we hold that the trial court must instruct the jury on the defense of consent when evidence is produced which, under all of the circumstances, could reasonably be viewed by the jury as an indication of affirmative and freely given consent to sexual penetration by the alleged victim. The focus remains on the accused's conduct in determining whether or not the accused has overcome the alleged victim, resulting in sexual penetration against his or her will.... [The court concluded that the defendant produced sufficient evidence to be entitled to a jury instruction on consent.]

[In] refusing Koperski's proffered jury instructions regarding consent, the trial court expressed the view that making consent a separate element or aspect of the case was confusing. Instead of an instruction regarding Koperski's theory of defense, the trial court thought it sufficient to simply not prohibit Koperski from arguing the issue of consent in his closing statement to the jury.

Contrary to the trial court's intuition, failing to instruct the jury regarding Koperski's consent theory of defense was in fact a source of confusion as evidenced by the jury's question to the court during deliberations asking whether it could even consider the issue of consent....

Reversed and remanded with directions.

PROBLEM

1. *Arguing the Consent Defense.* K.O. and her friend Marti went to a nightclub. They planned to stay at a friend's apartment afterwards, but when they arrived there at 2:00 a.m., the friend was not home. Marti called her friend Koperski, and he said they could spend the night in the house where he was living with three men. When K.O and Marti arrived, the house was full of party guests celebrating Koperski's birthday. K.O. felt sick and fell asleep on the couch in the living room. After the guests left, Marti and Koperski's three roommates retired for the night. Koperski decided to check on K.O. He woke her up and kissed her. She kissed him back with French kisses. Then Koperski jumped on top of K.O. and simulated intercourse by grinding his hips. Koperski is 6 feet tall and weighs 185 pounds. K.O. is 5 feet 1 inch tall and weighs 130 pounds. K.O testified that she stopped kissing Koperski, told him no repeatedly from this point on, and tried to push him

away repeatedly. Koperski pulled her pants down and K.O. couldn't get up because he was kneeling on them. After he penetrated her, she began crying and he apologized. Koperski testified that after he jumped on her, K.O. moved her hips when he moved his hips. He thought she was trying to pull down his pants so he pulled hers down. When he stood up, she made no attempt to leave so he lay down on her. Before he tried to penetrate her, she muttered no. He asked her if she was just teasing. She did not answer. When he penetrated her she said no again, and so he stopped and apologized.

a. *Persuading the Jury about Consent.* Assume that Koperski's jury will receive the two consent instructions requested by the defense counsel. What arguments will be made by each side at his new trial to persuade the jury to convict (or acquit) the defendant of sexual assault?

b. *Raising a Reasonable Doubt about Lack of Consent.* Assume that Koperski is prosecuted in a state where the prosecutor is required to prove "lack of consent" beyond a reasonable doubt as an element of the sexual assault crime. What arguments will be made by each side to persuade the jury to convict (or acquit) the defendant? How are these arguments different from the ones that would be made at his new trial in Nebraska?

2. MENS REA AND THE MISTAKE DEFENSE

When the "lack of consent" element is removed from a reform statute defining the rape crime, it would be logical for a court to reject the relevance of the defendant's claim of mistake concerning that missing element. For example, even though the *Koperski* Court approved the judicial recognition of the "affirmative defense of consent" when the Nebraska statute had no "lack of consent" element, the *Koperski* opinion also, in a separate holding, refused to recognize the defendant's proposed alternate defense of a "mistaken belief in the victim's consent", reasoning as follows:

> The purpose of the 1975 revision of Nebraska's former rape [statute] was to make our law, with respect to sexual assault, gender neutral and treat the offense as one involving assaultive conduct, not sexual activity. Thus, [the new statute] sought to shift the focus of the inquiry away from an examination of what the victim did or should have done and instead concentrate on the conduct of the assailant.

> In that regard, this court, as well as the courts of other jurisdictions construing similar legislative enactments, have removed or limited the many evidentiary impediments made applicable to the former crime of rape which distinguished it from other assaultive offenses. For example, courts and legislatures have either abandoned or severely limited the requirement of corroboration of a victim's testimony, the requirement that the

victim must offer palpable resistance, the requirement of prompt reporting, the spousal exemption, and evidence of a victim's prior sexual conduct. See *State in Interest of M.T.S.*, 129 N.J. 422, 609 A.2d 1266 (1992).

The common thread running through each of these abrogated impediments to proof is that, formerly, each was thought to be an essential evidentiary precaution so as to test whether the victim had consented to sexual penetration. Moreover, each, in effect, served to protect an accused's subjective belief that the victim had consented to sexual penetration, even when such belief was predicated on a mistake of fact whether reasonable or not. Abrogation of these impediments to proof necessarily means that an accused's subjective or mistaken belief as to a victim's consent is a harm which the 1975 legislative enactment sought to preclude.

[The defendant] argues that an accused's subjective belief that consent has been given to sexual penetration should act as a complete defense to [first degree sexual assault] if, and only if, this subjective belief is also objectively reasonable. However, no statutory authority exists for [this proposition]. If the element of the accused's subjective belief as to the alleged victim's state of mind is to be established as a defense to the crime of first degree sexual assault, then it should be done by our Legislature which has the power to define crimes and offenses.

State v. Koperski, 254 Neb. 624, 578 N.W.2d 837, 845 (1998).

For the many reform statutes that retain a "lack of consent" element, courts must determine whether the legislature intended to recognize the mistake defense. When a particular mental state is expressly required for the "lack of consent" element, it is easy for courts to infer the kind of mistaken belief defense that the legislature intended to make available. But many reform statutes are silent as to the mental state for this element. Thus, courts must make policy decisions about whether to recognize the mistaken belief defense, and how to define the evidence that will justify a jury instruction on that defense in particular cases. Their decisions are influenced by the policies embodied in other features of a state's rape statutes and case law interpretations of the crime.

REYNOLDS v. STATE

664 P.2d 621 (Alaska App. 1983).

SINGLETON, JUDGE.

Randall C. Reynolds was convicted of sexual assault in the first [degree]. He received a five-year sentence. [He] challenges the constitutionality of [the sexual assault statute]. [He] contends that the statutory definitions make the offense so broad that it does not distinguish between serious and harmless conduct thereby depriving him of substantive due process.

[It] is necessary to briefly consider the history of our [statute]. At common law, rape ... was a general intent crime. [It] was not necessary for the state to prove that the defendant knew or should have known that the victim did not consent. The potential harshness of this rule was mitigated by the common law requirement that in order for the state to prove the absence of consent, it must show that the victim "resisted to the utmost."

[More] recent cases [in other jurisdictions] have substantially diluted the requirement of "resistance to the utmost," increasing the risk that a jury might convict a defendant under circumstances where lack of consent was ambiguous. To counteract this risk, some courts [have] held that the defendant is entitled to an instruction on reasonable mistake of fact. *See People v. Mayberry*, 15 Cal.3d 143, 125 Cal.Rptr. 745, 542 P.2d 1337 (Cal. 1975). The [*Mayberry*] instruction reads as follows:

> It is a defense to a charge of forcible rape that the defendant entertained a reasonable belief that the female person voluntarily consented to engage in sexual intercourse. If from all the evidence you have a reasonable doubt whether the defendant reasonably and in good faith believed she voluntarily consented to engage in sexual intercourse, you must give the defendant the benefit of that doubt and acquit him of said charge.

Under [*Mayberry*], when a defendant argues consent as a defense, the state must prove that he intentionally engaged in intercourse and was at least negligent regarding his victim's lack of consent.

[The sexual assault statute defines the crime as follows: "the offender engages in sexual penetration with another person without the consent of that person." The element "without consent" is defined as follows: "with or without resisting, [a person] is coerced by the use of force against a person or property, or by the express or implied threat of imminent death, imminent physical injury or imminent kidnapping." The term "force" is defined as "any bodily impact, restraint or confinement or the threat of [same]," and the term "physical injury" is defined as "physical pain or an impairment of physical condition."]

Alaska has dispensed with any requirement that the victim resist at all.... Thus, the legislature has substantially enhanced the risk of conviction in ambiguous circumstances by eliminating the requirement that the state prove "resistance" and by substantially broadening the definitions of "force" and "physical injury." We are satisfied, however, that the legislature counteracted this risk through its treatment of *mens rea*. It did this by shifting the focus of the jury's attention from the victim's resistance or actions to the defendant's understanding of the totality of the circumstances. . . . No specific mental state is mentioned in [the sexual assault statute] governing [the element] of "consent". Therefore, the state must prove that the defendant acted "recklessly" regarding his [victim's] lack of consent. This requirement serves to protect the defendant against conviction for first-degree sexual assault where the circumstances are ambiguous at the time he has intercourse with the complaining witness. While the legislature has substantially reduced the state's burden of proof regarding the *actus reus* of the offense, it has at the same time made it easier for the defendant to argue the defense of mistake of fact. The Alaska rule is more favorable to Reynolds than the *Mayberry* [rule]. This follows from the distinction the code draws between negligence and recklessness. [The] test for recklessness is a subjective one—the defendant must actually be aware of the risk [and the] test for criminal negligence is an objective one—the defendant's culpability stems from his failure to perceive the risk.

In order to prove a violation of [the sexual assault statute,] the state must prove that the defendant knowingly engaged in sexual intercourse and recklessly disregarded his victim's lack of consent. Construed in this way, the statute does not punish harmless conduct and is neither vague nor overbroad.

[The] judgment [is] affirmed.

PROBLEM

The Morgan Problem. Three army buddies, including Morgan, are drinking one night with Joe, who is their superior officer. Joe proposes that they should go to his house and have sex with his wife. He tells them falsely that his wife likes to have multiple sex partners who engage in rough sex. He tells them falsely that their use of force will excite his wife, and he promises them that they can ignore her protests because she will be making those protests as part of her game. The three men go to Joe's house and each has forcible intercourse with Joe's wife over her repeated verbal protests. Assume that the three men are prosecuted for sexual assault in Alaska using the statute in *Reynolds*. How will the defense counsel argue to the jury that the men lacked the mens rea for the crime? How will the prosecutor argue that the defendants had the necessary mens rea? *Compare Regina v. Morgan*, 2 All E.R. 347 (H.L. 1975).

PEOPLE v. WILLIAMS

4 Cal.4th 354, 841 P.2d 961, 14 Cal.Rptr.2d 441 (1992) (In Bank).

ARABIAN, JUSTICE.

[Williams and Deborah were residents of a homeless shelter. Deborah is 5′ 1″ and 28 years old, and Williams is 6′ 1″ and 52 years old; Williams weighs 170 pounds more than Deborah. According to Deborah's testimony, Williams invited her to have coffee and proposed that they go to a place where they could watch television. He took Deborah to a hotel where he rented a room for $20 and asked the clerk for a sheet. Upon entering the room, Deborah noticed that there was no television, told Williams that he should get his money back, and tried to leave the locked room. Williams "hollered" at her that "he didn't spend $20 for nothing," punched her in the eye, and told her to get on the bed. When she said refused, he pushed her down, told her to take off her pants, and warned her that he did not like to hurt people. Deborah removed her pants because she was afraid. During sexual intercourse, Deborah screamed and tried to push Williams off, but the disparity in their sizes made this impossible. Afterwards, Williams offered her $50 but Deborah refused to take it. When she left the hotel, she went to the shelter to get directions to the nearest police station, and reported the rape there. Her "eye was so swollen she could hardly see out of it," and she suffered pains in her neck and ribs.]

[According to Williams's testimony, "prior to entering the hotel room he neither wanted nor expected to have sex," but "when he entered the room, Deborah hugged and kissed him and removed her clothes, whereupon [he] began to remove his clothes." She fondled his genitals and after sexual intercourse she told him she needed $50. When he refused to give her money, she threatened to tell a priest at the shelter and said she knew how to "fix" Williams. He admitted that he hit Deborah in the face at this point because he was angry. As they dressed, he asked her why she did not wipe away his sperm, and she told him that, "she wanted to preserve it as evidence."]

[Williams was charged with forcible rape, defined as "an act of sexual intercourse accomplished with a person not the spouse of the perpetrator," where "it is accomplished against a person's will by means of force, violence, duress, menace, or fear of immediate and unlawful bodily injury on the person or another."] The trial [judge] refused [to] give [a *Mayberry*] instruction [regarding the defendant's claim of a] reasonable and good faith but mistaken belief as to consent. A jury found Williams guilty [and he] was sentenced to eight years in state prison. [The Court of Appeal reversed, finding "there was substantial evidence in support of defendant's request for a *Mayberry* instruction."] . . .

[In] *People v. Flannel*, 25 Cal.3d 668, 684–85, 160 Cal.Rptr.84, 603 P.2d 1 (1979) we [explained] that a trial court must give a requested instruction only when the defense is supported by "substantial evidence," that is, evidence sufficient to "deserve consideration by the jury," not "whenever *any* evidence is presented, no matter how weak."

[A] mistake of fact occurs when one perceives facts differently from how they actually exist. [Here] there was no substantial evidence supporting a *Mayberry* instruction. [The] testimony [of Williams], if believed, established actual consent.... [The] testimony [of Deborah], if believed, would preclude any reasonable belief of consent. These wholly divergent accounts create no middle ground from which Williams could argue he reasonably misinterpreted Deborah's conduct. There was no substantial evidence of equivocal conduct warranting an instruction as to reasonable and good faith, but mistaken, belief of consent to intercourse....

We conclude that there was no substantial evidence warranting an instruction on reasonable and good faith but mistaken belief of consent to sexual intercourse in this case. Accordingly, we reverse the judgment of the Court of Appeal.

NOTE

Criticisms of the "equivocal conduct" test. Some other states follow the "equivocal conduct" test established in *Williams*, but it has been criticized for different reasons. Justice Kennard argued in *Williams* that the test is "too amorphous", and that a *Mayberry* instruction should be given only in cases where: 1) the amount of force used is slight; 2) there is evidence to support a reasonable belief in consent to the use of force; and 3) a substantial passage of time between the use or threat of force and the act of intercourse would provide evidence to support a reasonable belief that the victim's participation in intercourse was not coerced. By contrast, it has been argued that the "equivocal conduct" test virtually eliminates the mistake defense according to the following logic. If defendants with the strongest claims of consent "are precluded from presenting the defense to the jury" when they testify "to conduct that could be characterized as 'unequivocal'", then the only defendants who will receive *Mayberry* instructions will be those whose evidence of equivocal conduct will negate the reasonableness of their beliefs in consent. These defendants will be "doomed to certain conviction" because their evidence of "equivocal" consent is too weak. See Rosanna Cavallaro, *A Big Mistake: Eroding the Defense of Mistake of Fact about Consent in Rape*, 86 J. Crim. L. & Criminology 815, 838–839 (1996). In Cavallaro's view, the *Williams* court's limitation of *Mayberry* represents "a boomerang back from misgivings" in the pre-reform era "about juries who might too easily convict" to misgivings in the reform era about "juries who might too readily acquit." *Id.* at 858–859.

PROBLEMS

1. *Mayberry Instruction for Koperski.* Assume that the Nebraska statute in *Koperski* included the element of lack of consent, and that the Nebraska Supreme Court follows the *Williams* approach by allowing a *Mayberry* instruction only when the defendant shows evidence of "equivocal conduct" as to

consent. On the facts of *Koperski*, should the jury receive a *Mayberry* instruction? Argue both sides.

2. *Comparing Consent and Mistaken Belief in Consent.* Vicki attended a holiday party where the host, Nat, invited her to come to his beach house when the party is over. She turned him down, but when the party ended, Nat picked Vicki up, announced that they were "going to the beach," and carried her out to his car, followed by his friend Joe. When Vicki protested, saying, "Put me down!," the other partygoers did not intervene, and Vicki later testified that she did not physically resist because she thought that Nat was "just horsing around." When they got to the beach house, Nat gave Vicki and Joe a tour, and then when they arrived at the bedroom on the second floor, Nat and Joe took off their clothes. Vicki became frightened as Nat walked towards her, but as she backed away, she tripped and fell backwards down on to the bed. Nat quickly lifted up Vicki's skirt, pulled down her underwear, and had sexual intercourse with her. Joe watched them and then he had sexual intercourse with Vicki in the same manner. Vicki later testified that she did not physically or verbally resist Nat or Joe because she felt humiliated and frightened. But as soon as Nat drove Vicki back to where she parked her car near Nat's house in the city, Vicki drove to the police station and reported the rape. Compare *Commonwealth v. Sherry*, 386 Mass. 682, 437 N.E.2d 224 (1982).

   a. *Defense of Consent.* Assume that Nat was charged under a statute that defines rape as "an act of sexual intercourse where it is accomplished by means of force, violence, or fear of immediate and unlawful bodily injury on the person of another." Note that there is *no* "lack of consent" element. Assume that Nat's defense counsel *requested and obtained* the same jury instructions on the affirmative defense of consent as the defendant requested in *Koperski*. How will each side argue that Nat should be convicted (or acquitted) of rape?

   b. *Defense of Reasonable Mistaken Belief in Consent.* Assume that Nat was charged under a rape statute that *does* include a "lack of consent" element. Nat's defense counsel *requested and obtained* a *Mayberry* instruction. Now how will each side argue that Nat should be convicted (or acquitted) of rape? As a policy matter, why might the trial judge refuse to endorse *Mayberry* and deny the instruction on the defense of mistaken belief?

3. MARITAL RAPE EXEMPTION

At the time the Model Penal Code was proposed, most states used the marital rape exemption, and the M.P.C. drafters proposed that the exemption should be retained and extended to unmarried persons living together as spouses. The 1980 Commentary explains the M.P.C position as follows:

> [In] the case of intercourse coerced by force or threat of physical harm [the] law already authorizes a penalty for assault.

[The] issue is whether the still more drastic sanctions of rape should apply. The answer depends on whether the injury caused by forcible intercourse by a husband is equivalent to that inflicted by someone else. The gravity of the crime of forcible rape derives not merely from its violent character but also from its achievement of a particularly degrading kind of unwanted intimacy. Where the attacker stands in an ongoing relation of sexual intimacy, that evil, as distinct from the force used to compel submission, may well be thought qualitatively different. [That], in any event, is the conclusion long endorsed by the law of rape and carried forward in the Model Penal Code provision.

Model Penal Code § 213.1, Comment (8)(c), at 345–346 (1980).

But during the rape reform era, state courts and legislatures limited or abandoned the marital rape exemption. *See* WAYNE R. LaFAVE, CRIMINAL LAW (3d ed. 2000), § 7.20, at 779–781. When 40 states still retained some form of the exemption in 1984, one court invalidated it on equal protection grounds as gender-based discrimination. In *People v. Liberta*, 64 N.Y.2d 152, 166–167, 474 N.E.2d 567, 575, 485 N.Y.S.2d 207, 215 (1984), the court criticized the M.P.C defense of the exemption as follows:

The fact that rape statutes exist [is] a recognition that the harm caused by a forcible rape is different, and more severe, than the harm caused by an ordinary assault. [There] is no evidence to support the argument that marital rape has less severe consequences than other rape. On the contrary, numerous studies have shown that marital rape is frequently quite violent and generally has *more* severe, traumatic effects on the victim than other rape. [We] agree with the other courts which have analyzed the [marital rape] exemption, which have been unable to find any present justification for it.

The use of statutory interpretation to reject the marital rape exemption is illustrated by *Jones v. State*, 348 Ark. 619, 74 S.W.3d 663 (2002). The *Jones* defendant argued that the Arkansas legislature had adopted the common law of England when enacting the criminal code, and had thereby adopted the marital rape exemption in common law. However, the *Jones* Court noted that in 1976, the legislature enacted new rape statutes with the preface that: "The provisions of this code shall govern any prosecution for any offense defined by this code and committed after January 1, 1976." The court also observed that the language of the "forcible compulsion" rape statute "is neutral both as to gender and as to relationship, if any, between the perpetrator and the victim." Therefore, the court concluded that "[b]ecause the statute controls, the common law of England is irrelevant." *Id.* at 625–626, 667–668.

4. RAPE AND THE DEATH PENALTY

In the 1960s, civil rights litigation was undertaken in a number of states in order to challenge the constitutionality of the death penalty for rape on equal protection grounds. See M. Meltsner, Cruel and Unusual: The Supreme Court and Capital Punishment, 73–105 (1973). This litigation relied on empirical evidence concerning race discrimination, and the 1980 Revised Comments of the Model Penal Code summarize the history of race discrimination and the rape crime as follows:

> White [men's sexual] imposition upon black women may have been common in the old South. It is the reverse case that tended to dominate the public mind and that assumed a distinctive role in the regional consciousness. [This] reaction also explains the disproportionate tendency of Southern and Border states to punish rape as a capital offense. In 1925, the following states authorized the death penalty for rape: Alabama, Arkansas, Delaware, Florida, Georgia, Kentucky, Louisiana, Maryland, Mississippi, Missouri, Nevada, North Carolina, Oklahoma, South Carolina, Tennessee, Texas, Virginia, West Virginia. There has also been a long history in those jurisdictions of a *de jure* or *de facto* limitation of the death penalty for rape to black offenders. The Georgia Penal Code of 1811 set the penalty for rape at 16 years imprisonment, but the Code applied only to free whites. Blacks were subject to punishment of death under Georgia [statutes]. Even [after] *de jure* discrimination in rape penalties was [abolished], blacks continued to be subject disproportionately to the death penalty for rape. [The Wolfgang and Reidel study published in 1973 showed that] in a 20–year period in 11 southern states, seven times as many blacks were sentenced to death as [whites]. [The Justice Department statistics of 1971 showed that] 89.9 per cent of those executed for rape since 1930 have been non-white, almost double the percentage of blacks among those persons executed for [murder].

Model Penal Code § 213.1, Comment (3)(a), at 281–282 n. 27 (1980).

The litigation of the 1960s led to the Supreme Court's invalidation of death penalty sentencing procedures as "arbitrary" under the Eighth Amendment in *Furman v. Georgia*, 408 U.S. 238 (1972). At the time, statutes in 17 jurisdictions allowed capital punishment for rape. After *Furman*, 35 states enacted new capital homicide statutes, and only six Southern states enacted new capital rape statutes. In *Gregg v. Georgia*, 428 U.S. 153, 179 (1976), the Court validated the post-*Furman* homicide statutes whose procedural safeguards complied with *Furman*'s dictates. Then in *Coker v. Georgia*, 433 U.S. 584 (1977), the Court invalidated a death sentence for rape on Eighth Amendment "disproportionality" grounds, without reference to either the pre-*Furman* equal protection challenges or the evidence of race discrimination. The *Coker* defendant received a death sentence for the rape of an adult woman, and the Court limited its holding to this crime. But the Court also reasoned more broadly that rape cannot be compared to murder "in terms of moral depravity and of the injury to the person and to the public," and concluded that it is "disproportionate" and "excessive "to impose the death penalty, "which 'is unique in its severity and irrevocability,' [upon] the rapist who, as such, does not take human life." *Coker*, 433 U.S. at 598.

In *Kennedy v. Louisiana*, 128 S.Ct. 2641 (2008), the Court addressed the issue left open in *Coker* and held that the death penalty is "disproportionate" and "excessive" for the crime of child rape. The Court's narrow reasoning emphasized that the Eighth Amendment's "evolving standards of decency" required this determination, as evidenced by the consensus of 45 jurisdictions, that did not make child rape a capital crime in 2008. More broadly, the Court expanded upon *Coker*'s logic, and ruled that any "nonhomicide crimes against individual persons" cannot be punished with the severe and irrevocable penalty of death, because such crimes "cannot be compared" in their "severity and irrevocability" with "intentional first degree murder." *Kennedy*, 128 S.Ct. at 2660. See Chapter 14 *infra*.

B. ALTERNATIVE RAPE FORMULAS: DECEPTION AND DRUGS

At common law, the crime of rape included the act of sexual intercourse with a sleeping, unconscious, or drugged woman, because such victims were incapable of giving consent or resisting unwanted sexual acts. Modern statutes and judicial doctrines have expanded these definitions of rape further, but courts sometimes prefer that legislatures take the responsibility for designing the formulas for rape by deception or drugs.

1. RAPE BY DECEPTION

SULIVERES v. COMMONWEALTH

449 Mass. 112, 865 N.E.2d 1086 (2007).

In *Commonwealth v. Goldenberg*, 338 Mass. 377, 155 N.E.2d 187 (1959), we concluded that it is not rape when consent to sexual intercourse is obtained through fraud or deceit. In the present case, the Commonwealth asks us to overrule the *Goldenberg* decision and hold that misrepresentations can in fact substitute for the requisite force. [The] crime of rape is defined in G.L. c. 265, § 22(b): "Whoever has sexual intercourse ... with a person and compels such person to submit by force and against his will, or compels such person to submit by threat of bodily injury, shall be punished. . . ." This definition has changed over time, but the requirement that the act be "by force and against [the] will" of the victim has remained constant for two hundred years.

[The] *Goldenberg* case involved a woman who had gone to the defendant, a physiotherapist, to procure an abortion. The defendant told her that, as part of the procedure, he "had to have intercourse" with her and that it would "help it some way." He then proceeded to have intercourse with her. We noted that "it could not be found beyond a reasonable doubt that the intercourse was without her consent," and that the evidence "negatived the use of force." Thus, the only way the defendant could have been convicted was if his fraudulent representation that the intercourse was medically necessary could both invalidate the consent and supply the requisite "force." We concluded, however, that "[f]raud cannot be allowed to supply the place of the force which the statute makes mandatory"[.]

We turn now to the facts of the present case. [After a mistrial, the defendant filed a motion to dismiss the indictment, and brought this appeal from the denial of that motion.] On the night in question, the defendant had sexual intercourse with the [victim] by impersonating her longtime boy friend, his brother. [The victim testified that] while she was asleep alone in the bedroom she shared with her boy friend, the defendant entered the room, and she awoke. In the dark room, [she] assumed that the defendant was her boy friend returning home from work, and addressed him by her boy friend's name. [The defendant] got into the bed and had intercourse with her. [She was not asleep as shown by her intelligible conversation with him prior to the intercourse.] During the intercourse, she believed that the man was her boy friend, and had she known it was the defendant, she "would have never consented." [We] assume that the defendant fraudulently induced the complainant to have intercourse. However, [the] rule of *Goldenberg* [compels] the conclusion that there was no evidence of rape in this case, and we decline to overrule the *Goldenberg* decision.

[The] crime of rape is defined by statute as nonconsensual intercourse achieved "by force." The Commonwealth contends that the defendant's fraud should be allowed to satisfy the requirement of force [and thereby] asks us to read "force" out of the statute in cases involving misrepresentation as to identity. Yet we have never suggested that force is not an element of the crime, or that "by force" is synonymous with lack of consent. [No] portion of the statutory language may be deemed superfluous [and so] we are not free, any more than we were in the *Goldenberg* case, to adopt the Commonwealth's proposed interpretation.

We assume that, when it enacts legislation, the Legislature is not only aware of existing statutes, but is also aware of the prior state of the law as explicated by the decisions of this court. Thus, we find it significant that the Legislature has not seen fit to overrule the *Goldenberg* decision in forty-eight years, during which the rape statute was amended three times [and] scholarship and attitudes regarding rape changed considerably.... The Legislature is free to amend the rape statute or create a new substantive offense to encompass the conduct at issue, as many other States have done. However, where the Legislature has chosen not to do so, "[i]t is not for this court ... to rewrite the clear intention expressed by the statute." *Commonwealth v. Leno*, 415 Mass. 835, 841, 616 N.E.2d 453 (1993).

[The] Commonwealth attempts to distinguish the *Goldenberg* decision on the ground that it involved "fraud in the inducement" while the present case is one of "fraud in the factum." We find this argument unpersuasive. [The] term "fraud in the factum" typically refers to "the rare case when there has been fraud as to the essential nature of [a legal] instrument or an essential element of it." *Federico v. Brockton Credit Union*, 39 Mass.App.Ct. 57, 63, 653 N.E.2d 607 (1995). "Fraud in the inducement," by contrast, occurs "when a misrepresentation leads another to enter into a transaction with a false impression of the risks, duties, or obligations involved," but there is no fraud as to the essential nature of the transaction. In the context of rape, by analogy, "fraud in the factum" must mean that the victim is defrauded as to the nature of the act performed, rather than the reason for doing it. [Black's Law Dictionary 686 (8th ed. 2004)] Compare *Boro v. Superior Court*, 163 Cal.App.3d 1224, 1228, 210 Cal.Rptr. 122 (1985) (fraud in factum where victim consents to doctor's penetration of her with medical instrument but he then penetrates her with his penis), with *State v. Bolsinger*, 709 N.W.2d 560, 564 (Iowa 2006) (fraud in inducement where defendant touched victims' genitals on pretext of medical examination because they were "touched in exactly the manner represented to them"). In the present case, there is no claim that the [victim] did not know she was consenting to a sex act; rather, just as in the *Goldenberg* case, her consent was induced by fraud as to the circumstances surrounding the act. Thus, the present case involves "fraud in the inducement," as did *Goldenberg*, and is squarely controlled by that decision.

[The] defendant's motion for a required finding of not guilty should have been granted. This case is remanded to the county court for entry of an appropriate order ... barring a subsequent retrial[.]

Note

Legislative definitions of rape by fraud. The *Suliveres* Court recognized that other state legislatures have defined "fraud" as a basis for sexual assault crimes. These statutes take different approaches to defining the scope of the fraud concept. For example, the Michigan sexual conduct crime includes sexual penetration of another "through concealment", and the Tennessee rape crime applies to sexual penetration "accomplished by fraud." See Mich. Comp. Laws Ann. § 750.520b (West Supp. 2007); Tenn. Code Ann. § 39–13–503 (LexisNexis 2006). The more narrow California rape crime includes sexual intercourse "[w]here a person submits under the belief that the person committing the act is the victim's spouse, and this belief is induced by any artifice, pretense, or concealment practiced by the accused, with intent to induce the belief." Cal. Pen. Code § 261(5) (West Supp. 2007). However, the same statute illustrates how a legislature may seek to avoid the distinction illustrated by the contrasting holdings of *Boro* and *Bolsinger* described in *Suliveres*. In 2002, the California rape definition was amended in § 289(d)(4) to include sexual penetration when the victim "is unconscious of the nature of the act", which occurs when the victim is "not aware, knowing, perceiving, or cognizant of the essential characteristics of the act due to the perpetrator's fraudulent representation that the sexual penetration served a professional purpose when it served no professional purpose."

PROBLEM

Judicial Interpretation of "Force" as Fraud. The unwillingness of the *Suliveres* Court to define "force" as "fraud" appears to illustrate the inherent limitations of statutory interpretation as a vehicle for rape reform. By contrast, courts have been willing to define "force" as "constructive" force, and prosecutors have been allowed to prove "force" through evidence of "fear", or "resistance", or "lack of consent." Describe the policy reasons, not discussed in the *Suliveres* opinion, that can be used to explain the reluctance of courts to expand the definition of "force" to encompass "fraud" as illustrated by the facts of *Suliveres*.

2. RAPE BY DRUGS

It is common for rape statutes to apply where a victim is incapable of giving consent because of unconsciousness, or physical or mental helplessness. For example, the California rape statute applies where sexual intercourse occurs and "where a person is prevented from resisting by any intoxicating or anaesthetic substance, or any controlled substance, and this condition was known, or reasonably should have been known by the accused" or "where a person is unconscious or asleep [and this is known by the accused]." See Calif. Penal Code § 261(a)(3) & (4)(A) (2003). Some drugs can cause a victim to become unconscious and then, after a rape occurs, to have amnesia about what happened before and after they became unconscious. These circumstances may make it difficult for a prosecutor to obtain sufficient evidence to convict a defendant accused of rape of a drugged victim.

In *Sera v. Norris*, 400 F.3d 538 (8th Cir. 2005), the court upheld the defendant's convictions for multiple rapes of one victim, where the crime was defined as sexual intercourse "with a physically helpless person", even though the victim could not testify that an act of sexual intercourse occurred. The defendant was married but dating the victim, and when they took three trips together, the victim remembered that the defendant gave her two alcoholic drinks during each trip, just before she lost her memory of what happened next. Following one of the trips, the defendant's wife found a bottle of Rohypnol in his suitcase, "a so-called 'date rape drug'" that can cause "hypnosis, total muscle relaxation, and loss of memory" in the form of "anterograde amnesia." A person who has taken the drug "can be talking and functioning yet still not be able to remember what is happening", and alcohol magnifies the effects of the drug, causing a deeper state of unconsciousness. A divided court in *Sera* found sufficient circumstantial evidence for a jury to infer that a rape occurred during each trip, based on the similarity of the victim's experiences and drug symptoms, the defendant's access to the drug, and a videotape which showed the defendant raping the unconscious victim during the first trip. However, the defendant's federal habeas corpus action required only "limited and deferential review" of the state court's "not unreasonable" affirmance of his conviction.

C. STATUTORY RAPE

When the American common law absorbed the English "statutory" crime of sexual intercourse with a female under 10, the term "statutory rape" became the name of the crime. Consent was no defense because a child victim was presumed to be incapable of consent, and mistake as to the victim's age was no defense. By the 1950s, most statutes had raised the age of the victim to 16 or 17, and consensual sex acts with victims under 18 years old were covered in some jurisdictions. This change was troubling for judges who did not want to impose harsh penalties for the crime of consensual sex *between* underage teenagers, especially when only boys were subject to prosecution. In the 1960s, a few courts chose to recognize the defense of reasonable mistake as to the victim's age, as endorsed in the Model Penal Code for cases involving underage defendants and some victims. By 1980 the crime applied only to victims under 16 in most states; in the ensuing decades, states adopted gender neutral statutes, and provisions resembling the M.P.C. requirement of a four-year age gap when victims and defendants are between 10 and 16 years of age. This gap was "chosen to reflect the prevailing pattern of secondary education" so that "felony sanctions for mutually consensual behavior" would not apply to school "romancers." M.P.C. § 213.3(1)(a); Comment (2), at 386. Yet these legislative strategies did not relieve courts from resolving difficult policy questions concerning the appropriate scope of the statutory rape crime.

IN RE G.T.

170 Vt. 507, 758 A.2d 301 (2000).

DOOLEY, J.

The trial court's findings are not contested on appeal. G.T. [was a fourteen-year-old boy who] lived across the street from M.N., a twelve-year-old girl. The two had been friends, but had never had sexual contact with each other prior to the incident in question. One night in October 1995, while G.T. and M.N. were watching a television movie in M.N.'s house, G.T. began kissing M.N. on the mouth. G.T. then pulled M.N.'s legs out straight, pulled her shorts down, pulled his pants down, and got on top of her. He continued kissing her with his hands on her shoulders. M.N., who had never previously had intercourse, felt what she believed was G.T.'s penis in her vagina. G.T. asked if it hurt, but did not stop when M.N. said it hurt. Although she was not afraid of him, M.N. was not sure what G.T. would have done if she had pushed him off of her. G.T.'s actions were interrupted when M.N.'s mother and boyfriend unexpectedly returned to the house. They saw G.T. scramble up off M.N., but did not observe sexual contact. They ordered G.T. out of the house. M.N. began crying and ran upstairs. She revealed to her mother what had occurred.

On these facts, the State alleged that G.T. had committed statutory rape and, therefore, had engaged in a delinquent act. [This crime is defined in § 3252(a)(3) as follows: "A person who engages in a sexual act with another person and . . . [t]he other person is under the age of 16. . . ." A sexual act is defined as "any intrusion, however, slight, by any part of a person's body or any object into the genital or anal opening of another."] [The] family court [agreed with the prosecutor,] adjudicated G.T. a delinquent child, and this appeal followed.

[The State argues that the plain meaning of the statute is that the crime covers all persons, including those under sixteen, who engage in a sexual act with anyone under 16.] G.T. argues [that] the Legislature intended that the perpetrator be a person of sixteen years of age or older. Although G.T. recognizes that the plain meaning of the term might not contain that limitation, he argues that the context does require such a limitation.

[W]e have held that statutory rape is a strict liability offense, for which the only elements are the age of the "victim" and the presence of a sexual act. [U]nder the State's theory, both G.T. and M.N. have necessarily committed the crime, and all consensual sexual activity between teenagers is a felony for both participants. Given the prevalence of such activity, see Vermont Dep't of Health, Vermont Youth Risk Behavior Survey 53–54 (1997) (among students in the eleventh grade, the year in which they generally turn sixteen, fifty-six percent of males and fifty percent of females report having had sexual intercourse) and the potential sentence of twenty years in jail, G.T. argues that such a construction creates absurd, irrational or unjust results. . . .

We find [two reasons] to [question] the apparent plain meaning of § 3252(a)(3) in this context. The first is that the Legislature has taken other actions which appear inconsistent with the plain meaning of [the statute]. [Under Vermont law, statutory rape qualifies as "sexual abuse",] and [a] "child who is sexually abused [by] any person" is an "abused or neglected child." [The statutory duty to report suspected "abuse" of a child] to the Department of Social and Rehabilitation Services (SRS) within twenty-four hours [is imposed on school personnel, health care providers, mental health professionals, social workers, police, and others]. Failure to make such a report is a misdemeanor, subject to [criminal prosecution and a fine].

Under the State's theory in this case, if two persons under sixteen years of age commit consensual, mutual sexual acts with each other, they are both guilty of statutory rape. Thus, under the child abuse reporting laws, [many] professionals who learn of the acts must report them to SRS or risk prosecution. SRS must notify each child's parents and list both children in the child abuse registry as victims and perpetrators. [We have previously] noted the irony of maintaining confidential the fact and detail of a juvenile delinquency adjudication, while placing and disseminating information about the same juvenile in the child abuse registry. Here the tension goes beyond irony. We seriously doubt that the Legislature intended to label a juvenile under sixteen years of age who engages in a sexual act a child abuser for life. . . .

The second reason [to question the apparent plain meaning] is that the State's construction of [the statutory rape statute] involves a breadth of prosecutorial discretion that raises serious concerns about whether the resulting prosecutions are consistent with equal protection of the law. In this case, the prosecutor was candid that he believed G.T. had violated [the forcible rape statute,] which [applies to]: "A person who engages in a sexual act with another person and compels the other person to participate in a sexual act: without the consent of the other person; or by threatening or coercing the other person." [The prosecutor] chose to charge the case under [the statutory rape statute only] because it creates a strict liability offense which is easy to prove. Because sexual conduct is private, prosecution necessarily arises from complaints. The prosecutor added at argument that the Windham County State's Attorney's office receives numerous complaints to prosecute teenagers under [the statutory rape crime], usually from parents, but does so only when there is evidence of coercion or a lack of true consent.

[Although] we have only a limited record here, we note that the selective enforcement of the underlying statute has the hallmarks that other courts have relied upon to find discriminatory prosecution. [W]e [question] a statutory interpretation that necessarily results in this kind of enforcement administration. It is one thing to give discretion in enforcing a legislatively defined crime; it is quite another to give to prosecutors the power to define the crime. [The] preferable response to this kind of discretion is to reduce it by narrowing the ambit of the [statutory rape] statute.

[Therefore,] we construe [the statutory rape crime] as inapplicable in cases where the alleged perpetrator is also a victim under the age of [sixteen]. We [believe] that the statute is intended as a shield for minors and not a sword against them.

[Reversed.]

Johnson, J., dissenting.

[Under] the majority's holding, a fifteen-year-old minor cannot be found delinquent for the statutory rape of, say, a nine- or ten-year-old minor. The majority [assumes] that this will not impose any great burden on prosecutors because they can always seek an adjudication of delinquency based on an allegation of forcible rape[.] [The] majority fails to acknowledge that there will be instances, not unlike the present case, where the coercion is subtle and results from the different age, mental capacity, or maturity of the participants engaged in the conduct. [There] will be [cases] in which forcible rape will be difficult to prove. . . .

[The] majority's concern regarding the breadth of prosecutorial discretion is speculative in nature. There is not the slightest indication that any abuse of that discretion occurred in this case or is occurring generally. [Under] the facts of this case, [the] prosecutor acted properly in filing a petition of delinquency alleging statutory rape against only G.T. and not M.N. As the trial court stated, even though the difference between the two juveniles in this case was only two years, those two years between twelve and fourteen often encompass significant differences in psychological growth, cognitive skills, and sexuality. . . .

Our duty [is] to give effect to the intent of the Legislature. That intent is clear in this case. [Indeed,] Vermont "has long recognized an obligation to protect its children from others *and from themselves*." [*State v.*] *Barlow*, 160 Vt. [527,] 528, 630 A.2d [1299,] 1301 (1993) (emphasis added). The salutary purposes of the statutory rape law identified by this Court—reducing teen-age pregnancy, preventing venereal disease and damage to reproductive organs, and protecting minors who may be unable to give considered consent or who may

have a heightened vulnerability to physical and psychological harm—
are furthered regardless of the age of the alleged perpetrator. See *id.*
at 528, 530, 630 A.2d at 1300–1301 (recognizing that minors often
lack experience, perspective, and judgment to avoid choices that
could be detrimental to themselves and others).

I am authorized to say that Justice Gibson joins in this dissent.

NOTES

1. *Consequences of juvenile delinquency finding.* The majority opinion
noted that even though G.T. could not receive the adult penalty, he could be
placed in a "treatment, rehabilitative, or educational institution or facility"
and that the "adjudication of delinquency becomes part of the juvenile's
record available to the court in a future sentencing proceeding." The
dissenters observed that the goal of the M.P.C.'s age-gap proposal was to
protect juveniles from "the family court's power to intervene in the lives of
those adjudged to be delinquents." *In re G.T.*, 170 Vt. at 520, 509 n.2, 531–
532, 758 A.2d at 309, 303 n.2, 317–318.

2. *Reasonable mistake as to age.* State courts continue to debate the
question whether to recognize the reasonable mistake as to age defense for
statutory rape. Some sharply divided courts reject the defense on the
grounds that silence as to mens rea in a statutory rape statute should be
interpreted as evidence of legislative intent to impose strict liability. The
dissenters in these cases argue that this interpretation conflicts with the
presumption against strict liability for felony crimes with significant penalties.
See, *e.g.*, *State v. Martinez*, 14 P.3d 114 (Utah App. 2000); *State v. Anthony*, 351
N.C. 611, 528 S.E.2d 321 (2000); *State v. Yanez*, 716 A.2d 759 (R.I. 1998). In
defending a strict liability interpretation for statutes that apply only to
younger victims, such as those under 14, some courts have emphasized the
need to protect from them the severe physical and psychological consequences of sexual acts. See *People v. Douglas*, 381 Ill.App.3d 1067, 320
Ill.Dec. 163, 886 N.E.2d 1232 (2008) (following *Yanez*). Compare Catherine
L. Carpenter, *On Statutory Rape, Strict Liability, and the Public Welfare Offense
Model*, 53 Am. U. L. Rev. 312 (2003) (arguing that the judicial critiques of
strict liability for statutory rape are outmoded).

3. *Equal Protection and "Romeo and Juliet" statutes.* A Kansas provided for
more lenient punishment for the crimes of "voluntary sexual intercourse,
sodomy, or lewd touching when, at the time of the incident, (1) the victim is
a child of 14 or 15; (2) the offender is less than 19 years of age and less than
4 years older than the victim; (3) the victim and offender are the only ones
involved; and (4) the victim and offender are members of the opposite sex."
Limon, an 18–year–old male, was convicted of voluntary sodomy when he
engaged in a consensual act with M.A.R., a 15–year–old male. Limon and
M.A.R. are not members of the opposite sex and so Limon could not receive
the benefits of being charged under the "Romeo and Juliet" statute, which
exempts defendants from the stigma of sex offender registration, and

establishes a presumption for a sentence of probation for a first offender, with a maximum sentence of five months in jail. When Limon challenged the "opposite-sex" clause as a violation of equal protection, the court invalidated the clause in *State v. Limon*, 280 Kan. 275, 122 P.3d 22 (2005), holding that it established a "discriminatory classification" and furthered no legitimate state interest under the rational basis test. The court relied on *Lawrence v. Texas*, 539 U.S. 558 (2003) (holding that sodomy law applying to persons of the same sex violates due process) and *Romer v. Evans*, 517 U.S. 620 (1996) (relying on equal protection to invalidate state constitutional amendment prohibiting government protection of "homosexual, lesbian, bisexual orientation, conduct, practices or relationships").

PROBLEMS

1. *Revising the Vermont Statute.* Assume that you are the legal counsel to the state legislative committee in Vermont that is considering various options for possible revisions of the statutory rape statute after the *In re G.T.* decision. Four options are being considered: a) revising the statute to codify explicitly the majority's holding in *In re G.T.*; b) revising the statute to codify explicitly the dissent's holding in *In re G.T.*; c) codifying a reasonable mistake as to age defense when the defendant and the victim are between 10 and 16 years old; and d) adopting a four-year age gap requirement when both the offender and victim are under 16 and older than 10. Describe the pros and cons of each option and explain your recommendations as to which option(s) should be adopted.

2. *Drafting the Limon Opinion.* Assume that you are the law clerk for the Kansas Supreme Court judge who is writing the *Limon* opinion invalidating the "opposite-sex" clause described in Note 3 *supra*. Your research shows that the original draft of the "Romeo and Juliet" statute contained no opposite-sex clause when it was proposed by the Kansas Sentencing Commission in order to address concerns "raised by judges" about the sentencing of parties "in a mutual relationship" where "parents or other parties initiate prosecution." The Kansas County & District Attorneys Association (KCDAA) opposed the draft law on the grounds that: 1) "there are predatory relationships out there, regardless of the proximity in age between predator and victim" and so any "cases truly involving Romeo and Juliet are better left to prosecutor discretion"; 2) the goal of statutory rape prosecutions is to prevent teen pregnancy, which can occur without an age gap between predator and victim. The Kansas legislators ignored the opposition of the KCDAA, voted for the draft law, and sent it to conference committee. At this point, the opposite-sex clause was added to the law for unknown reasons.

Your judge tells you that the constitutionality of the opposite-sex clause was upheld by the lower appellate court based on three state interests that satisfied the rational basis test: 1) protection of teenagers against "coercive relationships"; 2) protection of teenagers from "increased health risks that accompany sexual activity"; and 3) "promotion of parental responsibility and procreation." In applying the rational basis test, the lower court held that the opposite-sex clause is neither *under-inclusive* (insufficiently broad to effectively accommodate the state's interest), nor *over-inclusive* (burdening a wider range of individuals than necessary). Your judge asks you to draft the arguments for the *Limon* opinion that will overrule the lower court decision and explain why the opposite-sex clause *cannot* satisfy the rational basis test, based on the legislative history of the statute and the four possible state interests identified by the lower court.

3. *Consensual Sex with Student.* A Connecticut statute defines sexual assault to include sexual intercourse and oral sexual conduct between "a school employee" and a "person who is a student enrolled in a school in which the actor works or a school under the jurisdiction of the local or regional board of education which employs the actor...." The age of the student and the consensual nature of the relationship are immaterial. A defendant challenged this statute's application to his acts of consensual sexual intercourse with students who were over the age of consent (16) under the statutory rape law. He argued that the *Lawrence* decision (see Note 3 *supra*) recognized "that the right of privacy includes the right to engage in private noncommercial consensual sexual intercourse with persons over the age of consent." The court assumed *arguendo* that *Lawrence* recognized this due process right, but held that this right did not encompass the defendant's acts, and that the statute satisfied the rational basis test. What arguments support this holding? See *State v. McKenzie–Adams*, 281 Conn. 486, 915 A.2d 822 (2007).

D.   PROOF LIMITATIONS

During the rape reform era, significant innovations in evidence law for rape trials evolved in statutes and case law. "Rape shield" statutes were enacted in all states and in Rule 412 of the Federal Rules of Evidence to prohibit, with some exceptions, the admission of evidence of prior sexual conduct by victims with persons other than the defendant. Expert witnesses were allowed to testify about "rape trauma syndrome" to explain victim behavior to juries. The prosecution's "fresh complaint" witnesses were subjected to fewer restrictions as the prompt reporting requirement eroded. Defendants were required by most courts to show a compelling need to obtain a mental health examinations of victims. Some state courts and legislatures also adopted evidence rules modeled on Federal Rules 413 and 414 which allow prosecutors to obtain sexual assault convictions by offering evidence of the defendant's prior sexual offenses.

1.   EVIDENCE BARRED BY RAPE SHIELD STATUTES

The first rape shield statute was part of the 1975 Michigan rape reform statute; within three years, 30 states had adopted such laws and Congress adopted Federal Rule 412. Rape shield laws eliminate the common law presumption that a victim's prior sexual conduct is relevant to prove her lack of credibility and willingness to consent to forcible sex. The opposite presumption, that such evidence is not generally relevant in a rape trial, is expressed in rape shield laws, either through a statutory list of exclusions and exceptions or through the delegation of case-by-case determinations of relevancy to the discretion of trial judges. Both types of rape shield laws require that even non-excluded evidence will not be admissible unless its probative value outweighs its potential prejudicial effect. When defendants challenge the exclusion of rape-shield evidence as a violation of their Sixth Amendment rights to a fair trial and confrontation of witnesses, courts will apply the interpretations of these rights that have been established in the rape-shield context. The complexity and variety of state and federal rape shield rules has spawned a constant stream of litigation and legislative change.

STATE v. ALBERTS

722 N.W.2d 402 (Iowa 2006).

[The victim R.M. is 22 years old and the defendant Alberts is the 42-year-old uncle of her boyfriend Jesse. In the past, R.M. had attended family gatherings with Jesse where Alberts was present. One night in October, R.M. attended a party at a Cedar Rapids bar, and Alberts happened to be there. R.M. drank several beers and a shot of tequila, and struck up a conversation with Alberts. At closing time, R.M. decided to go with Alberts to his family's lake house, where she ate some food but then quickly vomited. When she told Alberts that she felt ill and needed to "sleep this off", Alberts followed her into a bedroom. There he sat on the bed while R.M. took off her skirt, got into the bed, and fell asleep. Sometime later, R.M. woke up to find Alberts sucking her breasts. She pretended to be asleep while he had oral sex and sexual intercourse with her. Then Alberts left and slept in another bedroom. In the morning, Alberts drove R.M. to her home, and as soon as Jesse arrived, R.M. told him about what happened. He drove her to the hospital, where she reported the rape. At his trial, Alberts admitted that he had sex with R.M, but claimed that it was consensual. He was convicted of third degree sexual abuse.]

[Before trial, the defense counsel and prosecutor debated the admissibility of evidence and the trial judge granted the prosecutor's motion in limine to exclude evidence of a "skinny dipping" incident involving R.M. at a Fourth of July party, when her boyfriend's brother Josh discovered her in the Cedar River with her arms around a man named Chris Slach. Each of the three witnesses to this incident gave deposition testimony. Josh testified that after he appeared on the river bank, R.M. left the water, crying, and told Josh, "Thank God you saw me. I didn't know what to do out there. . . . I couldn't get away from him. I didn't know what to do." However, R.M. testified that Sach never "forced himself" on her, and that "he got close to me and asked me if he could kiss me, and I said, 'No, I have a boyfriend.'" Sach said that it was R.M.'s idea to go skinny-dipping, that she took her clothes off first and encouraged him to do the same, and that R.M. put her arms around him. He corroborated R.M.'s testimony that she declined his kiss. Both R.M. and Sach testified that there was no sexual contact or activity between them. The incident occurred at midnight and the two of them had never previously spoken.]

During argument on the motion in limine, Alberts contended this [incident] was relevant because R.M.'s statement to Josh [was] similar to her response [to] her sexual encounter with Alberts [when she reported the rape to Jesse]. [Alberts] claimed that this evidence [of R.M.'s statements to Josh] was important to his case because it supported his theory that R.M. accused men of improper sexual conduct in order to shift blame away from her supposed infidelity. He also claimed this incident was particularly relevant because it reflected on the credibility of the only other witness to the alleged rape—R.M.

Alberts argued the rape-shield law was not applicable to this situation because there was no sexual contact and therefore no "past sexual behavior." Alternatively, he argued that if this was sexual activity or sexual behavior, then it was admissible under the false-claim exception to the rape-shield law. The [trial judge] excluded any evidence pertaining to the skinny-dipping incident [without explanation]. . . .

Rule 5.412 prohibits introduction of reputation or opinion evidence of a complainant's "past sexual behavior" [defined as "sexual behavior other than the sexual behavior with respect to which sexual abuse is alleged."] [In *State v. Baker*, 679 N.W.2d 7, 10 (Iowa 2004),] [w]e recently clarified this definition:

> "past sexual behavior" means a volitional or non-volitional physical act that the victim has performed for the purpose of the sexual stimulation or gratification of either the victim or another person or an act that is sexual intercourse, deviate sexual intercourse or sexual contact, or an attempt to engage in such an act, between the victim and another person.

[At] the outset, we concede the difficulty in determining what sexual behavior is for purposes of our rape-shield law. In *State v. Zaehringer*, 280 N.W.2d 415 (Iowa 1979), we were asked to determine the applicability of the rape-shield law [to] nude posing [and we reasoned:]

> [Posing] nude does not in and of itself [connote] sexual activity or conduct. Absent a showing or implication of sexual activity of some sort accompanying the posing, [the rape-shield exclusion] does not come into play....

[*Id.*] at 420. Just like nudity alone is not sexual, skinny-dipping in and of itself is not sexual behavior. But in this case, the skinny-dipping incident should be deemed sexual behavior based on the circumstances described.... Based on [the deposition testimony of R.M., Slach, and Josh], the skinny-dipping was likely a precursor to sexual activity. This is evidenced by Slach asking for a kiss. To say it was not sexual behavior would be to say a circumstance where the complaining witness was thwarted in her attempt to meet someone [other than the defendant] for an amorous rendezvous was not sexual behavior. Such a result would be contrary to the purpose of the rape-shield law, which is to protect the victim's privacy, encourage the reporting and prosecution of sex offenses, and prevent the parties from delving into distractive, irrelevant matters. Thus, this particular episode of skinny-dipping is covered by the rape-shield law unless R.M. made a related false allegation of sexual misconduct.

In *Baker*, we held prior false claims of sexual activity do not fall within the coverage of our rape-shield law [because they are] not sexual behavior. We [now] hold that a criminal defendant wishing to admit such [false-claim] evidence must first make a threshold showing to the trial judge outside the presence of the jury that (1) the complaining witness made the statements and (2) the statements are false, based on a preponderance of the evidence.... [In this case,] the court failed to take the additional step of determining whether R.M. made a false claim of sexual misconduct [which] would make the rape-shield law not applicable [to the evidence of the skinny-dipping incident].

[The] State [now argues that irrespective of whether] the skinny-dipping incident [is] covered under [the rape-shield law,] it was properly excluded under general considerations of relevancy[.] ... [The] State contends the skinny-dipping incident was irrelevant because it has nothing to do with whether R.M. consented to the sexual encounter with Alberts. We disagree.... R.M.'s statements to Josh, if she did say them, are relevant for two reasons. First, they reflect on her credibility as a witness. Second, the alleged statements may reveal a motive to lie. If a fact-finder were to conclude she made untruthful statements to preserve her boyfriend's perception of her virtue when she was discovered skinny-dipping with another man, the fact-finder might reasonably conclude she's also untruthful with respect to her allegations that Alberts raped her for the same reason.

[We] do not find that any [dangers of prejudice] potentially outweighed the probative value of this evidence. This evidence would not have been [misleading] to the jury because R.M. would have had ample opportunity to deny or explain her allegedly untruthful statements. Finally, while it may have been embarrassing for R.M. to testify about going skinny-dipping, this is not the kind of unfair prejudice that will outweigh the probative value of clearly relevant evidence.

[Alberts] was entitled to a hearing in order to prove R.M. made a prior false claim of sexual misconduct [that would be admissible at trial, and we] must now decide whether the trial court's failure to conduct such a hearing requires us to reverse and remand for a new trial. [There] was no physical evidence of an assault [and no] other witnesses [to the assault]. The jury's assessment of the relative credibility of R.M. and Alberts was the key to the conviction, thereby enhancing the relevance of the allegedly false prior allegation. By denying Alberts the opportunity to prove [that R.M.] made a prior false claim of sexual misconduct, the court hampered Alberts' ability to argue that R.M. accused another man of improper conduct to disguise her own questionable behavior. This error may have unduly prejudiced Alberts' defense and therefore requires us to remand the case [for a new trial, including a hearing on the false-claim evidence].

NOTES

1. *Purposes of rape shield laws.* The main goal of rape shield laws is "to prevent a sexual assault trial from degenerating into an attack upon the [victim's] reputation rather than focusing on the relevant legal issues[.]" *Commonwealth v. Jones*, 826 A.2d 900 (Pa. Super. 2003). One court summarized the relevant policy concerns as follows:

> Rape shield laws were adopted in response to anachronistic and sexist views that a woman who had sexual relations in the past was more likely to have consented to sexual relations with a specific criminal defendant. Those attitudes resulted in two rape trials at the same time— the trial of the defendant and the trial of the rape victim based on her past sexual conduct. It has been said that the victim of a sexual assault is assaulted twice—once by the criminal justice system. The protections in rape shield laws recognized that intrusions into the irrelevant sexual history of a victim were not only prejudicial and embarrassing but also a practical barrier to many victims reporting sexual crimes.

State v. Sheline, 955 S.W.2d 42 (Tenn. 1997). The presumption that sexual history evidence will cause the jury to be unfairly prejudiced against the victim and the prosecution derives from the experience of prosecutors in the pre-reform era. After the enactment of the Michigan rape shield statute, judges and attorneys in Michigan perceived that this law enhanced the prosecution's opportunity to obtain rape convictions. See JEANNE C. MARSH, ALISON GEIST, & NATHAN CAPLAN, RAPE AND THE LIMITS OF LAW REFORM 59–65 (1982).

2. *Rape-shield exceptions.* The "exclusions and exceptions" model of rape shield laws is illustrated by Federal Rule 412, which provides the exclusion of sexual-behavior evidence with these exceptions: A) a "specific instance of sexual behavior" by the victim to prove that a person other than the accused was the source of semen, injury, or other physical evidence; B) a "specific instance of sexual behavior" by the victim with respect to the person accused of the sexual misconduct, offered by the accused to prove consent or by the prosecution; C) evidence the exclusion of which would violate the constitutional rights of the defendant. Some courts have established judge-made exceptions to rape shield statutes, and the "false claim of sexual misconduct" doctrine in *Alberts* is one example. See Denise R. Johnson, *Prior False Allegations of Rape: Falsus in Unio Falsus in Omnibus*, 7 Yale J.L. & Feminism 243 (1995).

3. *Prior sexual "conduct" or "behavior" as including statements and fantasies.* In 1994, the term "prior sexual conduct" in Federal Rule 412 was amended to replace the word "conduct" with "behavior." According to the Advisory Committee Notes, "prior sexual behavior" of the victim "connotes all activities that involve actual physical conduct" and "the word 'behavior' should be construed to include activities of the mind, such as fantasies or dreams." In arguing that the term "prior sexual conduct" in a state statute should be interpreted to emulate the newer federal definition of "prior sexual behavior", one judge reasoned as follows:

> As recently as 1970, *Wigmore on Evidence* suggested that every woman who claimed she had been raped should be subjected to a psychological evaluation. The reason for this claim was, "The unchaste (let us call it) mentality finds incidental but direct expression in the narration of imaginary sex incidents of which the narrator is the heroine or victim.". . . . This language suggests the attitude that some women accuse men of rape because they have conflated sexual fantasy with criminal violence.

> The Rape Shield Statute represents an express rejection of such attitudes. We now recognize the scarring effects of sexual assault, and the burden placed on victims by testifying about such a deeply personal invasion. . . . [E]vidence of past sexual acts with others has little probative value of whether a victim consented to have sex with a defendant in the present [and] this lack of probative force extends to evidence about a victim's sexual fantasies. Requiring a victim to testify about sexual fantasies can be as intrusive as testifying about prior sexual acts.

People v. Garcia, 179 P.3d 250, 261 (Colo.App. 2007) (Bernard, J., specially concurring). However, the *Garcia* majority rejected this argument because "[t]he fantasy could be established without revealing whether the victim had ever acted it out" and so inquiry into such statements would not subject the victim "to a fishing expedition into her past sexual conduct." *Garcia*, 179 P.3d at 255. State courts remain divided as to whether prior sexual "conduct" or "behavior" should include oral or written statements about previous sexual activity, sexual thoughts or sexual fantasies.

4. *Sixth Amendment challenges.* In *Michigan v. Lucas*, 500 U.S. 145 (1991), the Supreme Court determined that courts should make case-by-case determinations as to whether the exclusion of evidence under a rape shield statute violates the Sixth Amendment. For example, Federal Rule 412 requires a defendant to give notice (15 days before trial) regarding rape-shield-related evidence that the defendant will seek to introduce at trial. In *LaJoie v. Thompson*, 217 F.3d 663 (9th Cir. 2000), the court exercised the discretion allowed by *Lucas* and held on the facts that the trial judge violated the Sixth Amendment by excluding evidence submitted after the 15-day deadline that was otherwise admissible under the rape shield statute. Some courts use a five-factor test to determine whether evidence that violates a rape shield law should be admissible under the Sixth Amendment: 1) whether there is a clear showing that the victim committed the prior acts; 2) whether the circumstances of the prior acts closely resemble those of the present case; 3) whether the prior acts are clearly relevant to a material issue, such as identity, intent, or bias; 4) whether the evidence is necessary to the defendant's case; 5) whether the probative value of the evidence outweighs its prejudicial effect. See, *e.g.*, *State v. Stephen F.*, 144 N.M. 360, 188 P.3d 84 (N.M. 2008); *State v. Harris*, 272 Wis.2d 80, 680 N.W.2d 737 (2004).

PROBLEMS

1. *False Claim of Sexual Misconduct.* The *Alberts* Court did not decide whether R.M.'s statement about the skinny-dipping incident should be admissible under the "false claim" exception to the rape shield statute. The trial judge will hold a hearing on this issue, and the defendant must show by a preponderance of the evidence that R.M. made a statement that was a "false" claim of sexual misconduct.

   a. *Arguments at the Hearing.* What arguments can the defense counsel make to satisfy the burden imposed by the *Alberts* Court for obtaining admission of the evidence concerning the skinny-dipping incident? What counter-arguments can the prosecutor make in rebuttal?

   b. *Rejecting Alberts.* Assume that a different state supreme court is considering: i) whether to adopt the "false claim" doctrine recognized by the Iowa Supreme Court in *Alberts*; and ii) how to define this doctrine if it is adopted. What policy arguments can be made by a prosecutor to support the position that the *Alberts* doctrine should be rejected or defined more narrowly?

2. *Prior Sexual Conduct with Defendant.* Even when a victim's prior sexual conduct with a defendant is admissible under rape-shield laws, such evidence will not be admitted unless the trial judge also determines that its probative value outweighs its prejudicial effect.

a. *Evidence in Alberts.* The trial judge in *Alberts* admitted evidence that R.M. and her boyfriend Jesse went with a friend to the same Cedar Rapids bar three weeks before the reported rape. They happened to see Alberts there, and the four danced together as a group. R.M. also danced "provocatively" with Alberts. Then R.M. and Jesse smoked marijuana with Alberts in the cab of his truck, and as they were leaving, R.M. unhooked her bra under her shirt and hung it on the rear view mirror. What arguments did the defense counsel make in *Alberts* to persuade the trial judge to find that: i) this evidence fit the category of R.M.'s "past sexual behavior with the accused" under the Iowa rape shield statute; and ii) this evidence was admissible because it was more probative than prejudicial?

b. *Question and Photograph.* Assume that the marital rape exemption is not recognized under state law and that a defendant is charged with sexual assault upon his wife, which crime includes the act of engaging in oral sex by means of a "threat of physical injury to any person." At the defendant's trial, his wife testifies that two months after she left her husband and moved into a trailer with her children, he broke into it, threatened her with a box cutter, and threatened to harm the children if she refused to perform an oral sex act. She complied only because she was afraid of her husband's threats. During cross-examination, the defense counsel seeks to question the victim about a photograph taken by the defendant before his wife left him. In the photograph, the wife assumes the pose of performing the same type of oral sex act that is subject of the rape crime. The defense counsel asks the judge: 1) to allow the wife to be asked, Did you pose for a photograph while having oral sex with your husband?; and ii) to allow the photograph to be admitted into evidence. The prosecutor's position is that the probative value of the victim's admission to posing for the photograph and the photograph itself are outweighed by the prejudicial impact they would have upon the jury. How should the trial court resolve the issues here? See *Jones v. State*, 348 Ark. 619, 74 S.W.3d 663 (2002).

3. *Prior Acts of Prostitution.* Assume that the victim R.S. testifies that she was walking home late at night when she saw a car that she thought she recognized as belonging to a friend who might give her a ride. She approached the car, and when the Gregory rolled down the window, she realized that she did not know him. When he offered her a ride home, she hesitated and then accepted. Gregory drove to a deserted parking lot, punched R.S. when she tried to get out of the car, and then put on a condom and forced her to have sexual intercourse. When Gregory removed the condom, R.S. noticed that it had broken. Then Gregory opened the car door and pushed R.S. outside. When Gregory was arrested and charged with forcible rape, the broken condom was found in his car. He testified that he had consensual sex with R.S. in exchange for money, and that she had demanded more money when she discovered that the condom had broken. He refused to pay more, they argued, and he pushed her out of his car.

Assume that Gregory's defense counsel seeks to introduce evidence of R.S.'s two convictions for prostitution in 1996 and 1997 for acts committed while working for an escort service. The trial judge rules that these convictions are inadmissible under the rape shield statute because they involved prior sexual conduct with people other than the defendant. Gregory is convicted and he appeals.

a. *Always Admissible.* On appeal Gregory's defense counsel argues that as a policy matter, under the rape shield statute any convictions for prostitution should always be admissible, because the convictions are a matter of public record and so there is little risk that the victim will be unduly embarrassed by their admission. What reasoning could the appellate court use to reject this argument? See *State v. Gregory*, 158 Wash.2d 759, 147 P.3d 1201 (2006).

b. *Admissible on the Facts.* On appeal Gregory's defense counsel argues that the 1996 and 1997 convictions should be interpreted as "relevant" because they are: i) evidence of R.S.'s consent to sexual activity in the past, which without more, makes it more probable that she consented to sexual activity with Gregory; ii) evidence that R.S. had a motive to lie and falsely accuse Gregory of rape. What reasoning could the appellate court use to reject these two arguments? See *id.*

c. *Post–Crime Acts.* Assume that R.S. was convicted of a third act of prostitution for her work for an escort service, and that this act occurred after the victim's encounter with Gregory and before the defendant's rape trial began. Assume that it is unclear whether the rape statute's exclusion of "prior sexual conduct" evidence is meant to exclude sex acts by the victim that occur after the crime as well as those that occur before the crime. If Gregory's defense counsel argues that as a policy matter, the post-crime sexual conduct by R.S. should be admissible under the ambiguous rape shield statute because it is not "prior sexual conduct" occurring before the crime, how should the trial court rule on this question? See *Commonwealth v. Jones*, 826 A.2d 900 (Pa.Super. 2003).

4. *Virginity Evidence.* After the victim reported a rape crime to the police and agreed to a "rape kit exam", a doctor found a "small laceration or tear of her vaginal opening." At trial, the doctor testified that the injury of the vaginal tear "was consistent with non-consensual sex." Witnesses testified that the victim, a woman in her mid-twenties, had fallen asleep at a party due to her intoxication; the victim testified that she did not remember much before she was awakened by the defendant's act of sexual intercourse with her. The defendant testified that the victim consented to the act. The defendant was charged with sexual assault, defined as "knowingly inflict[ing] sexual penetration on a victim [when he] knows that the victim is incapable of appraising the nature of the victim's conduct." At trial, the *prosecutor* sought to introduce the victim's testimony about her sexual history, arguing "that it was relevant to establish that the defendant was the source of her vaginal injury." When the prosecutor asked, "Had you had sexual intercourse with anybody other than the defendant on that day?", the victim

answered, "No." But when the prosecutor asked the victim, "Had you *ever* had sexual intercourse before that day?", the defense counsel objected. If allowed to answer, the victim would have said, No. But the defense counsel argued that: 1) although the statute is silent as to whether the victim's *lack* of sexual history is inadmissible evidence, the court should interpret the statute as prohibiting "virginity" evidence; and 2) even if the rape shield statute does *not* bar this testimony, it should be excluded because it is not probative of the fact that the defendant was the source of the victim's injury, and it is excessively prejudicial to the defendant in the eyes of the jury. How should court resolve these issues? Compare *Fletcher v. People*, 179 P.3d 969 (Colo. 2007) (En Banc).

2. RAPE TRAUMA SYNDROME

During the 1980s, prosecutors started to use the testimony of expert witnesses concerning "rape trauma syndrome," which phenomenon was identified during the 1970s in a study by professors of nursing and sociology. This evidence is widely used in rape trials today, and its relevance is based on its potential usefulness to explain post-rape victim behavior that may seem otherwise inexplicable to jurors who are unfamiliar with the psychological effects of rape. However, courts continue to confront the question as to how expert testimony should be limited to avoid the presentation of unreliable evidence and the risk that jurors will abandon their fact-finding responsibility by deferring to expert testimony.

STATE v. KINNEY
171 Vt. 239, 762 A.2d 833 (2000).

Dooley, J.

[The] State called Dr. Jan Tyler to testify about rape trauma syndrome and the characteristics and conduct of rape victims. The admissibility of this testimony was first contested in pretrial proceedings when the State made an offer of proof indicating Dr. Tyler would testify about rape trauma syndrome and "the behavioral patterns of victims of sexual assault." The State noted that the expert witness would have no contact with the victim and would not offer an opinion on whether the victim was raped by defendant. Defendant challenged the evidence as inadmissible [and cited the federal criteria for assessing the reliability of scientific evidence] under *Daubert v. Merrell Dow Pharmaceuticals, Inc.*, 509 U.S. 579 (1993). The court [rejected] the challenge....

Dr. Tyler testified that rape trauma syndrome is associated with post-traumatic stress disorder—that is, it is a set of behaviors and symptoms experienced by victims of trauma [who] commonly experience symptoms such as nightmares, anxiety, and fear as a result of the trauma. Victims of rape, in particular, may experience symptoms such as difficulty in interpersonal relationships, guilt, shame, and sexual dysfunction.

Dr. Tyler also testified that studies have shown that victims of rape are more likely to resist their attacker by making verbal protests than by struggling or screaming, and that victims are less likely to resist if force is used or threatened. Furthermore, she said that it is not unusual for victims to delay in reporting a rape, especially if the attacker is an acquaintance, and that a rape victim may be more likely to report to a friend first, rather than to someone with whom she is having an intimate relationship. This delay in reporting is related to the feelings of guilt and shame experienced due to the trauma of the rape. Dr. Tyler then testified to statistics regarding the rate of false reporting of rape. Finally, she testified that, although she had no statistics, she thought it would not be unusual for a victim of rape to fall asleep immediately after the assault, due to the physical exertion and psychological responses to the trauma such as denial and withdrawal.

[We] acknowledge that we have never explicitly ruled upon the admissibility of evidence of rape trauma syndrome. [We] concur with the trial court that expert evidence of rape trauma syndrome and the associated typical behavior of adult rape victims is admissible to assist the jury in evaluating the evidence, and frequently to respond to defense claims that the victim's behavior after the alleged rape was inconsistent with the claim that the rape occurred. As with child sexual abuse victims, the jury may be at a loss to understand the behavior of a rape victim. See D. McCord, *The Admissibility of Expert Testimony Regarding Rape Trauma Syndrome in Rape Prosecutions*, 26 B.C. L. Rev. 1143, 1177 (1985). For example, the defense made much of the fact that defendant's parents were close by [sleeping in their bedroom] when the sexual contact took place [in the defendant's bedroom] but [they] heard no signs of a struggle, that the victim appeared to be sleeping peacefully in defendant's bed the next morning, and that she failed to immediately tell her boyfriend she had been raped. Dr. Tyler's testimony explained why a rape victim might exhibit these behaviors.

For the purpose the evidence was used here, it is sufficiently reliable to be admitted. Rape trauma syndrome is professionally recognized as a type of post-traumatic stress disorder, and the behavioral characteristics of rape victims has been the subject of numerous professional studies. As the trial court noted in this case, Dr. Tyler was prepared to address some of the studies that formed the bases for her opinions if the defendant raised them in cross-examination.

We note that the evidence here was of a type that the danger of improper usage or excessive prejudice was at a minimum. The expert never interviewed the victim and offered no opinion whether the victim suffered from rape trauma syndrome or exhibited any of the behavior of a rape victim. Thus, there was little risk that Dr. Tyler would be seen [by the jury] as a truth detector.

We do not, however, have the same view of the expert's testimony about the incidence of false reporting by rape victims. The prosecutor asked Dr. Tyler whether "there are any data on the issue of false reporting that you are aware of?" She answered:

> False reporting, the percentages are very low. About two percent. That's about the same as any other crime that's committed. In other words, the number of people who would report a burglary that didn't happen is about the same as people who would report a rape, with one difference. The statistics for the rape include those reports that are made and then either withdrawn by the victim for whatever reason, either they were false or there's a fear of going through the legal system, or they're being pressured by other persons. Those also include reports that the police will not arrest on because they don't feel they have enough evidence. And they also include those that don't get to trial because the prosecutor feels it's not a winnable case. So when you get down to literal false reporting of this really never happened, it's very small.

In short, Dr. Tyler testified that at least 98% of the rapes reported actually occurred.

In *State v. Percy*, 146 Vt. [475,] 484, 507 A.2d [955,] 960 [(1986)], a rape case in which defendant claimed [both] amnesia caused by insanity and consent of the victim, three psychiatrists testified for the State that rapists typically claim consent or amnesia. We reversed defendant's conviction in part because of the admission of this testimony. We concluded that explanations or excuses offered by other rapists were not relevant, and, in any event, the prejudicial effect of the testimony outweighed the probative value because the jury could have convicted defendant because "he fit the mold" and not because of the evidence in the case.

Similarly, in [*State v.*] *Catsam*, 148 Vt. [366,] 371, 534 A.2d [184,] 188 [(1987)], we found inadmissible an expert's opinion that child victims of sexual abuse do not make up stories of the abuse. As in this case, the evidence was offered as part of the expert's explanation of the typical behavior of victims. We concluded that the expert testimony was tantamount to an expert opinion that the victim was telling the truth and that it invaded the proper role of the jury.

Dr. Tyler's testimony on the rate of false reporting clearly went over the line as explained in *Percy* and *Catsam*. The jury could infer from her testimony that scientific studies have shown that almost no woman falsely claims to have been raped and convict defendant on that basis. [However, the defendant failed to preserve an objection to this testimony, and so it must be determined whether its admission was "plain error", which is found "only in exceptional circumstances where the failure to recognize it would result in a miscarriage of justice."]

This case exhibits none of the hallmarks of [a "plain error" case]. Dr. Tyler never testified about the story or credibility of the victim because she had never interviewed, or even met, the victim. . . . Further, defense counsel was able to reduce the prejudicial effect of the testimony of the low incidence of false reporting by cross-examination. Finally, the prosecutor did not highlight this testimony in closing argument. . . .

[Affirmed.]

NOTE

Daubert, Rule 702, and rape trauma syndrome evidence. The *Kinney* Court did not find it necessary to consider the criteria for the admissibility of scientific evidence under Rule 702 of the Federal Rules of Evidence, or the Supreme Court's interpretation of those criteria in *Daubert.* Instead, *Kinney* relied on state law precedents concerning post-traumatic stress disorder evidence to uphold the admissibility of rape trauma syndrome (R.T.S.) evidence. Rule 702 now provides that:

> If scientific, technical, or other specialized knowledge will assist the trier of fact to understand the evidence or to determine a fact in issue, a witness qualified as an expert by knowledge, skill, experience, training, or education, may testify thereto in the form of an opinion or otherwise, if (1) the testimony is based upon sufficient facts or data, (2) the testimony is the product of reliable principles and methods, and (3) the witness has applied the principles reliably to the facts of the case.

The three enumerated conditions in Rule 702 were added in 2000 to express the reliability concerns identified in the 1993 *Daubert* opinion and its progeny. The *Daubert* Court identified four additional questions to guide federal trial judges in making admissibility decisions about the validity of expert evidence: 1) has it been tested or can it be tested; 2) has it been subjected to peer review and publication; 3) has the known rate or potential rate of error been determined, and do standards exist for controlling the technique's operation; 4) has it been generally accepted within the relevant scientific community. One scholar has noted that if R.T.S. evidence were to be analyzed under the *Daubert* factors, "it would not pass the test." However, such evidence "has passed muster with every court considering the evidence since 1989." Janet C. Hoeffel, *The Gender Gap: Revealing Inequities in Admission of Social Science Evidence in Criminal Cases*, 24 U. Ark. L. Rev. 41, 55 (2001).

1. *Prosecutor's Preparation of Expert.* Assume you are a prosecutor in Vermont who is preparing an expert witness who will testify about rape trauma syndrome. Explain to your expert what kinds of testimony may be presented and what testimony must be avoided according to *Kinney*.

2. *Defense Counsel's Cross-examination of Expert.* Assume you are a defense counsel in Vermont who is preparing to cross-examine an expert witness who will testify about rape trauma syndrome. What questions will you ask in order to attempt to cast doubt on the testimony? What testimony will provoke you to object?

3. FRESH COMPLAINT TESTIMONY

Originally, the common law required the victims of all violent crimes to make a "hue and cry" in order for a criminal prosecution to be brought. Over time, this requirement was abandoned except in rape cases. Courts reasoned that the failure of a rape victim to "promptly" report the crime to the police could justify the inference that her claim of rape was fabricated. Thus, defense counsel could challenge the credibility of a rape victim at trial by using cross-examination to reveal her failure to make a prompt report. The "fresh complaint" doctrine evolved as an avenue for the prosecution to rebut the inference of fabrication and rehabilitate the credibility of victims who did not make a prompt report to police. If a victim disclosed the rape in a "fresh complaint" to a non-police witness, soon after the crime, then this fact could be offered by a prosecutor, but the scope of testimony concerning such a disclosure was limited in these ways: 1) a witness could testify only to the fact of the victim's disclosure and could not describe: a) the victim's actual words or demeanor during the disclosure, b) the time frame of the disclosure, or c) the circumstances giving rise to the disclosure; 2) the victim could testify only as to the identity of the witness to whom the disclosure was made, and could not describe the actual words of the disclosure; 3) the victim's delay in disclosure would result in the exclusion of any testimony about that disclosure. During the rape reform era, as the "prompt report" requirement eroded, courts also abandoned some of the old restrictions in the "fresh complaint" doctrine.

Revised "First Complaint" Doctrine. You are the law clerk for a state court judge who is drafting the opinion that will rename the "fresh complaint" doctrine as the "first complaint" doctrine, and revise it four ways. First, a trial judge will allow the jury to hear the testimony of only the *first* witness to whom the rape victim discloses the crime, and that witness may testify as to: a) the actual words used in the victim's disclosure; b) the victim's demeanor;

c) the time frame of the disclosure; and d) the circumstances giving rise to the disclosure. Second, a rape victim's testimony may describe both the words of the disclosure to the "first complaint" witness and the circumstances concerning the timing of the disclosure. Third, any delay by the victim in reporting the rape to that witness will not be grounds for excluding testimony about the disclosure by either the victim or the witness. Instead, the jury will be allowed to consider the fact of such a delay in weighing the credibility of the victim's testimony. Fourth, trial judges will have the discretion to allow the jury to hear the testimony of one witness who heard the victim's disclosure, when that witness was not the very first person to hear it; in this situation, that witness will serve as a "substitute" for the "first complaint" witness.

Now your judge asks you to draft the reasoning for the opinion, announcing the rules for the "first complaint" doctrine, and explaining how legislative and judicial changes in rape-reform statutes and doctrines support each of the four revisions of the old "fresh complaint" doctrine. In your draft, the judge also asks you to describe a few examples of the circumstances under which the testimony of a "substitute" witness should be allowed. See *Commonwealth v. King*, 445 Mass. 217, 834 N.E.2d 1175 (2005); *Commonwealth v. Murungu*, 450 Mass. 441, 879 N.E.2d 99 (2008).

4. MENTAL HEALTH EXAMINATION OF VICTIM

HAMILL v. POWERS

164 P.3d 1083 (Okla Crim.App. 2007).

[The] State alleges that the [adult victim] was incapable of consenting to sexual relations due to mental retardation. [The rape crime was defined as "rape committed upon a person incapable through mental illness or any unsoundness of mind of giving legal consent regardless of the age of the person committing the crime."] Before filing charges, the State employed a licensed counselor to examine the [victim] and administer intelligence tests to her. The counselor testified at [the] preliminary hearing and gave his opinion about the [victim's] ability to understand and make decisions about sexual matters.

[The defendant] claims that he has a clear legal right to have the [victim] examined by an expert secured by the defense, because the State intends to use its own expert evaluation to prove that the [victim] lacked the ability to consent to sexual relations. [The] State argues that [the defendant] can sufficiently prepare his defense by reviewing the conclusions of the State's expert, and the various records upon which that expert relied, in addition to his personal interview with the [victim]. [The trial court denied the defendant's request on the theory that it had no authority to permit the examination, and the defendant filed a petition for a writ of mandamus to direct the trial court to grant the defendant's request.]

[There] is no general constitutional right to discovery in a criminal case. [Although] the Due Process Clause "has little to say regarding the amount of discovery which the parties must be afforded, . . . it does speak to the balance of forces between the accused and his accuser." *Wardius v. Oregon*, 412 U.S. 470, 474 (1973). [We] have often used writs of prohibition and mandamus to clarity what "due process" requires with regard to particular pretrial discovery issues. . . .

[If] the [victim] here were to sue [the defendant] in a civil action based on the alleged sexual assault, [the defendant] would almost certainly be entitled, under Oklahoma's civil discovery rules, to have her undergo the same type of psychological examination he seeks in this criminal prosecution. [Moreover,] when the criminally accused intends to offer evidence of his own mental condition to support an insanity defense at trial, this Court has never questioned the [trial] court's inherent authority to "level the playing field" by permitting the State to evaluate [a defendant] with its own mental-health experts. Surely, the criminally accused, facing a serious loss of liberty, is entitled to the same quality of discovery granted to every other type of litigant in our justice system.

While the circumstances warranting such action are admittedly rare, most jurisdictions at least recognize the trial court's authority to order a psychological examination of the complaining witness, even in the absence of express statutory provision. [Some courts] hold that a defendant is entitled to conduct such an evaluation if he demonstrates sufficient compelling circumstances, [which exist when] the [victim's] mental state bears directly on an essential element of the charge, and [when] the State intends to offer the testimony of its own expert to support that element of proof at trial. [Both these compelling circumstances exist here, and so we hold that] due process requires that the accused be afforded the opportunity for pretrial investigation of substantially similar quality [as that afforded the prosecution].

For the reasons given above, the petition for writ of mandamus should be, and is hereby, granted.

Note

Opposition to Mental Health Examinations of Victims. In *Nobrega v. Commonwealth*, 271 Va. 508, 628 S.E.2d 922 (2006), the court ruled that a trial judge has no authority to require the complaining witness in a rape prosecution to be examined by an "independent" mental health expert at the request of the defendant. The defendant argued that he should have a due process right to request the trial judge to order a mental health examination of the victim, his eleven-year-old daughter, because: 1) the state's case hinged on the victim's uncorroborated testimony and so the examination was vital to his defense; 2) the victim's medical records showed that she "had been diagnosed with various psychological disorders" but "no current, accurate and independent" evaluation existed to allow the defendant to determine her "capacity to differentiate reality from imagination"; and 3) the purpose of the examination was to determine the victim's competency to testify as a witness at trial. The trial judge denied the defendant's request, giving no weight to his first two arguments, and rejecting the third argument on the grounds that if the requested examination were granted, then: 1) the defendant "would inevitably call [the expert witness] to testify regarding the results of the examination"; 2) the expert's testimony would "usurp the responsibility of the trial court to determine the child's competency to testify"; and 3) the expert also would usurp the responsibility of the fact-finder "to determine the child's credibility as a witness." *Nobrega*, 271 Va. at 512–514, 628 S.E.2d at 923–924.

On appeal, the *Nobrega* Court upheld the trial judge's decision, reasoning that under the common law, trial judges are vested with the discretion to determine the competency of witnesses and to consider expert opinions for that purpose only if they choose to do so. The court was "unpersuaded by the defendant's contention that a majority of jurisdictions have adopted a 'compelling need' test to authorize [trial courts to order mental health] examinations." Instead, the court held that "it is a matter properly left to the [legislature] to consider as an issue of public policy" whether to grant trial courts such authority. The *Nobrega* Court emphasized that: 1) defendants already have "adequate safeguards" available "to the accused to test the competency of the complaining witness without a court-ordered mental health examination"; and 2) such examinations of rape victims would conflict with a variety of policies expressed in rape law reforms. *Nobrega*, 271 Va. at 517–518, 628 S.E.2d at 925–926.

PROBLEM

Defending Nobrega Position. Assume that you are a prosecutor in another state with no precedent on the issue in *Nobrega*, and you want to persuade your state supreme court to adopt the *Nobrega* Court's position. Describe the arguments that you can make: 1) to identify the "adequate safeguards" that already exist to test the competency of rape victims, that is, their capacity accurately to observe, remember, and communicate facts; 2) to explain the ways in which mental health examinations for rape victims would conflict with various policies of rape law reforms; and 3) to distinguish the *Hamill* decision as inapposite in a case like *Nobrega*.

5. ADMISSIBILITY OF DEFENDANT'S PRIOR SEX CRIMES

Ordinarily a prosecutor may not introduce evidence of a defendant's "prior crimes, wrongs, or acts" in order to prove "the character of a person in order to show action in conformity therewith." This longstanding rule also appears in state evidence codes and in Rule 404(b) of the Federal Code of Evidence. The rationale for this ban on "propensity" evidence is that the jury may give it too much weight and convict a defendant based on the conclusion that the defendant is a "bad person." There are well-settled exceptions to this ban that apply when prior crimes evidence is offered as proof of "motive, opportunity, intent, preparation, plan, knowledge, identity, or absence of mistake or accident." *Id.*

In 1995 Congress adopted Rules 413 and 414 in order to nullify the operation of Rule 404(b) in sexual offense cases. Under Rule 413, evidence of the commission of a prior sexual assault crime is admissible and "may be considered for its bearing on any matter to which it is relevant." Rule 414 creates the same rule for child molestation offenses. The new rules are controversial because they did not originate in a proposal by the Advisory Committee on the Federal Rules of Evidence of the Judicial Conference. Instead, Congress enacted the rules in the Violent Crime Control and Law Enforcement Act of 1994. The Act provided that the Judicial Conference could comment on the new evidence rules before the law took effect. When the Advisory Committee expressed opposition to the rules, along with most contributors to the Committee's review process, Congress ignored these views and the new rules went into effect.

Although some states have chosen to adopt new evidence rules modeled on Rules 413 and 414, other states have not. For example, in 2004 the Maryland legislature "considered and rejected bills to admit into evidence prior sex crimes evidence to show propensity in cases involving sexual misconduct with a minor.... Both bills received unfavorable reports and died in committee." *Hurst v. State*, 400 Md. 397, 417–418, 929 A.2d 157, 168 (2007). The *Hurst* Court endorsed that rejection and then examined the question whether propensity evidence should be admitted under one of the traditional 404(b) exceptions recognized in Maryland law. The prosecutor in *Hurst* sought to present the testimony of a rape victim that she did not consent to a sex act with the defendant twenty-one years earlier (which testimony led to his prior rape conviction). The *Hurst* Court concluded that that the prosecutor's only purpose for this testimony was to rebut the defendant's testimony that the victim of the rape crime charged in *Hurst* consented to sex acts with him. Given the lack of sufficient similarity between the two crimes and the time lapse between them, the prior-crime witness's testimony did not fit into any of the exceptions.

Concern about the fairness of the admission of propensity evidence under Federal Rules 413 and 414 is reflected in the consensus among federal courts that such evidence remains subject to scrutiny under Rule 403, which requires courts to balance the probative value of the evidence against its prejudicial effect. One example of such scrutiny is provided by the Ninth Circuit's list of factors to consider when evaluating the admissibility of prior sex offenses under Rule 403: (1) "the similarity of the prior acts to the acts charged," (2) the "closeness in time of the prior acts to the acts charged," (3) "the frequency of the prior acts," (4) the "presence or lack of intervening circumstances," and (5) "the necessity of the evidence beyond the testimonies already offered at trial." This list of factors is not exclusive. See *United States v. LeMay*, 260 F.3d 1018, 1028 (9th Cir. 2001). The Tenth Circuit has identified additional factors, which include (1) how clearly the prior act has been proved; (2) how probative the evidence is of the material fact it is admitted to prove; (3) how seriously disputed the material fact is; (4) whether the government can avail itself of any less prejudicial evidence; (5) how likely it is such evidence will contribute to an improperly-based jury verdict; (6) the extent to which such evidence will distract the jury from the central issues of the trial; and (7) how time consuming it will be to prove the prior conduct. *See United States v. Enjady*, 134 F.3d 1427, 1433 (10th Cir. 1998).

CHAPTER 11

JUSTIFICATION DEFENSES

■ ■ ■

A defense is broadly defined as "any set of identifiable conditions or circumstances that may prevent conviction for an offense." This formulation is very broad since it includes both "legal" as well as "factual" defenses. A "factual" defense is usually one where the jury determines its value, such as self-defense. A "legal" defense would include such matters as delay or double jeopardy which are normally questions of law. While such "legal" defenses can be thought of as having the same effect as a factual defense, i.e., leading to acquittal or conviction on a lesser charge, this chapter will be devoted to the factual defenses tried to a jury. It should be noted that defenses related to specific offenses are discussed in conjunction with those offenses.

Even though a defendant has committed all of the elements of a crime, conviction may be inappropriate if the defendant's actions were either "justifiable" or "excusable." Justifications and excuses are similar because both exculpate a person based on the defendant's blamelessness. Justified conduct adheres to the criminal law's rules of conduct and therefore should be encouraged, or at least tolerated, in similar future situations. A decision whether conduct is justified will focus on a person's act and its circumstances, rather than on the person. Under special justifying circumstances, the harm caused by justified behavior will be viewed as being outweighed by the need to avoid an even greater harm or to promote a greater societal interest. For example, for the justification of self-defense, the defender's right to bodily integrity, combined with the wrongfulness of the physical harm threatened, entitle a person to use physical force against another even though such force is normally not condoned.

A. SELF–DEFENSE

At common law, a defendant was privileged to use force against another person when such force was necessary to defend against the threat of imminent unlawful force being used against her by the other person. The justified use of force to defend against physical harm provides a complete defense to intentional crimes like murder, voluntary manslaughter, assault and battery, and attempted murder.

The force used or threatened against the defendant must be unlawful, i.e., criminal or tortious. The force must also be physical. Thus, provoking words are an insufficient justification for self-defense. The common law also required that a person may use only a proportional amount of force when she believes that she is in immediate danger of unlawful bodily harm so that the use of such force is necessary to avoid the danger. Only a person who is not the aggressor has this right.

1. GENERAL PRINCIPLES

Generally at common law, in order for a defendant to obtain a self-defense instruction, the evidence must establish that at the time the defendant used physical force, she actually believed that the force was necessary to protect herself from another person's imminent use of unlawful physical force *and* her belief was reasonable under the circumstances. If her belief is unreasonable, she cannot claim self-defense. A defendant can use deadly force only when she reasonably believes that deadly force is necessary to defend against violent crimes that may cause death or serious physical injury, such as robbery, kidnapping, or rape.

PEOPLE v. WESLEY
76 N.Y.2d 555, 561 N.Y.S.2d 707, 563 N.E.2d 21 (Ct.App. 1990).

HANCOCK, J. Defendant was convicted after a jury trial of second degree manslaughter, second degree assault, and fourth degree criminal possession of a weapon. His sole contention on appeal is that the court's jury charge on the defense of justification under section 35.15 employed an improper standard for determining the reasonableness of defendant's belief that it was necessary to use deadly physical force. We agree with defendant that the trial court's instruction failed to satisfy fully the requirements as explained in *People v. Goetz*, 497 N.E.2d 41, 506 N.Y.S.2d 18 (1986). Section 35.15 requires an assessment of reasonableness which must be determined from the point of view of the particular defendant under the standard of a reasonable person in defendant's circumstances at the time of the incident. Accordingly, there should be a reversal and a new trial.

Defendant, a 19-year-old college student, was on the porch of a house in Buffalo with Diane Jackson, Jelean McMillan, and Arlene Woods. Woods, who had a knife in her possession, got into an argument with Jackson. The argument continued as Jackson and Woods walked away from each other. Suddenly, Woods doubled back after Jackson and threatened to stab her. Defendant managed to get the knife away from Woods and placed it in a paper bag.

At about that time, three male teen-agers arrived on the scene. Despite defendant's pleas to be left alone, Stone, Robinson and others continued shouting epithets at defendant as he walked down the street. Stone and Robinson also threatened defendant, saying "We'll kick your ass".

Stone left the scene for a few minutes and returned carrying a stick (sometimes referred to as a pipe), 2 to 2½ feet in length and 1 to 3 inches in diameter. After more argument, Stone struck defendant with the stick, and defendant stabbed him in the chest. Stone fell to the ground and dropped the stick. Robinson then picked up the stick and began chasing defendant out of the area where the stabbing had taken place. When Robinson returned, he had been stabbed in the hand. Stone died as a result of the stab wound. Defendant was arrested several hours later.

At the precharge conference, the Trial Judge declined to give the defense's proposed justification charge, stating that the proposed charge was not required under *People v Goetz*. The Judge told both attorneys that he would charge in accordance with *Goetz*, but was unable at that time to state the precise language. The following is that portion of the court's charge under section 35.15 which pertains to the requirement of reasonableness:

> You have heard the conflicting stories told by the witnesses as to what actually happened, and you must consider these stories under the rules of law as I have explained them to you. Having decided in your own minds that what truly occurred, you must then decide whether there was legal justification for the Defendant's alleged acts. In order to find justification for the Defendant's acts, you must find that he believed his conduct necessary to defend himself from what he reasonably believed to be an unprovoked physical assault against himself even if he was mistaken in his conclusion that the victim was about to assault him. As long as he reasonably believed that such assault was about to take place, he was justified in using physical force to repel such an assault. If from all of the testimony you have heard, you believe that the victim's conduct was provoked by the Defendant himself with an intent to cause a physical injury to the victim, or that the Defendant was the initial aggressor in the altercation, then such conduct was not legally justifiable to warrant a verdict of not guilty.

The defense exception [to the court's charge] stated, among other things, that the charge "did not direct the jury to place themselves, or a reasonable person in [defendant's] place, and the *Goetz* decision states ... a reasonable person ... is now the standard, but there still is that subjective element ... *and you're looking at it from [defendant's] point of view*" (emphasis added). The jury convicted defendant of second degree manslaughter, second degree assault, and fourth degree criminal possession of a weapon.... The Appellate Division affirmed [the convictions] and a Judge of this Court granted defendant leave to appeal.

In *People v Goetz*, we concluded that section 35.15 "retains an objective element" for assessing the reasonableness of defendant's belief in the necessity for use of deadly force. But, in rejecting the argument that the standard of reasonableness should be purely subjective, we emphasized that the statute requires a determination of reasonableness that is both subjective and objective. The critical focus must be placed on the particular defendant and the circumstances actually confronting him at the time of the incident, and what a reasonable person in those circumstances and having defendant's background and experiences would conclude.

To determine whether a defendant's conduct was justified under Penal Law §§ 35.15, a two-step inquiry is required. The jury must first determine whether defendant actually believed that deadly physical force was necessary. If the People fail to meet their burden of proving that defendant did not actually believe that the use of deadly physical force was necessary, then the jury must move to the second step of the inquiry and assess the reasonableness of this belief.

We held in *Goetz* that Penal Law §§ 35.15 requires a jury to consider both subjective and objective factors in determining whether a defendant's conduct was reasonable. We stated that "a determination of reasonableness must be based on the 'circumstances' facing a defendant or his 'situation'. [A] jury should be instructed to consider this type of evidence in weighing the defendant's actions." Evidence of a defendant's "circumstances" includes relevant knowledge that the defendant may have had about the victim, the physical attributes of all those involved in the incident, and any prior experiences that the defendant may have had "which could provide a reasonable basis for a belief that another person's intentions were to injure or rob him or that the use of deadly force was necessary."

In this case, the jury was never instructed that they should assess the reasonableness of defendant's belief that he was in deadly peril by judging the situation from the point of view of defendant as though they were actually in his place. They were never told, in words or substance, that in deciding the question of reasonableness they "must consider the circumstances [that] defendant found himself in" as well as defendant's background and other characteristics and the attributes of the other persons involved. The Trial Judge's repetition of the word "reasonable" and the phrase "reasonably believed" was not sufficient to inform the jurors that they should assess defendant's circumstances from defendant's position. The charge did not direct the jury's attention to the factors that we outlined in *Goetz* as critical to the jury's consideration of the defendant's circumstances, and did not inform the jurors that they should mentally place themselves in defendant's circumstances when judging reasonableness.

We are unpersuaded by the People's contention that a subjective element was sufficiently injected into the charge on reasonableness in the court's instruction that the jury must consider "the conflicting stories told by the witnesses" in deciding what truly occurred. This instruction was no more than a reiteration of the general charge to the jury on its duty to resolve conflicts in the testimony and it was not related to the particular instruction on justification which followed.

The People's alternative argument that the deficiency in the justification charge should be treated as harmless error is unavailing. Consideration of the factors required by *Goetz*, including defendant's background and characteristics and the circumstances confronting him at the time of the incident—given the heightening tensions and the threats and epithets—might have been significant in the jury's assessment of the reasonableness of defendant's belief that he was in peril. In view of the sharply conflicting testimony of the witnesses, we cannot say that the proof of guilt was so forceful and compelling that, had a proper and complete justification instruction been given, the result would not have been different.

Accordingly, the order of the Appellate Division should be reversed and a new trial ordered.

NOTES

1. *Nature of force and imminence.* Generally, under either the common law or the Model Penal Code, the amount of force must be related to the threatened harm which the person is trying to avoid. Non-deadly physical force may be used by a person who believes that another person is about to inflict illegal bodily harm upon her. Deadly force may be used only by a person who believes that another person is about to inflict unlawful death or serious bodily injury on her. It is never reasonable to use deadly force against non-deadly aggression.

The defendant must believe that the use of force by another was imminent (or, as the Model Penal Code states, "immediately necessary ... on the present occasion"). If the aggressor's force is not imminent, the defendant may have had alternative ways to protect herself from that force. The failure to meet the imminence requirement is frequently raised by the prosecution in cases of homicides by battered defendants against their abusing spouses or partners.

2. *M.P.C. revisions on self-defense.* The Model Penal Code contains the following provisions relating to the use of force in self-defense.

§ 03.04   Use of Force in Self–Protection

(1) **Use of Force Justifiable for Protection of the Person**. Subject to the provisions of this Section and of Section 3.09, the use of force upon

or toward another person is justifiable when the actor believes that such force is immediately necessary for the purpose of protecting himself against the use of unlawful force by such other person on the present occasion.

(2) **Limitations on Justifying Necessity for Use of Force**

(a) The use of force is not justifiable under this Section:

(i) to resist an arrest which the actor knows is being made by a peace officer, although the arrest is unlawful; or

(ii) to resist force used by the occupier or possessor of property or by another person on his behalf, where the actor knows that the person using the force is doing so under a claim of right to protect the property, except that this limitation shall not apply if:

(1) the actor is a public officer acting in the performance of his duties or a person lawfully assisting him therein or a person making or assisting in a lawful arrest; or

(2) the actor has been unlawfully dispossessed of the property and is making a re-entry or recaption justified by Section 3.06; or

(3) the actor believes that such force is necessary to protect himself against death or serious bodily harm.

(b) The use of deadly force is not justifiable under this Section unless the actor believes that such force is necessary to protect himself against death, serious bodily harm, kidnapping or sexual intercourse compelled by force or threat; nor is it justifiable if:

(i) the actor, with the purpose of causing death or serious bodily harm, provoked the use of force against himself in the same encounter; or

(ii) the actor knows that he can avoid the necessity of using such force with complete safety by retreating or by surrendering possession of a thing to a person asserting a claim of right thereto or by complying with a demand that he abstain from any action which he has no duty to take, except that:

(1) the actor is not obliged to retreat from his dwelling or place of work, unless he was the initial aggressor or is assailed in his place of work by another person whose place of work the actor knows it to be; and

(2) a public officer justified in using force in the performance of his duties or a person justified in using force in his assistance or a person justified in using force in making an arrest or preventing an escape is not obliged to desist from efforts to perform such duty, effect such arrest or prevent such escape because of resistance or threatened

resistance by or on behalf of the person against whom such action is directed.

(c) Except as required by paragraphs (a) and (b) of this Subsection, a person employing protective force may estimate the necessity thereof under the circumstances as he believes them to be when the force is used, without retreating, surrendering possession, doing any other act which he has no legal duty to do or abstaining from any lawful action.

(3) **Use of Confinement as Protective Force**. The justification afforded by this Section extends to the use of confinement as protective force only if the actor takes all reasonable measures to terminate the confinement as soon as he knows that he safely can, unless the person confined has been arrested on a charge of crime.

§ 3.11   Definitions

[U]nless a different meaning plainly is required:

(1) "unlawful force" means force, including confinement, which is employed without the consent of the person against whom it is directed and the employment of which constitutes an offense or actionable tort or would constitute such offense or tort except for a defense (such as the absence of intent, negligence, or mental capacity; duress; youth; or diplomatic status) not amounting to a privilege to use the force. Assent constitutes consent, within the meaning of this Section, whether or not it otherwise is legally effective, except assent to the infliction of death or serious bodily harm.

(2) "deadly force" means force which the actor uses with the purpose of causing or which he knows to create a substantial risk of causing death or serious bodily harm. Purposely firing a firearm in the direction of another person or at a vehicle in which another person is believed to be constitutes deadly force. A threat to cause death or serious bodily harm, by the production of a weapon or otherwise, so long as the actor's purpose is limited to creating an apprehension that he will use deadly force if necessary, does not constitute deadly force.

(3) "dwelling" means any building or structure, though movable or temporary, or a portion thereof, which is for the time being the actor's home or place of lodging.

3.   *Imminence and necessity.* The rationale for the imminence requirement is that the defendant had no alternative under the circumstances but to use force against the aggressor, *i.e.*, action taken in the absence of an imminent threat may not be necessary. In his treatise, Professor Paul Robinson poses the following problem to illustrate imminence requirement.

Suppose A kidnaps and confines D with the announced intention of killing him one week later. D has an opportunity to kill A and escape each morning as A brings him his daily ration. Taken literally, the *imminent* requirement would prevent D from using deadly force in self-defense until A is standing over him with a knife, but that outcome seems inappropriate. The proper inquiry is not the immediacy of the threat but the immediacy of the response necessary in defense. If a threatened harm is such that it cannot be avoided if the intended victim waits until the last moment, the principle of self-defense must permit him to act earlier—as early as is required to defend himself entirely.

2 PAUL ROBINSON, CRIMINAL LAW DEFENSES § 1331(c)(1) (1984).

4. *Immediate threat.* What is the appropriate role for the imminence requirement—that the defendant is responding to the imminent use of unlawful force, or that the defendant is using force when and to the extent it is immediately necessary? Some jurisdictions effectively relocate the word "immediately" to modify the "use" of force (instead of the "necessity" for the force) and substitute the word "imminent" for "immediately," so that action taken in the absence of an immediate threat may be unnecessary. For example, in *Commonwealth v. Lindsey*, 396 Mass. 840, 489 N.E.2d 666 (1986), the defendant was convicted of unlawful carrying of a firearm on his person. The court upheld the trial court's refusal to give a self-defense instruction:

> The defendant shot Michel shortly after 7 A.M. on August 31, 1983, at the Fields Corner MBTA station in the Dorchester section of Boston. The two, who had been employees of an ice cream manufacturing company, had exchanged angry words at work a few days before the shooting. Subsequently, on Monday, August 29, Michel had challenged the defendant to a fight and, when the defendant declined, had pursued him, charging the defendant with a knife. The defendant fended Michel off and escaped. That same day the defendant complained to the police and sought a complaint at the Dorchester District Court against Michel for assault and battery with a dangerous weapon. On the next day, fellow employees told the defendant that Michel was claiming that he would "get" the defendant.

> When the defendant left his home in Cambridge for work on Wednesday (August 31), he carried a firearm although he was not licensed to do so, because he "was afraid of getting stabbed." Michel approached the defendant, who stood waiting for a bus at the MBTA station. At a distance of ten feet, Michel pulled a knife from his jacket. The defendant backed up and told Michel to forget it and to drop the knife, but Michel continued to advance "very fast." When Michel was six feet away and still advancing, the defendant, in fear for his life and acting to protect himself, drew his gun and fired at Michel. The defendant then went home not knowing whether Michel had been hit and called a lawyer, who accompanied him to a police station. Although Michel testified to a considerably different version of the incidents described by the defendant, several disinterested witnesses substantially corroborated the defendant's testimony. . . .

> . . . The evidence in this case warranted the conclusion that, once Michel made his armed attack, there was no way the defendant could

have avoided the confrontation and that the defendant used his weapon in reasonable apprehension of death or serious bodily injury. The evidence did not, however, raise a reasonable doubt whether the defendant was acting out of necessity at all times when he carried the firearm from his home in Cambridge to the Field's Corner MBTA station and back. The defendant was not responding to an immediate and serious threat throughout that entire period. The judge was not required, therefore, to give an instruction [on] self-defense.

Were we to establish an exception [to the unlawful carrying crime] for an unlicensed person to carry a firearm in public if he reasonably believed he was likely to be threatened with serious bodily harm, ... such an exception would provide a way out which, if believed, would exonerate every unlicensed person who wants to carry a gun. Such a person wants to carry a gun precisely because he fears that at some time he might be threatened with serious bodily injury.

PROBLEMS

1. *Pre-emptive Strike.* Ivan believes that he has the ability to ascertain, in advance, who is going to attack him. When Ivan senses that an attack is imminent, he launches a "preemptive strike" against his "assailant." One day, Ivan is walking down Third Street in Louisville, Kentucky, when he spots Joe Johnson walking his dog. Ivan, convinced that Joe is about to attack him, lays into Joe with his fists. Suppose that the facts reveal that Joe is a kindly soul who never attacks anybody, and who had absolutely no intention of attacking Ivan on that day. Does Ivan have the right to claim defense of self under:

   a. The common law?

   b. The M.P.C.?

Does the preposterousness of Ivan's beliefs affect his ability to claim self-defense under either the common law or the M.P.C.?

2. *The Broken Bottle.* Defendant pulls into a gas station in the heart of a large metropolitan area. While defendant is pumping gas, he is approached by an impoverished man wearing rags, who asks for money. The man asks very politely ("Gee, mister, is there any chance that you could spare some money for some food. If so, I'd really appreciate it. Thank you."). However, the man is carrying a broken whiskey bottle in his hand and the bottle is pointed towards defendant. Can defendant respond by using force in self-defense? If so, what kind of force can he use?

3. *The Silver Flash.* On two prior occasions, Pat had been robbed at gunpoint by two unknown individuals. She contends that as a result of those robberies, she has developed post-traumatic stress syndrome. Pat is driving her car down a rural road when Joe approaches in another vehicle. Joe begins shouting profanities at Pat. Pat then sees a silver flash which she thinks is a gun. Does the flash give Pat the right to act in self-defense? May

she use deadly force (by firing a warning shot at Joe, which accidentally enters through the car's windshield, striking Joe's hand)?

4. *More on the Silver Flash.* In the prior problem, would it matter that the "silver flash" was Joe's silver cigarette lighter which he took out because he wanted to smoke a cigarette? What if it was a revolver?

5. *The Subway Vigilante.* Bart boards a New York subway train. Because he had been mugged on a prior occasion, Bart carries a loaded .38 caliber pistol inside his coat. Among the passengers of this particular subway car are four youths. They appear "rough looking" and Bart reasonably assumes that they are gang members. Although two of the youths are carrying screwdrivers inside their coats (for use in breaking into video game coin boxes), Bart cannot see screwdrivers. In which of the following situations would Bart have the right to utilize self-defense?

    a. *Asking for Money.* While three youths are standing on the other side of the subway car, one youth approaches Bart and asks him for money.

    b. *Give Me Money.* While three youths are standing on the other side of the subway car, one youth approaches Bart and orders him to give up some money.

    c. *Demand from All Four.* All four youths crowd around Bart in a menacing manner and one gruffly orders him to give them some money.

See People v. Goetz, 68 N.Y.2d 96, 497 N.E.2d 41, 506 N.Y.S.2d 18 (1986).

6. *More on the Subway Vigilante.* In the prior problem in subpart c., suppose that Bart feels threatened by the youths and decides to act in self-defense. Now, consider the type and scope of force that he might permissibly use:

    a. *Deadly Force.* May Bart respond with deadly force (the gun in his pocket) or must he use only non-deadly force?

    b. *Flashing the Gun.* Would it be permissible for Bart to "flash" the gun (show it) to the youths in a threatening manner which suggests that he will use the gun if they do not desist? What if the youths respond in a hostile manner and pull out their own weapons? May Bart shoot?

    c. *Shooting at Backs.* If Bart decides to shoot, and the youths turn and start to run, must Bart stop shooting once the youths turn their backs to him? What significance do you attach to the fact that Bart is riding on a moving subway car with the youths?

    d. *After Victim Retreats.* May Bart shoot at a fourth youth who has retreated to back of the subway car and who has his back to Bart?

7. *The Estranged Boyfriend.* One morning, Dan received a phone call from his sister, Maggie, who was screaming and crying, stating that she was scared for her life. Maggie stated that her estranged boyfriend, Chris, who had a history of violence towards her and others, had come to her house,

kicked in her door and destroyed most of her possessions. Because Chris had promised to return, Maggie asked her brother to move her remaining possessions out of her house while she sought safety. She warned her brother that Chris was carrying a loaded weapon. Dan went to Maggie's house to move her belongings. While he was there, Chris returned to the house in a rather "unpleasant" mood. Chris stated that if Dan didn't leave the house, he would shoot him with the gun in his car. At that point, Chris moved toward the front door intending to get the gun from his car. In response, Dan stabbed Chris in the stomach.

Dan was charged with aggravated assault. In claiming self defense, he stated that for numerous reasons he feared for his life. Dan said that he believed that Chris was going to get his gun and that he would use it to shoot Dan. Dan was aware of Chris's past violence towards Maggie and others. In fact, Chris had recently told Dan that he had shot a man. Further, Dan was frightened because Maggie had warned him that Chris might hurt him. As a result, Dan believed that Chris had a gun in his car and intended to carry out his threat to shoot Dan.

The lower court refused to instruct the jury regarding the issue of self-defense. The court stated that Dan could not have reasonably believed that force was necessary to defend himself because there was no evidence that Chris had used or attempted to use deadly force. Was the lower court correct to refuse to give an instruction on self-defense?

8. *Imminent Attack of Batterer.* After numerous beatings by a spouse or partner, a battered defendant may decide to kill at a time when there is not an immediate threat of another beating, but a great likelihood of additional beatings in the future. What does the imminence requirement mean for battered spouses or partners? Does the imminence requirement suggest that they must wait for their partners to beat them before killing? Would a statute requiring the defensive use of force to be "immediately necessary" enable a court to instruct on self-defense in the battered spouse or partner situation? See *Bechtel v. State*, 840 P.2d 1 (Okl.Crim.App. 1992).

STATE v. DANIELS

210 Mont. 1, 682 P.2d 173 (1984).

Sheehy, Justice.

Nolan T. Daniels, a 43-year-old ranch hand, had lived in the Beaverhead County area for about ten years, until 1981, during which time he did ranch work and tended bar. Jimmy John Nolan, the victim in this case, was also a ranch hand and a resident of the Beaverhead County area at the time of the shooting. In previous years, Daniels and Jimmy John had crossed paths, sometimes to express ... hostile feelings for one another. Their animosity was well known in the community.

On Sunday, June 7, [Daniels] met Scott Tarver, an acquaintance, in a downtown Dillon bar. The two decided to go to Dell for a roping event. Tarver, who had been drinking since early morning (his not unusual custom), bought a fifth of whiskey for the trip.

As they drove to Dell, Daniels and Tarver discussed Daniels' involvement in a fight which took place approximately six months earlier in Dell. According to Daniels, Tarver then asked Daniels if he had any guns, making some comment about his willingness to protect Daniels if the need arose. Daniels gave Tarver a .38 pistol which remained in the front seat of the car throughout the ensuing incident.

Once in Dell, the two stopped at the Airport Bar for a drink. They had stopped at the Dell Hotel but were refused admittance by the bartender, who obviously felt that because Jimmy John was inside, Daniels' presence would cause a disturbance. At the roping event, Daniels and Tarver met another acquaintance who agreed to meet them at the Airport Bar.

When Daniels and Tarver pulled into the parking lot of the Dell Airport Bar, Jimmy John Nolan was standing by the driver's side of his pickup truck. One witness testified that Jimmy John hollered something at Daniels as he drove in. Daniels testified that when he saw Jimmy John gesturing at him, he stopped his car. Jimmy John's pickup faced the bar and [Daniel's car] was parked approximately 15 feet from the truck, angled from the rear of the passenger side of the truck. Tarver got out of the [car], and walked to the wheel-well area of the truck on the passenger side. Daniels got out and approached Jimmy John. Daniels and Jimmy John became involved in a physical confrontation or wrestling match. At some point, Jimmy John reached for a pair of horseshoe nippers from the bed of his truck and struck Daniels on the head. The blow lacerated Daniels' scalp and cracked his skull causing him to bend over and turn away from Jimmy John. Daniels then walked back to his car, and after getting his keys from the driver's side of his automobile, went to his trunk, and removed a .357 pistol. He walked back toward Jimmy John, brought the gun up and started shooting. He fired four shots as Jimmy John turned and fell dead. After handing the gun to Tarver, Daniels walked into the bar where, bleeding profusely, he waited for the ambulance and law enforcement officers.

Daniels claims that as he approached Jimmy John, Jimmy John grabbed him and tore a necklace which Daniels was wearing from his neck and that he was immediately struck by Jimmy John with the horseshoe nippers. Tarver's testimony was that the two wrestled for a few moments until, when Jimmy John got winded he pushed Daniels away, saying he had had enough. Tarver said that Daniels came back with an open pocket knife toward Jimmy John and that Jimmy John struck Daniels over the head then with the horseshoe nippers. The pocket knife was never found nor introduced into evidence.

Daniels' defense during the trial was justification or self-defense. His testimony about the incident indicated that he had gotten out of the automobile, went to Jimmy John, who grappled with him, tore off his necklace, and then struck him with the nippers. Daniels denied that he used any knife in the incident. In connection with his defense of self-defense, the issue of whether Daniels was an aggressor was, of course, important.

Daniels raises issues in this case related to instructions which we must discuss for purposes of retrial. The District Court instructed the jury as to use of force in defense of person in accordance with the statute, and gave a further instruction outlining the necessity for reasonableness in the use of such justifiable force. However, he defined the word "imminent" as follows:

> " 'Imminent' means threatening to occur immediately, near at hand, impending; as used in relation to self-defense, it means such an appearance of threatening or impending injury as would put a reasonable and prudent man to his instant defense."

This instruction limited improperly the purpose and intent of the word "imminent" in section 45–3–102, MCA, which reads as follows:

> "*Use of force in defense of person.* A person is justified in the use of force or threat to use force against another when and to the extent that he reasonably believes that such conduct is necessary to defend himself [. . .] against such other's *imminent* use of unlawful force . . ." (Emphasis added.)

In the quoted statute, the word "imminent" applies to the assailant, the aggressor; the person imminently threatened is entitled to use force against the aggressor "when and to the extent that he reasonably believes that such conduct is necessary." The effect of the instruction in this case defining "imminent" is that the person *defending* himself must act instantly. This is a limitation not to be found in the statute defining justifiable use of force. The threatened person is entitled to act "*when* and to the extent that he reasonably believes that such conduct is necessary." (Emphasis added.) This may or may not be instantly. It depends upon the reasonableness of the circumstances.

Daniels' conviction of mitigated deliberate homicide is reversed [on other grounds], and the cause remanded to the District Court for a new trial.

PROBLEMS

1. *The Intruder at the Cabin.* Allen and his wife Mary went to their secluded cabin by the lake, arriving after sunset. When they entered the cabin, they saw evidence of a burglary. They checked around the area. While outside, on their way back into the house, they heard loud stomping near the cabin stairs. It sounded like branches shaking. The couple repeatedly

called out "Who are you? Identify yourself." They received no answer. Allen then took out and loaded a .22 rifle. After again asking who was there and receiving no answer, Allen fired several warning shots. A voice responded to the shots. While Allen called for emergency help on his CB radio, Mary stood at the door with the gun. When she heard a sound outside, she shouted "He's coming" to her husband. She shouted more warnings from the doorway and then fired more warning shots. Those shots resulted in the death of a man outside. At her trial, Mary claimed self-defense. The judge instructed the jury that self-defense is justifiable only if the victim is attempting to kill or to inflict great bodily harm upon the defendant. Does the requirement of imminent danger justify this instruction? Would circumstances other than an actual attempted attack give a defendant a reasonable expectation of imminent danger?

2. *Battered Spouse Syndrome.* Jerry was killed by a single gunshot wound to his left temple while asleep in his bed. His wife, Kimberly, confessed that she had fired the shot, claiming that she acted in self-defense because of physical and sexual abuse that he had inflicted upon her. Further, she claimed that he had threatened to abuse her daughter, his stepdaughter. To support her claim, Kimberly offered substantial evidence to support her defense, including witnesses and experts. Kimberly claims that she acted under a belief that she needed to act for self-protection, a belief that was formed as a result of "battered spouse syndrome." Was the threat to Kimberly imminent or immediate? How does the defense of "battered spouse syndrome" affect the requirement that the threatened force be imminent or immediate?

3. *More on Battered Spouse Syndrome.* Laura was charged with the murder of her live-in boyfriend, Nathan. Prior to her relationship with Nathan, Laura had been in a ten-year marriage in which there was long history of violent abuse by Laura's husband. There was no evidence of any domestic abuse between Laura and Nathan. On the afternoon of the murder, Laura and Nathan got into a heated argument. During the exchange, Laura, grabbed a .25 caliber pistol and fatally shot Nathan. Laura was charged with murder and she pled self-defense. Laura claimed that as a result of her violent marriage, she suffered from battered spouse syndrome. Should the judge instruct the jury on self-defense and the issue of battered spouse syndrome? Does it matter that Nathan was not Laura's abuser?

4. *The Fight.* Although Marvin and Ted had mutual friends, they had a history of hostility between them. One day they found themselves at the same social function. As usual, they found themselves arguing. In the heat of the argument, Marvin pulled out a knife and cut Ted. A fist fight ensued, and Marvin lost consciousness from Ted's blows. Ted continued to punch and kick Marvin, even after others tried to restrain him. Marvin never regained consciousness and eventually died as a result of his injuries. Ted was charged with manslaughter and claimed self-defense. The trial court instructed the jury that in order for Ted to successfully claim self-defense, the actions he used must have been necessary to save himself from danger.

Were *all* of Ted's actions necessary to save himself from danger? At what point did Ted's actions become unnecessary? Does it matter that Marvin lost consciousness? Can a necessary act subsequently become unnecessary?

5. *More on the Fight.* In the prior problem, if the defendant's belief in the need for deadly force is reasonable, can he still claim self-defense when he was mistaken in his belief? Model Penal Code § 3.04(1) provides that self-defense is permitted when the defendant "believes" that force is immediately necessary to protect against unlawful force. Does the § 3.04(1) language provide a defendant with self-defense solely upon the defendant's subjective belief that such force was appropriate? Is it important to know how reasonable or careless the defendant was in concluding that the force was necessary? How does M.P.C. § 3.09(2) affect the analysis?

6. *The Abusive Mother.* Jimmy is a 16-year-old who has been physically abused by his mother for ten years. One morning she tells him that she is going to the basement to find her "whipping stick" because he deserves to be punished. The mother has used this stick on Jimmy many times over the years, and has sometimes seriously hurt him with it. Under these circumstances, in which of the following situations may Jimmy kill his mother in self-defense:

a. The mother has merely threatened to go the basement, but has not yet gone.

b. The mother is heading for the basement stairs.

c. The mother has descended into the basement and is coming back up the stairs with the stick in hand.

See M.P.C. § 3.04(1).

7. *Zoe and Her Attackers.* Zoe left her apartment on crutches late one night and was immediately followed by two men. As she walked past several stores, she noticed the reflections of the men in the store windows. Once she passed the stores and headed into the park, the men tried to grab her. Because she believed they were trying to rape her, she grabbed a knife from her purse, stabbed both of them and escaped. If Zoe is later charged with assault, can she claim self-defense for her use of deadly force? See § 3.04(2)(b).

8. *The School Incident.* One day after school, April started playfully shoving her friend Dar. After April pushed her a third time, the short-tempered Dar told April that she'd had enough of her, pulled out a knife, and started toward April. Can April use a gun to prevent Dar from stabbing her?

9. *A Parolee's Perception.* Jack had been an inmate at a state prison for most of his life. After he is paroled, he is standing at a bus stop. When a man standing next to Jack reaches into his pocket, Jack perceives that the man is about to kill him. Jack pulls out a gun and shoots the man. Despite Jack's perception, a "reasonable person" would not have perceived that the other man was a threat. Under the M.P.C., can Jack argue that he had the right to

act in self-defense? Could a jury conclude that there was no right to act in self-defense?

EXERCISES

1. *Rules in State Code.* In your state, look at the criminal statute that provides for self-defense. Compare it with the Model Penal Code defense. Are important statutory terms defined? What do the Model Penal Code and your state's statute provide with regard to the following aspects of the defense?

    a. The imminence of the threat;

    b. The seriousness of the harm threatened;

    c. The nature of the harm threatened;

    d. The unlawfulness of the threat;

    e. The availability of the defense to an aggressor; and

    f. The source of the threat.

2. *Nature of Force.* As to the extent of the harm caused by the defendant, what do the Model Penal Code and your state's statute provide about the following levels of force used by the defendant, e.g.,

    a. The seriousness of the force used in relation to the harm threatened, e.g., the use of deadly force; and

    b. The availability of less harmful, but equally effective, alternatives to avoiding the threat, e.g., calling the police to arrest a trespasser?

2. SELF–DEFENSE BY AN AGGRESSOR

CONNELL v. COMMONWEALTH

34 Va.App. 429, 542 S.E.2d 49 (2001).

FRANK, JUDGE.

In the early morning hours of January 7, 1998, Jon Lord (victim) was shot by appellant in the parking lot of the Hyatt Hotel in Richmond. Judy Wiesler, a witness for the Commonwealth, testified she met the victim and Jeff Krupnicka on the evening of January 6, 1998 at the Hyatt Hotel in Richmond. Then, Wiesler and the victim rode with Krupnicka to the Playing Field to get something to eat and play pool. At the Playing Field, the three were sitting at a table when appellant sat down at the table. None of the three knew appellant. Appellant made fun of the victim's pastel-colored tie by saying it looked feminine and made the victim appear gay. Wiesler testified that appellant's tone was sarcastic and insulting. Appellant then commented in a sarcastic tone that Krupnicka had a Yankee accent and looked homosexual because of the earring in his ear. Wiesler then left the table and went to play pool. A couple of minutes later,

Wiesler looked up and saw the victim throw appellant's pack of cigarettes on the floor. Appellant then walked away from the table and left the Playing Field. Wiesler said that she, the victim, and Krupnicka played pool after appellant left and "blew off" the incident.

Wiesler, the victim, and Krupnicka left the Playing Field at 1:45 a.m. on January 7, 1998, and returned to the parking lot at the Hyatt Hotel. At the Hyatt Hotel, the victim and Wiesler exited Krupnicka's vehicle and started walking toward their parked cars. They noticed a four-wheel drive vehicle pull into the parking lot behind Krupnicka's car. Appellant got out of the four-wheel drive vehicle with a pistol in one hand and a shotgun in the other. Appellant started to walk toward Wiesler, the victim, and Krupnicka, yelling obscenities. Appellant had the pistol pointed down and the shotgun pointed up in the air. Appellant told Wiesler she was not going to get hurt and to walk away because she was not involved. Wiesler walked toward the street and was halfway across the street when she heard a shot. Wiesler turned around and saw the victim holding appellant against the four-wheel drive vehicle. The victim had his hands around appellant's shirt collar. Appellant was still holding the shotgun. Wiesler heard more shots and started to walk back to the Hyatt parking lot. Appellant and the victim started struggling with each other and fell below Wiesler's line of sight. After hearing three more shots, Wiesler looked around the corner of a car and saw the victim lying on the ground. The victim was screaming that he had been shot, and appellant was standing over him with both guns in his hands. Appellant told the victim he was an idiot and he was going to have to take him to the hospital. Krupnicka drove his car up to appellant and hit appellant in the back of his legs, causing appellant to stumble forward. Appellant said Krupnicka was crazy and that Wiesler was an idiot for hanging out with the victim and Krupnicka. Appellant then ran to his car and drove off. [Jeff Krupnicka testified to essentially the same facts as Wiesler]

Appellant testified he was playing pool in the Playing Field, when he first noticed Wiesler, the victim, and Krupnicka loudly having fun at a nearby table. He testified that as he was leaving the Playing Field, he "noticed the victim's necktie and actually paid him a compliment on it." The victim responded, "I wear this tie to pick up [f _ _ _ _ _ _] like you." Appellant considered the comment humorously "in the manner [the victim] intended it" and sat at their table at their invitation. After he introduced himself[,] all three of the group introduced themselves to him. They began a friendly conversation that later led to an argument. Appellant was intimidated and shocked when the victim threatened him. After the victim pushed him, appellant paid his bill and drove home, where he had another alcoholic drink. He then decided that he would "scare the hell out of [the group]" and "get an apology" from them. He retrieved a rifle and a shotgun. A handgun was already in his car. He then returned to the Playing Field.

He waited for Krupnicka, the victim, and Wiesler to leave and followed them to the Hyatt Hotel parking lot. Appellant parked behind Krupnicka's car and got out of his vehicle. He was carrying the shotgun and the pistol. He walked to the front of his car and demanded an apology from Krupnicka and the victim. The victim then began to walk toward him. Appellant told Wiesler to leave, that she was not involved, and he did not want her to get hurt. Appellant testified he warned the victim to stay back. He tucked the pistol in his pants and then pointed the shotgun in the air to fire a warning shot over the victim's head. Appellant testified he never pointed the shotgun at the victim, did not say he was going to kill the victim, and did not walk toward the victim. The victim continued walking toward appellant and appellant fired a second warning shot and said, " 'Stay back.' " Appellant realized the victim was not going to stop, so he turned to run and ran into the front of his car. The victim then grabbed appellant and appellant tossed away the shotgun. A struggle ensued between the two men. Appellant testified the victim put him in a headlock that included his left arm. The victim hoisted appellant into the air and told him he was going to kill him. The victim then dragged appellant around the side of appellant's vehicle. Appellant's feet were dragging across the ground and he did not have his weight under him. He stated that he " 'was like a rag doll in [the victim's] hands.' " Appellant stated that it was at this point that he fired the shot into the victim's side, which ultimately resulted in the victim's death. The victim maintained his hold on appellant and appellant shot him in the right thigh. The victim fell to the ground and appellant tried to get away from the victim. Fearing the victim was going to grab the pistol, appellant shot him a third time in the left shoulder. Appellant testified that he told the victim he would not leave him and would get him to the hospital. Appellant fled the scene after Krupnicka tried to run over him with his vehicle. . . .

A defendant is entitled to have the jury instructed only on those theories of the case that are supported by evidence. The evidence to support an instruction "must be more than a scintilla." . . .

Appellant contends the trial court erred in failing to give the jury appellant's proffered instruction on excusable homicide. We agree.

Excusable self-defense may be asserted when the accused, who was at some fault in precipitating the confrontation with the victim, abandons the fight and retreats as far as he or she safely can.

Once the accused abandons the attack and retreats as far as he or she safely can, he or she may kill his or her adversary if there is "a reasonably apparent necessity to preserve his [or her] own life or save himself [or herself] from great bodily harm." *Bailey v. Commonwealth*, 200 Va. 92, 96, 104 S.E.2d 28, 31 (1958).

Appellant's evidence established he provoked the violence in the hotel parking lot by following the victim, Krupnicka, and Wiesler to that location. He testified that he fired two warning shots over the victim's head when the victim began to advance toward him. He put the pistol on safety and tucked it into his pants. He also twice warned the victim to stay back. Then, he turned to run and ran into the front of his vehicle, which gave the victim the opportunity to catch him. This testimony established more than a mere scintilla of evidence that appellant retreated as far as possible before the victim apprehended him. At this point, appellant tossed his shotgun away. We believe this testimony established more than a mere scintilla of evidence that appellant abandoned the fight.

The victim was 6'1" tall and weighed over 200 pounds, while appellant is 5'6" tall and weighs 180 pounds. Appellant testified the victim hoisted him into the air and told him he was going to kill him. The victim headlocked appellant and dragged appellant. Appellant testified that the victim again told him he was going to kill him. Appellant said he did not have his weight under him and "was like a rag doll in [the victim's] hands." Appellant also testified he was fearful the victim would shoot him with the shotgun. At this point, appellant fired the fatal shot into the victim's side with the pistol. This evidence provided more than a scintilla of evidence that appellant killed the victim out of a reasonably apparent necessity to preserve his own life, and was sufficient to support an instruction on excusable homicide. Therefore, we find the trial judge erred in refusing to instruct the jury on excusable homicide. We reverse appellant's convictions and remand for a new trial if the Commonwealth be so advised.

NOTES

1. *Threat by aggressor.* When an aggressor unjustifiably threatens to harm the defendant, the right of self-protection is triggered. For example, in *Tate v. State*, 981 S.W.2d 189 (Tex.Crim.App. 1998), the appellate court reversed a homicide conviction due to an erroneous evidentiary ruling. To help prove his claim of self-defense, the defendant offered the testimony of his aunt who testified about a conversation that the deceased (the father of the defendant's girlfriend) had with the aunt a month or two before his death. She testified that the deceased told her that the animosity that existed within his family may "cause [him] to kill the little son of a bitch (the defendant) some day." The appellate court found that this evidence was probative of the deceased's state of mind and indicated a possible motive behind the confrontation between the deceased and the defendant on the evening of the homicide. The court held that if the evidence was offered to

show that the deceased was the aggressor, it was admissible even if the defendant had no knowledge of deceased's statement at the time of the homicide.

2. *Raising self-defense claim.* In *State v. Graves*, 97 Wash.App. 55, 982 P.2d 627 (1999), the court reversed a juvenile's assault conviction because he was entitled to raise the claim of self-defense. When the father, Graves, located his teenage son, Ricco, who had left home without permission for a few days, Graves told his son that he had to do chores around the house "to make up for the lost time." When Ricco refused, the father came into his room angrily, and Ricco testified that: "He came on me, and I thought he was going to do something." Ricco wrestled his father onto the bed in order to "[g]et him off me," and his father grabbed him and placed him in a headlock. Graves admitted that he initiated both incidents of physical contact. The *Graves* Court held that Ricco offered sufficient evidence to raise the claim of self-defense. The trial court erroneously ruled that a parent may use reasonable force to discipline a child, which use precludes the eligibility of the child to make a self-defense claim.

3. *Unlawful aggression.* A defendant is justified in using force against *unlawful* aggression. For example, if a police officer uses justified force to arrest a suspect, the arrestee cannot invoke self-defense. For example, in *United States v. Branch*, in Part A.4. *infra*, the defendant was not justified in starting "a firefight solely on the ground that the police sent too many well-armed officers to arrest him." The police conduct, no matter how provocative, was lawful.

4. *Excessive defensive force.* When a person starts a fight without justification and the victim responds with justifiable force, the initial aggressor cannot claim self-defense against the victim's use of force. However, when a victim uses excessive force to respond, the law regards that force as unlawful and the initial aggressor can defend against that force. The rationale is that, while the initial aggressor is accountable for her original unlawful force, she is not criminally liable for defending herself against a disproportionate return of force by the victim.

5. *Separate encounters.* An initial aggressor in a first encounter can also claim self-defense when he withdraws in good faith from any further confrontation with the victim and notifies the victim of that withdrawal. At that point, the initial aggressor is restored to the right of self-defense. The key issue for application of this exception is whether the second encounter between a defendant and the victim was separate and distinct from the first encounter or a continuation of the first encounter. As a matter of law, if there were separate encounters, then no qualifying jury instruction on the initial aggressor issue should be given. Only a self-defense instruction should be given. But if the evidence supports either the single or separate encounter theories, then jury instructions on both issues are appropriate. See, e.g., *Stepp v. Commonwealth*, 608 S.W.2d 371 (Ky. 1980).

6. *Provocation exception.* Self-defense also is unavailable to a defendant who provoked the use of force by the ultimate victim, when intending to kill

or seriously injure the victim, even though the defendant reasonably believed that it was necessary to use force to protect himself from harm. The rationale for this rule is that a defendant should not be permitted to contrive or provoke a situation in order to justify her own counterattack. Unlike the initial aggressor exception, the provocation exception may apply to a defendant who is a mental *or* physical aggressor. In addition, this qualification applies only when the prosecution can prove that the defendant intended from the beginning to kill or seriously injure the victim. Moreover, although this exception is silent on whether self-defense is available if the accused withdraws following the provocative act and before the victim retaliates, a person who provokes a fight with the intent to kill or seriously injure may claim self-protection if she withdraws from the encounter and effectively communicates to the other person her intent to do so, and if the latter nevertheless continues to threaten the use of unlawful physical force.

PROBLEMS

1. *Hatfields and McCoys.* George Hatfield lived in the same building as Thomas McCoy. There was a history of bad blood between George and Thomas. One evening, while Thomas, who lived on the third floor of the building, was in the hallway outside George's second floor apartment, George emerged from his apartment and shot Thomas in the left leg with a sawed-off shotgun, causing a serious wound. George admitted that he shot Thomas, but claimed self-defense. At trial, George testified that two days before he shot Thomas, Thomas had challenged him to come out of the apartment and had fired shots outside his door. He stated that this incident led him to believe that Thomas intended to kill him. George stated that when he heard Thomas in the hallway outside his apartment door, he believed that Thomas had come for him and was armed. The trial court agreed that George had a claim of self-defense and charged the jurors on that theory, instructing them that if they found "beyond a reasonable doubt that the defendant was, in fact, the aggressor, meaning that he was the first to use physical force, then the state has succeeded in disproving the defense of self-defense." Was this instruction appropriate? Did the court properly define initial aggressor?

2. *Looking for Trouble.* The victim Jane left the premises after the first encounter with the defendant Della, which was a shoving match, and returned "looking for trouble" ten to fifteen minutes later. When Jane returned, Della was in her truck with the motor running, about to go home. At the second encounter, the victim had two guns, one of which was a shotgun she was pointing at the Della. Della knocked away the shotgun with one hand and then killed Jane with a pistol that she pulled from her pocket. The court instructed the jury on both self-defense and the initial aggressor issue. Were there two separate and distinct encounters? Was it appropriate to instruct the jury on the initial aggressor issue?

3. *The Poker Game Incident.* Arnie arrived at an acquaintance's house for a "friendly" poker game. The players at the game barred Arnie from

playing. Angered, Arnie pulled a .22 caliber pistol from his belt and threatened several players. Seeing that his actions were not going to get him invited to play the game, Arnie lowered the gun and stepped back. Thereafter, Shawn, lunged at Arnie and attempted to take away the gun. During the scuffle, Shawn was shot and killed. Arnie was charged with manslaughter, but claimed self-defense. The trial court instructed the jury that if Arnie provoked Shawn to use physical force, then Arnie's use of force for his own protection was unlawful. Was the trial judge correct that if Arnie provoked the fight with the intent to kill or inflict serious bodily injury, he could not thereafter use physical force to protect himself?

4. *More on the Poker Game.* In the prior problem, suppose that Arnie had thrown the gun down and was running away when Shawn came after him. Then Shawn chased Arnie down, scuffled with him, and ultimately killed Arnie. Were Shawn's actions permissible under the M.P.C.?

5. *The Diner Incident.* After seeing a movie, Rick and his wife Sarah stopped at a diner to eat dinner. Seeing Paul's car in the parking lot, Rick parked next to Paul's car, beat on the window, and spoke in a derogatory manner to Paul's girlfriend. Paul got out of his car and told Rick to leave them alone. As Paul tried to reenter his car, Rick went after him, shoving him hard. A brutal fist fight ensued. By everyone's account, Paul was winning, having pinned Rick to the concrete, while continuing to hit him. Rick removed an electrician's knife from his pocket and slashed Paul. The two men stood up and Rick told Paul to stop. Paul continued the fist fight and subsequently died of head injuries. Rick was indicted for murder but claimed self-defense. The trial judge instructed the jury that self-defense is available to one who has in good faith endeavored to decline any further struggle if the killing was absolutely necessary to save his own life. Was the judge's instruction correct?

3. DUTY TO RETREAT

At common law, a person who could safely retreat was not required to run away before using nondeadly force. Perhaps in the frontier spirit, many jurisdictions also allowed a defendant to use deadly force for self-protection even though she could have retreated safely without using the lethal force. Even the minority of states requiring a duty to retreat (as the Model Penal Code requires) impose that duty only when the defendant knows that she can retreat in complete safety. As the following case indicates, a defendant need not retreat from her home before using deadly force. For battered spouses, this rule may be especially important.

WEIAND v. STATE
732 So.2d 1044 (Fla. 1999).

PARIENTE, J. [Should] the law impose a duty to retreat from the residence before a defendant may justifiably resort to deadly force in self-defense against a co-occupant, if that force is necessary to prevent death or great bodily harm?

Kathleen Weiand was charged with first-degree murder for the 1994 shooting death of her husband Todd Weiand. Weiand shot her husband during a violent argument in the apartment where the two were living together with their seven-week-old daughter. At trial, Weiand claimed self-defense and presented battered spouse syndrome evidence [in] support of her claim. Weiand testified that her husband had beaten and choked her throughout the course of their three-year relationship and had threatened further violence if she left him.

Two experts, including Dr. Lenore Walker, a nationally recognized expert on battered women, testified that Weiand suffered from "battered woman's syndrome." Dr. Walker detailed Weiand's history of abuse by her husband and testified about the effect of the abusive relationship on Weiand. Based on her studies, her work with Weiand and Weiand's history of abuse, Dr. Walker concluded that when Weiand shot her husband she believed that he was going to seriously hurt or kill her.

Dr. Walker opined that there were several reasons why Weiand did not leave the apartment that night during the argument, despite apparent opportunities to do so: she felt that she was unable to leave because she had just given birth seven weeks earlier; she had been choked unconscious; she was paralyzed with terror; and experience had taught her that threats of leaving only made her husband more violent.

At the charge conference following the close of the evidence, defense counsel requested that the following standard jury instruction be given: "If the defendant was attacked in [her] own home or on [her] own premises, [she] had no duty to retreat and had the lawful right to stand [her] ground and meet force with force, even to the extent of using force likely to cause death or great bodily harm if it was necessary to prevent either death or great bodily harm."

[T]he trial court refused the request to give this "defense of home" instruction. Instead, the trial court only gave the instruction applicable in all self-defense cases regarding the duty to retreat: "The fact that the defendant was wrongfully attacked cannot justify her use of force likely to cause death or great bodily harm if by retreating she could have avoided the need to use that force."

During closing arguments, the prosecutor used this standard instruction to the State's advantage by emphasizing Weiand's duty to retreat. The prosecutor stressed as "critical" that the killing could not be considered justifiable homicide unless Weiand had exhausted every reasonable means to escape the danger, including fleeing her home: "She had to exhaust every reasonable means of escape prior to killing him. Did she do that? No. Did she use the phone that was two feet away? No. Did she go out the door where her baby was sitting next to? No. Did she get in the car that she had driven all over town drinking and boozing it up all day? No." The jury found Weiand guilty of second-degree murder and the trial court sentenced her to eighteen years' imprisonment.

Under Florida statutory and common law, a person may use deadly force in self-defense if he or she reasonably believes that deadly force is necessary to prevent imminent death or great bodily harm. Even under those circumstances, however, a person may not resort to deadly force without first using every reasonable means within his or her power to avoid the danger, including retreat. The duty to retreat emanates from common law, rather than from our statutes.

There is an exception to this common law duty to retreat "to the wall," which applies when an individual claims self-defense in his or her own residence. An individual is not required to retreat from the residence before resorting to deadly force in self-defense, so long as the deadly force is necessary to prevent death or great bodily harm.

The privilege of nonretreat from the home, part of the "castle doctrine," has early common law origins. In *Hedges* [*v. State*, 172 So.2d 824 (Fla. 1965)], this Court applied the privilege of nonretreat from the residence where the attacker was not an intruder but an invitee with the defendant's permission to be on the premises. In that case, the defendant and the victim had maintained a long-term intimate relationship, and on the morning of the shooting the victim was an invitee, lawfully in the defendant's home. In instructing the jury on the law of self-defense, the trial court informed the jury that the defendant was required to use "all reasonable means within his power and consistent with his own safety to avoid the danger and avert the necessity of taking human life." The trial court [erroneously] failed to instruct the jury that the defendant was under no duty to retreat from her residence.

Eighteen years later, in [*State v.*] *Bobbitt*, [415 So.2d 724 (Fla. 1982)], this Court considered whether the privilege of nonretreat from the home should also apply where the defendant killed her co-occupant husband in self-defense, after being attacked without provocation. This Court rejected the extension of *Hedges* under those circumstances: "[T]he privilege not to retreat, premised on the maxim that every man's home is his castle which he is entitled to protect from invasion, does not apply here where both Bobbitt and her husband had equal rights to be in the 'castle' and neither had the legal right to eject the other."

Justice Overton, in a strongly-worded dissent, disagreed with the majority's decision because it was contrary to a "basic premise in our law that the home is a special place of protection and security." He further criticized the distinction made by the majority that authorized the privilege of nonretreat instruction in cases like *Hedges*, where the aggressor was an invitee with a legal right to be on the premises, but not where the aggressor was a co-occupant.

At the time we rendered our decision in *Bobbitt* in 1982, we were in a minority of jurisdictions that refused to extend the privilege of nonretreat from the residence where the aggressor was a co-occupant. Since our decision in *Bobbitt*, an even greater number of jurisdictions have declined to impose a duty to retreat from the residence.[9]

We now conclude that it is appropriate to recede from *Bobbitt* and adopt Justice Overton's well-reasoned dissent in that case. We join the majority of jurisdictions that do not impose a duty to retreat from the residence when a defendant uses deadly force in self-defense, if that force is necessary to prevent death or great bodily harm from a co-occupant.

There are two distinct reasons for our conclusion. First, we can no longer agree with *Bobbitt*'s minority view that relies on concepts of property law and possessory rights to impose a duty to retreat from the residence. Second, based on our increased understanding of the plight of victims of domestic violence in the years since our decision in *Bobbitt*, we find that there are sound policy reasons for not imposing a duty to retreat from the residence when a defendant resorts to deadly force in self-defense against a co-occupant. The more recent decisions of state supreme courts confronting this issue have recognized that imposing a duty to retreat from the residence has a potentially damaging effect on victims of domestic violence claiming self-defense.

In refusing to extend the privilege of nonretreat in *Bobbitt*, we held that "the privilege not to retreat [does] not apply here where both *Bobbitt* and her husband had equal rights to be in the 'castle' and neither had the legal right to eject the other." Thus, our decision in *Bobbitt* appears to have been grounded upon the sanctity of property and possessory rights, rather than the sanctity of human life.

In light of our decision in *Hedges*, our holding in *Bobbitt* created a distinction that resulted in the privilege of nonretreat applying when the defendant is defending herself against an invitee, with a legal right to be on the premises, but not when defending herself against a co-occupant, who also had a legal right to be on the premises. Justice Overton illustrated the effect of this "illogical distinction" in his dissenting opinion in *Bobbitt*:

> Under the majority opinion, a woman killing her paramour in her home has more protection under the law than a woman who

9. Of those jurisdictions imposing a duty to retreat before resorting to deadly force, eleven states have declined to find a duty to retreat from the residence when attacked by a co-occupant or invitee. Similarly, the Model Penal Code, which recognizes a duty to retreat under most circumstances, does not impose a duty to retreat when necessary to defend against death or great bodily harm from a co-occupant of the dwelling.

kills her husband in her home. More difficult still to understand is the application of the majority's rule to the situation where a mother is attacked in her home by a nineteen-year-old son. If the son is living in the home, the mother has a duty to retreat before she can use deadly force, but, if the son is not residing in the home, the mother has no duty to retreat before such force is used.

Bobbitt's distinction based on possessory rights may be important in the context of defending the home. However, the privilege of nonretreat from the home stems not from the sanctity of property rights, but from the time-honored principle that the home is the ultimate sanctuary. As has been asked rhetorically, if the duty to retreat from the home is applied to a defendant attacked by a co-occupant in the home, "whither shall he flee, and how far, and when may he be permitted to return?" *Jones v. Alabama*, 76 Ala. 8, 16 (1884)....

[M]uch has changed in the public policy of this State, based on increased knowledge about the plight of domestic violence victims. It is now widely recognized that domestic violence "attacks are often repeated over time, and escape from the home is rarely possible without the threat of great personal violence or death." *Thomas*, 673 N.E.2d at 1343.... Studies show that women who retreat from the residence when attacked by their co-occupant spouse or boyfriend may, in fact, increase the danger of harm to themselves due to the possibility of attack after separation. According to Dr. Lenore Walker, "[t]he batterer would often rather kill, or die himself, than separate from the battered woman." Lenore E. Walker, Terrifying Love: Why Battered Women Kill and How Society Responds 65 (1989).

Experts in the field explain that separation or retreat can be the most dangerous time in the relationship for the victims of domestic violence because "[v]iolence increases dramatically when a woman leaves an abusive relationship." Executive Office of the Governor, The Governor's Task Force on Domestic Violence, The First Report at 55 (January 31, 1994) (hereinafter First Report). A leading expert in the field cites one study which revealed that forty-five percent of the murders of women "were generated by the man's 'rage over the actual or impending estrangement from his partner.'" Donald G. Dutton, The Batterer: A Psychological Profile 15 (1995).

The imposition of a duty to retreat from one's residence when faced with a violent aggressor has the most significant impact on women because an overwhelming majority of victims of domestic violence are women. According to the statistics compiled by the Governor's Task Force on Domestic Violence, seventy-three percent of domestic violence victims are women. See First Report, supra at 47. Domestic violence is the single major cause of injury to women, more frequent than auto accidents, rapes, and muggings combined. "Over four thousand women die annually at the hands of their abuser," and in 1995, of all female homicide victims, thirty-nine percent were killed during domestic violence incidents. These studies and other similar findings in the intervening years since *Bobbitt* provide proof of Justice Overton's observation that retaining a duty to retreat from the home "clearly penalizes spouses, and particularly wives, in defending themselves from an aggressor spouse." *State v. Rippie*, 419 So.2d 1087, 1087 (Fla. 1982) (Overton, J., dissenting).

There is a common myth that the victims of domestic violence are free to leave the battering relationship any time they wish to do so, and that the " 'beatings' could not have been too bad for if they had been, she certainly would have left." *State v. Kelly*, 478 A.2d 364 (1984). A jury instruction placing a duty to retreat from the home on the defendant may serve to legitimize the common myth and allow prosecutors to capitalize upon it. The prosecutor capitalized on the jury instruction and the common myth in this case when she questioned the believability of Weiand's claims and asked the jury why Weiand did not "go out the door?" and why she did not "get in the car?" before resorting to violence. To re-affirm *Bobbitt* with its duty to retreat from the home would undermine our reasons for approving expert testimony on battered woman's syndrome.

While there may be more opportunities for violence in the domestic setting, no empirical data has been presented, either through expert testimony or studies, demonstrating any correlation between eliminating a duty to retreat from the home and an increase in incidents of domestic violence. In contrast, a duty to retreat from the home adversely affects victims of domestic violence by placing them at greater risk of death or great bodily harm. In addition, failing to inform the jurors that the defendant had no duty to retreat from the residence when attacked by a co-occupant may actually reinforce commonly held myths concerning domestic violence victims. . . .

[W]e conclude that Justice Overton's "middle ground" instruction, as set forth in his dissent in *Bobbitt*, satisfies any concern that eliminating a duty to retreat might invite violence. This instruction imposes a limited duty to retreat within the residence to the extent reasonably possible, but no duty to flee the residence. Accordingly, we adopt the following instruction:

> If the defendant was attacked in [his/her] own home, or on [his/her] own premises, by a co-occupant [or any other person lawfully on the premises] [he/she] had a duty to retreat to the extent reasonably possible without increasing [his/her] own danger of death or great bodily harm. However, the defendant was not required to flee [his/her] home and had the lawful right to stand [his/her] ground and meet force with force even to the extent of using force likely to cause death or great bodily harm if

it was necessary to prevent death or great bodily harm to [himself/herself].

It is our increased knowledge of the complexities of domestic violence that provides the impetus for reconsidering our decision in *Bobbitt*. However, in deciding whether the privilege of nonretreat instruction is available we consider it inappropriate to distinguish between victims of domestic violence and other defendants who have been attacked by a co-occupant in the residence. This was the position espoused in Justice Overton's dissent.

[T]he privilege of nonretreat instruction should be equally available to all those lawfully residing in the premises, provided, of course, that the use of deadly force was necessary to prevent death or great bodily harm. Because this instruction will apply to both invitees and co-occupants alike, we recede from *Hedges* to the extent that *Hedges* does not require a middle-ground instruction for invitees. . . .

In conclusion, we hold that there is no duty to retreat from the residence before resorting to deadly force against a co-occupant or invitee if necessary to prevent death or great bodily harm, although there is a limited duty to retreat within the residence to the extent reasonably possible. Thus, we answer the certified question, as rephrased, in the negative, recede from *Bobbitt*, recede in part from *Hedges*, and adopt the middle-ground jury instruction proposed by Justice Overton in his dissent in *Bobbitt*.

PROBLEMS

1. *Retreat from Batterer.* Does *Weiand* afford the same legal protection to a person defending against an invitee and a person defending against a co-inhabitant? Does the decision put more emphasis on the social relationships between the parties than on the legal status of the defendant-aggressor as, for example, an invitee or co-inhabitant? How does *Weiand* help victims of domestic abuse? Explain.

2. *Scope of Privilege of Nonretreat.* Does the *Weiand* Court's rule allow for misuse by abuse victims? Does the court's opinion contain an "imminence" requirement? Can the rule be invoked during "peacetime" in the home to justify a preemptive strike against predicted future abuse by a batterer?

3. *Broken Bottle Reprise.* Consider the facts of Problem 2 after the *Wesley* opinion in Part A.1., *supra*. Assuming that the defendant has the right to use deadly force to protect himself, must he first attempt to retreat under the Model Penal Code? Under the circumstances, is retreat realistic?

4. *The Liquor Store Incident.* Adam and Janet left a liquor store after buying cigarettes. William followed Adam outside and repeatedly asked for money and cigarettes. Adam refused and told William to leave them alone. William persisted and continued to pursue them as they backed away. When William refused to go away, Adam removed a knife from Janet's purse and

stated, "You don't want to get cut. Just leave us alone." William stopped and Adam and Janet continued to back away. At about that time William's friend Raymond appeared on the scene and began walking toward the couple, asking, "Are you messing with William?" Adam and Janet continued to slowly back away from William and Raymond, and Adam displayed the knife to Raymond, stating "Leave us alone. We're getting out of here. We don't want any trouble." Raymond nevertheless continued to walk rapidly toward the couple with raised fists. When Raymond caught up with them, a fight ensued in which Raymond struck Adam and Adam stabbed Raymond. A short time later, Raymond died. At trial, the trial judge instructed the jury that Adam was entitled to use deadly force if he reasonably believed a lesser degree of force was inadequate to protect himself from an assault or an attempted assault. However, the trial judge would not instruct the jury that Adam had "no duty to retreat." Should this instruction have been given? Was Adam entitled to stand his ground or was he required to avoid the conflict? Was he required to try to flee the scene before using deadly force against Raymond? Would the result be different under the common law rather than under the M.P.C.?

5. *Urban Street Gangs and "Retreat."* Zeke and his friends, known gang members, were crossing a city street very late one evening. As they crossed the street, a car came speeding around the corner. The driver of the car, Lenny, quickly braked to allow the group to pass. Zeke and his friends, unhappy with Lenny's driving, angrily let him know how they felt. Lenny responded with equal unpleasantness. An argument ensued and Lenny pulled the car over. Zeke walked towards Lenny, still shouting profanities. Lenny pushed open the driver's side door and swung at Zeke, starting a fight. The two men struggled for a few minutes until Lenny fell to the ground, whereupon Zeke walked away. As Zeke was leaving, Lenny shouted, "I'll be back!" At that point, Zeke turned around, took out a knife, and swung it at Lenny, stabbing him. As a result of the stab wound, Lenny died. At his trial for murder, Zeke claims self-defense. Zeke's attorney sought to introduce expert testimony on the sociology of poverty, and culture of street fighters. If allowed, the expert would testify that for street fighters such as Zeke, there is no retreat. Should the judge admit this testimony to show that Zeke believed that he could not retreat? If Zeke is not required to retreat, is he justified in using deadly force?

6. *Sibling Rivalries.* Two brothers, Carey and Patrick, lived together at their mother's house. One afternoon, a quarrel ensued between the two brothers in the living room. The quarrel quickly escalated into a fight, which became violent and ended with Carey shooting Patrick. Carey is charged with murder and pleads self-defense. The state statute imposes a duty to retreat. Because Carey lived in the house, must he retreat? Does it make a difference that Patrick lived there also? Would it matter if Carey were the initial aggressor?

4. SELF–DEFENSE AGAINST LAW ENFORCEMENT OFFICIALS

An individual may seek to invoke the right to use self-defense to prevent the police from arresting him or her. Such a claim may arise when police use force or deadly force to effect an arrest, or when arrestees are not aware that it is police officers who are using such force against them.

UNITED STATES v. BRANCH

91 F.3d 699 (5th Cir. 1996).

HIGGINBOTHAM, CIRCUIT JUDGE.

The Branch Davidians are a 65-year-old sect originally affiliated with the Seventh Day Adventist Church. Their faith urges a life of Bible study with emphasis on an imminent, apocalyptic confrontation between the Davidians and the "beast." The group's leader, Vernon Howell, instructed members to arm themselves in preparation for the final battle. Howell changed his name to David Koresh in 1990 and preached that "if you can't kill for God, you can't die for God." He told his followers that the "beast" included the U.S. Government and, specifically, the ATF.

Koresh and other Davidians stockpiled weapons and ammunition. They fortified the compound called Mount Carmel, building a two-foot high concrete barrier and an underground bunker. Koresh used "Bible studies" to instruct the residents in the use of firearms. In short, the Davidians turned Mount Carmel into a small fortress.

The ATF discovered that the Davidians had amassed weapons, including fully automatic machineguns and hand grenades. ATF agents obtained an arrest warrant for Koresh and a search warrant for the Mount Carmel compound.

The ATF decided to execute the search and arrest warrant on February 28, 1993, but, as it was to learn, the element of surprise had been lost. Around 8:00 A.M., an undercover ATF agent, Roberto Rodriguez, visited the Davidian compound and spoke with Koresh. During the conversation, Koresh took a phone call. When he returned, a visibly shaken Koresh told Rodriguez, "Robert, neither the ATF or National Guard will ever get me. They got me once, they'll never get me again." Koresh then walked over to the windows and looked toward the farmhouse used by the undercover ATF agents. He turned to Rodriguez and said, "They're coming, Robert. The time has come." Rodriguez left the compound around 9:00 A.M. and advised the ATF that Koresh had learned of the raid at least forty-five minutes earlier. The ATF decided to proceed with the arrest and search warrants.

When the ATF's decision to continue was made, approximately 115 men, women, and children, ranging in age from 6 months to 70 years, resided at Mount Carmel. The ATF plan called for ATF agents, who were transported to the compound in two cattle trailers, to quickly ... encircle the compound, while National Guard helicopters conducted a diversionary raid on the rear of the Mount Carmel compound.

The plan quickly went awry. The helicopters did not arrive until after the ATF agents had begun unloading from the cattle trailers. As the agents unloaded, gunfire erupted from the compound. The agents returned fire. In the ensuing gunbattle, four agents and three Davidians were killed. Twenty-two ATF agents and four Davidians were wounded.

The FBI then surrounded the compound, and for 51 days law enforcement and the Davidians were at a stand-off. During the stand-off, approximately 30 Davidians left the compound and were taken into custody. On April 19, FBI agents attempted to end the stand-off by flooding the compound with gas, but the Davidians did not leave. Around noon, the Davidians set the compound on fire. Seventy-five of the remaining 84 occupants perished in the blaze.

A grand jury returned a superseding 10–count indictment against twelve of the surviving Davidians. The Government dismissed the charges against one of the twelve Davidians [pursuant] to a plea bargain. After a jury trial lasting nearly two months, the jury acquitted four of the Davidians on all counts on which they were charged. The jury also acquitted all eleven of the Davidians on Count 1, which alleged a conspiracy to murder federal agents. However, the jury found seven of the Davidians ... guilty on Count 3 for using or carrying a firearm during a crime of violence. The jury acquitted all eleven of the defendants on Count 2 for aiding and abetting the murder of federal agents but convicted [five] on the lesser-included offense of aiding and abetting the voluntary manslaughter of federal agents....

The district court sentenced the defendants to prison terms ranging from 15 to 40 years, along with fines and restitution. ...

The record ... belies the contention that the ATF agents used excessive force. The defendants raise three arguments: First, that the ATF fired the first shots on February 28; second, that regardless of who fired first, the ATF fired indiscriminately into the compound, endangering the lives of women and children; and, third, that excessive force was inherent in the nature of the raid ATF conducted. The evidence in the record does not support any of these claims. ...

... Moreover, even evidence that the ATF agents fired the first shot would not have been sufficient by itself to warrant the self-defense instruction. The ATF agents testified that ATF policy and training directed agents to fire only if they saw an individual threatening the agent's or someone else's life. Initiating gunfire in those circumstances would not be unreasonable.... [E]vidence that the ATF fired first without sufficient evidence that such fire was indiscriminate or otherwise excessive does not warrant a self-defense instruction.

The Davidians point out that several ATF agents testified that firing through walls and into windows in which there was no discernable threat would be unreasonable because of the danger to innocents and the possibility for escalation. Seizing on this, the Davidians point to Kathryn Schroeder's testimony that gunfire came through the window in her room at the beginning of the raid. In addition, the Davidians ... highlight Marjorie Thomas' video deposition in which she stated that a gunshot shattered the window in her loft on the third floor as she watched the helicopters approach the compound at the beginning of the raid.

This testimony will not support an inference that the ATF agents used excessive force. The pilots of the helicopters all testified that no shots were fired from the helicopters. Significantly, the unchallenged testimony is supported by the physical facts. The helicopters were unarmed, and the doors on the aircraft were closed, thereby preventing agents inside from firing on the compound. ...

Finally, the Davidians argue that excessive force was inherent in the nature of the ATF raid. According to the defendants, sending over seventy well-armed agents to arrest Koresh and execute a search warrant for a residence housing women and children was excessive. We disagree.

The execution of search and arrest warrants necessarily involves some degree of force. The ATF had cause to believe that the Davidians had amassed a large supply of weaponry, including grenades and fully automatic assault rifles. In light of this knowledge and the concern that other methods would endanger the lives of residents of the center, the ATF concluded that a "dynamic entry" raid was the proper method to execute the search and arrest warrants. This evidence will not support an inference of unreasonable force.

Nor is there evidence that the agents possessed an excessive amount of firepower under the circumstances. All of the agents carried 9 millimeter pistols and a limited supply of ammunition. Of the seventy-plus agents participating in the raid, only six agents carried AR–15 semiautomatic rifles capable of shooting rounds that could penetrate a wall. None of the weapons were fully automatic, though some could fire in two-round bursts. Indeed, as events bore out, the ATF possessed too little, not too much, firepower.

Surely, a citizen may not initiate a firefight solely on the ground that the police sent too many well-armed officers to arrest him. The suggestion that a defendant would be entitled to claim self-defense simply by pointing to the police's tactical decision to send twenty heavily-armed officers instead of two lightly-armed ones is untenable. We reject this invitation for individuals to forcibly resist arrest and then put their arresters on trial for the reasonableness of their tactical decisions.

We conclude that the district court did not err in refusing to instruct the jury on self-defense and the defense of another with regard to the voluntary manslaughter charge. . . .

PROBLEMS

1. *Assault on Undercover Officer.* Tom was walking down the street at 2:00 p.m., not bothering anyone, when an undercover officer approached him and tried to arrest him by handcuffing him. Tom, unaware that the man was a police officer, slugged the officer and ran two blocks before a police car knocked him off his feet. Can Tom claim self-defense to an assault charge? See M.P.C. § 3.04(2)(a)(i). Does it matter that Tom was in a high-crime area at the time?

2. *Knowing about Police Status.* Would the result have been different in the prior problem if Tom had known that the man was a police officer?

5. "IMPERFECT" OR "MISTAKEN" SELF–DEFENSE

At common law, a person who uses force against another person under an honest but unreasonable belief that the force is justified cannot claim self-defense. If a defendant is mistaken about the need to use force (or the amount of force) in self-defense, the mistake does not affect the defendant's ability to claim self-defense as long as the mistake is reasonable. On the other hand, if the mistake is unreasonable, self-defense is unavailable to the defendant, who therefore is criminally liable for her offense.

DURAN v. STATE
990 P.2d 1005 (Wyo. 1999).

GOLDEN, JUSTICE.

Duran and the victim lived together in Duran's apartment. On the evening of January 3, 1996, they drove to several local drinking establishments together and ordered drinks at each establishment. At some point in the early morning hours of January 4, 1996, they began to argue. Duran left the establishment and walked to her car, and the victim followed her. Duran testified the victim got upset when she started to get into the car, so she offered to walk home, but he rejected the offer and pushed her into the car, causing her to hit her head.

D slams

When the victim moved away from the car door, <u>Duran slammed and locked the doors</u>, but the victim grabbed a partially opened window and tried to get into the car. Duran testified that she was afraid because the victim had never acted that way before, and she thought he might hit her or throw her down again. She jumped into the driver's seat and started the car. When Duran drove off, the victim was on the hood of the car. Duran did not know how the victim got onto the hood of the car, but denied hitting him. Duran made several driving maneuvers to dislodge the victim from the car and was finally successful. Apparently, the windshield wiper that the victim was gripping broke off the car. When the victim fell off the car, <u>he hit his head on the pavement.</u>

V tries to get in car.

maneuver car to make him fall.

V hits head.

Duran continued driving, then returned to the scene after a short while and attempted to convince the victim to get up. The victim was unconscious in the roadway and could not comply. Officer Fife arrived on the scene and questioned Duran. She told him that she had an argument with the victim, and when she drove away, the victim ran alongside the car for seven or eight blocks, then jumped onto the hood of the car. She said she slammed on her brakes, and the victim fell off the hood. <u>The victim suffered injuries to his brain consistent with striking his head on a hard surface.</u> The brain injuries proved fatal. The victim died on January 5, 1996.

Brain injury

The State filed <u>an information charging Duran with one count of aggravated homicide by motor vehicle.</u> The information alleged that Duran drove a motor vehicle in a reckless manner and proximately caused the death of the victim. The trial court refused to give self-defense instructions proffered by Duran. <u>The jury found Duran guilty of aggravated vehicular homicide on October 17, 1996.</u> . . .

△ guilty

This case presents an issue of first impression in Wyoming concerning whether the affirmative defense of self-defense is available to a defendant charged with a reckless act. As such, the district court's ruling involves a question of law, which we review de novo. . . .

. . . The trial court refused to instruct the jury on self-defense, explaining:

The reason is that it appears to me that the evidence does not warrant a self-defense instruction because as I understand the Defendant's testimony, she intended at no time to inflict any injury and certainly not death on [the victim], rather that she was simply trying to avoid further confrontation with him.

. . .

So that she does not claim that she ever acted intentionally to inflict any harm on him, rather any harm to him was incidental and accidental in her point of view. So it's the view of the Court that the self-defense being an affirmative defense and this Defendant, having in her testimony denied any such act on her part, inflict injury on [the victim], self-defense is not an available defense.

This Court has not directly considered whether self-defense is an appropriate affirmative defense to a crime involving recklessness rather than an intentional act. Duran argues that *Small v. State*, 689 P.2d 420 (Wyo. 1984), *cert. denied*, 469 U.S. 1224, implied that self-defense is an appropriate defense to criminal recklessness. In *Small*, the defendant was charged with involuntary manslaughter. "Out of an abundance of caution, the trial court gave eight instructions on self-defense." Contrary to Duran's contention, the court did not imply that the self-defense instructions were necessary.

The [*Small*] trial court also instructed the jury that one of the necessary elements of involuntary manslaughter was that "the defendant acted recklessly." In another instruction the court defined "recklessly." The state proved to the satisfaction of the jury that appellant acted recklessly. The same evidence that proved appellant acted recklessly also proved that appellant did not act in self-defense since proof of recklessness under the facts of [*Small*] negate[d] self-defense. A finding of recklessness is inconsistent with, and precludes a finding of, self-defense.

Small continued its analysis, quoting a [Washington] case . . . with approval:

When recklessness is an element of the crime charged, and the court properly instructs the jury on the elements of recklessness, the jury must determine, before it may convict, that the accused knew of and disregarded a substantial risk that a wrongful act would occur and that such disregard was a gross deviation from the conduct of a reasonable person in the same situation. Such a finding is totally inconsistent with self-defense. A person acting in self-defense cannot be acting recklessly. Thus, if the jury is able to find that a defendant acted recklessly, it has already precluded a finding of self-defense.

Id. (quoting *State v. Hanton*, 94 Wash.2d 129, 614 P.2d 1280, 1282 (1980)).

In *Small*, this Court opined that "henceforth, when self-defense is properly raised the jury should be specifically instructed that the state has the burden to prove absence of self-defense beyond a reasonable doubt." However, based on the *Hanton* analysis, we determined that, although the trial court failed to instruct the jury that the state has the burden to prove the absence of self-defense beyond a reasonable doubt, the error was not reversible error. *Small* held that "the instructions, taken as a whole, adequately informed the jury of the state's burden of proof, including the negation of appellant's assertion of self-defense."

Rather than implying that self-defense is a proper defense to criminal recklessness, *Small* implies that the self-defense instructions were not necessary because a finding of recklessness precludes a finding of self-defense. If *Small* had determined that the self-defense instructions were necessary, it would have found reversible error for "failure to specifically instruct that the state has the burden to prove absence of self-defense beyond a reasonable doubt."

While Duran claims that the more persuasive approach finds self-defense is relevant to the "reckless" element of the offense, this Court is inclined to follow "[t]he majority of jurisdictions hold[ing] that self-defense requires intentional conduct." See *State v. Blanks*, 712 A.2d 698, 703 (1998) and cases cited therein. A charge of recklessness involves an unintentional act. The trial court gave proper instructions to the jury on the elements of the offense and the definitions of "recklessness" and "proximate cause." The jury had the applicable law before it. The trial court did not err in refusing to submit an instruction on self-defense to the jury. . . .

judgment affirmed.

LEHMAN, CHIEF JUSTICE, dissenting. I respectfully dissent. The majority holds that a theory of self-defense is unavailable to one who is charged with recklessly causing a result because "a charge of recklessness involves an unintentional act." This is not always the case, as Ms. Duran's dilemma illustrates. There is no question that Ms. Duran intended to dislodge "the victim" from the hood of the car. In fact, she intentionally slammed on her brakes to forcibly remove her attacker and allow her escape. She did not intend to hurt him, but she voluntarily chose to use whatever force was necessary. The question before the jury was whether that intention was a conscious disregard of "a substantial and unjustifiable risk" and her actions constituted "a gross deviation from the standard of conduct that a reasonable person would observe in the situation[.]"

I cannot distinguish this scenario from those in which we allow a criminal defendant to claim self-defense. Had Ms. Duran stated she intended to harm "the victim," and had the prosecutor decided to charge her with an intentional homicide, the jury could have considered the reasonableness of her actions in light of her subjective belief of imminent harm. Rather, because her state of mind is less culpable (or because the prosecutor charges her as such), the majority denies her an opportunity to demonstrate that, given her subjective belief, her intentional conduct was reasonable and the risk justifiable.

justifiable

This case sadly personifies the fundamental unfairness caused by confusing "an unintentional act" with what really is an unintentional consequence. Here, Ms. Duran's actions were not unintentional; the victim's death was unintentional. To further illustrate the point, imagine the defendant is faced with a deadly assailant and, in response, the intended victim points and shoots a gun at the attacker's legs, meaning to incapacitate him. However, the defendant's lack of

act. not unintentional the harm is unintf

skill causes the bullet to enter the assailant's heart, instantly killing him. Should the prosecutor choose to charge him with manslaughter, will we deny a claim of self-defense at trial? Under the majority holding, we do.

NOTES

1. *Reckless or negligent belief in justifiability of using force.* Section 3.09(2) of the Model Penal Code addresses the issue of mistake of law as to the force or legality of an arrest, as well as the reckless or negligent use of otherwise justifiable force. It states as follows:

> (2) When the actor believes that the use of force upon or toward the person of another is necessary for any of the purposes for which such belief would establish a justification under Sections 3.03 to 3.08 but the actor is reckless or negligent in having such belief or in acquiring or failing to acquire any knowledge or belief which is material to the justifiability of his use of force, the justification afforded by those Sections is unavailable in a prosecution for an offense for which reckless-ness or negligence, as the case may be, suffices to establish culpability.

Under the Model Penal Code, only an honest belief in the need for force is necessary for the defendant to claim self-defense successfully. Section 3.09(2) provides that a person who acts unreasonably in using force still may be liable for a crime such as manslaughter when her belief about the necessity of using force was based on a reckless or negligent mistake. An actual but unreasonable belief in the necessity for the use of force justifies an intentional act, but not a reckless or negligent act. A common example of a defendant's unreasonable belief is the use of force beyond that which is justified by the circumstances. The origins and purpose of imperfect self-defense are thoroughly reviewed in *State v. Faulkner*, 301 Md. 482, 483 A.2d 759 (1984).

2. *Using force against wrong person.* Section 3.09(3) of the Model Penal Code also addresses the situation where a defendant is justified in using force against one person but is reckless or negligent toward innocent persons in using that force. For example, if Holmes intentionally fires several shots at Moriarty in self-defense but injures Watson, an innocent person, Holmes may be charged with reckless or negligent assault for his conduct.

3. *No lesser crime.* What happens if the charged crime does not include a lesser crime with a lesser culpable mental state equal to the mental state possessed by the defendant at the time she committed the offense? For example, assume that a defendant tried unsuccessfully to shoot and kill another person in the honest but negligent belief that the shooting was necessary to protect herself against deadly force. The defendant would not be guilty of attempted murder because her honest belief would be a complete defense to attempted murder which requires the intent to kill. Moreover, the defendant would not be guilty of a lesser version of attempted homicide, because in most jurisdictions, no crime exists for a negligent attempt.

Problems

1. *Imperfect Self–Defense for Non–Homicide Crimes.* Does imperfect self-defense apply to homicide law only or to other crimes such as assault? In *Bryant v. State*, 83 Md.App. 237, 574 A.2d 29 (1990), the court stated that "[o]utside of homicide law, the concept doesn't exist. . . . With respect to all other crimes, the defendant is either guilty or not guilty. He either acted in self-defense or he did not. There is no 'in between.' Under the circumstances, the judge was correct in declining to give an instruction on the subject of imperfect self-defense with respect to the charges of statutory maiming, assault with intent to disable, and assault and battery." What are the pros and cons of the rule described in *Bryant*?

2. *Effect of M.P.C. § 3.09(2).* What is the purpose of § 3.09(2) of the Model Penal Code? Does it limit the effect of the Code's subjective belief provisions on self-defense and other justification defenses? Is the provision relevant to (1) whether a defendant was reckless or negligent in believing that she needed to act for self-protection; or (2) whether she was reckless or negligent with respect to the result of her conduct, e.g., whether her act would cause the death or injury to another person? In another words, is it the defendant's act which determines whether her crime is classified as intentional or unintentional or her state of mind about the result of her act? See *Elliott v. Commonwealth*, 976 S.W.2d 416 (Ky. 1998).

3. *Unreasonable Belief Manslaughter Instruction.* In *State v. McAvoy*, 331 N.C. 583, 417 S.E.2d 489 (1992), the court found that an honest but unreasonable belief that deadly force is necessary does not reduce an intentional homicide charge to an unintentional charge such as manslaughter. "Defendant is entitled to an instruction on voluntary manslaughter due to the use of excessive force while otherwise acting in defense of a family member and in defense of home or due to defendant's being the aggressor. He is not entitled to an instruction on self-defense or voluntary manslaughter due to an honest but unreasonable belief in the necessity (real or apparent) to kill." Is the court's distinction relating to the propriety of a manslaughter instruction sensible? Explain.

4. *The High School Reunion.* Grant attended a high school reunion dance and drank beer for about eight hours. Eli was hired to close the place. At the conclusion of the dance, everyone departed except Eli, two other employees, and Grant, who was waiting for his designated driver. Eli, aware that Grant was highly intoxicated, took him by the arm and "walked" him out when his ride arrived. Grant was not ready to end the festivities, and vehemently protested. Grant swung at Eli, hitting him in the head with a bag containing Grant's last remaining beer. Eli was able to land a left hook on Grant's jaw, knocking him to the ground. When Grant made an attempt to get up, Eli kicked him in the chest and proceeded to stomp and kick Grant repeatedly. Grant was able to get into the car and go home. When Grant got home, his wife noticed a large knot on the back of his head and he passed

out. He was taken to the hospital and died the next day. Eli was indicted for murder and claimed self-defense. Is an instruction regarding the use of self-defense proper in this case? Would Eli have a reasonable belief that his *use* of force was justified? Would Eli have a reasonable belief that the *degree* of force that he used was justified? Assume that the jury found that Eli had been unreasonable. Must the jury now find him guilty of murder, or may it convict him of a lesser charge?

5. *The Fight.* In the prior problem, assume that Eli was indicted for negligent homicide. Is he entitled to a jury instruction on self-defense?

6. *Responding to a Drive–By Shooting.* Beth shot into an occupied car under the erroneous belief that she needed to shoot the driver in order to protect her family from a drive-by shooting. She was charged with felony murder. The underlying offense was the shooting into an occupied car. She asserts a claim of imperfect self-defense to the felony murder theory of liability. Is a claim of imperfect self-defense available to a charge of felony murder?

7. *Gang Rivalries.* One group of ("red") gang members is walking through a pedestrian mall when it is attacked by another group of ("blue") gang members who are shooting at them. The red gang that is under attack has one gang member who is carrying an automatic weapon. In fear for his life, this gang member whips out the automatic weapon and begins firing bullets indiscriminately. A public school principal, who was looking for a child who had left school, was killed. Under the M.P.C., is the gang member who fired the automatic weapon entitled to invoke self-defense? See *People v. Russell*, 91 N.Y.2d 280, 670 N.Y.S.2d 166, 693 N.E.2d 193 (1998).

EXERCISES

1. *State Code Rules.* In your state, look at the criminal statutes for an imperfect or mistaken defense provision. Compare it with the Model Penal Code defense. Are important statutory terms defined? What do the Model Penal Code and your state statute provide with regard to the following aspects of the defense?

    a.   Must the mistake be reasonable?

    b.   May the mistake be about the maximum harm authorized?

    c.   May the mistake relate to whether defendant's conduct was justified?

    d.   What other mistakes are the subject of the statute?

    e.   Does the provision excuse all crimes, or only some crimes, e.g., only intentional crimes, or only violent crimes?

2. *Charging Decision.* Assume that you practice law in a jurisdiction with the following homicide scheme: intentional murder; reckless plus extreme indifference to human life murder; reckless manslaughter; and negligent homicide. Assume further that your jurisdiction allows imperfect self-defense

to be asserted against lesser homicide offenses. In the following situations, the defendant has killed another person, but claims that she was acting in self-defense. What is the appropriate charge?

a.   Defendant used deadly force and intended to kill. She also believed that the use of deadly force was necessary for self-protection; her belief was reasonable.

b.   Defendant used deadly force and intended to kill. She did not believe that the use of deadly force was necessary for self-protection.

c.   Defendant used deadly force and intended to kill. She also believed that the use of deadly force was necessary for self-protection; her belief was not reasonable; she recklessly concluded that she needed to use deadly force.

d.   Defendant used deadly force and intended to kill. She also believed that the use of deadly force was necessary for self-protection; her belief was not reasonable; she negligently concluded that she needed to use deadly force.

e.   Defendant used deadly force and acted recklessly with extreme indifference to human life. She also believed that the use of deadly force was necessary for self-protection; her belief was reasonable.

f.   Defendant used deadly force and acted recklessly with extreme indifference to human life. She did not believe that the use of deadly force was necessary for self-protection.

g.   Defendant used deadly force and acted recklessly with extreme indifference to human life. She also believed that the use of deadly force was necessary for self-protection; her belief was not reasonable. She recklessly concluded that she needed to use deadly force.

h.   Defendant used deadly force and acted recklessly with extreme indifference to human life. She also believed that the use of deadly force was necessary for self-protection; her belief was not reasonable. She negligently concluded that she needed to use deadly force.

i.   Defendant used deadly force, acted negligently, believed that deadly force was necessary, and her belief was reasonable.

j.   Defendant used deadly force, acted negligently, did not believe that deadly force was necessary.

k.   Defendant used deadly force, acted negligently, believed that deadly force was necessary, and negligently concluded that deadly force was necessary.

B.   DEFENSE OF OTHERS

Self-defense also extends to the right of a defendant to defend another person. Many of the same common-law self-defense doctrines apply to the defense of another.

STATE v. BEELEY

653 A.2d 722 (R.I. 1995).

MURRAY, JUSTICE. [Beeley was convicted of burglary and simple assault. Beeley and John had been playing cards at a friend's house.] Beeley drove John to 80 Evergreen Drive in East Providence where he lived in an apartment with his wife, Julie Perry (Julie). By then it was approximately four o'clock in the morning. John invited Beeley to spend the night at the apartment since it was so late. Beeley dropped off John at the entrance to the apartment building and then went to park his car.

The testimony in the record is contradictory as to what occurred next. John testified that he used his key to gain entry into the apartment through the front door, which was locked. Upon entering the apartment, John walked toward the bedroom and came face-to-face with his wife, Julie, in the hallway. Julie turned on the hallway light and John observed a man sleeping in the bed. John began screaming at Julie and asked her, "Who was in the bed?" Julie responded, "You know who it is." John recognized the man as Robert Harding (Harding). Harding was not wearing any clothes. The two men began wrestling and moved toward the door of the apartment. Harding attempted to force John out of the apartment through the door. John yelled out to Beeley who was waiting outside the apartment. Beeley entered through the doorway and pulled John out of the apartment. John testified that he waited outside of the apartment with Beeley for the police to arrive who had been called by Julie. John then went around to the window of the apartment, opened it, yelled to Julie "How could you do this to me?" and threw a plant on the ground.

Julie and Harding offered a different version of the events. Julie testified that on May 20, 1991, Harding was sleeping on the couch in the living room of the apartment. At approximately four o'clock in the morning she was awakened by "noise." From her bedroom she observed John standing in the hallway. Julie testified that she was sure that John had gained entry into the apartment through a living room window because plant pots located on the window sill were broken. Julie and John began arguing and Harding woke up. John kicked Harding in the face several times as he sat on the couch. As the two men struggled, Julie called the police. John hollered to Beeley "somebody is in here" and then unlocked the door. Beeley entered the apartment, punched Harding in the face, and then left with John.

Harding corroborated Julie's testimony and indicated that as he was locked in combat with John, both tried to open the door. Harding testified that as he attempted to push John out the door, John unlocked the door. Initially Harding testified that John had opened

used Key

the door, but later on cross-examination he recalled that he opened the door after John had unlocked it. John then called out to Beeley and Beeley entered and hit Harding in the face. Harding indicated that this was the first time he had ever met Beeley. Harding sustained facial injuries; however, it is unclear from the record whether Harding's injuries were caused by the single punch executed by Beeley or by the altercation with John.

[margin note: unclear where injuries came from.]

Beeley testified that as he waited outside the apartment, he could hear John and Julie yelling. He walked to the door and banged on it but did not attempt to open it. The door opened and then slammed shut. When the door opened again, Beeley could see Harding who was naked grabbing John by the waist. Beeley did not know Harding and did not know what Harding was doing in the apartment. John was crying, and he yelled to Beeley, "This is the guy." Beeley hit Harding once to break his hold on John. Beeley observed Julie on the telephone, talking to the police. He then grabbed John and pulled him out of the apartment. Beeley and John waited outside for the police to arrive. Beeley further testified that he did not know how John gained entry into the apartment.

[The court reversed Beeley's burglary conviction and proceeded to discuss his contention about the assault conviction.] We next consider Beeley's contention that he is entitled to a new trial on the charge of simple assault. Beeley contends that the trial justice erred in instructing the jury that one acting to defend another has only a derivative right of self-defense, and that his or her actions are not judged by the reasonableness of his or her own conduct and perceptions.

[margin note: trial judge erred saying it's derivative.]

It is undisputed that Beeley hit Harding as Beeley entered the apartment. Beeley's defense to the charge of simple assault upon Harding was that when he entered the apartment, he saw John being held by a naked man (Harding) and speculated that the latter was an intruder who may have raped Julie. Beeley, in an attempt to break Harding's hold on John, executed a single punch at Harding. Beeley contends that he was therefore justified in assaulting Harding. . . .

The trial justice . . . . instructed the jury with respect to defense of another and explained that

> [O]ne who comes to the aid of another person must do so at his own peril and should be excused only when that other person would be justified in defending himself. Thus, if you find that Mr. Perry was not the aggressor and was justified in defending himself from the acts of Mr. Harding, then Mr. Beeley is then excused from any criminal responsibility for coming to the aid of Mr. Perry if Mr. Beeley in so doing did not use excessive force. However, if you find that Mr. Perry was in fact the aggressor and was not justified in his actions and was inflicting punches and

kicks on Mr. Harding, then Mr. Beeley acted at his own peril and his actions would not be justified. ... Our Supreme Court has said on repeated occasions, an intervening person stands in the shoes of the person that he is aiding.

The issue before us is whether an intervenor in an altercation between private individuals should be judged by his or her own reasonable perceptions or whether he or she stands in the shoes of the person that he or she is defending.

This court has addressed the issue of defense of another on several occasions. The cases have involved a defendant-intervenor aiding another in the context of an arrest situation. In *State v. Small*, 410 A.2d 1336 (1980), we held that the defendant did not have the right to use force against a police officer in circumstances in which it was obvious that the third person had no such right. Thereafter, in *State v. Gelinas*, 417 A.2d 1381 (R.I.1980), this court adopted the rule that "one who comes to the aid of an arrestee must do so at his own peril and should be excused only when the individual would himself be justified in defending himself from the use of excessive force by the arresting officer." ... [W]e have not extended the *Gelinas* rule to altercations between private individuals in a non-arrest situation.

A review of the relevant authorities reveals that there are two rules followed by American jurisdictions. The first rule, adopted by the trial justice in the instant case, is sometimes referred to as the "alter ego" rule, and it holds that the right to defend another is coextensive with the other's right to defend himself or herself. The other view, which follows the Model Penal Code, is that as long as the defendant-intervenor reasonably believes that the other is being unlawfully attacked, he or she is justified in using reasonable force to defend him or her. ... Under this section in order for the defense to be raised successfully, three conditions must be met. First, the force must be such as the actor could use in defending himself or herself from the harm that he or she believes to be threatened to the third person. In other words, the actor may use the same amount of force that he or she could use to protect himself or herself. Second, the third person must be justified in using such protective force in the circumstances as the actor believes them to be. Thus, if the third person was resisting an arrest by a known police officer, he or she would have no defense and, if the circumstances were known to the actor, the actor would have no defense either. Finally, the actor must believe that his or her intervention is necessary for the protection of the third party.

This view, which has been adopted in the new state criminal codes, is in our opinion the better view. We favor the doctrine which judges a defendant upon his or her own reasonable perceptions as he or she comes to the aid of the apparent victim. The justification should, of course, be based upon what a reasonable person might

RPP objective standard.

consider to be the imminence of serious bodily harm. As one court expressed it, not only as a matter of justice should one "not be convicted of a crime if he selflessly attempts to protect the victim of an apparently unjustified assault, but how else can we encourage by-standers to go to the aid of another who is being subjected to assault?" *State v. Fair*, 211 A.2d 359 (N.J. 1965). Moreover, to impose liability upon the defendant-intervenor in these circumstances is to impose liability upon him or her without fault.

Encourage Bystanders.

not @ fault.

In sum, it seems to this court preferable to predicate the justification on the actor's own reasonable beliefs. We are of the opinion that an intervenor is justified in using reasonable force to defend another as long as the intervenor reasonably believes that the other is being unlawfully attacked. This rule is "predicated on the social desirability of encouraging people to go to the aid of third parties who are in danger of harm as a result of unlawful actions of others." *Commonwealth v. Monico*, 366 N.E.2d 1241, 1244 (Mass. 1977). As we noted in *Gelinas*, there is an "important social goal of crime prevention, a duty of every citizen." 417 A.2d at 1385 n. 5.

social goal: crime prevention

Applying the foregoing to the instant case, we conclude that the trial justice incorrectly instructed the jury with respect to the charge of assault against Beeley. The rule that we adopted in *Gelinas*, applied to a defendant-intervenor in an arrest situation. The trial justice's application of the *Gelinas* rule in his instructions to the jury in the instant case was therefore incorrect. Accordingly, we vacate Beeley's conviction on the assault charge.

TC incorrect b/c Gelinas

Beeley's appeal is sustained in regard to the charge of breaking and entering for the reasons set out above. Likewise, his appeal in regard to the assault charge is sustained since the court is persuaded that the trial justice's charge to the jury was erroneous. The judgments of conviction are vacated. The case is remanded to the Superior Court for a new trial on the assault charge consistent with this opinion.

remanded

NOTES

1. *Alter ego rule.* At common law, a defendant could use force in defense of another when she reasonably believed such force was necessary to protect the other person from immediate unlawful force. Under the Model Penal Code, the defendant must believe that use of force is necessary. The defendant as a mistaken intervenor can use physical force, as long as her belief is not reckless or negligent.

The criminal law generally treats differently the use of deadly force to protect another. At common law, the defendant's right to use deadly force was no greater than that of the party sought to be protected (also known as the "alter ego" rule). When an intervenor puts herself in the same position as the person to be protected, she acts at her own peril. The person sought to be protected must have reasonably believed that such deadly force was necessary. A mistaken belief by the defendant, even if not reckless or negligent, as to the circumstances is material to the availability of the defense. Because the defendant "stood in the shoes" of the protected person, if the protected person would not in fact have been privileged to use deadly force, the defendant's conduct was likely to be regarded as reckless or negligent. On the other hand, it should be noted that while the protected party may not have had the right to use deadly self-defense—and thus the intervenor likewise would not have the right to use force—the circumstances may be such that the intervenor *herself* may have had the right to defend if attacked.

2. *M.P.C. revisions of defense of others.* The Model Penal Code rejects the "alter ego" rule, and treats the issue of mistake in the same manner as discussed *supra* with regard to self-defense. In addition, the Model Penal Code provides a justification defense in § 3.08 for defendants who intentionally use physical force based upon parental authority, authority to maintain public order and safety, or authority to dispense medical treatment.

§ 3.05   Use of Force for the Protection of Other Persons

(1) Subject to the provisions of this Section and of Section 3.09, the use of force upon or toward the person of another is justifiable to protect a third person when:

(a) the actor would be justified under Section 3.04 in using such force to protect himself against the injury he believes to be threatened to the person whom he seeks to protect; and

(b) under the circumstances as the actor believes them to be the person whom he seeks to protect would be justified in using such protective force; and

(c) the actor believes that his intervention is necessary for the protection of such other person.

(2) Notwithstanding Subsection (1) of this Section:

(a) when the actor would be obliged under Section 3.04 to retreat, to surrender the possession of a thing or to comply with a demand before using force in self-protection, he is not obliged to do so before using force for the protection of another person, unless he knows that he can thereby secure the complete safety of such other person; and

(b) when the person whom the actor seeks to protect would be obliged under Section 3.04 to retreat, to surrender the possession of a thing or to comply with a demand if he knew that he could obtain complete safety by so doing, the actor is obliged to try to cause him to do so before using force in his protection if the actor knows that he can obtain complete safety in that way; and

(c) neither the actor nor the person whom he seeks to protect is obliged to retreat when in the other's dwelling or place of work to any greater extent than in his own.

3.08 Use of Force by Persons With Special Responsibility for Care, Discipline or Safety of Others

The use of force upon or toward the person of another is justifiable if:

(1) the actor is the parent or guardian or other person similarly responsible for the general care and supervision of a minor or a person acting at the request of such parent, guardian or other responsible person and:

(a) the force is used for the purpose of safeguarding or promoting the welfare of the minor, including the prevention or punishment of his misconduct; and

(b) the force used is not designed to cause or known to create a substantial risk of causing death, serious bodily harm, disfigurement, extreme pain or mental distress or gross degradation; or

(2) the actor is a teacher or a person otherwise entrusted with the care or supervision for a special purpose of a minor and:

(a) the actor believes that the force used is necessary to further such special purpose, including the maintenance of reasonable discipline in a school, class or other group, and that the use of such force is consistent with the welfare of the minor; and

(b) the degree of force, if it had been used by the parent or guardian of the minor, would not be unjustifiable under Subsection (1)(b) of this Section; or

(3) the actor is the guardian or other person similarly responsible for the general care and supervision of an incompetent person; and:

(a) the force is used for the purpose of safeguarding or promoting the welfare of the incompetent person, including the prevention of his misconduct, or, when such incompetent person is in a hospital or other institution for his care and custody, for the maintenance of reasonable discipline in such institution; and

(b) the force used is not designed to cause or known to create a substantial risk of causing death, serious bodily harm, disfigurement, extreme or unnecessary pain, mental distress, or humiliation; or

(4) the actor is a doctor or other therapist or a person assisting him at his direction, and:

(a) the force is used for the purpose of administering a recognized form of treatment which the actor believes to be adapted to promoting the physical or mental health of the patient; and

(b) the treatment is administered with the consent of the patient or, if the patient is a minor or an incompetent person, with the consent of his parent or guardian or other person legally competent to consent in his behalf, or the treatment is administered in an emergency when the actor believes that no one competent to consent can be consulted and that a reasonable person, wishing to safeguard the welfare of the patient, would consent; or

(5) the actor is a warden or other authorized official of a correctional institution, and:

(a) he believes that the force used is necessary for the purpose of enforcing the lawful rules or procedures of the institution, unless his belief in the lawfulness of the rule or procedure sought to be enforced is erroneous and his error is due to ignorance or mistake as to provisions of the Code, any other provision of the criminal law or the law governing the administration of the institution; and

(b) the nature or degree of force used is not forbidden by Article 303 or 304 of the Code; and

(c) if deadly force is used, its use is otherwise justifiable under this article; or

(6) the actor is a person responsible for the safety of a vessel or an aircraft or a person acting at his direction, and:

(a) he believes that the force used is necessary to prevent interference with the operation of the vessel or aircraft or obstruction of the execution of a lawful order, unless his belief in the lawfulness of the order is erroneous and his error is due to ignorance or mistake as to the law defining his authority; and

(b) if deadly force is used, its use is otherwise justifiable under this Article; or

(7) the actor is a person who is authorized or required by law to maintain order or decorum in a vehicle, train or other carrier or in a place where others are assembled, and:

(a) he believes that the force used is necessary for such purpose; and

(b) the force used is not designed to cause or known to create a substantial risk of causing death, bodily harm, or extreme mental distress.

3. *Support for alter ego rule.* A minority of courts still apply an "alter ego" rule, by which the right to defend another person is applicable only if the other person in fact had the right to protect herself. In *Leeper v. State*, 589 P.2d 379 (Wyo. 1979), the wife of a combatant claimed defense of another when she killed the person who was fighting with her husband. The appellate court rejected the need for a jury instruction on the defense of another at trial, and reasoned as follows

One asserting the justification of defense of another steps into the position of the person defended. Defense of another takes its form and content from defense of self. The defender is not justified in using force unless he or she reasonably believes the person defended is in immediate danger of unlawful bodily harm, and that the force is reasonable and necessary to prevent that threat. The defender can only use that degree of force necessary to relieve the risk of harm. This defense does not allow the defender to do more than the one defended.

The rule allows defense from unlawful attacks, and under the traditional defense, a defender was not justified in coming to the defense of an aggressor or one who initiated the battle. As the rights of the defender are coterminous with the right of the defense of self, and as one who initiated a battle had no right to self-defense absent abandonment, withdrawal or retreat available or communicated, one who defends an aggressor does so at his or her peril. The law, we think, is also that where two engage unlawfully in a mutual fight, of whatever character, the law does not authorize anyone to take sides and aid one to overcome his adversary. Where both agree to fight, both are aggressors. Earl Leeper and Johannsen mutually agreed to settle their differences by combat. Both voluntarily left the bar. Which of the two initially gave the invitation appears to us immaterial in such a case. . . . Judith made no effort to dissuade the combatants. After they left the barroom, she thought for two or three minutes without comment. Then she rose, removed the weapon from her purse while still at the bar and without knowledge of the battle, and walked out the door. She requested no help and did not call for assistance. She was calm and collected, gave her warning and fired.

Judith Leeper was not, under these facts, justified in using deadly force in defense of her husband as he would not have been justified. Earl was a mutual combatant. A difficult situation might arise if the two had agreed to use nondeadly force, and Johannsen had escalated the battle to a mortal level, but the facts, as the jury was entitled to find them, do not support that conclusion. Earl was on the ground, face down, but Johannsen at the time of the fatal shot was not in attack. He was standing over him. Afterward, Earl arose immediately and with Judith's help attempted to revive Johannsen. All witnesses testified Earl appeared to have suffered no visible injury, no marks on his person, or torn clothing. The jury was entitled to believe Earl was not in great peril of death or great bodily harm, and deadly force was unjustified by him or on his behalf. As the killing was unjustified, and as all the evidence shows no heat of passion, the conviction on murder in the second degree appears valid. Indeed, Judith testified that she believed Earl dead. If she is to be believed, this fact, together with the other facts, would indicate a revengeful mind. Indeed, the absence of a passionate character under such circumstances could have been considered as evidence of malice.

We hold that where two persons have mutually engaged in combat of a nondeadly nature, as the jury was entitled to believe here, no one is justified to defend by use of deadly force. To do so is murder. The State has satisfied the essential elements of the crime, and the instructions given without objection are proper. The conviction is affirmed.

Problems

1. *Social Policy and Defense of Others.* Is the objective alter ego rule preferable to the subjective rule adopted in *Beeley*? Which approach does Section 3.05 of the Model Penal Code adopt? As a matter of social policy, is it a good idea to encourage people to come to the aid of others? Is such a policy more likely to be promoted based on the intervenor's own perceptions rather than on ability of the defended person to use force? Does the *Beeley* standard encourage impulsive or unlawful interference with other persons' activities? If social policy favors intervention based upon the defendant's own perceptions about whether assistance is necessary, why does the court retain the alter ego rule for interveners in the arrest situation? Explain.

2. *Defending Family Members.* Abby was charged with the murder of her husband, Dan. In her defense, she claims that she was defending her son, Tim, from his stepfather. Abby alleges that Dan always disliked Tim and the two had never gotten along. One afternoon, Abby came home to find Tim standing with his back to the corner with Dan pointing a pistol at him. Abby grabbed a knife from the counter and stabbed Dan in the back, killing him. Unfortunately, Dan was not going to shoot Tim. The gun was not loaded and Dan was merely showing Tim how to protect himself. In light of her mistake, does Abby have the "defense of others" under:

    a.   The common law "alter ego" rule?

    b.   The M.P.C.?

3. *Police Abuse.* After police officers responded to a fight between defendant and a neighbor at a trailer park, the defendant struck one of the officers and broke his jaw because he thought the officer was assaulting his wife. All the witnesses except the defendant and his wife testified that the officer was escorting defendant's wife to a spot near her husband with little more force than one would use in escorting a person to a waiting car. Defendant and his wife testified that the officer had the defendant's spouse in a hammer lock and that she was in great pain. Under the circumstances, should the court approve a defense-of-others instruction because the defendant and his wife testified about the use of excessive force? Wasn't the defendant's wife in fact the victim of excessive force at the time of the defendant's assault on the officer? *See Batson v. State*, 113 Nev. 669, 941 P.2d 478 (1997).

4. *The Fight over Property.* Jake was charged with aggravated assault for stabbing Henry during an altercation. In his defense, Jake claimed that his actions were legally justified under the theory of defense of others. Jake

claimed that he and his wife Mary went to their acquaintance Cathy's house to retrieve property that they claimed was theirs. His wife approached Cathy, who immediately attacked her. Jake contended that he heard his wife scream "Help. She's killing me," and he ran to protect her. When Jake tried to help Mary, Henry tackled him. Jake and Henry struggled and Jake begged Henry to let him go because he feared that his wife was in serious danger. He told Henry that he feared for his wife's life and, if Henry didn't let him go, he would have to hurt him. Jake pulled a knife and stabbed Henry, but Henry continued to fight him. Jake proceeded to stab Henry several more times. Jake's story was corroborated by witnesses. At the close of the evidence, the judge instructed the jury on self-defense, but refused to allow the jury to consider the issue of whether Jake's actions were justified under a theory of defense of others. Did the trial court rule correctly under:

    a.   The common law?

    b.   The M.P.C.?

If Jake was not in imminent danger and his attack was against his own assailant and not his wife's assailant, can he claim a defense-of-others justification? May a defendant use deadly force against a fourth person in order to utilize the defense-of-others justification against a third person? Does the fact that Jake used deadly force change your decision?

    5.   *The Trio.* John and Gwyneth had been friends for a long time, though they had never been romantically involved. John became very upset when he learned that Gwyneth was seeing Manny, a man whom he hated. John had repeatedly threatened Manny with violence, including death. One afternoon, Manny and Gwyneth were driving with a friend when John passed them in his car. John followed them and the trio pulled off the side of the road. John pulled up behind them, and Manny and Gwyneth got out to talk to him while their friend stayed in the car. John cursed at Manny and asked to speak to Gwyneth alone. Manny then walked around to the front of the car. While Gwyneth was standing at John's car window speaking to him, they began arguing, John grabbed Gwyneth and threatened to kill her. Gwyneth hollered to Manny, "He's got a gun!" In response, Manny fatally shot John. At his murder trial, Manny claimed defense of another. The trial judge instructed the jury that Manny was justified in shooting John if the jury reasonably believed that John was threatening Gwyneth with unlawful deadly force and if Manny reasonably believed that the degree and use of deadly force would be immediately necessary to protect Gwyneth from John's threatened and unlawful force and *that a reasonable person in Manny's situation would not have retreated.* Was Manny required to retreat before using deadly force to protect Gwyneth? If the theory of defense of others is based on the theory of self-defense, and the jurisdiction in question requires retreat for self-defense, would retreat also be necessary in the case of defense of others? Does it matter whether Manny reasonably believed that Gwyneth could not retreat?

6. *Chasing a Child.* Mike, a 26-year-old man, is charged with assault for forcefully kicking his 68-year-old neighbor, Andy. According to Mike, his wife informed him that Andy was chasing their six-year-old daughter Maggie from his yard. Apparently Maggie had been in Andy's yard "playing" with his dogs. Mike claims that his daughter was frightened and that he was afraid that she would be harmed. According to Maggie, she was not standing near her father or Andy when the actual incident occurred, although Andy had been chasing her. Mike claimed that he was justified in his actions towards Andy because he used force in defense of a third person. The trial judge refused to instruct the jury on the issue of defense of a third person, claiming that the evidence indicated that harm to Maggie was not a possibility. In determining whether the issue of defense of another should be presented to the jury, should the judge decide whether the third party could have actually been harmed? Is the correct standard whether the defendant reasonably believed that the third party could have been harmed? What if this state had adopted the alter ego rule? Would Mike have been justified in defending Maggie if there was no possibility for her to be injured? Does it matter that Maggie is Mike's daughter?

EXERCISES

1. *State Code Rules.* In your state, look at the criminal statutes for a defense. Compare it with the Model Penal Code defense. Are important statutory terms defined? Is there a separate section for the use of force by persons with special responsibility for the care, discipline or safety of specified other persons? What do the Model Penal Code and state statute provide with regard to the following aspects of the defense?

    a.   The imminence of the threat;

    b.   The seriousness of the harm threatened;

    c.   The nature of the harm threatened;

    d.   The target of the threat;

    e.   The unlawfulness of the threat;

    f.   The source of the threat; and

    g.   Whether there is one provision dealing with any defense of others situation, or whether there is a scheme like the Model Penal Code, with one general provision, supplemented by specific examples of authorized use of force by persons with special responsibility for the care, discipline or safety of others.

2. *Nature of Force.* As to the extent of the harm caused by the defendant, what do the Model Penal Code and state statute provide about the extent of harm caused by the defendant, e.g.,

    a.   The seriousness of the harm in relation to the harm threatened, e.g., the use of deadly force; and

b.   The availability of less harmful but equally effective alternatives to avoiding the threat, e.g., calling the police?

C.   DEFENSE OF PROPERTY

When an individual defends his property with deadly force rather than his person, difficult questions arise concerning the scope of this right.

STATE v. ANDERSON

972 P.2d 32 (Okl.Crim.App. 1998).

LUMPKIN, JUDGE: [Anderson was charged with Murder in the First Degree and Shooting with Intent to Kill. The trial judge ruled that Anderson, although only a visitor in the Alvey and Wilson residence, qualified as an occupant under the Oklahoma's "Make My Day" Law. The jury subsequently returned not guilty verdicts on all charges. The state reserved as a question of law whether the term "occupant," as used in the "Make My Day" Law, included people other than the homeowner or any continuous resident of the premises. This question is one of first impression.]

The only facts from Appellee's trial that now concern us are that he was an invited guest in the home of Joe Alvey and Chris Wilson; that the victims, Joe Younger and Chris Harris, forcibly broke into Alvey and Wilson's home, and that Appellee shot the victims.

§ Title 21 O.S.1991, 1289.25, also known as the "Make My Day" Law, provides:

A.   The Legislature hereby recognizes that the citizens of the State of Oklahoma have a right to expect absolute safety within their own homes.

B.   Any occupant of a dwelling is justified in using any degree of physical force, including but not limited to deadly force, against another person who has made an unlawful entry into that dwelling, and when the occupant has a reasonable belief that such other person might use any physical force, no matter how slight, against any occupant of the dwelling.

C.   Any occupant of a dwelling using physical force, including but not limited to deadly force, pursuant to the provisions of subsection B of this section, shall have an affirmative defense in any criminal prosecution for an offense arising from the reasonable use of such force and shall be immune from any civil liability for injuries or death resulting from the reasonable use of such force.

D.   The provisions of this section and the provisions of the Oklahoma Self–Defense Act, Sections 1 through 25 of this act, shall not be construed to require any person using a pistol pursuant to the provisions of this section to be licensed in any manner.

This statute does not contain a list of definitions. Lacking a specific statutory definition, we must look to the common ordinary meaning of the term "occupant." Webster's II defines "occupant" as "1. One that occupies a place or position, esp. a resident. 2. One who is the first to take possession of previously unowned land or premises." Webster's II New Riverside University Dictionary, (1984). The State argues that under these definitions, and those of "occupancy" and "occupy," section 1289.25 refers only to a person who has a possessory or privacy interest in the premises. While we find these definitions instructive, we do not find they answer the questions before us.

Looking to other statutory uses of the term "occupant," we do not find a requirement for a possessory or privacy interest. The use of the term "occupied" similarly implies no possessory interest.

While dictionary definitions, statutory references and case law from Oklahoma and other jurisdictions are helpful in our analysis, the interpretation of the Legislature's intent in Section 1289.25 is ultimately based upon the words in the statute itself. Reading the statute in its entirety, we find it a study in contradiction or compromise. The preamble seems to clearly set forth the intent of the law—"that the citizens of the State of Oklahoma have a right to expect absolute safety within their own homes." However, the terms "resident," "homeowner" or other such restrictive terms were not used in the remainder of the statute. Likewise, the all encompassing term "any person" was not used. Therefore, we are left with the term "occupant," a term with no specific statutory definition. That term is used three times in subsection B. It is the third use of the term "occupant" which leads us to the conclusion that the law was intended to protect anyone legally inside the dwelling, and not just the legal residents of the dwelling. Reading the statute in that manner, any person legally in the dwelling is justified in using any degree of physical force, including but not limited to deadly force, against another person who has made an unlawful entry into that dwelling, and when the person legally inside the dwelling has a reasonable belief that such other person might use any physical force, no matter how slight, against any person legally in the dwelling. To read it in any other manner would permit only residents or homeowners to protect only other residents or homeowners. Invited guests or employees would be left to fend for themselves. This type of application would lead to many absurd results and is not supported by any statements of legislative intent. There are many fact situations which illustrate this point, but we will look at just two.

The baby-sitter comes to the homeowner's residence to watch the children while the parents (the homeowners) are away. If someone breaks into the house making an unlawful entry, is the baby-sitter allowed to protect herself and the children in her care? Under the State's interpretation of the statute, the baby-sitter would not be able to use any physical force, including deadly force, against the intruder because she was not the homeowner or resident. We do not believe the Legislature intended to exclude someone in that position from using physical or deadly force to protect him or herself and those in his or her charge. Another scenario involves that of the invited guest. An unlawful entry is made into the home, the homeowners or residents are either away from the house or unable to defend themselves and only the invited guest is able to muster a defense. Is the invited guest allowed to use any physical force, including deadly force, against the intruder? We think so. Under the State's interpretation of the statute, the invited guest would not be able to so defend him or herself. While these are just two of many situations which could arise, they adequately illustrate the practical application of the statute. These situations also point out how our interpretation of the statute is consistent with the other laws on self-defense and defense of another.

Under Section 1289.25, the person inside the dwelling does not have to determine the intruder's intentions. An unlawful entry and the reasonable belief that the intruder might use any physical force is sufficient to permit the person inside the dwelling to use any physical force, including deadly force, against the person making the unlawful entry. Under Section 1289.25, persons legally inside a dwelling have the right to expect safety and freedom from unlawful intrusion. With the enactment of Section 1289.25 it appears the Legislature was trying to create a place of absolute safety and freedom—the home, whether it be your own home or one in which you are legally present.

The State's argument that including visitors in the term "occupant" will result in some sort of carnage is groundless. The statute has been on the books for approximately a decade without incident. It contains sufficient safeguards to prevent abuse. Under the statute, if the occupant does not "reasonably believe" that the intruder intends to use force, then he or she is not justified in using deadly force. This statute merely tells those who would break into other people's homes that they do so at their own risk. When one is going about his or her business, in the safety of a dwelling, and is suddenly surprised by an intruder breaking into the dwelling, we find the Legislature intended to give the benefit of the doubt to the law-abiding occupant rather than the law breaking intruder. When one intrudes into a dwelling that is not his, the extent of his wrongdoing should not depend on the legal relationship between the dwelling and those lawfully inside it. When one intrudes into the dwelling of another, the harm is the violation of the sanctity of the dwelling itself, not merely to a particular person's property interest. An invited guest in a dwelling has just a much right to expect safety therein as the owner.

Granted, as with many of our laws, this statute applies to the "good guys" as well as the "bad guys." While the persons legally inside the residence may be engaged in illegal activity, or may have occupations which are illegal, if they are legally inside the residence and an intruder illegally enters the dwelling, they are entitled to use any physical force, including deadly force, against the intruder. Whether the use of this force exonerates them from the result of the use of that force, i.e., murder, shooting with intent to kill, etc. would be for a jury to decide under the appropriate instructions.

Therefore, we find the Legislature intended for the term "occupant" as used in § 21 O.S.1991, 1289.25 to include visitors, i.e. persons legally inside the dwelling. . . .

CHAPEL, P.J., dissenting. I dissent. [T]he "Make My Day" Law provides in Subsection A that it is intended to protect citizens "within their own home." I would therefore limit the application of the Act. In view of Subsection A, I am of the opinion that the word "occupant" which appears in Subsections B and C refers only to residents of a dwelling and no others.

NOTES

1. *Preventing a property crime.* As with self-defense and the defense of others, the common law distinguishes between the use of non-deadly force and deadly force by a defendant in the defense of property. As a practical matter, the primary use of this defense is to give a defendant some privilege for her force so that she is not viewed as the initial aggressor. When a defendant reasonably believes it is immediately necessary to use non-deadly force against another to protect property possessed by her or by another for whose protection she acts, she can do so in order to prevent commission of crimes such as criminal trespass or a burglary; or criminal mischief or theft of tangible, movable property. Because the defense is available to prevent a property crime, once an offense is completed, the privilege to use force apparently ends.

A defendant can use deadly force in defense of property in limited circumstances at common law. Generally, only non-deadly force can be used to protect personal property. Deadly force is available to a defendant to prevent forcible entry of a dwelling only if the defendant reasonably believes that the trespasser intends to commit a felony once inside.

2. *M.P.C. and defense of property.* The Model Penal Code's provisions on defense of property are set forth in § 3.06.

§ 3.06 Use of Force for the Protection of Property

(1) **Use of Force Justifiable for Protection of Property.** Subject to the provisions of this Section and of Section 3.09, the use of force upon

or toward the person of another is justifiable when the actor believes that such force is immediately necessary:

(a) to prevent or terminate an unlawful entry or other trespass upon land or a trespass against or the unlawful carrying away of tangible, movable property, provided that such land or movable property is, or is believed by the actor to be, in his possession or in the possession of another person for whose protection he acts; or

(b) to effect an entry or re-entry upon land or to retake tangible movable property, provided that the actor believes that he or the person by whose authority he acts or a person from whom he or such other person derives title was unlawfully dispossessed of such land or movable property and is entitled to possession, and provided, further, that:

(i) the force is used immediately or on fresh pursuit after such dispossession; or

(ii) the actor believes that the person against whom he uses force has no claim of right to the possession of the property and, in the case of land, the circumstances, as the actor believes them to be, are of such urgency that it would be an exceptional hardship to postpone the entry or re-entry until a court order is obtained.

(2) **Meaning of Possession.** For the purposes of Subsection (1) of this Section:

(a) a person who has parted with the custody of property to another who refuses to restore it to him is no longer in possession, unless the property is movable and was and still is located on land in his possession;

(b) a person who has been dispossessed of land does not regain possession thereof merely by setting foot thereon;

(c) a person who has a license to use or occupy real property is deemed to be in possession thereof except against the licensor acting under claim of right.

(3) **Limitations on Justifiable Use of Force**.

(a) Request to Desist. The use of force is justifiable under this Section only if the actor first requests the person against whom such force is used to desist from his interference with the property, unless the actor believes that:

(i) such request would be useless; or

(ii) it would be dangerous to himself or another person to make the request; or

(iii) substantial harm will be done to the physical condition of the property which is sought to be protected before the request can effectively be made.

(b) Exclusion of Trespasser. The use of force to prevent or terminate a trespass is not justifiable under this Section if the actor knows that the exclusion of the trespasser will expose him to substantial danger of serious bodily harm.

(c) Resistance of Lawful Re-entry or Recaption. The use of force to prevent an entry or re-entry upon land or the recaption of movable property is not justifiable under this Section, although the actor believes that such re-entry or recaption is unlawful, if:

> (i) the re-entry or recaption is made by or on behalf of a person who was actually dispossessed of the property; and

> (ii) it is otherwise justifiable under paragraph (1)(b) of this Section.

(d) Use of Deadly Force. The use of deadly force is not justifiable under this Section unless the actor believes that:

> (i) the person against whom the force is used is attempting to dispossess him of his dwelling otherwise than under a claim of right to its possession; or

> (ii) the person against whom the force is used is attempting to commit or consummate arson, burglary, robbery or other felonious theft or property destruction and either:

>> (1) has employed or threatened deadly force against or in the presence of the actor; or

>> (2) the use of force other than deadly force to prevent the commission or the consummation of the crime would expose the actor or another in his presence to substantial danger of serious bodily harm.

(4) **Use of Confinement as Protective Force**. The justification afforded by this Section extends to the use of confinement as protective force only if the actor takes all reasonable measures to terminate the confinement as soon as he knows that he can do so with safety to the property, unless the person confined has been arrested on a charge of crime.

(5) **Use of Device to Protect Property**. The justification afforded by this Section extends to the use of a device for the purpose of protecting property only if:

> (a) the device is not designed to cause or known to create a substantial risk of causing death or serious bodily harm; and

> (b) the use of the particular device to protect the property from entry or trespass is reasonable under the circumstances, as the actor believes them to be; and

> (c) the device is one customarily used for such a purpose or reasonable care is taken to make known to probable intruders the fact that it is used.

(6) **Use of Force to Pass Wrongful Obstructor**. The use of force to pass a person whom the actor believes to be purposely or knowingly and unjustifiably obstructing the actor from going to a place to which he may lawfully go is justifiable, provided that:

(a) the actor believes that the person against whom he uses force has no claim of right to obstruct the actor; and

(b) the actor is not being obstructed from entry or movement on land which he knows to be in the possession or custody of the person obstructing him, or in the possession or custody of another person by whose authority the obstructor acts, unless the circumstances, as the actor believes them to be, are of such urgency that it would not be reasonable to postpone the entry or movement on such land until a court order is obtained; and

(c) the force used is not greater than would be justifiable if the person obstructing the actor were using force against him to prevent his passage.

PROBLEMS

1. *Reasonable Force in Anderson.* In *Anderson,* why does the court conclude that the amount of force used by an "occupant" does not have to be reasonable? What is the effect of the opinion on the use of any force by an occupant? Do you agree that the amount of force used should not have to depend on an occupant's reasonable belief that an intruder intends either to commit some crime or do harm to a person within the dwelling? Explain.

2. *Noise at the Window.* Defendant is at home at night when he hears noise at a window and investigates. Consider whether he can use force, including deadly force, in the following situations:

a. *Unsure Whether Burglar Has Weapon.* Defendant's investigation reveals that a burglar is trying to enter his house. Defendant is unsure whether the burglar is carrying a deadly weapon.

b. *Small Child.* Defendant's investigation reveals that a small child (5 years old) is trying to break into the house. Does it matter whether defendant knows (or does not know) whether the child has a firearm? Would it matter that defendant lives in a rough neighborhood where even young children frequently commit crimes with weapons?

c. *Fourth Grader.* Defendant's investigation reveals that a 10-year-old child is trying to break into the house. Again, does it matter whether defendant knows (or does not know) whether the child has a firearm, or whether defendant lives in a rough neighborhood where even young children frequently commit crimes with weapons?

d. *Large Man.* Defendant sees a large man trying to raise his window from the outside. Defendant, who by that time has grabbed his gun, fires twice, killing the man. On further investigation, defendant realizes that the "intruder" was not a burglar but his next door neighbor who was trying to play a prank. Did defendant have the right to use deadly force?

3. *Silent Burglar Alarm.* Lee has an expensive collection of automobiles (Corvettes, Ferraris, and Bentleys) that he keeps in a warehouse located approximately 40 feet from his house. Since Lee has experienced problems with break-ins and vandalism at the warehouse, he has installed a silent burglar alarm (one that alerts him, but not the intruder) at the warehouse. One night about 2:30am, the burglar alarm goes off. Lee quickly grabs a gun and rushes out to the warehouse. He finds a man with a flashlight in the warehouse. Is he free to use deadly force without making any inquiry or a request to desist?

4. *Security Devices.* In the prior problem, assume that there is no burglar alarm and that Lee does not go out to the warehouse with a gun. Instead, because of ongoing problems with vandalism, Lee decides to use various "security devices" to protect his property. Assume that a burglar enters the property and is injured by one the devices. Which of the following devices are permissible:

   a. *Vicious Dogs.* Lee keeps several large ferocious dogs in the warehouse, and posts warnings stating "Vicious Dogs – Keep Out."

   b. *Non-deadly Electric Fence.* Lee installs an electric fence on the perimeter of his land around his warehouse and posts a sign warning intruders to "keep out." The fence will provide a painful, but non-deadly, shock to intruders.

   c. *Scattered Toys.* Lee scatters his kids' toys all over the grounds knowing that they constitute a "hazard" to anyone who might be on the property around the warehouse.

   d. *Trap Gun.* Lee sets up a trap gun aimed at the door of the warehouse. Anyone who enters without disarming the trap gun is likely to be shot and killed.

5. *Curious Boy.* In the prior problem, would it make any difference if the "intruder" was a 10-year-old neighborhood child who entered Lee's land and his warehouse out of curiosity, but was injured by each of Lee's "security devices"?

6. *Distracted Robber.* Late one night, defendant, a clerk, is behind the counter of a convenience store when a robber enters the store with a gun. The robber points the gun at defendant and tells him, "This is a stick-up. I'm not going to hurt you if you cooperate. Just put the money in the bag and I'll leave quietly." As defendant is putting the money in the bag, a customer walks into the store. The robber turns around to confront the customer, thereby taking his eyes off of the defendant. The robber tells the customer, "This is a stick-up. Hit the floor and you won't get hurt." While the robber is distracted, the defendant grabs a gun from below the counter

and kills the robber. Under the M.P.C., was defendant allowed to use deadly force?

EXERCISES

1. *State Code Rules.* In your state, look at the criminal statutes for a defense of property provision. Compare it with the Model Penal Code defense. Are important statutory terms defined? What do the Model Penal Code and state statute provide with regard to the following aspects of the defense?

   a.   The imminence of the threat;

   b.   The seriousness of the harm threatened;

   c.   The nature of the harm threatened, e.g., specific crimes such as burglary, arson, trespass, interference with property; or instead property concepts like dispossession of movable property;

   d.   The target of the threat, e.g., real property, personal property, property in the defendant's possession, property in the possession of another for whose protection the defendant acts;

   e.   The unlawfulness of the threat; and

   f.   The source of the threat.

2. *Nature of Harm.* As to the extent of the harm caused by the defendant, what do the Model Penal Code and state statute provide with regard to the extent of harm caused by the defendant, e.g.,

   a.   The seriousness of the harm in relation to the harm threatened, e.g., the use of deadly force; and

   b.   The availability of less harmful but equally effective alternatives to avoiding the threat, e.g., calling the police to arrest a trespasser?

D.   LAW ENFORCEMENT DEFENSE

Under the common law, a law enforcement official could use any force reasonably appearing to be necessary to arrest a felon, and any non-deadly force to arrest a person charged with a misdemeanor. A private citizen called to assist a law enforcement official could use the force available to the officer.

In *Tennessee v. Garner*, 471 U.S. 1 (1985), the Supreme Court held that the use of deadly force to prevent the escape of an apparently unarmed suspected felon is constitutional under the Fourth Amendment only if it is "necessary to prevent the escape and the officer has probable cause to believe that the suspect poses a significant threat of death or serious physical injury to the officer or others."

The use of deadly force to prevent the escape of all felony suspects, whatever the circumstances, is constitutionally unreasonable. It is not better that all felony suspects die than that they escape. Where the suspect poses no immediate threat to the officer and no threat to others, the harm resulting from failing to apprehend him does not justify the use of deadly force to do so. It is no doubt unfortunate when a suspect who is in sight escapes, but the fact that the police arrive a little late or are a little slower afoot does not always justify killing the suspect. A police officer may not seize an unarmed, nondangerous suspect by shooting him dead. . . .

Where the officer has probable cause to believe that the suspect poses a threat of serious physical harm, either to the officer or to others, it is not constitutionally unreasonable to prevent escape by using deadly force. Thus, if the suspect threatens the officer with a weapon or there is probable cause to believe that he has committed a crime involving the infliction or threatened infliction of serious physical harm, deadly force may be used if necessary to prevent escape, and if, where feasible, some warning has been given. . . .

Nor do we agree with petitioners and appellant that the rule we have adopted requires the police to make impossible, split-second evaluations of unknowable facts. We do not deny the practical difficulties of attempting to assess the suspect's dangerousness. However, similarly difficult judgments must be made by the police in equally uncertain circumstances. Nor is there any indication that in States that allow the use of deadly force only against dangerous suspects, the standard has been difficult to apply or has led to a rash of litigation involving inappropriate second-guessing of police officers' split-second decisions. Moreover, the highly technical felony/misdemeanor distinction is equally, if not more, difficult to apply in the field. An officer is in no position to know, for example, the precise value of property stolen, or whether the crime was a first or second offense. Finally, as noted above, this claim must be viewed with suspicion in light of the similar self-imposed limitations of so many police departments. . . .

Because the *Garner* holding is constitutionally based, it applies to all state and federal law enforcement officials. Does *Garner* permit an officer to use deadly force when a person charged with a misdemeanor refuses to submit to an officer's arrest and instead tries to use deadly force against the officer?

———

What happens when an innocent bystander is harmed when the crime victim attempts to stop the perpetrators of the crime?

PEOPLE v. PENA

169 Misc.2d 75, 641 N.Y.S.2d 794 (1996).

DONNINO, JUSTICE. On February 18, 1995 at about 7:45 p.m., the defendant was operating the family bodega when two men entered. One of the two men appeared to position himself as a lookout while the other one pointed a shotgun at the defendant and robbed him. There were two other employees in the different parts of the store who observed portions of the robbery. The perpetrator with the shotgun was described as [a] male, wearing a dark green ski jacket and a black hat or "hood" or an item "like a ski mask" though the face was not covered; the other perpetrator was described as a male, dressed in a black hat, and a black coat or jacket.

The perpetrators exited the store, which was located at 178th Street and Webster Ave., and headed west on 178th Street toward the next block, Valentine Ave., and Echo Park, which was on the west side of Valentine Ave. The defendant testified that as the perpetrators left the store:

> I just thought about stopping them. It was the second time [in] less than a month that we had been robbed. I didn't think twice about it. I grabbed a weapon . . . [and] I went outside.

> As far as I was concerned, they were the same ones, the same size, the same black hood. I yelled out to them, hey. The taller one, the one in the dark hood turned around towards me and he was like trying to get something out of his coat. I thought I had seen the shotgun again. I thought that it was going to be used against me. So, I shot first, I fired first.

The defendant's recollection was that he fired five or six uninterrupted bullets at the two people who were on the sidewalk on 178th Street heading toward Valentine Ave. Those two, he said, were the only two people he saw on the sidewalk. After firing the shots, he returned to the bodega.

The friend of the person who was killed and who was accompanying the deceased at the time testified that neither he nor his friend engaged in the robbery. They were walking west on 178th Street toward Valentine Ave., heard multiple shots, ran toward Valentine Ave. and Echo Park, and his friend fell mortally wounded in the middle of Valentine Ave. When the friend of the deceased first heard the shots, he saw two men running in back of him; one of them was wearing a black ski jacket. The friend of the deceased was wearing a black ski jacket and a black ski hat; the deceased was wearing a light colored coat. The eyewitness did not think the deceased and his friend were the ones in the street based on the relative size of the people, but, he could make no facial distinctions and identifications.

In charging the Grand Jury on justification, the District Attorney effectively took the position that a victim of a robbery who properly used deadly physical force to arrest a robber who was in immediate flight from the robbery but did so in such a manner as to kill an innocent passerby could be held criminally liable for the death of the passerby. So charged, the Grand Jury indicted the defendant for depraved indifference murder, reckless manslaughter, [and other crimes]. The charge to the Grand Jury was in error. New York [statutory] law provides that the citizen who properly uses deadly physical force to arrest a robber who is in immediate flight from the robbery and in so doing unintentionally injures or kills a passerby is not criminally liable for that tragic death.

The applicable statute permits the "use" of deadly physical force when the user reasonably believes deadly physical force is necessary to effect the arrest of a person who has committed robbery and who is in immediate flight therefrom. ...Thus, the statutory language justifies the use of force upon "another" person when necessary to effect the arrest of "a" person. That construction means that the person upon whom the use of force is directed need not be the person sought to be arrested. For example, in apprehending "a" person who in fact has committed the requisite felony, force may have to be used against "another" person who may be attempting to prevent the arrest. If the Legislature meant to limit the use of force to the robber, the statutory language would have been written to reflect that the person against whom the force was being directed had to be the person sought to be arrested. Plainly, therefore, the requirement that the actor be seeking to arrest a person who in fact committed the requisite felony is a predicate to the use of the force and not a restriction on whom the force is used against. ...

While the Legislature did not explain why it drew a distinction between a police and peace officer and a citizen, there is one explanation to be found in part in the statute itself. The officer need not be correct in his/her reasonable belief that the person the officer is seeking to arrest committed an enumerated felony; nor is the officer restricted to using the deadly physical force to effect the arrest of a person who is in immediate flight from the commission of the felony. Before using deadly physical force, the citizen must be correct in his/her reasonable belief that the person he/she is seeking to arrest committed an enumerated felony and that such person is in immediate flight from the commission of the enumerated felony. Given that the police and peace officer is specially trained, *inter alia*, in the responsible use of firearms under trying circumstances, and that he/she was being authorized to use that deadly physical force on a much broader scale than the citizen, the Legislature wanted some statutory incentive for the police to act responsibly in the use of their broad power to use deadly physical force by holding them responsible for reckless conduct. In fact, those who opposed the legislation did so on the grounds that the legislation accorded too much authority to the police to use force. For the citizen who could not be presumed to have had training in the use of deadly physical force, and who would be acting often under stress, on the spur of the moment, in response to the commission of an enumerated felony and while the felon was in immediate flight from that felony, and who would often otherwise be a responsible member of the community, the Legislature chose not to hold that citizen accountable for an otherwise justifiable use of force that resulted in injury or death to the wrong person. Reasonable people may disagree with that decision, but the Legislature made its choice among the options presented and whether we agree or disagree with the law across the board or in its application to a particular situation, we are bound to accept the legislative direction.

NOTE

M.P.C. and law enforcement defense. The Model Penal Code limits the use of deadly force to the four conditions listed in § 3.07(2)(b). The section also describes the use of force that may be used to prevent an escape and to prevent crime.

§ 3.07   Use of Force in Law Enforcement

(1) **Use of Force Justifiable to Effect an Arrest.** Subject to the provisions of this Section and of Section 3.09, the use of force upon or toward the person of another is justifiable when the actor is making or assisting in making an arrest and the actor believes that such force is immediately necessary to effect a lawful arrest.

(2) **Limitations on the Use of Force.**

(a) The use of force is not justifiable under this Section unless:

(i) the actor makes known the purpose of the arrest or believes that it is otherwise known by or cannot reasonably be made known to the person to be arrested; and

(ii) when the arrest is made under a warrant, the warrant is valid or believed by the actor to be valid.

(b) The use of deadly force is not justifiable under this Section unless:

(i) the arrest is for a felony; and

(ii) the person effecting the arrest is authorized to act as a peace officer or is assisting a person whom he believes to be authorized to act as a peace officer; and

(iii) the actor believes that the force employed creates no substantial risk of injury to innocent persons; and

(iv) the actor believes that:

(1) the crime for which the arrest is made involved conduct including the use or threatened use of deadly force; or

(2) there is a substantial risk that the person to be arrested will cause death or serious bodily harm if his apprehension is delayed.

(3) **Use of Force to Prevent Escape from Custody**. The use of force to prevent the escape of an arrested person from custody is justifiable when the force could justifiably have been employed to effect the arrest under which the person is in custody, except that a guard or other person authorized to act as a peace officer is justified in using any force, including deadly force, which he believes to be immediately necessary to prevent the escape of a person from a jail, prison, or other institution for the detention of persons charged with or convicted of a crime.

(4) **Use of Force by Private Person Assisting an Unlawful Arrest**.

(a) A private person who is summoned by a peace officer to assist in effecting an unlawful arrest, is justified in using any force which he would be justified in using if the arrest were lawful, provided that he does not believe the arrest is unlawful.

(b) A private person who assists another private person in effecting an unlawful arrest, or who, not being summoned, assists a peace officer in effecting an unlawful arrest, is justified in using any force which he would be justified in using if the arrest were lawful, provided that (i) he believes the arrest is lawful, and (ii) the arrest would be lawful if the facts were as he believes them to be.

(5) **Use of Force to Prevent Suicide or the Commission of a Crime**.

(a) The use of force upon or toward the person of another is justifiable when the actor believes that such force is immediately necessary to prevent such other person from committing suicide, inflicting serious bodily harm upon himself, committing or consummating the commission of a crime involving or threatening bodily harm, damage to or loss of property or a breach of the peace, except that:

(i) any limitations imposed by the other provisions of this Article on the justifiable use of force in self-protection, for the protection of others, the protection of property, the effectuation of an arrest or the prevention of an escape from custody shall apply notwithstanding the criminality of the conduct against which such force is used; and

(ii) the use of deadly force is not in any event justifiable under this Subsection unless:

(1) the actor believes that there is a substantial risk that the person whom he seeks to prevent from committing a crime will cause death or serious bodily harm to another

unless the commission or the consummation of the crime is prevented and that the use of such force presents no substantial risk of injury to innocent persons; or

(2) the actor believes that the use of such force is necessary to suppress a riot or mutiny after the rioters or mutineers have been ordered to disperse and warned, in any particular manner that the law may require, that such force will be used if they do not obey.

(b) The justification afforded by this Subsection extends to the use of confinement as preventive force only if the actor takes all reasonable measures to terminate the confinement as soon as he knows that he safely can, unless the person confined has been arrested on a charge of crime.

PROBLEMS

1. *Police or Citizens.* Generally, a private person who acts on her own can use only nondeadly force to arrest someone she suspects of committing a crime. She may use deadly force to arrest someone who in fact committed a felony or in some states a violent felony. Do you agree with the New York legislature's distinctions in *Pena* between police and citizen justifications for using deadly force?

2. *Comparing Pena and M.P.C.* How would the *Pena* case be resolved under the M.P.C. § 3.07 or § 3.06(3)(d)? Would the New York court's holding or a ruling under the M.P.C. be preferable? Explain the pros and cons of each approach.

3. *Police Chase.* If Pena had called out to the police, who then began to chase the perpetrators, could the police have used deadly force under the holding in *Pena*? Under the M.P.C.?

4. *Force to Capture Escapee.* After an officer arrests a suspect, assume that the arrested person tries to escape from the patrol car during the trip to the police station. Under the M.P.C., what determines whether the officer can use non-deadly force to capture the escapee? Deadly force? What force, if any, can a jailer use when a person arrested for littering tries to escape from the jail after spending a day there without being able to obtain his release? Do the standards for the use of force differ if this person already was serving a short sentence after being convicted of littering?

5. *Nondeadly Force.* It appears clear that the defendant in *Pena* could have used either deadly or non-deadly force under the holding of the case. Under the M.P.C., could he have justifiably used non-deadly force?

6. *Interference.* A dog catcher is trying to catch an unleashed dog, but the dog's owner tries to stop him. At common law or under the M.P.C., can the dog catcher use any type of force to prevent the owner from interfering with the dog catcher doing her job of enforcing the leash laws?

7. *Fleeing Drug Suspect.* An undercover police officer is buying drugs in a sting operation from a seller, and after receiving the drugs, the officer announces his true identity and tells the seller that he is "under arrest." A struggle ensues in which the seller tries to take the officer's gun away from him. When the seller is unsuccessful in obtaining the gun, he turns and runs. Although the officer yells "halt," the seller keeps running. May the officer shoot the seller in the back? Would it matter whether:

     a. Unbeknownst to the officer, the seller is carrying a revolver (surprisingly, since he tried to wrest the officer's revolver away from him rather than going for his own weapon).

     b. It is common for drug sellers to carry guns.

8. *Handcuffed Suspect.* Two police officers arrest Taylor in a small apartment. After they handcuff Taylor, placing his arms behind his back, Taylor manages to grab a small carpet knife. As best he can, given the handcuffs and the position of his arms, Taylor advances towards the officers using the knife in a threatening manner. Even though the officers repeatedly order Taylor to "halt," he continues advancing towards them. May the officers use deadly force to halt Taylor's advance?

9. *Kicking an Arrestee.* Angie was Ricky's nosey neighbor. One night Angie called the police and told them to come and arrest Ricky because he was playing his music too loud on his front porch. Without obtaining a warrant, Officer Hamlin went to the address, entered Ricky's porch, saw that Ricky was making a lot of noise, and told him that he was investigating a neighborhood disturbance. Ricky refused to follow Hamlin's order to reduce the volume of the music. At this point, Officer Hamlin placed his hand on Ricky's arm and told him that he was under arrest for a breach of the peace. Ricky refused to come along, pulled back his arm, and retreated to his front door. When Officer Hamlin reached for Ricky's arms, Ricky clenched his fist and raised it towards the officer. Hamlin then kicked Ricky when Ricky began advancing towards the officer. More squad cars arrived and Ricky was arrested. Ricky was charged with interfering with a police officer. Does Ricky have a valid claim that Hamlin used excessive force against him?

EXERCISE

State Code Rules. In your state, look at the criminal statutes for a law enforcement authority provision. Compare it with the Model Penal Code defense. Are important statutory terms defined? On the scope of its coverage, what do the Model Penal Code and state statute provide with regard to the following aspects of the defense?

     a. The application of the defense to any private person summoned by a peace officer to assist;

     b. The limitations, if any, on the use of any force or force likely to cause death or serious physical injury;

c. The relevance of an arrest made pursuant to an invalid warrant;

d. The application of the defense to an arrest made by a private person;

e. The use of force to prevent an escape from custody or a penal institution; and

f. Its application to the prevention of suicide or the commission of a crime.

E. CHOICE–OF–EVILS OR NECESSITY DEFENSE

STATE v. CULP

900 S.W.2d 707 (Tenn.Crim.App. 1994).

HAYES, JUDGE. This is an appeal as of right from a conviction for felony escape. . . . The appellant was tried and convicted for the sale of a Schedule II controlled substance in the Circuit Court. . . . on October 21, 1992. At the trial's conclusion, the appellant, while being escorted from the courthouse, walked away from the custody of the deputy sheriff who was escorting him.

Later that evening, the Lauderdale County Sheriff's Department received information indicating that the appellant could be found at a particular location in Brownsville, Tennessee. This information was relayed to the Haywood County Sheriff's Department. An investigator for the sheriff's department proceeded to the location described where he found the appellant. As he approached the appellant, the appellant turned and ran. After a short chase, the appellant fell and was apprehended.

[T]he Lauderdale County Grand Jury indicted the appellant on one count of felony escape. The appellant was tried by a jury [which] returned a verdict of guilty. It is from this verdict that the appellant now appeals.

The appellant contends that the trial court erred in refusing to admit evidence relating to the defense of duress. Appellant filed a notice stating that he intended to rely on the defense of duress under the provisions of Tenn.Code Ann. 39–11–504. The appellant intended to prove at trial that he was in fear of his life in the Lauderdale County Jail, and that is why he escaped on October 21, 1992. In support of this theory, the appellant proposed to introduce testimony and other evidence of the following acts: (1) the September, 1992 beating of the appellant's girlfriend by the former Sheriff, Jerry Crain; (2) the detention of the appellant without clothes on September 4, 1992; (3) threats made toward the appellant on September 9, 1992 by the former Sheriff's son; (4) an assault made upon the appellant by a sheriff's deputy in September, 1992; and (5) the beating of several Lauderdale County inmates by other inmates in January or February of 1993.

Although the parties and the trial court referred to the defense submitted by the appellant as "duress," the defense actually raised by the appellant is more akin to "necessity" than "duress." In *People v. Lovercamp*, 43 Cal.App.3d 823, 118 Cal.Rptr. 110 (1974), the issue was the appropriate elements required to establish the defense of "necessity" in an escape case. [N]ecessity is now a statutorily recognized defense in this state.... We will therefore address appellant's arguments in terms of the defense of necessity rather than duress.[2]

In the case before us, the trial court held that, even if proved, the evidence "doesn't go to any of the requirements that the defendant is required to show in the affirmative defense ..." under the *Lovercamp* test. The trial court was incorrect [because] neither duress nor necessity are affirmative defenses. Both are "defenses." If admissible evidence fairly raises either defense, the trial court must submit the defense to the jury and the prosecution must "prove beyond a reasonable doubt that the defense does not apply." Thus, unlike an affirmative defense, the defendant need not prove either duress or necessity by a preponderance of the evidence.

[T]he question before this court is whether the evidence presented in the appellant's offer of proof tended to establish the defense of necessity. The first step in this inquiry is determining the elements necessary to establish the defense of necessity in an escape case.

[T]he defense of necessity is available when: (1) the person reasonably believes the conduct is immediately necessary to avoid imminent harm; and (2) the desirability and urgency of avoiding the harm clearly outweigh, according to ordinary standards of reasonableness, the harm sought to be prevented by the law proscribing the conduct.

In *Lovercamp*, the California Supreme Court recognized that the defense of necessity should be available in cases of escape. However, in order to keep from being "exposed to the spectacle of multitudes of prisoners leaping over the walls screaming rape," the court held that the defense must be "extremely limited." Id. 118 Cal.Rptr. at 115. Accordingly, the court ruled that the following five conditions must be met in order to establish the defense of necessity in an escape case:

---

2. Common law historically distinguished between the defense of duress and necessity. Duress was said to excuse criminal conduct where the actor was under an unlawful threat of imminent death or serious bodily injury, which threat caused the actor to engage in conduct violating the literal terms of the criminal law. While the defense of duress covered the situation where the coercion had its source in the actions of other human beings, the defense of necessity, or choice of evils, traditionally covered the situation where forces beyond the actor's control rendered illegal conduct the lesser of two evils. *United States v. Bailey*, 444 U.S. 394 (1980).

(1) The prisoner is faced with a specific threat of death, forcible sexual attack or substantial bodily injury in the immediate future;

(2) There is no time for a complaint to the authorities or there exists a history of futile complaints which make any result from such compliance illusory;

(3) There is no time or opportunity to resort to the courts;

(4) There is no evidence of force or violence used towards prison personnel or other "innocent" persons in the escape; and

(5) The prisoner immediately reports to the proper authorities when he has attained a position of safety from the immediate threat.

[Before the necessity defense statute was enacted, the five *Lovercamp* elements were used to define the defense in Tennessee case law.] We conclude that the second and fifth elements of the *Lovercamp* test are still viable [proof requirements] under our [new] statutory scheme [defining] the defense of necessity. Both elements are essentially logical extensions of the statutory requirements that the "person believes the conduct is immediately necessary to avoid imminent harm." Tenn.Code.Ann. 39–11–609(1). The second [element] is directly related to the immediate necessity of an escape. If the prisoner can remove the threat of imminent harm through administrative or other official channels, then there is no immediate necessity to flee from incarceration.

The fifth element is directly related to statutory requirement that the conduct be "necessary to avoid imminent harm." After the prisoner has escaped the threat or condition that created the threat of imminent harm, the necessity to continue flight from detention has abated. At this point, the defense of necessity should no longer be available.

Although we find the remaining factors in the *Lovercamp* test to be persuasive for policy reasons, we decline to adopt them. To do so would be to cast a greater burden upon a defendant than is required by the criminal code. These remaining *Lovercamp* factors do not fit within the statutory definition of necessity. Only the legislature may enact criminal laws.

For all the above reasons, we hold that in order to establish the defense of necessity in an escape case, the following conditions must be met:

(1) The person reasonably believes the conduct is immediately necessary to avoid imminent harm;

(2) The desirability and urgency of avoiding the harm clearly outweigh, according to ordinary standards of reasonableness,

the harm sought to be prevented by the law proscribing the conduct;

(3) There is no time for a complaint to the authorities or there exists a history of futile complaints which make any result from such compliance illusory; and

(4) The prisoner immediately reports to the proper authorities when he has attained a position of safety from the immediate threat.

In applying the above rules to the offer of proof in the instant case, we conclude that the evidence submitted in the appellant's offer of proof tends to establish several of the necessary elements of necessity. The evidence is therefore relevant and should have been admitted by the trial court.

The trial court found that there was no imminent danger to the appellant, since by the time he committed the escape, a new sheriff had assumed office in Lauderdale County. We are not at liberty to conclude, however, that the change in sheriffs removed the alleged threat to the appellant's safety. This is a question of fact that is more proper for the jury to decide than the trial court.

We cannot conclude that the trial court's refusal to admit evidence relevant to the defense of necessity was harmless beyond a reasonable doubt.

[T]he appellant's conviction is reversed. This case is remanded for a new trial consistent with this opinion.

NOTES

1. *Attempt to surrender.* In *Spakes v. State*, 913 S.W.2d 597 (Tex.Crim. App. 1996), the court rejected the requirement that the defense of necessity must include an attempt to surrender once the immediate threat justifying the escape has ceased. The Texas statute on necessity did not explicitly include such a provision, and the court characterized the matter as an "impermissible addendum" to the statutory requirement. In dissent, Judge Keller stated:

> Under the majority's analysis, a convict is free to stay at large forever, so long as his initial departure was immediately necessary to avoid imminent harm. I disagree. ... The necessity defense is really the ultimate catch-all provision for criminal defenses. It is used to judge extreme situations that ought to constitute a defense but have not been specifically provided for by the legislature. ... Although the issue appears to be one of first impression in Texas, the Court's opinion is at odds with the majority of jurisdictions that have addressed the issue. Most jurisdictions (thirty) require an attempt to surrender or report to the authorities (assuming there is time to do so) as a precondition for asserting justification-type defenses. ... Before today, only two states

had unequivocally taken the position that an attempt to report or surrender is not an absolute requirement for invoking a justification-type defense: Michigan [and] South Dakota. The American Law Institute, in its commentary on the Model Penal Code [views] the surrender requirement as dictated by the balancing prong of the necessity defense. I believe that the harm the escapee seeks to avoid never clearly outweighs the harm the law seeks to prevent unless the escapee subsequently surrenders or attempts to do so (as long as he has the opportunity).

. . .

2. *Choice of evils and imminence.* The defense of choice of evils, or necessity, has long occupied the attention of the commentators because it raises the policy question whether it is better to allow crime to go unpunished where the crime was committed to avoid a greater and more serious harm. While the defense is far from theoretical, as a practical matter, some prosecutors will not bring a charge when a minor infraction was committed to avoid a greater harm. For example, a defendant may plead the choice of evils defense to a charge of speeding through a school zone in order to get a dying person to a hospital.

The common law necessity defense requires that there be a threat of imminent injury. It must be shown that defendant's conduct was necessitated by a specific and imminent threat of injury to his or her person under circumstances which left him or her no reasonable and viable alternative other than the violation of the law. For example, a defendant may argue that he is entitled to an instruction on necessity or choice of evils because he escaped from jail to save his own life. Courts usually reject the claim that problems such as illness, loss of weight, severe chest pains, and denial of medical attention justified the lesser evil of escape, because incarceration is not regarded as a specific and imminent threat to his person. The common-law defense may be unavailable (1) when its assertion is inconsistent with other justification defenses or other law; or (2) as a justification for an intentional homicide.

3. *M.P.C. and choice of evils.* The Model Penal Code version of a choice of evils defense is somewhat broader than the traditional common law view.

§ 3.02 Justification Generally—Choice of Evils

(1) Conduct which the actor believes to be necessary to avoid a harm or evil to himself or to another is justifiable, provided that:

    (a) the harm or evil sought to be avoided by such conduct is greater than that sought to be prevented by the law defining the offense charged; and

    (b) neither the Code nor other law defining the offense provides exceptions or defenses dealing with the specific situation involved; and

    (c) a legislative purpose to exclude the justification claimed does not otherwise plainly appear.

(2) When the actor was reckless or negligent in bringing about the situation requiring a choice of harms or evils or in appraising the necessity for his conduct, the justification afforded by this Section is unavailable in a prosecution for any offense for which recklessness or negligence, as the case may be, suffices to establish culpability.

PROBLEMS

1. *Spakes Debate.* Did the *Spakes* Court in Note 1, *supra*, get the right result? What policy arguments support the majority's position? Is the dissent's position more persuasive? Explain.

2. *Drug Possession.* Why would a defendant assert a choice-of-evils defense to drug possession charges? In order to strengthen an allegation of medical necessity, should a defendant present evidence she did not have reasonable alternatives to using the drugs as a means of medical treatment?

3. *Regina v. Dudley & Stephens.* Consider the facts of the case of *Regina v. Dudley & Stephens* in Chapter 1. In that case, stranded sailors killed a cabin boy and ate his remains in order to avoid starvation. Would the common law defense of necessity have justified their actions? What about the M.P.C. choice-of-evils defense?

4. *Protecting Unborn Fetuses.* Defendant, who believes that abortion is equivalent to murder, trespasses at clinic where abortions are performed and destroys the surgery room. Can she use the defense of necessity on the theory that the doctors at the clinic were taking lives? Does it matter whether the trespasser claims no knowledge of a specific impending act of legal harm to a person, but does claim a threat to others based on the clinic's regular business activities? Is it possible that the trespass might have the opposite effect, causing a difficult event in the life of a woman to become worse? If a defendant claims that her actions were necessary to prevent illegal abortions, is a factual question presented? Is it relevant that a defendant could have sought an injunction to prevent any unlawful action at a clinic in advance of the date she trespassed? See *McMillan v. City of Jackson*, 701 So.2d 1105 (Miss. 1997).

5. *Anti–Nuclear Protest.* Security guards arrested Noah at a missile assembly plant on a United States Air Force base. A search of Noah revealed a variety of tools and a can of spray paint. Political slogans had been painted throughout the plant and pieces of equipment were damaged. Noah admitted to causing the damage at the plant. He stated that he intended to destroy all of the missiles at the plant in order to prevent nuclear war and world starvation. Should Noah be allowed to claim the choice of evils defense under either the common law or the M.P.C.? Was Noah attempting to prevent an imminent harm? Were there other options to prevent this harm? Would Noah's actions have prevented the harm that he sought to avoid?

6. *Medicinal Marijuana.* Hannah has suffered from muscular dystrophy for five years. The doctors have given her a diagnosis of less than six months

to live. Over the years, the doctors have prescribed various medications to relieve the excruciating pain that Hannah suffers. A few months ago, Hannah began using marijuana for medicinal purposes. However, she was arrested and convicted on marijuana possession. As her defense, Hannah claimed necessity. Does the law of necessity apply in medical cases such as Hannah's? Is Hannah faced with a clear and imminent harm? Will smoking the marijuana be effective in abating her harm? Are there other legal alternatives that will be effective in abating this harm? Does it matter whether the legislature has enacted a law to preclude the defense by making the smoking of marijuana illegal in *any* case? Does it matter whether the legislature has made the smoking of marijuana legal for a patient suffering from terminal cancer?

7. *Starving and Stealing.* Defendant has been hiking in the back woods of Wyoming for weeks. The weather is very cold (20 degrees below zero) and he is starving. Near death, he comes upon a remote cabin that is unoccupied. Defendant breaks into the cabin, starts a fire in the fireplace, and eats some of the owner's food. Does the choice-of-evils defense apply?

8. *Taking Money from Cars.* Defendant is a homeless person who begs on the street. When his begging is unsuccessful and defendant finds himself starving, he breaks into cars to steal money for food. He then returns to being a law-abiding citizen until he runs out of food again (whereupon he breaks into cars again). One night, defendant is apprehended breaking into a car. Can he claim the choice-of-evils defense?

9. *Financial Emergencies?* Defendant is arrested and charged with the crime of illegal possession of narcotics based on evidence showing that he was growing marijuana in his attic. Defendant claims that he was heavily in debt (due to his tendency to spend to excess), and faced bankruptcy and foreclosure on his farm. May defendant invoke the M.P.C. choice-of-evils defense on the basis that his cultivation of marijuana was a lesser evil than the circumstances he was facing, and that therefore he was justified in choosing to violate the drug law?

10. *The Speeding Motorist.* Dan is driving at 70 mph in a 35 mph zone. Unexpectedly, a group of children walk out in front of Dan's car. Making a quick calculation of "evils," Dan swerves onto the sidewalk (figuring that it is better to damage property (or, perhaps, to injure a single pedestrian) than to run over a group of children). Unfortunately, Dan runs over and kills a pedestrian. Charged with involuntary manslaughter, Dan makes a choice-of-evils claim. Should Dan prevail?

EXERCISES

1. *State Code Rules.* In your state, look at the criminal statutes for a choice of evils provision. Compare it with the Model Penal Code defense. Are important statutory terms defined? On the extent of the threat to the defendant, what do the Model Penal Code and state statute provide with respect to the following aspects of the defense?

a.   The imminence of the threat;

b.   The seriousness of the harm threatened;

c.   The nature of the harm threatened, e.g., physical, economic, emotional or other;

d.   The target of the threat, e.g., the defendant, a relative, friend, or business associate;

e.   The unlawfulness of the threat; and

f.   The source of the threat.

2. *Nature of Harm.* As to the extent of the harm caused by the defendant, what do the Model Penal Code and state statute provide about the extent of harm caused by the defendant, such as the seriousness of the harm in relation to the harm threatened, and the availability of less harmful but equally effective alternatives to avoiding the threat?

F. PROVING JUSTIFICATION DEFENSES

There are certain procedural and factual issues which must be addressed before a defense "goes to the jury." A defense must be supported by a factual record and ultimately requires a jury instruction which informs the jury how to consider the defense.

"Burden" questions in criminal cases can be divided into three separate issues. The first burden is a "burden of pleading" which requires that the defendant plead the defense. The second type of burden is known as the "burden of production," requiring a party to present certain evidence to raise a claim and obtain a jury instruction. When a defense is at issue, the defense lawyer usually bears the burden of production. The third type of burden is the "burden of persuasion" which requires the jury to find against a party if "enough" proof has not been introduced.

Burden of Production. The prosecution has the burden of production to establish the elements of the crime. The defendant has the burden of production in offering evidence in support of a defense. Unless the defendant satisfies the burden, the judge is not required to instruct on a defense. A defendant has a right to have every issue of fact raised by the evidence and material to the defense submitted to the jury under proper instructions by the court. In *Mathews v. United States*, 485 U.S. 58 (1988), the Supreme Court found that, as a "general proposition[,] a defendant is entitled to an instruction as to any recognized defense for which there exists evidence sufficient for a reasonable jury to find in his favor."

Burden of Persuasion. The burden of persuasion is on the prosecution to establish the elements of the crime. If the prosecution fails to meet its burden, the judge must grant a motion for acquittal. The standard for this burden is proof beyond a reasonable doubt. The rules regarding the standard and burden of persuasion with respect to elements of the crime are constitutionally grounded.

In *Mullaney v. Wilbur*, 421 U.S. 684 (1975), the Court held that a provision which placed the burden of persuasion on the defendant to prove "heat of passion" was unconstitutional since, in effect, the defendant thereby was required to negate malice, which was an element of the crime. However, in *Patterson v. New York* 432 U.S. 197 (1977), the Court upheld a provision which required the defendant to prove "extreme emotional disturbance." The apparent distinction between the two decisions is that the defendant may be required to prove a true affirmative defense which provides exoneration or reduces the degree of the offense, but may not be required simply to disprove an element of the crime.

UNITED STATES v. BRANCH

91 F.3d 699 (5th Cir. 1996).

HIGGINBOTHAM, CIRCUIT JUDGE.

[The facts are found in the opinion in Section A, Part 4, of this chapter.]

The district court instructed the jury that to convict the defendants of murder under Count 2, it had to find beyond a reasonable doubt that "the Defendant under consideration did not act in self-defense or defense of another." The court explained self-defense and the defense of another, and then turned to the lesser-included offense of voluntary manslaughter.

[Four defendants] argued that self-defense is also a defense to voluntary manslaughter, requested an instruction to that effect, and objected at the charge conference to its omission.

We review the district court's refusal to give the proposed instruction for abuse of discretion. "As a general proposition a defendant is entitled to an instruction as to any recognized defense for which there exists evidence sufficient for a reasonable jury to find in his favor," *Mathews v. United States*, 485 U.S. 58, 63 (1988), and we presume an abuse of discretion "where the district court 'refuse[s] a charge on a defense theory for which there is an evidentiary foundation and which, if believed by the jury, would be legally sufficient to render the accused innocent.' " The court may, however, refuse to give a requested instruction that lacks sufficient foundation in the evidence.

We review the record cognizant that the "merest scintilla of evidence" in the defendant's favor does not warrant a jury instruction regarding an affirmative defense for which the defendant bears the initial burden of production. Under *Mathews*, there must be "evidence sufficient for a reasonable jury to find in [the defendant's] favor." We have insisted that the evidence be sufficient to raise a factual question for a reasonable jury.

Our decisions leave no doubt that while a particular piece of evidence standing alone may support inferences that warrant an instruction, those inferences may evaporate after reviewing the entire record. ... A district court cannot refuse to give an instruction for which there is sufficient evidence in the record for a reasonable juror to harbor a reasonable doubt that the defendant did not act in self defense, but the district court is not required "to put the case to the jury on a basis that 'essentially indulges and even encourages speculations.' " *United States v. Collins*, 690 F.2d 431 (5th Cir. 1982).

The dissent measures the evidence in the record by an incorrect standard, misled [by] statements [in our precedents] that the district court must instruct the jury on a defense for which there is "any foundation in the evidence." The measure of "any evidence" never commanded allegiance.... Indeed, in *United States v. Stowell*, 953 F.2d 188 (5th Cir.), we explained:

> Although we have on several occasions before and after *Mathews* observed that the court must charge the jury on a defense theory when there is any evidence to support it, this language is admittedly incomplete. Its shorthand implies that a mere scintilla of evidence in support of a defense theory requires the giving of an instruction on that theory at the defendant's request. Of course, any evidence in support of a defensive theory must be sufficient for a reasonable jury to rule in favor of the defendant on that theory. This is what we meant when we stated in this case that a court may decide as a matter of law that the evidence ... fails to raise a factual question for the jury.

Similarly, Judge Posner in *United States v. Perez*, 86 F.3d 735, 736 (7th Cir. 1996), interpreted *Mathews* as rejecting the notion that "any evidence," no matter how weak or insufficient, entitled the defendant to an instruction on an affirmative defense....

In short, it is not enough that an item of evidence viewed alone and unweighed against all the evidence supports an inference that a defendant acted in self defense. The critical distinction is that a single item of evidence can be overwhelmed by other evidence in the record.

The distinction is neither academic nor prissy; it defines the character of appellate review of the criminal trial, reflecting our effort to curb any tendency of criminal appeals to become a lawyer's sporting search for "error." The jury plays a central role at trial, but the threshold to the jury room has never been so low as the dissent would have it. This is not word play; there is a vast difference in concept between the requirement of sufficient evidence and a scintilla. There is an equally large difference in their application.... In short, a scintilla rule can, in application, turn a criminal trial and the review of a conviction into a sporting contest for lawyers. When the contended-for inference becomes an absurdity in light of all the facts adduced at trial, we invade no province of the jury in refusing to pretend it has probative value....

We hold that the district court was not obligated to give the proposed self-defense instruction and did not err in the instruction it gave. It is true, as a general proposition, that self-defense and the related defense of another are affirmative defenses to both murder and voluntary manslaughter.[3] However, these general principles must accommodate a citizen's duty to accede to lawful government power and the special protection due federal officials discharging official duties. . . .

NOTE

Standards for giving instructions. How much evidence is necessary to require a jury instruction on self-defense? Three standards have been identified. The "scintilla" standard is based on the theory that any amount of evidence is deserving of an instruction. A higher standard is the "substantial evidence" standard, which not facetiously has been defined as more than a scintilla. The *Branch* court applied an even higher standard—the "sufficient evidence" standard which requires proof must exist that is sufficient to raise a factual question for a reasonable jury. Several circuit courts of appeal apply contradictory standards even within their own circuit.

PROBLEMS

1. *Judicial Discretion.* What considerations should affect a judge's decision whether to give a requested self-defense jury instruction? Explain.

2. *Denial of Instruction in Branch.* How did the political context of the *Branch* prosecution affect the Fifth Circuit's decision about the sufficiency of the evidence? Does the opinion reflect an implicit policy judgment about the use of self-defense during an arrest by law enforcement officers? If the jury was instructed on self-defense for the murder charge in *Branch*, what is the reason for not similarly instructing the jury on the manslaughter charge?

3. *Excessive Force.* Sixteen-year-old Lanchester Whitlow threatened to "beat up" eighteen-year-old Gerald Mickens if Mickens refused to pay off his debt to Whitlow. One afternoon, 1999, Mickens escorted his fifteen-year-old girlfriend, Sherea Upshaw, northbound on College Avenue to her home. Meanwhile, Whitlow and his sixteen-year-old friend, Marcus Lewis, walked southbound and encountered the couple. As the parties approached one another, no words were exchanged. Then Whitlow punched Mickens in the face once and Lewis also struck him. Mickens then stepped back and drew a

---

3. Self-defense is an affirmative defense on which the defendant bears the initial burden of production. If and only if the defendant has met his burden of production, the Government bears the burden of persuasion and must negate self-defense beyond a reasonable doubt.

gun. Lewis had seen Mickens' hand in his pocket earlier, but was not alarmed by the fact until Mickens drew the gun. Lewis ran from Mickens when he saw the gun; Whitlow remained motionless. After hearing one shot, Lewis turned around in time to see Mickens fire a second shot in the vicinity of where Whitlow lay on the ground. Whitlow died from gunshot wounds to the head and abdomen. Was there sufficient evidence from which a reasonable juror could conclude beyond a reasonable doubt that Mickens used excessive force and could not have entertained a good faith belief that he was in danger of death or great bodily harm? See *Mickens v. State*, 742 N.E.2d 927 (Ind. 2001).

G.   CONSTITUTIONAL DEFENSES

In the past few years, there have been constitutional challenges to a variety of sexual offense statutes based on the decision in *Lawrence v. Texas*, 539 U.S. 558 (2003). The *Lawrence* Court struck down a Texas statute prohibiting "deviate sexual intercourse" that made it a crime for two persons of the same sex to engage in certain intimate sexual conduct. In doing so, the Court stated that:

> [This case involves] two adults who, with full and mutual consent from each other, engaged in sexual practices common to a homosexual lifestyle. The petitioners are entitled to respect for their private lives. The State cannot demean their existence or control their destiny by making their private sexual conduct a crime. Their right to liberty under the Due Process Clause gives them the full right to engage in their conduct without intervention of the government. "It is a promise of the Constitution that there is a realm of personal liberty which the government may not enter." *Casey, supra,* at 847. The Texas statute furthers no legitimate state interest which can justify its intrusion into the personal and private life of the individual.

Justice Scalia dissented:

> Our opinions applying the doctrine known as "substantive due process" hold that the Due Process Clause prohibits States from infringing *fundamental* liberty interests, unless the infringement is narrowly tailored to serve a compelling state interest. *Washington v. Glucksberg,* 521 U.S., at 721. We have held repeatedly, in cases the Court today does not overrule, that *only* fundamental rights qualify for this so-called "heightened scrutiny" protection—that is, rights which are " 'deeply rooted in this Nation's history and tradition,' " See *Reno v. Flores,* 507 U.S. 292 (1993). All other liberty interests may be abridged or abrogated pursuant to a validly enacted state law if that law is rationally related to a legitimate state interest.

The Court today does not ... describe homosexual sodomy as a "fundamental right" or a "fundamental liberty interest," nor does it subject the Texas statute to strict scrutiny. Instead, having failed to establish that the right to homosexual sodomy is " 'deeply rooted in this Nation's history and tradition,' " the Court concludes that the application of Texas's statute to petitioners' conduct fails the rational-basis test....

The Texas statute undeniably seeks to further the belief of its citizens that certain forms of sexual behavior are "immoral and unacceptable,"—the same interest furthered by criminal laws against fornication, bigamy, adultery, adult incest, bestiality, and obscenity. *Bowers* [*v. Hardwick*, 478 U.S. 186 (1986)] held that this *was* a legitimate state interest. The Court today reaches the opposite conclusion. The Texas statute, it says, "furthers *no legitimate state interest* which can justify its intrusion into the personal and private life of the individual." The Court embraces instead Justice Stevens' declaration in his *Bowers* dissent, that "the fact that the governing majority in a State has traditionally viewed a particular practice as immoral is not a sufficient reason for upholding a law prohibiting the practice." This effectively decrees the end of all morals legislation. If, as the Court asserts, the promotion of majoritarian sexual morality is not even a *legitimate* state interest, none of the above-mentioned laws can survive rational-basis review.

One example of a post-*Lawrence* decision is *PHE, Inc. v. State*, 877 So.2d 1244 (Miss. 2004), where the court upheld a law prohibiting "knowingly selling, advertising, publishing or exhibiting any three-dimensional device designed or marketed as useful primarily for the stimulation of human genitalia ('sexual devices') is illegal". The court rejected a challenge to this statute based on state constitutional "privacy" grounds, and reasoned as follows:

"The positive law of this state affords each person a substantial zone of freedom which, at his election, he may keep private. This zone surrounds person and place and without his consent may not be invaded by other persons ... or by the state." *Pro-Choice Miss. v. Fordice*, 716 So.2d 645, 654 (Miss. 1998).... The right to privacy includes the right to "autonomous bodily integrity." *Pro-Choice*, 716 So.2d at 653. "[A] right to privacy exists for citizens and that right entitles citizens 'to be left alone.' " *Miller v. State*, 636 So.2d 391, 394 (Miss.1994) (quoting Warren and Brandeis, *The Right to Privacy*, 4 Harv. L.Rev. 193, 195 (1890)). "It requires little awareness of personal prejudice and human nature to know that, generally speaking, no aspects of life [are] more personal and private than those having to do with one's sexual organs and reproductive system." *Young*, 572 So.2d at 382. "The right to privacy is so personal that its protection does not require the giving of a reason for its exercise. That one is a person, unique and individual, is enough." *In re Brown,* 478 So.2d at 1040.

We find that there is no "independent fundamental right of access to purchase [sexual devices]," just as the United States Supreme Court found that there was no independent fundamental right of access to purchase contraceptives. *Carey v. Population Servs. Int'l,* 431 U.S. 678 (1977). However, the plaintiffs argue that "such access is essential to the exercise of the constitutionally protected right [of privacy to engage in adult consensual sexual activities]."

People who are sexually dysfunctional (presumably those people who cannot achieve sexual enjoyment and fulfillment without a sexual device) should be treated by a physician or a psychologist. Sexual dysfunction may be caused by medicinal side effects, diabetes, hormonal problems, endocrine problems, cardiovascular illness, neurological impairments, psychological problems or hypertension. Miss. Code Ann. § 97–29–107(1)(b) (Rev. 2000) expressly provides that physicians and psychologists may prescribe sexual devices for their patients, and the patients may purchase the sexual devices from the physicians and psychologists. The novelty and gag gifts which the vendor plaintiffs sell have no medical purpose.

The only conclusion we can reach is that the sale of or access to sexual devices sold by novelty stores is not protected under the right to privacy guaranteed under the Mississippi Constitution.

For other examples of constitutional challenges to sexual offense statutes, see the state decisions in the Problems in Chapter 10, Part C.

CHAPTER 12

EXCUSES

■ ■ ■

Like justification defenses, excuses are general defenses applicable to all offenses and available even though the evidence shows that the elements of the offense are satisfied. However, excuse defenses are based on the person's lack of subjective blameworthiness. An excuse defense represents a legal conclusion that even though a person's conduct is wrong, criminal liability is inappropriate because some characteristic of the person or aspect of the person's situation vitiates the person's blameworthiness.

A. DURESS

The defense of duress is available to a defendant who receives an unlawful threat from another that causes the defendant to violate the criminal law because she reasonably believes that the only way to avoid imminent death or serious injury is to engage in that criminal act. The theory underlying this defense is that it is better for the defendant to commit a lesser harm than to be injured or lose her life. But because death is not a "lesser evil," duress is not generally recognized as a defense to intentional homicide. Duress is a defense when unlawful force is threatened against the defendant or a third person, and when the defendant could not reasonably be expected to resist that threat. The type of threatened force may be relatively minor, but the force must be directed against a person, not the property or reputation of the defendant or another.

In *Dixon v. United States*, 548 U.S. 1 (2006), the Court held that [*Not violation of Due P.*] assigning the defendant the burden of proving duress by a preponderance of the evidence does not violate Due Process:

> The duress defense . . . may excuse conduct that would otherwise be punishable, but the existence of duress normally does not controvert any of the elements of the offense itself. . . . [T]he defense of duress does not negate a defendant's criminal state of mind when the applicable offense requires a defendant to have acted knowingly or willfully; instead, it allows the defendant to "avoid liability . . . because coercive conditions or necessity ne-

gates a conclusion of guilt even though the necessary mens rea was present." [*United States v.*] *Bailey*, 444 U.S. 394 (1980).

The common law definition of the duress defense was expanded in the Model Penal Code. But some states continue to require evidence of imminent force and to use a reasonable person standard for determining whether the defendant should have resisted a threat.

ANGUISH v. STATE

991 S.W.2d 883 (Tex.App. 1999).

TIM TAFT, JUSTICE. A jury found appellant, Gaylord William Anguish, guilty of robbery and theft of an automobile. The jury assessed appellant's punishment for the robbery at five years in prison, and for the theft at two years in prison and a $1,000 fine. We address whether threats made four days before appellant committed the offenses constituted imminent threats necessary to raise the affirmative defense of duress. We affirm.

On December 3, 1990, appellant stole a van from a child care center. He drove the van to a drive-through bank window where he threatened to blow up the bank. The teller placed all the money she had, approximately $15,000, in the drawer. Appellant took the money and drove away. The bank's security guard followed appellant to an apartment complex parking lot and then arrested him.

[All] of appellant's points of error complain of actions by the trial court in excluding evidence that would have fully explained appellant's claims of duress as a defense to prosecution. . . .

[A] defendant who claims duress must establish that the threatened harm was conditioned on his committing the charged offense, as opposed to some other offense. Appellant testified that two men told him to rob a bank and that he and his family would be harmed if he did not. Appellant claimed this threat compelled him to commit the theft. The record contains no evidence, however, that the two men who threatened appellant directed him to steal a van to use in carrying out a drive-through robbery. We therefore conclude there is no link between the duress that appellant claims was exerted on him and his theft of the van. In the absence of any evidence that appellant was threatened with death or serious bodily injury conditioned on his committing theft of a motor vehicle, the trial court properly excluded any evidence of duress as to that offense. . . .

[To] place appellant's contentions in context, we will examine his claims of duress concerning the robbery crime, the portion of his claims that the trial court permitted him to present to the jury, and the portion of his claims that the trial court excluded. We will then analyze the trial court's ruling that appellant's evidence of the threat was inadmissible as irrelevant because the alleged threat was not an imminent threat of harm. . . .

Appellant claimed to have learned that a Federal Bureau of Investigation (FBI) agent was having an extra-marital affair, and that the FBI agent and his lover conspired to kill the lover's husband. After appellant attempted to confront the FBI agent with his knowledge of the matter, appellant's house was burglarized and he began receiving threatening telephone calls. He reported these incidents to the Harris County Sheriff's Department and the FBI, but neither agency took any action.

Four days before appellant committed the charged offenses, he was threatened by two men he found waiting for him in the back seat of his car. One man put a gun to appellant's head while the other showed appellant a photograph of his wife and daughter in bed. The men told appellant that they were watching him, threatened to kill his family, instructed him not to tell anyone, and then instructed him to rob a bank. Based upon law enforcement agencies' previous inaction, appellant believed that reporting the latest threat would be useless.

Appellant believed the men's motive for urging him to rob the bank was their desire to discredit him and discourage him from conducting future investigations of the FBI agent or the agent's lover. During the three years after the charged offenses, appellant suffered several additional burglaries, an attempted kidnapping, arson, and further telephone threats against him and his family.

Appellant was permitted to introduce evidence that: (1) although *Permitted Evidence* his house was burglarized twice and he received threatening telephone calls, his reports of these matters were not taken seriously by law enforcement agencies; (2) four days before appellant committed the charged offenses, two men threatened to harm him and his family if he did not rob a bank; and (3) he robbed the bank because he was afraid that the men would carry out their threats and he did not think that law enforcement agencies would help him.

[First,] appellant argues that the trial court erred by excluding the content of the two men's threats, including that they: (1) told him they were watching him; (2) instructed him to rob a bank; (3) threatened to kill his family; and (4) instructed him not to tell anyone about their threats. [Second,] appellant contends the trial court erred in excluding: [1] his testimony regarding his investigation of the affair between the FBI agent and his lover and their plot to kill her husband; and [2] his testimony about incidents of harassment that occurred after the commission of the charged offenses [which] could also have corroborated his claims of duress.

The trial court ruled that the threat appellant claims compelled him to commit the robbery was not an imminent threat and was therefore inadmissible evidence, based upon its lack of relevance.

Duress is an affirmative defense to prosecution when an accused establishes that he "engaged in the proscribed conduct because he was compelled to do so by threat of imminent death or serious bodily injury to himself or another." Tex. Penal Code Ann. § 8.05(a). When a trial court determines that the threat the accused contends compelled his commission of the offense was not imminent, the trial court properly excludes evidence of the threat.

The Court of Criminal Appeals has not construed the term "imminent" in the context of a section 8.05 duress claim, but has interpreted the term in the context of aggravated robbery and aggravated rape. In these contexts, the Court of Criminal Appeals has determined that an imminent threat is a present threat of harm.

Other courts of appeals have relied on this interpretation of imminence. We join in this interpretation and conclude that, in applying it to the affirmative defense of duress, an imminent threat has two components of immediacy. First, the person making the threat must intend and be prepared to carry out the threat immediately. Second, carrying out the threat must be predicated upon the threatened person's failure to commit the charged offense immediately.

In the present case, the alleged threat was made four days before appellant committed the robbery. The specific threat was that appellant rob a bank or he and his family would be killed. The record does not reflect that the persons making this threat either intended or were prepared to carry it out immediately. Further, there was no evidence that the persons making the threat gave appellant a time by which he was to commit the robbery, much less that he was to commit the robbery immediately. Therefore, the threat that appellant claims compelled him to commit the robbery fails on both components of immediacy. Accordingly, we conclude the threat was not an imminent threat, as required by section 8.05.

Appellant argues that this Court should extend the definition of imminent to include the situation of an accused who, when threatened, believes that no law enforcement agency will protect him. We acknowledge that in most situations where the threat is imminent, no law enforcement agency is able to provide protection. However, a threat is not rendered imminent solely because law enforcement agencies are unable to provide protection. We therefore decline to adopt appellant's extension of the definition of imminency.

Having found that the alleged threat against appellant was not of imminent death of serious bodily injury unless appellant immediately committed the bank robbery, we conclude that appellant's testimony concerning the threat was irrelevant, and thus inadmissible. Therefore, the trial court's rulings excluding appellant's testimony and quashing appellant's subpoenas were proper. . . .

We affirm the judgment of the trial court.

NOTES

1. *M.P.C. revisions of duress.* The Model Penal Code does not require that the threatened harm for duress must be imminent. However, the lack of an imminence requirement may lead to possible fabrication of the defense, especially when the defendant claims that an accomplice forced her to commit a crime. Note that duress is available under the M.P.C. for even intentional killings but is unavailable if the defendant recklessly or negligently placed herself in a position likely to subject her to coercion. The M.P.C. duress defense is defined as follows:

Section 2.09. Duress.

(1) It is an affirmative defense that the actor engaged in the conduct charged to constitute an offense because he was coerced to do so by the use of, or a threat to use, unlawful force against his person or the person of another, which a person of reasonable firmness in his situation would have been unable to resist.

(2) The defense provided by this Section is unavailable if the actor recklessly placed himself in a situation in which it was probable that he would be subjected to duress. The defense is also unavailable if he was negligent in placing himself in such a situation, whenever negligence suffices to establish culpability for the offense charged.

(3) It is not a defense that a woman acted on the command of her husband, unless she acted under such coercion as would establish a defense under this Section. [The presumption that a woman, acting in the presence of her husband, is coerced is abolished.]

(4) When the conduct of the actor would otherwise be justifiable under Section 3.02 [choice-of-evils defense], this Section does not preclude such defense.

2. *Timid personality.* Should the reasonable person or the individual defendant be the pertinent reference point for evaluating the effect of the coercive behavior? In *State v. VanNatta*, 149 Or.App. 587, 945 P.2d 1062 (1997), the defendant attempted to introduce evidence that his timid personality made him susceptible to coercion from others. The court affirmed the trial court's refusal to admit such evidence. The Oregon duress defense is available only if a defendant "was coerced to [commit the act] by use or threatened use of unlawful physical force . . . of such nature or degree to overcome earnest resistance." The court stated that such "resistance is a generalized standard; it is not measured by a defendant's individual personality traits. The trial court was correct that whether defendant was a timid individual easily coerced is not relevant to whether, at the time of the robbery, defendant was subjected to a physical force of such a degree as to overcome earnest resistance."

3. *Strict liability.* Is there any limit to the types of offenses which may be the subject of the duress claim? In *State v. Rios*, 127 N.M. 334, 980 P.2d 1068 (Ct.App. 1999), the court held that a defendant was entitled to assert duress to a drunk driving charge, after being threatened by an angry mob after leaving a bar. The strict liability nature of the offense was deemed to be irrelevant to the defendant's right to claim the duress defense.

4. *Borrowed money.* In *Williams v. State*, 101 Md.App. 408, 646 A.2d 1101 (1994), the court affirmed the trial court's refusal to instruct the jury on duress as a defense to attempted robbery and burglary. Williams borrowed money from a drug dealer's brother and made two "drug runs" to help repay his debt. He was briefly abducted by associates of the drug dealer who threatened to kill him if he could not take them to the "stash house." So Williams picked a house and pretended that it was the "stash house." Williams and his abductors committed burglary and attempted robbery while searching fruitlessly for the "stash." The *Williams* court concluded that even though the defendant was under duress to repay the debt, his "contributory actions barred the availability of the defense," reasoning as follows:

> Williams through his own recklessness made others aware of his connection with [the drug dealer], including his abductors. Williams was readily identifiable to those in the organization, including his abductors, and the abductors acted accordingly. This was a situation that would not have occurred but for Williams's association with the drug organization. Considering these facts and the applicable law, we conclude that Williams's assertion that the defense of duress applies is unavailing.

PROBLEMS

1. *Battered Spouse Syndrome.* What effect do cases like *VanNatta* in Note 2, *supra*, have on the ability of a defendant to introduce evidence of the battered spouse syndrome in order to prove duress? Compare *United States v. Willis*, 38 F.3d 170 (5th Cir. 1994) (evidence of the syndrome cannot support duress) with *United States v. Marenghi*, 893 F.Supp. 85 (D.Me. 1995) (syndrome testimony admissible). See Laura Kratky Dore, "Downward Adjustment and the Slippery Slope: The Use of Duress in Defense of Battered Offenders," 56 Ohio State L.J. 665 (1995). Under the M.P.C. duress defense, how can a defendant argue that syndrome testimony is relevant to a claim of duress?

2. *Placing Self in Coercive Situation.* Should the duress defense be unavailable when a defendant intentionally places herself in a position likely to subject her to coercion? Consider the following statutory version of a duress defense.

(1) A person is excused for his offense if, at the time of the offense, he:

(a) was coerced to perform the conduct by a threat that a person of reasonable firmness in the person's situation would have been unable to resist, and

(b) as a result, the person is not sufficiently able to control his conduct so as to be justly held accountable for it.

(2) Factors to be Considered in Determining Whether a Person of Reasonable Firmness in the Person's Situation Would Have Been Unable to Resist the Threat. In determining whether a person of reasonable firmness in the person's situation would have been unable to resist the threat coercing the person, as required by Subsection (1), the following factors are among those that shall be considered:

> (a) the imminence of the threat, the seriousness of the harm threatened, the nature of the harm threatened (e.g., physical, economic, emotional, or other), the object of the threat (e.g., the person himself, a relative, or business associate), the unlawfulness of the threat, and the source of the threat (e.g., an other person or natural forces);

> (b) the seriousness of the harm caused in relation to the harm threatened and the availability of less harmful but equally effective alternatives to avoiding the threat.

What are its advantages and disadvantages, compared with the M.P.C. provision in § 2.09 in Note 1, *supra*? In subsection (2), which factors relate to the extent of the threat? Which factors relate to the extent of the harm caused by the person?

3. *The Threat to Kill.* Jimmy was charged with robbery. At his trial, Jimmy claimed that Simon, a federal inmate who Jimmy had "worked" with during prior illegal activities numerous times in the past, sent a message to Jimmy that if he did not commit the robbery, he would be killed. Jimmy alleged that Simon sent an accomplice, Jay, to go with Jimmy to make sure that the robbery happened as planned. During the actual robbery, Jay waited in the car while Jimmy went inside a bank with a loaded pistol. If Jimmy is telling the truth, and Simon did threaten Jimmy and sent Jay to ensure that the robbery took place, is Jimmy entitled to an instruction on duress? Was Jimmy compelled to commit the crime by a threat of imminent death or serious bodily injury? If Jimmy had an opportunity to escape, was the threat imminent?

4. *Duress and Intentional Killings.* Suppose that in the prior problem, Simon had coerced Jimmy into committing an intentional murder. At common law, and under the Model Penal Code, is Jimmy entitled to a duress instruction?

5. *The Cocaine Transporter.* Juan was a taxi-cab driver in Bogotá, Columbia. One afternoon a passenger, Jose, offered him a job as a private car driver. When Juan met with Jose to discuss the job, Jose told him that the job had changed. Juan's job now was to swallow balloons filled with cocaine and travel to the United States, where a drug dealer would "receive" them in Los Angeles. When Juan declined this offer, Jose mentioned numerous facts about Juan's wife and children, facts that Juan had not previously told Jose. Jose told Juan to cooperate or else his wife and baby would be killed. Juan

was informed that he would be watched at all times during the plane trip, and if he failed to do as he was told, his wife and child would die. Believing that the Colombian police were corrupt and would not help him, Juan agreed to Jose's offer. Immediately upon reaching the United States, Juan was detained, his stomach was x-rayed, and the cocaine was discovered. At his trial, Juan claimed the duress defense. Should the jury be allowed to hear evidence regarding duress?

6. *The Fearful Pigeon.* Mickey, a convicted felon, was approached by Max, who had been charged with international drug conspiracy offenses. Max offered Mickey $10,000 and half a kilogram of cocaine for each witness that he managed to "silence." Mickey, who had not previously encountered Max before receiving Max's offer, promptly reported the offer to the federal authorities. After the authorities promised to keep Mickey's identity secret and to protect him if his identity were revealed, Mickey agreed to help the government gather evidence against Max. Mickey pretended to accept Max's offer. As a result of Mickey's work, the government was able to build a strong case against Max. Unfortunately Mickey's name was included by mistake in the indictment against Max. Thereafter, Mickey began receiving death threats. After learning that there was a contract out on his life, Mickey went to the government and begged them to take him into protective custody. He also sought the assistance of the local authorities and he even told his parole officer that he was using drugs so that his parole officer would send him back to jail. No one was willing to help him. He was constantly in fear of his life, either staying at friends' houses or sleeping on the streets. In fear of his life and not knowing what else to do, Mickey obtained of a twelve-gauge shotgun. Shortly afterwards, two federal officers came to see Mickey regarding the case against Max. When they finally found Mickey at a friend's house, he was carrying his shotgun. The officers arrested him for being a felon in possession of a firearm. At his trial, Mickey sought to present the death threat evidence in order to make out a duress defense. The trial judge determined that the defense was inapplicable because the danger was not immediate enough; no one was holding a gun to the defendant's head at the time he had the shotgun in his possession. Was the trial judge correct?

EXERCISE

State Code Rules. In your state, look at the criminal statutes for a duress provision. Compare it with the Model Penal Code defense. Are important statutory terms defined? Regarding the extent of the threat to the defendant, what do the Model Penal Code and state statute provide with respect to the following aspects of the defense?

     a.   The imminence of the threat;

     b.   The seriousness of the harm threatened;

     c.   The nature of the harm threatened, e.g., physical, economic, emotional or other;

    d.   The target of the threat, e.g., the defendant, a relative, friend, or business associate;

    e.   The unlawfulness of the threat; and

    f.   The source of the threat.

As to the extent of the harm caused by the defendant, what do the Model Penal Code and state statute provide about the extent of harm caused by the defendant, such as the seriousness of the harm in relation to the harm threatened, and the availability of less harmful but equally effective alternatives to avoiding the threat?

B. INSANITY

There is little justification for punishing those who commit crimes while insane. As the Second Circuit stated in *United States v. Freeman*, 357 F.2d 606, 615 (2d Cir. 1966):

> Those who are substantially unable to restrain their conduct are, by definition, undeterrable and their "punishment" is no example for others; those who are unaware of or do not appreciate the nature and quality of their actions can hardly be expected rationally to weigh the consequences of their conduct. Finally, what segment of society can feel its desire for retribution satisfied when it wreaks vengeance upon the incompetent?

1. THE TEST FOR INSANITY

Although there is general agreement that the insane should not be held criminally responsible for their conduct, it is difficult to define the defense of insanity.

a. *M'NAGHTEN* AND THE IRRESISTIBLE IMPULSE TEST

For many years, U.S. courts applied the insanity test articulated in *M'Naghten's Case*.

DANIEL M'NAGHTEN'S CASE
10 Cl. & F. 200, 8 Eng. Rep. 718 (House of Lords 1843).

LORD CHIEF JUSTICE TINDAL:

[Daniel M'Naghten shot at Sir Robert Peel's carriage intending to kill Peel. M'Naghten actually shot Edward Drummond, Peel's private secretary, who was the only person inside the carriage. At his trial, M'Naghten claimed that he killed Drummond under the influence of insane delusions, and the jury found him not guilty by reason of insanity. Because the verdict was unpopular, the House of Lords debated the decision and appended conclusions to the report of the original case.]

The first question proposed by your Lordships is this: "What is the law respecting alleged crimes committed by persons afflicted with insane delusion in respect of one or more particular subjects or personas, for instance, where at the time of commission of the alleged crime the accused knew he was acting contrary to law, but did the act complained of with a view, under the influence of insane delusion, of redressing or revenging some supposed grievance or injury, or of producing some supposed public benefit?"

In answer to which question, assuming that your Lordships' inquiries are confined to those persons who labour under such partial delusions only, and are not in other respects insane, we are of opinion that, notwithstanding the party accused did the act complained of with a view, under the influence of redressing or revenging some supposed grievance or injury, or of producing some public benefit, he is nevertheless punishable according to the nature of the crime committed, if he knew at the time of committing such crime that he was acting contrary to law; by which expression we understand your Lordships to mean the law of the land.

Your Lordships are pleased to inquire of us, secondly, "What are the proper questions to be submitted to the jury, where a person alleged to be afflicted with insane delusion respecting one or more subjects or persons, is charged with the commission of a crime (murder, for example), and insanity is set up as a defence?" And, thirdly, "In what terms ought the question to be left to the jury as to the prisoner's state of mind at the time when the act was committed?" And as these two questions appear to us to be more conveniently answered together, we have to submit our opinion to be, that the jurors ought to be told in all cases that every man is to be presumed to be sane, and to possess a sufficient degree of reason to be responsible for his crimes, until the contrary be proved to their satisfaction; and that to establish a defence on the ground of insanity, it must be clearly proved that, at the time of the committing of the act, the party accused was labouring under such a defect of reason, from disease of the mind, as not to know the nature and quality of the act he was doing; or, if he did know it, that he did not know he was doing what was wrong. The mode of putting the latter part of the question to the jury on these occasions has generally been, whether the accused at the time of doing the act knew the difference between right and wrong. . . . If the accused was conscious that the act was one which he ought not to do, and if that act was at the same time contrary to the law of the land, he is punishable; and the usual course therefore has been to leave the question to the jury, whether the party accused had a sufficient degree of reason to know that he was doing an act that was [wrong].

The fourth question which your Lordships have proposed to us is this:—"If a person under an insane delusion as to existing facts, commits an offence in consequence thereof, is he thereby excused?" To which question the answer must of course depend on the nature of the delusion: but, making the same assumption as we did before, namely, that he labours under such partial delusion only, and is not in other respects insane, we think he must be considered in the same situation as to responsibility as if the facts with respect to which the delusion exists were real. For example, if under the influence of his delusion, he supposes another man to be in the act of attempting to take away his life, and he kills that man, as he supposes, in self-defense, he would be exempt from punishment. If his delusion was that the deceased has inflicted a serious injury to his character and fortune, and he killed him in revenge for such supposed injury, he would be liable to punishment.

The question lastly proposed by your Lordships is—"Can a medical man conversant with the disease of insanity, who never saw the prisoner previously to the trial, but who was present during the whole trial and the examination of all the witnesses, be asked his opinion as to the state of the prisoner's mind at the time of the commission of the alleged crime, or his opinion whether the prisoner was conscious at the time of doing the act that he was acting contrary to law, or whether he was labouring under any and what delusion at the time?" In answer thereto, we state to your Lordships, that we think the medical man, under the circumstances supposed, cannot in strictness be asked his opinion in the terms above stated, because each of those questions involves the determination of the truth of the facts deposed to, which it is for the jury to decide, and the questions are not mere questions upon a matter of science, in which case such evidence is admissible. But where the facts are admitted or not disputed, and the question becomes substantially one of science only, it may be convenient to allow the question to be put in that general form, though the same cannot be insisted on as a matter of right.

CLARK v. ARIZONA

548 U.S. 735 (2006).

JUSTICE SOUTER delivered the opinion of the Court.

The case presents two questions: whether due process prohibits Arizona's use of an insanity test stated solely in terms of the capacity to tell whether an act charged as a crime was right or wrong; and whether Arizona violates due process in restricting consideration of defense evidence of mental illness and incapacity to its bearing on a claim of insanity, thus eliminating its significance directly on the issue of the mental element of the crime charged (known in legal short-hand as the *mens rea*, or guilty mind). . . .

[On] June 21, 2000, Officer Jeffrey Moritz of the Flagstaff Police responded [to] complaints that a pickup truck with loud music blaring was circling a residential block. [T]he officer turned on the emergency lights and siren of his marked patrol car [and pulled Clark over.] Less than a minute later, Clark shot the officer, who died soon [there]after. . . . Clark was charged with first-degree murder [for] intentionally or knowingly killing a law enforcement officer in the line of duty. . . . At trial, Clark did not contest the shooting and death, but relied on his undisputed paranoid schizophrenia at the time of the incident in denying that he had the specific intent to shoot a law enforcement officer or knowledge that he was doing so, as required by the statute. Accordingly, the prosecutor offered circumstantial evidence that Clark knew Officer Moritz was a law enforcement officer. [The] testimony for the prosecution indicated that Clark had intentionally lured an officer to the scene to kill him, having told some people a few weeks before the incident that he wanted to shoot police officers. . . .

In presenting the defense case, Clark claimed mental illness, which he sought to introduce for two purposes. First, he raised the affirmative defense of insanity, putting the burden on himself to prove by clear and convincing evidence, that "at the time of the commission of the criminal act [he] was afflicted with a mental disease or defect of such severity that [he] did not know the criminal act was wrong." Second, he aimed to rebut the prosecution's evidence of the requisite *mens rea*, that he had acted intentionally or knowingly to kill a law enforcement officer. The trial court ruled that Clark could not rely on evidence bearing on insanity to dispute the *mens rea*. The court cited *State v. Mott*, 187 Ariz. 536, 931 P.2d 1046 (en banc) (1997), which "refused to allow psychiatric testimony to negate specific intent," and held that "Arizona does not allow evidence of a defendant's mental disorder short of insanity . . . to negate the *mens rea* element of a crime."

As to his insanity, then, Clark presented testimony from classmates, school officials, and his family describing his increasingly bizarre behavior over the year before the shooting. Witnesses testified, for example, that paranoid delusions led Clark to rig a fishing line with beads and wind chimes at home to alert him to intrusion by invaders, and to keep a bird in his automobile to warn of airborne poison. There was lay and expert testimony that Clark thought Flagstaff was populated with "aliens" (some impersonating government agents), the "aliens" were trying to kill him, and bullets were the only way to stop them. A psychiatrist testified that Clark was suffering from paranoid schizophrenia with delusions about "aliens" when he killed Officer Moritz, and he concluded that Clark was incapable of luring the officer or understanding right from wrong and that he was thus insane at the time of the killing. In rebuttal, a psychiatrist for the State gave his opinion that Clark's paranoid schizophrenia did not keep him from appreciating the wrongfulness of his conduct, as shown by his actions before and after the shooting (such as circling the residential block with music blaring as if to lure the police to intervene, evading the police after the shooting, and hiding the gun). [The] judge then issued a special verdict of first-degree murder, expressly finding that Clark shot and caused the death of Officer Moritz beyond a reasonable doubt and that Clark had not shown that he was insane at the time. The judge noted that though Clark was indisputably afflicted with paranoid schizophrenia at the time of the shooting, the mental illness "did not ... distort his perception of reality so severely that he did not know his actions were wrong." For this conclusion, the judge expressly relied on "the facts of the crime, the evaluations of the experts, [Clark's] actions and behavior both before and after the shooting, and the observations of those that knew [Clark]." The sentence was life imprisonment without the possibility of release for 25 years. [The Court of Appeals affirmed the conviction and the Supreme Court of Arizona denied review. We affirm.]

Clark first says that Arizona's definition of insanity, being only a fragment of the Victorian standard from which it derives, violates due process. The landmark English rule [appears] in *M'Naghten's Case*, 10 Cl. & Fin. 200, 8 Eng. Rep. 718 (1843).... When the Arizona Legislature first codified an insanity rule, it adopted the full *M'Naghten* [statement]. In 1993, the legislature dropped the cognitive incapacity part [a person does not "know the nature and quality of the act he or she was doing"], leaving only moral incapacity as the nub of the stated definition. Under current Arizona law, a defendant will not be adjudged insane unless he demonstrates that "at the time of the commission of the criminal act [he] was afflicted with a mental disease or defect of such severity that [he] did not know the criminal act was wrong."

Clark challenges the 1993 amendment excising the express reference to the cognitive incapacity element. He [argues] that elimination of the *M'Naghten* reference to nature and quality " 'offends [a] principle of justice so rooted in the traditions and conscience of our people as to be ranked as fundamental,' " *Patterson* v. *New York*, 432 U. S. 197, 202 (1977).... History shows no deference to *M'Naghten* that could elevate its formula to the level of fundamental principle, so as to limit the traditional recognition of a State's capacity to define crimes and defenses. Even a cursory examination of the traditional Anglo–American approaches to insanity reveals significant differences among them, with four traditional strains variously combined to yield a diversity of American standards. The main variants are the cognitive incapacity, the moral incapacity, the volitional incapacity, and the product-of-mental-illness tests. The first two emanate from the alternatives stated in the *M'Naghten* rule. The volitional incapacity or irresistible-impulse test, which surfaced over two centuries ago (first in England, then in this country), asks whether a person was so lacking in volition due to a mental defect or illness that he could not have controlled his actions. And the product-of-mental-illness test was used as early as 1870, and simply asks whether a person's action was a product of a mental disease or defect.

Seventeen States and the Federal Government have adopted a recognizable version of the *M'Naghten* test with both its cognitive incapacity and moral incapacity components. One State has adopted only *M'Naghten*'s cognitive incapacity test, and 10 (including Arizona) have adopted the moral incapacity test alone. Fourteen jurisdictions, inspired by the Model Penal Code, have in place an amalgam of the volitional incapacity test and some variant of the moral incapacity test, satisfaction of either (generally by showing a defendant's substantial lack of capacity) being enough to excuse. Three States combine a full *M'Naghten* test with a volitional incapacity formula. And New Hampshire alone stands by the product-of-mental-illness test. The alternatives are multiplied further by variations in the prescribed insanity verdict: a significant number of these jurisdictions supplement the traditional "not guilty by reason of insanity" verdict with an alternative of "guilty but mentally ill." Finally, four States have no affirmative insanity defense, though one provides for a "guilty and mentally ill" verdict. These four, like a number of others that recognize an affirmative insanity defense, allow consideration of evidence of mental illness directly on the element of *mens rea* defining the offense.

With this varied background, it is clear that no particular formulation has evolved into a baseline for due process, and that the insanity rule, like the conceptualization of criminal offenses, is substantially open to state choice. Indeed, the legitimacy of such choice is the more obvious when one considers the interplay of legal concepts of mental illness or deficiency required for an insanity defense, with the medical concepts of mental abnormality that influence the expert opinion testimony by psychologists and psychiatrists commonly introduced to support or contest insanity claims. For medical definitions devised to justify treatment, like legal ones devised to excuse from conventional criminal responsibility, are subject to flux and disagreement. There being such fodder for reasonable debate about what the cognate legal and medical tests should be, due process imposes no single canonical formulation of legal insanity.

[Though] Clark is correct that the application of the moral incapacity test (telling right from wrong) does not necessarily require evaluation of a defendant's cognitive capacity to appreciate the nature and quality of the acts charged against him, his argument fails to recognize that cognitive incapacity is itself enough to demonstrate moral incapacity. Cognitive incapacity, in other words, is a sufficient condition for establishing a defense of insanity, albeit not a necessary one. As a defendant can therefore make out moral incapacity by demonstrating cognitive incapacity, evidence bearing on whether the defendant knew the nature and quality of his actions is both relevant and admissible. In practical terms, if a defendant did not know what he was doing when he acted, he could not have known that he was performing the wrongful act charged as a crime. Indeed, when the two-part rule was still in effect, the Supreme Court of Arizona held that a jury instruction on insanity containing the moral incapacity part but not a full recitation of the cognitive incapacity part was fine, as the cognitive incapacity part might be " 'treated as adding nothing to the requirement that the accused know his act was wrong.' " *State* v. *Chavez*, 143 Ariz. 238, 239, 693 P. 2d 893, 894 (1984). [We] are satisfied that neither in theory nor in practice did Arizona's 1993 abridgment of the insanity formulation deprive Clark of due process.

Clark's second claim of a due process violation challenges the rule adopted [by] *Mott*. This case ruled on the admissibility of testimony from a psychologist offered to show that the defendant suffered from battered women's syndrome and therefore lacked the capacity to form the *mens rea* of the crime charged against her. The state court held that testimony of a professional psychologist or psychiatrist about a defendant's mental incapacity owing to mental disease or defect was admissible, and could be considered, only for its bearing on an insanity defense; such evidence could not be considered on the element of *mens rea*, that is, what the State must show about a defendant's mental state (such as intent or understanding) when he performed the act charged against him.

Understanding Clark's claim requires attention to the categories of evidence with a potential bearing on *mens rea*. First, there is "observation evidence" in the everyday sense, testimony from those who observed what Clark did and heard what he said; this category would also include testimony that an expert witness might give about Clark's tendency to think in a certain way and his behavioral characteristics. This evidence may support a professional diagnosis of mental disease and in any event is the kind of evidence that can be relevant to show what in fact was on Clark's mind when he fired the gun. Observation evidence in the record covers Clark's behavior at home and with friends, his expressions of belief around the time of the killing that "aliens" were inhabiting the bodies of local people (including government agents), his driving around the neighborhood before the police arrived, and so on. Contrary to the dissent's characterization, observation evidence can be presented by either lay or expert witnesses.

Second, there is "mental-disease evidence" in the form of opinion testimony that Clark suffered from a mental disease with features described by the witness. As was true here, this evidence characteristically but not always comes from professional psychologists or psychiatrists who testify as expert witnesses and base their opinions in part on examination of a defendant, usually conducted after the events in question. The thrust of this evidence was that, based on factual reports, professional observations, and tests, Clark was psychotic at the time in question, with a condition that fell within the category of schizophrenia.

Third, there is evidence we will refer to as "capacity evidence" about a defendant's capacity for cognition and moral judgment (and ultimately also his capacity to form *mens rea*). This, too, is opinion evidence. Here, as it usually does, this testimony came from the same experts and concentrated on those specific details of the mental condition that make the difference between sanity and insanity under the Arizona definition. In their respective testimony on these details the experts disagreed: the defense expert gave his opinion that the symptoms or effects of the disease in Clark's case included inability to appreciate the nature of his action and to tell that it was wrong, whereas the State's psychiatrist was of the view that Clark was a schizophrenic who was still sufficiently able to appreciate the reality of shooting the officer and to know that it was wrong to do that.

. . . *Mott* itself imposed no restriction on considering evidence of the first sort, the observation evidence. We read the *Mott* restriction to apply, rather, to evidence addressing the two issues in testimony that characteristically comes only from psychologists or psychiatrists qualified to give opinions as expert witnesses: mental-disease evidence (whether at the time of the crime a defendant suffered from a mental disease or defect, such as schizophrenia) and capacity evidence (whether the disease or defect left him incapable of performing or experiencing a mental process defined as necessary for sanity such as appreciating the nature and quality of his act and knowing that it was wrong). *Mott* was careful to distinguish this kind of opinion evidence from observation evidence generally and even from observation evidence that an expert witness might offer, such as descriptions of a defendant's tendency to think in a certain way or his behavioral characteristics; the Arizona court made it clear that this sort of testimony was perfectly admissible to rebut the prosecution's evidence of *mens rea*. Thus, only opinion testimony going to mental defect or disease, and its effect on the cognitive or moral capacities on which sanity depends under the Arizona rule, is restricted. In this case, the trial court seems to have applied the *Mott* restriction to all evidence offered by Clark for the purpose of showing what he called his inability to form the required *mens rea*. Thus, the trial court's restriction may have covered not only mental-disease and capacity evidence as just defined, but also observation evidence offered by lay (and expert) witnesses who described Clark's unusual behavior. Clark's objection to the application of the *Mott* rule does not, however, turn on the distinction between lay and expert witnesses or the kinds of testimony they were competent to present. [All] Members of the Court agree that Clark's general attack on the *Mott* rule covers its application in confining consideration of capacity evidence to the insanity defense. [The] only issue properly before us is the challenge to *Mott* on due process grounds, comprising objections to limits on the use of mental-disease and capacity evidence. [We] consider the claim, as Clark otherwise puts it, that "Arizona's prohibition of 'diminished capacity' evidence by criminal defendants violates" due process....

[Clark] claims a right to require the factfinder in this case to consider testimony about his mental illness and his incapacity directly, when weighing the persuasiveness of other evidence tending to show *mens rea*, which the prosecution has the burden to prove. As Clark recognizes, however, the right to introduce relevant evidence can be curtailed if there is a good reason for doing that.... *Holmes* v. *South Carolina*, 547 U.S. 319 (2006). And if evidence may be kept out entirely, its consideration may be subject to limitation, which Arizona claims the power to impose here. State law says that evidence of mental disease and incapacity may be introduced and considered, and if sufficiently forceful to satisfy the defendant's burden of proof under the insanity rule it will displace the presumption of sanity and excuse from criminal responsibility. But mental-disease and capacity evidence may be considered only for its bearing on the insanity defense, and it will avail a defendant only if it is persuasive enough to satisfy the defendant's burden as defined by the terms of that defense. The mental-disease and capacity evidence is thus being channeled or restricted to one issue and given effect only if the defendant carries the burden to convince the factfinder of insanity; the evidence is not being excluded entirely, and the question is whether reasons for requiring it to be channeled and restricted are good enough to satisfy the standard of fundamental fairness that due process requires. We think they are.

The first reason supporting the *Mott* rule is Arizona's authority to define its presumption of sanity (or capacity or responsibility) by choosing an insanity definition, [and] by placing the burden of persuasion on defendants who claim incapacity as an excuse from customary criminal responsibility. No one [denies] that a State may place a burden of persuasion on a defendant claiming insanity.... But if a State is to have this authority in practice as well as in theory, it must be able to deny a defendant the opportunity to displace the presumption of sanity more easily when addressing a different issue in the course of the criminal trial. Yet, as we have explained, just such an opportunity would be available if expert testimony of mental disease and incapacity could be considered for whatever a factfinder might think it was worth on the issue of *mens rea*. Now, a State is of course free to accept such a possibility in its law. After all, it is free to define the insanity defense by treating the presumption of sanity as a bursting bubble, whose disappearance shifts the burden to the prosecution to prove sanity whenever a defendant presents any credible evidence of mental disease or incapacity. In States with this kind of insanity rule, the legislature may well be willing to allow such evidence to be considered on the *mens rea* element for whatever the factfinder thinks it is worth. What counts for due process, however, is simply that a State that wishes to avoid a second avenue for exploring capacity, less stringent for a defendant, has a good reason for confining the consideration of evidence of mental disease and incapacity to the insanity defense. It is obvious that Arizona's *Mott* rule reflects such a [choice].

A State's insistence on preserving its chosen standard of legal insanity cannot be the sole reason for a rule like *Mott*. An insanity rule gives a defendant already found guilty the opportunity to excuse his conduct by showing he was insane when he acted, that is, that he did not have the mental capacity for conventional guilt and criminal responsibility. But, [if] the same evidence that affirmatively shows he was not guilty by reason of insanity (or "guilty except insane") under Arizona law also shows it was at least doubtful that he could form *mens rea*, then he should not be found guilty in the first place; it thus violates due process when the State impedes him from using mental-disease and capacity evidence directly to rebut the prosecution's evidence that he did form *mens rea*.

Are there, then, characteristics of mental-disease and capacity evidence giving rise to risks that may reasonably be hedged by channeling the consideration of such evidence to the insanity issue on which, in States like Arizona, a defendant has the burden of persuasion? We think there are: in the controversial character of some categories of mental disease, in the potential of mental-disease evidence to mislead, and in the danger of according greater certainty to capacity evidence than experts claim for it.

To begin with, the diagnosis may mask vigorous debate within the profession about the very contours of the mental disease itself. See, *e.g.*, American Psychiatric Association, Diagnostic and Statistical Manual of Mental Disorders xxxiii (4th ed. text rev. 2000) (hereinafter DSM–IV–TR). And Members of this Court have previously recognized that the end of such debate is not imminent. [The] consequence of this professional ferment is a general caution in treating psychological classifications as predicates for excusing otherwise criminal conduct.

Next, there is the potential of mental-disease evidence to mislead jurors (when they are the factfinders) through the power of this kind of evidence to suggest that a defendant suffering from a recognized mental disease lacks cognitive, moral, volitional, or other capacity, when that may not be a sound conclusion at all. Even when a category of mental disease is broadly accepted and the assignment of a defendant's behavior to that category is uncontroversial, the classification may suggest something very significant about a defendant's capacity, when in fact the classification tells us little or nothing about the ability of the defendant to form *mens rea* or to exercise the cognitive, moral, or volitional capacities that define legal sanity. The limits of the utility of a professional disease diagnosis are evident in the dispute between the two testifying experts in this case; they agree that Clark was schizophrenic, but they come to opposite conclusions on whether the mental disease in his particular case left him bereft of cognitive or moral capacity. Evidence of mental disease, then, can easily mislead; it is very easy to slide from evidence that an individual with a professionally recognized mental disease is very different, into doubting that he has the capacity to form *mens rea*, whereas that doubt may not be justified. And of course, in the cases mentioned before, in which the categorization is doubtful or the category of mental disease is itself subject to controversy, the risks are even greater that opinions about mental disease may confuse a jury into thinking the opinions show more than they do. Because allowing mental-disease evidence on *mens rea* can thus easily mislead, it is not unreasonable to address that tendency by confining consideration of this kind of evidence to insanity, on which a defendant may be assigned the burden of persuasion.

There are, finally, particular risks inherent in the opinions of the experts who supplement the mental-disease classifications with opinions on incapacity: on whether the mental disease rendered a particular defendant incapable of the cognition necessary for moral judgment or *mens rea* or otherwise incapable of understanding the wrongfulness of the conduct charged. Unlike observational evidence bearing on *mens rea*, capacity evidence consists of judgment, and judgment fraught with multiple perils: a defendant's state of mind at the crucial moment can be elusive no matter how conscientious the enquiry, and the law's categories that set the terms of the capacity judgment are not the categories of psychology that govern the expert's professional thinking. [Even] when an expert is confident that his understanding of the mind is reliable, judgment addressing the basic categories of capacity requires a leap from the concepts of psychology, which are devised for thinking about treatment, to the concepts of legal sanity, which are devised for thinking about criminal responsibility. In sum, these empirical and conceptual problems add up to a real risk that an expert's judgment in giving capacity evidence will come with an apparent authority that psychologists and psychiatrists do not claim to have. We think that this risk, like the difficulty in assessing the significance of mental-disease evidence, supports the State's decision to channel such expert testimony to consideration on the insanity defense, on which the party seeking the benefit of this evidence has the burden of persuasion.

It bears repeating that not every State will find it worthwhile to make the judgment Arizona has made, and the choices the States do make about dealing with the risks posed by mental-disease and capacity evidence will reflect their varying assessments about the presumption of sanity as expressed in choices of insanity rules. The point here simply is that Arizona has sensible reasons to assign the risks as it has done by channeling the evidence.

Arizona's rule serves to preserve the State's chosen standard for recognizing insanity as a defense and to avoid confusion and misunderstanding on the part of jurors. For these reasons, there is no violation of due process [and] no cause to claim that channeling evidence on mental disease and capacity offends any " 'principle of justice so rooted in the traditions and conscience of our people as to be ranked as fundamental,' " *Patterson,* 432 U. S., at 202.

The judgment of the Court of Appeals of Arizona is, accordingly, affirmed.

It is so ordered.

[Justice Breyer concurred in part and dissented in part; he would have remanded the case to determine whether the Arizona law is consistent with the distinctions drawn by the majority.]

Justice Kennedy, with whom Justice Stevens and Justice Ginsburg join, dissenting.

[The] central theory of Clark's defense was that his schizophrenia made him delusional. He lived in a universe where the delusions were so dominant, the theory was, that he had no intent to shoot a police officer or knowledge he was doing so. It is one thing to say he acted with intent or knowledge to pull the trigger. It is quite another to say he pulled the trigger to kill someone he knew to be a human being and a police officer. If the trier of fact were to find Clark's evidence sufficient to discount the case made by the State, which has the burden to prove knowledge or intent as an element of the offense, Clark would not be guilty of first-degree murder under Arizona law. . . .

The trial court's exclusion was all the more severe because it barred from consideration on the issue of *mens rea* all this evidence, from any source, thus preventing Clark from showing he did not commit the crime as defined by Arizona law. [Arizona's] rule is problematic because it excludes evidence no matter how credible and material it may be in disproving an element of the offense. The Court's cases have noted the potential arbitrariness of *per se* exclusions and, on this rationale, have invalidated various state prohibitions. . . . If the rule does not substantially burden the defense, then it is likely permissible. Where, however, the burden is substantial, the State must present a valid reason for its *per se* evidentiary rule.

In the instant case Arizona's proposed reasons are insufficient to support its categorical exclusion. While the State contends that testimony regarding mental illness may be too incredible or speculative for the jury to consider, this does not explain why the exclusion applies in all cases to all evidence of mental illness. "A State's legitimate interest in barring unreliable evidence does not extend to *per se* exclusions that may be reliable in an individual case." States have certain discretion to bar unreliable or speculative testimony and to adopt rules to ensure the reliability of expert testimony. Arizona has done so, and there is no reason to believe its rules are insufficient to avoid speculative evidence of mental illness.... The risk of jury confusion also fails to justify the rule. The State defends its rule as a means to avoid the complexities of determining how and to what degree a mental illness affects a person's mental state. The difficulty of resolving a factual issue, though, does not present a sufficient reason to take evidence away from the jury even when it is crucial for the defense.... Even were the risk of jury confusion real enough to justify excluding evidence in most cases, this would provide little basis for prohibiting all evidence of mental illness without any inquiry into its likely effect on the jury or its role in deciding the linchpin issue of knowledge and intent. Indeed, Arizona has a rule in place to serve this very purpose.

Even assuming the reliability and jury-confusion justifications were persuasive in some cases, they would not suffice here. It does not overcome the constitutional objection to say that an evidentiary rule that is reasonable on its face can be applied as well to bar significant defense evidence without any rational basis for doing so.... The reliability rationale has minimal applicability here. The Court is correct that many mental diseases are difficult to define and the subject of great debate. Schizophrenia, however, is a well-documented mental illness, and no one seriously disputes either its definition or its most prominent clinical manifestations. The State's own expert conceded that Clark had paranoid schizophrenia and was actively psychotic at the time of the killing. The jury-confusion rationale, if it is at all applicable here, is the result of the Court's own insistence on conflating the insanity defense and the question of intent. Considered on its own terms, the issue of intent and knowledge is a straightforward factual question. A trier of fact is quite capable of weighing defense testimony and then determining whether the accused did or did not intend to kill or knowingly kill a human being who was a police officer. True, the issue can be difficult to decide in particular instances, but no more so than many matters juries must confront.

The Court says mental-illness evidence "can easily mislead," and may "tel[l] us little or nothing about the ability of the defendant to form *mens rea*." These generalities do not, however, show how relevant or misleading the evidence in this case would [be]. As explained above, the evidence of Clark's mental illness bears directly on *mens rea*, for it suggests Clark may not have known he was killing a human being. It is striking that while the Court discusses at length the likelihood of misjudgment from placing too much emphasis on evidence of mental illness, it ignores the risk of misjudging an innocent man guilty from refusing to consider this highly relevant evidence at all. . . . This testimony was relevant to determining whether Clark knew he was killing a human being. . . .

The fact that mental-illness evidence may be considered in deciding criminal responsibility does not compensate for its exclusion from consideration on the *mens rea* elements of the crime. [While] 13 States still impose significant restrictions on the use of mental-illness evidence to negate *mens rea*, a substantial majority of the States currently allow it. The fact that a reasonable number of States restrict this evidence weighs into the analysis, but applying the rule as a *per se* bar, as Arizona does, is so plainly unreasonable that it cannot be sustained. . . . While defining mental illness is a difficult matter, the State seems to exclude the evidence one would think most reliable by allowing unexplained and uncategorized tendencies to be introduced while excluding relatively well-understood psychiatric testimony regarding well-documented mental illnesses. It is unclear, moreover, what would have happened in this case had the defendant wanted to testify that he thought Officer Moritz was an alien. If disallowed, it would be tantamount to barring Clark from testifying on his behalf to explain his own actions. If allowed, then Arizona's rule would simply prohibit the corroboration necessary to make sense of Clark's explanation. In sum, the rule forces the jury to decide guilt in a fictional world with undefined and unexplained behaviors but without mental illness. This rule has no rational justification and imposes a significant burden upon a straightforward defense: He did not commit the crime with which he was charged. . . .

NOTES

1. *Insane delusion as to existing facts.* Because of the House of Lords' answer to the fourth question, some jurisdictions interpreted *M'Naghten* to apply to insane delusions only when "the imaginary state of facts would, if real, justify or excuse the act." These jurisdictions held that defendant "must be considered in the same situation as to responsibility as if the facts with respect to which the delusion exists were real." *See Parsons v. State*, 81 Ala. 577, 2 So. 854 (1887).

2. *Irresistible impulse.* As described in *Clark*, some jurisdictions supplement the *M'Naghten* test with the "irresistible impulse" test, which provides that, even if defendant knew the difference between right and wrong and knew that his act was wrong, defendant cannot be convicted if he acted under an "irresistible impulse." *Parsons v. State*, 81 Ala. 577, 2 So. 854 (1887), is the leading case: "We think it sufficient if the insane delusion [so] subverts his will as to destroy his free agency by rendering him powerless to resist by reason of the duress of the disease."

3. *Incompetency at the time of trial.* Insanity can be relevant at three different points in the criminal process. First, as in *M'Naghten*, individuals who commit criminal acts while insane cannot be convicted of those acts. Second, defendants who are insane at the time of their trials cannot be tried, and will be committed until they are sane enough to proceed. The defendant must "[have] sufficient present ability to consult with his lawyer with a reasonable degree of rational understanding—[and have] a rational as well as factual understanding of the proceedings against him." *Dusky v. United States*, 362 U.S. 402 (1960). Finally, defendants sentenced to capital punishment cannot be executed until they regain their sanity. *See Ford v. Wainwright*, 477 U.S. 399 (1986). In *Panetti v. Quarterman*, 127 S.Ct. 2842 (2007), the Court reaffirmed the principle that an incompetent defendant cannot be executed.

4. *Indefinite commitment.* In *Jackson v. Indiana*, 406 U.S. 715 (1972), a defendant was unable to understand the nature of the charges against him or to participate in his defense, and was ordered committed until he "is sane." Jackson's counsel claimed that the commitment amounted to a "life sentence" without conviction of a crime. The Court agreed noting that Jackson was subjected "to a more lenient commitment standard and to a more stringent standard of release" which condemned him "in effect to permanent institutionalization without the showing required for commitment or the opportunity for release." The Court found violations of equal protection and due process.

5. *Pleading insanity.* In order to invoke the sanity issue, defendant must plead the defense. Consider the Federal Rules of Criminal Procedure:

Rule 12.2. Notice of Insanity Defense or Expert Testimony of Defendant's Mental Condition

(a) **Defense of Insanity.** If a defendant intends to rely upon the defense of insanity at the time of the alleged offense, the defendant shall, within the time provided for the filing of pretrial motions or at such later time as the court may direct, notify the attorney for the government in writing of such intention and file a copy of such notice with the clerk. If there is a failure to comply with the requirements of this subdivision, insanity may not be raised as a defense. The court may for cause shown allow late filing of the notice or grant additional time to the parties to prepare for trial or make such other order as may be appropriate.

(b) **Expert Testimony of Defendant's Mental Condition.** If a defendant intends to introduce expert testimony relating to a mental disease or defect or any other mental condition of the defendant bearing upon the issue of guilt, the defendant shall, within the time provided for the filing of pretrial motions or at such later time as the court may direct, notify the attorney for the government in writing of such intention and file a copy of such notice with the clerk. The court may for cause shown allow late filing of the notice or grant additional time to the parties to prepare for trial or make such other order as may be appropriate.

(c) Mental Examination of Defendant. In an appropriate case the court may, upon motion of the attorney for the government, order the defendant to submit to an examination pursuant to 18 U.S.C. § 4241 or § 4242. No statement made by the defendant in the course of any examination provided for by this rule, whether the examination be with or without the consent of the defendant, no testimony by the expert based upon such statement, and no other fruits of the statement shall be admitted in evidence against the defendant in any criminal proceeding except on an issue respecting mental condition on which the defendant has introduced testimony.

(d) Failure To Comply. If there is a failure to give notice when required by subdivision (b) of this rule or to submit to an examination when ordered under subdivision (c) of this rule, the court may exclude the testimony of any expert witness offered by the defendant on the issue of the defendant's guilt.

In *United States v. Winn*, 577 F.2d 86 (9th Cir. 1978), a defendant failed to raise the insanity issue, and the court concluded that the trial court was not required to instruct the jury on that issue. "[T]he Government must bear the burden of proving sanity beyond a reasonable doubt." "Rule 12.2 is designed to insure that [the government has] ample opportunity to investigate the facts of an issue critical to the determination of guilt or innocence." *Compare Williams v. Florida*, 399 U.S. 78 (1970).

6. *Defendant's objection to defense.* In *State v. Jones*, 99 Wash.2d 735, 664 P.2d 1216 (En Banc 1983), the court held that an insanity plea could be imposed over the defendant's objection. However, in *Frendak v. United States*, 408 A.2d 364 (D.C.App. 1979), where the court also imposed an insanity plea over the defendant's objection, it was held that "the trial judge may not force an insanity defense on a defendant found competent to stand trial if the individual intelligently and voluntarily decides to forego that defense":

> [A] defendant may fear that an insanity acquittal [will] lead to confinement in a mental institution for a period longer than the potential jail sentence.... Second[,] [a] defendant may object to the quality of treatment or the type of confinement to which he [may] be subject in an institution for the mentally ill.... Third, a defendant [may] choose to avoid the stigma of insanity.... Fourth, [i]n some states, an adjudication of insanity may affect a person's legal rights, for example, the right to vote or serve on a federal jury, and may even restrict his or her ability to obtain a driver's license.... Finally, a defendant [may] oppose the imposition of an insanity defense because he or she views the crime as a political or religious protest which a finding of insanity would denigrate. In any event, a defendant [may] forego the defense because of a feeling that he or she is not insane, or that raising the defense would be equivalent to an admission of guilt. [T]hese reasons substantially outweigh the [goal of ensuring] that some abstract concept of justice is satisfied by protecting one who may be morally blameless from a conviction and punishment which he or she might choose to accept.

Because the defendant must bear [the] ultimate consequences of any decision, [if] a defendant has acted intelligently and voluntarily, a trial court must defer to his or her decision to waive the insanity defense.

The court held that "the trial court still must have the discretion to raise an insanity defense, sua sponte, when a defendant does not have the capacity to reject the defense." When a defendant refuses to plead insanity, and the judge interposes the defense against his wishes, a defendant is not automatically committed under federal law. *Lynch v. Overholser*, 369 U.S. 705 (1962).

7. *Can states abolish the insanity defense?* In the wake of the verdict in the John Hinckley case (he was accused of attempting to assassinate President Ronald Reagan, but was found not guilty by reason of insanity), some jurisdictions moved to abolish the insanity defense. *State v. Korell*, 213 Mont. 316, 690 P.2d 992 (1984), involved a Montana statute which abolished the not guilty by reason of insanity plea, but allowed evidence of mental illness or insanity to be admitted on the question whether defendant was fit to proceed to trial, whether defendant had the mens rea of the crime, and what sentence should be imposed. The court upheld the law and rejected arguments that abolition of the insanity defense violates the Eighth Amendment's prohibition of cruel and unusual punishment.

8. *Antipsychotic drugs.* In *Sell v. United States*, 539 U.S. 166 (2003), the Supreme Court held that the Constitution allows the government to administer antipsychotic drugs involuntarily to a mentally ill criminal defendant—in order to render that defendant competent to stand trial for serious, but nonviolent, crimes—in limited circumstances. Relying on its prior decisions in *Washington v. Harper*, 494 U.S. 210 (1990), and *Riggins v. Nevada*, 504 U.S. 127 (1992), the Court stated that:

> In *Harper,* this Court recognized that an individual has a "significant" constitutionally protected "liberty interest" in "avoiding the unwanted administration of antipsychotic drugs." [In] *Riggins,* the Court [suggested] that, in principle, forced medication in order to render a defendant competent to stand trial for murder was constitutionally permissible.... These two cases, *Harper* and *Riggins,* indicate that the Constitution permits the Government involuntarily to administer antipsychotic drugs to a mentally ill defendant facing serious criminal charges in order to render that defendant competent to stand trial, but only if the treatment is medically appropriate, is substantially unlikely to have side effects that may undermine the fairness of the trial, and, taking account of less intrusive alternatives, is necessary significantly to further important governmental trial-related interests.

This standard will permit involuntary administration of drugs solely for trial competence purposes in certain instances. But those instances may be rare. That is because the standard says or fairly implies the following: First, a court must find that *important* governmental interests are at stake. The Government's interest in bringing to trial an individual accused of a serious crime is important.... Second, the court must conclude that involuntary medication will *significantly further* those concomitant state interests. It must find that administration of the drugs is substantially likely to render the defendant competent to stand trial.... Third, the court must conclude that involuntary medication is *necessary* to further those interests.... Fourth, [the] court must conclude that administration of the drugs is *medically appropriate, i.e.,* in the patient's best medical interest in light of his medical condition ....

[In order to make this evaluation, the court should] focus upon such questions as: Why is it medically appropriate forcibly to administer antipsychotic drugs to an individual who (1) is *not* dangerous *and* (2) *is* competent to make up his own mind about treatment? Can bringing such an individual to trial *alone* justify in whole (or at least in significant part) administration of a drug that may have adverse side effects, including side effects that may to some extent impair a defense at trial? [Courts must also consider w]hether a particular drug will tend to sedate a defendant, interfere with communication with counsel, prevent rapid reaction to trial developments, or diminish the ability to express emotions are matters important in determining the permissibility of medication to restore competence, but not necessarily relevant when dangerousness is primarily at issue. We cannot tell whether the side effects of antipsychotic medication were likely to undermine the fairness of a trial in Sell's case.

9. *Mental illness and self-representation.* In *Indiana v. Edwards*, 128 S.Ct. 2379 (2008), the Supreme Court held that a State may deny the right of self-representation to a defendant "who is found mentally competent to stand trial if represented by counsel but not mentally competent to conduct that trial" *pro se* because the defendant still suffers from "severe mental illness." The Court reasoned that mental illness "is not a unitary concept" and that an individual may be "able to work with counsel at trial" but "unable to carry out the basic tasks needed to present his own defense without the help of counsel." The Court relied on an amicus brief from the American Psychiatric Association in support of this reasoning, and also emphasized that trial proceedings must "appear fair to all who observe them."

PROBLEMS

1. *Making Grapefruit Juice.* Rick squeezes Johnson's head until Johnson dies. At trial, the evidence shows that Rick was so mentally ill that he perceived that Johnson was a grapefruit rather than a person. In squeezing Johnson's head, Rick believed that he was creating grapefruit juice. Under *M'Naghten*, is Rick insane?

2. *Scope of F.R.Crim.Pro. Rule 12.2.* Consider Rule 12.2 in note 5, *supra*, in answering the following questions:

    a. Does Rule 12.2 cover only the insanity defense, or is it broader?

    b. Why does the defendant have the burden of notifying the prosecutor about the intent to rely on an insanity defense prior to trial? What is the nature of the required disclosure?

c. Do the notice of insanity rules present Fifth Amendment problems?

d. Does the defendant have a reciprocal right to discovery from the prosecution?

e. Is there any harm or advantage to the defendant of making the required disclosures under the rule?

3. *Bear Hunting.* Under the interpretation of *M'Naghten*, set forth in note 1, *supra*, suppose that Joan shoots her neighbor in New York City. At the time, Joan believed that it was bear season, that she was hunting bears, and that her neighbor was a bear. Under *M'Naghten*, can Joan be convicted of murder? Can Joan be convicted of hunting bears out of season or without a license?[1]

4. *"Legal Wrong" or "Moral Wrong"*? Nat is a patient at a state mental hospital who strangled his wife while he was out of the hospital on a one day pass. A clinical psychologist testified that Nat suffered from classical paranoid schizophrenia. A delusional product of this illness was his belief that the marriage vow "till death do us part" bestows on a marital partner a God-given right to kill the other partner who has violated or was inclined to violate the marital vows. Because the vows reflect the direct wishes of God, the killing is with complete moral and criminal impunity and is not wrongful because it is sanctified by the will and desire of God. Under the *M'Naghten* test, is Nat insane? In considering *M'Naghten*, and its requirement that a defendant must know that what he did was "wrong," is the court referring to "legal wrong" or "moral wrong?" Does the distinction matter in this case? How would you argue the insanity case for Nat? How might the State respond? *See People v. Skinner*, 39 Cal.3d 765, 217 Cal.Rptr. 685, 704 P.2d 752 (1985).

5. *God's Representative.* Ed entered a church with a shotgun and tried to kill a minister. At the time, Ed suffered from paranoid schizophrenia which caused him to hear voices and to be preoccupied with ideas that were quite real for him. Ed had a feeling of being God or a representative of God, who was present at the Last Supper, who had at various times been threatened or attacked by others who did not give him credit for his rightful position. At the time of the shooting, Ed felt that he was being "threatened" and he responded violently in order to protect himself. In fact, Ed believed that his actions were totally justified. He "sensed" that other persons were in his body displacing him. Ed found the situation intolerable and felt that he had to defend himself from what he described as "salvation level attacks." In shooting the minister, Ed believed that he rightfully deserved money and respect from the church which he was not getting. Therefore, Ed needed to eliminate this "sermon giver" (the minister) so that he could arrange for another who would respond and give Ed the money to which he was entitled. Was Ed insane under the *M'Naghten* test? How would you argue the

---

1. The authors are indebted to Professor Edward Hunvald for this hypothetical.

case for the Ed? How might the state respond? *See State v. Boan*, 235 Kan. 800, 686 P.2d 160 (1984).

6. *Satan's Agent.* Gil stabbed his stepmother in excess of 70 times, leaving the knife sticking in her heart. The body was left in the bathtub with no apparent attempt to conceal it. Later that day a police officer saw Gil downtown wearing only a pair of women's stretch pants, a woman's house-coat, a shirt and no shoes. Gil suffered from paranoid schizophrenia. He understood that, as a mechanical thing, he was killing his stepmother and knew it was against the law. However, at the time, he was preoccupied with the delusional belief that his stepmother was an agent of satan who was persecuting him, as were others like Yasser Arafat and the Ayatollah Khomeini. He believed he was directed by God to kill satan's angel and that he was obeying God's higher directive or law. Gil believed himself to be a messiah and compared himself with Jesus Christ. Gil felt God had directed him to send his stepmother from this life to another. He had no remorse over the killing, felt that it was justified by God, and believed that he was merely doing a service. "He felt he would generally be protected from any difficulties ... because 'God would not allow it to happen'." Was Gil insane under *M'Naghten? See State v. Cameron*, 100 Wash.2d 520, 674 P.2d 650 (En Banc 1983).

7. *Oustographs.* Don first received psychiatric treatment at age seven after being suspended from school for "viciously beating" other children. At age sixteen, he refused to go to school, and stayed in bed all day and out all night. He refused to bathe. When spoken to, he would not respond or would laugh hysterically. Don carried a bag around with him that he said "kept him company." He complained that the television talked back at him. At first Don insisted there was nothing wrong with him, but he eventually agreed to psychiatric treatment. During this period he was heavily medicated and "was like a zombie." Because the medication made Don drowsy, he stopped taking the medicine and refused to visit the out-patient clinic. As an adult, Don went to an FBI office and told the agent that people were sending messages to his brain "directing" him. Don said that there was a machine called an "oustograph" that could detect these matters. The FBI agent thought the defendant "had mental problems," and urged him to go to a psychiatric hospital for help. Later, Don was charged with murdering a police officer. At the time of his arrest, officers found a note that contained a meaningless string of words and phrases, including reference to an "oustograph." Don was "agitated" and "mumbled" continually to himself. A court psychiatrist diagnosed him as paranoid schizophrenia, a condition characterized by irrational thinking, inappropriate feelings, an overly suspicious nature, hostility, and delusions of grandeur and of persecution. He was prone to delusions that included persecution and grandeur, and suffered from auditory hallucinations. When arrested, Don spoke only in "gibberish" and claimed that he was speaking "Chinese" (a Chinese-speaking staff member disagreed). Gradually, under medication, Don's gibberish gave way to coherence and there was a lessening of inappropriate laughter and his tendency to talk

to the ceiling. Does the evidence establish insanity under M'Naghten? *See State v. Green*, 643 S.W.2d 902 (Tenn.Crim.App. 1982).

8. *Religious Beliefs and Murder.* While Ted and his wife were honeymooning in Canada, Ted was deported to the U.S. following a brawl. When his wife arrived 2 days later, he immediately "felt" that she had been unfaithful. Ted took his wife to a motel, beat her unconscious, and inflicted fatal stab wounds. Ted then tried to conceal his actions by placing the body in a blanket. He then borrowed a bucket and sponge, and cleaned the room of blood and fingerprints. Before leaving, Ted chatted with the motel manager over a beer. He left the motel and drove to a remote area 25 miles away where he hid the body. When he drove 200 miles farther away, he picked up two hitchhikers, told them of his crime, and enlisted their aid in disposing of his wife's car in a river. Although he confessed to murder, he claimed that he followed the Moscovite religious faith, and that a Moscovite is required to kill his wife if she commits adultery. Ted had a history of mental problems, for which he had been hospitalized in the past. Was Ted insane under *M'Naghten*? What relevance do you attach to the fact that Ted cleaned the room and concealed the body parts? *See State v. Crenshaw*, 98 Wash.2d 789, 659 P.2d 488 (En Banc 1983).

9. *Evil Spirits.* Near midnight, Lee sat in the kitchen reading his Bible. Later, he went to the bedroom where his wife was sleeping and stabbed her in the back just below the shoulder blade. When his wife awoke, Lee told her that she had been stabbed by an intruder. Lee told the police that he had gone to a grocery store, and that he returned to hear the front door slam. He claimed that he found his wife bleeding from a wound in her back. Several weeks later, Lee's wife found letters which stated that "[o]ur marriage was severed when I put the knife in your back," and that "I have gone to be with Jehovah in heaven for three and one-half days." Lee's wife confronted him by telephone, and he stated that God told him to stab her in order to sever the marriage bond. Lee was charged with attempted premeditated murder. At trial, a psychiatrist (Dr. Seig) stated that Lee had a plan, inspired by his relationship to God, to establish a multi-million dollar sports complex. This facility would enable him achieve his goal of teaching people the path to perfection. On the night of the stabbing, Lee was discouraged by inner "evil spirits" who questioned his wife's lack of encouragement and support. Dr. Seig diagnosed Lee as suffering either from an organic delusional disorder or paranoid schizophrenia. Either diagnosis would account for Lee's delusional belief that he had a privileged relationship and communication with God. Dr. Seig found that Lee was operating under this delusional system when he stabbed his wife, that these delusions caused him to believe that his act was morally justified, but that he was aware that the act of stabbing was contrary to law. Dr. Miller testified that Lee suffered from a psychotic delusion that it was his divine mission to kill his wife and that he was morally justified in stabbing her because God had told him to do so. Dr. Miller testified that Lee's mental illness made it impossible for him to distinguish right from wrong even though Lee was aware that such conduct

was legally wrong. Dr. Kaplan testified that Lee was suffering from paranoid schizophrenia and was laboring under the paranoid delusion that his wife stood in the way of his divine mission of completing the large sports complex, that Lee believed that the stabbing was the right thing to do, and that Lee, as a result of his mental illness, was unable to distinguish right from wrong with respect to the stabbing. Two other psychiatrists, Dr. Heron and Dr. Sundell, offered the opinion that Lee was suffering from paranoid schizophrenia and a paranoid delusion about God which so affected his cognitive ability as to render him incapable of distinguishing right from wrong as normal people would be able to do in accordance with societal standards of morality. Was Lee insane under *M'Naghten*? *See People v. Serravo*, 823 P.2d 128 (Colo. En Banc 1992).

10. *Sleep Deprivation*. In February, 2007, NASA Astronaut Lisa Marie Nowak was charged with attempted murder for her attack on another woman, an Air Force captain and love rival. The prosecution alleged that Nowak drove 900 miles from Houston to Florida, and that she carried a wig to disguise her appearance, a steel mallet, a knife, pepper spray, 4 feet of rubber tubing, latex gloves and garbage bags with her. The prosecution also alleged that she wore a diaper during her drive so that she would not have to take rest breaks. News reports suggested that Nowak was under a great deal of stress while attempting to manage her career, her marriage, and her children, and may have suffered from severe sleep deprivation. However, she had succeeded well enough to participate in a space mission. Was Nowak "insane" under *M'Naghten*?

11. *Suicide and Insanity*. A love-sick driver, Maria, is absolutely distraught over the fact that the objection of her affections spurned her sexual advances. As a result, Maria decides to commit suicide by crashing her vehicle into another vehicle. The driver does a "countdown" to the crash in text messages sent to the girl who spurned her affections. In the crash, Maria crosses the center line and runs head-on into an oncoming vehicle. The driver of the other vehicle is killed and a young girl is seriously injured. Maria survives and is prosecuted on homicide charges. Was Maria "insane" under *M'Naghten*?

b. OTHER TESTS

Because of dissatisfaction with the *M'Naghten* and irresistible impulse tests, the courts and the Model Penal Code drafters developed alternative tests.

UNITED STATES v. FREEMAN
357 F.2d 606 (2d Cir. 1966).

Kaufman, Circuit Judge:

[Charles Freeman was found guilty on two counts of selling narcotics. Freeman's defense was that, at the time of the alleged sale of narcotics, he did not possess sufficient capacity and will to be held responsible for the criminality of his acts. In rejecting this contention, the District Court relied upon the *M'Naghten* rules.]

[We] are now concerned with whether the Court [should] have applied a test less rigid [than] *M'Naghten*, so that the essential examination and psychiatric testimony could have been directed towards Freeman's capacity to exercise free will or appreciate the wrongfulness of his conduct, rather than being confined to the relatively narrow inquiry required by *M'Naghten*. . . .

M'Naghten and its antecedents can [be] seen as examples of the law's conscientious efforts to place in a separate category, people who cannot be justly held "responsible" for their acts. . . . By modern scientific standards the language of these early tests is primitive. In the 18th Century, psychiatry had hardly become a profession, let alone a science. Thus, these tests and their progeny were evolved at a time when psychiatry was literally in the Dark Ages.

In the pre-*M'Naghten* period, the concepts of phrenology and monomania were being developed and had significant influence on the right and wrong test. Phrenologists believed that the human brain was divided into thirty-five separate areas, each with its own peculiar mental function. The sixth area, for example, was designated "destructiveness." It was located, we are told, above the ear because this was the widest part of the skull of carnivorous animals. Monomania, on the other hand, was a state of mind in which one insane idea predominated while the rest of the thinking processes remained normal.

Of course, both phrenology and monomania are rejected today as meaningless medical concepts since the human personality is viewed as a fully integrated system. But, by an accident of history, the rule of *M'Naghten's* case froze these concepts into the common law just at a time when they were becoming obsolete. . . . M'Naghten's exculpation from criminal responsibility was most significant for several reasons. His defense counsel had relied in part upon Dr. Isaac Ray's historic work, MEDICAL JURISPRUDENCE OF INSANITY which had been published in 1838. This book [contained] many enlightened views on the subject of criminal responsibility in general and on the weaknesses of the right and wrong test in particular. Thus, for example, the jury was told that the human mind is not compartmentalized and that a defect in one aspect of the personality could spill over and affect other areas. As Chief Judge Biggs tells us in his Isaac Ray lectures compiled in THE GUILTY MIND, the court was so impressed with this and other medical evidence of M'Naghten's incompetency that Lord Chief Justice Tindal practically directed a verdict for the accused.

For these reasons, *M'Naghten's* case could have been the turning point for a new approach to more modern methods of determining criminal responsibility. But the Queen's ire was raised by the acquittal and she was prompted to intervene. Mid–19th Century England was in a state of social upheaval and there had been three attempts on the life of the Queen and one on the Prince Consort.... Queen Victoria was so concerned about M'Naghten's acquittal that she summoned the House of Lords to "take the opinion of the Judges on the law governing such cases." Consequently, the fifteen judges of the common law courts were called [into] extraordinary session under a not too subtle atmosphere of pressure to answer five prolix and obtuse questions on the status of criminal responsibility in England. Significantly, it was Lord Chief Justice Tindal who responded for fourteen of the fifteen judges, and thus articulated what has come to be known as the *M'Naghten* Rules or *M'Naghten* test. Rather than relying on Dr. Ray's monumental work which [had] impressed him at M'Naghten's trial, Tindal, with the Queen's breath upon him, reaffirmed [the] right-wrong test despite its 16th Century roots and the fact that [it] echoed such uninformed concepts as phrenology and monomania.... Dr. Ray's insights were [lost] to the common law for over one hundred years except in the small state of New Hampshire.

[T]he principal objection to *M'Naghten* is [that] it has several serious deficiencies which stem [from] its narrow scope. ... [W]e are told by eminent medical scholars that it does not permit the jury to identify those who can distinguish between good and evil but who cannot control their behavior. The result is that instead of being treated at appropriate mental institutions for a sufficiently long period to bring about a cure or sufficient improvement so that the accused may return with relative safety to himself and the community, he is ordinarily sentenced to a prison term as if criminally responsible and then released as a potential recidivist with society at his mercy. To the extent that these individuals continue to be released from prison because of the narrow scope of *M'Naghten*, that test poses a serious danger to society's welfare.

Similarly, [the] *M'Naghten's* test recognizes no degrees of incapacity. Either the defendant knows right from wrong or he does not and that is the only choice the jury is given. But such a test is grossly unrealistic; our mental institutions, as any qualified psychiatrist will attest, are filled with people who to some extent can differentiate between right and wrong, but lack the capacity to control their acts to a substantial degree....

A further fatal defect of the *M'Naghten* Rules stems from the unrealistically tight shackles which they place upon expert psychiatric testimony. When the law limits a testifying psychiatrist to stating his opinion whether the accused is capable of knowing right from wrong, the expert is thereby compelled to test guilt or innocence by a concept which bears little relationship to reality. He is required thus to consider one aspect of the mind as a "logic-tight compartment in

which the delusion holds sway leaving the balance of the mind intact."
. . .

The true vice of *M'Naghten* is [that] the ultimate deciders—the judge or the jury—will be deprived of information vital to their final judgment. [A] test which depends vitally on notions already discredited when *M'Naghten* was adopted can no longer be blandly accepted as representing the "moral sense of the community." To continue to apply such medically discarded concepts would be to follow a negative approach which is the result of a holdover of long outmoded attitudes rather than a policy decision grounded in reason or science.

Efforts to supplement or replace the *M'Naghten* Rules with a more meaningful and workable test have persisted for generations, with varying degrees of success. Perhaps the first to receive judicial approval, however, was more an added fillip to *M'Naghten* than a true substitute: the doctrine which permits acquittal on grounds of lack of responsibility when a defendant is found to have been driven by an "irresistible impulse" to commit his offense. . . . [W]e find the "irresistible impulse" test to be inherently inadequate and unsatisfactory. Psychiatrists have long questioned whether "irresistible impulses" actually exist; the more basic legal objection to the term "irresistible impulse" is that it is too narrow and carries the misleading implication that a crime impulsively committed must have been perpetrated in a sudden and explosive fit. Thus, the "irresistible impulse" test is unduly restrictive because it excludes the far more numerous instances of crimes committed after excessive brooding and melancholy by one who is unable to resist sustained psychic compulsion or to make any real attempt to control his conduct. In seeking one isolated and indefinite cause for every act, moreover, the test is unhappily evocative of the notions which underlay *M'Naghten*—unfortunate assumptions that the problem can be viewed in black and white absolutes and in crystal-clear causative terms. . . .

With the exception of New Hampshire, American courts waited until 1954 and Judge Bazelon's opinion for the District of Columbia Circuit in *Durham v. United States*,[48] for legal recognition that disease or defect of the mind may impair the whole mind and not a subdivided portion of it. The *Durham* court swept away the intellectual debris of a century and articulated a test which was as simple in its formulation as its sources were complex. A defendant is not criminally responsible, wrote Judge Bazelon, "if his unlawful act was the product of mental disease or mental defect."

[But] many students of the law recognized that the "product" test new rule, despite its many advantages, also possessed serious deficiencies. . . . The most significant criticism of *Durham*, however, is that it fails to give the fact-finder any standard by which to measure the

---

48. 94 U.S.App.D.C. 228, 214 F.2d 862 (1954).

competency of the accused. As a result, psychiatrists when testifying that a defendant suffered from a "mental disease or defect" in effect usurped the jury's function. This problem was strikingly illustrated in 1957, when a staff conference at Washington's St. Elizabeth's Hospital reversed its previous determination and reclassified "psychopathic personality" as a "mental disease." Because this single hospital provides most of the psychiatric witnesses in the District of Columbia courts, juries were abruptly informed that certain defendants who had previously been considered responsible were now to be acquitted. It seems clear that a test which permits all to stand or fall upon the labels or classifications employed by testifying psychiatrists hardly affords the court [or jury] the opportunity to perform its function of rendering an independent legal and social judgment.[51]

In 1953, a year before *Durham*, the American Law Institute commenced an exhaustive study of criminal conduct including the problem of criminal responsibility.... Gradually and painstakingly a new definition of criminal responsibility began taking shape as Section 4.01 of the Model Penal Code was evolved.... Section 4.01 provides that "A person is not responsible for criminal conduct if at the time of such conduct as a result of mental disease or defect he lacks substantial capacity either to appreciate the wrongfulness of his conduct or to conform his conduct to the requirements of law."[52]

[W]e believe this test to be the soundest yet formulated and we accordingly adopt it as the standard of criminal responsibility in the Courts of this Circuit.... The Model Penal Code formulation views the mind as a unified entity and recognizes that mental disease or defect may impair its functioning in numerous ways. The rule, moreover, reflects awareness that from the perspective of psychiatry absolutes are ephemeral and gradations are inevitable. By employing the telling word "substantial" to modify "incapacity," the rule emphasizes that "any" incapacity is not sufficient to justify avoidance of criminal responsibility but that "total" incapacity is also unnecessary. The choice of the word "appreciate," rather than "know" in the first branch of the test also is significant; mere intellectual awareness that conduct is wrongful, when divorced from appreciation or understanding of the moral or legal import of behavior, can have little significance. ...

---

51. To correct many of the deficiencies of *Durham*, the Washington, D.C. Court of Appeals amplified its definition of mental disorder for the purpose of making "it very clear that neither the court nor the jury is bound by ad hoc definitions or conclusions as to what experts state is a disease or defect." To reinforce its decision, the Court redefined mental disease and defect to include "any abnormal condition of the mind which substantially affects mental or emotional processes and substantially impairs behavior controls." *McDonald v. United States*, 114 U.S.App. D.C. 120, 312 F.2d 847, 851 (1962). It thus adopted a formulation which closely approximates the recommendation of the American Law Institute in its Model Penal Code.

52. American Law Institute, Model Penal Code (final draft) (1962). We have adopted the word "wrongfulness" in Section 4.01 as the American Law Institute's suggested alternative to "criminality" because we wish to include the case where the perpetrator appreciates that his conduct is criminal, but, because of a delusion, believes it to be morally justified.

[We believe that] the American Law Institute test—which makes no pretension at being the ultimate in faultless definition—is an infinite improvement over the *M'Naghten* Rules, even when, as had been the practice in the courts of this Circuit, those Rules are supplemented by the "irresistible impulse" doctrine. All legal definitions involve elements of abstraction and approximation which are difficult to apply in marginal cases. The impossibility of guaranteeing that a new rule will always be infallible cannot justify continued adherence to an outmoded standard, sorely at variance with enlightened medical and legal scholarship. . . .

Since Freeman's responsibility was determined under the rigid standards of the *M'Naghten* Rules, we are compelled to reverse his conviction and remand the case for a new trial in which the criteria employed will be those provided by Section 4.01 of the Model Penal Code. . . .

[Reversed and remanded].

Notes

1.   *Refusal to be evaluated by state psychiatrists.* In *State v. Richardson*, 276 Or. 325, 555 P.2d 202 (In Banc 1976), the court held that "when a defendant pleads not guilty by reason of insanity the state is entitled to a mental examination," and the privilege against self-incrimination does not protect a defendant against that examination: "if he [refuses], his affirmative defense of mental defect will be stricken." However, in *Motes v. State*, 256 Ga. 831, 353 S.E.2d 348 (1987), the court held that defendant was not required to submit to an examination if he proceeds without an expert: "If the defendant wants to introduce expert testimony, then the state must be allowed the same privilege and the defendant must cooperate. . . ."

2.   *Effect of an insanity acquittal.* A majority of the states preclude the jury from receiving information about the effect of the NGI verdict. *See Erdman v. State*, 315 Md. 46, 553 A.2d 244, 249–50 (1989). In *Shannon v. United States*, 512 U.S. 573 (1994), the Supreme Court held that a federal district court is not required to inform the jury of the consequences of rendering a "not guilty by reason of insanity" (NGI) verdict:

> [The] principle that juries are not to consider the consequences of their verdicts is a reflection of the basic division of labor in our legal system between judge and jury. The jury's function is to find the facts and to decide whether, on those facts, the defendant is guilty of the crime charged. The judge, by contrast, imposes sentence on the defendant after the jury has arrived at a guilty verdict. Information regarding the consequences of a verdict is therefore irrelevant to the jury's task. Moreover, providing jurors sentencing information invites them to ponder matters that are not within their province, distracts them from their factfinding responsibilities, and creates a strong possibility of confusion. [A]n instruction of some form may be necessary under certain

limited circumstances. If, for example, a witness or prosecutor states in the presence of the jury that a particular defendant would 'go free' if found NGI, it may be necessary for the district court to intervene with an instruction to counter such a misstatement . . . ."

In *Cordova v. People*, 817 P.2d 66 (Colo. En Banc 1991), the trial court overruled defendant's request for an informational instruction advising the jury of the consequences of a NGI verdict (that defendant would be committed). The court reversed: "In light of the manifest risk [of] the jury's mistaken belief that a verdict of not guilty by reason of impaired mental condition might result in the defendant's return to the community—a risk which the defendant's requested instruction was calculated to negate—[the] fairness of the trial [was] detrimentally affected by the trial court's erroneous ruling on the defendant's request for the informational instruction." *See also State v. Shickles*, 760 P.2d 291 (Utah 1988); *State v. Hamann*, 285 N.W.2d 180 (Iowa 1979).

3. *Right to a court-appointed psychiatrist.* In *Ake v. Oklahoma*, 470 U.S. 68 (1985), the Court held that: "when a defendant has made a preliminary showing that his sanity at the time of the offense is likely to be a significant factor at trial, the Constitution requires that a State provide access to a psychiatrist's assistance on this issue if the defendant cannot otherwise afford one." As the Court noted: "[W]ithout the assistance of a psychiatrist to conduct a professional examination on issues relevant to the defense, to help determine whether the insanity defense is viable, to present testimony, and to assist in preparing the cross-examination of a State's psychiatric witnesses, the risk of an inaccurate resolution of sanity issues is extremely high. With such assistance, the defendant is fairly able to present at least enough information to the jury, in a meaningful manner, as to permit it to make a sensible determination." Most requests for psychiatric assistance turn on whether defendant has made "a preliminary showing that his sanity at the time of the offense [was] likely to be a significant factor at trial." *See State v. Gambrell*, 318 N.C. 249, 347 S.E.2d 390 (1986). Even when the state must pay for a psychiatrist, "the Constitution does not give an indigent defendant the right to choose his own psychiatrist or even to receive funds to hire a private psychiatric expert. [The] appointment of State-employed psychiatrists may fulfill the state's constitutional obligation. Their employment by the state, we are satisfied, creates no conflict of interest which would disable them from fulfilling the constitutional requirements." *Id.*

4. *Burden of proof.* As noted in *Clark*, it is constitutionally permissible for the state to treat insanity as an affirmative defense and to saddle defendant with the burden of proof of "beyond a reasonable doubt." *See Leland v. Oregon*, 343 U.S. 790, *rehearing denied*, 344 U.S. 848 (1952). Even so, the state has the obligation to prove all elements of the criminal offense beyond a reasonable doubt including showing that defendant was capable of forming, and did in fact form, the required mens rea. *See Rivera v. Delaware*, 429 U.S. 877 (1976).

5. *Forcible medication.* In *In re Pray*, 133 Vt. 253, 336 A.2d 174 (1975), the defendant, while in state custody for trial purposes, was given thorazine four times a day, and tofranil and phenobarbital twice a day, and an occasional dosage of chlorohydrate. Without the medicine, he was not competent to stand trial. With the medicine, he was quiet, tractable, rational, well oriented, answered questions clearly, cooperative, and knew what was going on. He showed no effects of the depression on which his insanity defense was based. The Supreme Court reversed the conviction:

> At the very least, [the jury] should have been informed that he was under heavy, sedative medication, that his behavior in their presence was strongly conditioned by drugs administered to him at the direction of the State, and that his defense of insanity was to be applied to a basic behavior pattern that was not the one they were observing. In fact, it may well have been necessary, in view of the critical nature of the issue, to expose the jury to the undrugged, unsedated Gary Pray[,] insofar as safety and trial progress might permit. A life sentence ought not to rest on the shaky premise that an undisclosed behavioral alteration, brought about by the State, did not affect the jury's resolution of the issue of insanity. The matter must be retried.

6. *Bifurcation.* In some states, the insanity issue is bifurcated from guilt issues. In *Vardas v. Estelle*, 715 F.2d 206 (5th Cir. 1983), the defendant claimed that his due process rights were violated by the established Texas procedure allowing the issue of sanity to be tried contemporaneously with the issue of guilt or innocence. He claimed that he should have been granted a separate trial on the issue of insanity. The court rejected the argument. In *United States v. Bennett*, 460 F.2d 872, 148 U.S.App.D.C. 364 (D.C.Cir. 1972), defendant argued that:

> his entire defense was prejudiced by the intermingling at trial of his insanity defense and his defense on the merits. The prejudice, he asserts, was of two types. First, he argues that the introduction of evidence on the merits prejudiced his insanity defense because the jury was exposed to the 'unpleasant details' of the 'shocking sexual assault on a 13-year-old boy.' Second, his defense [was] prejudiced by the introduction of evidence, ostensibly relevant only to the issue of sanity, which was tantamount to a confession of guilt by appellant. The evidence [was] to the effect that Bennett's sanity was evidenced by his 'very good recollection of the events of the alleged events. He recalls minutely what happened prior to the offense, of the alleged offense, and following it. He expressed his own version of the story, his feeling about it....'

Although the court held that: "Bifurcation lies in the first instance within the 'sound discretion' of the trial court", it concluded that bifurcation is required when necessary to avoid prejudice.

7. *Diminished capacity distinguished.* In addition to the insanity defense, a defendant might also raise a "diminished capacity" defense. This defense addresses the question whether defendant had the capacity to form the mens

rea of the crime. In *United States v. Brawner*, 471 F.2d 969, 153 U.S.App.D.C. 1 (D.C.Cir. 1972) (En Banc), the court summarized this defense: "Expert testimony as to a defendant's abnormal mental condition may be received and considered, as tending to show [that] defendant did not have the specific mental state required for a particular crime or degree of crime—even though he was aware that his act was wrongful and was able to control it, and hence was not entitled to complete exoneration. . . ." The *Clark* court upheld Arizona's decision to bar the use of insanity evidence for a mens rea defense.

8. *The "guilty but mentally ill" verdict.* When John Hinckley attempted to assassinate President Ronald Reagan in Washington, D.C., he was acquitted on the grounds of insanity. *See United States v. Hinckley*, 525 F.Supp. 1342 (D.D.C. 1981), *aff'd*, 672 F.2d 115 (D.C.Cir. 1982). The verdict provoked a strong adverse public reaction and much legislative reform. A number of states made it more difficult to assert the insanity defense and others abolished the defense altogether. The verdict also enhanced the popularity of the so-called "guilty but mentally ill" verdict. Essentially, under this approach, a defendant is convicted of the crime but declared to be mentally ill. In theory, this verdict requires the state to determine whether psychiatric treatment is necessary or warranted. At the end of the criminal sentence, defendant must be released—unless the state is able to satisfy the standards for commitment.

9. *Psychiatric witnesses.* In *Jones v. State*, 289 So.2d 725 (Fla. 1974), a defendant offered the testimony of two psychiatrists and a psychologist based on a patient history of the defendant as they described it. The State objected to their testimony on the basis that defendant had not testified as to his own history. The court concluded that a "qualified expert may testify to his opinion concerning the defendant's mental condition based either upon (1) personal examination of the defendant made by the witness, or (2) the testimony in the case, if he has been in court and heard it all. (3) He may also give his opinion upon hypothetical questions propounded by counsel." In addition, "it is not necessary that the expert state the detailed circumstances of the examination before giving his finding. The facts and symptoms which he observed, and on which he bases his opinion, may be brought out on cross-examination." "The court below should have allowed the psychiatrists to testify as to their opinions without relating what the defendant told concerning the alleged facts of the case."

10. *Lay witnesses.* In *United States v. Milne*, 487 F.2d 1232 (5th Cir. 1973), a defendant sought to offer the testimony of three lay witnesses who described their interactions with him, his heavy drug use and his bizarre behavior. All of the witnesses had known the defendant for a year or more and had seen him nearly every day. The court overruled the trial court's decision to exclude the evidence: "[T]he lay opinion of a witness who is sufficiently acquainted with the person involved and has observed his conduct is admissible as to the sanity of such individual." "Insanity is a variance from usual or normal conduct. For that reason a lay witness should be required to testify as to unusual, abnormal or bizarre conduct before being

permitted to express an opinion as to insanity. [T]he trial judge must exercise a sound discretion in concluding whether or not a particular witness is qualified."

11. *Retrial of Andrea Yates.* In 2006, the murder conviction of Andrea Yates was reversed on appeal. Yates is the woman who murdered her five children by drowning them in a bathtub. On July 26, 2006 at her retrial, Andrea Yates was acquitted based on her insanity defense. One juror expressed concern that Yates was suffering from psychosis. Under Texas law, she must be institutionalized until a court decides that she is no longer deemed to be a threat to herself or to others. She was sent to a prison-like maximum security facility.

PROBLEMS

1. *The ALI Test.* Reconsider the *M'Naghten* problems after the after the *Clark* opinion. Would those problems be decided the same way under the ALI test in the Model Penal Code?

2. *Proving Insanity.* How does an attorney go about proving that a client was insane at the time of the alleged offense? In other words, what types of evidence might be offered in support of an assertion of insanity?

3. *Multiple Personalities.* Tara was charged with kidnapping a baby. Tara suffered from multiple personality disorder resulting from childhood physical and sexual abuse and two rapes. At the time of the kidnapping, Tara wanted to convince a former boyfriend that she was pregnant with his child. She had photographs made which made her appear pregnant. Later, she abducted a baby from a hospital nursery. One of Tara's alter personalities, "Rina," perhaps with another alter personality, "Bridget," controlled Tara's conduct at the time of the kidnapping. Her host or dominant personality, "Gidget," did not consciously participate in the abduction. Psychiatric experts disagreed as to whether the alter personality in control at the time of the offense ("Rina") was "unable to appreciate the nature and quality or the wrongfulness of [defendant's] acts." The experts agreed that "[e]ach of the personalities taken alone knew, or was very capable of knowing, what she was doing and of making moral judgments." Under the circumstances, was defendant insane and not criminally responsible for the kidnapping? How would you argue the case for the defendant? How would you argue the case for the state? *See United States v. Denny–Shaffer*, 2 F.3d 999 (10th Cir. 1993). *See also State v. Wheaton*, 121 Wash.2d 347, 850 P.2d 507 (En Banc 1993).

4. *Pathological Gambling Disorder.* A jewelry store manager was indicted for stealing jewelry from his employer. Defendant contends that a compulsion to gamble rendered him unable to resist becoming a thief and stealing to support his habit. The American Psychiatric Association's Diagnostic and Statistical Manual of Mental Disorders ¶ 312.31 (3d Ed.1980) contains the following description of pathological gambling:

The essential features are a chronic and progressive failure to resist impulses to gamble and gambling behavior that compromises, disrupts, or damages personal, family, or vocational pursuits. The gambling preoccupation, urge, and activity increase during periods of stress.... As the gambling increases, the individual is usually forced to lie in order to obtain money and to continue gambling, but hides the extent of the gambling. There is no serious attempt to budget or save money. When borrowing resources are strained, antisocial behavior in order to obtain money for more gambling is likely. Any criminal behavior—*e.g.*, forgery, embezzlement, or fraud—is typically nonviolent. There is a conscious intent to return or repay the money.

Was defendant "insane" under the ALI test? How would defense counsel argue the case? How might the State respond? *See United States v. Runnells*, 985 F.2d 554 (4th Cir. 1993); *United States v. Gould*, 741 F.2d 45 (4th Cir. 1984); *United States v. Torniero*, 735 F.2d 725 (2d Cir. 1984); *United States v. Lewellyn*, 723 F.2d 615 (8th Cir. 1983).

5. *XYY Chromosomes.* Defendant Karl, who possessed an extra male (Y) chromosome, was charged with attempted murder. Studies have shown that males who possess this extra Y chromosome, referred to as "47 XYY individuals", exhibit aggressive behavior as a causal result of this chromosomal abnormality. However, not all XYY individuals are by nature involuntarily aggressive. Some identified XYY individuals have not exhibited such behavior. Given this evidence, is Karl insane under the *M'Naghten* or ALI tests? *See People v. Tanner*, 13 Cal.App.3d 596, 91 Cal.Rptr. 656 (1970).

6. *Post-Traumatic Stress Disorder.* At the time of a double homicide, defendant was having flashbacks and believed he was in a combat situation during the Vietnam War. Psychiatric evidence revealed that defendant was suffering a dissociative flashback episode related to his Vietnam experience. He perceived himself as searching for Viet Cong guerrillas or documents, rather than robbing a tavern. Is defendant insane under the *M'Naghten* or ALI tests? *See State v. Coogan*, 154 Wis.2d 387, 391–92, 453 N.W.2d 186, 187 (Ct.App. 1990).

7. *More PTSD.* Expert testimony revealed that Sue was suffering PTSD at the time of a homicide. A psychologist testified that children who grow up in war-torn or violent areas can suffer post-traumatic stress disorder. Sue offered seventeen examples of violent events during her childhood that allegedly "caused the onset of PTSD." These included proof of the following: that she saw a friend shoot his gun in a drug house and was terrified; a man pulled a gun on Sue and her mother, and Sue stepped into the path of the gun; gang members shot at a friend while in Sue's presence; Sue was robbed; Sue's sister's boyfriend, a father-figure to Sue, was shot and paralyzed; Sue was robbed of her coat at gunpoint; Sue's cousin was killed in a drive-by shooting; Sue's uncle, a close friend, was shot and killed; Sue was robbed of jewelry at gunpoint; Sue was tied up and raped when she was fourteen years old; Sue's cousin was shot in a street fight and lost the use of her arm; Sue stepped in front of a man with a gun to protect her aunt; Sue was severely

beaten and robbed by a group of girls; Sue's mother shot a man, in front of Sue, because he was molesting Sue while giving her a bath; Sue was regularly beaten by her mother and father; her father shot at her mother "because there was too much salt in the gravy"; from age four to six, Sue saw her mother and father "regularly dine with loaded revolvers at their sides during family dinners to protect them from the violent outbursts of the other. Sue argues that she was unable to appreciate the wrongfulness of her conduct nor conform her conduct to the requirements of law. What will she have to show in order to prevail? What proof might be relevant to the claim?" *See State v. Morgan*, 195 Wis.2d 388, 536 N.W.2d 425 (1995).

8. *Traumatic Neurosis?* Paul was a married policeman with three sons and a daughter. He seemed to be a well-adjusted, happy, family man when his wife and infant daughter were brutally killed in an unprovoked attack by a drunken neighbor. Two years later, one day before Paul was to remarry, he robbed a bank. He was found to be suffering from a "traumatic neurosis" or "dissociative reaction", characterized by moods of depression and severe feelings of guilt, induced by the traumatic effect of the death of his wife and child and his belief that he was responsible for their deaths because he was not home. He had an unconscious desire to be punished by society to expiate his guilt feelings. The defense claimed that his mind was so destroyed or impaired that he was unable to resist the criminal acts. Paul was not psychotic, but he had been despondent, seemed to be lost in thought, and did not respond to questions directed to him. On one occasion, prior to the crime, Paul repeatedly beat the steering wheel of the police car while at the same time saying the name of his murdered wife. His's present wife testified that on two occasions he suddenly, and for no apparent reason, lapsed into crying spells and talked about committing suicide. During one such period, he pointed a gun at himself and the police took him to the station. After his release, he appeared jovial and acted as if nothing had happened. He expressed a desire to commit suicide because he now no longer had a reason for living. However, a police lieutenant testified that Paul's police work, as evidenced by his efficiency rating and his written duty reports, was, if anything, more effective than his service prior to the death of his wife. Was Paul "insane" under *M'Naghten* or the ALI test at the time of the robbery? *See United States v. Pollard*, 171 F.Supp. 474 (E.D.Mich. 1959).

9. *Murder by Burning.* Quinn was charged with the murder of his wife. The marriage was never happy, and he became increasingly violent. One day, Quinn went to a police station and told them he had burned his wife. He was very upset and agitated, pacing back and forth and sometimes refusing to answer questions. At one point he said, "Help her!" As they talked, the officers detected the smell of gasoline and noticed that Quinn's facial and neck hair was singed. He eventually told the officers that his wife was in a wildlife refuge, and was transported to the scene to help find the body. He shouted at the officers to hurry and to go faster, saying that his wife was hurt. The officers found the wife's badly burned body and a dented

gas can in the middle of a dirt road at the refuge. Medical testimony revealed that Quinn suffered from chronic and subchronic undifferentiated schizophrenia. However, the State's expert witnesses all testified that Quinn understood that he was burning his wife and that he knew it was wrong. Under the ALI test, was defendant insane? *See State v. Provost*, 490 N.W.2d 93 (Minn. 1992).

10. *Drug Addiction and Insanity.* Inga was indicted for knowingly and intentionally obtaining controlled narcotics by fraud. She claimed insanity on the basis that she was drug addicted and that the addiction deprived her of substantial capacity to conform her conduct to the requirements of the law. Defendant showed that she suffered from severe painful ailments, that various narcotics were prescribed for her pain, and that she became addicted to these drugs. She also offered expert testimony which showed that her drug addiction affected her brain both physiologically and psychologically. Was she insane under the ALI test if she knew that it was illegal to obtain drugs by fraud? *See United States v. Lyons*, 731 F.2d 243 (5th Cir. 1984).

11. *Battered Woman?* Sandy was charged with murdering her husband. During the marriage, Sandy had been subjected to physical abuse. After Sandy gave birth to a daughter, Ava, the husband became involved with another woman and moved to Florida. On one of his return trips, the husband went to Sandy's place of employment where he brandished a pocket knife and tried to choke her. Later, at her apartment, the husband pressed Sandy to move with him to Florida. She refused. He then took a weapon from his traveling bag and threatened to use it if she thwarted him. After he fell asleep on a couch in the living room, defendant took the gun intending to end her life. Deciding that suicide would be no solution, she returned to the living room to put the weapon back in the suitcase, but when her eyes fell upon her husband, she raised the weapon and fired until it was empty. Under the circumstances, can Sandy establish the defense of insanity under *M'Naghten* or the ALI test? Is there such a thing as "temporary insanity?" Did Sandy suffer from it? *See State v. Guido*, 40 N.J. 191, 191 A.2d 45 (1963). *See also State v. Myers*, 239 N.J.Super. 158, 570 A.2d 1260 (1990).

12. *Psychotic Episodes.* A stay-at-home mother, Nan, called 911 just after midnight and stated that "I've just killed my boys." She also stated that God ordered her to do it. When they arrived at the scene, police found a 6-year-old and 8-year-old boy in the front yard with their skulls smashed. They also found a 14-month-old baby, alive in his crib with a fractured skull. The evidence revealed that the mother had suffered from delusional psychotic disorder and had experienced three major psychotic episodes during the prior three years. Does the fact that Nan had the awareness to contact police after the killings suggest that she was not insane?

2. EFFECT OF AN INSANITY ACQUITTAL

What happens to a defendant who has been acquitted by reason of insanity? In some jurisdictions, the defendant is automatically committed to an mental hospital. In most jurisdictions, the decision to commit is discretionary. At the federal level, an acquittee may be held for up to 40 days. 18 U.S.C. § 4243. In *In re Rosenfield*, 157 F.Supp. 18 (D.D.C. 1957), defendant was found not guilty by reason of insanity and was committed to Saint Elizabeth's Hospital for the mentally ill under a statute requiring mandatory commitment of those acquitted on insanity grounds. Later, petitioner was conditionally released. The Court upheld the statute and the conditional release.

JONES v. UNITED STATES
463 U.S. 354 (1983).

JUSTICE POWELL delivered the opinion of the Court.

The question presented is whether petitioner, who was committed to a mental hospital upon being acquitted of a criminal offense by reason of insanity, must be released because he has been hospitalized for a period longer than he might have served in prison had he been convicted.

In the District of Columbia a criminal defendant [who] successfully invokes the insanity defense [is] committed to a mental hospital. The statute provides several ways of obtaining release. Within 50 days of commitment the acquittee is entitled to a judicial hearing to determine his eligibility for release, at which he has the burden of proving by a preponderance of the evidence that he is no longer mentally ill or dangerous. If he fails to meet this burden[,] the committed acquittee subsequently may be released, with court approval, upon certification of his recovery by the hospital chief of service. Alternatively, the acquittee is entitled to a judicial hearing every six months at which he may establish by a preponderance of the evidence that he is entitled to release.

Independent of its provision for the commitment of insanity acquittees, the District of Columbia also has adopted a civil-commitment procedure, under which an individual may be committed upon clear and convincing proof by the Government that he is mentally ill and likely to injure himself or others. The individual may demand a jury in the civil-commitment proceeding. Once committed, a patient may be released at any time upon certification of recovery by the hospital chief of service. Alternatively, the patient is entitled after the first 90 days, and subsequently at 6–month intervals, to request a judicial hearing at which he may gain his release by proving by a preponderance of the evidence that he is no longer mentally ill or dangerous. . . .

On September 19, 1975, petitioner was arrested for attempting to steal a jacket from a department store [and charged with] attempted petit larceny, a misdemeanor punishable by a maximum prison sentence of one year. The court ordered petitioner committed to St.

Elizabeth's, a public hospital for the mentally ill, for a determination of his competency to stand trial. On March 2, 1976, a hospital psychologist submitted a report to the court stating that petitioner was competent to stand trial, that petitioner suffered from "Schizophrenia, paranoid type," and that petitioner's alleged offense was "the product of his mental disease." [Petitioner subsequently pleaded] not guilty by reason of insanity. The Government did not contest the plea.... [The court] found petitioner not guilty by reason of insanity and committed him to St. Elizabeth's pursuant to § 24–301(d)(1).

On May 25, 1976, the court held the 50–day hearing required by § 24–301(d)(2)(A). A psychologist from St. Elizabeth's testified [that], in the opinion of the staff, petitioner continued to suffer from paranoid schizophrenia and that "because his illness is still quite active, he is still a danger to himself and to others." Petitioner's counsel [presented] no evidence. The court then found that "the defendant-patient is mentally ill and as a result of his mental illness, at this time, he constitutes a danger to himself or others." Petitioner was returned to St. Elizabeth's. Petitioner obtained new counsel and [a] second release hearing was held on February 22, 1977. By that date, petitioner had been hospitalized for more than one year, the maximum period he could have spent in prison if he had been convicted. On that basis, he demanded that he be released unconditionally or recommitted pursuant to the civil-commitment standards in § 21–545(b), including a jury trial and proof by clear and convincing evidence of his mental illness and dangerousness. The Superior Court denied petitioner's request for a civil-commitment hearing, reaffirmed the findings made at the May 25, 1976, hearing, and continued petitioner's commitment to St. Elizabeth's. [The District of Columbia Court of Appeals ultimately affirmed the judgment.] [We granted] certiorari and now affirm.

III

It is clear that "commitment for any purpose constitutes a significant deprivation of liberty that requires due process protection." Therefore, a State must have "a constitutionally adequate purpose for the confinement." Congress has determined that a criminal defendant found not guilty by reason of insanity in the District of Columbia should be committed indefinitely to a mental institution for treatment and the protection of society. Petitioner does not contest the Government's authority to commit a mentally ill and dangerous person indefinitely to a mental institution, but rather contends that "the petitioner's trial was not a constitutionally adequate hearing to justify an indefinite commitment."

Petitioner's argument rests principally on *Addington v. Texas*, [441 U.S. 418 (1979)], in which the Court held that the Due Process Clause requires the Government in a civil-commitment proceeding to demonstrate by clear and convincing evidence that the individual is mentally ill and dangerous. Petitioner contends that these due process standards were not met in his case because the judgment of not guilty by reason of insanity did not constitute a finding of present mental illness and dangerousness and because it was established only by a preponderance of the evidence. Petitioner then concludes that the Government's only conceivably legitimate justification for automatic commitment is to ensure that insanity acquittees do not escape confinement entirely, and that this interest can justify commitment at most for a period equal to the maximum prison sentence the acquittee could have received if convicted. Because petitioner has been hospitalized for longer than the one year he might have served in prison, he asserts that he should be released unconditionally or recommitted under the District's civil-commitment procedures.

We turn first to the question whether the finding of insanity at the criminal trial is sufficiently probative of mental illness and dangerousness to justify commitment. A verdict of not guilty by reason of insanity establishes two facts: (i) the defendant committed an act that constitutes a criminal offense, and (ii) he committed the act because of mental illness. Congress has determined that these findings constitute an adequate basis for hospitalizing the acquittee as a dangerous and mentally ill person. We cannot say that it was unreasonable and therefore unconstitutional for Congress to make this determination.

The fact that a person has been found, beyond a reasonable doubt, to have committed a criminal act certainly indicates dangerousness. Indeed, this concrete evidence generally may be at least as persuasive as any predictions about dangerousness that might be made in a civil-commitment proceeding. We do not agree with petitioner's suggestion that the requisite dangerousness is not established by proof that a person committed a non-violent crime against property. This Court never has held that "violence," however that term might be defined, is a prerequisite for a constitutional commitment.

Nor can we say that it was unreasonable for Congress to determine that the insanity acquittal supports an inference of continuing mental illness. It comports with common sense to conclude that someone whose mental illness was sufficient to lead him to commit a criminal act is likely to remain ill and in need of treatment. The precise evidentiary force of the insanity acquittal, of course, may vary from case to case, but the Due Process Clause does not require Congress to make classifications that fit every individual with the same degree of relevance. Because a hearing is provided within 50 days of the commitment, there is assurance that every acquittee has prompt opportunity to obtain release if he has recovered.

Petitioner also argues that, whatever the evidentiary value of the insanity acquittal, the Government lacks a legitimate reason for committing insanity acquittees automatically because it can introduce the insanity acquittal as evidence in a subsequent civil proceeding. This argument fails to consider the Government's strong interest in avoiding the need to conduct a *de novo* commitment hearing following every insanity acquittal—a hearing at which a jury trial may be demanded, and at which the Government bears the burden of proof by clear and convincing evidence. Instead of focusing on the critical question whether the acquittee has recovered, the new proceeding likely would have to relitigate much of the criminal trial. These problems accent the Government's important interest in automatic commitment. We therefore conclude that a finding of not guilty by reason of insanity is a sufficient foundation for commitment of an insanity acquittee for the purposes of treatment and the protection of society.

Petitioner next contends that his indefinite commitment is unconstitutional because the proof of his insanity was based only on a preponderance of the evidence, as compared to *Addington's* civil-commitment requirement of proof by clear and convincing evidence. In equating these situations, petitioner ignores important differences between the class of potential civil-commitment candidates and the class of insanity acquittees that justify differing standards of proof. The *Addington* Court expressed particular concern that members of the public could be confined on the basis of "some abnormal behavior which might be perceived by some as symptomatic of a mental or emotional disorder, but which is in fact within a range of conduct that is generally acceptable." In view of this concern, the Court deemed it inappropriate to ask the individual "to share equally with society the risk of error." But since automatic commitment under § 24–301(d)(1) follows only if the acquittee himself advances insanity as a defense and proves that his criminal act was a product of his mental illness, there is good reason for diminished concern as to the risk of error. More important, the proof that he committed a criminal act as a result of mental illness eliminates the risk that he is being committed for mere "idiosyncratic behavior." A criminal act by definition is not "within a range of conduct that is generally acceptable."

We therefore conclude that concerns critical to our decision in *Addington* are diminished or absent in the case of insanity acquittees. Accordingly, there is no reason for adopting the same standard of proof in both cases. "[D]ue process is flexible and calls for such procedural protections as the particular situation demands." The preponderance of the evidence standard comports with due process for commitment of insanity acquittees.[17]

The remaining question is whether petitioner nonetheless is entitled to his release because he has been hospitalized for a period

---

17. A defendant could be required to prove his insanity by a higher standard than a preponderance of the evidence....

longer than he could have been incarcerated if convicted. The Due Process Clause "requires that the nature and duration of commitment bear some reasonable relation to the purpose for which the individual is committed." The purpose of commitment following an insanity acquittal, like that of civil commitment, is to treat the individual's mental illness and protect him and society from his potential dangerousness. The committed acquittee is entitled to release when he has recovered his sanity or is no longer dangerous. And because it is impossible to predict how long it will take for any given individual to recover—or indeed whether he ever will recover—Congress has chosen, as it has with respect to civil commitment, to leave the length of commitment indeterminate, subject to periodic review of the patient's suitability for release.

In light of the congressional purposes underlying commitment of insanity acquittees, we think petitioner clearly errs in contending that an acquittee's hypothetical maximum sentence provides the constitutional limit for his commitment. A particular sentence of incarceration is chosen to reflect society's view of the proper response to commission of a particular criminal offense, based on a variety of considerations such as retribution, deterrence, and rehabilitation. The State may punish a person convicted of a crime even if satisfied that he is unlikely to commit further crimes.

Different considerations underlie commitment of an insanity acquittee. As he was not convicted, he may not be punished. His confinement rests on his continuing illness and dangerousness. Thus, under the District of Columbia statute, no matter how serious the act committed by the acquittee, he may be released within 50 days of his acquittal if he has recovered. In contrast, one who committed a less serious act may be confined for a longer period if he remains ill and dangerous. There simply is no necessary correlation between severity of the offense and length of time necessary for recovery. The length of the acquittee's hypothetical criminal sentence therefore is irrelevant to the purposes of his commitment.

We hold that when a criminal defendant establishes by a preponderance of the evidence that he is not guilty of a crime by reason of insanity, the Constitution permits the Government, on the basis of the insanity judgment, to confine him to a mental institution until such time as he has regained his sanity or is no longer a danger to himself or society. This holding accords with the widely and reasonably held view that insanity acquittees constitute a special class that should be treated differently from other candidates for commitment. We have observed before that "[w]hen Congress undertakes to act in areas fraught with medical and scientific uncertainties, legislative options must be especially broad and courts should be cautious not to rewrite [legislation]." This admonition has particular force in the context of legislative efforts to deal with the special problems raised by the insanity defense.

The judgment of the District of Columbia Court of Appeals is Affirmed.

JUSTICE BRENNAN, with whom JUSTICE MARSHALL and JUSTICE BLACKMUN join, dissenting.

[The] Government's interests in committing petitioner are [the] isolation, protection, and treatment of a person who may, through no fault of his own, cause harm to others or to himself. Whenever involuntary commitment is a possibility, the Government has a strong interest in accurate, efficient commitment decisions. Nevertheless, *Addington* held both that the Government's interest in accuracy was not impaired by a requirement that it bear the burden of persuasion by clear and convincing evidence, and that the individual's interests in liberty and autonomy required the Government to bear at least that burden. An acquittal by reason of insanity of a single, nonviolent misdemeanor is not a constitutionally adequate substitute for the due process protections [of] proof by clear and convincing evidence of present mental illness or dangerousness, with the Government bearing the burden of persuasion.... I cannot agree that the Government should be excused from the burden that *Addington* held was required by due process....

JUSTICE STEVENS, dissenting.

[A] plea of guilty, may provide a sufficient basis for confinement for the period fixed by the legislature as punishment for the acknowledged conduct, provided of course that the acquittee is given a fair opportunity to prove that he has recovered from his illness. But surely if he is to be confined for a longer period, the State must shoulder the burden of proving by clear and convincing evidence that such additional confinement is appropriate....

NOTES

1. *Civil commitment.* Prior to *Jones*, in order to civilly commit someone to a mental institution, the state was required to prove by clear and convincing evidence that he was presently mentally ill and dangerous to himself or to others. *See Addington v. Texas*, 441 U.S. 418 (1979). *Jones* suggests that such proof is not required when a defendant is found not guilty by reason of insanity. Was *Jones* correctly decided? Compare *State ex rel. Collins v. Superior Court*, 150 Ariz. 295, 723 P.2d 644 (1986).

2. *Post-prison commitment.* In *Baxstrom v. Herold*, 383 U.S. 107 (1966), when petitioner's prison term ended, he was committed to a hospital for the criminally ill. The Court held that petitioner had not been committed pursuant to proper procedures: "[P]etitioner was denied equal protection

[by] the statutory procedure under which a person may be civilly committed at the expiration of his penal sentence without the jury review available to all other persons civilly committed.... Petitioner was further denied equal protection [by] his civil commitment to an institution maintained by the Department of Correction beyond the expiration of his prison term without a judicial determination that he is dangerously mentally ill...."

3. *Medical treatment in mental hospital.* In *Rouse v. Cameron*, 373 F.2d 451 (D.C.Cir. 1966), defendant was acquitted on the grounds of insanity and confined to Saint Elizabeth's Hospital. When he received no psychiatric treatment, defendant sought habeas corpus. The court held that defendant was entitled to treatment, but not necessarily to release: "The purpose of involuntary hospitalization is treatment, not punishment. [C]ommitment rests upon [the] 'necessity for treatment of the mental condition which led to the acquittal by reason of insanity.' Absent treatment, the hospital is '[a] penitentiary where one could be held indefinitely for no convicted offense [even] though the offense of which he was previously acquitted [might] not have been [a serious felony] or might have been [a] misdemeanor.' " The court's holding was based on a statute which provided that a "person hospitalized [for] a mental illness shall [be] entitled to medical and psychiatric care and treatment." Interestingly, most insanity acquittees spend more time in mental hospitals than they would have spent in prison had they been convicted of the crime of which they were acquitted.

C. INFANCY AND INCAPACITY

Questions of mental capacity can also arise in contexts outside of insanity. For example, issues might arise regarding whether a child or a mentally retarded adult may be criminally liable, or may invoke a defense of incapacity.

IN RE DEVON T.
85 Md.App. 674, 584 A.2d 1287 (1991).

Moylan, Judge.

[The] juvenile appellant, Devon T., was charged with committing an act which, if committed by an adult, would have constituted the crime of possession of heroin with intent to distribute. [The trial court] found that Devon was delinquent. The heart of the case [was that] Devon was directed to empty his pockets by the security guard at the Booker T. Washington Middle School, under the watchful eye of the Assistant Principal, the search produced a brown bag containing twenty zip-lock pink plastic bags [which] contained heroin.... Devon [contends that] the State did not offer legally sufficient evidence to rebut his presumptive incapacity because of infancy.... At the time of the offense, Devon was 13 years, 10 months, and 2 weeks of age. He timely raised the infancy defense....

The case law and the academic literature alike conceptualize the infancy defense as but an instance of the broader phenomenon of a defense based upon lack of moral responsibility or capacity. The criminal law generally will only impose its retributive or deterrent sanctions upon those who are morally blameworthy—those who know they are doing wrong but nonetheless persist in their wrongdoing.

After several centuries of pondering the criminal capacity of children and experimenting with various cut-off ages, the Common Law settled upon its current resolution of the problem by late Tudor and early Stuart times. As explained by LaFave & Scott, *Criminal Law,* (2d ed. 1986), at 398, the resolution was fairly simple:

> At common law, children under the age of seven are conclusively presumed to be without criminal capacity, those who have reached the age of fourteen are treated as fully responsible, while as to those between the ages of seven and fourteen there is a rebuttable presumption of criminal incapacity.

The authors make clear that infancy was an instance of criminal capacity generally: "The early common law infancy defense was based upon an unwillingness to punish those thought to be incapable of forming criminal intent and not of an age where the threat of punishment could serve as a deterrent." [In] *Adams v. State,* 8 Md. App. 684, 262 A.2d 69 (1970), *cert. denied,* 400 U.S. 928 (1970) [, this court] recognized for the first time this venerable common law defense as part of the inherent law of Maryland. . . .

With the creation shortly after the turn of the present century of juvenile courts in America, diverting many youthful offenders from criminal courts into equity and other civil courts, the question arose as to whether the infancy defense had any pertinence to a juvenile delinquency adjudication. Under the initially prevailing philosophy that the State was acting in delinquency cases as *parens patriae* (sovereign parent of the country), the State was perceived to be not the retributive punisher of the child for its misdeeds but the paternalistic guardian of the child for its own best interests. Under such a regime, the moral responsibility or blameworthiness of the child was of no consequence. Morally responsible or not, the child was in apparent need of the State's rehabilitative intervention and the delinquency adjudication was but the avenue for such intervention. . . . This was the philosophy that persuaded this Court [in] *Matter of Davis* to forbear from extending the defense of infancy to juvenile court proceedings [as] inapposite. . . .

Over the course of the century, however, buffeted by unanticipated urban deterioration and staggering case loads, the reforming vision [faded]. Although continuing to stress rehabilitation over retribution more heavily than did the adult criminal courts, delinquency adjudications nonetheless took on, in practice if not in theory, many of the attributes of junior varsity criminal trials. The Supreme Court, in *In re Gault,* 387 U.S. 1 (1967), and *In re Winship,* 397 U.S. 358 (1970), acknowledged this slow but inexorable transformation of the juvenile court apparatus into one with increasingly penal overtones. It ultimately guaranteed, therefore, a juvenile charged with delinquency most of the due process protections afforded an adult charged with crime . . .

The infancy defense was not applied to all juvenile court proceedings but only to delinquency adjudications, where moral blameworthiness is an integral part of the wrongdoing. . . . With respect to other situations, where the conduct itself of the juvenile, irrespective of moral accountability, calls for some rehabilitative intervention on the part of the State, . . . the State may still file a petition alleging a Child in Need of Supervision (CINS) or a Child in Need of Assistance (CINA). . . .

In a juvenile delinquency adjudication, however, the defense of infancy is now indisputably available in precisely the same manner as it is available in a criminal trial. . . . The availability of such a defense raises several subsidiary questions. What precisely is the *probandum*—the quality of mind that has to be proved? To whom are allocated the burdens of proof (production and persuasion) with respect to that *probandum*? What are the standards or levels of proof necessary to carry those burdens?

With respect to the allocation of both burdens, the answer is clear. Once the question of criminal incapacity because of infancy is legitimately in the case, the unequivocal command of the due process clause is that the burdens of proof (assuming the proper generation of the issue) are allocated to the State. *In re Winship,* 397 U.S. 358, 364 (1970). It is equally clear, under *Winship,* that the State's constitutionally mandated standard of persuasion is that of beyond a reasonable doubt.

. . . Our attention [turns] to the two remaining questions: 1) what precisely is that quality of mind that constitutes criminal capacity in an infant? and 2) was the State's evidence in this case legally sufficient to satisfy its burden of production that the infant here possessed such mental capacity? . . . Here the issue of mental incapacity due to infancy was properly generated and before the court.

To overcome the presumption of incapacity, then, what precisely was that quality of Devon's mind as to which the State was required to produce legally sufficient evidence? It was required to produce evidence permitting the reasonable inference that Devon—the Ghost of *M'Naghten* speaks:—"at the time of doing the act knew the difference between right and wrong." . . .

When *Adams v. State* first incorporated the infancy defense into Maryland law, the opinion of Judge Morton made it very clear that the pivotal mental quality being examined was *M'Naghten*'s classic cognitive appreciation of the difference between right and wrong[.]

... In *In re William A.*, Judge Eldridge perceptively stressed that the critical mental faculty for rendering an infant morally responsible for his otherwise delinquent actions was that same cognitive or intellectual capacity that would enable an adult to entertain a criminal *mens rea*[.]

... In short, when Devon walked around the Booker T. Washington Middle School with twenty zip-lock bags of heroin, apparently for sale or other distribution, could Devon pass the *M'Naghten* test? Was there legally sufficient data before him to permit Judge Brown to infer that Devon knew the difference between right and wrong and knew, moreover, that what he was doing was wrong?

As we turn to the legal sufficiency of the evidence, it is important to know that the only mental quality we are probing is the cognitive capacity to distinguish right from wrong. Other aspects of Devon's mental and psychological make-up, such as his scholastic attainments, his I.Q., his social maturity, his societal adjustment, his basic personality, etc., might well require evidentiary input from psychologists, from parents, from teachers or other school authorities, etc. On knowledge of the difference between right and wrong, however, the general case law, as well as the inherent logic of the situation, has established that that particular psychic phenomenon may sometimes permissibly be inferred from the very circumstances of the criminal or delinquent act itself. Indeed, *Adams v. State* spoke of the fact that "the *surrounding circumstances must demonstrate* ... that the individual knew what he was doing and that it was wrong." (emphasis supplied). ...

The applicable common law on *doli incapax* with relation to the infancy defense establishes that on the day before their seventh birthday, no persons possess cognitive capacity. (0 per cent). It also establishes that on the day of their fourteenth birthday, all persons (at least as far as age is concerned) possess cognitive capacity. (100 per cent). On the time scale between the day of the seventh birthday and the day before the fourteenth birthday, the percentage of persons possessing such capacity steadily increases. The statistical probability is that on the day of the seventh birthday, at most a tiny fraction of one per cent will possess cognitive capacity. Conversely, on the day before the fourteenth birthday, only a tiny fraction of one per cent will lack such cognitive capacity. Assuming a steady rate of climb,[6] the mid-

---

6. The climb in cognitive capacity from the seventh birthday through the fourteenth birthday, of course, has not been charted with actuarial precision by the social sciences. The rise in maturity of the group as a whole may be a linear progression at a regular rate of climb. There may, however, be plateaus interrupting the upward progression. There might even be a parabolic curve, concentrating much of the statistical advance of the group as a whole into the last year or two rather than having it spread evenly across the course of the seven years. Whatever the configuration of the maturity chart, however, Devon had moved 98.2 per cent of the way, on the timeline of his life, from his seventh birthday to his fourteenth birthday.

point where fifty per cent of persons will lack cognitive capacity and fifty per cent will possess it would be at 10 years and 6 months of age. That is the scale on which we must place Devon.

We stress that the burden in that regard, notwithstanding the probabilities, was nonetheless on the State. The impact of the allocation of the burden of proof to the State is that the infant will enjoy the benefit of the doubt. The fact that the quantum of proof necessary to overcome presumptive incapacity diminishes in substantially the same ratio as the infant's age increases only serves to lessen the State's burden, not to eliminate it. The State's burden is still an affirmative one. It may not, therefore, passively rely upon the mere absence of evidence to the contrary.

We hold that the State successfully carried that burden. A minor factor, albeit of some weight, was that Devon was essentially at or near grade level in school. . . . That would tend to support his probable inclusion in the large majority of his age group rather than in a small and subnormal minority of it.

[The] juvenile master [was] in a position to observe first-hand Devon's receiving of legal advice from his lawyer, his acknowledgement of his understanding of it, and his acting upon it. His lawyer explained that he had a right to remain silent and that the master would not infer guilt from his exercise of that right. He acknowledged understanding that right. His lawyer also advised him of his right to testify but informed him that both the assistant state's attorney and the judge might question him about the delinquent act. Devon indicated that he wished to remain silent and say nothing. Although reduced to relatively simple language, the exchange with respect to the risk of self-incrimination and the privilege against self-incrimination forms a predicate from which an observer might infer some knowledge on Devon's part of the significance of incrimination. . . .

We turn, most significantly, to the circumstances of the criminal act itself. As we do so, we note the relevance of such circumstances to the issue at hand. R. Perkins & R. Boyce, *Criminal Law,* (3d ed. 1982), points out, at 938:

> The prosecution, in brief, cannot obtain the conviction of such a person without showing that he had such maturity in fact as to have a guilty knowledge that he was doing wrong. Conduct of the defendant such as concealing himself or the evidence of his misdeed may be such under all the circumstances as to authorize a finding of such maturity. . . .

Assuming a regular linear progression, [that] would mean that of all persons in Devon's particular age group, 98.2 per cent would be expected to possess cognitive capacity and 1.8 per cent would be expected to lack it. The State's burden, therefore, would not be to prove that Devon was precociously above average but only to satisfy the court that Devon fell within the upper 98.2 per cent of his age group and not within the subnormal 1.8 per cent of it. . . .

Just such a use of a secluded location or concealment was present in this case. The case broke when a grandmother, concerned enough to have had her own live-in grandson institutionalized, complained to the authorities at Booker T. Washington Middle School that several of her grandson's classmates were being truant on a regular basis and were using her home, while she was out working, as the "hide out" from which to sell drugs. Although the initial suspicion was directed toward Edward, it ultimately appeared that Edward and Devon were in the enterprise together. Children who are unaware that what they are doing is wrong have no need to hide out or to conceal their activities.

The most significant circumstance was the very nature of the criminal activity in which Devon engaged. It was not mere possession of heroin. It was possession of twenty packets of heroin with the intent to distribute.... There were no needle marks or other indications of personal use on Devon's body. Nothing ... gave any indication that this sixth grader, directly or indirectly, had the affluence to purchase drugs for himself in that amount. Indeed, [he] acknowledged that he had been selling drugs for two days when the current offense occurred. His motivation was "that he just wanted something to do."

The evidence [indicated] that Devon and Edward and several other students had been regularly using the absent grandmother's home as a base from which to sell drugs.... Devon and his companions were not innocent children unaware of the difference between games and crimes but "street wise" young delinquents knowingly involved in illicit activities. Realistically, one cannot engage in the business of selling drugs without some knowledge as to sources of supply, some pattern for receiving and passing on the money, some network of potential customers, and some *modus operandi* to avoid the eye of the police and of school authorities. It is almost inconceivable that such a crime could be engaged in without the drug pusher's being aware that it was against the law. That is, by definition, criminal capacity.

We hold that the surrounding circumstances here were legally sufficient to overcome the slight residual weight of the presumption of incapacity due to infancy....

Judgment affirmed; costs to be paid by appellant.

PROBLEM

Right from wrong. How does the *Devon T.* Court's use of the "knowing right from wrong" concept illustrate the different application of this doctrine outside the insanity context. Is reliance on this *M'Naughten* idea necessary? What substitute concept could be used instead?

CHAPTER 13

THEFT CRIMES

■ ■ ■

A. THE EVOLUTION OF THEFT LAW

The roots of the modern law of theft crimes lie in the fifteenth century when English judges invented the crimes of larceny and larceny by trick. Although the judges were willing to use legal fictions to expand the original larceny crime to some degree, it required legislation by Parliament to create the crimes of embezzlement and false pretenses in the late eighteenth century. These four crimes were adopted as the common law foundation of property crimes in state criminal codes, together with offenses such as receiving stolen property, robbery and burglary. Today most states use some version of the Model Penal Code's provisions on theft crimes, which are widely regarded as one of the most significant and successful M.P.C. reforms. Yet common law theft concepts remain important because they inform the interpretation of modern code provisions. Some state codes retain the definitions of common law theft crimes and other codes blend elements of these old crimes with elements of the revised M.P.C. versions. A knowledge of common law theft crimes is necessary for an understanding of the many changes the M.P.C. drafters sought to accomplish in simplifying and broadening the scope of the common law definitions. This chapter covers seven of the most important common law theft crimes and their five descendants in the M.P.C. and modern codes.

The broad goals of the M.P.C. drafters mirror those of the English judges whose opinions helped to expand the scope of theft law to encompass the evolving property harms that came to be recognized by society. The most significant revisions of the common law crimes were, first, the M.P.C.'s merger of larceny and embezzlement into the new crime of "theft by unlawful taking," and second, the similar merger of larceny by trick and false pretenses into the new crime of "theft by deception." These innovative crimes abandoned many of the common law elements that had become anachronistic technicalities. Another significant revision was the M.P.C. "consolidation" of many theft crimes in order to avoid the reversal of convictions where defendants conceded the illegality of their conduct on appeal but argued correctly that they had been convicted of the wrong crime. This consolidation took the form of a statutory rule that convictions may be affirmed if one of eight theft crimes is proved by the evidence, irrespective of the particular theft offense that was charged at trial.

NOTES

1. *The trend toward consolidation.* The M.P.C definition of consolidation is set forth in § 223.1(1) as follows:

> Conduct denominated theft in this Article constitutes a single offense. An accusation of theft may be supported by evidence that it was committed in any manner that would be theft under this Article, notwithstanding the specification of a different manner in the indictment or information, subject only to the power of the Court to ensure fair trial by granting a continuance or other appropriate relief where the conduct of the defense would be prejudiced by lack of fair notice or by surprise.

The M.P.C. provides for the consolidation of the following eight crimes under article § 223: Theft by unlawful taking or disposition; theft by deception; theft by extortion; theft of property lost, mislaid, or delivered by mistake; receiving stolen property; theft of services; theft by failure to make required disposition of funds received; and unauthorized use of automobiles and other vehicles. By 1980, 30 states had adopted the concept of consolidation of theft offenses. M.P.C. § 223.1, Comment (1)(b), at 135 (1980). Even when state codes do not provide for the consolidation of the same eight theft crimes as the M.P.C., it is common for states to consolidate the crimes of larceny and embezzlement (or theft by unlawful taking or disposition) and the crimes of larceny by trick and false pretenses (or theft by deception). Despite the modern trend toward consolidation, some states do not use this concept. One criticism of consolidation is that it deprives defendants of fair notice of the crime with which they are charged, and makes it difficult for them to adequately prepare to defend themselves against all possible theft crimes not charged at trial. See *Bruhn v. Commonwealth*, 37 Va.App. 537, 541, 559 S.E.2d 880, 882 (2002) (holding proof of embezzlement does not support a conviction under an indictment alleging larceny).

2. *Grading of theft offenses and proof of the value of property.* The punishment for theft crimes typically depends, in part, on the value of the property taken. For example, "grand larceny" (or "first degree larceny" or "felony larceny") applies to thefts of property valued at an amount exceeding a particular statutory limit. Usually the prosecutor must establish the market value of the property beyond a reasonable doubt, and "absent direct testimony of the market [value], proof may be established through the following factors: original market cost, manner in which the item has been used, its general condition and quality, and the percentage of depreciation since its purchase or construction." *Gilbert v. State*, 817 So.2d 980 (Fla.App. 2002)

(holding evidence insufficient to prove the market value of the property was over $300 where prosecutor asked owner only to testify as to "rough estimate" or "approximate cost" of the items).

B. PROPERTY THAT IS SUBJECT TO THEFT

Definitions of "property" that is subject to theft have changed over time as new forms of property have been recognized as valuable. Yet the tradition of strict construction of criminal statutes and the unpredictable evolution of technology have created an endless stream of issues for courts charged with the task of interpreting the meaning of "property" in particular statutory contexts.

UNITED STATES v. FARRAJ

142 F.Supp.2d 484 (S.D.N.Y. 2001).

MARRERO, DISTRICT JUDGE.

[In] the summer of 2000, Said Farraj was a paralegal with the law firm of Orrick, Harrington & Sutcliffe [LLP]. At the time, Orrick represented plaintiffs in a class action tobacco case [*Falise*]. In preparation for the *Falise* trial, the attorneys and paralegals at Orrick created a trial plan [of over 400 pages, including] "trial strategy, deposition excerpts and summaries, and references to anticipated trial exhibits." Only Orrick employees assigned to *Falise* were permitted access to the trial [plan]. [The record] does not reveal whether [Farraj] was included among such employees.

The Government charges that [Farraj], using the moniker "Fly-GuyNYt," e-mailed an 80–page excerpt of the [plan] to the *Falise* defendants' attorneys and offered to sell them the entire [plan]. An FBI agent posing as one of the Falise defendants' attorneys negotiated with [Farraj] via email—and ultimately agreed to purchase the [plan] for $2 million. On July 21, 2000, Yeazid, [Farraj's] brother, met with a second undercover FBI agent at a McDonald's restaurant in lower Manhattan to receive payment. Yeazid was arrested then and gave a statement to the FBI implicating his [brother].

The Government charges [that] by e-mailing the [excerpt] across state lines, [Farraj] violated 18 U.S.C. § 2314 [the National Stolen Property Act], which provides [that] "[w]hoever transports, transmits, or transfers in interstate or foreign commerce any goods, wares, merchandise, securities, or money, of the value of $5,000 or more, knowing the same to have been stolen, converted, or taken by fraud ... shall be fined under this title or imprisoned.... " [Farraj argues] that § 2314 applies only to the physical asportation of tangible goods or currency, not to "information" stored and transmitted electronically, such as the [plan] excerpt e-mailed [here]. Neither the Supreme

Court nor the Second Circuit has addressed this question directly, and this appears to be an issue of first impression in this District.

[The] Second Circuit has held that the phrase "goods, wares, or merchandise" is "a general and comprehensive designation of such personal property or chattels as are ordinarily a subject of commerce." *In re Vericker*, 446 F.2d 244, 248 (2d Cir. 1971) (Friendly, J.). [The] Second Circuit has at times determined that documents fall outside the scope of § 2314. At other times, however, the Second Circuit and other courts have held that documents may be considered "goods, wares, or merchandise" under § 2314. *See, e.g., United States v. Greenwald*, 479 F.2d 320 (6th Cir. 1973) (documents containing secret chemical formulae); *United States v. Bottone*, 365 F.2d 389 (2d Cir. 1966) (drug manufacturing processes); *United States v. Seagraves*, 265 F.2d 876 (3d Cir. 1959) (geophysical maps); *United States v. Caparros*, 1987 WL 8653 (S.D.N.Y. March 25, 1987) (secret business plans). . . . The [trial plan] at issue here . . . was the work product of a business relationship between client and attorney, and may thus be viewed as an ordinary subject of commerce, created for a commercial purpose and carrying inherent commercial value at least as to the persons directly interested in the matter.

[Farraj] argues that even if trial plans generally may be viewed as goods under § 2314, he is accused of transmitting an "intangible," an electronic form of the document, and therefore that it was not a good, but merely "information." [But the] text of § 2314 makes no distinction between tangible and intangible property, or between electronic and other manner of transfer across state lines. Indeed, in 1988, Congress amended § 2314 to include the term "transmits" to reflect its agreement with the Second Circuit and other courts which had held that § 2314 applied to money wire transfers, where the only interstate transportation took place electronically and where there was no transportation of any physical item. See Anti–Drug Abuse Act of 1988, Pub. L. 100–690, § 7507(a), 102 Stat. 4181, 4402 (1988); 134 Cong. Reg. S17367, S17370 (statement of Sen. Biden). [In *United States v. Gilboe*, 684 F.2d 235 (2d Cir. 1982)], the Second Circuit addressed the issue of electronic transfer for the first time and recognized that

> the manner in which funds were moved does not affect the ability to obtain tangible paper dollars or a bank check from the receiving account. . . . Indeed, we suspect that actual dollars rarely move between banks, particularly in international transactions. . . . The primary element of this offense, transportation, "does not require proof that any specific means of transporting were used."

684 F.2d at 238 (quoting *Pereira v. United States*, 347 U.S. 1, 9, 74 S.Ct. 358, 98 L.Ed. 435 (1954)).

The Second Circuit has also held that § 2314 was violated when the defendants stole documents containing some drug manufacturing process, copied and returned them, and then sent the copies abroad. *See Bottone*, 365 F.2d at 391–392. The court noted that it did not matter that the item stolen was not the same as that transported. Rather, as observed by Judge Friendly,

> where the physical form of the stolen goods is secondary in every respect to the matter recorded in them, the transformation of the information in the stolen papers into a tangible object never possessed by the original owner should be deemed immaterial. It would offend common sense to hold that these defendants fall outside the statute simply because, in efforts to avoid detection, their confederates were at pains to restore the original papers to [the employer] and transport only copies or notes.

Id. at 394.

[Similarly, the] court in *United States v. Riggs*, 739 F.Supp. 414 (N.D.Ill. 1990), held that the defendant violated § 2314 when he downloaded a text file containing proprietary information onto a home computer, and transferred it over a computer network to his co-defendant in another state, who then uploaded it onto a computer bulletin board. The court reasoned that just because the defendant stored the information on a computer, rather than printing it on paper, his acts were not removed from the purview of the statute:

> [I]n the instant case, if the information in [a] text file had been affixed to a floppy disk, or printed out on a computer printer, then [the defendant's] transfer of that information across state lines would clearly constitute the transfer of "goods, wares, or merchandise" within the meaning of § 2314. This court sees no reason to hold differently simply because [the defendant] stored the information inside a computer instead of printing it out on paper. In either case, the information is in a transferable, accessible, even salable form.

Id. at 421. The court noted that "reading a tangibility requirement into the definition of 'goods, wares, or merchandise' might unduly restrict the scope of § 2314, especially in this modern technological age," and recognized that although not tangible in a conventional sense, the stolen property was physically stored on a computer hard drive and could be viewed and printed out with the push of a button. *See id.* at 422. . . .

Weighing the scant authority at hand, the Court is persuaded that the view most closely analogous to Second Circuit doctrine is that which holds that the transfer of electronic documents via the internet across state lines does fall within the purview of § 2314. The indictment is therefore upheld and the motion to dismiss [the charge under § 2314] is denied.

NOTES

1. *Loading software as "physical" stealing of "goods."* The *Farraj* decision was followed in *United States v. Alavi*, 2008 WL 1971391 (D.Ariz. 2008), where the court recognized that conviction under § 2314 requires that an item "unlawfully obtained" and an item "eventually transported" must be identical, and " 'some prior physical taking of the subject goods' must have taken place to violate the statute." However, items covered by § 2314 "need not take a physical form independent of any computer medium." Therefore, this crime occurred when a defendant "physically stole a software program from his employer by loading it on to his computer, and then transported it in its electronic form" across state lines.

2. *Statutory definitions of property for purposes of theft crimes.* Here is an example of a statutory definition of "property" that is subject to theft crimes in Massachusetts:

> The term 'property', as used in this section, shall include money, personal chattels, a bank note, bond, promissory note, bill of exchange or other bill, order or certificate, a book of accounts for or concerning money or goods due or to become due or to be delivered, a deed or writing containing a conveyance of land, any valuable contract in force, a receipt, release or defeasance, a writ, process, certificate of title or duplicate certificate issued under chapter one hundred and eighty-five, a public record, anything which is of the realty or is annexed thereto, a security deposit received pursuant to section fifteen B of chapter one hundred and eighty-six, electronically processed or stored data, either tangible or intangible, data while in transit, telecommunications services, and any domesticated animal, including dogs, or a beast or bird which is ordinarily kept in confinement.

Mass. Gen. Laws. Ann. ch. 266, § 30(2) (West 2008). It is typical for common law definitions of property to enumerate a lengthy list of types of property, and the legislature must add new examples of property to the list whenever a prosecutor fails to persuade a court that it is covered by the existing statute. See *Commonwealth v. Mills*, 51 Mass.App.Ct. 366, 371–372, 745 N.E.2d 981, 987 (2001) (holding that the "release of the right to money" is not property under this statute). The terms "electronically processed or stored data" were added in 1983, the phrase "including dogs" was added in 1987, and the term "telecommunications services" was added in 1995.

3. *Common law exclusions of certain types of property.* At common law, some property was excluded from being the subject of larceny, such as domestic animals (treated as having no value), real estate (immovable property), and things connected to real estate, such as fixtures and growing crops. As the M.P.C. commentary observes, "there was understandable pressure not to expand [the] coverage" of larceny when it was a capital offense, and even when this status of the crime changed, many artificial limits on the definition of "property" remained. M.P.C. § 223.2, Comment (3), at 166 (1980).

4. *M.P.C. definitions of property.* The M.P.C definitions of "property" in § 223.0 apply to movable and immovable property alike:

(4) "movable property" means property the location of which can be changed, including things growing on, affixed to, or found in land, and documents although the rights represented thereby have no physical location. "Immovable property" is all other property.

(6) "property" means anything of value, including real estate, tangible and intangible property, contract rights, choses-in-action and other interests in or claims to wealth, admission or transportation tickets, captured or domestic animals, food and drink, electric or other power.

For the M.P.C. crime of "theft of services," the term "services" is defined under § 223.0 as including: "labor, professional services, transportation, telephone or other public service, accommodation in hotels, restaurants or elsewhere, admission to exhibitions, use of vehicles or other movable property."

PROBLEMS

1. *Taking a Shower.* A homeowner called the police to her house after she entered it and noticed that someone had turned on the television while she was out. The police found Martin, naked and hiding in a closet. He was charged with the crime of burglary under a statute that requires proof of his intent to commit "theft" inside the house, and "theft," in turn, requires proof of his intent to permanently deprive the owner of some "property." At his trial, Martin testified that he entered the house through an unlocked window and claimed that he did so because he wanted to take a shower. How can the prosecutor argue that he intended to deprive the owner of property? Explain. Compare *People v. Martinez*, 95 Cal.App.4th 581, 115 Cal.Rptr.2d 574 (2002).

2. *Images and Sounds.* An indictment alleges that a defendant committed the theft of "certain intellectual property contained in and on two video cassette tapes of a movie entitled Star Wars, which was the property of Twentieth Century–Fox Film Corporation." The indictment does not claim that the tapes were themselves stolen property. How can a prosecutor in Massachusetts argue that the images and sounds on the tapes qualify as "property" under the 2008 statute in Note 2 *supra*? Explain. How would the arguments change if the prosecution occurred before the amendments described in Note 2? Compare *Commonwealth v. Yourawski*, 384 Mass. 386, 425 N.E.2d 298 (1981).

3. *List of Informants.* Zoe is a DEA agent who is approached by Max, an apparent drug smuggler who proposes to pay Zoe for assisting him in an illegal venture. Max made an arrangement with four people in Texas to bring marijuana from Mexico into the United States, and he wants to find out if any of these people are DEA informants. Max offers to pay Zoe $10,000 per name for the information he seeks. The money is too good for

Zoe to refuse. So she goes to the computer in her DEA office and clicks on the links that give her access to a database with names of DEA informants. Zoe sees that none of the four people in Texas are informants, and when she relays this fact to Max, he gives her $40,000. Later when Max is caught, the DEA learns about Zoe's actions and she is convicted of the federal crime of "unauthorized sale of government property" under 18 U.S.C. § 641, which applies to anyone who "without authority, sells any record, voucher, money or thing of value of the United States or of any department or agency thereof. . . ." Compare *United States v. Girard*, 601 F.2d 69 (2d Cir. 1979).

    a. *"Government Property."* On appeal Zoe's defense counsel's position is Zoe did not sell "government property" because the language of the § 641 crime and relevant policy arguments would not justify an interpretation of the statute that would result in Zoe's conviction. Explain the arguments that the prosecutor will make to support the conviction.

    b. *"Goods, Wares, or Merchandise."* What if Zoe's defense counsel points to the *Farraj* decision by analogy, and argues that: 1) what Zoe sold would not qualify as "goods, wares, or merchandise" that are "ordinarily a subject of commerce" under the § 2341 crime; and 2) therefore, by analogy, the appellate court should conclude that what Zoe sold should not qualify as "government property" under the § 641 crime. What responses can the prosecutor make to these two arguments by defense counsel?

C. LARCENY & EMBEZZLEMENT (THEFT BY UNLAWFUL TAKING)

The Model Penal Code drafters proposed that larceny and embezzlement should be combined into the concept of "theft by unlawful taking or disposition" in § 223.2. This crime broadens liability by eliminating some of the anachronistic features of the common law predecessor crimes.

1. LARCENY

The original crime of larceny required a "trespassory" taking of property that violated the "possessory" right of the owner. There was also an "asportation" requirement, which meant that the property was supposed to be "carried away," although even a small movement sufficed. The required mental state was the "intent to steal," which implied an intent to deprive the owner permanently of the property.

a. "TRESPASSORY" TAKING FROM "POSSESSION"

In the fifteenth century and earlier, the meaning of a "taking" as an element of the judge-made crime of larceny "had no artificial meaning." As one scholar explains,

> Trespass as an essential element of larceny simply meant taking a chattel from one who had possession of it. [Anglo–Saxon] and early Norman economic conditions limited both the objects and the methods of theft. Movable property consisted of cattle, farm products, and furniture. [Since] theft of cattle by armed bands was by far the most important crime against property, it requires no stretch of imagination to see what was meant by "trespass" in the early law.

JEROME HALL, THEFT, LAW AND SOCIETY 6 (2d ed. 1952). Later, however, the meaning of "trespassory" taking became laden with legal fictions to allow the expansion of the larceny crime through judicial interpretation. In the *Carrier's Case* (1473), a larceny conviction was upheld by English judges who found a trespassory taking when the defendant was hired to take certain bales to one city, and instead carried the bales elsewhere, broke them open, and kept the contents. The owner was deemed to have retained possession of the contents, though not the packaging. Five hundred years later, judges who interpret common law statutes continue to rely on legal fictions to find that larceny occurs.

UNITED STATES v. MAFNAS

701 F.2d 83 (9th Cir. 1983).

PER CURIAM:

Appellant (Mafnas) was convicted in the U.S. District Court of Guam of stealing money from two federally insured banks in violation of 18 U.S.C. § 2113(b) which makes it a crime to "[take] with intent to steal ... any money belonging to [any bank]."

Mafnas was employed by the Guam Armored Car Service (Service), which was hired by the Bank of Hawaii and the Bank of America to deliver bags of money.... On three occasions Mafnas opened the bags and removed money. As a result he was convicted of three counts of stealing money from the banks.

This Circuit has held that [§ 2113(b)] applies only to common law larceny which requires a trespassory taking. Mafnas argues his taking was embezzlement rather than larceny as he had lawful possession of the bags, with the consent of the banks, when he took the money.

This problem arose centuries ago, and common law has evolved to handle it. The law distinguishes between possession and custody. R. Perkins and R. Boyce, Criminal Law 296–302 (1982), 3 Wharton's Criminal Law 346–57 (C. Torcia, 14th ed. 1980).

Ordinarily, ... if a person receives property for a limited or temporary purpose, he is only acquiring custody. Thus, if a person receives property from the owner with instructions to deliver it to the owner's house, he is only acquiring custody; therefore, his subsequent decision to keep the property for himself would constitute larceny.

The District Court concluded that Mafnas was given temporary custody only, to deliver the money bags to their various destinations. The later decision to take the money was larceny, because it was beyond the consent of the owner, who retained constructive possession until the custodian's task was completed. This rationale was used in *United States v. Pruitt*, 446 F.2d 513, 515 (6th Cir. 1971). There, Pruitt was employed by a bank as a messenger. He devised a plan with another person to stage a fake robbery and split the money which Pruitt was delivering for the bank. The Sixth Circuit found that Pruitt had mere custody for the purpose of delivering the money, and that his wrongful conversion constituted larceny.

Mafnas distinguishes *Pruitt* because the common law sometimes differentiates between employees, who generally obtain custody only, and others (agents), who acquire possession. Although not spelled out, Mafnas essentially claims that he was a bailee, and that the contract between the banks and Service resulted in Service having lawful possession, and not mere custody over the bags.

The common law also found an answer to this situation. A bailee who "breaks bulk" commits larceny. Under this doctrine, the bailee-carrier was given possession of a bale, but not its contents. Therefore, when the bailee pilfered the entire bale, he was not guilty of larceny; but when he broke open the bale and took a portion or all of the contents, he was guilty of larceny because his taking was trespassory and it was from the constructive possession of another. Either way, Mafnas has committed the common law crime of larceny, replete with trespassory taking.

Mafnas also cannot profit from an argument that any theft on his part was from Service and not from the banks. Case law is clear that since what was taken was property belonging to the banks, it was property or money "in the care, custody, control, management, or possession of any bank" within the meaning of [§ 2113(b)], notwithstanding the fact that it may have been in the possession of an armored car service serving as a bailee for hire.

Therefore, his conviction is affirmed.

NOTES

1. *The evolution of "trespassory" taking.* The expansion of the larceny crime by English judges came to a halt soon after the American Revolution, as described by the M.P.C. Commentary:

> [A]bout the end of the 18th century, a combination of circumstances caused the initiative in the further development of the criminal law [of theft] to pass from the courts to the legislature. Among these circum-

stances were the general advance in prestige and power of parliament and the conversion of the idea of "natural law" from an instrument for judicial defiance of monarchy to a restraining philosophy envisioning judges as interpreters of immemorial custom rather than framers of policy. Perhaps the most direct influence of all was a revulsion against capital punishment, which was the penalty for all theft offenses except petty larceny during much of the 18th century. The severity of this penalty [made] the judges reluctant to enlarge felonious [larceny].

M.P.C. § 223.2, Comment (1)(a), at 128–129 (1980). Parliament enacted statutes that established the crimes of embezzlement and false pretenses to punish conduct that did not fit the elements of larceny or its progeny crime, "larceny by trick." The American state codes and case law absorbed the nuances of the English definitions of these four theft offenses, and the boundaries between these crimes sometimes were so difficult to determine that it was not unusual for prosecutors to charge the wrong crime. When this occurred, defendants would win reversals of convictions and prosecutors would have to start over with the correct charge at a new trial.

2. *M.P.C. revisions.* The M.P.C. drafters reduced the multiple elements of larceny to the act of a person who unlawfully "takes" property, and abandoned the elements of asportation, trespass, and a taking from possession. The element of "intent to deprive permanently" was replaced with a more flexible definition of "purpose to deprive" another person of his or her property. The new title of the crime, "Theft by Unlawful Taking or Disposition", reflects the joinder of larceny and embezzlement; the latter crime is reflected in the alternate description of a person who "exercises unlawful control over property". The terms of § 223.2 provide as follows:

(1) **Movable Property.** A person is guilty of theft if he unlawfully takes, or exercises unlawful control over, movable property of another with purpose to deprive him thereof.

(2) **Immovable Property.** A person is guilty of theft if he unlawfully transfers immovable property of another or any interest therein with purpose to benefit himself or another not entitled thereto.

The M.P.C. defines "deprive" in § 223.0(1) as follows:

(a) to withhold property of another permanently or for so extended a period as to appropriate a major portion of its economic value, or with intent to restore only upon payment of reward or other compensation; or (b) to dispose of the property so as to make it unlikely that the owner will recover it.

PROBLEMS

1. *Mafnas and the M.P.C.* How would *Mafnas* be decided under Model Penal Code § 223.2 defining the crime of "theft by unlawful taking"? Explain.

2. *Depositing Same Check Twice.* Explain whether there is sufficient evidence to affirm the conviction of a defendant for the larceny type of theft

crime in *Mafnas* where the facts are as follows: "Sellers entered the Placer Savings and Loan Association, placed a check on the counter, endorsed it, and told the teller she wanted to cash it. The teller picked up the check, turned it over, and placed it on the counter to record information from the face of the check on a deposit slip. The teller entered the transaction in the bank's computer and handed $2,000 cash to Sellers. Sellers picked up her passbook and other papers and left. The next day Sellers deposited the same check in another bank." *See United States v. Sellers*, 670 F.2d 853 (9th Cir. 1982).

3. *Shoplifting Reconsidered.* A security officer in a J.C. Penney's store was behind an observation window when he saw Ellis concealing sportswear under her clothing and in her purse. The officer, who was holding his walkie-talkie radio transmitter, followed Ellis out of the store. When she was about 10 feet outside she turned and saw the officer directly approaching her, radio in hand. She then ran back into the store and she threw the sportswear under a rack displaying other clothing. Ellis was eventually caught by the officer. Is there sufficient evidence to convict her of larceny? Is there sufficient evidence to convict her of "theft by unlawful taking" under Model Penal Code § 223.2? Explain. *See State v. Ellis*, 618 So.2d 616 (La.App. 1993).

b.   THE CLAIM OF RIGHT DEFENSE

It would seem to be axiomatic that a person who honestly believes property belongs to him or to her cannot possess the "intent to deprive the owner permanently of the property." Thus it is common for states to endorse a "claim of right" defense to theft, either in codes or in case law. Most definitions of the defense require only an honest belief in a claim of right, and some definitions provide more extensive descriptions of the conditions that justify a jury instruction on the defense.

BINNIE v. STATE
321 Md. 572, 583 A.2d 1037 (1991).

CHARLES E. ORTH, JR., JUDGE:

[The defendant was convicted of the theft of property, and he claims on appeal that the trial judge erred by refusing to give an instruction concerning his mental state defense of "claim of right." The theft statute provides "it shall be a defense to theft if [t]he defendant acted in the honest belief that he had the right to obtain or exert control over the property as he did." Binnie testified that he found a dirty hat without a price tag on the floor of a department store. It did not look like the other hats for sale, and so he checked with a sales clerk, and asked her whether it was for sale. She laughed and said, "Well, I guess it is yours." Binnie walked out of the store while concealing the hat. A security guard testified that he watched

Binnie from behind a two-way mirror, saw him pick up a hat with a price tag from a sale table, and then saw him conceal it and try to leave the store with it inside his jacket. When confronted outside the store, Binnie admitted to the guard that he did not pay for it. He also stated that it was a "dumb thing" to take the hat but he refused to sign an acknowledgement that he had taken it wrongfully. Binnie testified that he had not seen the price tag that was located in the inside of the hat hidden by a band, and that the guard had refused to listen to his explanation.]

The claim of right defense springs from the notion that in cases of common law larceny the defendant must have had an intent to permanently deprive the owner of the property.... "[I]f the defendant can produce evidence that he was acting under an honest belief he had a 'claim of right', *this will be weighed by the trier of the facts in resolving the issue of whether the defendant possessed the requisite mens rea to commit the offense of theft*". [*Sibert v. State*, 301 Md. 141, 147, 482 A.2d 483 (1984)(emphasis in original).]

We pointed out in *Sibert* that "[n]either the theft statute nor the accompanying legislative history defines the phrase 'honest belief.'" Nevertheless, we found it "clear that this defense operates to negate the *mens rea* for the offense of theft, thereby providing a total defense." We looked to the commentary to the Model Penal Code (Official Draft and Revised Comments, 1980) which served as a model for portions of the Maryland theft statute, and opined that it was "particularly instructive as to the purpose for the inclusion of the honest belief defense in its draft."

First, the commentary notes that "it seems important to make it clear beyond doubt that an honest belief that the property does not belong to another should be a defense to theft." Second, the commentary states that recklessness or negligence should not serve as a basis for theft liability....

[We] must determine if the evidence adduced at the trial generated a jury issue as to whether Binnie "acted in the honest belief that he had the right to obtain or exert control over the property as he did." It is axiomatic that the weight of the evidence and the credibility of witnesses are always matters for the jury to determine when it is the trier of facts. In our view, Binnie's testimony was sufficient to support fairly the issue whether he acted in an honest belief within the contemplation of Art. 27, § 343(c)(2). Whether the jury sitting as a trier of fact would lend any credence to Binnie or give any weight to his testimony was for the jury's determination, not that of the trial judge. The contradictions between Binnie's evidence and that of [the security guard] went only to the weight of the evidence, not to its sufficiency.... If the jury believed Binnie, the honest belief defense was generated by his testimony and operated as a total defense to the charge. We observe that such an issue may be generated by the testimony of the defendant alone; it is not necessary that his testimony be corroborated. . . .

In short, under the circumstances and the factual situation presented by Binnie, it was within the province of the jury, not of the court, to determine whether Binnie should benefit from the honest belief defense, regardless of how dubious, suspect, farfetched, and incredible Binnie's account may have appeared to the trial judge. . . .

[When Binnie's counsel sought to argue the honest belief defense, the trial judge failed to give an instruction on this point.] We hold that the trial judge erred in his failure to give an instruction on the honest belief defense. The judgment of the Court of Special Appeals is reversed. Binnie is entitled to a new trial.

NOTES

1. *Honest belief need not be reasonable.* Only a few states require that a claim of right must be based on reasonable grounds. The overwhelming majority of states adhere to the M.P.C. view that only an honest belief is necessary because "theft has been and should be regarded as a crime of purposeful appropriation of the property interests of others." M.P.C. § 223.1, Comment (4), at 151–152 (1980).

2. *M.P.C. revisions.* The M.P.C. provisions reflect the rules endorsed in the case law of most states on the honest belief defense. The M.P.C provision on "Claim of Right" is set forth in § 223.1(3) as follows:

It is an affirmative defense to prosecution for theft that the actor:

(a) was unaware that the property or service was that of another; or

(b) acted under an honest claim of right to the property or service involved or that he had a right to acquire or dispose of it as he did; or

(c) took property exposed for sale, intending to purchase and pay for it promptly, or reasonably believing that the owner, if present, would have consented.

PROBLEMS

1. *Binnie and the M.P.C.* How would *Binnie* be decided under the relevant Model Penal Code provision governing a "claim of right" in § 223.1(3)? Explain.

2. *Car Parts.* Dabney noticed a Ford automobile that had caught fire and burned while it was parked on the roadside in Nacogdoches, Texas. The car stayed there for a month. What Dabney did not know was that its owner was waiting for an insurance adjuster to examine it. As the four weeks passed, Dabney noticed that some of the parts of car began to disappear, including the cylinder head. Finally, at the end of the month, Dabney decided that the car must have been abandoned. So he removed the

radiator, generator, and self-starter. He took these parts home and then he brought them to a local garage and offered to sell them. The garage owner got suspicious and called the police, who listened to Dabney's story and then arrested him for larceny. At Dabney's trial, his defense counsel requested this jury instruction: "You should acquit the defendant if you find that he acted under an *honest belief* that he had a claim of right to the car parts he took because he believed that the car had been abandoned by the owner, and so it was no longer 'the property of another person.'" The prosecutor objected to the wording of this instruction and requested that the phrase "*honest and reasonable belief*" should be used instead. Over the objection of defense counsel, the judge used the prosecutor's version of the instruction and Dabney was convicted. Compare *Jordan v. State*, 296 S.W. 585 (Tex.Crim. App. 1927).

a. *Honest Belief Instruction*. On appeal, you are Dabney's defense counsel and you recognize that there is no clear precedent on point in Texas. You want to argue that the court should endorse the defense counsel's version of the "honest belief" instruction in accord with the overwhelming majority of states. What arguments will you make to support your position?

b. *New Trial*. Assume that you win on appeal and Dabney gets a new trial where the jury receives the *honest belief* instruction. What arguments will you make to persuade the jury to acquit Dabney based on the honest belief defense?

2. EMBEZZLEMENT

The crime of embezzlement was produced by the inventive action of Parliament when judges refused to stretch the larceny crime to cover the conduct of embezzlers. The case that occasioned this refusal is *Bazeley's Case* (1799), where a person delivered property to a servant who acted on behalf of a master, and no larceny occurred when the servant misappropriated the property by "converting" it. This was because the servant had obtained "possession" of the property from the third party, and so could not be guilty of a "trespassory" taking from the possession of the master. The crime of embezzlement was designed to cover this non-larceny scenario, and early English and American statutes limited the categories of entrusted persons whose conduct was subject to prosecution. Ultimately, general embezzlement statutes expanded the concept of entrustment to cover a wide variety of defendants, and the crime came to be defined as the fraudulent conversion of the property of another by an entrusted person in lawful possession who had the intent to convert the property for his or her own use.

BATIN v. STATE

118 Nev. 61, 38 P.3d 880 (Nev. 2002).

LEAVITT, J.:

[In] 1993, Batin moved [from] the Philippines and began working as a dishwasher at the Nugget [Hotel and Casino]. After several years at the Nugget, Batin became a slot mechanic. Batin's job duties [included] fixing jammed coins and refilling the "hopper." Warren Reid Anderson, Batin's supervisor, explained that the "hopper" is the part of the slot machine that pays the coins back, and is separate from the "bill validator" component of the slot machine where the paper currency is kept. Anderson further testified that Batin had no duties with respect to the paper currency in the bill validator, except to safeguard the funds, and that the cash in the bill validator "wasn't to be touched." Likewise, Anderson testified that if a customer had a problem with a machine that required a cash refund "it would require supervisory backup in order to take any money out of a slot machine and pass it back to a [customer]."

As a slot mechanic, Batin was given an "SDS" card that was used to both access the inside of the slot machine and identify him as the employee that was opening the slot machine door. The computerized SDS system is physically connected to each slot machine and counts the paper currency placed into each machine's bill validator. The SDS actually records the different denominations of bills and runs numerous reports concerning the currency. The SDS also registers every time that the slot machine door is open or closed. If the power is turned off to a particular slot machine, the SDS system will only record the opening and closing of the door; it cannot track what happens inside the machine.

Lori Barrington, soft count supervisor, explained that after the money is counted by SDS, it is then counted three more times by a minimum of three Nugget employees. Barrington further testified that there was not much variance between the amount of money SDS recorded that the casino was supposed to have and the amount of money the casino actually had. In fact, out of 1100 slot machines, there were perhaps three errors per month totaling approximately $100.00 in variance.

In March and early June 1999, however, there were larger discrepancies discovered between the amount of money that the SDS recorded had been put into the slot machines and the amount of money the slot machine actually contained. Kathleen Plamabeck, the Nugget's Internal Auditor, testified to several shortages from four different slot machines, totaling approximately $40,000.00.

In reviewing the SDS reports, Plambeck testified that she found a pattern of conduct. Namely, prior to the time that a shortage had been detected on a slot machine, Batin inserted his SDS card into the slot machine, opened the door, turned off the power, and thereafter closed the door on the machine. Plambeck found this pattern of conduct unusual because it was not necessary to turn off the slot machine for most repairs, and no one other than Batin had been turning off the power on the slot machines with the cash shortages. Batin testified at trial, however, that he turned off the power on the slot machines so that he would not be electrocuted and that he had always turned off the power prior to working on the slot machines.

James Carlisle, an agent with the Nevada Gaming Control Board, investigated Batin and discovered that he gambled regularly at three local casinos, and that he lost tens of thousands of dollars. When Carlisle questioned Batin about how he was able to afford to gamble such large sums of money, Batin could not or did not answer. At trial, however, Batin testified that he was able to afford to gamble large sums of money because he won often.

Although Batin adamantly denied taking the money, Batin was arrested and charged [with] embezzlement. The information alleged that Batin had been entrusted with money by his employer and converted the money for a purpose other than that for which it was entrusted. After a jury trial, Batin was convicted [of] embezzlement.

[Batin] contends that his convictions for embezzlement should be reversed because there was insufficient evidence of an essential element of the crime. We agree.

[The] key distinguishing element of the crime of embezzlement is the element of entrustment. In order to be guilty of embezzlement, a defendant must have been entrusted with lawful possession of the property prior to its conversion. For purposes of proving embezzlement, the lawful possession need not be actual; rather, the State may show that a defendant had constructive possession of the property converted. This court has defined constructive possession as " 'both the power and the intention at a given time to exercise dominion or control over a thing, either directly or through another person or persons.' " [*Palmer v. State*, 112 Nev. 763, 768, 920 P.2d 112, 115 (1996) (quoting *Black's Law Dictionary* 1163 (6th ed. 1990)).] In proving constructive possession, a showing that a defendant was given mere access to the property converted is insufficient. Often, an individual is entrusted with access to a particular place or thing without being given dominion and control over the property therein. This is particularly true in instances, like the present one, where the individual is expressly told that he is not allowed to touch the property in the place to which access is gained.

In the instant case, the record reveals that Batin was not entrusted with lawful possession, constructive or otherwise, of the currency he allegedly took from the bill validators. In fact, both Batin and his supervisor testified that Batin had no job duties whatsoever involving this currency and that it "wasn't to be touched." Further, Batin had absolutely no power to exercise control over this currency, as Batin was required to contact his supervisor for any job task involving possession of the currency inside the bill validator, such as a cash refund to a [customer].

[In] light of the foregoing, we are compelled to reverse Batin's conviction. The State failed to prove the entrustment element of the crime of embezzlement beyond a reasonable [doubt].

MAUPIN, C.J., with whom BECKER, J., agrees, dissenting.

[In] viewing the evidence in a light most favorable to the State, we conclude that there is ample evidence to support the jury's verdict that Batin had constructive possession of the paper currency inside the bill validator. The State proffered evidence that Batin's employer entrusted him with an SDS card, which allowed Batin to access the bill validator inside the slot machine where the currency was kept. Moreover, Batin's job, as prescribed by his employer, included safeguarding the funds contained inside the bill validator when he made a slot machine repair and when supervising non-employee slot machine repairmen. In safeguarding the currency inside the bill validator, Bain was entrusted with dominion and control over that currency in a manner sufficient to support the jury's finding that Batin had constructive possession over the funds that he converted.

Accordingly, because we conclude that there was sufficient evidence of the crime of embezzlement, we would affirm the judgment of conviction.

NOTES

1. *The entrustment relationship.* Modern common law embezzlement statutes often contain lists of the types of entrustment relationships covered by the embezzlement crime. For example, a Mississippi embezzlement statute provides:

> If any director, agent, clerk, servant, or officer of any incorporated company, or if any trustee or factor, carrier or bailee, or any clerk, agent or servant of any private person, shall embezzle or fraudulently secrete, conceal, or convert to his own use, or make way with, or secrete with intent to embezzle or convert to his own use, any goods, rights in action, money, or other valuable security, effects, or property of any kind or description which shall have come or been intrusted to his care or possession by virtue of his office, place, or employment, either in mass or otherwise, he shall be guilty of embezzlement, and upon conviction thereof, shall be imprisoned in the penitentiary not more than ten years, or fined not more than one thousand dollars and imprisoned in the county jail not more than one year, or either.

Miss. Code Ann. § 97–23–19 (Rev. 2000). However, the omission of a particular type of relationship from such a statute may not prevent a court from finding that the relationship qualifies for the embezzlement crime, if that relationship is covered by some broad term in the statute. *See, e.g., Alexander v. State*, 2002 WL 16823 at *2 (Miss.App. 2002) (holding that employee is covered by embezzlement statute because of "agency" relationship created on the facts, so conviction affirmed where defendant received money to wash car and kept the car instead of returning it at the time promised).

2. *The intent to convert.* The mental state for common law embezzlement is the intent to convert the owner's property to the defendant's own use. Usually prosecutors must argue that such an intent should be inferred from the circumstances. Where an employee fails to pay over money belonging to his employer, this may not be sufficient to convict the employee of embezzlement. *See, e.g., Waymack v. Commonwealth*, 4 Va.App. 547, 358 S.E.2d 765 (1987). But a defendant need not make use of embezzled property to be convicted, and a defendant's claim that his employer's money belongs to him may provide sufficient evidence of the intent to convert. *See State v. Kier*, 2002 WL 1042041 at *5 (Ohio App. 2002) (affirming conviction where salesperson sold a customer an item for cash, put the cash in his own pocket, did not properly enter the transaction into the store computer, and did not give the customer a receipt).

3. *M.P.C. revisions.* The M.P.C. drafters reduced the elements of embezzlement to the conduct of "exercis[ing] unlawful control" over property. For movable property, the required mental state is the "purpose to deprive" the owner, and for immovable property, the mental state is the "intent to benefit" onself. The M.P.C. abandoned the elements of "entrustment" and the "intent to convert." *See* M.P.C. § 223.2(1) & (2), set forth *supra* in Note 2 of Part C.1.

PROBLEMS

1. *Batin and Larceny.* Was there sufficient evidence in *Batin* to convict the defendant of larceny? Explain. Was there sufficient evidence to convict him of "theft by unlawful taking" under Model Penal Code § 223.2? Explain.

2. *Farraj and Common Law Crimes.* Assume that the defendant in the *Farraj* case (in Part A of this chapter, *supra*) was authorized to have access to the trial plan described in *Farraj*. When he e-mailed the 80–page excerpt of the trial plan, did Farraj commit the crime of common law embezzlement? Would there be sufficient evidence to convict Farraj under Model Penal Code § 223.2 for the crime of "theft by unlawful taking"? Explain.

3. *Making Change.* Sandy is a housekeeper at a B & B in Panama City, Florida. One day the owner of the B & B, Rina, gives Sandy $2,000 in a cash bundle to take to the bank in order to obtain some small bills. The bundle is wrapped in paper and it consists of twenty $100 bills. Rina asks Sandy to

bring back 100 twenty dollar bills in order to make change for customers. Sandy goes to the bank and obtains just what Rina wanted, 100 twenty dollar bills wrapped in paper. Then Sandy is overcome by temptation, keeps the cash for herself, and runs off from her job at the B & B. She is arrested after Rina reports the crime. Sandy is charged with larceny and convicted. How can the prosecutor defend the conviction?

4. *The Money Drawer*. Jade owned a jewelry store in Houston and she suspected her employee Kim of taking money from sales to customers and keeping it for herself. So Jade sent two private detectives, Dominick and Della, to the jewelry store with "marked bills" to enable them to determine whether Jade's suspicions were correct. Dominick and Della came to the store separately, and Della pretended to shop for jewelry while Dominick told Kim that he wanted to buy a particular necklace. Dominick gave Kim a large cash sum that covered the cost of the necklace. In exchange, Kim handed Dominick a receipt and took the cash. Then Dominick left the store and Della stayed there and pretended to be looking at jewelry. Della saw Kim drop the wad of cash into the open money drawer of the cash register, during a moment when another store clerk opened the drawer for a transaction. Then a few minutes later, Kim removed $100 from the money drawer but Della never saw Kim ring up the transaction for Dominick's purchase. What arguments can be made that Kim committed embezzlement?

D. LARCENY BY TRICK & FALSE PRETENSES (THEFT BY DECEPTION)

After English judges expanded the larceny concept to include "larceny by trick", they refused to expand this crime to cover defendants who took not only possession but also title to property. The statutory crime of "false pretenses" was used to fill this liability gap. The Model Penal Code combined both of these crimes into the concept of "theft by deception" in § 223.3, which simplifies and broadens the coverage of the common law predecessor crimes.

1. LARCENY BY TRICK

The crime of "larceny by trick" enabled prosecutors to convict defendants who "trespassed against possession" by telling lies to obtain possession of property, instead of taking it by stealth. The crime is illustrated by *Pear's Case* (1779) where the defendant hired a horse with the understanding that the horse would be returned to the owner. But the defendant actually intended to sell the horse at the time of the hire and later did "convert" the horse by selling it and keeping the proceeds. The defendant was not a servant, employee, bailee or other agent, but he had obtained temporary lawful possession of the horse. Judges decided to call this conduct "larceny" by reasoning that the false promise to return the horse was a "trick" that could be treated as a "trespass", thus making the defendant's conduct a "taking from possession." As the owner's act of parting with possession was based on fraud, this act could not create lawful "possession" in the taker.

NOTE

The crime of failing to return rental property. Some states have created special statutes to deal with conduct that resembles larceny by trick. Such statutes may include specific provisions to address issues that arise often in a particular context, such as the theft of rental cars. For example, two Missouri statutes provides as follows:

> A person commits the crime of failing to return leased or rented property if, with the intent to deprive the owner thereof, he purposefully fails to return leased or rented personal property to the place and within the time specified in an agreement in writing. REV. STAT. MO. § 578.150.1 (2000).

> It shall be prima facie evidence of the crime of failing to return leased or rented property when a person who has leased or rented personal property of another willfully fails to return or make arrangements acceptable with the lessor to return the personal property to its owner at the owner's place of business within ten days after proper notice following the expiration of the lease or rental agreement, except that if the motor vehicle has not been returned within seventy-two hours after the expiration of the lease or rental agreement, such failure to return the motor vehicle shall be prima facie evidence of the intent of the crime of failing to return leased or rented property. REV. STAT. MO. § 578.150.2 (2000).

See State v. Smith, 81 S.W.3d 657 (Mo.App. 2002) (affirming conviction where defendant failed to return rental vehicle allegedly stolen by another).

2. FALSE PRETENSES

Just as the crime of ordinary larceny reached its theoretical limit, so also the crime of larceny by trick reached its limit when the English judges found that the latter crime did not occur when an owner actually parted with title to property instead of possession. However, the judges filled this liability gap by reinterpreting case law that defined the statutory crime of "false pretenses" and found that "false pretenses" prosecutions could be brought against defendants who fraudulently obtained title. This statutory crime came to encompass the making of false representations about present or past facts which cause the victim to pass title to his or her property, when the defendant knew that the representations were false and intended to defraud the victim.

STATE v. MILLER

590 N.W.2d 45 (Iowa 1999).

NEUMAN, JUSTICE.

[During] her tenure as a prisoner at the women's reformatory, Monzelle Miller engaged in extensive correspondence and phone calls with a number of men she "met" through advertisements in "singles" newspapers. This appeal focuses on her simultaneous relationships with three men aged seventy-two, sixty-nine, and thirty-six.

Miller's correspondence with the men began on a casual, friendly basis. Their letters soon progressed, however, to mutual expressions of affection, long-term commitment, and promises of explicit sexual gratification. . . . All three victims believed Miller planned to move in with them upon her release from prison.

Sprinkled among the many promises of devotion upon her release were requests for cash and personal items. The men responded with certified checks, money orders and catalog purchases billed to their personal credit cards. Their testimony revealed some equivocation about whether they regarded the transactions as gifts or loans. It is plain, however, that each man believed Miller needed financial assistance and each one regarded his help as an investment in their future.

At some point, prison officials got wind of a scam afoot within the prison. When the institution began returning the checks to their senders, Miller told her pen pals to direct their largess to her "attorney," David Porter. Porter was not in fact an attorney but one of Miller's confederates. The record reveals that the sum funneled through Porter for Miller's benefit totaled roughly $14,000.

[After] Miller [was] released from prison [she] failed to follow through on her promises to join any of her correspondents. An examination of Miller's prison account deposits yielded names and addresses of men taken in by Miller's scheme. [She] admitted writing the letters and extending promises of love, and even marriage, to her correspondents. She acknowledged having sought and received sums of money from them but contended the men were no more than "perverts who wanted her to write and talk dirty to them." She conceded, however, that her overall conduct was "kind of deceiving."

The State charged Miller with three counts of second-degree theft by deception, a class "D" felony, as an habitual offender. Iowa Code section 714.1(3) states that a person commits theft when she "[o]btains the labor or services of another, or a transfer of possession, control, or ownership of the property of another, or the beneficial use of property of another, by deception." Pertinent to this appeal, "deception" is defined in alternative ways at section 702.9 as follows:

    1. Creating or confirming another's belief or impression as to the existence or nonexistence of a fact or condition which is false and which the actor does not believe to be true.

    2. Failing to correct a false belief or impression as to the existence or nonexistence of a fact or condition which the actor previously has created or confirmed.

    . . .

    5. Promising payment, the delivery of goods, or other performance which the actor does not intend to perform or knows the actor will not be able to perform. Failure to perform, standing alone, is not evidence that the actor did not intend to perform. . . .

[A] jury found Miller guilty as charged. At trial, and now on appeal, Miller alleges error in the court's marshaling instruction to the jury. Following the format outlined in Iowa Criminal Jury Instruction 1400.10, the court described the factual premise for the State's charge this way:

> Between March 16, 1995, through December 10, 1996, the Defendant did misrepresent her financial needs *and/or romantic intentions to* [named victims].

Miller contends that criminal culpability cannot rest on deceit regarding "romantic intentions." The State [argues] that this case does not fall within any exceptions recognized by Iowa's statutes. For the reasons that follow, we agree.

    Our theft-by-deception statute was enacted in 1976 to replace earlier statutes variously criminalizing "false pretenses, frauds, and other cheats." *State v. Hogrefe*, 557 N.W.2d 871, 876–77 (Iowa 1996). Patterned after the Model Penal Code, section 714.1(3) "clarified the legislature's intent to criminalize every instance of a person obtaining another person's property by deception." "Theft by deception," we said in *Hogrefe*, "is meant as a catch-all crime to encompass the full and ever changing varieties of deception." When the alleged deception relates to unfulfilled promises,

> the inquiry centers on (1) whether the defendant intended to perform or (2) whether the defendant knew he or she would not be able to perform. Proof as to either prong depends in most cases on circumstantial evidence.

Hogrefe, 557 N.W.2d at 878. . . .

    [Miller argues that] it would be contrary to public policy and legislative will to criminalize insincerity in [matters of romantic intentions]. . . . [But] the record plainly reveals that Miller has not been prosecuted for merely breaking promises of romantic intention, but for deliberately using her false promises as a vehicle for parting her victims from their money. Defense counsel strenuously urges that the latter practice is not uncommon among single persons, and that by criminalizing the conduct here the State puts many failed relationships in jeopardy of prosecution. We are not so persuaded.

Miller admitted being "trained" by another inmate in the technique of writing letters that would reach the men on an emotional level, paving the way for later financial requests. Moreover, the record is replete with proof of her deliberate intent to mislead the men from the outset. For example, she sent her victims purported photos of herself which were actually of a woman not even of the same race, proof that she had no intent to ever meet the men face-to-face. The requests she made for financial assistance—*e.g.*, to pay for surgery, car licenses, lawyer's fees, and traffic fines—were not legitimate inmate expenses. And Miller did not use the payments for such purposes. The record reveals that much of the money was forwarded to her mother and other family members; the remainder held by Porter was used to purchase Miller a vehicle. Finally, it appears plain that Miller had no intent, or ability, to simultaneously follow through on her promises of marital/sexual bliss with three separate victims. But more importantly, these misrepresentations of "romantic intention" were motivated solely by Miller's desire to make her victims more vulnerable to misrepresentations of a financial sort.

In sum, we believe the challenged jury instruction enjoys substantial support in the law and in this record. Accordingly, we affirm the judgments entered upon the jury's verdicts.

Affirmed.

NOTE

M.P.C. revisions. The goal of the M.P.C.'s merger of larceny by trick and false pretenses was to replace these crimes with a broader one. The concept of "deception" was created in order to replace the element of "false pretense or representation," and was meant to include deceptions concerning matters excluded by the common law. *See* M.P.C. § 223.3, Comment (1), at 181 (1980). The M.P.C. provision on "Theft by Deception" has been emulated by many states; for example, the *Miller* Court described the Iowa statute as a "nearly wholesale adoption of the Model Penal Code's language." It is set forth in § 223.3 as follows:

> A person is guilty of theft if he purposely obtains property of another by deception. A person deceives if he purposely:
>
> (1) creates or reinforces a false impression, including false impressions as to law, value, intention or other state of mind, but deception as to a person's intention to perform a promise shall not be inferred from the fact alone that he did not subsequently perform the promise; or
>
> (2) prevents another from acquiring information which would affect his judgment of a transaction; or

(3) fails to correct a false impression which the deceiver previously created or reinforced, or which the deceiver knows to be influencing another to whom he stands in a fiduciary or confidential relationship; or

(4) fails to disclose a known lien, adverse claim or other legal impediment to the enjoyment of property which he transfers or encumbers in consideration for the property obtained, whether such impediment is or is not valid, or is or is not a matter of official record.

The term "deceive" does not, however, include falsity as to matters having no pecuniary significance, or puffing by statements unlikely to deceive ordinary persons in the group addressed.

The M.P.C. defines the term "obtain" in § 223.0(5) to mean:

(a) in relation to property, to bring about a transfer or purported transfer of a legal interest in the property, whether to the obtainer or another; or (b) in relation to labor or service, to secure performance thereof.

PROBLEMS

1. *Romantic Intentions.* Which of the three types of deception in the *Miller* statute describes the defendant's conduct? Explain. Did her conduct also fit the requirement of the common law false pretenses crime that a defendant must make false representations about past or present facts? Or were Miller's false representations about future facts and therefore outside the scope of that crime? Explain.

2. *Two Checking Accounts.* Dawn Tovar was convicted of "theft by deception" under the Iowa statute set forth in *Miller.* She owned a company called "Dawn's Floors" and in mid-September she agreed to install carpet on October 1 for Margot and told her that the job would cost $1,200.00. Dawn also told Margot that she always required customers to pay 50% of the fee as a deposit. When Margot wrote out a check for $600.00, Margot asked Dawn whether she should make the check out to Dawn's Floors, and Dawn told her to leave the payee line on the check blank. Then Dawn took the check and wrote her own name, Dawn Tovar, on the payee line in Margot's presence. She explained to Margot that her bank was "changing over" her accounts and so she needed a check made out to herself and not to her company. This was a false statement. Margot assumed that the $600.00 deposit would be used by Dawn to cover half the cost of the carpet job but Dawn did not explicitly describe the use that would be made of the deposit. On October 1, Margot did not receive any contact from Dawn, so Margot called Dawn to find out what had happened to the carpet. Dawn explained that her carpet installer had quit, which was true. She promised to call Margot back to reschedule the installation as soon as a replacement worker could be hired. Then on October 10, Margot received a letter from Dawn's lawyer, informing her that Dawn had filed for bankruptcy. Margot contacted the police and Dawn's prosecution for "theft by deception" followed. At her trial, Dawn

testified, "If Margot had written out her check to Dawn's Floors then probably that money would have been taken by my bank or by the Iowa Revenue people, and then I could not have received the cash that I needed to keep my business going. I needed to get a check written to me so I could get carpet supplies and stay open for business." Assume that the trial judge convicts Dawn on the theory that: 1) she created a false belief and 2) she promised delivery without the intent to perform. Dawn appeals her conviction on the grounds that there is insufficient evidence to support it. What arguments will the defense counsel make on appeal? *See State v. Tovar*, 580 N.W.2d 768 (Iowa 1998).

3. *The Knowing Victim.* A security guard saw Finch take the sales tag off a baby dress that was on sale and switch it with the tag of another dress that was not on sale. So the guard notified the cashier that Finch was coming through the check out line and should be charged the price indicated on the erroneous tag, unless Finch asked her to check the correctness of the price. The cashier noticed that the price tag on the dress had been removed and reinserted, but she charged Finch the erroneous "sale" price and Finch left the store. Then Finch was stopped by the security guard, who called the police so that she could be arrested. Finch testified that she never switched the price tags. The Kansas definition of "theft by deception" is "obtaining by deception control over property." "Obtaining" is defined as "to bring about a transfer of interest in or possession of property," and "deception" is defined as "knowingly and willfully making a false statement or representation, express or implied, pertaining to a present or past existing fact." Finch is convicted of "theft by deception" and appeals, arguing that actual reliance by the victim on the deception should be an implied element required to sustain the conviction. It is clear that Finch could not have been convicted of common law false pretenses as defined in the pre–1970 Kansas statute, because of the lack of reliance by the victim. But the Kansas legislature enacted a "consolidated" theft statute in 1970 that adopts the new "theft by deception" crime with which Finch is charged. Should the actual reliance element be retained? If so, must Finch's conviction be reversed? Explain. See *State v. Finch*, 223 Kan. 398, 573 P.2d 1048 (1978).

E. RECEIVING STOLEN PROPERTY

The conduct of "receiving stolen goods" was made a statutory crime in England in the nineteenth century. State codes originally defined the crime with four traditional elements to cover defendants who "receive" property, "knowing" the property is "stolen," with the "intent to deprive the owner." Even though the meaning and scope of each of these elements has expanded in many states, most definitions of the crime retain some version of each of these four elements.

STATE v. McCOY

116 N.J. 293, 561 A.2d 582 (1989).

POLLOCK, J.

[Defendant pled guilty to receiving a stolen automobile.] Thereafter, in providing a factual basis for his plea, defendant described the events of December 10:

> THE DEFENDANT: I was walking down the street and my friend came around the corner. Keith Martin came around the corner in the car and he called me over there to him. So I came to the car. I was getting ready to enter the car. I put my hands on the car. As soon as I put my hands on the car, the cop told me freeze, so I ran.
>
> THE COURT: Okay. [Mr.] McCoy, did you have any reason to believe that the car was or might be stolen?
>
> THE DEFENDANT: Yes, I did.
>
> THE COURT: Did you think the car was or was likely to be stolen?
>
> THE DEFENDANT: Yes.
>
> THE COURT: He says he wasn't in the car.
>
> [THE ASSISTANT PROSECUTOR]: Were you about to get into the car, Mr. McCoy?
>
> THE DEFENDANT: Yes, I was.
>
> [THE DEFENDANT'S ATTORNEY]: What were you about to get into the car for?
>
> THE DEFENDANT: I was going to ride around in it.
>
> [THE DEFENDANT'S ATTORNEY]: Knowing that the car was stolen?
>
> THE DEFENDANT: Yes.

[Defendant] appealed his conviction on the grounds that there was an insufficient factual basis to support the [plea]. [The Appellate Division] concluded [that] the facts were insufficient to establish that defendant had "received" the stolen automobile.

[Defendant] was charged under *N.J.S.A.* 2C:20–7a, which provides:

> A person is guilty of theft if he knowingly receives or brings into this State movable property of another knowing that it has been stolen, or believing that it is probably stolen.... "Receiving" means acquiring possession, control or title, or lending on the security of the property.

"Possession" is defined in *N.J.S.A.* 2C:2–1c as "an act, within the meaning of this section, if the possessor knowingly procured or received the thing possessed or was aware of his control thereof for a sufficient period to have been able to terminate his possession."

The key elements of the offense are knowing that the property is stolen and possession. When entering his plea, the defendant explicitly stated that he knew the automobile was stolen. Hence, our attention shifts to the question of possession.

[In] defining "possession" before the adoption of the New Jersey Penal Code, we stated that "[I]t ... signifies an intentional control and dominion." [*State v. Labato*, 7 N.J. 137, 148, 80 A.2d 617 (1951).] We recognized that "[possession signifies] the ability to affect physically and care for the item during a span of time." *State v. Brown*, 80 N.J. 587, 597, 404 A.2d 1111 (1979). [In] adopting the Penal Code, the drafters stated that the definition of "possession" in *N.J.S.A.* 2C:2–1c was to be "in accord" with our prior [definitions]. *II New Jersey Penal Code, Final Report of the New Jersey Criminal Law Revision Commission* Commentary at 39–40 (1971).

Possession, moreover, can be actual or constructive. Here, for example, the driver was in actual possession of the stolen automobile. [However,] "[p]hysical or manual control of the proscribed item is not required as long as there is an intention to exercise control over it manifested in circumstances where it is reasonable to infer that the capacity to do so exists." *Brown, supra,* 80 N.J. at 597, 404 A.2d 1111. Thus, constructive possession exists when a person intentionally obtains a measure of control or dominion over the stolen goods although they are under the physical control of another. Finally, possession may be exercised jointly by two or more persons at the same time. [*Id.*] Consequently, the question in the present case becomes whether defendant's relationship to the car was sufficient to permit a finding that he shared possession with the driver.

[A] defendant's words or conduct, as well as other evidence, may sufficiently substantiate his or her relationship to the stolen property to support an inference of possession. Thus, when police observed the defendant unloading beer from a stolen truck and defendant fled when approached by the police, the evidence was sufficient for the jury to infer that the defendant had the requisite intention and control to be in constructive possession of the truck. *State v. Bozeyowski*, 77 N.J. Super. 49, 57–58, 185 A.2d 393 (App.Div. 1962). Similarly, in *State v. Alexander*, 215 N.J.Super. 522, 529, 522 A.2d 464 (App.Div. 1987), the defendant was riding in a stolen vehicle within six hours after its theft, lived in close proximity to the place of the theft, and gave the police false information. This evidence was sufficient for the jury to infer that the defendant constructively possessed the [automobile].

[An] inference of possession may arise from a passenger's presence in a stolen automobile when that presence is coupled with additional evidence that the passenger knew the driver, knew that the vehicle was stolen, and intended to use the vehicle for his or her own benefit and enjoyment. Those facts could lead a jury to infer that it is more probable than not that the passenger had both the intention and the capacity to control the stolen vehicle. A jury might infer that such a passenger could exert control over the vehicle, an inference that would support a finding of constructive possession. Although a jury might reject the inference in a contested case, the facts would be sufficient to support a plea of guilty to possession of a stolen automobile.

[When] a defendant is outside the car, proof of his or her possession is more problematic. Here, for example, the defendant was arrested before he entered the stolen automobile. The facts reveal nothing more than that he had placed his hands on the automobile with the intent "to ride around in it," knowing the driver, and knowing that the automobile was stolen. We believe that those facts are insufficient to support an inference that at the time of his arrest defendant could have exercised dominion and control over the automobile. In brief, the evidence was insufficient to support a conviction for receipt of a stolen automobile. Consequently, defendant must be allowed to withdraw his plea.

NOTES

1. *The meaning of "receiving."* The M.P.C. commentary observes that common law courts had "stretched" the concept of "receiving" to include both "possession" and "constructive possession," as demonstrated in *McCoy*. The M.P.C. definition of "receiving" sought to broaden and clarify the common law by defining receiving as including "acquiring possession, control or title," and included "lending on security" in order to cover pawnbrokers. The M.P.C. also covers defendants who "retain" stolen property, so as to punish those who receive property innocently and then later learn the property is stolen and choose to keep it. *See* M.P.C. § 223.6, Comment 2, at 235 (1980).

2. *"Knowledge" that property is stolen.* The defendant in *McCoy* conceded that he knew the car was stolen, but this knowledge element usually must be inferred from circumstantial evidence. Most states use the M.P.C. formula that requires prosecutors to prove only that the defendant believed the property probably is stolen. Even in states where the mental state element is described as "knowledge" that property is stolen, the consensus in case law is that proof of "positive knowledge" is not required. For example, possession of stolen property that is still wrapped in the original store packaging can demonstrate knowledge. *See Panajotov v. Commonwealth*, 2002 WL 1163453 at *2–3 (Va.App. 2002) (affirming conviction where defendant possessed nine

stolen clocks and was caught after returning one clock to the store in exchange for cash). Other suspicious circumstances or suspicious comments and behavior by the defendant may supply the necessary inference of knowledge.

3. *Requirement that property must be "stolen."* The M.P.C. eliminated the common law requirement that property must be "stolen" in order to avoid the liability gap that could occur when goods lose their stolen character in a sting operation and when the crime of attempting to receive stolen goods may be unavailable because of the defense of legal impossibility. *See* M.P.C. § 223.6, Comment 4(b), at 239–240 (1980). However, some states retain the requirement that property must be stolen, and one court explained this preference as follows:

> The elimination of the requirement [would] create a situation [of] a victimless crime. [Without the requirement] it is possible that no person or business entity has been criminally injured. [Also the elimination of the requirement] would, in fact, shift the burden of proof to the defendant to show that his possession of an item was legitimate before the [prosecutor] has established that the defendant's possession was even suspect, much less criminal. That would be directly contrary to the most basic principle of criminal jurisprudence—the presumption of innocence.

Commonwealth v. Stafford, 424 Pa.Super. 591, 623 A.2d 838 (1993), *aff'd*, 539 Pa. 278, 652 A.2d 297 (1995) (noting that an attempt prosecution is appropriate when goods are not stolen).

4. *The intent to deprive the owner.* Originally the crime of receiving stolen property applied to property that was stolen through larceny, but gradually it came to apply to the receipt of goods stolen by any means of theft. The M.P.C. and most states use the latter definition, even though the term "stolen," a characteristic traditionally associated with the larceny crime, is retained in the title of the crime in most states. *See* M.P.C. § 223.6, Comment 4(c), at 240 (1980). Most states also require that a defendant possess the "intent to deprive the owner" of the property, but the M.P.C. requires instead that the prosecutor prove that the defendant did not possess the intent to restore the property. *See* M.P.C. § 223.6, Comment 4(a), at 237 (1980).

5. *M.P.C. revisions.* The M.P.C. provision on "Receiving Stolen Property" is set forth in § 223.6 as follows:

> (1) **Receiving.** A person is guilty of theft if he purposely receives, retains, or disposes of movable property of another knowing that it has been stolen, or believing that it has probably been stolen, unless the property is received, retained, or disposed with purpose to restore it to the owner. "Receiving" means acquiring possession, control or title, or lending on the security of the property.
>
> (2) **Presumption of Knowledge**. The requisite knowledge or belief is presumed in the case of a dealer who:

(a) is found in possession or control of property stolen from two or more persons on separate occasions; or

(b) has received stolen property in another transaction within the year preceding the transaction charged; or

(c) being a dealer in property of the sort received, acquires it for a consideration which he knows is far below its reasonable value.

"Dealer" means a person in the business of buying or selling goods including a pawnbroker.

PROBLEMS

1. *A Ride Home.* Moehring and Dan were friends who went to a party, fell asleep when it got late, and then woke up with no ride home. They started hitchhiking down Route 17 in Virginia; after one hour, no one had stopped to pick them up. Dan spotted a gas station on the other side of the two-lane highway, and noticed that one truck driver had left his engine running while he went in to the station to pay for gas. Without consulting Moehring, Dan dashed across the highway, jumped in the truck, and drove away. The truck's owner ran out of the station but couldn't catch Dan. Then the owner shouted out to Moehring, asking him for Dan's name, but Moehring said he didn't know it. A few minutes later, Dan decided to go back for Moehring, and found him on the road, still hitchhiking. Dan picked him up and drove him home. Both were arrested later and Dan was charged with larceny. Moehring was charged with receiving stolen property. Is there sufficient evidence to convict him, assuming that the Virginia court uses *McCoy* to interpret the crime? What arguments will be made by both sides? Is there sufficient evidence to convict him under M.P.C. § 223.6? Explain. *Compare Moehring v. Commonwealth*, 223 Va. 564, 290 S.E.2d 891, 893 (1982).

2. *Cab Passenger with a Box.* Norm is a "gypsy cab" driver in New York City. He rents a car for several months at a time and offers to transport people for money, just like a regular taxi driver. He is known to people in the neighborhood he frequents, and he knows many people as well. One day Norm picks up a man and a woman who agree to pay his fare. Norm recognizes the man as someone who has been convicted in the past of petty theft crimes. The man is holding a large box on his lap, and he tells Norm that the box contains stolen goods. Norm responds by saying, "I don't want to know what you have got in that box. So just stop talking about it." When Norm arrives at the couple's destination, the police arrest the couple, who are under surveillance. The stolen goods are discovered when the large box is opened, and Norm is arrested at that point, and charged with the crime of "receiving stolen property knowing it to be stolen." After his conviction, Norm appeals on the grounds that there is insufficient evidence of all the elements of the crime. What arguments will be made by both sides?

F. ROBBERY AND CARJACKING

Robbery is defined traditionally as a taking by means of violence. The harms of robbery include the violence done to a victim, the potential that such violence may lead to a breach of the peace, and the loss of property. Common law robbery required the same elements as common law larceny and two additional elements. These are the taking of property from the person or presence of the victim, by means of force or by putting the victim in fear of violence. In recent decades, legislatures have created the crime of "carjacking" in order to provide for higher penalties for robberies that take the form of a violent taking of an automobile. This crime has created a variety of statutory interpretation problems, and courts disagree as to whether carjacking is a specialized form of robbery or a unique crime.

UNITED STATES v. LAKE

150 F.3d 269 (3d Cir. 1998).

ALITO, CIRCUIT JUDGE

[The] events that led to Lake's prosecution occurred at Little Magen's Bay in St. Thomas, United States Virgin Islands. The road to the beach at Little Magen's Bay ends at the top of a hill [where a parking area is located]. There is a steep path bordered by vegetation and rocks that leads from the [parking area] down to the beach, and the [parking area] cannot be seen from the beach.

On the day in question, Lake hitchhiked to Little Magen's Bay and encountered Milton Clarke, who was sitting on the beach reading a newspaper. Lake asked whether Clarke owned a white car parked up on the road. Clarke said that he did, and Lake initially walked away. However, Lake returned a few moments later and asked to borrow the car. When Clarke refused, Lake stated that it was an emergency. Clarke again refused ... Lake walked off and sat on a rock while Clarke anxiously watched him out of the corner of his eye but Lake soon returned [and] asked if he could have a drink from Clarke's cooler. Clarke said: "[D]on't you get it? Leave me alone." Lake then lifted up his shirt, showed Clarke the handle of a gun, and said: "[Y]ou know what that is?" Clarke stood up and started backing away, but Lake pulled the gun from his waist band, put it against Clarke's face, and demanded the car keys. Clarke said that he did not have the keys and started walking toward the water with Lake following. Clarke waded into waist-deep water, and Lake walked out onto a promontory overlooking the water.

While Clarke was in the water, his friend, Pamela Croaker, appeared on the beach. Clarke shouted a warning, prompting Lake to approach Croaker. Lake demanded that Croaker surrender her car keys, and Croaker said: "I don't even know you. Why would I give you the keys to the car?" Lake then grabbed the keys, and the two wrestled for possession of the keys. When Croaker saw the gun, she surrendered the keys but asked to keep her house keys. Lake went up the steep path to the parking area where Croaker had parked her car out of sight of the beach. Lake then drove away in Croaker's car after leaving her house keys on the hood of Clarke's car. [Both] Croaker and Clarke followed [Lake] up the path, but when they arrived [at the top], he was driving away. [Later] that day, the police apprehended Lake in the stolen car at a McDonald's restaurant....

[Lake argues] that the evidence was insufficient to show that he violated the carjacking statute, 18 U.S.C. § 2119, and thus [insufficient to show] that he committed the predicate offense needed to support his [firearms] conviction. [He was convicted of carrying a firearm during and in relation to a crime of violence, namely carjacking.] Under the carjacking statute, the prosecution must prove that the defendant (1) "with intent to cause death or serious bodily harm" (2) took a motor vehicle (3) that had been "transported, shipped, or received in interstate or foreign commerce" (4) "from the person or presence of another" (5) "by force and violence or by intimidation." Lake contends that the evidence in this case was insufficient to prove elements one [and four].

[We] see no merit in Lake's contention that the evidence was insufficient to show that he intended to cause death or serious bodily injury. [The] carjacking victim, Pamela Croaker, testified that Lake waved the gun in front of her and ordered her to give him the keys to her car. When she hesitated, she testified, Lake placed the gun close to her head and again told her to surrender the keys. Based on this testimony, a rational jury could find that Lake had the intent to kill or cause serious bodily injury to Croaker if she did not comply with his demands, and we have previously held that such a conditional intent is sufficient to satisfy the carjacking [statute].

[Lake] maintains that the evidence did not show that he took Croaker's car "from [her] person or presence," as [the carjacking statute] demands. Lake argues that he took her keys, not her car, from her person or presence and that the car was not in Croaker's presence when he took it because she could not see or touch the car at that moment.

The carjacking statute's requirement that the vehicle be taken "from the person or presence of the victim" "tracks the language used in other federal robbery statutes." Under these statutes, "property is in the presence of a person if it is 'so within his reach, observation or control, that he could if not overcome by violence or prevented by fear, retain his possession of it.' " *United States v. Burns*, 701 F.2d 840, 843 (9th Cir. 1983).

[Here] Lake took Croaker's car keys at gunpoint on the beach and then ran up the path and drove away in her car. Croaker pursued Lake but did not reach the parking area in time to stop him. Applying the definition of "presence" noted above, we conclude that a rational jury could have found that Croaker could have prevented the taking of her car if she had not been fearful that Lake would shoot or otherwise harm her. Croaker testified that the sight of Lake's gun caused her great fear.... Although Croaker did not say in so many words that she hesitated for some time before pursuing Lake up the path, the sequence of events laid out in her testimony supports the inference that this is what occurred.... [Croaker] did not start to run up the path until Clarke emerged from the water.... Clarke related that he "caught up to [Croaker] at the bottom of the paved driveway" and that the two of them proceeded up the path together. They reached the parking area in time for Croaker to see Lake driving away in her car but not in time to stop him.... [A] rational jury could infer that Croaker hesitated before pursuing Lake due to fear and that if she had not hesitated she could have reached the parking area in time to prevent Lake from taking her car without employing further force, violence, or intimidation. We do not suggest this inference was compelled, but because such an inference was rational, we hold that the evidence was [sufficient].

In sum, we hold that the evidence was sufficient to establish all of the elements of the carjacking [statute].

BECKER, CHIEF JUDGE, dissenting.

When the defendant took the car keys from his victim, Pamela Croaker, Ms. Croaker's car was, in city terms, a block away, up the hill, out of sight. Under these circumstances, I would join an opinion upholding Lake's conviction for "keyjacking," or for both key robbery and grand larceny. I cannot, however, agree that he is guilty of carjacking. The majority draws upon federal robbery statutes to explicate how the vehicle (as opposed to its keys) may be considered to have been taken from the "person or presence of the victim." ... [My] polestar is the plain meaning of words, and in my lexicon, Ms. Croaker's car cannot fairly be said to have been taken from her person or presence, hence I respectfully dissent.

The robbery statutes upon which the carjacking statute is based do not themselves define the phrase "from the person or presence of the victim." Webster's New International Dictionary defines presence as "the vicinity of, or area immediately near one." However, rather than relying on the plain meaning, the majority turns to a construction of the phrase "person or presence" adopted by the Ninth Circuit in *United States v. Burns*, 701 F.2d 840 (9th Cir. 1983), where, in construing a federal robbery statute, that court reasoned that "property is in the presence of a person if it is 'so within his reach, inspection, observation or control, that he could if not overcome by violence or prevented by fear, retain his possession of it.'" Based on this definition, the majority concludes that a rational jury "could infer that Croaker hesitated before pursuing Lake due to fear and that if she had not hesitated she could have reached the parking area in time to prevent Lake from taking her car without employing further force, violence, or intimidation." This proves too much. If it is true that had Croaker not hesitated out of fear she could have followed Lake up the steep path leading from the secluded beach to the road, then it is equally true (barring physical limitations) that she could have followed him up that path and then halfway across St. Thomas. The fact that Croaker's car was nearby is thus not relevant; if she could have followed Lake up the hill, she could have followed him anywhere. I am aware, of course, that the craft of judging requires line-drawing, but I simply do not see how that endeavor can be principled when it is predicated on open-ended definitions of key statutory terms, especially where those terms admit of plain [meaning].

NOTES

1. *Interpreting the elements of carjacking.* In 1991, the conduct that became known as carjacking came to the attention of the public when one victim died after being dragged for two miles during a carjacking in Maryland. Congress then enacted the Anti Car Theft Act of 1992, which covers anyone who "takes" a motor vehicle "or attempts to do so." Many states enacted carjacking statutes, and the interpretation of these statutes has been the subject of controversy in some jurisdictions. Initially, the federal carjacking statute was construed as a general intent crime, but it was amended in 1994 to require "the intent to cause death or serious bodily harm." Therefore, the federal crime is now viewed as a specific intent crime. *See, e.g., United States v. Rivera–Gomez*, 67 F.3d 993 (1st Cir. 1995).

By contrast, some state statutes have been construed as general intent crimes that are easier to prove than the traditional robbery crime. In *Harris v. State*, 353 Md. 596, 728 A.2d 180 (1999), the court adopted a general intent interpretation of a statute that was silent as to mental state. The *Harris* Court emphasized that the Maryland legislators wanted to "proscribe actions which although already crimes (such as robbery), are deemed to be of such an aggravated nature as to require specific legislation and punishment," and that they believed that "the existing penalties are wholly inadequate for the gravity of the offense," and that prosecutors need additional tools "to place carjackers behind bars, and [to send] a strong signal to carjackers that the penalties for carjacking are severe." *Harris*, 353 Md. at 608, 728 A.2d at 185–186. However, the dissenting judges in *Harris* emphasized that it did not make sense for a severe penalty to be imposed for a general intent crime when lesser crimes like robbery are specific intent crimes. *Id.* at 617 (Bell, J., dissenting) (arguing that the implicit mental state for carjacking should be the specific "intent to deprive the owner of the car temporarily, without regard to the intended duration of the deprivation").

2. *Presence or person of the victim in carjacking or robbery.* The federal carjacking statute in *Lake* borrowed the "person or presence" element from the federal robbery statute. But most states accept the M.P.C. view that the element of "person or presence of the victim" should be eliminated from the crime of robbery. As the M.P.C. Commentary explains,

> It is enough that there be actual force or the threat of immediate force. The [person or presence] requirement [excludes] some cases that should be covered and adds little by way of narrowing the scope of the offense in any appropriate manner.

M.P.C. § 222.1, Comment (3)(d), at 112 (1980). One example of improperly excluded cases is where a "threat may be to one person in order to receive property from another who is not then present." *Id.*

3. *State reactions to M.P.C. revisions of common law robbery.* Most states do not follow the M.P.C. proposal that "serious" bodily injury or a threat of "serious" bodily injury should be required for robbery. Instead, most state codes use the concept of bodily injury. *See* M.P.C. § 222.1, Comment (2)(a), at 106–108 (1980). Many states do accept the M.P.C. view that the asportation requirement (derived from the elements of larceny) should be abandoned for robbery, so that it is irrelevant whether the defendant obtains any property during a robbery. Many states also expand the scope of the robbery crime as proposed by the M.P.C. to cover conduct "in the course of committing a theft," and thereby treat what would otherwise be attempted robbery as robbery. *See* M.P.C. § 222.1, Comment (2)(a), at 99–104 (1980).

4. *M.P.C. revisions of robbery.* The M.P.C provision on "Robbery" is set forth in § 222.1 as follows:

> (1) **Robbery Defined.** A person is guilty of robbery if, in the course of committing a theft, he:
>
>> (a) inflicts serious bodily injury upon another; or
>>
>> (b) threatens another with or purposely puts him in fear of immediate serious bodily injury; or
>>
>> (c) commits or threatens immediately to commit any felony of the first or second degree.
>
> An act shall be deemed "in the course of committing a theft" if it occurs in an attempt to commit theft or in flight after the attempt or commission.
>
> (2) **Grading.** Robbery is a felony of the second degree, except that it is a felony of the first degree if in the course of committing the theft the actor attempts to kill anyone, or purposely inflicts or attempts to inflict serious bodily injury.

Note that Robbery is not one of the theft crimes consolidated with the crimes of section 223 of the M.P.C. under § 223.0.

PROBLEMS

1. *Limiting Principle for Lake.* Assume that you are the prosecutor in *Lake*, making the oral argument in the Third Circuit before the case is decided. In your argument, you rely on the same theory of "presence" as the *Lake* majority, arguing that Croaker's car at the top of the hill was "within her control" even when she was on the beach, because she could have "retained possession" of her car by chasing the defendant and stopping him from driving her car, if she had not been "prevented by fear" from doing so. Assume that Chief Judge Becker asks you this question during oral argument that foreshadows his argument in the *Lake* dissent: "I am concerned that your definition of 'presence' has no limiting principle. Are you arguing that the victim's car would have been 'within her control' and therefore 'within her presence' under your definition, if she had parked her car in her driveway at home, two miles away from the beach, and then walked to the beach, where she encountered Mr. Lake and surrendered her car keys when he threatened her with a gun?" Explain how you would defend the *Lake* majority's definition of "presence" and persuade Chief Judge Becker that there are ways to create reasonable limitations as to the meaning of "control" and "presence" in future cases.

2. *No Asportation Requirement in Carjacking Crime.* Assume that Jorge is sitting in his parked car in Ghirardelli Square in San Francisco. The car's engine is on and the driver's window is rolled down. Eliza approaches Jorge from the sidewalk, points a gun at him, and demands that Jorge get out of his car and leave the engine running. Jorge gets out. But when Eliza gets into the driver's seat, before she can take the car out of park and put it into drive, the engine suddenly quits. Eliza jumps out of the car and flees, but she is apprehended and convicted of the crime of carjacking. The 1993 California statute defines this crime as: "The felonious taking of a motor vehicle in the possession of another, from his or her person or immediate presence, or from the person or immediate presence of a passenger of the motor vehicle, against his or her will and with the intent to either permanently or temporarily deprive the person in possession, accompanied by means of force or fear." On appeal, Eliza's defense counsel argues that the term "felonious" in the carjacking statute should be construed to have the same meaning as the term "felonious" in the larceny and robbery statutes enacted in 1888. The California courts hold that the term "feloniously" in those statutes includes the common law concept of "asportation", which requires some actual physical movement of the property, even if slight, to show that the property was "carried away." Thus, Eliza's defense counsel contends that since Eliza did not cause Jorge's car to make even the slightest movement, no "asportation" occurred and so there was no "felonious" taking under the carjacking statute.

Assume that the following discoveries about California law are made by the prosecutor who must defend Eliza's conviction. First, it appears that the carjacking statute is based on the robbery statute, which is based on the larceny statute. But even though some elements in each statute also appear in one or both of the other statutes, each statute also contains unique elements. Second, the legislative history of the carjacking statute shows that the legislature enacted this crime, among other reasons, to deter the thrill-seeking use of carjacking as an initiation rite for aspiring gang members. Third, even though the phrase "against his or her will" appears in all three statutes, the California Supreme Court has held that this phrase means different things in the robbery and carjacking statutes. Specifically, an infant or child passenger can be a victim of a carjacking, even though he or she is too young to give or withhold consent to the taking, but an infant or a child cannot be the victim of a robbery. Based on these discoveries, what arguments can the prosecutor make to support the position that Eliza should be convicted because the term "felonious" in the carjacking statute should *not* be interpreted to include "asportation"? See *People v. Lopez*, 31 Cal.4th 1051, 79 P.3d 548, 6 Cal.Rptr.3d 432 (2003).

3. *Snatching Property.* Assume that a Florida robbery statute is defined as the "taking of property from the person of another" when "in the course of the taking there is the use of force or putting in fear." Assume that the term "force" is not defined in the statute, and that Florida precedents do not provide a clear definition. Therefore, it is unclear whether the crime of robbery covers the conduct of a defendant who comes up behind a person without being seen, quickly grabs or "snatches" a purse that is hanging loosely from the victim's hand, and then runs off with it before the victim realizes what happened. Should the snatching of property, by no more force than is necessary to remove the property from an unresisting victim, qualify as robbery under the Florida statute? Explain the pro and con arguments here. How would such a case be resolved under the M.P.C. § 222.1? See *Robinson v. State*, 692 So.2d 883 (Fla. 1997); *Owens v. State*, 787 So.2d 143 (Fla.App. 2001).

G. BURGLARY

Common law burglary created a special kind of attempt crime to cover the conduct of breaking and entering a dwelling at night with the purpose of committing a crime inside. That crime might be theft in many cases, but burglary also encompassed the intent to commit any felony. Modern burglary statutes have broadened the burglary concept, and usually cover daytime intrusions into occupied structures or vehicles. Such statutes also use degrees of the crime with greater punishments for aggravating factors, such as the possession of a deadly weapon or the attempt to inflict bodily injury.

IN THE MATTER OF T.J.E.
Sx426 N.W.2d 23 (S.D. 1988).

WUEST, CHIEF JUSTICE.

[T.J.E.,] age 11, entered a retail store during business hours with her aunt. While in the store, T.J.E. took and ate a piece of candy from a display and left with her aunt without paying for the candy. T.J.E. was stopped outside of the store by the manager and ultimately admitted to him that she had eaten a piece of candy without paying for it. [Her aunt offered to pay for it but the manager called the police.]

[The state] subsequently filed a petition in the circuit court alleging T.J.E. to be a delinquent child.... After an adjudicatory hearing the circuit court sustained the allegations of second degree burglary. [This crime covers "[a]ny person who *enters* or *remains* in an occupied structure with intent to commit any crime therein."]

[First, we] find no proof in the record that at the time T.J.E. entered the store with her aunt she had the intent to commit a crime inside. We decline to interpret the impulsive act of this 11 year old child in taking candy after entering the store as evincing an intent *at the time of her entry* to commit theft. This clearly distinguishes this case from our affirmance of a burglary conviction in *State v. Shult*, 380 N.W.2d 352 (S.D. 1986), where the defendant took an item of merchandise from a convenience store. In *Shult*, there was an admission by him that at the time he entered the store he had the specific intent to commit theft therein. There is no such evidence in the present case.

[Second, the] circuit court did find that T.J.E. *remained* in the store with the intent to commit theft, thereby committing second degree burglary by *remaining* in an occupied structure with the intent to commit a crime therein.

A literal reading of the word "remains" in the statute would support this finding and would end the need for further inquiry. However, where the literal meaning of a statute leads to absurd or unreasonable conclusions, ambiguity exists. To interpret the word "remains" in [the statute] to hold a person commits second degree burglary whenever he is present in an occupied structure with the intent to commit a crime therein would make every shoplifter a burglar. It would make the commission of any crime indoors, no matter how severe, subject to a felony burglary charge. We do not believe the legislature intended such absurd results when it amended the burglary statutes in 1976.

Because the history of our state burglary statutes makes reference to the state of California, we have previously looked to that state for guidance in interpretation of our own burglary provisions. Therefore, we once again turn to California for assistance with our present inquiry.... [The] supreme court of that state has discussed the type of presence in a building or structure necessary for commission of burglary. *People v. Gauze*, 15 Cal.3d 709, 125 Cal.Rptr. 773, 775, 542

P.2d 1365, 1367 (1975). The California court has interpreted the law of burglary in that state as retaining the principle that burglary must be committed by a person who has no right to be in the building or structure burglarized. . . .

We conclude, therefore, that the word "remains" in the second degree burglary statute means to *unlawfully* remain in a structure. Therefore, second degree burglary was not committed in this case where T.J.E. entered an occupied structure and *after* entry, while *lawfully* remaining in the structure, formed the intent to commit an offense therein. This distinction between criminal intent at the point of entry and formation of such intent after entry while lawfully within a structure was noted long ago in *People v. Brittain*, 142 Cal. 8, 75 P. 314 (1904):

> [i]t would be an impeachment [of] common sense . . . to say that a thief who enters a store with intent to steal does so with the owner's consent or upon his invitation. It is true the thief must have clothes and food, and may enter a store to [buy] them; and *if, after he enters, he changes his mind, and [decides] to steal, and not purchase his supplies, it would be larceny.* But if it be proven that he entered with intent to steal, the law will not, in the face of such proof, shield him from punishment as a burglar on the assumption that he has the consent and invitation of the proprietor to so enter.

(emphasis added).

We find that state failed to establish that T.J.E. either entered or *unlawfully* remained in an occupied structure with the intent to commit a crime therein. Therefore, the evidence was insufficient to sustain the allegations in state's delinquency petition. Accordingly, we reverse the circuit court's adjudication and disposition of T.J.E. as a juvenile delinquent.

HENDERSON, JUSTICE (specially concurring).

[If] an eleven year old takes a chocolate Easter egg, a few days before Easter, and without paying for it, eats it, and walks out of the store, has he/she committed second-degree burglary under the statutes of South Dakota? SDCL 22–30A–17 (shoplifting) was not considered by the State. [The] State and trial court seized upon, and employed, a second-degree burglary charge. [The] preposterous result witnessed in Tripp County by the prosecution of this little girl, was a type of horror/nonsensical situation envisioned in my dissent in [*Schult*]:

> This second-degree burglary statute has a sweep whereby any and all crimes in occupied structures are amalgamated together by the same punishment depending upon the whim of the prosecutor. Prosecutors must have some channels of discretion and restraint.

[380 N.W.2d at 358]

T.J.E. was found to be a delinquent [child]. Thereupon, she was [placed] on probation with five conditions of probation [to govern a period of three months]. Such a finding and punishment [is] contrary to common sense and justice. This prosecutor chose to prosecute under a felony, the child having eaten a chocolate Easter egg, rather than prosecuting for a Class 2 misdemeanor. Not only does it violate common sense, but in my opinion, it violates the Eighth Amendment to the United States Constitution which provides a guarantee against cruel and unusual punishment. *Solem v. Helm*, 463 U.S. 277, 103 S.Ct. 3001, 77 L.Ed.2d 637 (1983). [The] maximum penalty for second-degree burglary [by an adult defendant] in South Dakota is a maximum sentence of 15 years and a $15,000 fine. (SDCL 22–6–1(5)). [For] a child to go through [a delinquency] proceeding and counseling and trips to a court services officer, can be humiliating, degrading, and self-defeating. In common language, a little girl should not have been treated this way. This was a de minimis act. This case should not have reached the circuit court and Supreme Court levels. It could have been treated in an informal setting.

[Therefore,] I would reverse this adjudication that T.J.E. is a delinquent [child]. She should have, initially, been treated as a possible shoplifter with store manager and parent(s) having a conference. [Prosecutors] should use a prosecutorial function to a better advantage than displayed here.... It is difficult not to scoff at this type of justice and not to feel sorry for the little girl and her aunt who were caught up in the capricious law enforcement on a given day in Tripp County. Law, in the end, does have to make sense.

Notes

1. *The expansive modern definitions of burglary.* By contrast with other types of theft, the M.P.C. drafters did not seek to expand the burglary definitions that existed when the M.P.C. was drafted, but rather to limit them. Like the judges in *T.J.E.*, the M.P.C. commentary notes that "a greatly expanded burglary statute authorizes the prosecutor and the courts to treat as burglary behavior that is distinguishable from theft [only] on purely artificial grounds." M.P.C. § 222.1, Comment (1), at 63 (1980). The M.P.C. drafters sought to define the burglary crime so as to narrow its scope and bring it closer to "the distinctive situation for which it was originally devised," namely the "invasion of premises under circumstances that are likely to terrorize occupants." *Id.*, Comment (2), at 67 (1980). Notably, the M.P.C. drafters rejected the burglary definitions of many states that include unoccupied structures or vehicles. The M.P.C. also requires "unprivileged entries" so as to exclude shoplifters like T.J.E. from burglary, because privileged entries "involve no surreptitious intrusion, no element of aggravation of the crime that the actor proposes to carry out." *Id.*, Comment (3)(a),

at 69 (1980). Many states use the M.P.C. mental state which requires a "purpose to commit a crime" instead of an intent to commit theft or an intent to commit a felony, on the theory that it may be difficult for police to prove exactly what crime was contemplated at the time of entry. Note that Burglary is not one of the theft crimes consolidated with the crimes of section 223 of the M.P.C. under § 223.0.

2. *M.P.C. revisions.* The M.P.C provision on "Burglary" is set forth in § 222.1 as follows:

(1) **Burglary Defined.** A person is guilty of burglary if he enters a building or occupied structure, or separately secured or occupied portion thereof, with purpose to commit a crime therein, unless the premises are at the time open to the public or the actor is licensed or privileged to enter. It is an affirmative defense to prosecution for burglary that the building or structure was abandoned.

(2) **Grading.** Burglary is a felony of the second degree if it is perpetrated in the dwelling of another at night, or if, in the course of committing the offense, the actor:

(a) purposely, knowingly or recklessly inflicts or attempts to inflict bodily injury on anyone; or

(b) is armed with explosives or a deadly weapon.

Otherwise, burglary is a felony of the third degree. An act shall be deemed "in the course of committing" an offense if it occurs in an attempt to commit the offense or in flight after the attempt or commission.

M.P.C. § 221.0(1) provides that "occupied structure" means "any structure, vehicle or place adapted for overnight accommodation of persons, or for carrying on business therein, whether or not a person is actually present."

3. *M.P.C. "lesser" burglary crime of criminal trespass.* The M.P.C provision on "Criminal Trespass" is set forth in § 222.2 as follows:

(1) **Buildings and Occupied Structures.** A person commits an offense if, knowing that he is not licensed or privileged to do so, he enters or surreptitiously remains in any building or occupied structure, or separately secured or occupied portion thereof. An offense under this Subsection is a misdemeanor if it is committed in a dwelling at night. Otherwise it is a petty misdemeanor.

. . .

(3) **Defenses.** It is an affirmative defense to prosecution under this Section that:

(a) a building or occupied structure involved in an offense under Subsection (1) was abandoned; or

(b) the premises were at the time open to members of the public and the actor complied with all lawful conditions imposed on access to or remaining in the premises; or

(c) the actor reasonably believed that the owner of the premises, or other person empowered to license access thereto, would have licensed him to enter or remain.

PROBLEMS

1. *Defining Night.* According to Blackstone, the harm of burglary was the causing of a "forcible invasion" against the "right of habitation" at night, "when all the creation, except beasts of prey, are at rest" and "when sleep has disarmed the owner, and rendered his castle defenseless." Yet defining the required element of "night" was difficult. Blackstone reported that according to the most ancient rule, "the day was accounted to begin only at sunrising and to end immediately upon sunset." But he viewed the "better opinion" as this one: "if there be daylight [or twilight] enough, begun or left, to discern a [person's] face withal it is no burglary." WILLIAM BLACKSTONE, 4 COMMENTARIES, *224. Describe the strengths and weaknesses of these two rules, and explain how the M.P.C. drafters could justify the proposed definition of "night" as "the period between thirty minutes past sunset and thirty minutes before sunrise," all year round. See M.P.C. § 221.0(2).

2. *Evolving Definitions of Burglary.* Assume that Gil makes weekly visits to the General Store in Bismarck, South Dakota, to make deliveries of milk at midnight. Otto the owner has given Gil a key to open the back door of the store that leads to the storage room, so that Gil can put the bottles of milk away in the walk-in refrigerator in that room. After several months of making deliveries, Gil happens to see something new, a large stack of cases of cans of root beer in the storage room. After putting the milk in the storage room as usual, Gil picks up three cases of root beer and carries them out the back door without leaving any money to pay for it. As Gil walks toward his truck, he has the bad luck to encounter Otto, who is out walking his dog in the parking area behind the General Store. Gil is arrested and charged with second degree burglary. *Compare State v. Burdick,* 712 N.W.2d 5 (S.D. 2006).

a. *1862 Dakota Territory Statute.* If Gil's conduct occurred in 1862, he would have been charged simply with burglary, as there were no degrees of the crime, which was defined as follows: "If a person break and enter the dwelling house of another in the night time, with intent to commit larceny, he shall be deemed guilty of burglary, and imprisoned for between five and ten years." What arguments would Gil's defense counsel make to obtain Gil's acquittal under this statute?

b. *1976 South Dakota Statute.* Assume that Gil's conduct occurred in 1988 *after* the *T.J.E.* decision interpreting the 1976 second degree burglary crime which was the basis for the delinquency proceeding against the defendant in *T.J.E.* Assume that Gil was charged with the same crime, which was defined as follows: "entering or remaining in an occupied or unoccupied structure at any time with the intent to commit any crime." What arguments would Gil's defense counsel make to obtain Gil's acquittal under this statute?

c. *1989 Amended Statute.* Assume that Gil's conduct occurred in 1989 *after* the South Dakota legislature responded to the 1988 *T.J.E.* decision by amending the second degree burglary statute to define the crime as follows: "Any person who enters or remains in an occupied or unoccupied structure with the intent to commit any crime, except that of shoplifting, shall be deemed guilty of second degree burglary." The crime of shoplifting is defined as follows: "Any person who takes merchandise displayed for sale in a store without the consent of the owner and with the intention of converting it to the person's use without paying the purchase price for the merchandise shall be deemed guilty of shoplifting." If Gil is charged under the 1989 burglary statute, what arguments would Gil's defense counsel make to obtain Gil's acquittal under this statute? What counter-arguments would the prosecutor make to obtain Gil's conviction?

d. *2005 Amended Statute.* Assume that Gil's conduct occurred in 2005 *after* the legislature amended the second degree burglary statute again to define the crime as follows: "Any person who enters or remains in an occupied or unoccupied structure with the intent to commit any crime, shall be guilty of second degree burglary, unless the structure is open to the public at the time, or the person is licensed or privileged at the time to enter or remain in the structure." If Gil is charged under the 2005 burglary statute, what arguments would Gil's defense counsel make to obtain Gil's acquittal under this statute?"

3. *Pry Marks on Window.* A statute defines burglary as being committed when a person "enters any building, including a house, with intent to commit larceny or any felony." One day a neighbor of the Floreas family saw Valencia with a screwdriver in his hand. He removed a window screen from a bathroom window and tried unsuccessfully to open the window itself. The neighbor called the police. Valencia was arrested and the police found what appeared to be rub marks on the bathroom window that could have been made by his hands as he tried to open the window. They also found several pry marks on the frame of the bedroom window that could have been made by the screwdriver. A pair of black gloves and a screwdriver with a bent blade and shank were found in Valencia's pocket. If Valencia is charged with burglary, is there sufficient evidence to convict him? See *People v. Valencia*, 28 Cal.4th 1, 46 P.3d 920, 120 Cal.Rptr.2d 131 (2002).

4. *Structure with Three Walls.* Vic owns a house and his large enclosed workshop is located behind his house. On one side of his workshop he has built a "four stall lean-to" in order to provide sheltered parking for individuals using the workshop. The workshop wall is the north side of the lean-to. Two other sides have walls and there is a roof, but the south side of the lean-to is totally open. The lean-to has a dirt floor. Vic parks his own truck in the lean-to, and he has motion detectors installed all around the lean-to with an alarm system. One night after midnight the alarm goes off, and when Vic discovers Sara near his lean-to, she claims that she was looking for a car jack because she has a flat tire on her car, which she has parked a few blocks

away. Nothing was taken from Vic's truck or from the lean-to. However, Sara's footprints are in the dirt inside the lean-to, and her nearby parked car does not have a flat tire. Sara is charged with "burglary" under a Nebraska statute that provides: "Burglary is knowingly and without authority entering into or remaining within any building, manufactured home, mobile home, tent or other structure which is not a dwelling, with intent to commit a felony therein." At trial the defense counsel makes a motion to have the charge dismissed on the grounds the lean-to was not a "structure" under the burglary statute. The judge denies the motion and Sara is convicted. On appeal, Sara argues that the judge erred in refusing to dismiss the charge. How will the prosecutor argue that the lean-to qualifies as a structure under the burglary statute, and how will the defendant argue that it does not? See *State v. Moler*, 269 Kan. 362, 2 P.3d 773 (2000).

5. *Intent to Rob Different Location.* Assume that Joe is convicted of common law burglary for entering the dwelling of Merrill with the intent to commit theft. The facts showed that Joe, by exhibiting a handgun and threatening the victim, forced his way into the home of Richard Merrill, president of the First City National Bank of Houston. Once inside, Joe pulled out a cassette tape player and played a tape explaining that Joe was part of a group whose plan to take Merrill to his bank and force him to withdraw an unspecified sum of money. However, Merrill's wife managed to summon the police and Joe was arrested. Joe claims on appeal that a burglary conviction is proper only if he had the intent to steal from Merrill's home. The prosecutor claims that the crime includes the intent to steal from any location irrespective of connection with or proximity to the entered premises. Which interpretation of the common law crime is appropriate? How would this case be resolved under M.P.C. § 222.1? Explain. See *Robles v. State*, 664 S.W.2d 91 (Tex.Crim.App. 1984).

CHAPTER 14

SENTENCING

■ ■ ■

Ordinarily it is a relatively simple matter to ascertain a defendant's potential "exposure" to a sentence under a given criminal provision. All statutory crimes contain an express or implied penalty. In the vast majority of cases, the actual punishment is contained in the definition of the offense by reference to statutes defining ranges of imprisonment terms and fines. In some instances, a punishment for a violation of one statute is determined by reference to the "classification" of the crime in a particular category or misdemeanor.

This chapter covers selected sentencing topics that involve complex modern constitutional doctrines. After an introduction concerning non-capital sentences, the Supreme Court's proportionality doctrine is examined in the capital and non-capital contexts. The chapter concludes with a study of the Court's Sixth Amendment doctrine recognizing the right to have the jury determine facts that are essential to a criminal sentence. This is the doctrine that caused the invalidation of the mandatory use of the Federal Sentencing Guidelines.

A. NON–CAPITAL SENTENCES

Fines and Costs. The punishment for a violation of the law may include a fine in addition to or, in some cases, instead of imprisonment. Due to certain constitutional limitations, an indigent person usually may not be imprisoned for failure to pay the fine or costs.

The procedure for the collection of fines is governed largely by statute. Fines cannot be imposed upon any person determined by the court to be indigent. While incarceration is a possibility for an intentional refusal to pay, the court must explore non-imprisonment alternative means of satisfaction of a fine, when a non-indigent defendant encounters financial hardships that prevent timely payment. See *Bearden v. Georgia*, 461 U.S. 660 (1983). In instances where the defendant seeks to appeal a fine, the trial judge may grant a stay of the payment and require bail.

In some jurisdictions, the sentencing court may issue a criminal garnishment order for all fines, court costs, restitution, and reimbursement charges, combining them in a single order of garnishment. Any convicted person owing such fees, either before or after his or her release from incarceration, is subject to a lien upon his or her interest, present or future, in any real property.

The costs associated with litigation are also governed by statute. It appears that the defendant is responsible for the payment of costs only upon conviction. However, court costs cannot be imposed upon an indigent defendant, and the defendant cannot be incarcerated for failure to pay costs. See *Bearden v. Georgia*, 461 U.S. 660 (1983).

Recently, states have begun to provide that the sentencing court may order a person incarcerated to reimburse the state or local government for the costs of incarceration. The sentencing court determines the amount to be paid, based on the actual per diem, per person, cost of incarceration, the cost of medical services provided to a prisoner (less any copayment paid by the prisoner), and the prisoner's ability to pay all or part of the incarceration costs.

Restitution. By statute, a person convicted of certain types of crimes such as a crime involving the taking of, injury to, or destruction of property can be ordered to restore the property or its value to the victim. An order of restitution may defer payment until the person is released from custody. However, the decision by a trial judge not to use this remedy does not deprive the victim of a civil action for the injury sustained.

Forfeiture or Confiscation of Property. A person convicted of certain types of crimes (such as those involving controlled substances, intoxicating liquors, eavesdropping devices, deadly weapons, gambling devices, and obscene matter) can be ordered to forfeit property used in connection with commission of the offense. Forfeitures, as payments in kind, are "fines" if they constitute punishment for an offense. *Austin v. United States*, 509 U.S. 602 (1993). Thus, forfeiture orders may include vehicles and realty used to facilitate commission of drug trafficking, because such orders serve as punishment under the Eighth Amendment's Excessive Fines Clause. In *Alexander v. United States*, 509 U.S. 544 (1993), as part of his punishment for violating federal obscenity laws and RICO, the defendant was ordered to forfeit his businesses and almost $9 million acquired through racketeering activity. The Supreme Court found that the forfeiture was a permissible criminal punishment, not a prior restraint on speech, because it merely prevented him from financing his activities with assets derived from his prior racketeering offenses.

Under the Due Process Clause, the Government must provide notice and a meaningful opportunity to be heard before seizing real property subject to civil forfeiture. See *United States v. James Daniel*

Good Real Property, 510 U.S. 43 (1993). However, due process does not preclude forfeiture of property used for unlawful purposes by a defendant who does not own that property. See *Bennis v. Michigan*, 516 U.S. 442 (1996).

Probation and Conditional Discharge. Probation is granted when the sentencing court suspends the execution of a sentence of imprisonment conditionally and releases the defendant under the supervision of a probation officer. Some jurisdictions grant "conditional discharge" when a defendant is released without supervision. These forms of release are regarded as "legislative clemencies," granted as a matter of grace, not constitutional rights.

Eligibility requirements for probation or conditional discharge usually prohibit the use of these sentences after convictions for capital offenses, recidivist-status offenses, serious felonies involving the use of a firearm or a sex-related offense against a minor. Otherwise, many states require that a defendant be considered for probation or conditional discharge unless the court finds imprisonment to be necessary to protect the public.

Conditions of release are usually stated in writing and furnished to the defendant. All defendants are required to refrain from committing another offense, and to comply with other conditions (such as restitution) which the court deems to be reasonably necessary to enable the defendant to lead a law-abiding life. In addition to reasonable conditions, a court may require a defendant to submit to a period of imprisonment in the local jail at times to be determined by the court. This is known as a "split sentence." Finally, the court may initiate proceedings to determine whether to revoke the release because of a violation of its conditions.

Home Incarceration. Many states now permit defendants convicted of minor offenses to serve all or part of a definite term of imprisonment under conditions of home incarceration. Some provisions prohibit home incarceration for minor offenders with outstanding criminal charges or a recent conviction for a violent crime. The sentencing judge may have discretion to order home incarceration as another type of "split sentence" for the defendant to serve part of the sentence at home and part of it in jail. As with probation and conditional discharge, a defendant under home incarceration signs an agreement to abide by all of the conditions for confinement.

Continuous Confinement for a Definite Term or Indeterminate Term. About two-thirds of the states use indeterminate sentences. An indeterminate sentence is set within statutory limits, with the parole board having responsibility for deciding precisely when the defendant is eligible for early release. A determinate sentence (also known as "flat time,") is for a fixed period without the possibility of early release;

supervision often accompanies the release that follows a determinate sentence.

B.   DEATH AS A PUNISHMENT

1.   THE PROBLEM OF PROPORTIONALITY

KENNEDY v. LOUISIANA

128 S.Ct. 2641 (2008).

JUSTICE KENNEDY delivered the opinion of the Court.

... Patrick Kennedy seeks to set aside his death sentence under the Eighth Amendment. He was charged [with] the aggravated rape of his then–8-year-old stepdaughter. [P]etitioner was convicted and sentenced to death under a state statute authorizing capital punishment for the rape of a child under 12 years of age. This case presents the question whether the Constitution bars [a state] from imposing the death penalty for the rape of a child where the crime did not result, and was not intended to result, in death of the victim....

Petitioner's crime was one that cannot be recounted in these pages in a way sufficient to capture in full the hurt and horror inflicted on his victim or to convey the revulsion society, and the jury that represents it, sought to express by sentencing petitioner to death. At 9:18 a.m. on March 2, 1998, petitioner called 911 to report that his stepdaughter, referred to here as L. H., had been raped.... L.H. was transported to the Children's Hospital. An expert in pediatric forensic medicine testified that L. H.'s injuries were the most severe he had seen from a sexual assault in his four years of practice....

The State charged petitioner with aggravated rape of a child under La. Stat. Ann. § 14:42 and sought the death penalty.... The jury unanimously determined that petitioner should be sentenced to death. The Supreme Court of Louisiana affirmed. The court rejected petitioner's reliance on *Coker v. Georgia*, 433 U.S. 584 (1977), noting that, while *Coker* bars the use of the death penalty as punishment for the rape of an adult woman, it left open the question which, if any, other nonhomicide crimes can be punished by death consistent with the Eighth Amendment. Because "children are a class that need special protection," the state court reasoned, the rape of a child is unique in terms of the harm it inflicts upon the victim and our society.

The court acknowledged that petitioner would be the first person executed for committing child rape since La. Stat. Ann. § 14:42 was amended in 1995 and that Louisiana is in the minority of jurisdictions that authorize the death penalty for the crime of child rape. But following the approach of *Roper v. Simmons*, 543 U.S. 551 (2005), and *Atkins v. Virginia*, 536 U.S. 304 (2002), it found significant not the "numerical counting of which [S]tates ... stand for or against a particular capital prosecution," but "the direction of change." Since 1993, the court explained, four more States—Oklahoma, South Carolina, Montana, and Georgia—had capitalized the crime of child rape and at least eight States had authorized capital punishment for other nonhomicide crimes. By its count, 14 of the then–38 States permitting capital punishment, plus the Federal Government, allowed the death penalty for nonhomicide crimes and 5 allowed the death penalty for the crime of child rape.... The state court next asked whether "child rapists rank among the worst offenders." It noted the severity of the crime; that the execution of child rapists would serve the goals of deterrence and retribution; and that, unlike in *Atkins* and *Roper,* there were no characteristics of petitioner that tended to mitigate his moral culpability. It concluded: "[S]hort of first-degree murder, we can think of no other non-homicide crime more deserving [of capital punishment]." ... On this reasoning the Supreme Court of Louisiana rejected petitioner's argument that the death penalty for the rape of a child under 12 years is disproportionate and upheld the constitutionality of the statute.... We granted certiorari.

The Eighth Amendment, applicable to the States through the Fourteenth Amendment, provides that "[e]xcessive bail shall not be required, nor excessive fines imposed, nor cruel and unusual punishments inflicted." The Amendment proscribes "all excessive punishments, as well as cruel and unusual punishments that may or may not be excessive." *Atkins,* 536 U.S., at 311, n. 7. The Court explained in *Atkins* and *Roper* that the Eighth Amendment's protection against excessive or cruel and unusual punishments flows from the basic "precept of justice that punishment for [a] crime should be graduated and proportioned to [the] offense." *Weems v. United States,* 217 U.S. 349, 367 (1910). Whether this requirement has been fulfilled is determined not by the standards that prevailed when the Eighth Amendment was adopted in 1791 but by the norms that "currently prevail." *Atkins, supra,* at 311. The Amendment "draw[s] its meaning from the evolving standards of decency that mark the progress of a maturing society." *Trop v. Dulles,* 356 U.S. 86, 101 (1958) (plurality opinion). This is because "[t]he standard of extreme cruelty is not merely descriptive, but necessarily embodies a moral judgment. The standard itself remains the same, but its applicability must change as the basic mores of society change." *Furman v. Georgia,* 408 U.S. 238, 382 (1972) (Burger, C. J., dissenting).

Evolving standards of decency must embrace and express respect for the dignity of the person, and the punishment of criminals must conform to that rule. [P]unishment is justified under one or more of three principal rationales: rehabilitation, deterrence, and retribution. It is the last of these, retribution, that most often can contradict the law's own ends.... When the law punishes by death, it risks its own sudden descent into brutality, transgressing the constitutional commitment to decency and restraint.

[C]apital punishment must "be limited to those offenders who commit 'a narrow category of the most serious crimes' and whose extreme culpability makes them 'the most deserving of execution.'" *Roper, supra,* at 568. Though the death penalty is not invariably unconstitutional, the Court insists upon confining the instances in which the punishment can be imposed.

Applying this principle, we held in *Roper* and *Atkins* that the execution of juveniles and mentally retarded persons are punishments violative of the Eighth Amendment because the offender had a diminished personal responsibility for the crime. The Court further has held that the death penalty can be disproportionate to the crime itself where the crime did not result, or was not intended to result, in death of the victim. In *Coker,* 433 U.S. 584, for instance, the Court held it would be unconstitutional to execute an offender who had raped an adult woman. And in *Enmund v. Florida,* 458 U.S. 782 (1982), the Court overturned the capital sentence of a defendant who aided and abetted a robbery during which a murder was committed but did not himself kill, attempt to kill, or intend that a killing would take place. On the other hand, in *Tison v. Arizona,* 481 U.S. 137 (1987), the Court allowed the defendants' death sentences to stand where they did not themselves kill the victims but their involvement in the events leading up to the murders was active, recklessly indifferent, and substantial.

In these cases the Court has been guided by "objective indicia of society's standards, as expressed in legislative enactments and state practice with respect to executions." *Roper,* 543 U.S., at 563. . . . Consensus is not dispositive. Whether the death penalty is disproportionate to the crime committed depends as well upon the standards elaborated by controlling precedents and by the Court's own understanding and interpretation of the Eighth Amendment's text, history, meaning, and purpose.

Based both on consensus and our own independent judgment, our holding is that a death sentence for one who raped but did not kill a child, and who did not intend to assist another in killing the child, is unconstitutional under the Eighth and Fourteenth Amendments.

The existence of objective indicia of consensus against making a crime punishable by death was a relevant concern in *Roper, Atkins, Coker,* and *Enmund,* and we follow the approach of those cases here. The history of the death penalty for the crime of rape is an instructive beginning point. . . . In 1925, 18 States, the District of Columbia, and the Federal Government had statutes that authorized the death penalty for the rape of a child or an adult. Between 1930 and 1964,

455 people were executed for those crimes. To our knowledge the last individual executed for the rape of a child was Ronald Wolfe in 1964.... In 1972, *Furman* invalidated most of the state statutes authorizing the death penalty for the crime of rape; and in *Furman's* aftermath only six States reenacted their capital rape provisions. Three States—Georgia, North Carolina, and Louisiana—did so with respect to all rape offenses. Three States—Florida, Mississippi, and Tennessee—did so with respect only to child rape. All six statutes were later invalidated under state or federal law.

Louisiana reintroduced the death penalty for rape of a child in 1995. Under the current statute, any anal, vaginal, or oral intercourse with a child under the age of 13 constitutes aggravated rape and is punishable by death. Mistake of age is not a defense, so the statute imposes strict liability in this regard. Five States have since followed Louisiana's lead.

By contrast, 44 States have not made child rape a capital offense. As for federal law, Congress in the Federal Death Penalty Act of 1994 expanded the number of federal crimes for which the death penalty is a permissible sentence, including certain nonhomicide offenses; but it did not do the same for child rape or abuse....

... When *Atkins* was decided in 2002, 30 States, including 12 noncapital jurisdictions, prohibited the death penalty for mentally retarded offenders; 20 permitted it. When *Roper* was decided in 2005, the numbers disclosed a similar division among the States: 30 States prohibited the death penalty for juveniles, 18 of which permitted the death penalty for other offenders; and 20 States authorized it. Both in *Atkins* and in *Roper,* we noted that the practice of executing mentally retarded and juvenile offenders was infrequent. Only five States had executed an offender known to have an IQ below 70 between 1989 and 2002, and only three States had executed a juvenile offender between 1995 and 2005.

The statistics in *Enmund* bear an even greater similarity to the instant case. There eight jurisdictions had authorized imposition of the death penalty solely for participation in a robbery during which an accomplice committed murder, and six defendants between 1954 and 1982 had been sentenced to death for felony murder where the defendant did not personally commit the homicidal assault. These facts, the Court concluded, "weigh[ed] on the side of rejecting capital punishment for the crime."

The evidence of a national consensus with respect to the death penalty for child rapists, as with respect to juveniles, mentally retarded offenders, and vicarious felony murderers, shows divided opinion but, on balance, an opinion against it. Thirty-seven jurisdictions—36 States plus the Federal Government—have the death penalty. As mentioned above, only six of those jurisdictions authorize the death penalty for rape of a child.... [I]t is of significance that, in 45 jurisdictions, petitioner could not be executed for child rape of any kind. That number surpasses the 30 States in *Atkins* and *Roper* and the 42 States in *Enmund* that prohibited the death penalty under the circumstances those cases considered.

[The] state courts that have confronted the precise question before us have been uniform in concluding that *Coker* did not address the constitutionality of the death penalty for the crime of child rape.... We conclude on the basis of this review that there is no clear indication that state legislatures have misinterpreted *Coker* to hold that the death penalty for child rape is unconstitutional. The small number of States that have enacted this penalty, then, is relevant to determining whether there is a consensus against capital punishment for this crime.

[The Louisiana Attorney General] insists that the six States where child rape is a capital offense, along with the [five] States that have proposed but not yet enacted applicable death penalty legislation, reflect a consistent direction of change in support of the death penalty for child rape. Consistent change might counterbalance an otherwise weak demonstration of consensus. But ... no showing of consistent change has been made in this case.

[It] is not our practice, nor is it sound, to find contemporary norms based upon state legislation that has been proposed but not yet enacted.... Here, the total number of States to have made child rape a capital offense after *Furman* is six. This is not an indication of a trend or change in direction comparable to the one supported by data in *Roper*. The evidence here bears a closer resemblance to the evidence of state activity in *Enmund,* where we found a national consensus against the death penalty for vicarious felony murder despite eight jurisdictions having authorized the practice.

[Statistics] about the number of executions may inform the consideration whether capital punishment for the crime of child rape is regarded as unacceptable in our society. These statistics confirm our determination from our review of state statutes that there is a social consensus against the death penalty for the crime of child rape.

Nine States—Florida, Georgia, Louisiana, Mississippi, Montana, Oklahoma, South Carolina, Tennessee, and Texas—have permitted capital punishment for adult or child rape for some length of time between the Court's 1972 decision in *Furman* and today. Yet no individual has been executed for the rape of an adult or child since 1964, and no execution for any other nonhomicide offense has been conducted since 1963.

After reviewing the authorities informed by contemporary norms, including the history of the death penalty for this and other nonhomicide crimes, current state statutes and new enactments, and the number of executions since 1964, we conclude there is a national consensus against capital punishment for the crime of child rape....

We turn, then, to the resolution of the question before us, which is informed by our precedents and our own understanding of the Constitution and the rights it secures. [First,] [i]t must be acknowledged that there are moral grounds to question a rule barring capital punishment for a crime against an individual that did not result in death. These facts illustrate the point. Here the victim's fright, the sense of betrayal, and the nature of her injuries caused more prolonged physical and mental suffering than, say, a sudden killing by an unseen assassin. The attack was not just on her but on her childhood. For this reason, we should be most reluctant to rely upon the language of the plurality in *Coker*, which posited that, for the victim of rape, "life may not be nearly so happy as it was" but it is not beyond repair. Rape has a permanent psychological, emotional, and sometimes physical impact on the child. We cannot dismiss the years of long anguish that must be endured by the victim of child rape.

It does not follow, though, that capital punishment is a proportionate penalty for the crime.... Evolving standards of decency that mark the progress of a maturing society counsel us to be most hesitant before interpreting the Eighth Amendment to allow the extension of the death penalty, a hesitation that has special force where no life was taken in the commission of the crime. It is an established principle that decency, in its essence, presumes respect for the individual and thus moderation or restraint in the application of capital punishment.

To date the Court has sought to define and implement this principle, for the most part, in cases involving capital murder. One approach has been to insist upon general rules that ensure consistency in determining who receives a death sentence. At the same time the Court has insisted, to ensure restraint and moderation in use of capital punishment, on judging the "character and record of the individual offender and the circumstances of the particular offense as a constitutionally indispensable part of the process of inflicting the penalty of death."

The tension between general rules and case-specific circumstances has produced results not all together satisfactory. This has led some Members of the Court to say we should cease efforts to resolve the tension and simply allow legislatures, prosecutors, courts, and juries greater latitude. For others the failure to limit these same imprecisions by stricter enforcement of narrowing rules has raised doubts concerning the constitutionality of capital punishment itself.

Our response to this case law, which is still in search of a unifying principle, has been to insist upon confining the instances in which capital punishment may be imposed.

Our concern here is limited to crimes against individual persons. We do not address, for example, crimes defining and punishing treason, espionage, terrorism, and drug kingpin activity, which are offenses against the State. As it relates to crimes against individuals, though, the death penalty should not be expanded to instances where the victim's life was not taken.

The same distinction between homicide and other serious violent offenses against the individual informed the Court's analysis in *Enmund,* 458 U.S. 782, where the Court held that the death penalty for the crime of vicarious felony murder is disproportionate to the offense. The Court repeated there the fundamental, moral distinction between a "murderer" and a "robber," noting that while "robbery is a serious crime deserving serious punishment," it is not like death in its "severity and irrevocability."

Consistent with evolving standards of decency and the teachings of our precedents we conclude that, in determining whether the death penalty is excessive, there is a distinction between intentional first-degree murder on the one hand and nonhomicide crimes against individual persons, even including child rape, on the other. The latter crimes may be devastating in their harm, as here, but "in terms of moral depravity and of the injury to the person and to the public," *Coker,* 433 U.S., at 598, they cannot be compared to murder in their "severity and irrevocability."

In reaching our conclusion we find significant the number of executions that would be allowed under respondent's approach. The crime of child rape, considering its reported incidents, occurs more often than first-degree murder. Approximately 5,702 incidents of vaginal, anal, or oral rape of a child under the age of 12 were reported nationwide in 2005; this is almost twice the total incidents of intentional murder for victims of all ages (3,405) reported during the same period. . . . As a result of existing rules, only 2.2% of convicted first-degree murderers are sentenced to death. But under Louisiana's approach, the 36 States that permit the death penalty could sentence to death all persons convicted of raping a child less than 12 years of age. This could not be reconciled with our evolving standards of decency and the necessity to constrain the use of the death penalty.

It might be said that narrowing aggravators could be used in this context, as with murder offenses, to ensure the death penalty's restrained application. We find it difficult to identify standards that would guide the decisionmaker so the penalty is reserved for the most severe cases of child rape and yet not imposed in an arbitrary way. Even were we to forbid, say, the execution of first-time child rapists, or require as an aggravating factor a finding that the perpetrator's instant rape offense involved multiple victims, the jury still must balance, in its discretion, those aggravating factors against mitigating circumstances. In this context, which involves a crime that in many cases will overwhelm a decent person's judgment, we have no confidence that the imposition of the death penalty would not be so arbitrary as to be "freakis[h]," *Furman*, 408 U.S., at 310 (Stewart, J., concurring). We cannot sanction this result when the harm to the victim, though grave, cannot be quantified in the same way as death of the victim. . . .

Our concerns are all the more pronounced where, as here, the death penalty for this crime has been most infrequent. We have developed a foundational jurisprudence in the case of capital murder to guide the States and juries in imposing the death penalty. Starting with *Gregg*, we have spent more than 32 years articulating limiting factors that channel the jury's discretion to avoid the death penalty's arbitrary imposition in the case of capital murder. Though that practice remains sound, beginning the same process for crimes for which no one has been executed in more than 40 years would require experimentation in an area where a failed experiment would result in the execution of individuals undeserving of the death penalty. Evolving standards of decency are difficult to reconcile with a regime that seeks to expand the death penalty to an area where standards to confine its use are indefinite and obscure.

Our decision is consistent with the justifications offered for the death penalty. *Gregg* instructs that capital punishment is excessive when it is grossly out of proportion to the crime or it does not fulfill the two distinct social purposes served by the death penalty: retribution and deterrence of capital crimes.

As in *Coker*, here it cannot be said with any certainty that the death penalty for child rape serves no deterrent or retributive function. . . . This argument does not overcome other objections, however. The incongruity between the crime of child rape and the harshness of the death penalty poses risks of overpunishment and counsels against a constitutional ruling that the death penalty can be expanded to include this offense. . . .

There is an additional reason for our conclusion that imposing the death penalty for child rape would not further retributive purposes. In considering whether retribution is served, among other factors we have looked to whether capital punishment "has the potential . . . to allow the community as a whole, including the surviving family and friends of the victim, to affirm its own judgment that the culpability of the prisoner is so serious that the ultimate penalty must be sought and imposed." *Panetti v. Quarterman*, 127 S.Ct. 2842 (2007). In considering the death penalty for nonhomicide offenses this inquiry necessarily also must include the question whether the death penalty balances the wrong to the victim.

It is not at all evident that the child rape victim's hurt is lessened when the law permits the death of the perpetrator. . . . In cases like this the key testimony is not just from the family but from the victim herself. During formative years of her adolescence, made all the more daunting for having to come to terms with the brutality of her experience, L.H. was required to discuss the case at length with law enforcement personnel. In a public trial she was required to recount once more all the details of the crime to a jury as the State pursued the death of her stepfather. And in the end the State made L.H. a central figure in its decision to seek the death penalty, telling the jury in closing statements: "[L. H.] is asking you, asking you to set up a time and place when he dies."

Society's desire to inflict the death penalty for child rape by enlisting the child victim to assist it over the course of years in asking for capital punishment forces a moral choice on the child, who is not of mature age to make that choice. The way the death penalty here involves the child victim in its enforcement can compromise a decent legal system; and this is but a subset of fundamental difficulties capital punishment can cause in the administration and enforcement of laws proscribing child rape.

There are, moreover, serious systemic concerns in prosecuting the crime of child rape that are relevant to the constitutionality of making it a capital offense. The problem of unreliable, induced, and even imagined child testimony means there is a "special risk of wrongful execution" in some child rape cases. *Atkins, supra,* at 321.... Similar criticisms pertain to other cases involving child witnesses; but child rape cases present heightened concerns because the central narrative and account of the crime often comes from the child herself. She and the accused are, in most instances, the only ones present when the crime was committed....

With respect to deterrence, if the death penalty adds to the risk of non-reporting, that, too, diminishes the penalty's objectives. Underreporting is a common problem with respect to child sexual abuse. [O]ne of the most commonly cited reasons for nondisclosure is fear of negative consequences for the perpetrator, a concern that has special force where the abuser is a family member. The experience of the *amici* who work with child victims indicates that, when the punishment is death, both the victim and the victim's family members may be more likely to shield the perpetrator from discovery, thus increasing underreporting. As a result, punishment by death may not result in more deterrence or more effective enforcement.

In addition, by in effect making the punishment for child rape and murder equivalent, a State that punishes child rape by death may remove a strong incentive for the rapist not to kill the victim. Assuming the offender behaves in a rational way, as one must to justify the penalty on grounds of deterrence, the penalty in some respects gives less protection, not more, to the victim, who is often the sole witness to the crime....

Each of these propositions, standing alone, might not establish the unconstitutionality of the death penalty for the crime of child rape. Taken in sum, however, they demonstrate the serious negative consequences of making child rape a capital offense. These considerations lead us to conclude, in our independent judgment, that the death penalty is not a proportional punishment for the rape of a child.

Our determination that there is a consensus against the death penalty for child rape raises the question whether the Court's own institutional position and its holding will have the effect of blocking further or later consensus in favor of the penalty from developing. The Court, it will be argued, by the act of addressing the constitutionality of the death penalty, intrudes upon the consensus-making process. By imposing a negative restraint, the argument runs, the Court makes it more difficult for consensus to change or emerge. The Court, according to the criticism, itself becomes enmeshed in the process, part judge and part the maker of that which it judges.

These concerns overlook the meaning and full substance of the established proposition that the Eighth Amendment is defined by "the evolving standards of decency that mark the progress of a maturing society." *Trop,* 356 U.S., at 101. Confirmed by repeated, consistent rulings of this Court, this principle requires that use of the death penalty be restrained. The rule of evolving standards of decency with specific marks on the way to full progress and mature judgment means that resort to the penalty must be reserved for the worst of crimes and limited in its instances of application. In most cases justice is not better served by terminating the life of the perpetrator rather than confining him and preserving the possibility that he and the system will find ways to allow him to understand the enormity of his offense. Difficulties in administering the penalty to ensure against its arbitrary and capricious application require adherence to a rule reserving its use, at this stage of evolving standards and in cases of crimes against individuals, for crimes that take the life of the victim.

The judgment of the Supreme Court of Louisiana upholding the capital sentence is reversed. This case is remanded for further proceedings not inconsistent with this opinion. It is so ordered.

Justice ALITO, with whom THE CHIEF JUSTICE, Justice SCALIA, and Justice THOMAS join, dissenting.

[In] assessing current norms, the Court relies primarily on the fact that only 6 of the 50 States now have statutes that permit the death penalty for this offense. But this statistic is a highly unreliable indicator of the views of state lawmakers and their constituents. [D]icta in this Court's decision in *Coker v. Georgia,* 433 U.S. 584 (1977), has stunted legislative consideration of the question whether the death penalty for the targeted offense of raping a young child is consistent with prevailing standards of decency. The *Coker* dicta gave state legislators and others good reason to fear that any law permitting the imposition of the death penalty for this crime would meet precisely the fate that has now befallen the Louisiana statute that is currently before us, and this threat strongly discouraged state legislators—regardless of their own values and those of their constituents—from supporting the enactment of such legislation....

For the past three decades, these interpretations have posed a very high hurdle for state legislatures considering the passage of new laws permitting the death penalty for the rape of a child. The enactment and implementation of any new state death penalty statute—and particularly a new type of statute such as one that specifically targets the rape of young children—imposes many costs.... When a capital sentence is imposed under the new law, there is the burden of keeping the prisoner on death row and the lengthy and costly project of defending the constitutionality of the statute on appeal and in collateral proceedings. And if the law is eventually overturned, there is the burden of new proceedings on remand. Moreover, conscientious state lawmakers, whatever their personal views about the morality of imposing the death penalty for child rape, may defer to this Court's dicta, either because they respect our authority and expertise in interpreting the Constitution or merely because they do not relish the prospect of being held to have violated the Constitution and contravened prevailing "standards of decency." Accordingly, the *Coker* dicta gave state legislators a strong incentive not to push for the enactment of new capital child-rape laws even though these legislators and their constituents may have believed that the laws would be appropriate and desirable.... Because of the effect of the *Coker* dicta, the Court is plainly wrong in comparing the situation here to that in *Atkins* or *Roper*....

[I]n just the past few years, despite the shadow cast by the *Coker* dicta, five States have enacted targeted capital child-rape laws. If, as the Court seems to think, our society is "[e]volving" toward ever higher "standards of decency," these enactments might represent the beginning of a new evolutionary line.... Such a development would not be out of step with changes in our society's thinking since *Coker* was decided. During that time, reported instances of child abuse have increased dramatically; and there are many indications of growing alarm about the sexual abuse of children. In 1994, Congress enacted the Jacob Wetterling Crimes Against Children and Sexually Violent Offender Registration Program, 42 U.S.C. § 14071 (2000 ed. and Supp. V), which requires States receiving certain federal funds to establish registration systems for convicted sex offenders and to notify the public about persons convicted of the sexual abuse of minors. All 50 States have now enacted such statutes. In addition, at least 21 States and the District of Columbia now have statutes permitting the involuntary commitment of sexual predators, and at least 12 States have enacted residency restrictions for sex offenders. . . .

[The] Court argues that statistics about the number of executions in rape cases support its perception of a "national consensus," but here too the statistics do not support the Court's position. . . . The Court [fails] to mention that in Louisiana, since the state law was amended in 1995 to make child rape a capital offense, prosecutors have asked juries to return death verdicts in four cases. This 50% record is hardly evidence that juries share the Court's view that the death penalty for the rape of a young child is unacceptable under even the most aggravated circumstances.

[Neither] Congress nor juries have done anything that can plausibly be interpreted as evidencing the "national consensus" that the Court perceives. . . . I do not suggest that six new state laws necessarily establish a "national consensus" or even that they are sure evidence of an ineluctable trend. . . . But they might also have been the beginning of a strong new evolutionary line. We will never know, because the Court today snuffs out the line in its incipient stage. . . .

That sweeping holding is also not justified by the Court's concerns about the reliability of the testimony of child victims. First, the Eighth Amendment provides a poor vehicle for addressing problems regarding the admissibility or reliability of evidence, and problems presented by the testimony of child victims are not unique to capital cases. Second, concerns about the reliability of the testimony of child witnesses are not present in every child-rape case. In the case before us, for example, there was undisputed medical evidence that the victim was brutally raped, as well as strong independent evidence that petitioner was the perpetrator. Third, if the Court's evidentiary concerns have Eighth Amendment relevance, they could be addressed by allowing the death penalty in only those child-rape cases in which the independent evidence is sufficient to prove all the elements needed for conviction and imposition of a death sentence. . . . A State wishing to permit the death penalty in child-rape cases could impose an analogous corroboration requirement. . . .

The Court's final—and, it appears, principal—justification for its holding is that murder, the only crime for which defendants have been executed since this Court's 1976 death penalty decisions, is unique in its moral depravity and in the severity of the injury that it inflicts on the victim and the public. . . . With respect to the question of moral depravity, is it really true that every person who is convicted of capital murder and sentenced to death is more morally depraved than every child rapist? Consider the following two cases. In the first, a defendant robs a convenience store and watches as his accomplice shoots the store owner. The defendant acts recklessly, but was not the triggerman and did not intend the killing. In the second case, a previously convicted child rapist kidnaps, repeatedly rapes, and tortures multiple child victims. Is it clear that the first defendant is more morally depraved than the second? . . . The rape of any victim inflicts great injury, and "[s]ome victims are so grievously injured physically or psychologically that life *is* beyond repair." *Coker,* 433 U.S., at 603 (opinion of Powell, J.). . . . The deep problems that afflict child-rape victims often become society's problems as well. Commentators have noted correlations between childhood sexual abuse and later prob- lems such as substance abuse, dangerous sexual behaviors or dysfunc- tion, inability to relate to others on an interpersonal level, and psychiatric illness. . . . The harm that is caused to the victims and to society at large by the worst child rapists is grave. It is the judgment of the Louisiana lawmakers and those in an increasing number of other States that these harms justify the death penalty. . . . Conclusory references to "decency," "moderation," "restraint," "full progress," and "moral judgment" are not enough. . . . The party attacking the constitutionality of a state statute bears the "heavy burden" of estab- lishing that the law is unconstitutional. That burden has not been discharged here, and I would therefore affirm the decision of the Louisiana Supreme Court.

NOTES

1. *Military death penalty for child rape.* In *Kennedy v. Louisiana,* 129 S.Ct. 1 (2008), the Supreme Court issued a rare opinion explaining the denial of the petition for rehearing in *Kennedy.* The petition was based on information about the military death penalty for child rape, "not cited by either party, nor by any of the numerous *amici* in the case", which was "first brought to the Court's attention after the opinion had issued, in a letter signed by 85 Members of Congress." *Id.* at *2 (Scalia, J, statement respecting the denial of rehearing). This information related to the fact that "military law has included the death penalty for rape of a child or adult victim since at least 1863", although the death penalty "has not been carried out against a military offender for almost 50 years". In 2006, Congress revised the military's sexual-assault statutes to make adult rape and child rape separate crimes; although Congress did not set the maximum penalty for these crimes, it left in place the existing penalty as the "interim maximum punishment", which the President later left in place by executive order. The Court determined that: 1) "authorization of the death penalty in the military sphere does not indicate that the penalty is constitutional in the civilian context"; 2) the *Kennedy* case did not raise the issue of the constitutionality of the military death penalty for rape; and 3) the existence of the death penalty for rape in the Manual for Courts Martial "does not draw into question our conclusions that there is a consensus against the death penalty for the crime in the civilian context". *Id.* at *1–2 (Kennedy, J., statement respecting the denial of rehearing [joined by four justices in the *Kennedy* majority]). Justices Thomas and Alito voted to grant the petition for rehearing. Justice Scalia and Chief Justice Roberts voted to deny it because "the views of the

American people on the death penalty for child rape were … irrelevant to the majority's decision", although, in their view, the information about the military death penalty "utterly destroys the majority's claim to be discerning a national consensus and not just giving effect to the majority's own preference." *Id.* at *2 (Scalia, J, statement respecting the denial of rehearing).

2. *Evolution of concerns about administration of the death penalty.* The Supreme Court first upheld the use of "guided discretion" sentencing procedures for imposing the death penalty in *Gregg v. Georgia*, 428 U.S. 153 (1976) and two companion cases from Texas and Florida; in two other companion cases, the Court invalidated "mandatory" sentencing procedures in *Woodson v. North Carolina*, 428 U.S. 280 (1976) and *Roberts v. Louisiana*, 428 U.S. 325 (1976). The *Gregg* Court identified three criteria relating to the Eighth Amendment's "evolving standard of decency" concept that emerged in *Furman v. Georgia*, 408 U.S. 238 (1972), as a core value underlying the prohibition on "cruel and unusual punishment": 1) the need for punishment to be consistent with contemporary standards of acceptable punishment; 2) the need to avoid the operation of unguided, standardless jury discretion that could result in the arbitrary imposition of death sentences; and 3) the need to insure that death sentences would be imposed based on the "individualized" consideration, by the jury, of the character and record of a defendant and of the circumstances of his offense. See *Gregg*, 428 U.S. at 299–304. In *Woodson* and *Roberts*, the mandatory schemes were invalidated because they violated these three criteria; by contrast, the "guided discretion" scheme in *Gregg*, which was modeled on a Model Penal Code proposal, was upheld because it satisfied the three criteria. These procedural features of the Georgia scheme were praised by the *Gregg* majority as creating safeguards against the arbitrary sentencing condemned in *Furman*: 1) "a bifurcated proceeding at which the sentencing authority is appraised of the information relevant to the imposition of sentence", namely, a traditional trial on the issue of guilt, followed by a sentencing hearing on the issue of a life or death sentence; 2) the presentation of mitigating circumstances by the defendant at the sentencing hearing; 3) the requirement of a finding identifying a reason for the imposition of a death sentence, as through the selection of an "aggravating" circumstance from a statutory list; and 4) the provision for appellate court review of a death sentence. From these doctrinal beginnings, the Court constructed a complex doctrinal edifice of Eighth Amendment law concerning the procedural "fairness" of particular death penalty procedures; some of the features of this jurisprudence are described in the summary in Part 2, *infra*, of procedures in a "typical capital case."

Since *Gregg*, even those who are supportive of the death penalty as an appropriate punishment have remained concerned about the manner in which it is used. Responding to growing criticism about the administration of the death penalty, a dozen states have commissioned studies of their penalty system to examine racial and geographic disparities within states, as well as serious problems with court-appointed lawyers and the appeals process. For example, Illinois Governor George H. Ryan appointed the Illinois Commission on Capital Punishment in March 2000 after declaring a moratorium on the execution of death row inmates two months earlier. The Commission's report issued two years later recommended 85 reforms to the capital punishment system in Illinois. The report has fueled a new phase of the nationwide debate on the death penalty. Before leaving office in January, 2003, Governor Ryan commuted the death sentences of 167 of the state's death row inmates, and pardoned four inmates. The Commission recommendations included:

a. Creating a statewide review panel to conduct a pre-trial review of prosecutorial decisions to seek capital punishment. The panel would be comprised of four prosecutors and a retired judge.

b. Significantly reducing the current list of death eligibility factors from twenty to five including: murder of a peace officer or firefighter; murder in a correctional facility; the murder of two or more persons; the intentional murder of a person involving torture; and any murder committed by a suspected felon in order to obstruct the justice system.

c. Prohibiting a death sentence in a case where the conviction is based solely on uncorroborated single eyewitness or accomplice testimony or the uncorroborated testimony of jail house informants.

d. Recommending other reforms concerning the use of jail house informants who purport to have information about the case or statements allegedly made by the defendant, including the requirements that a preliminary hearing must be conducted by the court as to the reliability of such witnesses and their proposed testimony, that benefits conferred for such testimony must be fully disclosed, and that the background of such witnesses must be disclosed early to the defense.

e. Videotaping the entire interrogation of homicide suspects at a police station, and not merely the confession.

f. Allowing trial judges to concur or reverse a jury's death sentence verdict. This will allow the trial judge to take into account potential improper influences such as passion and prejudice that may have influenced a jury's verdict, to consider potential residual doubt about the defendant's absolute guilt, and to consider trial strategies of counsel, credibility of witnesses and the actual presentation of evidence, which may differ from what was anticipated in making pretrial rulings in either admitting or excluding evidence.

g. Requiring the Illinois Supreme Court to review all death sentences to determine whether the sentence is excessive or disproportionate to the penalty imposed in similar cases, whether death was the appropriate sentence given aggravating and mitigating factors, and whether the sentence was imposed due to some arbitrary factor.

h. Supporting the Illinois Supreme Court's recommendation for a capital case trial bar and requiring judges to be pre-certified before presiding over capital cases. As part of regular training for judges and counsel, as suggested by the Illinois Supreme Court and the Commission, improvements must be made in disseminating information and creating manuals and check lists to be used by counsel and the courts. There must also be better reporting of information concerning capital cases so that the fairness and accuracy of the capital punishment system can be adequately assessed.

i. To eliminate confusion and improper speculation, juries should be instructed as to all the possible sentencing alternatives before they consider the appropriateness of imposing a death sentence.

j. Like defendants in any other criminal case, capital defendants should be afforded the opportunity to make a statement to those who will be deciding whether to impose the ultimate punishment allowed by the state, a sentence of death.

3. *Discrimination in death sentences.* The Supreme Court rejected a constitutional challenge to Georgia's death penalty system based on evidence of race discrimination in *McCleskey v. Kemp*, 481 U.S. 279 (1987). The *McCleskey* defendant relied on a study showing that defendants who killed white victims were 4.3 times as likely to receive a death sentence as those who killed black defendants, and for some categories of cases, "the white-victim average death-sentence rate is at least 100 percent higher than the black-victim rate." David C. Baldus, George Woodworth, Charles A. Pulaski, Jr. Equal Justice and the Death Penalty: A Legal and Empirical Analysis. 383 (1990). But the *McCleskey* majority held that the study did not "demonstrate a constitutionally significant risk of racial bias" under either Eighth or Fourteenth Amendments precedents. The Court emphasized two "concerns" that informed its holding: 1) if the Court accepted the claim of bias in the capital sentencing system, then it "could soon be faced with similar claims as to other types of penalty", as "there is no limiting principle to the type of challenge brought by McCleskey"; 2) the arguments about race discrimination "are best presented to the legislative bodies." *Id.* at 315–319.

In 2008 there were roughly 3400 death row inmates in the United States, and studies after *McCleskey* continued to show evidence of race discrimination. In 2003, a Maryland study showed that murder defendants "in a majority black county are 26 times more likely" to receive a death sentence than those in other counties; a Virginia study showed that the rate at which prosecutors "in high-density population (typically urban) localities" "sought the death penalty in capital-eligible cases was 200 percent lower than was observed in medium density localities", and that "location, more than any other factor is most strongly associated with a prosecutor's decision" to seek death. Paul Marcus, *Capital Punishment in the United States, and Beyond*, 31 Melbourne Univ. L. Rev. 837, 859–862 (2007). In February 2008, the Houston Chronicle reported that more than one third of the executions since 1976 (242 out of 693) had occurred in Texas, and 61 of the executed inmates in Texas had received the death sentence in Harris County (Houston). "If this were a state, it would rank third nationally behind Texas and

Virginia ... [but] Harris County has more people awaiting execution compared with only 30 in Virginia." http://www.chron.com/content/chronicle/special01/penalty (Feb. 12, 2008).

4. *Shifts in attitudes toward the death penalty.* The recent trends in the numbers of death sentences and executions has been summarized as follows:

> The number of executions per year has varied greatly throughout U. S. history, but has dropped considerably in recent years. During the 1930s and 1940s, well over 100 individuals were executed each year. In peak years since 1976, just over 300 people were sentenced to death each year.... In recent years, the year in which the most individuals were executed was 1999, with 98 death sentences carried out. That number has been steadily declining since [and dropped to 47 in 2007.] Whereas 317 people were sentenced to death in 1996[,] in recent years, death sentences per year have only been about a third of that 1996 figure.

Marcus, *supra* Note 3, at 846. According to polling data, public support for the death penalty is dropping. For example, 80 per cent of respondents in a 1994 poll were "in favor of the death penalty for a person convicted of murder", but in 2004 it was 64 per cent. In 2007, New Jersey "became the first state to abolish the death penalty through the legislative process", and "New York and Massachusetts have chosen not to re-enact their death penalty statutes." *Id.* at 847–848 & nn. 52–56.

2. THE TYPICAL CAPITAL CASE

The procedures for the trial of capital cases has been fashioned in response to federal precedent on the issue. The government must establish at least one aggravating circumstance beyond a reasonable doubt in order to impose the death penalty. Current capital punishment provisions are the product of a lengthy series of court opinions, beginning with *Furman v. Georgia*, 408 U.S. 238 (1972) and *Gregg v. Georgia*, 428 U.S. 153 (1976).

In *California v. Brown*, 479 U.S. 538 (1987), the Court summarized its precedents as establishing two prerequisites for a valid death sentence. First, "death penalty statutes [must] be structured so as to prevent the penalty from being administered in an arbitrary and unpredictable fashion. ... Second, ... the capital defendant generally must be allowed to introduce any relevant mitigating evidence." The prosecution must give defense counsel adequate notice that it will seek the death penalty. The defendant's guilt is initially determined at a "guilt" phase, and if the defendant is found guilty, a second hearing (the "penalty" phase) is conducted to determine the punishment. If the guilt phase of the proceeding is tried without a jury, the judge alone presides over the penalty phase. Likewise, if a jury has found guilt, the penalty phase is conducted as soon as possible before the same jury. When a defendant pleads guilty to a capital offense, the defendant may demand that a jury be impanelled to determine punishment.

At a pretrial conference, the defendant may allege that a sentence of death is being sought on the basis of race. The defendant must state with particularity how the evidence supports a claim that racial considerations played a significant part in the decision to seek a death sentence in his or her case. Relevant evidence may include statistical evidence or other evidence that death sentences were sought significantly more frequently either upon persons of one race than upon persons of another race, or as punishment for capital offenses against persons of one race than as punishment for capital offenses against persons of another race. The defendant has the burden of proving by clear and convincing evidence that race was the basis of the decision to seek the death penalty. The prosecution may offer evidence in rebuttal of the claims or evidence of the defendant. If the court finds that race was the basis of the decision to seek the death sentence, the court orders that a death sentence cannot be sought in that case.

In *Zant v. Stephens*, 462 U.S. 862 (1983), the Court held that all evidence may be introduced in a capital sentencing hearing as long as it is relevant, reliable and not prejudicial. Evidence is relevant to punishment if it is relevant to a statutory aggravating circumstance or to a statutory or other mitigating circumstance raised by the defendant. See *Bell v. Ohio*, 438 U.S. 637 (1978).

Each jurisdiction may define the aggravating circumstances which must be proved before the death penalty can be imposed. A common aggravating circumstance is that the defendant has been previously convicted of a capital offense. See *Romano v. Oklahoma*, 512 U.S. 1 (1994). A prior conviction cannot be used as an aggravating circumstance, however, if an appeal of the conviction is pending.

A second typical aggravating circumstance is that the defendant committed murder or kidnapping while engaged in the commission of a serious felony such as arson, robbery, burglary, or rape. See *Schiro v. Farley*, 510 U.S. 222 (1994). A third example of an aggravating circumstance is that the defendant killed more than one person. A fourth is that the defendant knowingly created a great risk of death to two or more persons in a public place by means of a destructive device or weapon normally hazardous to more than one person. This aggravator is not improper merely because it duplicates one of the elements of the homicide. See *Lowenfield v. Phelps*, 484 U.S. 231 (1988).

A fifth aggravating circumstance describes defendants who either pay for or receive remuneration for a murder. This circumstance also may apply to persons who commit murder and expect to profit from the victim's death. Many statutes contain no minimum level of profit, but the evidence may permit the jury to infer that it would be substantial, and thereby demonstrate the motive for the crime.

A sixth type of aggravating circumstance concerns the murder of a prison employee by a defendant who was a prisoner at the time of the homicide. The murder must have occurred while the prison employee was engaged in the performance of duties. In recent years, states have included: 1) the intentional killing of a state or local public official or police officer, sheriff or deputy sheriff while the official was engaged in the lawful performance of duties, and 2) a killing of a victim who has obtained an emergency protective order or a domestic violence order, or any other order designed to protect the victim from the defendant (such as an order issued as a condition of a bond, conditional release, probation, parole, or pretrial diversion).

As a practical matter the defense may introduce proof of any mitigating circumstances for consideration by the jury. See *California v. Brown*, 479 U.S. 538 (1987). The purpose of the mitigating factors is to allow a jury to give individualized consideration to a defendant, and independent weight to aspects of his or her character, record, and offense, that may call for a penalty of life instead of death. See *Lockett v. Ohio*, 438 U.S. 586 (1978). Typical statutory mitigating circumstances include: the defendant did not have a significant history of prior criminal activity, the defendant was under extreme mental or emotional disturbance, the victim participated in the act, the defendant believed he had a moral justification for the conduct, the defendant was only an accomplice, the defendant acted under duress, the defendant suffered from some diminished capacity, and the defendant was young and/or under the domination of an older person. Evidence of statutory mitigating circumstances should be admitted regardless of its cumulative effect.

At the conclusion of all the evidence in the penalty phase, the parties have the right of closing argument with the defense usually having the right to make the final argument. Because of the nature of the hearing there are additional areas of defense objection not usually available in a regular trial. Of particular note is the prohibition against minimizing the jury's responsibility in assessing the death penalty. See *Romano v. Oklahoma*, 512 U.S. 1 (1994). For example, a prosecutor cannot argue to the jury that the ultimate responsibility for determining the appropriateness of a death sentence rests not with the jury but with an appellate court. See *Caldwell v. Mississippi*, 472 U.S. 320 (1985).

Most states use the following format for instructions during the penalty phase. First, with regard to the statutory aggravating and mitigating circumstances, the judge must charge only those factors raised by the proof. See *Delo v. Lashley*, 507 U.S. 272 (1993). Second, the judge must instruct the jury as to the authorized sentences, and explain that imposition of the death penalty is permitted only if it finds the existence of at least one aggravating circumstance beyond a reasonable doubt. In addition, the Court should instruct on the manner in which aggravating and mitigating circumstances are weighed. For example, in *Kansas v. Marsh*, 548 U.S. 163 (2006), the Court approved the procedure by which the death penalty is imposed if the jury finds that aggravating circumstances are either in equipoise with or not outweighed by mitigating circumstances. Finally, the judge should instruct the jury on the necessity of unanimity and define the meaning of "mitigating circumstances." See *Penry v. Lynaugh*, 492 U.S. 302 (1989).

If the jury finds at least one aggravating circumstance beyond a reasonable doubt, its recommendation as to punishment of death must include a written designation of the aggravating circumstance. If the jury does not find at least one aggravating circumstance, the judge cannot impose a sentence of death. In this situation, the judge can impose a sentence of life. When a sentence of death is not imposed, any error committed during the proceeding is subject to a harmless error analysis. An appeal is automatic in cases in which the death penalty is imposed. If a death sentence is set aside because of an error in the penalty phase only, then only a new penalty phase hearing will occur.

E*XERCISE*

State Death Penalty Procedures. Check the statutes in your state to learn whether the death penalty is available as a punishment for homicide. If the death penalty is not used, locate a state in which it is permitted and find the following provisions:

a. *Notice.* What is the notice provision for informing the defendant that the prosecution will seek the death penalty? How far in advance of trial must the notice occur? Is there a provision for notifying the defendant that the prosecution has decided not to seek the death penalty?

b. *Aggravating Factors.* How many aggravating factors can be the basis for seeking the death penalty? How often has the list changed? Have any factors been removed by the legislature or ruled too vague by the courts? Do recent additions reflect increased concerns about particular issues? If so, which ones?

c. *Mitigating Factors.* Are specific mitigating factors listed in the statute? How often has the list changed? Have any factors been removed by the legislature? Do recent additions reflect new concerns about a defendant's background that a jury should know?

d. *Weighing Factors.* If the jury finds the presence of an aggravating factor, is the death penalty the only possible punishment, or can life imprisonment still be considered? Even if the jury finds the presence of an aggravating factor, can the mitigating evidence offset the aggravating factor so that the death penalty is not imposed?

e. *Other Factors.* Can you think of additional aggravating or mitigating factors that the legislature should recognize?

C.   PROPORTIONALITY IN NON–CAPITAL CASES

EWING v. CALIFORNIA

538 U.S. 11 (2003).

JUSTICE O'CONNOR announced the judgment of the Court and delivered an opinion in which The CHIEF JUSTICE and JUSTICE KENNEDY join.

In this case, we decide whether the Eighth Amendment prohibits the State of California from sentencing a repeat felon to a prison term of 25 years to life under the State's "Three Strikes and You're Out" law.

I

A

California's three strikes law reflects a shift in the State's sentencing policies toward incapacitating and deterring repeat offenders who threaten the public safety. [In March 1993,] Assembly Bill 971, the legislative version of what would later become the three strikes law [was introduced and the] Assembly Committee on Public Safety defeated the bill only weeks later. Public outrage over the defeat sparked a voter initiative to add Proposition 184, based loosely on the bill, to the ballot in the November 1994 general election.

On October 1, 1993, while Proposition 184 was circulating, 12-year-old Polly Klaas was kidnapped from her home in Petaluma, California. Her admitted killer, Richard Allen Davis, had a long criminal history that included two prior kidnapping convictions. Davis had served only half of his most recent sentence (16 years for kidnapping, assault, and burglary). Had Davis served his entire sentence, he would still have been in prison on the day that Polly Klaas was kidnapped.... California thus became the second State to enact a three strikes law.... Between 1993 and 1995, 24 States and the Federal Government enacted [such] laws....

B

California's current three strikes law consists of two virtually identical statutory schemes "designed to increase the prison terms of repeat felons." ... If the defendant has one prior "serious" or "violent" felony conviction, he must be sentenced to "twice the term otherwise provided as punishment for the current felony conviction." If the defendant has two or more prior "serious" or "violent" felony convictions, he must receive "an indeterminate term of life imprisonment." Defendants sentenced to life under the three strikes law become eligible for parole on a date calculated by reference to a "minimum term," which is the greater of (a) three times the term otherwise provided for the current conviction, (b) 25 years, or (c) the term determined by the court pursuant to § 1170 for the underlying conviction, including any enhancements.

Under California law, certain offenses may be classified as either felonies or misdemeanors. These crimes are known as "wobblers." Some crimes that would otherwise be misdemeanors become "wobblers" because of the defendant's prior record. For example, petty theft, a misdemeanor, becomes a "wobbler" when the defendant has previously served a prison term for committing specified theft-related crimes. Other crimes, such as grand theft, are "wobblers" regardless of the defendant's prior record. Both types of "wobblers" are triggering offenses under the three strikes law only when they are treated as felonies. Under California law, a "wobbler" is presumptively a felony and "remains a felony except when the discretion is actually exercised" to make the crime a misdemeanor.

In California, prosecutors may exercise their discretion to charge a "wobbler" as either a felony or a misdemeanor. Likewise, California trial courts have discretion to reduce a "wobbler" charged as a felony to a misdemeanor either before preliminary examination or at sentencing to avoid imposing a three strikes sentence. In exercising this discretion, the court may consider "those factors that direct similar sentencing decisions," such as "the nature and circumstances of the offense, the defendant's appreciation of and attitude toward the offense, . . . [and] the general objectives of sentencing."

California trial courts can also vacate allegations of prior "serious" or "violent" felony convictions, either on motion by the prosecution or *sua sponte*. In ruling whether to vacate allegations of prior felony convictions, courts consider whether, "in light of the nature and circumstances of [the defendant's] present felonies and prior serious and/or violent felony convictions, and the particulars of his background, character, and prospects, the defendant may be deemed outside the [three strikes'] scheme's spirit, in whole or in part." Thus, trial courts may avoid imposing a three strikes sentence in two ways: first, by reducing "wobblers" to misdemeanors (which do not qualify as triggering offenses), and second, by vacating allegations of prior "serious" or "violent" felony convictions.

C

On parole from a 9–year prison term, petitioner Gary Ewing walked into the pro shop of the El Segundo Golf Course in Los

Angeles County on March 12, 2000. He walked out with three golf clubs, priced at $399 apiece, concealed in his pants leg. A shop employee, whose suspicions were aroused when he observed Ewing limp out of the pro shop, telephoned the police. The police apprehended Ewing in the parking lot.

Ewing ... was charged with, and ultimately convicted of, one count of felony grand theft of personal property in excess of $400. As required by the three strikes law, the prosecutor formally alleged, and the trial court later found, that Ewing had been convicted previously of four serious or violent felonies [for] three burglaries [and] robbery ...

At the sentencing hearing, Ewing asked the court to reduce the conviction for grand theft, a "wobbler" under California law, to a misdemeanor so as to avoid a three strikes sentence. Ewing also asked the trial court to exercise its discretion to dismiss the allegations of some or all of his prior serious or violent felony convictions[.] ... Before sentencing Ewing, the trial court took note of his entire criminal history, including the fact that he was on parole when he committed his latest offense. The court also heard arguments from defense counsel and a plea from Ewing himself.

In the end, the trial judge determined that the grand theft should remain a felony. The court also ruled that the four prior strikes for the three burglaries and the robbery in Long Beach should stand. As a newly convicted felon with two or more "serious" or "violent" felony convictions in his past, Ewing was sentenced under the three strikes law to 25 years to life. The California Court of Appeal ... rejected Ewing's claim that his sentence was grossly disproportionate under the Eighth Amendment.... The Supreme Court of California denied Ewing's petition for review, and we now affirm.

II

A

The Eighth Amendment, which forbids cruel and unusual punishments, contains a "narrow proportionality principle" that "applies to noncapital sentences." We have most recently addressed the proportionality principle as applied to terms of years in a series of cases beginning with *Rummel v. Estelle*, [445 U.S. 263, 100 S.Ct. 1133, 63 L.Ed.2d 382 (1980)].

In *Rummel*, we held that it did not violate the Eighth Amendment for a State to sentence a three-time offender to life in prison with the possibility of parole. Like Ewing, Rummel was sentenced to a lengthy prison term under a recidivism statute. Rummel's two prior offenses were a 1964 felony for "fraudulent use of a credit card to obtain $80 worth of goods or services," and a 1969 felony conviction for "passing a forged check in the amount of $28.36." His triggering offense was a conviction for felony theft—"obtaining $120.75 by false pretenses."

This Court ruled that "[h]aving twice imprisoned him for felonies, Texas was entitled to place upon Rummel the onus of one who is simply unable to bring his conduct within the social norms prescribed by the criminal law of the State." The recidivism statute "is nothing more than a societal decision that when such a person commits yet another felony, he should be subjected to the admittedly serious penalty of incarceration for life, subject only to the State's judgment as to whether to grant him parole." We noted that this Court "has on occasion stated that the Eighth Amendment prohibits imposition of a sentence that is grossly disproportionate to the severity of the crime." But "[o]utside the context of capital punishment, successful challenges to the proportionality of particular sentences have been exceedingly rare." Although we stated that the proportionality principle "would ... come into play in the extreme example ... if a legislature made overtime parking a felony punishable by life imprisonment," we held that "the mandatory life sentence imposed upon this petitioner does not constitute cruel and unusual punishment under the Eighth and Fourteenth Amendments."

In *Hutto v. Davis*, 454 U.S. 370, 102 S.Ct. 703, 70 L.Ed.2d 556 (1982) (per curiam), the defendant was sentenced to two consecutive terms of 20 years in prison for possession with intent to distribute nine ounces of marijuana and distribution of marijuana. We held that such a sentence was constitutional [under *Rummel*].

Three years after *Rummel*, in *Solem v. Helm*, 463 U.S. 277, 279, 103 S.Ct. 3001, 77 L.Ed.2d 637 (1983), we held that the Eighth Amendment prohibited "a life sentence without possibility of parole for a seventh nonviolent felony." The triggering offense in *Solem* was "uttering a 'no account' check for $100." We specifically stated that the Eighth Amendment's ban on cruel and unusual punishments "prohibits ... sentences that are disproportionate to the crime committed," and that the "constitutional principle of proportionality has been recognized explicitly in this Court for almost a century." The *Solem* Court then explained that three factors may be relevant to a determination of whether a sentence is so disproportionate that it violates the Eighth Amendment: "(i) the gravity of the offense and the harshness of the penalty; (ii) the sentences imposed on other criminals in the same jurisdiction; and (iii) the sentences imposed for commission of the same crime in other jurisdictions."

Applying these factors in *Solem*, we struck down the defendant's sentence of life without parole. We specifically noted the contrast between that sentence and the sentence in *Rummel*, pursuant to which the defendant was eligible for parole. Indeed, we explicitly declined to overrule *Rummel*: "[O]ur conclusion today is not inconsistent with *Rummel v. Estelle*."

Eight years after *Solem*, we grappled with the proportionality issue again in *Harmelin* [*v. Michigan*, 501 U.S. 957 (1991)]. *Harmelin* was not a recidivism case, but rather involved a first-time offender convicted of possessing 672 grams of cocaine. He was sentenced to life in prison without possibility of parole. A majority of the Court rejected Harmelin's claim that his sentence was so grossly disproportionate that it violated the Eighth Amendment. The Court, however, could not agree on why his proportionality argument failed. Justice Scalia, joined by The Chief Justice, wrote that the proportionality principle was "an aspect of our death penalty jurisprudence, rather than a generalizable aspect of Eighth Amendment law." He would thus have declined to apply gross disproportionality principles except in reviewing capital sentences.

Justice Kennedy, joined by two other Members of the Court, concurred in part and concurred in the judgment. Justice Kennedy specifically recognized that "[t]he Eighth Amendment proportionality principle also applies to noncapital sentences." He then identified four principles of proportionality review—"the primacy of the legislature, the variety of legitimate penological schemes, the nature of our federal system, and the requirement that proportionality review be guided by objective factors"—that "inform the final one: The Eighth Amendment does not require strict proportionality between crime and sentence. Rather, it forbids only extreme sentences that are 'grossly disproportionate' to the crime." Justice Kennedy's concurrence also stated that *Solem* "did not mandate" comparative analysis "within and between jurisdictions."

The proportionality principles in our cases distilled in Justice Kennedy's concurrence guide our application of the Eighth Amendment in the new context that we are called upon to consider.

B

. . .

[When] the California Legislature enacted the three strikes law, it made a judgment that protecting the public safety requires incapacitating criminals who have already been convicted of at least one serious or violent crime. . . . California's justification is no pretext. Recidivism is a serious public safety concern in California and throughout the Nation. According to a recent report, approximately 67 percent of former inmates released from state prisons were charged with at least one "serious" new crime within three years of their release. . . .

The State's interest in deterring crime also lends some support to the three strikes law. We have long viewed both incapacitation and deterrence as rationales for recidivism statutes: "[A] recidivist statute['s] . . . primary goals are to deter repeat offenders and, at some point in the life of one who repeatedly commits criminal offenses serious enough to be punished as felonies, to segregate that person from the rest of society for an extended period of time." *Rummel, supra.* Four years after the passage of California's three strikes law, the recidivism rate of parolees returned to prison for the commission of a new crime dropped by nearly 25 percent. . . .

III

Against this backdrop, we consider Ewing's claim that his three strikes sentence of 25 years to life is unconstitutionally disproportionate to his offense of "shoplifting three golf clubs." We first address the gravity of the offense compared to the harshness of the penalty. At the threshold, we note that Ewing incorrectly frames the issue. The gravity of his offense was not merely "shoplifting three golf clubs." Rather, Ewing was convicted of felony grand theft for stealing nearly $1,200 worth of merchandise after previously having been convicted of at least two "violent" or "serious" felonies. Even standing alone, Ewing's theft should not be taken lightly. His crime was certainly not "one of the most passive felonies a person could commit." To the contrary, the Supreme Court of California has noted the "seriousness" of grand theft in the context of proportionality review.

That grand theft is a "wobbler" under California law is of no moment. Though California courts have discretion to reduce a felony grand theft charge to a misdemeanor, it remains a felony for all purposes "unless and until the trial court imposes a misdemeanor sentence." . . .

In weighing the gravity of Ewing's offense, we must place on the scales not only his current felony, but also his long history of felony recidivism. Any other approach would fail to accord proper deference to the policy judgments that find expression in the legislature's choice of sanctions. . . . Ewing's sentence is justified by the State's public-safety interest in incapacitating and deterring recidivist felons, and amply supported by his own long, serious criminal record. Ewing has been convicted of numerous misdemeanor and felony offenses, served nine separate terms of incarceration, and committed most of his crimes while on probation or parole. His prior "strikes" were serious felonies including robbery and three residential burglaries. To be sure, Ewing's sentence is a long one. But it reflects a rational legislative judgment, entitled to deference, that offenders who have committed serious or violent felonies and who continue to commit felonies must be incapacitated. The State of California "was entitled to place upon [Ewing] the onus of one who is simply unable to bring his conduct within the social norms prescribed by the criminal law of the State." Ewing's is not "the rare case in which a threshold comparison of the crime committed and the sentence imposed leads to an inference of gross disproportionality."

We hold that Ewing's sentence of 25 years to life in prison, imposed for the offense of felony grand theft under the three strikes law, is not grossly disproportionate and therefore does not violate the Eighth Amendment's prohibition on cruel and unusual punishments. The judgment of the California Court of Appeal is affirmed.

JUSTICE BREYER, with whom JUSTICE STEVENS, JUSTICE SOUTER, and JUSTICE GINSBURG join, dissenting.

The constitutional question is whether the "three strikes" sentence imposed by California upon repeat-offender Gary Ewing is "grossly disproportionate" to his crime.... In *Solem v. Helm*, the Court found grossly disproportionate a somewhat longer sentence imposed on a recidivist offender for triggering criminal conduct that was somewhat less severe. [T]he differences are not determinative, and the Court should reach the same ultimate conclusion here.

I

This Court's precedent sets forth a framework for analyzing Ewing's Eighth Amendment claim. The Eighth Amendment forbids, as "cruel and unusual punishments," prison terms (including terms of years) that are "grossly disproportionate." In applying the "gross disproportionality" principle, courts must keep in mind that "legislative policy" will primarily determine the appropriateness of a punishment's "severity," and hence defer to such legislative policy judgments....

If courts properly respect those judgments, they will find that the sentence fails the test only in rare instances.... And they will only " 'rarely' " find it necessary to " 'engage in extended analysis' " before rejecting a claim that a sentence is "grossly disproportionate."

To implement [Justice Kennedy's *Harmelin*] approach, courts faced with a "gross disproportionality" claim must first make "a threshold comparison of the crime committed and the sentence imposed." If a claim crosses that threshold—itself a rare occurrence—then the court should compare the sentence at issue to other sentences "imposed on other criminals" in the same, or in other, jurisdictions. The comparative analysis will "validate" or invalidate "an initial judgment that a sentence is grossly disproportionate to a crime." [The] case before us is a "rare" case—one in which a court can say with reasonable confidence that the punishment is "grossly disproportionate" to the crime.

II

Ewing's claim crosses the gross disproportionality "threshold." First, precedent makes clear that Ewing's sentence raises a serious disproportionality question. Ewing is a recidivist. Hence the two cases most directly in point are those in which the Court considered the constitutionality of recidivist sentencing: *Rummel* and *Solem*. Ewing's claim falls between these two cases. It is stronger than the claim presented in *Rummel*, where the Court upheld a recidivist's sentence as constitutional. It is weaker than the claim presented in *Solem*, where the Court struck down a recidivist sentence as unconstitutional.

Three kinds of sentence-related characteristics define the relevant comparative spectrum: (a) the length of the prison term in real time, i.e., the time that the offender is likely actually to spend in prison; (b) the sentence-triggering criminal conduct, i.e., the offender's actual behavior or other offense-related circumstances; and (c) the offender's criminal history.

In *Rummel*, the Court held constitutional (a) a sentence of life imprisonment with parole available within 10 to 12 years, (b) for the offense of obtaining $120 by false pretenses, (c) committed by an offender with two prior felony convictions (involving small amounts of money). In *Solem*, the Court held unconstitutional (a) a sentence of life imprisonment without parole, (b) for the crime of writing a $100 check on a nonexistent bank account, (c) committed by an offender with six prior felony convictions (including three for burglary). Which of the three pertinent comparative factors made the constitutional difference?

The third factor, prior record, cannot explain the difference. The offender's prior record was worse in *Solem*, where the Court found the sentence too long, than in *Rummel*, where the Court upheld the sentence. The second factor, offense conduct, cannot explain the difference. The nature of the triggering offense—viewed in terms of the actual monetary loss—in the two cases was about the same. The one critical factor that explains the difference in the outcome is the length of the likely prison term measured in real time. In *Rummel*, where the Court upheld the sentence, the state sentencing statute authorized parole for the offender, Rummel, after 10 or 12 years. In *Solem*, where the Court struck down the sentence, the sentence required the offender, Helm, to spend the rest of his life in prison.

Now consider the present case. The third factor, offender characteristics—i.e., prior record—does not differ significantly here from that in *Solem*. . . .

The difference in length of the real prison term—the first, and critical, factor in *Solem* and *Rummel*—is considerably more important. Ewing's sentence here amounts, in real terms, to at least 25 years without parole or good-time credits. That sentence is considerably shorter than Helm's sentence in *Solem*, which amounted, in real terms, to life in prison. Nonetheless Ewing's real prison term is more than twice as long as the term at issue in *Rummel*, which amounted, in real terms, to at least 10 or 12 years. And, Ewing's sentence, unlike *Rummel*'s (but like Helm's sentence in *Solem*), is long enough to consume the productive remainder of almost any offender's life. (It means that Ewing himself, seriously ill when sentenced at age 38, will likely die in prison.)

The upshot is that the length of the real prison term—the factor that explains the *Solem/Rummel* difference in outcome—places Ewing closer to *Solem* than to *Rummel*, though the greater value of the golf clubs that Ewing stole moves Ewing's case back slightly in *Rummel*'s direction. Overall, the comparison places Ewing's sentence well within the twilight zone between *Solem* and *Rummel*—a zone where the argument for unconstitutionality is substantial, where the cases themselves cannot determine the constitutional outcome.

Second, Ewing's sentence on its face imposes one of the most severe punishments available upon a recidivist who subsequently engaged in one of the less serious forms of criminal conduct.... [Some] well-publicized instances of shoplifting suggest that the offense is often punished without any prison sentence at all. On the other hand, shoplifting is a frequently committed crime; but "frequency," standing alone, cannot make a critical difference. Otherwise traffic offenses would warrant even more serious punishment.

This case, of course, involves shoplifting engaged in by a recidivist. One might argue that any crime committed by a recidivist is a serious crime potentially warranting a 25–year sentence. But this Court rejected that view in *Solem*, and in *Harmelin*, with the recognition that "no penalty is *per se* constitutional."

Third, some objective evidence suggests that many experienced judges would consider Ewing's sentence disproportionately harsh. The United States Sentencing Commission (having based the federal Sentencing Guidelines primarily upon its review of how judges had actually sentenced offenders) does not include shoplifting (or similar theft-related offenses) among the crimes that might trigger especially long sentences for recidivists.

III

[A] comparison of Ewing's sentence with other sentences requires answers to two questions. First, how would other jurisdictions (or California at other times, i.e., without the three strikes penalty) punish the same offense conduct? Second, upon what other conduct would other jurisdictions (or California) impose the same prison term? Moreover, since hypothetical punishment is beside the point, the relevant prison time, for comparative purposes, is real prison time, i.e., the time that an offender must actually serve.

Sentencing statutes often shed little light upon real prison time. That is because sentencing laws normally set maximum sentences, giving the sentencing judge discretion to choose an actual sentence within a broad range, and because many States provide good-time credits and parole, often permitting release after, say, one-third of the sentence has been served. Thus, the statutory maximum is rarely the sentence imposed, and the sentence imposed is rarely the sentence that is served. For the most part, the parties' briefs discuss sentencing statutes. Nonetheless, that discussion, along with other readily available information, validates [the point] that Ewing's sentence, comparatively speaking, is extreme.

As to California itself, we know the following: First, between the end of World War II and 1994 (when California enacted the three strikes law), no one like Ewing could have served more than 10 years in prison. We know that for certain because the maximum sentence for Ewing's crime of conviction, grand theft, was for most of that period 10 years. We also know that the time that any offender actually served was likely far less than 10 years. This is because statistical data shows that the median time actually served for grand theft (other than auto theft) was about two years, and 90 percent of all those convicted of that crime served less than three or four years.

Second, statistics suggest that recidivists of all sorts convicted during that same time period in California served a small fraction of Ewing's real-time sentence. On average, recidivists served three to four additional (recidivist-related) years in prison, with 90 percent serving less than an additional real seven to eight years.

Third, we know that California has reserved, and still reserves, Ewing-type prison time, i.e., at least 25 real years in prison, for criminals convicted of crimes far worse than was Ewing's. Statistics for the years 1945 to 1981, for example, indicate that typical (nonrecidivist) male first-degree murderers served between 10 and 15 real years in prison, with 90 percent of all such murderers serving less than 20 real years. Moreover, California, which has moved toward a real-time sentencing system (where the statutory punishment approximates the time served), still punishes far less harshly those who have engaged in far more serious conduct. . . .

As to other jurisdictions, we know the following: The United States, bound by the federal Sentencing Guidelines, would impose upon a recidivist, such as Ewing, a sentence that, in any ordinary case, would not exceed 18 months in prison. . . .

With three exceptions, we do not have before us information about actual time served by Ewing-type offenders in other States. We do know, however, that the law would make it legally impossible for a Ewing-type offender to serve more than 10 years in prison in 33 jurisdictions, as well as the federal courts, more than 15 years in 4 other States, and more than 20 years in 4 additional States. In nine other States, the law might make it legally possible to impose a sentence of 25 years or more—though that fact by itself, of course, does not mean that judges have actually done so. . . .

In sum, ... Ewing's sentence ... is grossly disproportionate to the triggering offense conduct—stealing three golf clubs—Ewing's recidivism notwithstanding. . . .

NOTES

1. *Forfeitures and proportionality.* Proportionality limitations apply to forfeitures as well. In *United States v. Bajakajian*, 524 U.S. 321 (1998), the defendant was arrested while trying to take $357,144 on a flight to Cyprus, because he had failed to report that he possessed or had control of more than $10,000. At a bench trial, the trial court found the entire amount subject to forfeiture under a criminal forfeiture statute. The court, however, ordered only $15,000 forfeited, reasoning that forfeiture of more than that amount would be "grossly disproportional" to Bajakajian's culpability and thus unconstitutional under the Excessive Fines Clause. The court expressly found that all of the money came from a lawful source and was to be used for a lawful purpose. The Supreme Court upheld the forfeiture order. After concluding that the forfeiture qualified as a "fine," the Court turned to the question of excessiveness. Bajakajian's crime was "solely a reporting offense," and the harm Bajakajian's caused was "minimal" in the sense that the government would be deprived only of the information that the $357,144 left the country. Therefore, full forfeiture would be "grossly disproportional" to the gravity of the offense.

2. *Enhanced sentences for recidivists.* Recidivist offender statutes like the one applied in *Ewing* are used by about half the states. A defendant may be sentenced to a maximum of life imprisonment upon proof of a requisite number of prior convictions for certain felony crimes. A person cannot be convicted as a recidivist unless a term of imprisonment is imposed as punishment for the underlying charge. Recidivist provisions do not create an independent offense but merely serve to enhance the punishment for a crime committed by a person who qualifies as a recidivist. A conviction for a capital offense is not subject to enhancement.

A defendant is entitled to notice of being charged as a recidivist before the trial of the underlying substantive offense. A separate indictment or complaint meets this requirement, just as does a separate count charging the substantive offense to which it refers. It is common practice for the indictment or complaint to specify the nature, time and place of the prior conviction.

Assuming the defendant is properly charged as a recidivist, then the trial initially takes place on the underlying felony and no mention is made of the prior convictions, except for impeachment. The determination of whether the defendant is a recidivist must occur in a separate proceeding from the trial on the underlying felony. The defendant is not entitled to separate juries for the guilt and penalty phases. The evidence at the penalty hearing is very narrow, and the only function of the jury is to hear proof of prior convictions and to determine if a defendant's record of recidivism warrants punishment. Accordingly, courts deny the defendant an opportunity to introduce evidence of mitigation. During the hearing, the prosecution must prove every element of the recidivist charge beyond a reasonable doubt. A defendant charged with being a recidivist may plead guilty to the charge.

In many jurisdictions, there are two degrees of recidivist status, the elements of which are indistinguishable except for the number of previous felony convictions required. For example, a recidivist in the second degree must have been convicted of one previous felony before committing the current felony. A recidivist in the first degree must have been convicted of two or more previous felonies prior to committing the current felony. Except for prior convictions, any fact increasing sentence beyond the statutory maximum for the crime of conviction must be proved beyond a reasonable doubt. See *Apprendi v. New Jersey*, in Part D, *infra*.

For both degrees of recidivist status, the defendant's prior conviction must have occurred prior to the date of the commission of the current felony. Likewise, for first degree status, the second felony must have been committed after the conviction for the first felony. For example, if a defendant is convicted and paroled, then commits another felony and is again incarcerated and released, upon committing a third felony, he has two prior felony convictions and is a first-degree offender. However, if the defendant's second conviction did not occur until after commission of the third felony, he has one prior felony conviction and second-degree offender status. A prior conviction must be for a felony in the sentencing jurisdiction; if the defendant has been convicted of a crime in another state which is a felony in the sentencing jurisdiction, that conviction counts as a prior felony conviction for purposes of the recidivist statute. The prior conviction must have included imposition of a sentence of one year or more.

A defendant who is indicted as a recidivist may challenge the validity of any prior conviction. The defendant must file a motion to suppress any evidence of prior convictions before trial, alleging that a prior conviction was obtained by constitutionally impermissible means. At a hearing on the motion to suppress, the burden is on the prosecution to prove the judgments of conviction for each of the prior offenses. This burden is sustained by a duly authenticated record of a judgment and conviction. When a defendant is found to be a recidivist, the sentence for the principal crime is replaced and enhanced by an indeterminate sentence.

Typically, if a defendant is found to be a recidivist in the second degree, the sentence imposed is "for the next highest degree than the offense for which [he was] convicted." For example, if the principal conviction is for a Class B felony, the enhanced sentence may be for a Class A felony. Then the sentence ranges for a first degree recidivist may range from twenty to fifty years or life imprisonment for the principal conviction of a Class A or Class B felony, and ten to twenty years for a Class C or Class D felony.

3. *Limitations on sentencing.* Suppose the defendant is convicted of a felony and is sentenced to twenty years, but then the defendant is successful

in obtaining a new trial and is convicted again. Could the judge or jury sentence the defendant to thirty years? The answer, in non-capital cases, depends on who is imposing the sentence. In *North Carolina v. Pearce*, 395 U.S. 711 (1969), the Court held that, absent other factors, a defendant could not be given a higher sentence at a retrial following the reversal of a conviction. In the context of jury sentencing where a different jury imposes a higher sentence at retrial than the jury in the initial trial, the correlating control and the threat are both absent. The foregoing principles are not applicable to capital cases. When a defendant is sentenced to life and succeeds in obtaining a new trial, he or she is no longer subject to the death penalty at any retrial. *Bullington v. Missouri*, 451 U.S. 430 (1981). This proposition, grounded on double jeopardy, applies even if a jury trial is waived. However, if an appellate court corrects a mistaken legal interpretation of an aggravating factor which does not alter the validity of the punishment, a retrial after a reversal for the trial error can result again in a death sentence. *Poland v. Arizona*, 476 U.S. 147 (1986).

Pearce does not totally prohibit a greater sentence at retrial in another situation. Where the same judge imposes the sentence at each trial, a higher sentence may be fixed if the judge finds a "change of circumstances." In *Wasman v. United States*, 468 U.S., 559 (1984), the defendant had been charged with another criminal offense at the time of the original sentence, and then had been convicted of this offense by the time of the higher sentence. The Court found that a conviction which took place after the original sentence could be considered even though the conduct took place prior to the initial sentence. The Court concluded that a judge may justify an increased sentence by affirmatively identifying relevant conduct or events that occurred subsequent to the original sentencing proceeding.

When the legislature increases the punishment for a crime, the defendant receives the benefit of being sentenced under the old law with the lesser punishment. This result is mandated by the proposition that such an increase is a prohibited *ex post facto* law. *Lindsey v. Washington*, 301 U.S. 397 (1937).

EXERCISE

State Code Rules. Check the statutes in your state to learn whether an enhanced sentence is available for recidivists. If the enhanced sentences are is not used, locate a state in which it is permitted and find the following:

a. *Notice.* What is the notice provision for informing the defendant that the prosecution will seek an enhanced sentence? How far in advance of trial must the notice occur? Is there a provision for notifying the defendant that the prosecution has decided not to seek an enhanced sentence?

b. *Prior Felony.* Can a prior felony conviction be used both to create an offense or enhance a punishment of the second crime and again to enhance the punishment as a recidivist? For example, possession of a handgun by a convicted felon requires proof of a prior felony. Can that same prior felony also be used to enhance the penalty for the current possessory offense?

c. *Age of Defendant.* Is there a minimum age for the defendant in order to receive an enhanced recidivist sentence? Is there a minimum age for the defendant when he committed the prior crimes for which enhanced sentencing is now sought?

d. *Felony Elsewhere.* Is the prior felony conviction limited to a felony in your state, or can a felony conviction anywhere be considered? Does it matter whether the felony in another jurisdiction is not considered a felony in your state?

e. *Age of Felony Conviction.* Is there a limit on the age of the prior felony conviction, e.g., within five years prior to the date of the commission of the current felony?

f. *Proof.* How does the prosecution prove the prior felony conviction?

g. *Degrees of Sentence.* Is there more than one degree or type of enhanced recidivist sentencing?

D. SENTENCING AND THE SIXTH AMENDMENT

After the defendant has been convicted, the case should proceed to sentencing without unreasonable delay. However, it is customary to postpone sentencing for a short period of time to enable the court to obtain a presentence report. Normally, the judge who presided at the trial will conduct the sentencing. Following a felony or misdemeanor conviction, the judge must consider the defendant for probation or conditional discharge as an alternative to imprisonment. If the record at sentencing does not clearly reflect a consideration of sentencing alternatives, the case must be remanded for proper sentencing.

Regardless of whether the defendant is eligible for alternative sentencing, the court cannot impose a sentence for a felony other than a capital offense without the consideration of a presentence report. The report must be prepared by a probation officer, must include an analysis of the defendant's background and may include a victim impact statement under appropriate circumstances. *Payne v. Tennessee*, 501 U.S. 808 (1991). Before imposing sentence, the trial court must review the report and advise the defendant or defense counsel of the contents of the report. If the defendant wishes to controvert the contents of any report, the court must afford a fair opportunity and a reasonable period of time to challenge its contents. However, the court need not disclose the sources of confidential information contained in the report.

WILLIAMS v. NEW YORK

337 U.S. 241 (1949).

MR. JUSTICE BLACK delivered the opinion of the Court.

[A state statute required that the court "shall cause the defendant's previous criminal record to be submitted to it, . . . and may seek any information that will aid the court in determining the proper treatment of such defendant [for sentencing purposes]." Williams argued that his sentence violated due process, because it was provided by witnesses he had not confronted or cross-examined.]

The narrow contention here makes it unnecessary to set out the facts at length. The record shows a carefully conducted trial lasting more than two weeks in which appellant was represented by three appointed lawyers who conducted his defense with fidelity and zeal. The evidence proved a wholly indefensible murder committed by a person engaged in a burglary. . . .

The case presents a serious and difficult question. The question relates to the rules of evidence applicable to the manner in which a judge may obtain information to guide him in the imposition of sentence upon an already convicted defendant. Within limits fixed by statutes, New York judges are given a broad discretion to decide the type and extent of punishment for convicted defendants. . . . To aid a judge in exercising this discretion intelligently the New York procedural policy encourages him to consider information about the convicted person's past life, health, habits, conduct, and mental and moral propensities. The sentencing judge may consider such information even though obtained outside the courtroom from persons whom a defendant has not been permitted to confront or cross-examine. It is the consideration of information obtained by a sentencing judge in this manner that is the basis for appellant's broad constitutional challenge to the New York statutory policy. . . .

Undoubtedly the New York statutes emphasize a prevalent modern philosophy of penology that the punishment should fit the offender and not merely the crime. The belief no longer prevails that every offense in a like legal category calls for an identical punishment without regard to the past life and habits of a particular offender. . . . Today's philosophy of individualizing sentences makes sharp distinctions for example between first and repeated offenders. Indeterminate sentences, the ultimate termination of which are sometimes decided by nonjudicial agencies have to a large extent taken the place of the old rigidly fixed punishments. The practice of probation which relies heavily on non-judicial implementation has been accepted as a wise policy. Execution of the United States parole system rests on the discretion of an administrative parole board. Retribution is no longer the dominant objective of the criminal law. Reformation and rehabilitation of offenders have become important goals of criminal jurisprudence. . . .

Under the practice of individualizing punishments, investigation techniques have been given an important role. Probation workers making reports of their investigations have not been trained to prosecute but to aid offenders. Their reports have been given a high value by conscientious judges who want to sentence persons on the best available information rather than on guesswork and inadequate information. To deprive sentencing judges of this kind of information would undermine modern penological procedural policies that have been cautiously adopted throughout the nation after careful consideration and experimentation. We must recognize that most of the information now relied upon by judges to guide them in the intelligent imposition of sentences would be unavailable if information were restricted to that given in open court by witnesses subject to cross-examination. And the modern probation report draws on information concerning every aspect of a defendant's life. The type and extent of this information make totally impractical if not impossible open court testimony with cross-examination. Such a procedure could endlessly delay criminal administration in a retrial of collateral issues.

The considerations we have set out admonish us against treating the due-process clause as a uniform command that courts throughout the Nation abandon their age-old practice of seeking information from out-of-court sources to guide their judgment toward a more enlightened and just sentence. New York criminal statutes set wide limits for maximum and minimum sentences. Under New York statutes a state judge cannot escape [the] grave responsibility of fixing sentence. In determining whether a defendant shall receive a one-year minimum or a twenty-year maximum sentence, we do not think the Federal Constitution restricts the view of the sentencing judge to the information received in open court. The due-process clause should not be treated as a device for freezing the evidential procedure of sentencing in the mold of trial procedure. So to treat the due-process clause would hinder if not preclude all courts—state and federal—from making progressive efforts to improve the administration of criminal justice. . . .

Affirmed.

MR. JUSTICE MURPHY, dissenting. . . . The record before us indicates that the judge exercised his discretion [to impose a sentence] in reliance on material made available to him in a probation report, consisting almost entirely of evidence that would have been inadmissible at the trial. Some, such as allegations of prior crimes, was irrelevant. Much was incompetent as hearsay. All was damaging, and none was subject to scrutiny by the defendant.

Due process of law includes at least the idea that a person accused of crime shall be accorded a fair hearing through all the stages of the proceedings against him. I agree with the Court as to the value and humaneness of liberal use of probation reports as developed by modern penologists, but, in a capital case, against the unanimous recommendation of a jury, where the report would concededly not have been admissible at the trial, and was not subject to examination by the defendant, I am forced to conclude that the high commands of due process were not obeyed.

Notes

1. *Right of allocution.* Formal sentencing consists of the pronouncement of a sentence in accordance with the previous plea or adjudication of guilt at trial. Any pending motions which may affect the need for sentencing should be decided before the sentence is pronounced. The defendant should be accorded the common law right of allocution, so that he or she may speak up and identify any reason why the sentence should not be pronounced or why a particular sentence is appropriate. This right thus affords regularity to the proceedings and reduces the likelihood of a subsequent attack on the judgment. If the sentence is predicated upon a contested adjudication, the defendant must be advised of rights regarding appeal.

2. *Sentencing considerations.* In making a sentencing determination, the judge should consider the presentence report, sentencing alternatives (if any), evidence concerning the nature and characteristics of the criminal conduct, and the question whether to impose any multiple sentences to run concurrently or consecutively. In addition, the judge may consider the defendant's untruthfulness or refusal to cooperate with law enforcement authorities. The judge "must be permitted to consider any and all information that reasonably might bear on the proper sentence for the particular defendant, given the crime committed." *Wasman v. United States*, 468 U.S. 559 (1984).

APPRENDI v. NEW JERSEY

530 U.S. 466 (2000).

Justice Stevens delivered the opinion of the Court.

[A New Jersey hate crime statute provided for an "extended term" of imprisonment if the trial judge found, by a preponderance of the evidence, that "[t]he defendant in committing the crime acted with a purpose to intimidate an individual or group of individuals because of race, color, gender, handicap, religion, sexual orientation or ethnicity." The extended term authorized by the hate crime law is imprisonment for "between 10 and 20 years." After his indictment, Apprendi agreed to plead guilty to possession of a firearm for an unlawful purpose, punishable by five to ten years. The plea agreement allowed the prosecution to request that the sentence be enhanced due to a biased purpose. After an adversarial hearing, the trial court concluded that the crime was motivated by racial bias and relied on the "extended term" statute to sentence the defendant.]

. . . The question presented is whether the Due Process Clause of the Fourteenth Amendment requires that a factual determination authorizing an increase in the maximum prison sentence for an offense from 10 to 20 years be made by a jury on the basis of proof beyond a reasonable doubt. . . .

. . . Our answer to that question was foreshadowed by our opinion in *Jones v. United States*, 526 U.S. 227 (1999), construing a federal statute. We there noted that "under the Due Process Clause of the Fifth Amendment and the notice and jury trial guarantees of the Sixth Amendment, any fact (other than prior conviction) that increases the maximum penalty for a crime must be charged in an indictment, submitted to a jury, and proven beyond a reasonable doubt." The Fourteenth Amendment commands the same answer in this case involving a state statute.

[At] stake in this case are constitutional protections of surpassing importance: the proscription of any deprivation of liberty without "due process of law," Amdt. 14, and the guarantee that "[i]n all criminal prosecutions, the accused shall enjoy the right to a speedy and public trial, by an impartial jury," Amdt. 6. . . .

Any possible distinction between an "element" of a felony offense and a "sentencing factor" was unknown to the practice of criminal indictment, trial by jury, and judgment by court as it existed during the years surrounding our Nation's founding. As a general rule, criminal proceedings were submitted to a jury after being initiated by an indictment containing "all the facts and circumstances which constitute the offence, . . . stated with such certainty and precision, that the defendant . . . may be enabled to determine the species of offence they constitute, in order that he may prepare his defence accordingly . . . and that there may be no doubt as to the judgment which should be given, if the defendant be convicted." J. Archbold, Pleading and Evidence in Criminal Cases 44 (15th ed. 1862). The defendant's ability to predict with certainty the judgment from the face of the felony indictment flowed from the invariable linkage of punishment with crime. . . .

[Just] as the circumstances of the crime and the intent of the defendant at the time of commission were often essential elements to be alleged in the indictment, so too were the circumstances mandating a particular punishment. "Where a statute annexes a higher degree of punishment to a common-law felony, if committed under particular circumstances, an indictment for the offence, in order to bring the defendant within that higher degree of punishment, must expressly charge it to have been committed under those circumstances, and must state the circumstances with certainty and precision. [2 M. Hale, Pleas of the Crown *170]." Archbold, Pleading and Evidence in Criminal Cases, at 51. If, then, "upon an indictment under the statute, the prosecutor prove the felony to have been committed, but fail in proving it to have been committed under the circumstances specified in the statute, the defendant shall be convicted of the common-law felony only." *Id*. at 188. . . .

We should be clear that nothing in this history suggests that it is impermissible for judges to exercise discretion—taking into consideration various factors relating both to offense and offender—in imposing a judgment within the range prescribed by statute. We have often noted that judges in this country have long exercised discretion of this nature in imposing sentence within statutory limits in the individual case. . . . As in *Williams* [*v. New York*, 337 U.S. 241 (1949)], our periodic recognition of judges' broad discretion in sentencing—since the 19th-century shift in this country from statutes providing fixed-term sentences to those providing judges discretion within a permissible range, has been regularly accompanied by the qualification that that discretion was bound by the range of sentencing options prescribed by the legislature. . . .

We do not suggest that trial practices cannot change in the course of centuries and still remain true to the principles that emerged from the Framers' fears "that the jury right could be lost not only by gross denial, but by erosion." But practice must at least adhere to the basic principles undergirding the requirements of trying to a jury all facts necessary to constitute a statutory offense, and proving those facts beyond reasonable doubt. As we made clear in [*In re*] *Winship*, [397 U.S. 358 (1970)], the "reasonable doubt" requirement "has [a] vital role in our criminal procedure for cogent reasons." . . . [We] require this, among other, procedural protections in order to "provid[e] concrete substance for the presumption of innocence," and to reduce the risk of imposing . . . deprivations [of liberty] erroneously. If a defendant faces punishment beyond that provided by statute when an offense is committed under certain circumstances but not others, it is obvious that both the loss of liberty and the stigma attaching to the offense are heightened; it necessarily follows that the defendant should not—at the moment the State is put to proof of those circumstances—be deprived of protections that have, until that point, unquestionably attached. Since *Winship*, we have made clear beyond peradventure that *Winship*'s due process and associated jury protections extend, to some degree, "to determinations that [go] not to a defendant's guilt or innocence, but simply to the length of his sentence." *Almendarez–Torres*, 523 U.S., at 251, (Scalia, J., dissenting). . . .

It was in *McMillan v. Pennsylvania*, 477 U.S. 79 (1986), that this Court, for the first time, coined the term "sentencing factor" to refer to a fact that was not found by a jury but that could affect the sentence imposed by the judge.... Articulating for the first time, and then applying, a multifactor set of criteria for determining whether the *Winship* protections applied to bar such a system, we concluded that the Pennsylvania statute did not run afoul of our previous admonitions against relieving the State of its burden of proving guilt, or tailoring the mere form of a criminal statute solely to avoid *Winship*'s strictures.

We did not, however, there budge from the position that (1) constitutional limits exist to States' authority to define away facts necessary to constitute a criminal offense, and (2) that a state scheme that keeps from the jury facts that "expos[e] [defendants] to greater or additional punishment," may raise serious constitutional concern....

[Moreover,] ... *Almendarez-Torres v. United States*, 523 U.S. 224 (1998), represents at best an exceptional departure from the historic practice that we have described.... Because Almendarez–Torres had admitted the three earlier convictions for aggravated felonies—all of which had been entered pursuant to proceedings with substantial procedural safeguards of their own—no question concerning the right to a jury trial or the standard of proof that would apply to a contested issue of fact was before the Court. Although our conclusion in that case was based in part on our application of the criteria we had invoked in *McMillan*, the specific question decided concerned the sufficiency of the indictment. More important, ... our conclusion in *Almendarez-Torres* turned heavily upon the fact that the additional sentence to which the defendant was subject was "the prior commission of a serious crime." ... Both the certainty that procedural safeguards attached to any "fact" of prior conviction, and the reality that Almendarez–Torres did not challenge the accuracy of that "fact" in his case, mitigated the due process and Sixth Amendment concerns otherwise implicated in allowing a judge to determine a "fact" increasing punishment beyond the maximum of the statutory range.

Even though it is arguable that *Almendarez-Torres* was incorrectly decided, and that a logical application of our reasoning today should apply if the recidivist issue were contested, Apprendi does not contest the decision's validity and we need not revisit it for purposes of our decision today to treat the case as a narrow exception to the general rule we recalled at the outset. Given its unique facts, it surely does not warrant rejection of the otherwise uniform course of decision during the entire history of our jurisprudence.

In sum, our reexamination of our cases in this area, and of the history upon which they rely, confirms the opinion that we expressed in *Jones*. Other than the fact of a prior conviction, any fact that increases the penalty for a crime beyond the prescribed statutory maximum must be submitted to a jury, and proved beyond a reasonable doubt. With that exception, we endorse the statement of the rule set forth in the concurring opinions in that case: "[I]t is unconstitutional for a legislature to remove from the jury the assessment of facts that increase the prescribed range of penalties to which a criminal defendant is exposed. It is equally clear that such facts must be established by proof beyond a reasonable doubt."

The New Jersey statutory scheme that Apprendi asks us to invalidate allows a jury to convict a defendant of a second-degree offense based on its finding beyond a reasonable doubt that he unlawfully possessed a prohibited weapon; after a subsequent and separate proceeding, it then allows a judge to impose punishment identical to that New Jersey provides for crimes of the first degree, based upon the judge's finding, by a preponderance of the evidence, that the defendant's "purpose" for unlawfully possessing the weapon was "to intimidate" his victim on the basis of a particular characteristic the victim possessed. In light of the constitutional rule explained above, and all of the cases supporting it, this practice cannot stand.

[This] Court has previously considered and rejected the argument that the principles guiding our decision today render invalid state capital sentencing schemes requiring judges, after a jury verdict holding a defendant guilty of a capital crime, to find specific aggravating factors before imposing a sentence of death. *Walton v. Arizona*, 497 U.S. 639, 647–649 (1990); *id.*, at 709–714 (Stevens, J., dissenting). For reasons we have explained, the capital cases are not controlling:

> "[Once] a jury has found the defendant guilty of all the elements of an offense which carries as its maximum penalty the sentence of death, it may be left to the judge to decide whether that maximum penalty, rather than a lesser one, ought to be imposed. . . . The person who is charged with actions that expose him to the death penalty has an absolute entitlement to jury trial on all the elements of the charge." *Almendarez–Torres*, 523 U.S., at 257, n. 2, (Scalia, J., dissenting).

[Accordingly], the judgment of the Supreme Court of New Jersey is reversed, and the case is remanded for further proceedings not inconsistent with this opinion.

JUSTICE O'CONNOR, with whom The CHIEF JUSTICE, JUSTICE KENNEDY, and JUSTICE BREYER join, dissenting.

[None] of the history contained in the Court's opinion requires the rule it ultimately adopts. The history cited by the Court can be divided into two categories: first, evidence that judges at common law had virtually no discretion in sentencing, and, second, statements from a 19th-century criminal procedure treatise that the government must charge in an indictment and prove at trial the elements of a statutory offense for the defendant to be sentenced to the punishment attached to that statutory offense. The relevance of the first category of evidence can be easily dismissed. Indeed, the Court does not even claim that the historical evidence of nondiscretionary sentencing at common law supports its "increase in the maximum penalty" rule. Rather, almost as quickly as it recites that historical practice, the Court rejects its relevance to the constitutional question presented here due to the conflicting American practice of judges exercising sentencing discretion and our decisions recognizing the legitimacy of that American practice.

. . . [Apparently,] then, the historical practice on which the Court places so much reliance consists of only two quotations taken from an 1862 criminal procedure treatise. . . . Taken together, the statements from the Archbold treatise demonstrate nothing more than the unremarkable proposition that a defendant could receive the greater statutory punishment only if the indictment expressly charged and the prosecutor proved the facts that made up the statutory offense, as opposed to simply those facts that made up the common-law offense. In other words, for the defendant to receive the statutory punishment, the prosecutor had to charge in the indictment and prove at trial the elements of the statutory offense. . . . This case, however, concerns the distinct question of when a fact that bears on a defendant's punishment, but which the legislature has not classified as an element of the charged offense, must nevertheless be treated as an offense element. The excerpts drawn from the Archbold treatise do not speak to this question at all. The history on which the Court's opinion relies provides no support for its "increase in the maximum penalty" rule. . . .

[The] Court appears to hold that the Constitution requires that a fact be submitted to a jury and proved beyond a reasonable doubt only if that fact, as a formal matter, extends the range of punishment beyond the prescribed statutory maximum. A State could, however, remove from the jury (and subject to a standard of proof below "beyond a reasonable doubt") the assessment of those facts that define narrower ranges of punishment, within the overall statutory range, to which the defendant may be sentenced. Thus, apparently New Jersey could cure its sentencing scheme, and achieve virtually the same results, by drafting its weapons possession statute in the following manner: First, New Jersey could prescribe, in the weapons possession statute itself, a range of 5 to 20 years' imprisonment for one who commits that criminal offense. Second, New Jersey could provide that only those defendants convicted under the statute who are found by a judge, by a preponderance of the evidence, to have acted with a purpose to intimidate an individual on the basis of race may receive a sentence greater than 10 years' imprisonment.

The Court's proffered distinction of *Walton v. Arizona*, [497 U.S. 639 (1990)] suggests that it means to announce a rule of only this limited effect. The Court claims the Arizona capital sentencing scheme is consistent with the constitutional principle underlying today's decision because Arizona's first-degree murder statute itself authorizes both life imprisonment and the death penalty.... In real terms, however, the Arizona sentencing scheme removes from the jury the assessment of a fact that determines whether the defendant can receive that maximum punishment. The only difference, then, between the Arizona scheme and the New Jersey scheme we consider here—apart from the magnitude of punishment at stake—is that New Jersey has not prescribed the 20–year maximum penalty in the same statute that it defines the crime to be punished. It is difficult to understand, and the Court does not explain, why the Constitution would require a state legislature to follow such a meaningless and formalistic difference in drafting its criminal statutes.

Under another reading of the Court's decision, it may mean only that the Constitution requires that a fact be submitted to a jury and proved beyond a reasonable doubt if it, as a formal matter, *increases* the range of punishment *beyond that which could legally be imposed absent that fact*. A State could, however, remove from the jury (and subject to a standard of proof below "beyond a reasonable doubt") the assessment of those facts that, as a formal matter, decrease the range of punishment *below that which could legally be imposed absent that fact*. Thus, consistent with our decision in *Patterson* [*v. New York*, 432 U.S. 197 (1977)], New Jersey could cure its sentencing scheme, and achieve virtually the same results, by drafting its weapons possession statute in the following manner: First, New Jersey could prescribe, in the weapons possession statute itself, a range of 5 to 20 years' imprisonment for one who commits that criminal offense. Second, New Jersey could provide that a defendant convicted under the statute whom a judge finds, by a preponderance of the evidence, not to have acted with a purpose to intimidate an individual on the basis of race may receive a sentence no greater than 10 years' imprisonment....

Given the pure formalism of the above readings of the Court's opinion, one suspects that the constitutional principle underlying its decision is more far reaching. The actual principle underlying the Court's decision may be that any fact (other than prior conviction) that has the effect, *in real terms*, of increasing the maximum punishment beyond an otherwise applicable range must be submitted to a jury and proved beyond a reasonable doubt. The principle thus would apply not only to schemes like New Jersey's, under which a factual determination exposes the defendant to a sentence beyond the prescribed statutory maximum, but also to all determinate-sentencing schemes in which the length of a defendant's sentence within the statutory range turns on specific factual determinations (e.g., the federal Sentencing Guidelines)....

[The] concerns animating the Sixth Amendment's jury trial guarantee, if they were to extend to the sentencing context at all, would apply with greater strength to a discretionary-sentencing scheme than to determinate sentencing. In the former scheme, the potential for mischief by an arbitrary judge is much greater, given that the judge's decision of where to set the defendant's sentence within the pre-scribed statutory range is left almost entirely to discretion. In contrast, under a determinate-sentencing system, the discretion the judge wields within the statutory range is tightly constrained. Accordingly, our approval of discretionary-sentencing schemes, in which a defendant is not entitled to have a jury make factual findings relevant to sentencing despite the effect those findings have on the severity of the defendant's sentence, demonstrates that the defendant should have no right to demand that a jury make the equivalent factual determinations under a determinate-sentencing scheme.

The Court appears to hold today, however, that a defendant is entitled to have a jury decide, by proof beyond a reasonable doubt, every fact relevant to the determination of sentence under a determinate-sentencing scheme. If this is an accurate description of the constitutional principle underlying the Court's opinion, its decision will have the effect of invalidating significant sentencing reform accomplished at the federal and state levels over the past three decades.

[It] is ironic that the Court, in the name of constitutional rights meant to protect criminal defendants from the potentially arbitrary exercise of power by prosecutors and judges, appears to rest its decision on a principle that would render unconstitutional efforts by Congress and the state legislatures to place constraints on that very power in the sentencing context.

Finally, perhaps the most significant impact of the Court's decision will be a practical one—its unsettling effect on sentencing conducted under current federal and state determinate-sentencing schemes. As I have explained, the Court does not say whether these schemes are constitutional, but its reasoning strongly suggests that they are not. Thus, with respect to past sentences handed down by judges under determinate-sentencing schemes, the Court's decision threatens to unleash a flood of petitions by convicted defendants seeking to invalidate their sentences in whole or in part on the authority of the Court's decision today. Statistics compiled by the United States Sentencing Commission reveal that almost a half-million cases have been sentenced under the Sentencing Guidelines since 1989 ... [and] federal criminal prosecutions represented only about 0.4% of the total number of criminal prosecutions in federal and state courts.... Because many States, like New Jersey, have determinate-sentencing schemes, the number of individual sentences drawn into question by the Court's decision could be colossal.

[We should] evaluate New Jersey's sentence-enhancement statute by analyzing the factors we have examined in past cases. [The] magnitude of the New Jersey sentence enhancement, as applied in petitioner's case, is constitutionally permissible.... The 10–year increase in the maximum penalty to which petitioner was exposed falls well within the range we have found permissible. [T]he New Jersey statute gives no impression of having been enacted to evade the constitutional requirements that attach when a State makes a fact an element of the charged offense. For example, New Jersey did not take what had previously been an element of the weapons possession offense and transform it into a sentencing factor.

In sum, New Jersey "simply took one factor that has always been considered by sentencing courts to bear on punishment"—a defendant's motive for committing the criminal offense—"and dictated the precise weight to be given that factor" when the motive is to intimidate a person because of race....

Justice BREYER, with whom The Chief Justice joins, dissenting.

[It] is important for present purposes to understand why judges, rather than juries, traditionally have determined the presence or absence [of] sentence-affecting facts in any given case. And it is important to realize that the reason is not a theoretical one, but a practical one. It ... reflect[s] an ... administrative need for procedural compromise. There are, to put it simply, far too many potentially relevant sentencing factors to permit submission of all (or even many) of them to a jury. As the Sentencing Guidelines state the matter,

> "[a] bank robber with (or without) a gun, which the robber kept hidden (or brandished), might have frightened (or merely warned), injured seriously (or less seriously), tied up (or simply pushed) a guard, a teller or a customer, at night (or at noon), for a bad (or arguably less bad) motive, in an effort to obtain money for other crimes (or for other purposes), in the company of a few (or many) other robbers, for the first (or fourth) time that day, while sober (or under the influence of drugs or alcohol), and so forth." Sentencing Guidelines, Part A, at 1.2.

The Guidelines note that "a sentencing system tailored to fit every conceivable wrinkle of each case can become unworkable and seriously compromise the certainty of punishment and its deterrent effect." Ibid. To ask a jury to consider all, or many, such matters would do the same....

[The] majority ... makes no constitutional objection to a legislative delegation to a commission of the authority to create guidelines that determine how a judge is to exercise sentencing discretion. But if the Constitution permits Guidelines, why does it not permit Congress similarly to guide the exercise of a judge's sentencing discretion? That is, if the Constitution permits a delegatee (the commission) to exercise sentencing-related rulemaking power, how can it deny the delegator (the legislature) what is, in effect, the same rulemaking power?

The majority appears to offer two responses. First, it argues for a limiting principle that would prevent a legislature with broad authority from transforming (jury-determined) facts that constitute elements of a crime into (judge-determined) sentencing factors, thereby removing procedural protections that the Constitution would otherwise require. ("[C]onstitutional limits" prevent States from "defin[ing] away facts necessary to constitute a criminal offense"). The majority's cure, however, is not aimed at the disease.

[The] solution to the problem lies, not in prohibiting legislatures from enacting sentencing factors, but in sentencing rules that determine punishments on the basis of properly defined relevant conduct, with sensitivity to the need for procedural protections where sentencing factors are determined by a judge (for example, use of a "reasonable doubt" standard), and invocation of the Due Process Clause where the history of the crime at issue, together with the nature of the facts to be proved, reveals unusual and serious procedural unfairness.

Second, the majority, in support of its constitutional rule, emphasizes the concept of a statutory "maximum." . . . From a defendant's perspective, the legislature's decision to cap the possible range of punishment at a statutorily prescribed "maximum" would affect the actual sentence imposed no differently than a sentencing commission's (or a sentencing judge's) similar determination. Indeed, as a practical matter, a legislated mandatory "minimum" is far more important to an actual defendant. A judge and a commission, after all, are legally free to select any sentence below a statute's maximum, but they are not free to subvert a statutory minimum.

[I] am willing, consequently, to assume that the majority's rule would provide a degree of increased procedural protection in respect to those particular sentencing factors currently embodied in statutes. I nonetheless believe that any such increased protection provides little practical help and comes at too high a price. For one thing, by leaving mandatory minimum sentences untouched, the majority's rule simply encourages any legislature interested in asserting control over the sentencing process to do so by creating those minimums. That result would mean significantly less procedural fairness, not more. . . . For another thing, this Court's case law, prior to *Jones*, led legislatures to believe that they were permitted to increase a statutory maximum sentence on the basis of a sentencing factor. . . . [T]he rationale that underlies the Court's rule suggests a principle—jury determination of all sentencing-related facts—that, unless restricted, threatens the workability of every criminal justice system (if applied to judges) or threatens efforts to make those systems more uniform, hence more fair (if applied to commissions). . . .

NOTES

1. *Mandatory minimums.* Soon after *Apprendi* was decided, scores of challengers attempted to take advantage of what Justice O'Connor had termed a "watershed change in constitutional law." In *Harris v. United States*, 536 U.S. 545 (2002), the Court held that *Apprendi* is inapplicable to mandatory minimum sentences. Under federal law, carrying a firearm in relation to a drug trafficking offense requires a mandatory minimum sentence of five years. The judge, rather than jury, in Harris's case found that he had carried a gun and sentenced him to seven years. Justice Kennedy's opinion first decided that the mandatory minimum provision was a sentence enhancement provision rather than a separate offense. This view affirmed *McMillan v. Pennsylvania*, 477 U.S. 79 (1986), which permitted a legislature to specify a condition for a mandatory minimum without making the condition an element of the crime. *Apprendi* did not apply to the mandatory minimum concept at issue because that sentencing decision required a jury determination beyond a reasonable doubt for any fact that increased the penalty for a crime above the prescribed statutory *maximum* sentence. A "judge may impose the minimum, the maximum, or any other sentence within the range without seeking further authorization from" a jury.

2. *Findings for death sentence.* By contrast, the Court in *Ring v. Arizona*, 536 U.S. 584 (2002), concluded that it violated *Apprendi* for a sentencing judge sitting without a jury to find an aggravating circumstance necessary for imposition of the death penalty. When the judge made that finding, the defendant was exposed to a penalty greater than that authorized by the jury's verdict alone, in violation of *Apprendi*.

The Court stated in *Schriro v. Summerlin*, 542 U.S. 348 (2004), that *Ring* did not apply retroactively to defendants whose convictions were already final when *Ring* was decided. New substantive rules generally apply retroactively; new procedural rules like the *Ring* holding apply retroactively only if they implicate the fundamental fairness and accuracy of the proceeding. *Ring* altered only the method of deciding whether the defendant was subject to the death penalty and therefore was not a "watershed rule of criminal procedure."

3. *Indictment allegations.* The failure of a federal indictment to allege a drug quantity that was necessary for and could result in an enhanced statutory maximum sentence violates *Apprendi*. In *United States v. Cotton*, 535 U.S. 625 (2002), the defendants never objected to this error at trial, thereby requiring a plain error analysis. However, the Court found that the error did not seriously affect the fairness, integrity, or public reputation of judicial proceedings and therefore did not constitute plain error requiring a reversal of the conviction.

UNITED STATES v. BOOKER

543 U.S. 220 (2005).

JUSTICE STEVENS delivered the opinion of the Court in part [in which JUSTICE SCALIA, JUSTICE SOUTER, JUSTICE THOMAS, and JUSTICE GINSBURG join].

The question presented . . . is whether an application of the Federal Sentencing Guidelines violated the Sixth Amendment. In each case, the courts below held that binding rules set forth in the Guidelines limited the severity of the sentence that the judge could lawfully impose on the defendant based on the facts found by the jury at his trial. In both cases the courts rejected, on the basis of our decision in *Blakely v. Washington*, 542 U.S. 296, 124 S.Ct. 2531 (2004), the Government's recommended application of the Sentencing Guidelines because the proposed sentences were based on additional facts that the sentencing judge found by a preponderance of the evidence. We hold that both courts correctly concluded that the Sixth Amendment as construed in *Blakely* does apply to the Sentencing Guidelines. In a separate opinion authored by Justice Breyer, the Court concludes that in light of this holding, two provisions of the Sentencing Reform Act of 1984 (SRA) that have the effect of making the Guidelines mandatory must be invalidated in order to allow the statute to operate in a manner consistent with congressional intent.

I

Respondent Booker was charged with possession with intent to distribute at least 50 grams of cocaine base (crack). Having heard evidence that he had 92.5 grams in his duffel bag, the jury found him guilty of violating 21 U.S.C. § 841(a)(1). That statute prescribes a minimum sentence of 10 years in prison and a maximum sentence of life for that offense.

Based upon Booker's criminal history and the quantity of drugs found by the jury, the Sentencing Guidelines required the District Court Judge to select a "base" sentence of not less than 210 nor more than 262 months in prison. See United States Sentencing Commission, Guidelines Manual §§ 2D1.1(c)(4), 4A1.1 (Nov.2003) (hereinafter USSG). The judge, however, held a post-trial sentencing proceeding and concluded by a preponderance of the evidence that Booker had possessed an additional 566 grams of crack and that he was guilty of obstructing justice. Those findings mandated that the judge select a sentence between 360 months and life imprisonment; the judge imposed a sentence at the low end of the range. Thus, instead of the sentence of 21 years and 10 months that the judge could have imposed on the basis of the facts proved to the jury beyond a reasonable doubt, Booker received a 30-year sentence. [The Seventh

Circuit held that the sentence violated the Sixth Amendment under *Apprendi*.]

II

It has been settled throughout our history that the Constitution protects every criminal defendant "against conviction except upon proof beyond a reasonable doubt of every fact necessary to constitute the crime with which he is charged." *In re Winship*, 397 U.S. 358, 364, (1970). It is equally clear that the "Constitution gives a criminal defendant the right to demand that a jury find him guilty of all the elements of the crime with which he is charged." *United States v. Gaudin*, 515 U.S. 506, 511, (1995). These basic precepts, firmly rooted in the common law, have provided the basis for recent decisions interpreting modern criminal statutes and sentencing procedures....

In *Blakely v. Washington*, 542 U.S. 296, 124 S.Ct. 2531 (2004), we dealt with a determinate sentencing scheme similar to the Federal Sentencing Guidelines. There the defendant pleaded guilty to kidnapping, a class B felony punishable by a term of not more than 10 years. Other provisions of Washington law, comparable to the Federal Sentencing Guidelines, mandated a "standard" sentence of 49–to–53 months, unless the judge found aggravating facts justifying an exceptional sentence. Although the prosecutor recommended a sentence in the standard range, the judge found that the defendant had acted with " 'deliberate cruelty' " and sentenced him to 90 months.

... The application of Washington's sentencing scheme violated the defendant's right to have the jury find the existence of " 'any particular fact' " that the law makes essential to his punishment. That right is implicated whenever a judge seeks to impose a sentence that is not solely based on "facts reflected in the jury verdict or admitted by the defendant." We rejected the State's argument that the jury verdict was sufficient to authorize a sentence within the general 10-year sentence for Class B felonies, noting that under Washington law, the judge was required to find additional facts in order to impose the greater 90-month sentence. Our precedents, we explained, make clear "that the 'statutory maximum' for *Apprendi* purposes is the maximum sentence a judge may impose solely on the basis of the facts reflected in the jury verdict or admitted by the defendant." The determination that the defendant acted with deliberate cruelty, like the determination in *Apprendi* that the defendant acted with racial malice, increased the sentence that the defendant could have otherwise received. Since this fact was found by a judge using a preponderance of the evidence standard, the sentence violated Blakely's Sixth Amendment rights.

As the dissenting opinions in *Blakely* recognized, there is no distinction of constitutional significance between the Federal Sentencing Guidelines and the Washington procedures at issue in that case. This conclusion rests on the premise, common to both systems, that the relevant sentencing rules are mandatory and impose binding requirements on all sentencing judges.

If the Guidelines as currently written could be read as merely advisory provisions that recommended, rather than required, the selection of particular sentences in response to differing sets of facts, their use would not implicate the Sixth Amendment. We have never doubted the authority of a judge to exercise broad discretion in imposing a sentence within a statutory range. See *Apprendi*, 530 U.S., at 481, 120 S.Ct. 2348; *Williams v. New York*, 337 U.S. 241, 246, 69 S.Ct. 1079, 93 L.Ed. 1337 (1949). Indeed, everyone agrees that the constitutional issues presented by these cases would have been avoided entirely if Congress had omitted from the SRA the provisions that make the Guidelines binding on district judges; it is that circumstance that makes the Court's answer to the second question presented possible. For when a trial judge exercises his discretion to select a specific sentence within a defined range, the defendant has no right to a jury determination of the facts that the judge deems relevant.

The Guidelines as written, however, are not advisory; they are mandatory and binding on all judges. While subsection (a) of § 3553 of the sentencing statute lists the Sentencing Guidelines as one factor to be considered in imposing a sentence, subsection (b) directs that the court "shall impose a sentence of the kind, and within the range" established by the Guidelines, subject to departures in specific, limited cases. Because they are binding on judges, we have consistently held that the Guidelines have the force and effect of laws. See, e.g., *Mistretta v. United States*, 488 U.S. 361, 391, 109 S.Ct. 647, 102 L.Ed.2d 714 (1989); *Stinson v. United States*, 508 U.S. 36, 42, 113 S.Ct. 1913, 123 L.Ed.2d 598 (1993).

The availability of a departure in specified circumstances does not avoid the constitutional issue, just as it did not in *Blakely* itself. The Guidelines permit departures from the prescribed sentencing range in cases in which the judge "finds that there exists an aggravating or mitigating circumstance of a kind, or to a degree, not adequately taken into consideration by the Sentencing Commission in formulating the guidelines that should result in a sentence different from that described." 18 U.S.C.A. § 3553(b)(1) (Supp.2004). At first glance, one might believe that the ability of a district judge to depart from the Guidelines means that she is bound only by the statutory maximum. Were this the case, there would be no *Apprendi* problem. Importantly, however, departures are not available in every case, and in fact are unavailable in most. In most cases, as a matter of law, the Commission will have adequately taken all relevant factors into account, and no departure will be legally permissible. In those instances, the judge is bound to impose a sentence within the Guidelines range. It was for this reason that we rejected a similar argument in *Blakely*, holding that although the Washington statute allowed the judge to impose a sentence outside the sentencing range for " 'substantial and compelling reasons,' " that exception was not available for *Blakely* himself. The sentencing judge would have been reversed had he invoked the departure section to justify the sentence. . . .

In his dissent, Justice Breyer argues on historical grounds that the Guidelines scheme is constitutional across the board. He points to traditional judicial authority to increase sentences to take account of any unusual blameworthiness in the manner employed in committing a crime, an authority that the Guidelines require to be exercised consistently throughout the system. This tradition, however, does not provide a sound guide to enforcement of the Sixth Amendment's guarantee of a jury trial in today's world.

It is quite true that once determinate sentencing had fallen from favor, American judges commonly determined facts justifying a choice of a heavier sentence on account of the manner in which particular defendants acted. *Apprendi*, 530 U.S., at 481, 120 S.Ct. 2348. In 1986, however, our own cases first recognized a new trend in the legislative regulation of sentencing when we considered the significance of facts selected by legislatures that not only authorized, or even mandated, heavier sentences than would otherwise have been imposed, but increased the range of sentences possible for the underlying crime. Provisions for such enhancements of the permissible sentencing range reflected growing and wholly justified legislative concern about the proliferation and variety of drug crimes and their frequent identification with firearms offences.

The effect of the increasing emphasis on facts that enhanced sentencing ranges, however, was to increase the judge's power and diminish that of the jury. It became the judge, not the jury, that determined the upper limits of sentencing, and the facts determined were not required to be raised before trial or proved by more than a preponderance. . . .

III

The Government advances three arguments in support of its submission that we should not apply our reasoning in *Blakely* to the Federal Sentencing Guidelines. It contends that *Blakely* is distinguishable because the Guidelines were promulgated by a commission rather than the Legislature; that principles of *stare decisis* require us to follow four earlier decisions that are arguably inconsistent with *Blakely*; and that the application of *Blakely* to the Guidelines would conflict with separation of powers principles reflected in *Mistretta v. United States*, 488 U.S. 361, (1989). These arguments are unpersuasive. . . .

IV

[We] recognize . . . that in some cases jury factfinding may impair the most expedient and efficient sentencing of defendants. But the interest in fairness and reliability protected by the right to a jury trial—a common-law right that defendants enjoyed for centuries and that is now enshrined in the Sixth Amendment—has always outweighed the interest in concluding trials swiftly. As Blackstone put it:

> [H]owever convenient these [new methods of trial] may appear at first (as doubtless all arbitrary powers, well executed, are the most convenient) yet let it be again remembered, that delays, and little inconveniences in the forms of justice, are the price that all free nations must pay for their liberty in more substantial matters; that these inroads upon this sacred bulwark of the nation are fundamentally opposite to the spirit of our constitution; and that, though begun in trifles, the precedent may gradually increase and spread, to the utter disuse of juries in questions of the most momentous concerns. 4 Commentaries on the Laws of England 343–344 (1769).

Accordingly, we reaffirm our holding in *Apprendi*: Any fact (other than a prior conviction) which is necessary to support a sentence exceeding the maximum authorized by the facts established by a plea of guilty or a jury verdict must be admitted by the defendant or proved to a jury beyond a reasonable doubt.

JUSTICE BREYER delivered the opinion of the Court in part. [in which THE CHIEF JUSTICE, JUSTICE O'CONNOR, JUSTICE KENNEDY, and JUSTICE GINSBURG join].

. . . We answer the question of remedy by finding the provision of the federal sentencing statute that makes the Guidelines mandatory incompatible with today's constitutional holding. We conclude that this provision must be severed and excised, as must one other statutory section which depends upon the Guidelines' mandatory nature. So modified, the Federal Sentencing Act, see Sentencing Reform Act of 1984 makes the Guidelines effectively advisory. It requires a sentencing court to consider Guidelines ranges, but it permits the court to tailor the sentence in light of other statutory concerns as well.

I

We answer the remedial question by looking to legislative intent. We seek to determine what "Congress would have intended" in light of the Court's constitutional holding. In this instance, we must determine which of the two following remedial approaches is the more compatible with the legislature's intent as embodied in the 1984 Sentencing Act.

One approach, that of Justice Stevens' dissent, would retain the Sentencing Act (and the Guidelines) as written, but would engraft onto the existing system today's Sixth Amendment "jury trial" requirement. The addition would change the Guidelines by preventing the sentencing court from increasing a sentence on the basis of a fact that the jury did not find (or that the offender did not admit).

The other approach, which we now adopt, would (through severance and excision of two provisions) make the Guidelines system advisory while maintaining a strong connection between the sentence imposed and the offender's real conduct—a connection important to the increased uniformity of sentencing that Congress intended its Guidelines system to achieve. Both approaches would significantly alter the system that Congress designed. But today's constitutional holding means that it is no longer possible to maintain the judicial factfinding that Congress thought would underpin the mandatory Guidelines system that it sought to create and that Congress wrote into the Act[.] Hence we must decide whether we would deviate less radically from Congress' intended system (1) by superimposing the constitutional requirement announced today or (2) through elimination of some provisions of the statute....

In today's context—a highly complex statute, interrelated provisions, and a constitutional requirement that creates fundamental change—we cannot assume that Congress, if faced with the statute's invalidity in key applications, would have preferred to apply the statute in as many other instances as possible. Neither can we determine likely congressional intent mechanically. We cannot simply approach the problem grammatically, say, by looking to see whether the constitutional requirement and the words of the Act are linguistically compatible.

Nor do simple numbers provide an answer. It is, of course, true that the numbers show that the constitutional jury trial requirement would lead to additional decisionmaking by juries in only a minority of cases. Prosecutors and defense attorneys would still resolve the lion's share of criminal matters through plea bargaining, and plea bargaining takes place without a jury. Many of the rest involve only simple issues calling for no upward Guidelines adjustment. And in at least some of the remainder, a judge may find adequate room to adjust a sentence within the single Guidelines range to which the jury verdict points, or within the overlap between that range and the next highest.

But the constitutional jury trial requirement would nonetheless affect every case. It would affect decisions about whether to go to trial. It would affect the content of plea negotiations. It would alter the judge's role in sentencing. Thus we must determine likely intent not by counting proceedings, but by evaluating the consequences of the Court's constitutional requirement in light of the Act's language, its history, and its basic purposes.

While reasonable minds can, and do, differ about the outcome, we conclude that the constitutional jury trial requirement is not compatible with the Act as written and that some severance and excision are necessary.... In essence, in what follows, we explain both (1) why Congress would likely have preferred the total invalidation of the Act to an Act with the Court's Sixth Amendment requirement engrafted onto it, and (2) why Congress would likely have preferred the excision of some of the Act, namely the Act's mandatory language, to the invalidation of the entire Act. That is to say, in light of today's holding, we compare maintaining the Act as written with jury factfinding added (the dissenters' proposed remedy) to the total invalidation of the statute, and conclude that Congress would have preferred the latter. We then compare our own remedy to the total invalidation of the statute, and conclude that Congress would have preferred our remedy.

II

Several considerations convince us that, were the Court's constitutional requirement added onto the Sentencing Act as currently written, the requirement would so transform the scheme that Congress created that Congress likely would not have intended the Act as so modified to stand. First, the statute's text states that "[t]he court" when sentencing will consider "the nature and circumstances of the offense and the history and characteristics of the defendant." 18 U.S.C.A. § 3553(a)(1). In context, the words "the court" mean "the judge without the jury," not "the judge working together with the jury." A further statutory provision, by removing typical "jury trial" evidentiary limitations, makes this clear. See § 3661 (ruling out any "limitation ... on the information concerning the [offender's] background, character, and conduct" that the "court ... may receive"). The Act's history confirms it. This provision is tied to the provision of the Act that makes the Guidelines mandatory. They are part and parcel of a single, unified whole—a whole that Congress intended to apply to all federal sentencing....

Second, Congress' basic statutory goal—a system that diminishes sentencing disparity—depends for its success upon judicial efforts to determine, and to base punishment upon, the real conduct that underlies the crime of conviction. That determination is particularly important in the federal system where crimes defined as, for example, "obstruct[ing], delay[ing], or affect[ing] commerce or the movement of any article or commodity in commerce, by ... extortion," 18 U.S.C. § 1951(a), or, say, using the mail "for the purpose of executing" a "scheme or artifice to defraud," § 1341, can encompass a vast range of very different kinds of underlying conduct. But it is also important even in respect to ordinary crimes, such as robbery, where an act that meets the statutory definition can be committed in a host of different ways. Judges have long looked to real conduct when sentencing. Federal judges have long relied upon a presentence report, prepared by a probation officer, for information (often unavailable until after the trial) relevant to the manner in which the convicted offender committed the crime of conviction. . . .

The Sentencing Guidelines [assume] that Congress intended this system to continue. That is why, among other things, they permit a judge to reject a plea-bargained sentence if he determines, after reviewing the presentence report, that the sentence does not adequately reflect the seriousness of the defendant's actual conduct.

To engraft the Court's constitutional requirement onto the sentencing statutes, however, would destroy the system. It would prevent a judge from relying upon a presentence report for factual information, relevant to sentencing, uncovered after the trial. In doing so, it would, even compared to pre-Guidelines sentencing, weaken the tie between a sentence and an offender's real conduct. It would thereby undermine the sentencing statute's basic aim of ensuring similar sentences for those who have committed similar crimes in similar ways. . . .

[Yet the] basic goal [of Congress] in passing the Sentencing Act was to move the sentencing system in the direction of increased uniformity. That uniformity does not consist simply of similar sentences for those convicted of violations of the same statute—a uniformity consistent with the dissenters' remedial approach. It consists, more importantly, of similar relationships between sentences and real conduct, relationships that Congress' sentencing statutes helped to advance. . . .

Third, the sentencing statutes, read to include the Court's Sixth Amendment requirement, would create a system far more complex than Congress could have intended. How would courts and counsel work with an indictment and a jury trial that involved not just whether a defendant robbed a bank but also how? Would the indictment have to allege, in addition to the elements of robbery, whether the defendant possessed a firearm, whether he brandished or discharged it, whether he threatened death, whether he caused bodily injury, whether any such injury was ordinary, serious, permanent or life threatening, whether he abducted or physically restrained anyone, whether any victim was unusually vulnerable, how much money was taken, and whether he was an organizer, leader, manager, or supervisor in a robbery gang? See USSG §§ 2B3.1, 3B1.1. If so, how could a defendant mount a defense against some or all such specific claims should he also try simultaneously to maintain that the Government's evidence failed to place him at the scene of the crime? Would the indictment in a mail fraud case have to allege the number of victims, their vulnerability, and the amount taken from each? How could a judge expect a jury to work with the Guidelines' definitions of, say, "relevant conduct," which includes "all acts and omissions committed, aided, abetted, counseled, commanded, induced, procured, or willfully caused by the defendant; and [in the case of a conspiracy] all reasonably foreseeable acts and omissions of others in furtherance of the jointly undertaken criminal activity"? §§ 1B1.3(a)(1)(A)–(B). How would a jury measure "loss" in a securities fraud case—a matter so complex as to lead the Commission to instruct judges to make "only . . . a reasonable estimate"? § 2B1.1, comment., n. 3(C). How would the court take account, for punishment purposes, of a defendant's contemptuous behavior at trial—a matter that the Government could not have charged in the indictment? § 3C1.1.

Fourth, plea bargaining would not significantly diminish the consequences of the Court's constitutional holding for the operation of the Guidelines. Rather, plea bargaining would make matters worse. Congress enacted the sentencing statutes in major part to achieve greater uniformity in sentencing, i.e., to increase the likelihood that offenders who engage in similar real conduct would receive similar sentences. The statutes reasonably assume that their efforts to move the trial-based sentencing process in the direction of greater sentencing uniformity would have a similar positive impact upon plea-bargained sentences, for plea bargaining takes place in the shadow of (i.e., with an eye towards the hypothetical result of) a potential trial.

That, too, is why Congress, understanding the realities of plea bargaining, authorized the Commission to promulgate policy statements that would assist sentencing judges in determining whether to reject a plea agreement after reading about the defendant's real conduct in a presentence report (and giving the offender an opportunity to challenge the report). See 28 U.S.C. § 994(a)(2)(E); USSG § 6B1.2(a). This system has not worked perfectly; judges have often simply accepted an agreed-upon account of the conduct at issue. But compared to pre-existing law, the statutes try to move the system in the right direction, i.e., toward greater sentencing uniformity.

The Court's constitutional jury trial requirement, however, if patched onto the present Sentencing Act, would move the system backwards in respect both to tried and to plea-bargained cases. In respect to tried cases, it would effectively deprive the judge of the ability to use post-verdict-acquired real-conduct information; it would prohibit the judge from basing a sentence upon any conduct other than the conduct the prosecutor chose to charge; and it would put a defendant to a set of difficult strategic choices as to which prosecutorial claims he would contest. The sentence that would emerge in a case tried under such a system would likely reflect real conduct less completely, less accurately, and less often than did a pre-Guidelines, as well as a Guidelines, trial. Because plea bargaining inevitably reflects estimates of what would happen at trial, plea bargaining too under such a system would move in the wrong direction. That is to say, in a sentencing system modified by the Court's constitutional requirement, plea bargaining would likely lead to sentences that gave greater weight, not to real conduct, but rather to the skill of counsel, the policies of the prosecutor, the caseload, and other factors that vary from place to place, defendant to defendant, and crime to crime. Compared to pre-Guidelines plea bargaining, plea bargaining of this kind would necessarily move federal sentencing in the direction of diminished, not increased, uniformity in sentencing. It would tend to defeat, not to further, Congress' basic statutory goal.

Such a system would have particularly troubling consequences with respect to prosecutorial power. Until now, sentencing factors have come before the judge in the presentence report. But in a sentencing system with the Court's constitutional requirement engrafted onto it, any factor that a prosecutor chose not to charge at the plea negotiation would be placed beyond the reach of the judge entirely. Prosecutors would thus exercise a power the Sentencing Act vested in judges: the power to decide, based on relevant information about the offense and the offender, which defendants merit heavier punishment. . . .

For all these reasons, Congress, had it been faced with the constitutional jury trial requirement, likely would not have passed the same Sentencing Act. It likely would have found the requirement incompatible with the Act as written. Hence the Act cannot remain valid in its entirety. Severance and excision are necessary.

III

We now turn to the question of which portions of the sentencing statute we must sever and excise as inconsistent with the Court's constitutional requirement. Although, as we have explained, we believe that Congress would have preferred the total invalidation of the statute to the dissenters' remedial approach, we nevertheless do not believe that the entire statute must be invalidated. Most of the statute is perfectly valid.

[We] must sever and excise two specific statutory provisions: the provision that requires sentencing courts to impose a sentence within the applicable Guidelines range (in the absence of circumstances that justify a departure), see 18 U.S.C. § 3553(b)(1), and the provision that sets forth standards of review on appeal, including de novo review of departures from the applicable Guidelines range, see § 3742(e). With these two sections excised (and statutory cross-references to the two sections consequently invalidated), the remainder of the Act satisfies the Court's constitutional requirements. As the Court today recognizes in its first opinion in these cases, the existence of § 3553(b)(1) is a necessary condition of the constitutional violation. . . .

Without the "mandatory" provision, the Act nonetheless requires judges to take account of the Guidelines together with other sentencing goals. The Act nonetheless requires judges to consider the Guidelines "sentencing range established for . . . the applicable category of offense committed by the applicable category of defendant," the pertinent Sentencing Commission policy statements, the need to avoid unwarranted sentencing disparities, and the need to provide restitution to victims. And the Act nonetheless requires judges to impose sentences that reflect the seriousness of the offense, promote respect for the law, provide just punishment, afford adequate deterrence, protect the public, and effectively provide the defendant with needed educational or vocational training and medical care.

[D]espite the absence of § 3553(b)(1), the Act continues to provide for appeals from sentencing decisions (irrespective of whether the trial judge sentences within or outside the Guidelines range in the exercise of his discretionary power under § 3553(a)). We concede that the excision of § 3553(b)(1) requires the excision of a different, appeals-related section, namely § 3742(e), which sets forth standards of review on appeal. That section contains critical cross-references to the (now-excised) § 3553(b)(1) and consequently must be severed and excised for similar reasons.

Excision of § 3742(e), however, does not pose a critical problem for the handling of appeals. That is because, as we have previously held, a statute that does not explicitly set forth a standard of review may nonetheless do so implicitly. See *Pierce v. Underwood*, 487 U.S. 552, 558–560 (1988) (adopting a standard of review, where "neither a clear statutory prescription nor a historical tradition" existed, based on the statutory text and structure, and on practical considerations). We infer appropriate review standards from related statutory language, the structure of the statute, and the "sound administration of justice." *Pierce, supra*, at 559–560. And in this instance those factors, in addition to the past two decades of appellate practice in cases involving departures, imply a practical standard of review already familiar to appellate courts: review for "unreasonable [ness]." 18 U.S.C. § 3742(e)(3). . . .

Finally, the Act without its "mandatory" provision and related language remains consistent with Congress' initial and basic sentencing intent. Congress sought to "provide certainty and fairness in meeting the purposes of sentencing, [while] avoiding unwarranted sentencing disparities . . . [and] maintaining sufficient flexibility to permit individualized sentences when warranted." 28 U.S.C. § 991(b)(1)(B); see also USSG § 1A1.1, application note (explaining that Congress sought to achieve "honesty," "uniformity," and "proportionality" in sentencing (emphases deleted)). The system remaining after excision, while lacking the mandatory features that Congress enacted, retains other features that help to further these objectives. . . .

As we have said, the Sentencing Commission remains in place, writing Guidelines, collecting information about actual district court sentencing decisions, undertaking research, and revising the Guidelines accordingly. See 28 U.S.C.A. § 994. The district courts, while not bound to apply the Guidelines, must consult those Guidelines and take them into account when sentencing. See 18 U.S.C.A. §§ 3553(a)(4), (5). . . .

We do not doubt that Congress, when it wrote the Sentencing Act, intended to create a form of mandatory Guidelines system. But, we repeat, given today's constitutional holding, that is not a choice that remains open. Hence we have examined the statute in depth to determine Congress' likely intent in light of today's holding. And we have concluded that today's holding is fundamentally inconsistent with the judge-based sentencing system that Congress enacted into law. In our view, it is more consistent with Congress' likely intent in enacting the Sentencing Reform Act (1) to preserve important elements of that system while severing and excising two provisions (§§ 3553(b)(1) and 3742(e)) than (2) to maintain all provisions of the Act and engraft today's constitutional requirement onto that statutory scheme.

Ours, of course, is not the last word: The ball now lies in Congress' court. The National Legislature is equipped to devise and install, long-term, the sentencing system, compatible with the Constitution, that Congress judges best for the federal system of justice. . . .

V

In respondent Booker's case, the District Court applied the Guidelines as written and imposed a sentence higher than the maximum authorized solely by the jury's verdict. The Court of Appeals held *Blakely* applicable to the Guidelines, concluded that Booker's sentence violated the Sixth Amendment, vacated the judgment of the District Court, and remanded for resentencing. We affirm the judgment of the Court of Appeals and remand the case. On remand, the District Court should impose a sentence in accordance with today's opinions, and, if the sentence comes before the Court of Appeals for review, the Court of Appeals should apply the review standards set forth in this opinion. . . .

As these dispositions indicate, we must apply today's holdings—both the Sixth Amendment holding and our remedial interpretation of the Sentencing Act—to all cases on direct review. See *Griffith v. Kentucky*, 479 U.S. 314, 328 (1987) ("[A] new rule for the conduct of criminal prosecutions is to be applied retroactively to all cases . . . pending on direct review or not yet final, with no exception for cases in which the new rule constitutes a 'clear break' with the past"). That fact does not mean that we believe that every sentence gives rise to a Sixth Amendment violation. Nor do we believe that every appeal will lead to a new sentencing hearing. That is because we expect reviewing courts to apply ordinary prudential doctrines, determining, for example, whether the issue was raised below and whether it fails the "plain-error" test. It is also because, in cases not involving a Sixth Amendment violation, whether resentencing is warranted or whether it will instead be sufficient to review a sentence for reasonableness may depend upon application of the harmless-error doctrine.

It is so ordered.

[Justice Breyer's *Booker* dissent repeated the argument from his *Apprendi* dissent that the jury trial right permits judges to find "sentencing facts." Justice Stevens also dissented, arguing that the prosecution should be permitted to empanel juries to find "sentencing facts" that would increase a sentence above the maximum term of a presumptive range. Justice Scalia's dissenting opinion criticized the severance remedy, preferring a reasonableness standard.]

NOTES

1. *Effect of Booker.* Immediately after *Booker*, officials from the United States Sentencing Commission, the Department of Justice, and the Congress were cautious about whether further legislative action was necessary. However, the instant impact of *Booker* was to throw into disarray the appeals of hundreds of federal criminal cases. Defendants sentenced *before Booker* comprised the largest group potentially seeking a new sentencing hearing. No appellate court has held that *Booker* is retroactive, thereby relieving the potential for added litigation in the federal courts. See, e.g., *Padilla v. United States*, 416 F.3d 424, 427 (5th Cir. 2005); *Humphress v. United States*, 398 F.3d 855, 860 (6th Cir. 2005); *Wilson v. United States*, 414 F.3d 829, 831–32 (7th Cir. 2005); *Never Misses a Shot v. United States*, 413 F.3d 781, 783–84 (8th Cir. 2005).

A second, smaller group of federal defendants were sentenced after *Blakely v. Washington* indicated a potential *Apprendi* problem with the Federal Sentencing Guidelines. Some post-*Blakely* courts continued to apply (erroneously, as it turned out) the Guidelines as mandatory; some used them as advisory without considering the statutory factors like age, poor upbringing, education, mental health, drug addiction and other factors previously thought to be inapplicable under the Guidelines.

2. *Appellate review of sentences after Booker.* What about cases that were on appeal at the time *Booker* was decided? In *United States v. Crosby*, 397 F.3d 103 (2d Cir. 2005) the court set out a procedure for a limited remand on sentences invalid under *Booker*. As long as the trial court retains jurisdiction of the case, the trial judge may make a finding of whether she would have imposed a materially different sentence and, if she would have done so, she keeps the case and resentences the defendant. If the case is already on appeal, the circuit court reviews for "plain error" by the sentencing court when the defendant did not raise an objection. If a defendant raised an objection and the Guidelines calculation was correct, but erroneously imposed because the Guidelines' use was mandatory, the circuit court remands

to the trial court for resentencing in conformity with *Booker*. In a deeply divided *en banc* opinion, the Ninth Circuit chose to follow the *Crosby* approach. *United States v. Ameline*, 409 F.3d 1073 (9th Cir. 2005).

Not every circuit has agreed with the *Crosby* approach. For example, in *United States v. Rodriguez*, 398 F.3d 1291 (11th Cir. 2005), the court held that when the defendant did not raise the *Booker* issue, he must establish a "reasonable probability" that the trial judge would have imposed a different sentence had the Guidelines not been mandatory. That decision brought a swift rebuke from the Seventh Circuit in *United States v. Paladino*, 401 F.3d 471 (7th Cir. 2005).

3. *Appellate advice for prospective trial court sentencing.* For future cases, the circuits have attempted to prescribe a sentencing method, now that the mandatory nature of the Guidelines is unconstitutional:

> [A]t this point, we can identify several essential aspects of *Booker* that concern the selection of sentences. First, the Guidelines are no longer mandatory. Second, the sentencing judge must consider the Guidelines and all of the other factors listed in section 3553(a). Third, consideration of the Guidelines will normally require determination of the applicable Guidelines range, or at least identification of the arguably applicable ranges, and consideration of applicable policy statements. Fourth, the sentencing judge should decide, after considering the Guidelines and all the other factors set forth in section 3553(a), whether (i) to impose the sentence that would have been imposed under the Guidelines, i.e., a sentence within the applicable Guidelines range or within permissible departure authority, or (ii) to impose a non-Guidelines sentence. Fifth, the sentencing judge is entitled to find all the facts appropriate for determining either a Guidelines sentence or a non-Guidelines sentence.

United States v. Crosby, 397 F.3d 103 (2d Cir. 2005).

4. *What is a "reasonable" sentence?* Justice Breyer's opinion reasoned that the remedy for the constitutional violation was to make the Guidelines advisory and to replace *de novo* appellate review of sentences with a reasonableness standard of review. Appellate courts may apply a presumption of reasonableness to within-guidelines sentences. See *Rita v. United States*, 127 S.Ct. 2456 (2007). However, this does not mean that courts may adopt a presumption of unreasonableness for nonguidelines sentences. Judges may impose a nonguidelines sentence on the basis of policy disagreements with the guidelines. *Kimbrough v. United States*, 128 S.Ct. 558 (2007).

In *Gall v. United States*, 128 S.Ct. 586 (2007), the Court held that "while the extent of the difference between a particular sentence and the recommended Guidelines range is surely relevant, courts of appeals must review all sentences—whether inside, just outside, or significantly outside the Guidelines range—under a deferential abuse of discretion standard." The Court "reject[ed] ... an appellate rule that requires 'extraordinary' circumstances to justify a sentence outside the Guidelines range." The *Gall* Court explained the duties of the sentencing and appellate courts:

[A] district court should begin all sentencing proceedings by correctly calculating the applicable Guidelines range.... Accordingly, after giving both parties an opportunity to argue for whatever sentence they deem appropriate, the district judge should then consider all of the [Guidelines] factors to determine whether they support the sentence requested by a party. In so doing, he may not presume that the Guidelines range is reasonable. He must make an individualized assessment based on the facts presented. If he decides that an outside-Guidelines sentence is warranted, he must consider the extent of the deviation and ensure that the justification is sufficiently compelling to support the degree of the variance.... [A] major departure should be supported by a more significant justification than a minor one. After settling on the appropriate sentence, he must adequately explain the chosen sentence to allow for meaningful appellate review and to promote the perception of fair sentencing.

Regardless of whether the sentence imposed is inside or outside the Guidelines range, the appellate court must review the sentence under an abuse-of-discretion standard. It must first ensure that the district court committed no significant procedural error, such as failing to calculate (or improperly calculating) the Guidelines range, treating the Guidelines as mandatory, failing to consider the [statutory] factors, selecting a sentence based on clearly erroneous facts, or failing to adequately explain the chosen sentence-including an explanation for any deviation from the Guidelines range. Assuming that the district court's sentencing decision is procedurally sound, the appellate court should then consider the substantive reasonableness of the sentence imposed under an abuse-of-discretion standard. When conducting this review, the court will, of course, take into account the totality of the circumstances, including the extent of any variance from the Guidelines range. If the sentence is within the Guidelines range, the appellate court may, but is not required to, apply a presumption of reasonableness. But if the sentence is outside the Guidelines range, the court may not apply a presumption of unreasonableness. It may consider the extent of the deviation, but must give due deference to the district court's decision that the [statutory] factors, on a whole, justify the extent of the variance. The fact that the appellate court might reasonably have concluded that a different sentence was appropriate is insufficient to justify reversal of the district court.

For an application of the *Gall* standard to a below-the-Guidelines sentence, see *United States v. Cutler*, 520 F.3d 136 (2d Cir. 2008). The court carefully examined both the trial court's sentencing procedure as well as the factual underpinnings and reasonableness of the ultimate sentences.